95775P 16 95 / 8 —

THE OXFORD AUTHORS

General Editor: Frank Kermode

SAMUEL JOHNSON was born in 1709 in Lichfield, Staffordshire. The son of an impecunious bookseller, he experienced poverty throughout the first part of his life, and, in spite of his formidable mental endowments, was able to attend Pembroke College, Oxford, for only a year. After moving to London in 1737, he earned his living by miscellaneous journalism for many years, until his *Rambler* essays and the first historical dictionary of the English language brought him fame. A government pension of £300 a year relieved him from necessity, and in the later part of his life he came to be regarded as the greatest literary figure of his time in England. Among his most noted works are his poem 'The Vanity of Human Wishes', his periodical essays, his moral tale *Rasselas*, his edition of Shakespeare's plays, and his long series of *Prefaces, Biographical and Critical*, to the works of the English poets. He died in 1784 and was buried in Westminster Abbey.

DONALD GREENE is retired Leo S. Bing Professor of English in the University of Southern California. His books include *The Politics of Samuel Johnson* (1960), (with James L. Clifford) *Samuel Johnson: A Survey and Bibliography of Critical Studies* (1970), and an edition of Johnson's *Political Writings* (1977).

FRANK KERMODE, retired King Edward VII Professor of English Literature at Cambridge, is the author of many books, including *Romantic Image*, *The Sense of an Ending*, *The Classic*, *The Genesis of Secrecy*, *Forms of Attention*, and *History and Value*; he is also co-editor with John Hollander of *The Oxford Anthology of English Literature*.

D0950392

THE OXFORD AUTHORS

SAMUEL JOHNSON

EDITED BY
DONALD GREENE

Oxford   New York
OXFORD UNIVERSITY PRESS

Oxford University Press, Great Clarendon Street, Oxford OX2 6DP

Oxford New York

Athens Auckland Bangkok Bogota Buenos Aires Calcutta
Cape Town Chennai Dar es Salaam Delhi Florence Hong Kong Istanbul
Karachi Kuala Lumpur Madrid Melbourne Mexico City Mumbai
Nairobi Paris São Paolo Singapore Taipei Tokyo Toronto Warsaw

and associated companies in
Berlin Ibadan

Oxford is a registered trade mark of Oxford University Press

Introduction, Notes, and editorial matter © Donald Greene 1984

First published 1984

All rights reserved. No part of this publication may be reproduced,
stored in a retrieval system, or transmitted, in any form or by any means,
without the prior permission in writing of Oxford University Press.
Within the UK, exceptions are allowed in respect of any fair dealing for the
purpose of research or private study, or criticism or review, as permitted
under the Copyright, Designs and Patents Act, 1988, or in the case of
reprographic reproduction in accordance with the terms of the licences
issued by the Copyright Licensing Agency. Enquiries concerning
reproduction outside these terms and in other countries should be
sent to the Rights Department, Oxford University Press,
at the address above

This book is sold subject to the condition that it shall not, by way
of trade or otherwise, be lent, re-sold, hired out or otherwise circulated
without the publisher's prior consent in any form of binding or cover
other than that in which it is published and without a similar condition
including this condition being imposed on the subsequent purchaser

British Library Cataloguing in Publication Data
Data available

Library of Congress Cataloging in Publication Data
Johnson, Samuel, 1709–1784.
Samuel Johnson.
(The Oxford authors)
Bibliography: p.
Includes index.
I. Greene, Donald Johnson. II. Title.
PR3522.G73 1984   828'.609   83–17280
ISBN 0-19-281340-4

13 15 17 19 20 18 16 14

Printed in Great Britain by
Cox & Wyman Ltd, Reading, Berkshire

CONTENTS

An asterisk (*) indicates an excerpt or abridgement. Dates are generally those of publication, if occurring in Johnson's lifetime; otherwise, of composition.

INTRODUCTION

ONE reason why Samuel Johnson, more than any other major figure of English literature, is better known as a 'personality' than as the great writer he was has been the difficulty of access to the large and varied canon of his writings. This is being remedied by the steady, if slow, appearance of the first full scholarly edition of his works. But it will be some time before that edition is complete, and in any case it is likely to be of most use to the specialist. The aim of the present volume is to provide the discerning general reader, as well as students of English literature, with a substantial sampling of Johnson's achievement as a writer: to bring him into contact with Johnson's wide-ranging curiosity about the world and its inhabitants; his intense concern for their problems and the penetrating insight he brought to them; and the verbal artistry with which he set down his observations and reflections on the human condition.

The biography of Johnson has become a field of specialization in itself, and it would be useless here to try to summarize what its many practitioners have discovered, or thought they have discovered, about his life and his psychology. (Without detracting from the excellence of some of this work, it may still be useful to repeat Johnson's remark, when pressed for an introduction to some writer much in the public eye, 'The best part of every author is in general to be found in his book, I assure you.') In fact, the outline of Johnson's life, like that of most dedicated professional writers, is not a very eventful one. He was born in 1709, in Lichfield, Staffordshire, to an impecunious fifty-two-year-old bookseller and his forty-year-old wife. He received the traditional classical education at the Lichfield grammar school, and was able to attend Pembroke College, Oxford, for a little more than a year before poverty made him withdraw. There followed some locust years in the Midlands, with Johnson trying his hand unsuccessfully at schoolmastering, and undertaking sporadic ventures in writing. There was a strange marriage with a widow twenty years older than he, whose modest fortune he invested in a boarding school, which soon failed. At last, in 1737, accompanied by his former pupil, young David Garrick, he made his way to London, to try to make a living in Grub Street by his pen.

Then came a decade of ill-paid miscellaneous journalism, the bulk of it for the pioneering 'first magazine', the *Gentleman's*, which

Johnson helped to convert from a rather dreary collection of reprints from current newspapers to the prototype of the modern 'intellectual' journal, designed to inform and stimulate the minds of the educated and educable general public. When he was about forty, his name began to be known, with the moderate *succès d'estime* of his long poem 'The Vanity of Human Wishes' and his blank-verse tragedy *Irene*, written long before, but only now produced, through Garrick's influence.

In the 1750s, with his acclaimed series of *Rambler* essays and his great *Dictionary of the English Language*, Johnson began to be recognized as one of the most important literary figures of his time. There was still financial hardship. The payment for the *Dictionary* had been exhausted during the eight years of work on it, and Johnson undertook the editorship of the *Literary Magazine*—an appointment which lasted for only a few months because of his intransigent opposition to the popular Seven Years War—and two other sets of periodical essays, *The Adventurer* and *The Idler*. The decade also saw the deaths of the two people dearest to him, his wife in 1752—there had been no children—and his mother in 1759. To pay for the expenses of his mother's last illness, he wrote ('in the evenings of a week') his fine *conte philosophique*, *Rasselas*.

When he was fifty-three, he was relieved of financial worry by the award of an annual pension from the new government of George III and Lord Bute (a good deal of mystery still surrounds the pension: that Johnson had written much in virulent opposition to the Whig regimes of Walpole and the Pelhams in the previous reign is surely not irrelevant). The pension of £300 (multiplied by perhaps twenty-five to arrive at its current equivalent) also relieved him from some incentive to effort, and it was not until after much prodding that his edition of Shakespeare, announced nine years before, appeared in 1765. A related effect may have been the intensification of the periods of severe depression to which he was subject. From the worst of these, in 1766, he was rescued by a new-found friend, the charming and intellectual Hester Thrale, wife of a wealthy brewer. For the rest of his life he cultivated friendships, often with the young—the amusing, if erratic Scot, James Boswell, the learned and solemn Bennet Langton, the young Oxford professor Robert Chambers, to whom he secretly gave much help when Chambers was faced with the formidable task of preparing a course of lectures in English law in succession to the *Commentaries* of his predecessor in the Vinerian chair, Sir William Blackstone. At the famous 'Club' which he and Sir Joshua Reynolds

founded in 1765 (the second of three dining clubs organized by
Johnson), he took part in the brilliant conversational exchanges
reported by Boswell, with men like Burke and Gibbon. He travelled
a good deal, spending many summers in his native Midlands, with
his stepdaughter Lucy Porter in Lichfield, and his old schoolfellows
the surgeon Edmund Hector in Birmingham and John Taylor,
rector of Ashbourne, Derbyshire. In 1773 he made his astonishing
tour, with Boswell, of the remote and scarcely-known Highlands
of Scotland, and later travelled with the Thrales through Wales and
France.

He now wrote, not to earn his living, but as occasion and impulse
offered: in the 1770s, four hard-hitting pamphlets in defence of
actions of the government of the day; an account of his travels in
Scotland; fifty-two *Prefaces*, *Biographical and Critical* (commonly but
inaccurately called *The Lives of the Poets*) for an anthology of English
verse brought out by a syndicate of London booksellers. Though he
suffered from a multitude of ailments throughout his life, and was
given in a hypochondriacal way to self-diagnosis and treatment, he
was basically robust—his tall, muscular frame is not done justice to by
Reynolds's most frequently reproduced portrait, which overempha-
sizes his obesity—and he lived to the respectable age of seventy-five,
dying in December 1784.

This brief sketch can be supplemented by the Chronology
(p. xxix), and of course by the many biographies. What follows is a more
detailed account of Johnson's career as a writer, attempting to show how
the various pieces printed in the body of this volume fit into his *oeuvre* as
a whole.

Before 1730. Like other skilled writers, Johnson began to compose
early. A good deal of his juvenilia has been preserved. Six pieces of
Latin composition survive—'themes', in which a gnomic quotation
from a Latin author is set by a schoolmaster (or college tutor), on
which the pupil has to write a page or so of Latin prose (and, with the
two preserved from his Pembroke days, a quatrain of Latin verse).
They are of some interest: a diatribe against European exploitation of
distant lands; one (p. 39) based on the lines from Juvenal's tenth
satire that Johnson was later to render in 'The Vanity of Human
Wishes' as 'This pow'r has praise, that virtue scarce can warm,/Till
fame supplies the universal charm'; one on a tag from Macrobius's
Saturnalia (so that the credit Johnson gained for quoting Macrobius
when entering Pembroke perhaps belongs rather to the schoolmaster

who set him the assignment). They also show young Johnson's Latin not to have been impeccable.

Much more that has survived is verse—sometimes English, sometimes Latin; some obviously deriving from schoolwork (translations from Horace, Virgil, and Homer), some 'original'. His earliest known poem, 'On a Daffodil' (Romantic critics would have stared), was written when he was about fifteen; it is not very good, and contains the kind of 'traditional imagery'—'lambent zephyrs', 'Sol's bright chariot'—he was later to deplore. A religious poem, 'On the Feast of St Simon and St Jude', in the six-line *Song to David* stanza, and a version, in heroic couplets, of Addison's Latin 'Battle of the Pygmies and Cranes' show increasing competence. A good example of this early work is the translation of Horace, *Odes*, ii. 20 (p. 1), where the quatrain form imposes an economy suitable to that of Horace's Latin. There are conventional poems of compliment to ladies, some perhaps done at the request of friends, which Johnson continued to write in the 1740s. The best is 'To Miss ——, On Her Playing upon the Harpsichord' (p. 9), which has a fascinating 'metaphysical' quality.

For all that Johnson is usually thought of as a prose writer, poetry was dear to his heart, and he composed much of it, especially in his youth and in old age, when he whiled away insomniac nights by turning the lyrics of the Greek *Anthology* into Latin verse. His first publication, written when he was nineteen and a Pembroke undergraduate, was a translation of Pope's *Messiah* into Latin dactylics, published in John Husbands's *Miscellany of Poems*, 1731, to which Pope himself is said to have given the highest praise. Johnson's collected poetry runs to a good-sized volume. Much of it displays his talent for 'light' and epigrammatic verse, sometimes made extemporaneously, of which a sampling is included here. In considering Johnson as a poet, it is well to keep in mind T. S. Eliot's magisterial pronouncement, concerning the Charles XII passage in 'The Vanity of Human Wishes', 'If these lines are not poetry, I do not know what is.'

1730–1740. During Johnson's peregrinations in the Midlands, he may have contributed to Thomas Warren's *Birmingham Journal*. Nothing known to be by him has survived from it, but there is a presage of Johnson's later extensive involvement in journalism. What *has* survived from his Birmingham days is his translation (or rather adaptation), from the French version by Joachim LeGrand, of the Portuguese Jesuit Jerome Lobo's *Voyage to Abyssinia*, together with LeGrand's 'dissertations' appended to it. The 400-page volume touches on some highly controversial matters, mentioned in Johnson's preface (p. 41). The attempt by the Portuguese Jesuit mission in the early seventeenth century to 'convert' the Ethiopians, who had long had their own brand of Christianity, was denounced by Protestants as a cynical power-play by Portugal to protect its commercially profitable sea-route to India. Johnson comes down firmly on the Protestant side, and, though paying tribute to Lobo's honesty as an observer, spares no emphasis in reprobating Roman Catholic missionary methods. He is said to have been able to finish the work only through the efforts of Hector, who took down the words Johnson dictated as he lay in bed, too depressed to rise. For this substantial task, Johnson received five guineas.

Once in London, however, and attached to the *Gentleman's Magazine*, Johnson found plenty to do—its shrewd proprietor, Edward Cave, believed in getting full value out of his employees. Among Johnson's contributions to the *GM* were several short biographies: of the Venetian Fra Paolo Sarpi, a considerable amount of whose great *History of the Council of Trent*, written from an anti-Papal point of view, Johnson translated (only three paragraphs of the translation survive); of Sir Francis Drake and the Cromwellian Admiral Robert Blake, whose successful exploits against the Spanish and Dutch were perhaps intended to shame Sir Robert Walpole's feeble efforts in the War of Jenkins's Ear; of the scholarly prodigy Jean-Philippe Barretier and the great Dutch scientist Boerhaave, both recently dead. They are of course derivative—Johnson had no opportunity for original research—but they are competent journalism. The life of Boerhaave is given here (p. 54), partly because it has been said, with some justice, that much in Boerhaave's life formed a personal ideal for Johnson's.

Throughout his life Johnson was concerned with human attitudes towards death; the two essays on epitaphs given here (pp. 51, 96) testify to that concern. A significant early piece in the *GM* is 'The State of Affairs in Lilliput' (p. 44), which introduces Cave's ingenious device for evading Parliament's ban on the reporting of its debates; the popularity of such pseudo-debates contributed much to the prosperity of Cave's journal and its rival, the *London Magazine*, in the hectic political climate of the years preceding the downfall of Walpole. Though one can't be absolutely sure, recent scholars agree that Johnson had a large share in this introductory diatribe. The hair-raising suggestion of an uprising in which the royal family and the ministry are massacred is not inconsistent with Johnson's violently anti-government views at the time, and the opinions expressed about European aggression in other continents coincide with Johnson's throughout his life.

Johnson published much else outside the pages of the *GM*. The Swiftian tone of 'The State of Affairs in Lilliput' is continued in two anti-Walpolian pamphlets of 1739, *Marmor Norfolciense*, which it was reported impelled the ministry to issue a warrant for his arrest, and *A Complete Vindication of the Licensers of the Stage* (p. 71). The heavy-handed irony is better controlled in the latter—a mock defence of the Lord Chamberlain's office, under the Stage Licensing Act, 1737 (passed to protect the administration from such assaults), for refusing to license the performance of Henry Brooke's near-seditious *Gustavus Vasa*. Under the auspices of Cave, Johnson was involved in the controversy over Pope's 'Essay on Man' initiated by the Swiss theologian Jean-Pierre de Crousaz, whose *Examen* and *Commentaire* on the poem detected dangerous Leibnizian fatalism and deism in it. The *Examen* was translated by Johnson's colleague on the *GM*, Elizabeth Carter, and the *Commentaire* by Johnson. In his elaborate apparatus, Johnson gave an interlinear re-translation into English of the French translation of the *Essay* by Du Resnel on which Crousaz had relied, and had no difficulty showing that it shockingly mis-represented what Pope had written. A handful of his annotations are given here (p. 84); they provide early examples of the 'close reading' critical technique Johnson was later to apply to Shakespeare, Milton, Gray, and other English poets, as well as a good deal of significant moral and theological commentary.

The best known of Johnson's works during this decade is 'London' (p. 2), an 'imitation' of Juvenal's third satire ('variations on a theme' by Juvenal might be a better description of this and other contemporary 'imitations'). Pope again praised this exuberant work, which, full of standard anti-Walpole propaganda of the time, is best read in the context of *Marmor* and *A Complete Vindication*. In that context, the vexed questions 'Could Johnson have been sincere in his denunciation of London and praise of rural retirement?' and 'Was Thales Richard Savage, and did Johnson know him personally at the time?' lose some of their importance.

1740–1750. Savage, always a great self-publicist, died in 1743, and Cave and Johnson decided to take advantage of the publicity. In his *Life of Savage*, 1744 (abridged, p. 128), Johnson produced his first—

perhaps, strictly speaking, only—full-scale biography. Though much
of it derives from an earlier anonymous *Life of Savage*, a good deal
comes from personal knowledge. It has often been remarked how
Johnson sometimes seems to identify himself with Savage ('SLOW RISES
WORTH BY POVERTY DEPRESSED', as he wrote in 'London'), and yet can
distance himself from his subject and view Savage's near-paranoia
objectively. His passionate adoption of Savage's dubious tales about
his persecution by his supposed mother has given rise to speculation
about Johnson's relations with his own mother.

During this decade, Johnson began to withdraw from his connection
with the *GM*; in 1746 he signed the contract for the *Dictionary*.
Earlier, however—as well as contributing an interesting review of the
memoirs of old Sarah, Duchess of Marlborough (p. 113), a shrewd
comment on the limits of historical scepticism—he seems to have been
the chief writer of the *GM*'s debates in Parliament (that of 'Lilliput',
of course). These, totalling around half a million words, are the part of
Johnson's writing that has been most, and most unjustly, neglected.
Modern students agree that, whatever Johnson may have said later
about not letting the Whig dogs get the best of it, they are a fair
representation of the gist of the arguments the various speakers
actually used; they appear in Cobbett's *Parliamentary History*, the
precursor of Hansard, and are still quoted by historians, sometimes
unaware that the words are actually Johnson's. They contain some
splendid rhetoric. A small sample of it is given here (p. 103) from the
debate in the House of Commons on 13 February 1741, on a motion to
request the King to dismiss Walpole. So vicious is the attack upon
Walpole that the *GM* did not venture to print it until two years later,
when Walpole was safely out of power. It has not before been printed
in a collection of Johnson's writings.

For a considerable time Johnson was employed, along with William
Oldys, by the bookseller Thomas Osborne, who had bought the great
Harleian library collected by the Earls of Oxford (not to be confused
with the Harleian collection of *manuscripts*, which later became one of
the initial collections of the British Museum). How much Johnson
may have contributed to the descriptions of the books in the
formidable five-volume sale catalogue still needs study. But his
prefatory material to it, and to the selection of pamphlets from the
collection reprinted as the eight-volume *Harleian Miscellany* (p. 117),
provides a brilliant exposition of the importance of book-catalogues
and the preservation of 'ephemera', which every serious scholar
should ponder. Johnson also contributed a dozen brief but

interesting notes to pieces in the *Miscellany*. His apologue 'The Vision of Theodore' (p. 165), printed in *The Preceptor*, a manual of self-education published by Dodsley in 1748, for which Johnson also wrote the preface and which he may have had a hand in organizing, he is said to have called 'the best thing he ever wrote'.

Johnson had come to London in 1737 with a blank-verse tragedy, *Irene*, partly completed; as with Addison's *Cato*, the performance of such a play could lead to fame overnight. It did not however succeed in finding a producer until 1749, when Garrick, now patentee of the Theatre Royal, Drury Lane, staged it. It had the respectable run of nine nights, and earned Johnson £300. The plot, taken from Knolles's *General History of the Turks*, had been popular with earlier playwrights, and indeed is one that might have appealed to Racine. The central story is that of the beautiful Greek Christian, Irene, taken captive at the fall of Constantinople to the Turks in 1453, with whom the Sultan Mahomet falls passionately in love. He offers to make her his bride, on condition that she change her religion. She succumbs to the temptation, but in the end falls victim to a palace intrigue of Mahomet's followers, while her virtuous friend Aspasia, who holds firm to her religion, escapes to freedom with her faithful lover Demetrius. Johnson's handling of the complex psychology is skilled, but many have complained of the monotony of the versification, in which almost every blank-verse line is end-stopped. The scene given here is the climactic exchange between Mahomet and Irene (p. 21).

At the same time, Johnson's greatest poem, 'The Vanity of Human Wishes' (p. 12), was published, bearing (unusually) his name on the title-page. The density of its poetic texture, the richness of its imagery, make it necessary to read it slowly and thoughtfully. It is wrong to misread its title as 'the vanity of human life': the conclusion points out emphatically that a happy life *is* possible for those who adopt the higher values of faith, hope, and love rather than the merely 'human' ones of fame, wealth, and power. As in Eliot's *Waste Land* ('vanity' and 'waste' both derive from Latin *vanus*, 'empty'), the bulk of the poem pictures the dreary frustration of lives directed by mere this-worldly values, and concludes with the affirmation that another kind of life is possible.

1750–1760. This was Johnson's most prolific decade. Although Arthur Murphy stated, on what authority we do not know, that his semi-weekly *Rambler* essays had a circulation of only five hundred, far below that of *The Spectator*, recent study has shown that they were among the most popular of those reprinted, as they came out, by the provincial press. The twenty-four essays here (p. 175) (of the total of 208) give a sampling of their chief subject-matter—'interpersonal' relations, literary criticism (nos. 4 and 60, on the realistic novel and biography, are noteworthy), general human psychology and morality. He was one of four collaborators in *The Adventurer* (p. 261), in which his contributions maintain the general level of high seriousness of *The Rambler* (the striking conclusion of no. 85 helps us to understand many of Johnson's other pronouncements on the human condition). The weekly *Idler* essays (p. 277) are shorter and generally lighter, although nothing else he wrote exceeds in ferocity his denunciation of man's inhumanity to man in nos. 81 and no. 22 (original numbering), both inspired by the slaughter of the Seven Years War.

The beginning, in 1756, of that war, from which Great Britain emerged as a great imperial and commercial power, coincided with Johnson's appointment as editor of a new monthly, the *Literary Magazine, or Universal Review*. Although he contributed many incisive reviews to it (pp. 488–543), one of them his devastating refutation of Soame Jenyns's 'great chain of being' and 'whatever is, is right' theodicy, much of the journal was concerned with the war, which Johnson bitterly opposed. It opened with a long 'Introduction to the Political State of Great Britain', which traces with acidity the history of European colonial expansion. This was a prelude to the 'Observations' on the present war (p. 501), which apparently was too much for the proprietorship of the magazine: in the next number a new and patriotic hand took over the political commentary, though Johnson continued sporadic attacks on the war-makers in *The Idler* and the short-lived 'Observations' in the *Universal Chronicle*. As the war drew to a close, he published two compassionate postscripts, a defence against 'patriots' who objected to charity given to French prisoners of war (p. 547) and 'On the Bravery of the English Common Soldiers' (p. 549).

Other notable pieces from this busy period are his review of a study of the famous 'casket letters' which were supposed to establish the guilt of Mary, Queen of Scots (p. 551); the drily hostile life of the obstreperous Puritan Cheynel, one of Johnson's best pieces of short biography (p. 476); and one of several manifestoes he was called on to write for new periodicals (p. 544)—(as well as an experienced practical journalist, Johnson seems also to have been regarded as the principal theorist of journalism of the time). Included here, though we really have no idea when it was written, is one of the twenty-six sermons that have survived of the forty he is supposed to have written for clerical friends. Like the 'Debates', they have been unjustly neglected. They contain some of Johnson's most thoughtful and powerfully expressed theological and moral statements. No. 5 in the traditional numbering (p. 467), on 'the origin of evil', should be read in connection with the Soame Jenyns review.

Johnson's most famous publications of the decade were *The Rambler*, the *Dictionary of the English Language*, which he, with the help of six amanuenses, had laboured on for eight years, and *Rasselas*. Two common mistakes about the *Dictionary* should be avoided. One is that it was intended to be 'normative', and to 'fix the language'. Although he had expressed such a hope in the 1747 *Plan* addressed to Lord Chesterfield, in the 1755 Preface (p. 307) he firmly states that experience has proved this impossible: his task as a lexicographer is not to 'form, but register, the language'. The second is to follow Boswell's 'confused and erroneous' account—so called by Bishop Percy, who corrected it long ago—of how the *Dictionary* was compiled. According to Boswell, Johnson first wrote down the list of words it was to contain, composed definitions for them, and then sought in books written in English for 'authorities' to justify the definitions. Life would not be long enough to put together a dictionary in this fashion. In fact, as Percy describes it, Johnson's method was the empirical one of modern dictionary makers. First, the books were read; passages containing significant uses of words were marked, and given to the amanuenses to be copied on to slips, which were then assembled under the words exemplified in each. Then, from a study of the quotations containing a word, its various significations were discriminated, definitions formulated, and a selection of the protocol quotations chosen to exemplify each definition. (It has been estimated that the two large folio volumes contain over 116,000 quotations, and that these represent perhaps half of those originally assembled.) As the Preface says, 'all-purpose' verbs like *take* and *get* have very many different shades of meaning: under *take* Johnson lists no fewer than 134, a feat not unworthy of the *Dictionary*'s great successor, the *Oxford English Dictionary*.

Since many readers know little more of the *Dictionary* than a few 'quaint' or prejudiced definitions (without their supporting quotations), a few pages are given in facsimile (p. 329) in the hope of familiarizing them with the real nature of the work. It is well, too, to remember that it was not designed primarily to help the ordinary user to look up the spelling or meaning of 'hard words': that purpose was

served by the octavo abridgement Johnson brought out the next year
(the one thrown by Becky Sharp), which omits the quotations. As he
writes in the preface to the abridgement, the full *Dictionary*, 'like
those compiled by the academies of Italy and France', is for 'the use of
such as aspire to exactness of criticism or elegance of style'.

Rasselas (p. 335)—Johnson's original title for it was 'The Choice of
Life'— is probably Johnson's most widely-read work: hundreds of
editions and translations into many languages have circulated since its
publication in 1759. It teaches much the same lesson as the conclusion
of *The Adventurer*, no. 85: 'Some deficiency must be forgiven all,
because all are men. . . . It is, however, reasonable to have perfection
in our eye: that we may always advance towards it, though we know it
never can be reached.' As with Voltaire's *Candide*, so similar in form
and plot and written at almost the same time, whether its ending be
thought 'pessimistic' or not must depend on the reader's own
philosophy of life.

1760–1770. However later editions may have improved on it,
Johnson's edition of Shakespeare's plays, which finally appeared in
eight volumes in 1765 (Johnson having lost the list of subscribers who
had paid for it nine years earlier), is a notable advance on its
predecessors, those by Rowe, Pope, Hanmer, and Warburton. It is the
first 'variorum' edition, printing not only Johnson's own notes, but
those by earlier editors which he thinks useful to the interpretation of
a passage—as well as some he thinks are mistaken and should be
corrected. A few pages are given here in facsimile (p. 457), so that the
reader can see what is actually being done in it. The famous Preface
(p. 419) is perhaps Johnson's most beautifully written and memorable
piece of criticism. It has been argued that some of its doctrines, such
as the rejection of 'the unities' and of the distinction between the
genres of tragedy and comedy, are not so 'advanced' for the time as
used to be thought; though, as in *Ramblers* nos. 4 and 60, Johnson's
insistence on basing his critical principles on the psychology of
'reader' (or audience) 'response', unfashionable not so long ago, seems
to be becoming popular again. The best place to see 'Johnson's
criticism in action', a recent student maintains, is in the annotation—
the careful explication of Elizabethan language (not only was Johnson
the first editor of Shakespeare to have a historical dictionary of
English available: he had compiled it himself), and the record of his

own emotional responses to the plays and moving incidents in them. Space permits only a small sampling of it here (p. 462).

Only recently have students become aware of the large amount of time and energy Johnson spent in the 1760s helping Robert Chambers compose the course of lectures in the elements of English, or common, law he delivered to Oxford undergraduates. Johnson had come to know and befriend him when the seventeen-year-old Chambers came down from his native Newcastle to enrol as a law student in the Middle Temple (where Johnson was then living) and as an undergraduate at Lincoln College, Oxford. At Oxford he became a pupil of William Blackstone, the first holder of the chair of English law established by the will of Charles Viner, and at the age of twenty-nine was appointed to succeed Blackstone in that chair. Chambers, unnerved by the thought of competing with his formidable teacher (whose own Vinerian lectures began to be published in 1765, as his famous *Commentaries*), had great difficulty beginning to compose them, and called on Johnson for help, which was willingly given.

A manuscript of the series of fifty-six lectures written for George III, in the hands of professional scribes, was discovered only in the 1940s by the late E. L. McAdam in the British Museum, to which the King's library had been donated, and McAdam published some excerpts, which he thought were from Johnson's pen. The whole series, running to around 450,000 words, deserves to be published. It gives a lucid introduction to the common law, different in approach from Blackstone's but not unworthy of comparison with the *Commentaries*. The work is divided into four sections: an Introduction, dealing with general principles of jurisprudence; Public Law—i.e. the British constitution; Criminal Law; and Private (civil) Law, dealing chiefly with the law of property. What is given here (p. 570), printed in full for the first time, is the introductory lecture to the section on Criminal Law. The problem of distinguishing between Johnson's and Chambers's prose is perhaps harder than McAdam thought, but one recognizes Johnsonian ideas and expressions in the lecture.

Johnson's charming and poignant 'fairy tale' 'The Fountains' (p. 558), a kind of miniaturization of *Rasselas* or 'The Vanity of Human Wishes', was written for the volume of *Miscellanies*, 1766, which he organized for the benefit of the blind lady, Anna Williams, who shared his home.

1770–1784. In the 1770s Johnson demonstrated that the fire of his earlier diatribes against Walpole and the promoters of the Seven Years War was not extinguished, in four *Political Tracts* (collected under that title in 1776), in defence of various policies of the North administration. *The False Alarm*, 1770, ridiculed those who wished to make a major issue of the House of Commons's expulsion of John Wilkes; *Thoughts on the Late Transactions Respecting Falkland's Islands*, 1771, provided a clear historical account of the issue of sovereignty over the islands disputed between Britain and Spain (whose claim Argentina later took up), and a blistering condemnation of those who urged that the matter be settled by war rather than by the delicate diplomatic manoeuvres by which the ministry did in fact settle it (for the time being); *Taxation No Tyranny*, 1775, gave a closely reasoned legal and historical defence of the British claim, against the American revolutionaries, that Parliament had full power to legislate for British colonies. Given here (p. 580) is the shortest of them, *The Patriot*, written to assist his friend Henry Thrale's re-election as MP for Southwark, and to expose the falsity of his opponents' claim to 'patriotism' ('the last refuge of a scoundrel', as Johnson once memorably put it); in it the themes of the other pamphlets are repeated.

A Journey to the Western Islands of Scotland, 1775 (abridged, p. 593) gives a shrewdly and compassionately observed 'social anthropological' account of the little known Highland culture Johnson encountered on his memorable tour. An even more ambitious undertaking was the *Prefaces, Biographical and Critical, to the Works of the English Poets* that he wrote in his late sixties and early seventies for a syndicate of London booksellers, who planned their bulky anthology (sixty-eight volumes in all) of English poetry of around 1650 to 1750 in answer to what they thought a threat to their claim to copyright of it. They chose the poets to be anthologized, though Johnson got them to add James Thomson, Isaac Watts, and one or two others to the list. For the £300 they offered, they perhaps expected no more than the few perfunctory pages a modern publisher might expect from some 'celebrity' whom he commissions to write a preface to a reprint of an older work in hope of increasing the sales. Indeed, the short prefaces Johnson provided for the great majority of the poets in the list—most of them forgotten and forgettable, as the majority of fifty English poets drawn from any century would be—*are* fairly perfunctory, enlivened here and there by personal reminiscences, as when Johnson uses his preface to the works of Edmund 'Rag' Smith to pay a touching tribute to Gilbert Walmesley, who had befriended him when a boy, and to David Garrick, recently dead, who had shared Walmesley's hospitality. But the challenge of such major writers as Milton, Dryden, and Pope, or one like Cowley, who presented a special problem in the history of literary taste, impelled Johnson to provide long and important studies, which are still classics of literary criticism, inspiring the publishers to present him with an additional £100.

It is important to keep in mind that, apart from the reprinted *Life of Savage*, written thirty-five years earlier, they are *not* biographies pure and simple, even though Johnson called them 'my little Lives' and though the handy title *Lives of the Poets* (omitting the continuation 'and a Criticism on Their Works' which early editions carried) will probably continue to be used. In fact, the biographical parts of the prefaces have not worn so well as the critical. Later research on the lives of Milton, Swift, and Pope, say, has inevitably added to and corrected Johnson's sketches; and some of his most famous stories, such as that about Dryden's 'Cousin Swift, you will never be a poet', have been exploded. But they are always readable, and Johnson's psychological and moral judgements on the activities of his subjects are usually shrewd (admirers of Milton will of course disagree).

The dedicated student will not rest content without examining the whole collection. The sampling here includes, in full, one of the most satisfyingly organized of the longer prefaces, and one delightful for its abundance of dry, mildly satiric humour (even 'gay malevolence', in Johnson's phrase), as well as the vehicle for some of Johnson's most memorable critical dicta, 'Addison'. Its typical tripartite arrangement should be noted: a biographical narrative (pp. 643–62); a summing up, or 'character' of the subject (pp. 662–5); and a detailed critique of his writings (pp. 665–76). Also here is one of the best of the shorter prefaces, 'Collins'. In addition, there are the 'critical' sections (or significant parts of them) of 'Cowley', 'Milton', 'Dryden', 'Pope', 'Thomson', 'Watts', 'Gray', and 'Young'. The first twenty-four prefaces (including 'Cowley', 'Milton', and 'Dryden') were published in 1779, and the remaining twenty-eight in 1781.

Another late, often overlooked, critical statement (p. 588) is the preface to Thomas Maurice's translation of Sophocles' *Oedipus Tyrannus*. As Allen Hazen (who edited them) writes, although Carlyle called Johnson's letter to Chesterfield (p. 782) the 'blast of doom' to literary patronage, the many prefaces and dedications Johnson furnished (anonymously) for his less celebrated friends may have helped to keep the practice alive. The elegant dedication to George III of Charles Burney's *Account* of the great Handel festival in 1784 (p. 591) was probably the last thing Johnson wrote for publication.

In these late years Johnson also wrote some of his most effective poetry: the moving Latin poems (in the eighteenth century and earlier, poetic expressions of personal emotion often tended to be written in Latin rather than English) on the occasions of his extensive revision of the *Dictionary*, his visiting Skye, and revisiting the pool where his father had taught him to swim; the sardonic *carpe diem* poem addressed to Mrs Thrale's wastrel nephew, Sir John Lade; the poignant elegy on his old friend Levet (pp. 26–37).

Diaries and Letters (pp. 771–92). Only the briefest selection can be given here of Johnson's diary entries and of his letters. Although he made a holocaust of his private jottings before his death, enough has survived to fill a 400-page volume in the Yale edition of his *Works*. Given here are an excerpt from the too brief fragment of an autobiography, a few entries from the journals of his tours in Wales and France, and several of the 'meditations' (self-examinations such as Christians were recommended to undertake regularly) and prayers he composed at times of particular significance, usually New Year's Day, Holy Week, and his birthday.

Some 1,500 of Johnson's letters have survived. Their variety and interest have seldom been fully appreciated. Here are given his three famous denunciations, of Chesterfield, Macpherson, and Mrs Thrale, when she announced her second marriage to the Italian and Roman Catholic musician, Gabriel Piozzi. It is only fair to her to include her spirited reply to Johnson. There is an excerpt from one of the long letters to her from the Highlands—themselves almost a journal of the tour—which he drew on when composing the *Journey to the Western Islands*. There are some of the letters of fatherly advice and warning he wrote to young men such as Boswell and George Strahan, and a miscellany of others.

'To choose the best among many good is one of the most hazardous attempts of criticism': so Johnson wrote in his 'Preface' to Cowley, and every compiler of an anthology is keenly aware of the hazards. In this collection an attempt has been made to provide an adequate representation of the writings by which Johnson is traditionally best known: in full, 'London' and 'The Vanity of Human Wishes', the prefaces to the *Dictionary* and the edition of Shakespeare, the review of Soame Jenyns, *Rasselas*; and in substantial part, the periodical essays, the *Life of Savage*, the *Journey to the Western Islands of Scotland*, and the biographical and critical prefaces to the works of the English poets (*The Lives of the Poets*)—though the serious student will not be content with such excerpts, but will want to familiarize himself with the complete works.

Some readers, familiar only with these, may be alarmed at being urged to extend their Johnsonian horizons to include the fairly large sampling—though still only a fraction of the whole—of Johnson's hitherto less well-known writings, involving matters historical, scientific, bibliographical, legal, theological, political, about which, perhaps to their surprise, they will find Johnson highly knowledgeable, and on which he often held strong views, sometimes views by no means irrelevant today. But there is very little that Johnson ever wrote, on whatever subject, that does not furnish the reader with, as Johnson said of Bacon, 'the observations of a strong mind operating on life'. Edmund Wilson summed it up: 'That Johnson really was one of the best English writers of his time, that he deserved his great reputation, is a fact that we are likely to lose sight of.' If any have lost sight of it, or not yet become aware of it, this volume affords them an opportunity to verify Wilson's contention.

ACKNOWLEDGEMENTS

I am grateful to Arthur A. Houghton, Jr., for permission to print a Latin school exercise of Johnson's of which he owns the manuscript; to Mary Hyde, the British Library, the Bodleian Library, and Pembroke College, Oxford, for the opportunity at various times to consult manuscript material in their possession; to John Wain, sometime Professor of Poetry in the University of Oxford, for kindly undertaking an English verse translation of Johnson's Latin poem on Skye, and for permission to reprint earlier versions by him of two other Latin poems by Johnson; to J. M. Dent & Sons Ltd., for permission to reprint these poems from *Johnson on Johnson* in the Everyman's Library Series; to O M Brack, Jr., who has collaborated with me in editing various early prose pieces; to Thomas M. Curley for help with the Vinerian Lectures, which he is editing; to my colleague Paul K. Alkon for advice and encouragement; to my former students Gloria Sybil Gross and R. Barrie Walkley for valuable original insights into *Rasselas*; and to the far-flung community of Johnsonian scholars, centred on the *Johnsonian News Letter* and the Yale Edition of Johnson's Works, whose textual and interpretive contributions to modern Johnson scholarship I have drawn on so freely that space will not permit individual acknowledgements.

If a dedication were appropriate for such a volume as this, it would inevitably be to the memory of James Lowry Clifford, who did so much to create and sustain that community, and who, for all his fine work as a biographer of Johnson, always urged his pupils, 'Read *Johnson* before reading *about* him.'

D. G.

Los Angeles,
July 1983

POSTSCRIPT

This reprinting has afforded the opportunity to make a number of small amendments to the earlier impression, together with one not so small, the restoration to Chapter Two of *Rasselas* of three paragraphs that had been inadvertently transferred to Chapter Three; and to add my thanks for help in improving the quality of this edition to Professors Frank Kermode and John H. Middendorf of Columbia University and the vigilant editorial staff of the Oxford University Press. Two recent important Johnsonian publications should be mentioned: Joel J. Gold's fine edition of Johnson's translation and adaptation of Lobo's *Voyage to Abyssinia* (volume xv of the Yale Edition of Johnson's works), Yale University Press, 1985; and Thomas M. Curley's *editio princeps* of Sir Robert Chambers's (and Johnson's) Vinerian lectures, the successor to Blackstone's *Commentaries* (*A Course of Lectures on the English Law Delivered at the University of Oxford, 1767–1773*), Clarendon Press, Oxford, and the University of Wisconsin Press, 1986.

D. G.

Los Angeles,
April 1986

CHRONOLOGY

1709   Samuel Johnson born (7 September, OS; 18, NS) at Lichfield, Staffordshire.

1712   Taken to London to be touched by Queen Anne for 'the Evil' (scrofula). Nathanael Johnson (brother) born.

1717   Enters Lichfield Grammar School.

1726   Visits his cousin, the Revd Cornelius Ford, at Stourbridge, Worcestershire; attends school there.

1728   Enters Pembroke College, Oxford, in October; leaves December 1729.

1731   Michael Johnson (father) dies.

1732   Teaches for some months at Market Bosworth, Leicestershire.

1733   At Birmingham. Translates Lobo's *Voyage to Abyssinia* (published 1735).

1735   Marries Elizabeth Jervis (widow of Harry Porter, and mother of Jervis, Joseph, and Lucy Porter).

1736   Opens school at Edial, near Lichfield. Begins *Irene*.

1737   Nathanael Johnson dies. Moves to London (March) with David Garrick.

1738   Begins writing for *Gentleman's Magazine*. Publishes 'London', 'Life of Sarpi'; begins abortive translation of Sarpi's *History of the Council of Trent*.

1739   *Marmor Norfolciense*, *A Complete Vindication of the Licensers of the Stage* (anti-government pamphlets). 'Life of Boerhaave'; translation of Crousaz's *Commentary* on Pope's *Essay on Man*.

1740   Lives of Admiral Robert Blake, Sir Francis Drake, Jean-Philippe Barretier.

1741–4   'Life of Sydenham'. Contributions to *Harleian Miscellany* and catalogue of the Harleian library. 'Debates in the Senate of Lilliput' and other journalism for the *Gentleman's Magazine*. *Life of Savage*.

1745   Proposals (abortive) for an edition of Shakespeare. *Miscellaneous Observations on Macbeth*.

1746   Signs contract for *Dictionary*. Drafts *Plan of an English Dictionary* (published 1747, dedicated to Lord Chesterfield).

1749   'The Vanity of Human Wishes'. *Irene* performed and published.

1750   Forces William Lauder to withdraw his charge of plagiarism against Milton; prologue to *Comus* for benefit performance for Milton's granddaughter. Begins *The Rambler* (to 1752).

1752   Elizabeth ('Tetty') Johnson (wife) dies.

1753   Contributes to *The Adventurer*.

1755   Awarded honorary MA degree, Oxford. *Dictionary of the English Language* published.

1756   Edits *Literary Magazine*; contributes anti-war articles and much reviewing. Proposals for edition of Shakespeare to be published by subscription.

1758   Begins *The Idler* (to 1760).

1759   Sarah Johnson (mother) dies. *Rasselas*.

1762   Awarded annual pension of £300 by government.

1763   Meets James Boswell.

1765   Edition of Shakespeare published. Meets Mr and Mrs Henry Thrale. Honorary LL D, Trinity College, Dublin.

1766   Begins to assist Robert Chambers with Vinerian lectures on English law at Oxford. Severe depression; recovers with help of Mrs Thrale.

1770   *The False Alarm*.

1771   *Thoughts on Falkland's Islands*.

1773   Revised editions of *Dictionary* and Shakespeare published. Tours Scotland (August to November) with Boswell.

1774   Tours Wales with the Thrales. *The Patriot*.

1775   *Journey to the Western Islands of Scotland*. *Taxation No Tyranny*. Honorary DCL, Oxford. Visits France with the Thrales.

1777   Agreement with booksellers to write prefaces to works of English poets (*The Lives of the Poets*). Unsuccessful campaign to reprieve the Revd William Dodd, condemned to be hanged for forgery.

1779   First four volumes of *Prefaces* published.

1781   Henry Thrale dies. Last six volumes of *Prefaces* published.

1782   'On the Death of Dr Robert Levet'.

1783   Stroke, temporary loss of speech. Recovers; during winter of 1783–4 ill and depressed.

1784   Religious 'conversion', February. Hester Thrale marries Gabriel Piozzi. Dedication of Burney's *Account* of Handel festival. Dies 13 December. Buried in Westminster Abbey, 20 December.

NOTE ON THE TEXT

FOR the great majority of the shorter pieces in this volume, only one textual authority exists, their first printing. For much of his journalism Johnson probably did not have the opportunity to read proof, and the received text sometimes contains obvious errors, some clearly resulting from misreadings of Johnson's difficult hand. An attempt has been made here to correct them. Two pieces, the excerpt from the Chambers/Johnson Vinerian Lectures and the Latin school exercise, are here printed from manuscript.

Longer works which ran into more than one edition in Johnson's lifetime were sometimes extensively revised by him. The present editor acknowledges his indebtedness to the many scholars who have worked on the text of these, and has profited greatly from their editions, although he has sometimes been more conservative than some of them about attributing a variant reading to Johnson rather than to his printers. Of these texts, the editions principally relied on (though compared with others) are

'London'. Dodsley's *Collection of Poems*, 1748
'The Vanity of Human Wishes'. Dodsley's *Collection*, 1755
Life of Savage. 2nd edn., 1748
The Rambler. 4th (3rd collected) edn., 1756
The Adventurer. 2nd edn., 1754
The Idler. 2nd (1st collected) edn., 1761
Preface to *Dictionary*. 2nd edn., 1756
Rasselas. 2nd edn., 1759
Preface to Shakespeare. 4th edn., 1773
The Patriot. Political Tracts, 1776
Journey to the Western Islands. 1st edn. (with errata), 1775

Much textual study still needs to be done on the *Prefaces, Biographical and Critical* (*Lives of the Poets*). The text here follows that of G. Birkbeck Hill's edition of 1905, based, we are told, on the four-volume octavo edition of 1783. The text of the letters follows that of R. W. Chapman's edition, 1952. Both these editions are published by the Oxford University Press.

Generally the text has been modernized in spelling, punctuation, and the use of capital letters and italics (an exception has been made for the diary entries and letters, where Johnson's use of capitals has been preserved). But the occasional variant spelling, still in use, has been left unchanged. Johnson and his printers often used italics instead of inverted commas to indicate quoted material; the italics may add a nuance of emphasis that was perhaps intended, and have sometimes been preserved here. Long quotations have been printed in block form in smaller type. The use of commas in Johnson's time was highly erratic, and Johnson's printers were more lavish in their use of them than, to judge from his manuscripts, was Johnson himself. Many of them have been removed, especially when, contrary to modern usage, they set off a restrictive modifier, or intervene between a verb and its subject or object, practices that could mislead the modern reader.

The degree sign (°) indicates a note at the end of the book.

NOTE ON DICTION

Johnson's writings, like those of other eighteenth-century writers, have suffered from those who have read important words in his vocabulary in their twentieth-century instead of their eighteenth-century senses. A handful of such misreadings to beware of:

candour means, not *frankness*, but *good will, kindness*
discover, often not *find*, but *reveal, disclose*
disgusting, not *repulsive*, but *distasteful, boring*
eat (pronounced *et*) is often the past tense (now *ate*)
enthusiastic still has much of the (hostile) theological sense of someone
    pretending to speak with special divine inspiration
general, in Johnson's criticism, often not *abstract*, but *widely
    recognizable*
great, often *of high rank, powerful*, rather than *excellent*
meat, not necessarily *flesh*, but *food in general*
nature, in Johnson's criticism, often *reality*
prevalent, not *widespread*, but *predominating*
sentiments, not *feelings*, but *thoughts*
still, not *however*, but *always, continually*
vulgar, not *coarsely low*, but *commonplace*
want, not *desire*, but *lack*

Translation of Horace, *Odes*, ii. 20

Now with no weak unballast wing
    A poet double-formed I rise;
From th' envious world with scorn I spring,
    And cut with joy the wond'ring skies.

Though from no princes I descend,
    Yet shall I see the blest abodes,
Yet, great Maecenas, shall your friend
    Quaff nectar with th' immortal Gods.

See! how the mighty change is wrought!
    See how whate'er remained of man   10
By plumes is veiled; see! quick as thought
    I pierce the clouds a tuneful swan.

Swifter than Icarus I'll fly
    Where Lybia's swarthy offspring burns,
And where beneath th' inclement sky
    The hardy Scythian ever mourns.

My works shall propagate my fame,
    To distant realms and climes unknown,
Nations shall celebrate my name
    That drink the Phasis or the Rhone.   20

Restrain your tears and cease your cries,
    Nor grace with fading flowers my hearse;
I without funeral elegies
    Shall live for ever in my verse.

London

A POEM IN IMITATION OF JUVENAL'S THIRD SATIRE

Quis ineptae
Tam patiens urbis, tam ferreus ut teneat se?

JUVENAL

Though grief and fondness in my breast rebel,
When injured Thales bids the town farewell,°
Yet still my calmer thoughts his choice commend,
I praise the hermit, but regret the friend,
Resolved at length, from vice and London far,
To breathe in distant fields a purer air,
And, fixed on Cambria's solitary shore,
Give to St David one true Briton more.

For who would leave, unbribed, Hibernia's land,
Or change the rocks of Scotland for the Strand?   10
There none are swept by sudden fate away,
But all whom hunger spares, with age decay:
Here malice, rapine, accident, conspire,
And now a rabble rages, now a fire;
Their ambush here relentless ruffians lay,
And here the fell attorney prowls for prey;
Here falling houses thunder on your head,
And here a female atheist talks you dead.

While Thales waits the wherry that contains
Of dissipated wealth the small remains,   20
On Thames's banks, in silent thought we stood,
Where Greenwich smiles upon the silver flood:
Struck with the seat that gave Eliza birth,°
We kneel, and kiss the consecrated earth;
In pleasing dreams the blissful age renew,
And call Britannia's glories back to view;
Behold her cross triumphant on the main,
The guard of commerce, and the dread of Spain,
Ere masquerades debauched, excise oppressed,
Or English honour grew a standing jest.°   30

A transient calm the happy scenes bestow,
And for a moment lull the sense of woe.

At length awaking, with contemptuous frown,
Indignant Thales eyes the neighbouring town.
　Since worth, he cries, in these degenerate days,
Wants ev'n the cheap reward of empty praise;
In those curs'd walls, devote to vice and gain,
Since unrewarded Science toils in vain;
Since hope but soothes to double my distress,
And every moment leaves my little less;　　　　　40
While yet my steady steps no staff sustains,
And life still vigorous revels in my veins;
Grant me, kind heaven, to find some happier place,
Where honesty and sense are no disgrace;
Some pleasing bank where verdant osiers play,
Some peaceful vale with nature's paintings gay;
Where once the harassed Briton found repose,
And safe in poverty defied his foes;
Some secret cell, ye powers, indulgent give.
Let —— live here, for —— has learned to live.°　50
Here let those reign, whom pensions can incite
To vote a patriot black, a courtier white;
Explain their country's dear-bought rights away,
And plead for pirates in the face of day;
With slavish tenets taint our poisoned youth,
And lend a lie the confidence of truth.
　Let such raise palaces, and manors buy,
Collect a tax, or farm a lottery,
With warbling eunuchs fill a licensed stage,°
And lull to servitude a thoughtless age.　　　　　60
　Heroes, proceed! what bounds your pride shall hold?
What check restrain your thirst of power and gold?
Behold rebellious virtue quite o'erthrown,
Behold our fame, our wealth, our lives your own.
　To such, a groaning nation's spoils are giv'n,
When public crimes inflame the wrath of heav'n:
But what, my friend, what hope remains for me,
Who start at theft, and blush at perjury?
Who scarce forbear, though Britain's Court he sing,
To pluck a titled poet's borrowed wing;　　　　　70
A statesman's logic unconvinced can hear,
And dare to slumber o'er the *Gazetteer*;°
Despise a fool in half his pension dressed,

And strive in vain to laugh at H——y's jest.°
  Others with softer smiles, and subtler art,
Can sap the principles, or taint the heart;
With more address a lover's note convey,
Or bribe a virgin's innocence away.
Well may they rise, while I, whose rustic tongue
Ne'er knew to puzzle right, or varnish wrong,   80
Spurned as a beggar, dreaded as a spy,
Live unregarded, unlamented die.
  For what but social guilt the friend endears?
Who shares Orgilio's crimes, his fortune shares.
But thou, should tempting villainy present
All Marlborough hoarded, or all Villiers spent,°
Turn from the glittering bribe thy scornful eye,
Nor sell for gold, what gold could never buy,
The peaceful slumber, self-approving day,
Unsullied fame, and conscience ever gay.   90
  The cheated nation's happy fav'rites, see!
Mark whom the great caress, who frown on me!
London! the needy villain's general home,
The common shore of Paris and of Rome,°
With eager thirst, by folly or by fate,
Sucks in the dregs of each corrupted state.
Forgive my transports on a theme like this,
I cannot bear a French metropolis.
  Illustrious Edward! from the realms of day,
The land of heroes and of saints survey;   100
Nor hope the British lineaments to trace,
The rustic grandeur, or the surly grace,
But lost in thoughtless ease, and empty show,
Behold the warrior dwindled to a beau;
Sense, freedom, piety, refined away,
Of France the mimic, and of Spain the prey.
  All that at home no more can beg or steal,
Or like a gibbet better than a wheel;
Hissed from the stage, or hooted from the court,
Their air, their dress, their politics import;   110
Obsequious, artful, voluble, and gay,
On Britain's fond credulity they prey.
No gainful trade their industry can 'scape,
They sing, they dance, clean shoes, or cure a clap;

All sciences a fasting Monsieur knows,
And bid him go to hell, to hell he goes.

   Ah! what avails it, that, from slavery far,
I drew the breath of life in English air;
Was early taught a Briton's right to prize,
And lisp the tale of Henry's victories,   120
If the gulled conqueror receives the chain,
And flattery subdues when arms are vain?

   Studious to please, and ready to submit,
The supple Gaul was born a parasite:
Still to his interest true, where'er he goes,
Wit, bravery, worth, his lavish tongue bestows;
In every face a thousand graces shine,
From every tongue flows harmony divine.
These arts in vain our rugged natives try, ⎫
Strain out with faltering diffidence a lie, ⎬   130
And get a kick for awkward flattery. ⎭

   Besides, with justice, this discerning age
Admires their wondrous talents for the stage:
Well may they venture on the mimic's art,
Who play from morn to night a borrowed part;
Practised their master's notions to embrace,
Repeat his maxims, and reflect his face;
With every wild absurdity comply,
And view each object with another's eye;
To shake with laughter ere the jest they hear,   140
To pour at will the counterfeited tear,
And as their patron hints the cold or heat,
To shake in dog-days, in December sweat.

   How, when competitors like these contend,
Can surly virtue hope to fix a friend?
Slaves that with serious impudence beguile,
And lie without a blush, without a smile;
Exalt each trifle, every vice adore,
Your taste in snuff, your judgment in a whore;
Can Balbo's eloquence applaud, and swear   150
He gropes his breeches with a monarch's air.

   For arts like these preferred, admired, caressed,
They first invade your table, then your breast;
Explore your secrets with insidious art,
Watch the weak hour, and ransack all the heart;

Then soon your ill-placed confidence repay,
Commence your lords, and govern or betray.
  By numbers here from shame or censure free,
All crimes are safe, but hated poverty.
This, only this, the rigid law pursues,   160
This, only this, provokes the snarling muse.
The sober trader at a tattered cloak,
Wakes from his dream, and labours for a joke;
With brisker air the silken courtiers gaze,
And turn the varied taunt a thousand ways.
Of all the griefs that harass the distressed,
Sure the most bitter is a scornful jest;
Fate never wounds more deep the generous heart
Than when a blockhead's insult points the dart.
  Has heaven reserved, in pity to the poor,   170
No pathless waste, or undiscovered shore;
No secret island in the boundless main?
No peaceful desert yet unclaimed by Spain?
Quick let us rise, the happy seats explore,
And bear oppression's insolence no more.
This mournful truth is everywhere confessed,
SLOW RISES WORTH, BY POVERTY DEPRESSED:
But here more slow, where all are slaves to gold,
Where looks are merchandise, and smiles are sold;
Where won by bribes, by flatteries implored,   180
The groom retails the favours of his lord.
  But hark! th' affrighted crowd's tumultuous cries
Roll through the streets, and thunder to the skies;
Raised from some pleasing dream of wealth and power,
Some pompous palace, or some blissful bower,
Aghast you start, and scarce with aching sight
Sustain th' approaching fire's tremendous light;
Swift from pursuing horrors take your way,
And leave your little ALL to flames a prey;
Then through the world a wretched vagrant roam,   190
For where can starving merit find a home?
In vain your mournful narrative disclose,
While all neglect, and most insult your woes.
  Should heaven's just bolts Orgilio's wealth confound,
And spread his flaming palace on the ground,
Swift o'er the land the dismal rumour flies,

And public mournings pacify the skies;
The laureate tribe in servile verse relate,
How virtue wars with persecuting fate;
With well-feigned gratitude the pensioned band   200
Refund the plunder of the beggared land.
See! while he builds, the gaudy vassals come,
And crowd with sudden wealth the rising dome;
The price of boroughs and of souls restore,
And raise his treasures higher than before.
Now blessed with all the baubles of the great,
The polished marble, and the shining plate,
Orgilio sees the golden pile aspire,
And hopes from angry heav'n another fire.

Couldst thou resign the park and play content,   210
For the fair banks of Severn or of Trent;
There might'st thou find some elegant retreat,
Some hireling senator's deserted seat;°
And stretch thy prospects o'er the smiling land,
For less than rent the dungeons of the Strand;
There prune thy walks, support thy drooping flowers,
Direct thy rivulets, and twine thy bowers;
And, while thy grounds a cheap repast afford,
Despise the dainties of a venal lord:
There every bush with nature's music rings,   220
There every breeze bears health upon its wings;
On all thy hours security shall smile,
And bless thine evening walk and morning toil.

Prepare for death, if here at night you roam,
And sign your will before you sup from home.
Some fiery fop, with new commission vain,
Who sleeps on brambles till he kills his man;
Some frolic drunkard, reeling from a feast,
Provokes a broil, and stabs you for a jest.
Yet ev'n these heroes, mischievously gay,   230
Lords of the street, and terrors of the way,
Flushed as they are with folly, youth, and wine,
Their prudent insults to the poor confine;
Afar they mark the flambeau's bright approach,
And shun the shining train, and golden coach.

In vain, these dangers past, your doors you close,
And hope the balmy blessings of repose:

Cruel with guilt, and daring with despair,
The midnight murderer bursts the faithless bar;
Invades the sacred hour of silent rest,   240
And leaves, unseen, a dagger in your breast.

Scarce can our fields, such crowds at Tyburn die,
With hemp the gallows and the fleet supply.
Propose your schemes, ye Senatorian band,
Whose Ways and Means support the sinking land;°
Lest ropes be wanting in the tempting spring,
To rig another convoy for the K—g.

A single jail, in Alfred's golden reign,
Could half the nation's criminals contain;
Fair justice then, without constraint adored,   250
Held high the steady scale, but dropped the sword;
No spies were paid, no special juries known,°
Blest age! but ah! how different from our own!

Much could I add,—but see the boat at hand,
The tide retiring, calls me from the land:
Farewell!—When youth, and health, and fortune spent,
Thou fly'st for refuge to the wilds of Kent;
And tired like me with follies and with crimes,
In angry numbers warn'st succeeding times;
Then shall thy friend, nor thou refuse his aid,   260
Still foe to vice, forsake his Cambrian shade;
In virtue's cause once more exert his rage,
Thy satire point, and animate thy page.

Prologue to Garrick's *Lethe*

Prodigious madness of the writing race!
Ardent of fame, yet fearless of disgrace.
Without a boding tear, or anxious sigh,
The bard obdurate sees his brother die.
Deaf to the critic, sullen to the friend,
Not one takes warning by another's end.
Oft has our bard in this disastrous year
Beheld the tragic heroes taught to fear.
Oft has he seen the poignant orange fly,
And heard th'ill-omened catcall's direful cry.   10

Yet dares to venture on the dangerous stage
And weakly hopes to 'scape the critic's rage.
This night he hopes to show that farce may charm,
Though no lewd hint the mantling virgin warm,
That useful truth with humour may unite.
That mirth may mend, and innocence delight.

Epitaph on Claudy Phillips, a Musician

Phillips! whose touch harmonious could remove
The pangs of guilty power, and hapless love,
Rest here, distressed by poverty no more,
Find here that calm thou gav'st so oft before;
Sleep undisturbed within this peaceful shrine,
Till angels wake thee with a note like thine.

On Colley Cibber°

Augustus still survives in Maro's strain,
And Spenser's verse prolongs Eliza's reign;
Great George's acts let tuneful Cibber sing,
For Nature formed the poet for the King.

To Miss —— On Her Playing upon the Harpsichord

IN A ROOM HUNG WITH SOME FLOWER-PIECES OF HER OWN PAINTING

When Stella strikes the tuneful string
In scenes of imitated spring,
Where beauty lavishes her powers
On beds of never-fading flowers,
And pleasure propagates around
Each charm of modulated sound,
Ah! think not, in the dangerous hour,
The nymph fictitious, as the flower,
But shun, rash youth, the gay alcove,
Nor tempt the snares of wily love.

10

When charms thus press on every sense,
What thought of flight, or of defence?
Deceitful Hope, and vain Desire,
For ever flutter o'er her lyre,
Delighting, as the youth draws nigh,
To point the glances of her eye,
And forming, with unerring art,
New chains to hold the captive heart.
    But on these regions of delight,
Might Truth intrude with daring flight,   20
Could Stella, sprightly, fair and young,
One moment hear the moral song,
Instruction with her flowers might spring,
And wisdom warble from her string.
    Mark, when from thousand mingled dyes
Thou see'st one pleasing form arise,
How active light, and thoughtful shade,
In greater scenes each other aid;
Mark, when the different notes agree
In friendly contrariety,   30
How passion's well-accorded strife
Gives all the harmony of life.
Thy pictures shall thy conduct frame,
Consistent still, though not the same;
Thy music teach the nobler art
To tune the regulated heart.

Prologue°

SPOKEN AT THE OPENING OF THE THEATRE IN DRURY LANE

When Learning's triumph o'er her barbarous foes
First reared the stage, immortal SHAKESPEAR rose;
Each change of many-coloured life he drew,
Exhausted worlds, and then imagined new:
Existence saw him spurn her bounded reign,
And panting Time toiled after him in vain:
His powerful strokes presiding truth impressed,
And unresisted Passion stormed the breast.
    Then JONSON came, instructed from the school,

To please in method, and invent by rule; 10
His studious patience and laborious art,
By regular approach essayed the heart;
Cold Approbation gave the lingering bays,
For those who durst not censure, scarce could praise.
A mortal born he met the general doom,
But left, like Egypt's kings, a lasting tomb.

The wits of Charles found easier ways to fame,
Nor wished for Jonson's art, or Shakespear's flame;
Themselves they studied, as they felt, they writ,
Intrigue was plot, obscenity was wit. 20
Vice always found a sympathetic friend;
They pleased their age, and did not aim to mend.
Yet bards like these aspired to lasting praise,
And proudly hoped to pimp in future days.
Their cause was gen'ral, their supports were strong,
Their slaves were willing, and their reign was long;
Till Shame regained the post that Sense betrayed,
And Virtue called Oblivion to her aid.

Then crushed by rules, and weakened as refined,
For years the power of Tragedy declined; 30
From bard to bard, the frigid caution crept,
Till Declamation roared, while Passion slept.
Yet still did Virtue deign the stage to tread,
Philosophy remained, though Nature fled.
But forced at length her ancient reign to quit,
She saw great Faustus lay the ghost of wit:°
Exulting Folly hailed the joyful day,
And pantomime, and song, confirmed her sway.
But who the coming changes can presage,
And mark the future periods of the stage?— 40
Perhaps if skill could distant times explore,
New Behns, new Durfeys yet remain in store.
Perhaps, where Lear has raved, and Hamlet died,
On flying cars new sorcerers may ride.
Perhaps, for who can guess th' effects of chance?
Here Hunt may box, or Mahomet may dance.°

Hard is his lot that here by fortune placed
Must watch the wild vicissitudes of taste;
With every meteor of caprice must play,
And chase the new-blown bubbles of the day. 50

Ah! let not censure term our fate our choice,
The stage but echoes back the public voice.
The drama's laws the drama's patrons give,
For we that live to please, must please to live.
 Then prompt no more the follies you decry,
As tyrants doom their tools of guilt to die;
'Tis yours this night to bid the reign commence
Of rescued Nature, and reviving Sense:
To chase the charms of sound, the pomp of show,
For useful mirth, and salutary woe;   60
Bid scenic Virtue form the rising age,
And Truth diffuse her radiance from the stage.

The Vanity of Human Wishes

THE TENTH SATIRE OF JUVENAL IMITATED

Let observation with extensive view,
Survey mankind, from China to Peru;°
Remark each anxious toil, each eager strife,
And watch the busy scenes of crowded life;
Then say how hope and fear, desire and hate,
O'erspread with snares the clouded maze of fate,
Where wavering man, betrayed by venturous pride,
To tread the dreary paths without a guide,
As treacherous phantoms in the mist delude,
Shuns fancied ills, or chases airy good: 10
How rarely reason guides the stubborn choice,
Rules the bold hand, or prompts the suppliant voice;
How nations sink, by darling schemes oppressed,
When Vengeance listens to the fool's request.
Fate wings with every wish th' afflictive dart,°
Each gift of nature, and each grace of art,
With fatal heat impetuous courage glows,
With fatal sweetness elocution flows,
Impeachment stops the speaker's powerful breath,
And restless fire precipitates on death.°   20
 But scarce observed, the knowing and the bold
Fall in the general massacre of gold;

Wide-wasting pest! that rages unconfined,
And crowds with crimes the records of mankind;
For gold his sword the hireling ruffian draws,
For gold the hireling judge distorts the laws;
Wealth heaped on wealth, nor truth nor safety buys,
The dangers gather as the treasures rise.

Let history tell where rival kings command,
And dubious title shakes the madded land,   30
When statutes glean the refuse of the sword,
How much more safe the vassal than the lord;
Low skulks the hind beneath the rage of power,
And leaves the wealthy traitor in the Tower,
Untouched his cottage, and his slumbers sound,
Though confiscation's vultures hover round.

The needy traveler, serene and gay,
Walks the wild heath, and sings his toil away.
Does envy seize thee? crush th' upbraiding joy,
Increase his riches and his peace destroy;   40
Now fears in dire vicissitude invade,
The rustling brake alarms, and quivering shade,
Nor light nor darkness bring his pain relief,
One shows the plunder, and one hides the thief.

Yet still one general cry the skies assails,
And gain and grandeur load the tainted gales;
Few know the toiling statesman's fear or care,
Th' insidious rival and the gaping heir.

Once more, Democritus, arise on earth,°
With cheerful wisdom and instructive mirth,   50
See motley life in modern trappings dressed,
And feed with varied fools th' eternal jest:
Thou who couldst laugh where want enchained caprice,
Toil crushed conceit, and man was of a piece;
Where wealth unloved without a mourner died,
And scarce a sycophant was fed by pride;
Where ne'er was known the form of mock debate,
Or seen a new-made mayor's unwieldy state;
Where change of favourites made no change of laws,
And senates heard before they judged a cause;   60
How wouldst thou shake at Britain's modish tribe,
Dart the quick taunt, and edge the piercing gibe!
Attentive truth and nature to descry,

And pierce each scene with philosophic eye.
To thee were solemn toys or empty show,
The robes of pleasure and the veils of woe:
All aid the farce, and all thy mirth maintain,
Whose joys are causeless, or whose griefs are vain.

Such was the scorn that filled the sage's mind,
Renewed at every glance on humankind;   70
How just that scorn ere yet thy voice declare,
Search every state, and canvass every prayer.

Unnumbered suppliants crowd Preferment's gate,
Athirst for wealth, and burning to be great;
Delusive Fortune hears th' incessant call,
They mount, they shine, evaporate, and fall.°
On every stage the foes of peace attend,
Hate dogs their flight, and insult mocks their end.
Love ends with hope, the sinking statesman's door
Pours in the morning worshipper no more: 80
For growing names the weekly scribbler lies,
To growing wealth the dedicator flies,
From every room descends the painted face,
That hung the bright Palladium of the place,°
And smoked in kitchens, or in auctions sold,
To better features yields the frame of gold:
For now no more we trace in every line
Heroic worth, benevolence divine:
The form distorted justifies the fall,
And detestation rids th' indignant wall.   90

But will not Britain hear the last appeal,
Sign her foes' doom, or guard her favourites' zeal?
Through Freedom's sons no more remonstrance rings,
Degrading nobles and controlling kings;
Our supple tribes repress their patriot throats,
And ask no questions but the price of votes:
With weekly libels and septennial ale,°
Their wish is full to riot and to rail.

In full-blown dignity, see Wolsey stand,°
Law in his voice, and fortune in his hand: 100
To him the church, the realm, their powers consign,
Through him the rays of regal bounty shine,
Turned by his nod the stream of honour flows,
His smile alone security bestows:

Still to new heights his restless wishes tower,
Claim leads to claim, and power advances power;
Till conquest unresisted ceased to please,
And rights submitted, left him none to seize.
At length his sovereign frowns—the train of state
Mark the keen glance, and watch the sign to hate.   110
Where'er he turns he meets a stranger's eye,
His suppliants scorn him, and his followers fly;
At once is lost the pride of aweful state,
The golden canopy, the glittering plate,
The regal palace, the luxurious board,
The liveried army, and the menial lord.
With age, with cares, with maladies oppressed,
He seeks the refuge of monastic rest.
Grief aids disease, remembered folly stings,
And his last sighs reproach the faith of kings.   120
    Speak thou, whose thoughts at humble peace repine,
Shall Wolsey's wealth, with Wolsey's end be thine?
Or liv'st thou now, with safer pride content,
The wisest justice on the banks of Trent?°
For why did Wolsey near the steeps of fate,
On weak foundations raise th' enormous weight?
Why but to sink beneath misfortune's blow,
With louder ruin to the gulfs below?
    What gave great Villiers to th' assassin's knife,°
And fixed disease on Harley's closing life?   130
What murdered Wentworth, and what exiled Hyde,
By kings protected, and to kings allied?
What but their wish indulged in courts to shine,
And power too great to keep, or to resign?
    When first the college rolls receive his name,
The young enthusiast quits his ease for fame;
Through all his veins the fever of renown
Burns from the strong contagion of the gown;
O'er Bodley's dome his future labours spread,°
And Bacon's mansion trembles o'er his head.   140
Are these thy views? proceed, illustrious youth,
And Virtue guard thee to the throne of Truth!
Yet should thy soul indulge the generous heat,
Till captive Science yields her last retreat;
Should Reason guide thee with her brightest ray,

And pour on misty Doubt resistless day;
Should no false Kindness lure to loose delight,
Nor Praise relax, nor Difficulty fright;
Should tempting Novelty thy cell refrain,
And Sloth effuse her opiate fumes in vain;   150
Should Beauty blunt on fops her fatal dart,
Nor claim the triumph of a lettered heart;
Should no disease thy torpid veins invade,
Nor Melancholy's phantoms haunt thy shade;
Yet hope not life from grief or danger free,
Nor think the doom of man reversed for thee:
Deign on the passing world to turn thine eyes,
And pause awhile from letters, to be wise;
There mark what ills the scholar's life assail,
Toil, envy, want, the patron, and the jail.°   160
See nations slowly wise, and meanly just,
To buried merit raise the tardy bust.
If dreams yet flatter, once again attend,
Hear Lydiat's life, and Galileo's end.°

    Nor deem, when learning her last prize bestows,
The glittering eminence exempt from foes;
See when the vulgar 'scape, despised or awed,
Rebellion's vengeful talons seize on Laud.°
From meaner minds, though smaller fines content,
The plundered palace or sequestered rent;   170
Marked out by dangerous parts he meets the shock,
And fatal Learning leads him to the block:
Around his tomb let Art and Genius weep,
But hear his death, ye blockheads, hear and sleep.

    The festal blazes, the triumphal show,
The ravished standard, and the captive foe,
The senate's thanks, the gazette's pompous tale,
With force resistless o'er the brave prevail.
Such bribes the rapid Greek o'er Asia whirled,°
For such the steady Romans shook the world;   180
For such in distant lands the Britons shine,
And stain with blood the Danube or the Rhine;
This power has praise, that virtue scarce can warm,
Till fame supplies the universal charm.
Yet Reason frowns on war's unequal game,
Where wasted nations raise a single name,

And mortgaged states their grandsires' wreaths regret,
From age to age in everlasting debt;
Wreaths which at last the dear-bought right convey
To rust on medals, or on stones decay. 190
    On what foundation stands the warrior's pride,
How just his hopes let Swedish Charles decide;°
A frame of adamant, a soul of fire,
No dangers fright him, and no labours tire;
O'er love, o'er fear, extends his wide domain,
Unconquered lord of pleasure and of pain;
No joys to him pacific scepters yield,
War sounds the trump, he rushes to the field;
Behold surrounding kings their power combine,
And one capitulate, and one resign; 200
Peace courts his hand, but spreads her charms in vain;
'Think nothing gained,' he cries, 'till nought remain,
'On Moscow's walls till Gothic standards fly,°
'And all be mine beneath the polar sky.'
The march begins in military state,
And nations on his eye suspended wait;
Stern Famine guards the solitary coast,
And Winter barricades the realms of Frost;
He comes, not want and cold his course delay;—
Hide, blushing Glory, hide Pultowa's day: 210
The vanquished hero leaves his broken bands,
And shows his miseries in distant lands;
Condemned a needy supplicant to wait,
While ladies interpose, and slaves debate.°
But did not Chance at length her error mend?
Did no subverted empire mark his end?
Did rival monarchs give the fatal wound?
Or hostile millions press him to the ground?
His fall was destined to a barren strand,
A petty fortress, and a dubious hand;° 220
He left the name, at which the world grew pale,
To point a moral, or adorn a tale.
    All times their scenes of pompous woes afford,
From Persia's tyrant to Bavaria's lord.°
In gay hostility, and barbarous pride,
With half mankind embattled at his side,
Great Xerxes comes to seize the certain prey,

And starves exhausted regions in his way;
Attendant Flattery counts his myriads o'er,
Till counted myriads soothe his pride no more;   230
Fresh praise is tried till madness fires his mind,
The waves he lashes, and enchains the wind;°
New powers are claimed, new powers are still bestowed,
Till rude resistance lops the spreading god;
The daring Greeks deride the martial show,
And heap their valleys with the gaudy foe;
Th' insulted sea with humbler thoughts he gains,
A single skiff to speed his flight remains;
Th' incumbered oar scarce leaves the dreaded coast°
Through purple billows and a floating host.   240

    The bold Bavarian in a luckless hour,
Tries the dread summits of Caesarean power,
With unexpected legions bursts away,
And sees defenceless realms receive his sway;
Short sway! fair Austria spreads her mournful charms,°
The queen, the beauty, sets the world in arms;
From hill to hill the beacon's rousing blaze
Spreads wide the hope of plunder and of praise;
The fierce Croatian, and the wild Hussar,°
And all the sons of ravage crowd the war;   250
The baffled prince in honour's flattering bloom
Of hasty greatness finds the fatal doom,
His foes' derision, and his subjects' blame,
And steals to death from anguish and from shame.

    Enlarge my life with multitude of days,
In health, in sickness, thus the suppliant prays;
Hides from himself his state, and shuns to know
That life protracted is protracted woe.
Time hovers o'er, impatient to destroy,
And shuts up all the passages of joy: 260
In vain their gifts the bounteous seasons pour,
The fruit autumnal, and the vernal flower,
With listless eyes the dotard views the store,
He views, and wonders that they please no more;
Now pall the tasteless meats and joyless wines,
And Luxury with sighs her slave resigns.
Approach, ye minstrels, try the soothing strain,
Diffuse the tuneful lenitives of pain:

No sounds, alas, would touch th' impervious ear,
Though dancing mountains witnessed Orpheus near; 270
Nor lute nor lyre his feeble powers attend,
Nor sweeter music of a virtuous friend,
But everlasting dictates crowd his tongue,
Perversely grave, or positively wrong.
The still returning tale, and lingering jest,
Perplex the fawning niece and pampered guest,
While growing hopes scarce awe the gathering sneer,
And scarce a legacy can bribe to hear;
The watchful guests still hint the last offence,
The daughter's petulance, the son's expense, 280
Improve his heady rage with treacherous skill,
And mould his passions till they make his will.

Unnumbered maladies his joints invade,
Lay siege to life and press the dire blockade;
But unextinguished avarice still remains,
And dreaded losses aggravate his pains;
He turns, with anxious heart and crippled hands,
His bonds of debt, and mortgages of lands;
Or views his coffers with suspicious eyes,
Unlocks his gold, and counts it till he dies. 290

But grant the virtues of a temperate prime,
Bless with an age exempt from scorn or crime;
An age that melts with unperceived decay,
And glides in modest innocence away;
Whose peaceful day Benevolence endears,
Whose night congratulating Conscience cheers;
The general fav'rite as the general friend:
Such age there is, and who shall wish its end?

Yet even on this her load Misfortune flings,
To press the weary minutes' flagging wings: 300
New sorrow rises as the day returns,
A sister sickens, or a daughter mourns.
Now kindred Merit fills the sable bier,
Now lacerated Friendship claims a tear.
Year chases year, decay pursues decay,
Still drops some joy from withering life away;
New forms arise, and different views engage,
Superfluous lags the veteran on the stage,
Till pitying Nature signs the last release,

And bids afflicted worth retire to peace.   310
    But few there are whom hours like these await,
Who set unclouded in the gulfs of Fate.
From Lydia's monarch should the search descend,°
By Solon cautioned to regard his end,
In life's last scene what prodigies surprise,
Fears of the brave, and follies of the wise?
From Marlborough's eyes the streams of dotage flow,°
And Swift expires a driveller and a show.
    The teeming mother, anxious for her race,°
Begs for each birth the fortune of a face: 320
Yet Vane could tell what ills from beauty spring;°
And Sedley cursed the form that pleased a king.
Ye nymphs of rosy lips and radiant eyes,
Whom pleasure keeps too busy to be wise,
Whom joys with soft varieties invite,
By day the frolic, and the dance by night,
Who frown with vanity, who smile with art,
And ask the latest fashion of the heart,
What care, what rules your heedless charms shall save,
Each nymph your rival, and each youth your slave?   330
Against your fame with fondness hate combines,
The rival batters, and the lover mines.
With distant voice neglected Virtue calls,
Less heard and less, the faint remonstrance falls;
Tired with contempt, she quits the slippery reign,
And Pride and Prudence take her seat in vain.
In crowd at once, where none the pass defend,
The harmless Freedom, and the private Friend.
The guardians yield, by force superior plied;
By Interest, Prudence; and by Flattery, Pride.   340
Now beauty falls betrayed, despised, distressed,
And hissing Infamy proclaims the rest.
    Where then shall Hope and Fear their objects find?
Must dull Suspense corrupt the stagnant mind?°
Must helpless man, in ignorance sedate,
Roll darkling down the torrent of his fate?
Must no dislike alarm, no wishes rise,
No cries attempt the mercies of the skies?
Enquirer, cease, petitions yet remain,
Which heaven may hear, nor deem religion vain.   350

Still raise for good the supplicating voice,
But leave to heaven the measure and the choice,
Safe in his power, whose eyes discern afar
The secret ambush of a specious prayer.
Implore his aid, in his decisions rest,
Secure whate'er he gives, he gives the best.
Yet when the sense of sacred presence fires,
And strong devotion to the skies aspires,
Pour forth thy fervours for a healthful mind,
Obedient passions, and a will resigned;   360
For love, which scarce collective man can fill;
For patience sovereign o'er transmuted ill;
For faith, that panting for a happier seat,
Counts death kind Nature's signal of retreat:
These goods for man the laws of heaven ordain,
These goods he grants, who grants the power to gain;
With these celestial wisdom calms the mind,
And makes the happiness she does not find.

Irene°

(ACT II, SCENE vii)

MAHOMET: Wilt thou descend, fair daughter of perfection,
    To hear my vows, and give mankind a queen?
    Ah! cease, Irene, cease those flowing sorrows,
    That melt a heart impregnable till now,
    And turn thy thoughts henceforth to love and empire.
    How will the matchless beauties of Irene,
    Thus bright in tears, thus amiable in ruin,
    With all the graceful pride of greatness heightened,
    Amidst the blaze of jewels and of gold,
    Adorn a throne, and dignify dominion.   10

IRENE: Why all this glare of splendid eloquence,
    To paint the pageantries of guilty state?
    Must I for these renounce the hope of Heaven,
    Immortal crowns and fullness of enjoyment?

MAHOMET: Vain raptures all—For your inferior natures
    Formed to delight and happy by delighting,
    Heaven has reserved no future paradise,
    But bids you rove the paths of bliss, secure
    Of total death and careless of hereafter;
    While Heaven's high minister, whose awful volume   20
    Records each act, each thought of sovereign man,
    Surveys your plays with inattentive glance,
    And leaves the lovely trifler unregarded.

IRENE: Why then has Nature's vain munificence
    Profusely poured her bounties upon woman?
    Whence then those charms thy tongue has deigned to flatter,
    That air resistless and enchanting blush,
    Unless the beauteous fabric was designed
    A habitation for a fairer soul?

MAHOMET: Too high, bright maid, thou rat'st exterior grace;   30
    Not always do the fairest flowers diffuse
    The richest odours, nor the speckled shells
    Conceal the gem; let female arrogance
    Observe the feathered wanderers of the sky,
    With purple varied and bedropped with gold,
    They prune the wing, and spread the glossy plumes,
    Ordained, like you, to flutter and to shine,
    And cheer the weary passenger with music.

IRENE: Mean as we are, this tyrant of the world
    Implores our smiles, and trembles at our feet: 40
    Whence flow the hopes and fears, despair and rapture,
    Whence all the bliss and agonies of love?

MAHOMET: Why, when the balm of sleep descends on man,
    Do gay delusions, wandering o'er the brain,
    Sooth the delighted soul with empty bliss?
    To want give affluence? and to slavery freedom?
    Such are love's joys, the lenitives of life,
    A fancied treasure, and a waking dream.

IRENE: Then let me once, in honour of our sex,
    Assume the boastful arrogance of man.   50
    Th' attractive softness, and th' endearing smile,
    And powerful glance, 'tis granted, are our own;
    Nor has impartial Nature's frugal hand

Exhausted all her nobler gifts on you;
Do not we share the comprehensive thought,
Th' enlivening wit, the penetrating reason?
Beats not the female breast with generous passions,
The thirst of empire, and the love of glory?

MAHOMET: Illustrious maid, new wonders fix me thine,
Thy soul completes the triumphs of thy face.   60
I thought, forgive my fair, the noblest aim,
The strongest effort of a female soul,
Was but to choose the graces of the day;
To tune the tongue, to teach the eyes to roll,
Dispose the colours of the flowing robe,
And add new roses to the faded cheek.
Will it not charm a mind like thine exalted,
To shine the goddess of applauding nations,
To scatter happiness and plenty round thee,
To bid the prostrate captive rise and live,   70
To see new cities tower at thy command,
And blasted kingdoms flourish at thy smile?

IRENE: Charmed with the thought of blessing human kind,
Too calm I listen to the flattering sounds.

MAHOMET: O seize the power to bless—Irene's nod
Shall break the fetters of the groaning Christian;
Greece, in her lovely patroness secure,
Shall mourn no more her plundered palaces.

IRENE: Forbear—O do not urge me to my ruin!

MAHOMET: To state and power I court thee, not to ruin: 80
Smile on my wishes, and command the globe.
Security shall spread her shield before thee,
And Love enfold thee with his downy wings.
    If greatness please thee, mount th' imperial seat;
    If pleasure charm thee, view this soft retreat;
    Here every warbler of the sky shall sing;
    Here every fragrance breathe of every spring:
    To deck these bowers each region shall combine,
    And even our Prophet's gardens envy thine:
    Empire and love shall share the blissful day,   90
    And varied life steal unperceived away.

A New Prologue Spoken at the Representation of
Comus°

Ye patriot crowds, who burn for England's fame,
Ye nymphs, whose bosoms beat at MILTON'S name,
Whose generous zeal, unbought by flattering rhymes,
Shames the mean pensions of Augustan times;°
Immortal patrons of succeeding days,
Attend this prelude of perpetual praise!
Let Wit, condemned the feeble war to wage
With close malevolence, or public rage;
Let Study, worn with Virtue's fruitless lore,
Behold this theatre, and grieve no more.   10
This night, distinguished by your smile, shall tell,
That never Briton can in vain excel;
The slighted arts futurity shall trust,
And rising ages hasten to be just.
    At length our mighty bard's victorious lays
Fill the loud voice of universal praise,
And baffled spite, with hopeless anguish dumb,
Yields to renown the centuries to come.
With ardent haste, each candidate of fame
Ambitious catches at his towering name: 20
He sees, and pitying sees, vain wealth bestow
Those pageant honours which he scorned below:
While crowds aloft the laureate bust behold,
Or trace his form on circulating gold,
Unknown, unheeded, long his offspring lay,
And want hung threatening o'er her slow decay.
What though she shine with no MILTONIAN fire,
No favouring muse her morning dreams inspire;
Yet softer claims the melting heart engage,
Her youth laborious, and her blameless age: 30
Hers the mild merits of domestic life,
The patient sufferer, and the faithful wife,
Thus graced with humble virtue's native charms
Her grandsire leaves her in Britannia's arms,
Secure with peace, with competence, to dwell,
While tutelary nations guard her cell.
Yours is the charge, ye fair, ye wise, ye brave!
'Tis yours to crown desert—beyond the grave!

Verses for Baretti°

At sight of sparkling bowls or beauteous dames,
When fondness melts me, or when wine inflames,
I too can feel the rapture, fierce and strong;
I too can pour th' extemporary song:
But though the numbers for a moment please,
Though music thrills, or sudden sallies seize,
Yet, lay the sonnet for an hour aside,
Its charms are fled and all its powers destroyed.
What soon is perfect, soon alike is past;
That slowly grows, which must for ever last.

Parodies of Modern Ballad Imitations°

The tender infant meek and mild
    Fell down upon a stone;
The nurse took up the squealing child
    But yet the child squealed on.

*

I put my hat upon my head
    And walked into the Strand,
And there I met another man
    Whose hat was in his hand.

*

I therefore pray thee, Renny dear,°
    That thou wilt give to me,
With cream and sugar softened well,
    Another dish of tea.

Nor fear that I, my gentle maid,
    Shall long detain the cup,
When once unto the bottom I
    Have drunk the liquor up.

Yet hear, alas! this mournful truth,
    Nor hear it with a frown—
Thou canst not make the tea so fast
    As I can gulp it down.

10

Impromptu Translation of Benserade's 'Verses à son lit'°

In bed we 'laugh, in bed we cry,
And born in bed, in bed we die;
The near approach a bed may show
Of human bliss to human woe.

Epitaph on Hogarth°

The hand of him here torpid lies
    That drew th' essential form of grace;
Here closed in death th' attentive eyes
    That saw the manners in the face.

If genius warm thee, reader, stay,
    If merit touch thee, shed a tear;
Be vice and dullness far away—
    Great Hogarth's honoured dust is here.

ΓΝΩΘΙ ΣΕΑΥΤΟΝ°

(Post Lexicon Anglicanum Auctum et Emendatum)

Lexicon ad finem longo luctamine tandem
Scaliger ut duxit, tenuis pertaesus opellae,
Vile indignatus studium, nugasque molestas,
Ingemit exosus, scribendaque lexica mandat
Damnatis, poenam pro poenis omnibus unam.
    Ille quidem recte, sublimis, doctus, et acer,
Quem decuit majora sequi, majoribus aptum,
Qui veterum modo facta ducum, modo carmina vatum,
Gesserat et quicquid virtus, sapientia quicquid
Dixerat, imperiique vices, coelique meatus,
Ingentemque animo seclorum volverat orbem.
    Fallimur exemplis; temere sibi turba scholarum
Ima tuas credit permitti, Scaliger, iras.

10

Quisque suum nôrit modulum; tibi, prime virorum,
Ut studiis sperem, aut ausim par esse querelis,
Non mihi sorte datum; lenti seu sanguinis obsint
Frigora, seu nimium longo jacuisse veterno,
Sive mihi mentem dederit Natura minorem.

    Te sterili functum cura, vocumque salebris
Tuto eluctatum spatiis sapientia dia   20
Excipit aethereis, ars omnis plaudit amica,
Linguarumque omni terra discordia concors
Multiplici reducem circumsonat ore magistrum.

    Me, pensi immunis cum jam mihi reddor, inertis
Desidiae sors dura manet, graviorque labore
Tristis et atra quies, et tardae taedia vitae.
Nascuntur curis curae, vexatque dolorum
Importuna cohors, vacuae mala somnia mentis.
Nunc clamosa juvant nocturnae gaudia mensae,
Nunc loca sola placent; frustra te, somne, recumbens   30
Alme voco, impatiens noctis metuensque diei.
Omnia percurro trepidus, circum omnia lustro,
Si qua usquam pateat melioris semita vitae,
Nec quid agam invenio, meditatus grandia, cogor
Notior ipse mihi fieri, incultumque fateri
Pectus, et ingenium vano se robore jactans.
Ingenium, nisi materiem doctrina ministret,
Cessat inops rerum, ut torpet, si marmoris absit
Copia, Phidiaci foecunda potentia coeli.
Quicquid agam, quocunque ferar, conatibus obstat   40
Res angusta domi, et macrae penuria mentis.

    Non rationis opes animus, nunc parta recensens,
Conspicit aggestas, et se miratur in illis,
Nec sibi de gaza praesens quód postulet usus
Summus adesse jubet celsa dominator ab arce;
Non operum serie, seriem dum computat aevi,
Praeteritis fruitur, laetos aut sumit honores
Ipse sui judex, actae bene munera vitae;
Sed sua regna videns, loca nocte silentia late
Horret, ubi vanae species, umbraeque fugaces,   50
Et rerum volitant rarae per inane figurae.

    Quid faciam? tenebrisne pigram damnare senectam
Restat? an accingar studiis gravioribus audax?
Aut, hoc si nimium est, tandem nova lexica poscam?

Know Thyself

(After Enlarging and Correcting the English Dictionary)

Scaliger, when with scant sense of achievement he had scrawled
his lexicon's last page, after prolonged toil, loathing
the mindless menial grind, the small problems piled into
    mountains,
in hate groaning, he gave his thought to guide grave judges
that the penal system should prescribe for all hard prisoners
found guilty of devilment, the drudgery of making a dictionary—
one punishment, for the most impenitent, all punishments
    compounding!

How right he was, that rare man, erudite, lofty, rigorous,
worthy of weightier work, better able to serve the world
by enchanting the ear with antique heroisms, or the bards'
    ecstasies;
the shifting sands of governance, the swirl of the shining spheres
his mind could read and unriddle, and the vast earth's revolving.

A large example is dangerous. The dunciad of learned dolts
    presume
to glare and grumble, presenting their case, princely Scaliger
as if it were yours, master. Let each mind his measure!
I, at least, have realized that to be your rival (in rage
or in knowledge) was never part of my nature. Who can know
    why?
Is it the lazy flow of my chill blood, or the long idle years that I
    lost?
or was I just bundled into the world with a bad brain?

As soon as your sterile work was over, and the stiff word-stubble
you had pushed through, peerless Wisdom the goddesss into her
    pure
arcanum accepted you, while all the arts applauded,
and the world's words, their voices so long at variance,
now home from exile joyfully rang about you, gentle master, their
    joiner.

As for me, my task finished, I find myself still fettered to myself:
the dull doom of doing nothing, harsher than any drudgery,
stays with me, and the staleness of slow stagnation.
Cares beget cares, and a clamouring crowd of troubles
vex me, and vile dreams, the sour sleep of an empty mind.
What will refresh me? The rattle of all-night roisterers,   30
or the quiet of solitary spaces? Oh, sleep, sleep, I call,
lying where I fret at the lingering night, but fear day's cold finger.

Trembling, I trudge everywhere, peering, prying, into every-
    thing, trying
passionate to know if somewhere, anyhow, a path leads up to a
    more perfect pasture,
but glooming over grand schemes I never find my growing-point,
and am always forced finally to face myself, to own frankly
that my heart is illiterate, and my mind's strength an illusion
I labour to keep alive. Fool, a mind not fuelled by learning
slides into a morass. Stop the supply of marble
to Phidias our fertile sculptor, and where are his forms and faces?   40

Every endeavour, every avenue, ends in frustration always,
closed in by lack of cash, bound up by a costive mind.
Ah, when that mind reckons up its resources, the sheaves of
    reason
stacked high, matter for self-satisfaction, are conspicuously
    absent:
nor does creation's great king from his high castle
send down daily supplies to ensure its survival.

Regularly the years mount up, regularly the mind's works do not
    mount up:
as for the frills and the friendly honours, fruits of a useful life,
its own harsh judgment forbids it that harmless enjoyment.
Turning to survey its territory, that night-shadowed tundra,   50
the mind is full of fear—of ghosts, of the fleeting glimmer
of the thin shadows of nothing, the absence of shapes, the
    shimmer.

What then am I to do? Let my declining years go down to the
    dark?
Or get myself together, gather the last of my gall,
and hurl myself at some task huge enough for a hero?

And if that's too much, perhaps my friends might find me
some dull, decent job, undemanding: like making a
dictionary. . . .°

(Translated by John Wain)

Skia°

Ponti profundis clausa recessibus,
Strepens procellis, rupibus obsita,
  Quam grata defesso virentem
    Skia sinum nebulosa pandis.

His cura credo sedibus exulat;
His blanda certe pax habitat locis:
  Non ira, non moeror quietis
    Insidias meditatur horis.

At non cavata rupe latescere,
Menti nec aegrae montibus aviis   10
  Prodest vagari, nec frementes
    E scopulo numerare fluctus.

Humana virtus non sibi sufficit,
Datur nec aequum cuique animum sibi
  Parare posse, ut Stoicorum
    Secta crepet nimis alta fallax.

Exaestuantis pectoris impetum,
Rex summe, solus tu regis arbiter,
  Mentisque, te tollente, surgunt,
    Te recidunt moderante fluctus.   20

Skye

Held and defined by ocean's ultimate
reaches, storm-loud, rock-strewn,
how grateful to tired men's eyes
your cloud-layered bay, Skye.

Certain I am, from these dwellings
worry is banished: peace lives here:
not anger, not envy waylay
their quiet hours to work mischief.

But hiding in recesses of scooped-out
rock, or roaming untracked hills,   10
or, crag-perched, counting the loud waves: what
help there for a sick mind?

Within the island of his own
nature, no man has enough resources.
The Stoics, proud ranters, erred: the mind
needs help to find peace.

You, God, King, control the yearning
heart's energies. When you say *Rise!* those
waves tower into crests, when you say
Peace, they sink and lie sleeping.   20

(Translated by John Wain)

To Mrs Thrale°

ON HER COMPLETING HER THIRTY-FIFTH YEAR

Oft in danger yet alive
We are come to thirty-five;
Long may better years arrive,
Better years than thirty-five;
Could philosophers contrive
Life to stop at thirty-five,
Time his hours should never drive
O'er the bounds of thirty-five:
High to soar and deep to dive
Nature gives at thirty-five;   10
Ladies, stock and tend your hive,
Trifle not at thirty-five;
For howe'er we boast and strive,
Life declines from thirty-five;

He that ever hopes to thrive
Must begin by thirty-five:
And those who wisely wish to wive,
Must look on Thrale at thirty-five.

Lines in Hawkesworth's *The Rival*°

Thy mind, which voluntary doubts molest,
Asks but its own permission to be blest.

On Archaism in Poetry°

Whereso'er I turn my view,
All is strange, yet nothing new;
Endless labour all along,
Endless labour to be wrong;
Phrase that time has flung away,
Uncouth words in disarray:
Tricked in antique ruff and bonnet,
Ode and elegy and sonnet.

Parody of Thomas Warton

Hermit hoar, in solemn cell,
　　Wearing out life's evening gray,
Smite thy bosom, sage, and tell,
　　Where is bliss? and which the way?

Thus I spoke, and speaking sighed—
　　Scarce repressed the starting tear—
When the smiling sage replied,
　　'Come, my lad, and drink some beer'.

Prologue to Kelly's *A Word to the Wise*°

This night presents a play which public rage,
Or right, or wrong, once hooted from the stage;
From zeal or malice now no more we dread,
For English vengeance *wars not with the dead.*°
A generous foe regards, with pitying eye,
The man whom Fate has laid where all must lie.
To wit, reviving from its author's dust,
Be kind, ye judges, or at least be just:
Let no resentful petulance invade
Th' oblivious grave's inviolable shade.   10
Let one great payment every claim appease,
And him who cannot hurt, allow to please;
To please by scenes unconscious of offence,
By harmless merriment, or useful sense.
Where aught of bright, or fair, the piece displays,
Approve it only—'tis too late to praise.
If want of skill, or want of care, appear,
Forbear to hiss—the poet cannot hear.
By all, like him, must praise and blame be found
At best, a fleeting gleam, or empty sound.   20
Yet then shall calm reflection bless the night
When liberal pity dignified delight;
When Pleasure fired her torch at Virtue's flame,
And mirth was bounty with a humbler name.

An Extempore Elegy°

Here's a woman of the town,
    Lies as dead as any nail!
She was once of high renown—
    And so here begins my tale.

She was once as cherry plump,
    Red her cheek as Cath'rine pear,
Tossed her nose, and shook her rump,
    Till she made the neighbours stare.

But there came a country squire—
    He was a seducing pug!   10
Took her from her friends and sire,
    To his own house her did lug.

There she soon became a jilt,
    Rambling often to and fro;
All her life was naught but guilt,
    Till purse and carcase both were low.

Black her eye with many a blow,
    Hot her breath with many a dram.
Now she lies exceeding low,
    And as quiet as a lamb.   20

To Sir John Lade, on His Coming of Age°

('A SHORT SONG OF CONGRATULATION')

Long-expected one and twenty
    Lingering year at last is flown,
Pomp and pleasure, pride and plenty,
    Great Sir John, are all your own.

Loosened from the minor's tether,
    Free to mortgage or to sell,
Wild as wind, and light as feather,
    Bid the slaves of thrift farewell.

Call the Bettys, Kates, and Jennys,
    Every name that laughs at care,   10
Lavish of your grandsire's guineas,
    Show the spirit of an heir.

All that prey on vice and folly
    Joy to see their quarry fly,
Here the gamester light and jolly,
    There the lender grave and sly.

Wealth, Sir John, was made to wander,°
　Let it wander as it will;
See the jockey, see the pander,
　Bid them come, and take their fill.   20

When the bonny blade carouses,
　Pockets full, and spirits high,
What are acres? What are houses?
　Only dirt, or wet or dry.

If the guardian or the mother
　Tell the woes of wilful waste,
Scorn their counsel and their pother,
　You can hang or drown at last.

On the Death of Dr Robert Levet°

Condemned to Hope's delusive mine,
　As on we toil from day to day,
By sudden blasts, or slow decline,
　Our social comforts drop away.

Well tried through many a varying year,
　See Levet to the grave descend;
Officious, innocent, sincere,°
　Of every friendless name the friend.

Yet still he fills Affection's eye,
　Obscurely wise, and coarsely kind;   10
Nor, lettered Arrogance, deny
　Thy praise to merit unrefined.

When fainting Nature called for aid,
　And hovering Death prepared the blow,
His vig'rous remedy displayed
　The power of art without the show.

In Misery's darkest caverns known,
  His useful care was ever nigh,
Where hopeless Anguish poured his groan,
  And lonely Want retired to die.   20

No summons mocked by chill delay,
  No petty gain disdained by pride,
The modest wants of every day
  The toil of every day supplied.

His virtues walked their narrow round,
  Nor made a pause, nor left a void;
And sure th' Eternal Master found
  The single talent well employed.

The busy day, the peaceful night,
  Unfelt, uncounted, glided by;   30
His frame was firm, his powers were bright,
  Though now his eightieth year was nigh.

Then with no throbbing fiery pain,
  No cold gradations of decay,
Death broke at once the vital chain,
  And freed his soul the nearest way.

In Rivum a Mola Stoana Lichfeldiae Diffluentem°

Errat adhuc vitreus per prata virentia rivus,
  Quo toties lavi membra tenella puer;
Hic delusa rudi frustrabar brachia motu,
  Dum docuit blanda voce natare pater.
Fecerunt rami latebras, tenebrisque diurnis
  Pendula secretas abdidit arbor aquas.
Nunc veteres duris perière securibus umbrae,
  Longinquisque oculis nuda lavacra patent.
Lympha tamen cursus agit indefessa perennis,
  Tectaque qua fluxit, nunc et aperta fluit.   10
Quid ferat externi velox, quid deterat aetas,
  Tu quoque securus res age, Nise, tuas.

By the River, at Stowe Mill, Lichfield, Where the Streams Flow Together

Clear as glass the stream still wanders through
green fields.
           Here, as a boy, I bathed
my tender limbs, unskilled, frustrated, while
with gentle voice my father from the bank
taught me to swim.
              The branches made
a hiding-place: the bending trees concealed
the water in a daytime darkness.
                Now
hard axes have destroyed those ancient shades:
the pool lies naked, even to distant eyes.

But the water, never tiring, still runs on   10
in the same channel: once hidden, now overt,
always flowing.
           Nisus, you too, what time°
brings from outside, or wears away within
ignoring, do the things you have to do.

(Translated by John Wain)

Translation of Horace, *Odes*, iv. 7

The snow dissolved no more is seen,
The fields, and woods, behold, are green.
The changing year renews the plain,
The rivers know their banks again,
The spritely nymph and naked Grace
The mazy dance together trace.
The changing year's successive plan
Proclaims mortality to man.
Rough winter's blasts to spring give way,
Spring yields to summer's sovereign ray,   10
Then summer sinks in autumn's reign,
And winter chills the world again.

Her losses soon the moon supplies,
But wretched man, when once he lies
Where Priam and his sons are laid,
Is naught but ashes and a shade.
Who knows if Jove, who counts our score,
Will toss us in a morning more?
What with your friend you nobly share
At least you rescue from your heir.   20
Not you, Torquatus, boast of Rome,
When Minos once has fixed your doom,
Or eloquence, or splendid birth,
Or virtue shall replace on earth.
Hippolytus unjustly slain
Diana calls to life in vain,
Nor can the might of Theseus rend
The chains of hell that hold his friend.

A Latin School Exercise°

Quis enim virtutem amplectitur ipsam
Praemia si tollas?

Nihil magis Principi ex[pe]dit reipublicae studioso quam ut bonos titulis honoribusque augeat, in m[alos] severissime animadvertat. Ut enim omnes se conte[mp]tos videntes deterrentur, sic si factis dignas ferant mercedes, ad majora eodem transite ascender[e] conantur. Invicta et inexpugnabilis cupido no[s]tris inseritur pectoribus honoris et laudum, quam Naturam nobis sapientem (nihil enim frustra agit) indidisse credam ut ad facta laudabilia extimulet. Omnes fere artes, professores deseritis cumulando propagatas fuisse constat. Primi medici ad Deos relati sunt, et templa in illorum honorem aedificabantur. Etsi virtus ipsa sibi pretium est, tamen si desit gratia principis, si boni obscuris latescunt villis dum infames praeturas consulatusque adsequantur, alii illos vix imitabuntur. Constat artes non, nisi mag[nat]ibus excoluntur, florere, nec tanta, Tyrannis regnantibus, bellisque regnis ardentibus, ingenia, quan[t]a sub optimo principe, nascuntur. Omnes vero ad [r]egum exempla sese conformant, si ab illo spretae jacent musae ab aliis ibidem contemnuntur. Si[c] nisi ex suo exemplo populum ad relligionis Divorumque trahit observantiam, omnis pietas cito [s]ordebit. Primis Romanae reipublicae aetatibus, dum boni, ortu nihil aestimato, ad grande decus sublati sunt, virtus quotidie increvit, moribus vero postea depravatis, vitia seculis venientibus obruta est.

Sam: Johnson

[Translation]

For Who Embraces Virtue Herself, If You Take Away Rewards?

Nothing is more advantageous to a ruler concerned for the public welfare than that he promote good men by giving them titles and honours, and take the severest action against the bad. For as all are deterred by seeing themselves despised, so if they receive rewards worthy of their actions, they try to rise to higher things by the same route. An unsubdued and invincible desire of honour and praise is planted in our hearts, which I would believe wise Nature (for she does nothing in vain) has instilled in us to spur us to praiseworthy deeds.

Nearly all the arts, it is agreed, have been advanced by acquiring practitioners because of rewards. The first physicians were traced back to the gods, and temples were built in their honour. Although virtue is its own reward, yet if the favour of the prince is wanting, if good men remain in backwoods obscurity while the infamous obtain praetorships and consulships, others will scarcely imitate them. It is generally agreed that the arts do not flourish unless they are honoured by governors, nor do such great talents appear when tyrants rule and kingdoms are aflame with war as under a truly good ruler. But everyone will conform to the examples of kings; if the Muses are scorned by him, they will at the same time be despised by others. Thus unless by his own example he draws the people to respect of religion and the gods, all piety will quickly be debased. In the early days of the Roman republic, when good men, irrespective of their origin, were raised to high honour, virtue every day increased; but afterwards, when morals became depraved, it was overthrown by vice in later ages.

A Voyage to Abyssinia

BY FATHER JEROME LOBO, A PORTUGUESE JESUIT

. . . . .

WITH . . . FIFTEEN DISSERTATIONS ON VARIOUS SUBJECTS . . .
BY MR LE GRAND. FROM THE FRENCH

PREFACE

The following relation is so curious and entertaining, and the dissertations that accompany it so judicious and instructive, that the translator is confident his attempt stands in need of no apology, whatever censures may fall on the performance.

The Portuguese traveller, contrary to the general vein of his countrymen, has amused his reader with no romantic absurdities or incredible fictions: whatever he relates, whether true or not, is at least probable; and he who tells nothing exceeding the bounds of probability, has a right to demand that they should believe him who cannot contradict him.

He appears, by his modest and unaffected narration, to have described things as he saw them, to have copied nature from the life, and to have consulted his senses, not his imagination. He meets with no basilisks° that destroy with their eyes; his crocodiles devour their prey without tears; and his cataracts fall from the rock without deafening the neighbouring inhabitants.

The reader will here find no regions cursed with irremediable barrenness, or blest with spontaneous fecundity; no perpetual gloom or unceasing sunshine; nor are the nations here described either devoid of all sense of humanity, or consummate in all private and social virtues: here are no Hottentots without religion, polity, or articulate language; no Chinese perfectly polite, and completely skilled in all sciences: he will discover what will always be discovered by a diligent and impartial inquirer, that wherever human nature is to be found, there is a mixture of vice and virtue, a contest of passion and reason; and that the Creator doth not appear partial in his distributions, but has balanced in most countries their particular inconveniences by particular favours.

In his account of the mission, where his veracity is most to be suspected, he neither exaggerates over-much the merits of the Jesuits, if we consider the partial regard paid by the Portuguese to their countrymen, by the Jesuits to their society, and by the papists to their church; nor aggravates the vices of the Abyssinians; but if the reader will not be satisfied with a popish account of a popish mission, he may have recourse to the history of the church of Abyssinia, written by Dr Geddes,° in which he will find the actions and sufferings of the missionaries placed in a different light, though the same in which Mr Le Grand,° with all his zeal for the Roman church, appears to have seen them.

This learned dissertator, however valuable for his industry and erudition, is yet more to be esteemed for having dared so freely, in the midst of France,° to declare his disapprobation of the patriarch Oviedo's° sanguinary zeal, who was continually importuning the Portuguese to beat up their drums for missionaries who might preach the gospel with swords in their hands, and propagate, by desolation and slaughter, the true worship of the God of peace.

It is not easy to forbear reflecting with how little reason these men profess themselves the followers of Jesus, who left this great characteristic to his disciples, that they should be known by loving one another, by universal and unbounded charity and benevolence.

Let us suppose an inhabitant of some remote and superior region, yet unskilled in the ways of men, having read and considered the precepts of the gospel, and the example of our Saviour, to come down in search of the true church. If he would not inquire after it among the cruel, the insolent, and the oppressive; among those who are continually grasping at dominion over souls as well as bodies; among those who are employed in procuring to themselves impunity for the most enormous villainies, and studying methods of destroying their fellow-creatures, not for their crimes, but their errors; if he would not expect to meet benevolence engaged in massacres, or to find mercy in a court of inquisition—he would not look for the true church in the church of Rome.

Mr Le Grand has given, in one dissertation, an example of great moderation, in deviating from the temper of his religion; but, in the others, has left proofs that learning and honesty are often too weak to oppose prejudice. He has made no scruple of preferring the testimony of father Du Bernat to the writings of all the Portuguese Jesuits, to whom he allows great zeal, but little learning, without giving any other reason than that his favourite was a Frenchman. This is writing only to Frenchmen and to papists: a protestant would be desirous to know why he must imagine that father Du Bernat had a cooler head or more knowledge, and why one man, whose account is singular, is not more likely to be mistaken than many agreeing in the same account.

If the Portuguese were biased by any particular views, another bias equally powerful may have deflected the Frenchman from the truth; for they evidently write with contrary designs: the Portuguese, to make their mission seem more necessary, endeavoured to place in the strongest light the differences between the Abyssinian and Roman church; but the great Ludolfus,° laying hold on the advantage, reduced these later writers to prove their conformity.

Upon the whole, the controversy seems of no great importance to those who believe the holy Scriptures° sufficient to teach the way to salvation; but, of whatever moment it may be thought, there are no proofs sufficient to decide it.

His discourses on indifferent subjects will divert, as well as instruct; and if either in these, or in the relation of father Lobo, any argument shall appear unconvincing, or description obscure, they are defects incident to all mankind, which, however, are not rashly to be imputed to the authors, being sometimes, perhaps, more justly chargeable on the translator.

In this translation (if it may be so called) great liberties have been taken, which, whether justifiable or not, shall be fairly confessed, and let the judicious part of mankind pardon or condemn them.

In the first part, the greatest freedom has been used, in reducing the narration into a narrow compass; so that it is by no means a translation, but an epitome, in which, whether every thing either useful or entertaining be comprised, the compiler is least qualified to determine.

In the account of Abyssinia, and the continuation, the authors have been followed with more exactness; and as few passages appeared either insignificant or tedious, few have been either shortened or omitted.

The dissertations are the only part in which an exact translation has been attempted; and even in those, abstracts are sometimes given, instead of literal quotations, particularly in the first; and sometimes other parts have been contracted.

Several memorials and letters, which are printed at the end of the dissertations to secure the credit of the foregoing narrative, are entirely left out.

It is hoped that, after this confession, whoever shall compare this attempt with the original, if he shall find no proofs of fraud or partiality, will candidly overlook any failure of judgment.

The State of Affairs in Lilliput°

The public several years ago received a great deal of entertainment and instruction from Capt. Gulliver's elaborate and curious account of the newly discovered empire of Lilliput; a relation which (however rejected at its first appearance by some as incredible, and criticized by others as partial or ostentatious) has, with the success almost always attendant on probity and truth, triumphed over all opposition, gained belief from the most obstinate incredulity and established a reputation in the world which can fear no dimunition, nor admit of any increase.

It is much to be regretted that the ingenious traveller was diverted from his design of completing a full and accurate description of that unknown country, by bringing down its history from the earliest ages, explaining the laws and customs of the inhabitants, and delineating the works of art and productions of nature peculiar to that soil and people. Happy had it been for mankind had so noble and instructive a subject been cultivated and adorned by the genius of LEMUEL GULLIVER, a genius equally sublime and extensive, acute and sagacious, worthy to display the policy of the most refined, and celebrate the achievements of the most warlike nation. Then might the legislators of Lilliput have been produced as rivals in fame to Numa or Lycurgus; and its heroes have shone with no less lustre than Cadmus and Theseus.

Felix tanto argumento ingenium, felix tanto ingenio argumentum!°

But as the hope conceived by the public of seeing this immense undertaking successfully completed has been frustrated by indolence, business, or perhaps by the unexpected stroke of sudden death, we doubt not but our readers will be much pleased with an appendix to Capt. Gulliver's account, which we received last month, and which the late resolution of the House of Commons, whereby we are forbidden to insert any account of the proceedings of the British Parliament, gives us an opportunity of communicating in their room.

Some years after the publication of Capt. Gulliver's discoveries, in the midst of the clamour raised against them by ignorance, misapprehension, and malice, a grandson of the Captain's, fired with resentment at the indignities offered to his ancestor's character by men who, without the least regard to his celebrated veracity, dared to charge his relation with no less than premeditated, deliberate falsehood, resolved, as the most effectual method of vindicating his memory, to undertake a voyage to Lilliput, that he might be able at his return to confirm his grandfather's reports by ocular testimony, and forever silence those aspersions, which were, in his opinion, founded on nothing but extreme ignorance of both geography and human nature.

This voyage, by the assistance of some charts and observations which he found amongst his grandfather's papers, he successfully performed in the ship named the *Confidence*, and met, upon his discovering his name and family, with such a reception at the court of Lilliput as sufficiently showed that the memory of the Man-Mountain was far from being obliterated among them; and that time had in Lilliput the effect which it is observed to have on our side of the globe, of preserving and increasing a reputation built on great and illustrious actions, and of dissipating the whispers of malice and calumnies of faction. The accusations brought against the Captain by his enemies were cleared up, or forgot; and the grandson, at his arrival, found the preservation of Mildendo from the flames, and the conquest of the formidable navy of Blefuscu,° the subject of epic poems, and annual orations, the old man's constant topic of discourse, and the example by which their youth were animated to fidelity, presence of mind, and military prowess.

The hospitable and generous reception he found in the country gave him opportunities of informing himself more fully of the state of that part of the world; for which he came prepared by his grandfather's conversation, and a tolerable knowledge of the Lilliputian tongue, attained by the help of a grammar and a vocabulary, which, with other writings in that language, Captain Gulliver had left behind him.

Enabled by these concurrent advantages to make a speedy progress in his enquiries, he returned at the end of three years, not with a cargo of gold or silk or diamonds, but with histories, memoirs, tracts, speeches, treaties, debates, letters and instructions, which will be a sufficient compensation to mankind for the loss they have sustained by the negligence or untimely death of Captain Gulliver; and established a correspondence between Lilliput and the English colonies in the East-Indies, by which all the valuable writings published there, and all historical and political novelties, are to be annually transmitted to him.

This gentleman, notwithstanding that veneration for his grandfather which engaged him to take so long and tedious a voyage, upon no other motive than a desire of obliging the world to do justice to his character, has given the highest testimonies that truth is yet dearer to him than the reputation of his family, and that no mistaken piety can prevail upon him to palliate the mistakes, or conceal the errors which were the necessary effects of Capt. Gulliver's short stay, difficult situation, formidable appearance, and perplexed affairs.

The ready access to the great men of Lilliput, and familiarity with the Emperor himself, which the traditional regard paid to his grandfather's merit procured him, rendered it easy for him to make greater discoveries in three days than Capt. Gulliver had been able to do during his whole stay. He was particularly surprised in his first conference with the Emperor, to hear him mention many states and empires beside those of Lilliput and Blefuscu; and, upon observing that in his grandfather's account no other nations are taken notice of, he was told with great condescension by his Majesty that there had been lately discovered, in an old repository of archives, an edict of those times absolutely forbidding, under the pain and penalty of death, any person or persons to give the Man-Mountain the least information relating to the state of any other country; lest his ambition might prompt him to seize upon some defenceless part, either of his Lilliputian majesty's dominions, or of some weak prince, or petty state, and to erect an absolute dominion, which might in time perhaps become formidable to the state of Lilliput itself. 'Nor do I believe', said his Majesty, 'that your ancestor would have heard the name of Blefuscu, had not the necessities of state obliged the court unwillingly to discover it; and even in that emergence of affairs, they gave him so imperfect an account that he has represented Blefuscu as an island; whereas it is a very large empire on the continent, confining on other empires, kingdoms, and states, of which I'll order my geographer to communicate to you an accurate description.'

He had immediately recourse to the royal professor of geography, and found upon inspection that the maps of Lilliput and Blefuscu, and the neighbouring islands, kingdoms, and empires, were a perfect epitome of the map of Europe, and that these petty regions, with their dependencies, constitute a resemblance or compendium of our great world, just as the model of a building contains all the parts in the same disposition as the principal design.

This observation engaged him closely to his geographical studies, and the farther he advanced, the more he was convinced of the justness of the notion he had conceived of a world in miniature, inhabited by this pigmy race. In it he found all the four parts of our earth represented by correspondent countries, excepting that the Lilliputian world is not spherical, but must be considered as bearing the form° which the ancients attributed to our own. Neither need I acquaint the mathematical readers that, being enlightened by our sun, it does not admit of any diversity of zones or climates, but bears an exact analogy to our earth in its lands and seas, chains of mountains, tracts of deserts, and diversity of nations.

The people of Degulia, or the Lilliputian Europe, which name is derived from DEGUL, illustrious (a word now obsolete, and known only to antiquaries and etymologists), are, above those of the other parts of the world, famous for arts, arms, and navigation, and, in consequence of this superiority, have made conquests and settled colonies in very distant regions, the inhabitants of which they look upon as barbarous, though in simplicity of manners, probity, and temperance superior to themselves; and seem to think that they have a right to treat them as passion, interest, or caprice shall direct, without much regard to the rules of justice or humanity; they have carried this imaginary sovereignty so far that they have sometimes proceeded to rapine, bloodshed, and desolation. If you endeavour to examine the foundation of this authority, they neither produce any grant from a superior jurisdiction, nor plead the consent of the people whom they govern in this tyrannical manner; but either threaten you with punishment for abridging the Emperor's sovereignty, or pity your stupidity, or tell you in positive terms that *Power is right*. Some indeed pretend to a grant from a pontiff,° to whom, as they happen to be inclined, they sometimes pay an absolute submission, and as often deny common respect; but this grant is not worth examination, the pontiff from whom it is derived being equally at a loss to fix his own authority upon any solid ground; so that at best the Degulians' claim to these settlements is like the Mahometan world, which rests upon an elephant, which is supported by a stone, which is supported by nothing.

It is observable that their conquests and acquisitions in Columbia (which is the Lilliputian name for the country that answers our America) have very little contributed to the power of those nations which have, to obtain them, broke through all the ties of human nature.° They have indeed added extent to their territories, and procured new titles for their princes, but at the same time have exhausted their mother country of its inhabitants, and subjected themselves to a thousand insults, by possessing vast tracts of land, which are too spacious to be constantly garrisoned, and too remote to be occasionally and duly supplied.

Even Iberia,° a country at the southwest point of Degulia, whose inhabitants were the first discoverers of Columbia, though she boasts herself mistress of the richest and most fertile part of that quarter of the world, which she secured to herself by the most dreadful massacres and devastations, has not yet, in all the gold she has imported, received an equivalent for the numbers of her natives sent out to people those kingdoms her sword has wasted; so that the whole advantage of her mighty conquests is bulk without strength, and pride without power.

It must be observed to the honour of the Lilliputians, who have in all ages been famous for their politics, that they have the art of civilizing their remote dominions without doing much injury to their native country; for when any of their people have forfeited the rights of society, by robberies, seditions, or any other crimes which make it not safe to suffer them to live, and yet are esteemed scarce heinous enough to be punished with death, they send them to some distant colony for a certain number of years proportionate to their crimes. Of these Mr Gulliver, during his stay, saw ten thousand conveyed from the prisons of Mildendo in close lighters to ships that lay at anchor in the river to carry them to Columbia,° where they were disposed among the inhabitants, undoubtedly very much to the propagation of knowledge and virtue, and no less to the honour of their native country.

Another inconvenience of these new claims is that they are a constant source of discord and debate among the Degulian powers, some of which are perpetually disputing their titles to countries which neither has a right to, and which sometimes are defended by the natives against both. There not long since arose a quarrel of this kind between the Lilliputians and Iberians, who contested the limits of their Columbian (or American) acquisitions. The Lilliputians, contrary to the ancient genius of that martial people, made very liberal concessions, such as rather drew upon them the imputation of cowardice than procured them the praise of moderation; but the Iberians, insatiable in their ambition, resolved to insist on nothing less than the absolute uninterrupted possession of that whole quarter of the world. In pursuance of this resolution they seized, upon various pretences, all the Lilliputian shipping that ventured or were drove near their shores in the Columbian seas, confiscated their lading, and imprisoned, tortured, and starved their seamen.° The Lilliputians were patient under all these insults for a long time, but being at length awakened by frequent injuries were making, at Mr Gulliver's departure, preparations for war; the event of which is not yet come to his knowledge.

Our author, having satisfied his curiosity with regard to the geography of this petty world, began to enquire more nearly into the constitution and laws of Lilliput. But how great was his surprise when he found it so nearly to resemble our own! The executive power being lodged wholly in the Emperor; as the legislative is in the Emperor, the House of Hurgoes,° or Lords, whose honours and privileges are hereditary, and the House of Clinabs, or Commons, representatives elect of the body of the people, whose assemblies are continued by several sessions and adjournments or prorogations, for the space of seven moons,° after which their authority determines, and writs are issued for new elections.

Mr Gulliver, astonished at this wonderful conformity between the constitution of England and Lilliput, consulted Flibo Quibus, the royal historiographer, upon that subject, who gave him the following account:

'Tis now, according to the best chronologers, more than 392 moons° since the arrival of your illustrious ancestor Quinbus Flestrin, or the Man-Mountain, upon the confines of Lilliput, where he performed those achievements still recorded in our histories, and celebrated by our poets; but alas! he was at last disgraced and banished by the effects of the most undeserved calumny and malice.

After his departure, the people, who had been irritated against him by false reports, finding the same evil measures that were imputed to his advice still pursued, and all the calamities still subsisting which had been described as the effects of his stay amongst them, were on the sudden not only convinced of his innocence, but so exasperated against his enemies, by the remembrance of his wisdom, clemency, and valour, that they surrounded the royal palace, and demanded the heads of the Man-Mountain's accusers. The ministers, according to custom, ran for shelter to the royal authority; but far from appeasing the people by that artifice, they involved their master in the common destruction.

The people having set fire to the palace, and buried the whole royal family in its ruins, placed one Mulgo Malvin, who had been secretary to the Man-Mountain, upon the throne of Lilliput. This man new-modelled the form of government, according to the plan which his master had delivered to him and affirmed to be an exact account of the British constitution.

Our government [continued the Lilliputian] has in some particulars varied from its original. The Clinabs were at first elected every moon, but now continue in office seven moons; to which alteration many attribute the present venality and dependency discovered in their assemblies.° They were likewise anciently paid by the people they represented for their attendance on the public business; but of late it is more common for the Clinabs to pay the people for admitting them to attend. Our ancestors, in ancient times, had some regard to the moral character of the person sent to represent them in their national assemblies, and would have shown some degree of resentment, or indignation, had their votes been asked for a murderer, an adulterer, a known oppressor, an hireling evidence, an attorney, a gamester, or a pimp. They demanded likewise in those who stood candidates for the power of making laws some knowledge of the laws already made; but now neither the most flagrant immorality, nor the grossest ignorance, are, amongst some electors, any objections to the character of a man who solicits voices with gold in his hand.

Such was the answer of the learned Lilliputian which incited Mr Gulliver to pursue his search into their laws, customs, and history; if haply he might discover, since human nature generally operates alike in all parts of the world, by what means the government of Lilliput, which had been once established on so excellent a plan, became so miserably degenerate; while the government of Britain, its original, maintained inviolate the purity and vigour of its primitive constitution.

As we propose to publish every month such part of Mr Gulliver's papers as shall seem most proper to bring our readers acquainted with the history and present state of Lilliput, we have chose for this half year's entertainment the debates of the Lilliputian senate, and shall begin with a very important one upon occasion of the Iberian depredations already mentioned, and the measures to be pursued for redress, which debate, as indeed all others on such high affairs, was carried on with the greatest eloquence and spirit, in the 4th session of the 8th senate (or parliament) of Magna Lilliputia, held at Belfaborac in the 11th moon of the reign of the Emperor Gorgenti the Second.°

On Gay's Epitaph°

Mr Urban,

Matters of very small consequence in themselves are often made important by the circumstances that attend them. Little follies and petty weaknesses, of no moment in common life, may, when they enter into the characters of men in high stations, obstruct the happiness of a great part of mankind. A barbarous inscription or disproportioned busto deserves no notice on account of the statuary who carved it or the writer who composed it; they were only private follies in the study or the shop; but erected in a temple, or engraved on a column, they are considered as public works, and censured as a disgrace to a nation. For this reason I have been often offended with the trifling distich upon Mr Gay's monument in Westminster Abbey:

> Life is a jest, and all things show it;
> I thought so once, but now I know it.

I never heard when or where this wonderful couplet was composed, or to what happy genius we are indebted for it: the miserable poetry of the first line makes it unlikely that it could be a studied production, unless it were one of the first efforts of a romantic girl, or some dapper school-boy's imitation of

> *Παντα γελως, και παντα κονις, και παντα το μηδεν.*°

If I might be indulged in making conjectures on a question of such weight, I should conceive it to have been a drunken sally, which was perhaps, after midnight, applauded as a lively epigram, and might have preserved its reputation had it, instead of being engraved on a monument at Westminster, been scribbled in its proper place, the window of a brothel.

There are very different species of wit appropriated to particular persons and places; the smartness of a shoeboy would not be extremely agreeable in a chancellor, and a tavern joke sounds but ill in a church, from which it ought to be banished, if for no other reason, at least for that which forbids a drunken man to be introduced into sober company.

Yet, lest this epigram should have any secret merit which, though it has escaped the observation of negligent and vulgar readers, has entitled it to the place I have found it in possession of, we will consider it with a little more attention than I fear we shall discover it to deserve.

The design of epitaphs is rational and moral, being generally to celebrate the virtues of the dead, and to excite and awaken the reader to the imitation of those excellencies which he sees thus honoured and distinguished, of which kind almost every sepulchral monument affords us an example.

There is another kind, in which the person departed is represented as delivering some precept to those whom he has left behind him, or uttering some important sentence suitable to his present state, from which the reader is prepared to receive very strong impressions by the silence and solemnity of the place where such inscriptions are generally found, and by the serious and affecting thoughts which naturally arise at the sight of the receptacles of the dead, upon the transitory and uncertain nature of human pleasure, vanity, and greatness. Of this sort the most ancient and the best that I have met with is that ordered (if I forget not) by the great Sesostris° to be inscribed on his tomb,

$Eις εμε τις οραων, ευσεβης εστω.$

Let every man who looks upon me learn to be pious.

On this monument perhaps no man ever looked without being, at least for some time, wiser and better, and doubtless, by so striking an instruction, the libertine has been often checked in the height of his debaucheries, and the oppressor softened in the midst of his tyranny. Perhaps, as long life is often the effect of virtue, the tomb of Sesostris may have more than repaired the ravages of his arms. Of this latter kind is the important distich we are considering. Mr Gay, like the Egyptian king, calls upon us from the habitations of the dead; but in such a manner and for such ends as shows what was anciently believed, that departed souls still preserve the characters they supported on earth, and that the author of the *Beggar's Opera* is not yet on the level with Sesostris. I cannot help thinking upon the dialogue on this occasion between Oedipus and his Jocasta:

Was Laius used to lie?
Joc. O no! the most sincere, plain, honest man; one that abhorred a lie.
Oed. Then he has got that quality in hell.

Dryden°

Mr Gay has returned from the regions of death not much improved in his poetry, and very much corrupted in his morals; for he is come back with a lie in his mouth, *Life is a jest.*

Mankind, with regard to their notions of futurity, are divided into two parties: a very small one that believes, or pretends to believe, that the present is the only state of existence; and another, which acknowledges that in some life to come, men will meet rewards or punishments according to their behaviour in this world.

In one of the classes our poet must be ranked: if he properly belonged to the first, he might indeed think life a jest, and might live as if he thought so; but I must leave it to acuter reasoners to explain how he could in that case *know* it after death, being for my part inclined to believe that knowledge ceases with existence.°

If he was of the latter opinion, he must think life more than a jest, unless he thought eternity a jest too; and if these were his sentiments, he is by this time most certainly undeceived. These lines, therefore, are impious in the mouth of a Christian, and nonsense in that of an atheist.

But whether we consider them as ludicrous or wicked, they ought not to stand where they are at present; buffoonery appears with a very ill grace, and impiety with much worse, in temples and on tombs. A childish levity has of late infected our conversation and behaviour, but let it not make its way into our churches. Irreligion has corrupted the present age, but let us not inscribe it on marble, to be the ruin or scorn of another generation. Let us have some regard to our reputation amongst foreigners, who do not hold either fools or atheists in high veneration, and will imagine that they can justify themselves in terming us such from our own monuments. Let us therefore review our public edifices, and, where inscriptions like this appear, spare our posterity the trouble of erasing them.

PAMPHILUS.

The Life of Dr Herman Boerhaave°

LATE PROFESSOR OF PHYSIC IN THE UNIVERSITY OF LEYDEN IN
HOLLAND

The following account of the late Dr Boerhaave, so loudly celebrated, and so universally lamented through the whole learned world, will, we hope, be not unacceptable to our readers: we could have made it much larger by adopting reports, and inserting unattested facts; a close adherence to certainty has contracted our narrative, and hindered it from swelling to that bulk at which modern histories generally arrive.

Dr Herman Boerhaave was born on the last day of December 1668, about one in the morning, at Voorhout, a village two miles distant from Leyden: his father, James Boerhaave, was minister of Voorhout, of whom his son, in a small account of his own life, has given a very amiable character for the simplicity and openness of his behaviour, for his exact frugality in the management of a narrow fortune, and the prudence, tenderness, and diligence with which he educated a numerous family of nine children. He was eminently skilled in history and genealogy, and versed in the Latin, Greek, and Hebrew languages.

His mother was Hagar Daelder, a tradesman's daughter of Amsterdam, from whom he might, perhaps, derive an hereditary inclination to the study of physic, in which she was very inquisitive, and had obtained a knowledge of it not common in female students.

This knowledge, however, she did not live to communicate to her son; for she died in 1673, ten years after her marriage.

His father, finding himself encumbered with the care of seven children, thought it necessary to take a second wife, and in July 1674, was married to Eve du Bois, daughter of a minister of Leyden, who, by her prudent and impartial conduct, so endeared herself to her husband's children, that they all regarded her as their own mother.

Herman Boerhaave was always designed by his father for the ministry, and with that view instructed by him in grammatical learning and the first elements of languages; in which he made such a proficiency, that he was, at the age of eleven years, not only master of the rules of grammar, but capable of translating with tolerable accuracy, and not wholly ignorant of critical niceties.

At intervals, to recreate his mind and strengthen his constitution, it was his father's custom to send him into the fields, and employ him in agriculture, and such kind of rural occupations, which he continued through all his life to love and practise; and, by this vicissitude of study and exercise, preserved himself, in a great measure, from those distempers and depressions which are frequently the consequences of indiscreet diligence and uninterrupted application; and from which students, not well acquainted with the constitution of the human body, sometimes fly for relief to wine instead of exercise, and purchase temporary ease at the hazard of chronical distempers.

The studies of young Boerhaave were, about this time, interrupted by an accident, which deserves a particular mention, as it first inclined him to that science to which he was, by nature, so well adapted, and which he afterwards carried to so great perfection.

In the twelfth year of his age, a stubborn, painful, and malignant ulcer broke out upon his left thigh; which, for near five years, defeated all the art of the surgeons and physicians, and not only afflicted him with most excruciating pains, but exposed him to such sharp and tormenting applications, that the disease and remedies were equally insufferable. Then it was that his own anguish taught him to compassionate that of others, and his experience of the inefficacy of the methods then in use incited him to attempt the discovery of others more certain.

He began to practise at least honestly, for he began upon himself; and his first essay was a prelude to his future success; for having laid aside all the prescriptions of his physicians, and all the applications of his surgeons, he at last, by fomenting the part with salt and urine, effected a cure.

That he might, on this occasion, obtain the assistance of surgeons with less inconvenience and expense, he was brought, by his father, at fourteen, to Leyden, and placed in the fourth class of the public school, after having been examined by the master: here his application and abilities were equally conspicuous. In six months, by gaining the first prize in the fourth class, he was raised to the fifth; and, in six months more, upon the same proof of the superiority of his genius, rewarded with another prize, and translated to the sixth; from whence it is usual, in six months more, to be removed to the university.

Thus did our young student advance in learning and reputation, when, as he was within view of the university, a sudden and unexpected blow threatened to defeat all his expectations.

On the 12th of November, in 1682, his father died, and left behind him a very slender provision for his widow and nine children, of which the eldest was not yet seventeen years old.

This was a most afflicting loss to the young scholar, whose fortune was by no means sufficient to bear the expenses of a learned education, and who therefore now seemed to be summoned by necessity to some way of life more immediately and certainly lucrative; but, with a resolution equal to his abilities, and a spirit not to be depressed or shaken, he determined to break through the obstacles of poverty, and supply by diligence the want of fortune.

He therefore asked and obtained the consent of his guardians to prosecute his studies so long as his patrimony would support him, and, continuing his wonted industry, gained another prize.

He was now to quit the school for the university, but, on account of the weakness yet remaining in his thigh, was, at his own entreaty, continued six months longer under the care of his master, the learned Wynschotan, where he was once more honoured with the prize.

At his removal to the university, the same genius and industry met with the same encouragement and applause. The learned Triglandius, one of his father's friends, made soon after professor of divinity at Leyden, distinguished him in a particular manner, and recommended him to the friendship of Mr Van Apphen, in whom he found a generous and constant patron.

He became now a diligent hearer of the most celebrated professors, and made great advances in all the sciences, still regulating his studies with a view principally to divinity, for which he was originally intended by his father; and, for that reason, he exerted his utmost application to attain an exact knowledge of the Hebrew tongue.

Being convinced of the necessity of mathematical learning, he began to study those sciences in 1687, but without that intense industry with which the pleasure he found in that kind of knowledge induced him afterwards to cultivate them.

In 1690, having performed the exercises of the university with uncommon reputation, he took his degree in philosophy; and, on that occasion, discussed the important and arduous question of the distinct natures of the soul and body, with such accuracy, perspicuity, and subtlety, that he entirely confuted all the sophistry of Epicurus, Hobbes, and Spinoza, and equally raised the character of his piety and erudition.

Divinity was still his great employment, and the chief aim of all his studies. He read the Scriptures in their original languages; and, when difficulties occurred, consulted the interpretations of the most ancient fathers, whom he read in order of time, beginning with Clemens Romanus.

In the perusal of these early writers, he was struck with the profoundest veneration for the simplicity and purity of their doctrine, the holiness of their lives, and the sanctity of the discipline practised by them; but, as he descended to the lower ages, he found the peace of Christianity broken by useless controversies, and its doctrines sophisticated by the subtleties of the schools. He found the holy writers interpreted according to the notions of philosophers, and the chimeras of metaphysicians adopted as articles of faith. He found difficulties raised by idle curiosity, and fomented to bitterness and rancour. He saw the simplicity of the Christian doctrine corrupted by the private notions of particular parties, of which each adhered to its own philosophy, and orthodoxy was confined to the sect in power.

Having now exhausted his fortune in the pursuit of his studies, he found the necessity of applying to some profession that, without engrossing all his time, might enable him to support himself; and, having obtained a very uncommon knowledge of the mathematics, he read lectures in those sciences to a select number of young gentlemen in the university.

At length, his propension to the study of physic grew too violent to be resisted; and, though he still intended to make divinity the great employment of his life, he could not deny himself the satisfaction of spending some time upon the medicinal writers, for the perusal of which he was so well qualified by his acquaintance with the mathematics and philosophy.

But this science corresponded so much with his natural genius, that he could not forbear making that his business which he intended only as his diversion; and still growing more eager, as he advanced further, he at length determined wholly to master that profession, and to take his degree in physic, before he engaged in the duties of the ministry.

It is, I believe, a very just observation, that men's ambition is, generally, proportioned to their capacity. Providence seldom sends any into the world with an inclination to attempt great things, who have not abilities likewise to perform them. To have formed the design of gaining a complete knowledge in medicine by way of digression from theological studies would have been little less than madness in most men, and would have only exposed them to ridicule and contempt. But Boerhaave was one of those mighty capacities to whom scarce anything appears impossible, and who think nothing worthy of their efforts but what appears insurmountable to common understandings.

He began this new course of study by a diligent perusal of Vesalius,

Bartholine, and Fallopius; and, to acquaint himself more fully with the structure of bodies, was a constant attendant upon Nuck's public dissections in the theatre, and himself very accurately inspected the bodies of different animals.

Having furnished himself with this preparatory knowledge, he began to read the ancient physicians, in the order of time, pursuing his inquiries downwards, from Hippocrates through all the Greek and Latin writers.

Finding, as he tells us himself, that Hippocrates was the original source of all medicinal knowledge and that all the later writers were little more than transcribers from him, he returned to him with more attention, and spent much time in making extracts from him, digesting his treatises into method, and fixing them in his memory.

He then descended to the moderns, among whom none engaged him longer, or improved him more, than Sydenham, to whose merit he has left this attestation, *that he frequently perused him, and always with greater eagerness*.

His insatiable curiosity after knowledge engaged him now in the practice of chemistry, which he prosecuted with all the ardour of a philosopher, whose industry was not to be wearied, and whose love of truth was too strong to suffer him to acquiesce in the reports of others.

Yet did he not suffer one branch of science to withdraw his attention from others: anatomy did not withhold him from the prosecution of chemistry, nor chemistry, enchanting as it is, from the study of botany, in which he was no less skilled than in other parts of physic. He was not only a careful examiner of all the plants in the garden of the university, but made excursions, for his further improvement, into the woods and fields, and left no place unvisited where any increase of botanical knowledge could be reasonably hoped for.

In conjunction with all these inquiries, he still pursued his theological studies, 'and still', as we are informed by himself, 'proposed, when he had made himself master of the whole art of physic, and obtained the honour of a degree in that science, to petition regularly for a licence to preach, and to engage in the cure of souls'; and intended, in his theological exercise, to discuss this question, *Why so many were formerly converted to Christianity by illiterate persons, and so few at present by men of learning*.

In pursuance of this plan he went to Hardewich, in order to take the degree of doctor in physic, which he obtained in July, 1693, having performed a public disputation, *De utilitate explorandorum excrementorum in aegris, ut signorum.*

Then returning to Leyden, full of his pious design of undertaking the ministry, he found, to his surprise, unexpected obstacles thrown in his way, and an insinuation dispersed through the university, that made him suspected, not of any slight deviation from received opinions, not of any pertinacious adherence to his own notions in doubtful and disputable matters, but of no less than Spinozism, or, in plainer terms, of atheism itself.

How so injurious a report came to be raised, circulated, and credited, will be, doubtless, very eagerly inquired; and an exact relation of the affair will not only satisfy the curiosity of mankind, but show that no merit, however exalted, is exempt from being not only attacked, but wounded, by the most contemptible whispers. Those who cannot strike with force can, however, poison their weapon, and, weak as they are, give mortal wounds, and bring a hero to the grave: so true is that observation, that many are able to do hurt, but few to do good.

This detestable calumny owed its rise to an incident from which no consequence of importance could be reasonably apprehended. As Boerhaave was sitting in a common boat, there arose a conversation among the passengers upon the impious and pernicious doctrine of Spinoza, which, as they all agreed, tends to the utter overthrow of all religion. Boerhaave sat and attended silently to this discourse for some time, till one of the company, willing to distinguish himself by his zeal, instead of confuting the positions of Spinoza by argument, began to give a loose to contumelious language and virulent invectives; with which Boerhaave was so little pleased that at last he could not forbear asking him, whether he had ever read the author against whom he declaimed.

The orator, not being able to make much answer, was checked in the midst of his invectives, but not without feeling a secret resentment against him who had at once interrupted his harangue, and exposed his ignorance.

This was observed by a stranger who was in the boat with them; he inquired of his neighbour the name of the young man whose question had put an end to the discourse, and having learned it, set it down in his pocket-book, as it soon appeared, with a malicious design, for in a few days it was the common conversation at Leyden that Boerhaave had revolted to Spinoza.

It was in vain that his advocates and friends pleaded his learned and unanswerable confutation of all atheistical opinions, and particularly of the system of Spinoza, in his discourse of the distinction between soul and body. Such calumnies are not easily suppressed, when they are once become general. They are kept alive and supported by the malice of bad, and sometimes by the zeal of good men, who, though they do not absolutely believe them, think it yet the surest method to keep not only guilty, but suspected men out of public employments, upon this principle, that the safety of many is to be preferred before the advantage of few.

Boerhaave, finding this formidable opposition raised against his pretensions to ecclesiastical honours or preferments, and even against his design of assuming the character of a divine, thought it neither necessary nor prudent to struggle with the torrent of popular prejudice, as he was equally qualified for a profession, not indeed of equal dignity or importance, but which must undoubtedly claim the second place among those which are of the greatest benefit to mankind.

He therefore applied himself to his medicinal studies with fresh ardour and alacrity, reviewed all his former observations and inquiries, and was continually employed in making new acquisitions.

Having now qualified himself for the practice of physic, he began to visit patients, but without that encouragement which others, not equally deserving, have sometimes met with. His business was, at first, not great, and his circumstances by no means easy; but still, superior to any discouragement, he continued his search after knowledge, and determined that prosperity, if ever he was to enjoy it, should be the consequence, not of mean art, or disingenuous solicitations, but of real merit, and solid learning.

His steady adherence to his resolutions appears yet more plainly from this circumstance: he was, while he yet remained in this unpleasing situation, invited by one of the first favourites of King William III to settle at the Hague upon very advantageous conditions, but declined the offer. For having no ambition but after knowledge, he was desirous of living at liberty, without any restraint upon his looks, his thoughts, or his tongue, and at the utmost distance from all contentions and state parties. His time was wholly taken up in visiting the sick, studying, making chemical experiments, searching into every part of medicine with the utmost diligence, teaching the mathematics, and reading the Scriptures, and those authors who profess to teach a certain method of loving God.

This was his method of living to the year when he was recommended by Mr Van Berg to the university, as a proper person to succeed Drelincourt in the office of lecturer on the institutes of physic, and elected without any solicitations on his part, and almost without his consent, on the 18th of May.

On this occasion, having observed, with grief, that Hippocrates, whom he regarded not only as the father, but as the prince of physicians, was not sufficiently read or esteemed by young students, he pronounced an oration, *de commendando studio Hippocratico*; by which he restored that great author to his just and ancient reputation.

He now began to read public lectures with great applause, and was prevailed upon by his audience to enlarge his original design, and instruct them in chemistry.

This he undertook, not only to the great advantage of his pupils, but to the great improvement of the art itself, which had been hitherto treated only in a confused and irregular manner, and was little more than a history of particular experiments, not reduced to certain principles, nor connected one with another: this vast chaos he reduced to order, and made that clear and easy, which was before to the last degree perplexed and obscure.

His reputation began now to bear some proportion to his merit, and extended itself to distant universities; so that in 1703, the professorship of physic being vacant at Groningen, he was invited thither; but he chose to continue his present course of life, and therefore refused to quit Leyden.

This invitation and refusal being related to the governors of the University of Leyden, they had so grateful a sense of his regard for them, that they immediately voted an honorary increase of his salary, and promised him the first professorship that should be vacant.

On this occasion he pronounced an oration upon the use of mechanics in the science of physic, in which he endeavoured to recommend a rational and mathematical inquiry into the causes of diseases, and the structure of bodies; and to show the follies and weaknesses of the jargon introduced by Paracelsus, Helmont, and other chemical enthusiasts, who have obtruded idle dreams upon the world, and, instead of enlightening their readers with explications of nature, have darkened the plainest appearances, and bewildered mankind in error and obscurity.

Boerhaave had now for nine years read physical lectures, but without the title or dignity of a professor, when, by the death of Professor Hotten, the professorship of physic and botany fell to him of course.

On this occasion he asserted the simplicity and facility of the science of physic in opposition to those that think that obscurity contributes to the dignity of learning, and that to be admired it is necessary not to be understood.

His profession of botany made it part of his duty to superintend the physical garden, which he improved so much by the immense number of new plants which he procured that it was enlarged to twice its original extent.

In 1714, he was deservedly advanced to the highest dignities of the university, and, in the same year, made physician of St Augustine's Hospital in Leyden, into which the students are admitted twice a week, to learn the practice of physic.

This was of equal advantage to the sick and the students, for the success of his practice was the best demonstration of the soundness of his principles.

When he laid down his office of governor of the university in 1715, he made an oration upon the subject of *attaining to certainty in natural philosophy*; in which he declares himself in the strongest terms, a favourer of experimental knowledge, and reflects with just severity upon those arrogant philosophers who are too easily disgusted with the slow methods of obtaining true notions by frequent experiments; and who, possessed with too high an opinion of their own abilities, rather choose to consult their own imaginations, than inquire into nature, and are better pleased with the delightful amusement of forming hypotheses, than the toilsome drudgery of amassing observations.

The emptiness and uncertainty of all those systems, whether venerable for their antiquity, or agreeable for their novelty, he has evidently shown; and not only declared, but proved, that we are entirely ignorant of the principles of things, and that all the knowledge we have is of such qualities alone as are discoverable by experience, or such as may be deduced from them by mathematical demonstration.

This discourse, filled as it was with piety, and a true sense of the greatness of the Supreme Being, and the incomprehensibility of his works, gave such offence to a professor of Franeker, who having long entertained a high esteem for Descartes, considered his principles as the bulwark of orthodoxy, that he appeared in vindication of his darling author, and complained of the injury done him with the greatest vehemence, declaring little less than that the Cartesian system and the Christian must inevitably stand and fall together, and that to say we were ignorant of the principles of things was not only to enlist among the sceptics but to sink into atheism itself.

So far can prejudice darken the understanding, as to make it consider precarious and uncertain systems as the chief support of sacred and invariable truth.

This treatment of Boerhaave was so far resented by the governors of his university, that they procured from Franeker a recantation of the invective that had been thrown out against him. This was not only complied with, but offers were made him of more ample satisfaction; to which he returned an answer not less to his honour than the victory he gained, 'that he should think himself sufficiently compensated, if his warned adversary received no farther molestation on his account.'

So far was this weak and injudicious attack from shaking a reputation not casually raised by fashion or caprice, but founded upon solid merit, that the same year his correspondence was desired upon botany and natural philosophy by the Academy of Sciences at Paris, of which he was, upon the death of Count Marsigli, in the year 1728, elected a member.

Nor were the French the only nation by which this great man was courted and distinguished; for, two years after, he was elected Fellow of our Royal Society.

It cannot be doubted but, thus caressed and honoured with the highest and most public marks of esteem by other nations, he became more celebrated in his own university; for Boerhaave was not one of those learned men, of whom the world has seen too many, that disgrace their studies by their vices, and by unaccountable weaknesses make themselves ridiculous at home, while their writings procure them the veneration of distant countries, where their learning is known, but not their follies.

Not that his countrymen can be charged with being insensible of his excellencies till other nations taught them to admire him; for, in 1718, he was chosen to succeed Le Mort in the professorship of chemistry; on which occasion he pronounced an oration, *De chemia errores suos expurgante*, in which he treated that science with an elegance of style not often to be found in chemical writers, who seem generally to have affected not only a barbarous, but unintelligible phrase, and like the Pythagoreans of old, to have wrapped up their secrets in symbols and enigmatical expressions, either because they believed that mankind would reverence most what they least understood, or because they wrote not from benevolence, but vanity, and were desirous to be praised for their knowledge, though they could not prevail upon themselves to communicate it.

In 1722, his course both of lectures and practice was interrupted by the gout, which, as he relates it in his speech after his recovery, he brought upon himself, by an imprudent confidence in the strength of his own constitution, and by transgressing those rules which he had a thousand times inculcated to his pupils and acquaintance. Rising in the morning before day, he went immediately, hot and sweating, from his bed into the open air, and exposed himself to the cold dews.

The history of his illness can hardly be read without horror. He was for five months confined to his bed, where he lay upon his back without daring to attempt the least motion, because any effort renewed his torments, which were so exquisite that he was at length not only deprived of motion, but of sense. Here art was at a stand; nothing could be attempted, because nothing could be proposed with the least prospect of success. At length, having, in the sixth month of his illness, obtained some remission, he took simple medicines in large quantities, and at length wonderfully recovered.

Succos pressos bibit noster herbarum cichoreae, endiviae, fumariae, nasturtii aquatici, veronicae aquaticae latifoliae, copia ingenti: simul deglutiens abundantissime gummi ferulacea Asiatica.°

His recovery, so much desired, and so unexpected, was celebrated on January 11, 1723, when he opened his school again, with general joy, and public illuminations.

It would be an injury to the memory of Boerhaave not to mention what was related by himself to one of his friends, that when he lay whole days and nights without sleep, he found no method of diverting his thoughts so effectual as meditation upon his studies, and that he often relieved and mitigated the sense of his torments by the recollection of what he had read, and by reviewing those stores of knowledge which he had reposited in his memory.

This is, perhaps, an instance of fortitude, and steady composure of mind, which would have been for ever the boast of the Stoic schools, and increased the reputation of Seneca or Cato. The patience of Boerhaave, as it was more rational, was more lasting than theirs; it was that *Patientia Christiana*, which Lipsius,° the great master of the Stoical philosophy, begged of God in his last hours; it was founded on religion, not vanity; not on vain reasonings, but on confidence in God.

In 1727, he was seized with a violent burning fever, which continued so long, that he was once more given up by his friends.

From this time he was frequently afflicted with returns of his distemper, which yet did not so far subdue him as to make him lay aside his studies, or his lectures, till in 1729 he found himself so worn out, that it was improper for him to continue any longer the professorships of botany or chemistry, which he therefore resigned April 28, and upon his resignation spoke a *Sermo academicus*, or oration, in which he asserts the power and wisdom of the Creator from the wonderful fabric of the human body; and confutes all those idle reasoners who pretend to explain the formation of parts, or the animal operations, to which he proves, that art can produce nothing equal, nor any thing parallel. One instance I shall mention, which is produced by him, of the vanity of any attempt to rival the work of God. Nothing is more boasted by the admirers of chemistry, than that they can, by artificial heats and digestion, imitate the productions of nature. 'Let all these heroes of science meet together,' says Boerhaave; 'let them take bread and wine, the food that forms the blood of man, and by assimilation contributes to the growth of the body: let them try all their arts, they shall not be able from these materials to produce a single drop of blood.' So much is the most common act of nature beyond the utmost efforts of the most extended science!

From this time Boerhaave lived with less public employment indeed, but not an idle or a useless life; for, besides his hours spent in instructing his scholars, a great part of his time was taken up by patients, who came, when the distemper would admit it, from all parts of Europe to consult him, or did it by letters, which, in more urgent cases, were continually sent to inquire his opinion and ask his advice.

Of his sagacity, and the wonderful penetration with which he often discovered and described, at first sight of a patient, such distempers as betray themselves by no symptoms to common eyes, such wonderful relations have been spread over the world, as, though attested beyond doubt, can scarcely be credited. I mention none of them, because I have no opportunity of collecting testimonies, or distinguishing between those accounts which are well proved, and those which owe their rise to fiction and credulity.

Yet I cannot but implore, with the greatest earnestness, such as have been conversant with this great man, that they will not so far neglect the common interest of mankind, as to suffer any of these circumstances to be lost to posterity. Men are generally idle, and ready to satisfy themselves, and intimidate the industry of others by calling that impossible which is only difficult. The skill to which Boerhaave attained, by a long and unwearied observation of nature, ought therefore to be transmitted, in all its particulars, to future ages, that his successors may be ashamed to fall below him, and that none may hereafter excuse his ignorance by pleading the impossibility of clearer knowledge.

Yet so far was this great master from presumptuous confidence in his abilities, that in his examinations of the sick he was remarkably circumstantial and particular. He well knew that the originals of distempers are often at a distance from their visible effects; that to acquiesce in conjecture, where certainty may be obtained, is either vanity or negligence; and that life is not to be sacrificed, either to an affectation of quick discernment, or of crowded practice; but may be required, if trifled away, at the hand of the physician.

About the middle of the year 1737, he felt the first approaches of that fatal illness that brought him to the grave, of which we have inserted an account written by himself Sept. 8, 1738, to a friend at London; which deserves not only to be preserved, as an historical relation of the disease which deprived us of so great a man, but as a proof of his piety and resignation to the divine will.

Aetas, labor, corporisque opima pinguetudo, effecerant, ante annum, ut inertibus refertum, grave, hebes, plenitudine turgens corpus, anhelum ad motus minimos, cum sensu suffocationis, pulsu mirifice anomalo, ineptum evaderet ad ullum motum. Urgebat praecipue subsistens prorsus & intercepta respiratio ad prima somni initia : unde somnus prorsus prohibebatur, cum formidabili strangulationis molestia. Hinc hydrops pedum, crurum, femorum, scroti, praeputii, et abdominis. Quae tamen omnia sublata. Sed dolor manet in abdomine, cum anxietate summa, anhelitu suffocante, & debilitate incredibili: somno pauco, eoque vago, per somnia turbatissimo : animus vero rebus agendis impar. Cum his luctor fessus, nec emergo: patienter expectans Dei jussa, quibus resigno data, quae sola amo, & honoro unice.°

In this last illness, which was to the last degree lingering, painful, and afflictive, his constancy and firmness did not forsake him. He neither intermitted the necessary cares of life, nor forgot the proper preparations for death. Though dejection and lowness of spirit was, as he himself tells us, part of his distemper; yet even this, in some measure, gave way to that vigour which the soul receives from a consciousness of innocence.

About three weeks before his death he received a visit at his country-house from the Revd Mr Schultens, his intimate friend, who found him sitting without door, with his wife, sister, and daughter. After the compliments of form, the ladies withdrew, and left them to private conversation; when Boerhaave took occasion to tell him what had been, during his illness, the chief subject of his thoughts. He had never doubted of the spiritual and immaterial nature of the soul, but declared that he had lately had a kind of experimental certainty of the distinction between corporeal and thinking substances, which mere reason and philosophy cannot afford; and opportunities of contemplating the wonderful and inexplicable union of soul and body, which nothing but long sickness can give. This he illustrated by a description of the effects which the infirmities of his body had upon his faculties; which yet they did not so oppress or vanquish, but his soul was always master of itself, and always resigned to the pleasure of its Maker.

He related, with great concern, that once his patience so far gave way to extremity of pain, that, after having lain fifteen hours in exquisite tortures, he prayed to God that he might be set free by death.

Mr Schultens, by way of consolation, answered, that he thought such wishes, when forced by continued and excessive torments, unavoidable in the present state of human nature; that the best men, even Job himself, were not able to refrain from such starts of impatience. This he did not deny; but said, 'He that loves God ought to think nothing desirable but what is most pleasing to the supreme Goodness.'

Such were his sentiments, and such his conduct, in this state of weakness and pain: as death approached nearer, he was so far from terror or confusion, that he seemed even less sensible of pain, and more cheerful under his torments, which continued till the 23rd day of September 1738, on which he died, between four and five in the morning, in the 70th year of his age.

Thus died Boerhaave, a man formed by nature for great designs, and guided by religion in the exertion of his abilities. He was of a robust and athletic constitution of body, so hardened by early severities, and wholesome fatigue, that he was insensible of any sharpness of air, or inclemency of weather. He was tall, and remarkable for extraordinary strength. There was, in his air and motion, something rough and artless, but so majestic and great at the same time, that no man ever looked upon him without veneration, and a kind of tacit submission to the superiority of his genius.

The vigour and activity of his mind sparkled visibly in his eyes; nor was it observed that any change of his fortune, or alteration in his affairs, whether happy or unfortunate, affected his countenance.

He was always cheerful, and desirous of promoting mirth by a facetious and humorous conversation: he was never soured by calumny and detraction, nor ever thought it necessary to confute them; for 'they are sparks,' said he, 'which, if you do not blow them, will go out of themselves.'

Yet he took care never to provoke enemies by severity of censure; for he never dwelt on the faults or defects of others, and was so far from inflaming the envy of his rivals by dwelling on his own excellencies, that he rarely mentioned himself, or his writings.

He was not to be overawed or depressed by the presence, frowns, or insolence of great men, but persisted on all occasions in the right, with a resolution always present, and always calm. He was modest, but not timorous; and firm without rudeness.

He could, with uncommon readiness and certainty, make a conjecture of men's inclinations and capacity by their aspect.

His method of life was to study in the morning and evening, and to allot the middle of the day to his public business. He rose at four in the summer, and five in winter. His usual exercise was riding, till, in his latter years, his distempers made it more proper for him to walk: when he was weary, he amused himself with playing on the violin.

His greatest pleasure was to retire to his house in the country, where he had a garden of eight acres, stored with all the herbs and trees which the climate would bear; here he used to enjoy his hours unmolested, and prosecute his studies without interruption.

The diligence with which he pursued his studies is sufficiently evident from his success. Statesmen and generals may grow great by unexpected accidents, and a fortunate concurrence of circumstances, neither procured nor foreseen by themselves, but reputation in the learned world must be the effect of industry and capacity. Boerhaave lost none of his hours, but when he had obtained one science, attempted another; he added physic to divinity, chemistry to the mathematics, and botany to anatomy. He examined systems by experiments, and formed experiments into systems. He neither neglected the observations of others, nor blindly submitted to celebrated names. He neither thought so highly of himself as to imagine he could receive no light from books; nor so meanly as to believe he could discover nothing but what was to be learned from them. He examined the observations of other men, but trusted only to his own.

Nor was he unacquainted with the art of recommending truth by elegance, and embellishing philosophy with polite literature: he knew that but a small part of mankind will sacrifice their pleasure to their improvement; and those authors who would find many readers must endeavour to please while they instruct.

He knew the importance of his own writings to mankind; and lest he might, by a roughness and barbarity of style, too frequent among men of great learning, disappoint his own intentions, and make his labours less useful, he did not neglect the arts of eloquence and poetry. Thus was his learning at once various and exact, profound and agreeable.

He was not only skilled in the learned languages, and the tongues in which the Old Testament was written, but was able to converse in many of the modern languages, and to read others which he could not speak.

But his knowledge, however uncommon, holds, in his character, but the second place; his virtue was yet much more uncommon than his learning. He was an admirable example of temperance, fortitude, humility, and devotion. His piety, and a religious sense of his dependence on God, was the basis of all his virtues, and the principle of his whole conduct. He was too sensible of his weakness to ascribe any thing to himself, or to conceive that he could subdue passion, or withstand temptation, by his own natural power; he attributed every good thought, and every laudable action, to the Father of Goodness. Being once asked by a friend, who had often admired his patience under great provocations, whether he knew what it was to be angry, and by what means he had so entirely suppressed that impetuous and ungovernable passion, he answered, with the utmost frankness and sincerity, that he was naturally quick of resentment, but that he had, by daily prayer and meditation, at length attained to this mastery over himself.

As soon as he arose in the morning, it was, throughout his whole life, his daily practice to retire for an hour to private prayer and meditation; this, he often told his friends, gave him spirit and vigour in the business of the day; and this he therefore commended, as the best rule of life; for nothing, he knew, could support the soul in all distresses but a confidence in the Supreme Being, nor can a steady and rational magnanimity flow from any other source than a consciousness of the divine favour.

He asserted on all occasions the divine authority, and sacred efficacy, of the Holy Scriptures; and maintained that by them alone was taught the way of salvation, and that they only could give peace of mind. The excellency of the Christian religion was the frequent subject of his conversation. A strict obedience to the doctrine, and a diligent imitation of the example, of our blessed Saviour, he often declared to be the foundation of true tranquillity. He recommended to his friends a careful observation of the precept of Moses° concerning the love of God and man. He worshipped God as he is in himself, without attempting to inquire into his nature. He desired only to think of God what God has revealed of himself. There he stopped, lest by indulging his own ideas he should form a deity from his own imagination, and commit sin by falling down before him. To the will of God he paid an absolute submission, without endeavouring to discover the reason of his determinations; and this he accounted the first and most inviolable duty of a Christian. When he heard of a criminal condemned to die, he used to think, and often say, 'Who can tell whether this man is not better than I? Or, if I am better, it is not to be ascribed to myself, but to the goodness of God.'

So far was this man from being made impious by philosophy, or vain by knowledge, or by virtue, that he ascribed all his abilities to the bounty, and all his goodness to the grace of God. May his example extend its influence to his admirers and followers! May those who study his writings, imitate his life; and those who endeavour after his knowledge, aspire likewise to his piety!

He married, September 17, 1710, Mary Drolenveaux, the only daughter of a burgomaster of Leyden, by whom he had Joanna Maria, who survives her father, and three other children, who died in their infancy.°

A Complete Vindication of the Licensers of the Stage,

FROM THE MALICIOUS AND SCANDALOUS ASPERSIONS OF MR BROOKE,
AUTHOR OF *Gustavus Vasa*
WITH A PROPOSAL FOR MAKING THE OFFICE OF LICENSER MORE
EXTENSIVE AND EFFECTUAL. BY AN IMPARTIAL HAND°

It is generally agreed by the writers of all parties that few crimes are equal, in their degree of guilt, to that of calumniating a good and gentle, or defending a wicked and oppressive administration.

It is therefore with the utmost satisfaction of mind that I reflect how often I have employed my pen in vindication of the present ministry, and their dependents and adherents, how often I have detected the specious fallacies of the advocates for independence, how often I have softened the obstinacy of patriotism, and how often triumphed over the clamour of opposition.

I have, indeed, observed but one set of men upon whom all my arguments have been thrown away, which neither flattery can draw to compliance, nor threats reduce to submission, and who have, notwithstanding all expedients that either invention or experience could suggest, continued to exert their abilities in a vigorous and constant opposition of all our measures.

The unaccountable behaviour of these men, the enthusiastic resolution with which, after a hundred successive defeats, they still renewed their attacks, the spirit with which they continued to repeat their arguments in the senate, though they found a majority determined to condemn them, and the inflexibility with which they rejected all offers of places and preferments at last excited my curiosity so far that I applied myself to enquire with great diligence into the real motives of their conduct, and to discover what principle it was that had force to inspire such unextinguishable zeal, and to animate such unwearied efforts.

For this reason I attempted to cultivate a nearer acquaintance with some of the chiefs of that party, and imagined that it would be necessary for some time to dissemble my sentiments that I might learn theirs.

Dissimulation to a true politician is not difficult, and therefore I readily assumed the character of a proselyte, but found that their principle of action was no other than that which they make no scruple of avowing in the most public manner, notwithstanding the contempt and ridicule to which it every day exposes them, and the loss of those honours and profits from which it excludes them.

This wild passion, or principle, is a kind of fanaticism by which they distinguish those of their own party, and which they look upon as a certain indication of a great mind. *We* have no name for it *at court*,° but among themselves, they term it by a kind of cant-phrase, *a regard for posterity*.

This passion seems to predominate in all their conduct, to regulate every action of their lives, and sentiment of their minds; I have heard L—— and P——,° when they have made a vigorous opposition, or blasted the blossom of some ministerial scheme, cry out, in the height of their exultations, 'This will deserve the thanks of posterity!' And when their adversaries, as it much more frequently falls out, have outnumbered and overthrown them, they will say with an air of revenge, and a kind of gloomy triumph, 'Posterity will curse you for this.'

It is common among men under the influence of any kind of frenzy, to believe that all the world has the same odd notions that disorder their own imaginations. Did these unhappy men, these deluded patriots, know how little we are concerned about posterity, they would never attempt to fright us with their curses, or tempt us to a neglect of our own interest by a prospect of their gratitude.

But so strong is their infatuation that they seem to have forgotten even the primary law of self-preservation, for they sacrifice without scruple every flattering hope, every darling enjoyment, and every satisfaction of life to this *ruling passion*, and appear in every step to consult not so much their own advantage as that of *posterity*.

Strange delusion! that can confine all their thoughts to a race of men whom they neither know, nor can know; from whom nothing is to be feared, nor any thing expected; who cannot even bribe a special jury,° nor have so much as a single riband° to bestow.

This fondness for posterity is a kind of madness which at Rome was once almost epidemical, and infected even the women and the children. It reigned there till the entire destruction of Carthage, after which it began to be less general, and in a few years afterwards a remedy was discovered, by which it was almost entirely extinguished.

In England it never prevailed in any such degree; some few of the ancient barons° seem indeed to have been disordered by it, but the contagion has been for the most part timely checked, and our ladies have been generally free.

But there has been in every age a set of men much admired and reverenced, who have affected to be always talking of posterity, and have laid out their lives upon the composition of poems for the sake of being applauded by this imaginary generation.

The present poets I reckon amongst the most inexorable enemies of our most excellent ministry, and much doubt whether any method will effect the cure of a distemper which in this class of men may be termed not an accidental disease, but a defect in their original frame and constitution.

Mr Brooke, a name I mention with all the detestation suitable to my character, could not forbear discovering this depravity of his mind in his very prologue, which is filled with sentiments so wild, and so much unheard of among those who frequent levees and courts, that I much doubt whether the zealous licenser proceeded any further in his examination of his performance.

He might easily perceive that a man,

> Who bade his moral beam through every age,°

was too much a bigot to exploded notions to compose a play which he could license without manifest hazard of his office, a hazard which no man would incur untainted with the love of posterity.

We cannot therefore wonder that an author wholly possessed by this passion should vent his resentment for the licenser's just refusal, in virulent advertisements, insolent complaints, and scurrilous assertions of his rights and privileges, and proceed in defiance of authority to solicit a subscription.

This temper which I have been describing is almost always complicated with ideas of the high prerogatives of human nature, of a sacred unalienable birthright, which no man has conferred upon us, and which neither kings can take, nor senates give away, which we may justly assert whenever and by whomsoever it is attacked, and which, if ever it should happen to be lost, we may take the first opportunity to recover.

The natural consequence of these chimeras is contempt of authority, and an irreverence for any superiority but what is founded upon merit, and their notions of merit are very peculiar; for it is among them no great proof of merit to be wealthy and powerful, to wear a garter or a star, to command a regiment or a senate, to have the ear of the minister or of the king, or to possess any of those virtues and excellencies which among us entitle a man to little less than worship and prostration.

We may therefore easily conceive that Mr Brooke thought himself entitled to be importunate for a license, because, in his own opinion, he deserved one, and to complain thus loudly at the repulse he met with.

His complaints will have, I hope, but little weight with the public, since the opinions of the sect in which he is enlisted are exposed and shown to be evidently and demonstrably opposite to that system of subordination and dependence to which we are indebted for the present tranquillity of the nation, and that cheerfulness and readiness with which the two Houses concur in all our designs.

I shall however, to silence him entirely, or at least to show those of our party that he ought to be silent, consider singly every instance of hardship and oppression which he has dared to publish in the papers, and to publish in such a manner that I hope no man will condemn me for want of candour in becoming an advocate for the ministry, if I can consider his advertisements as nothing less than *an appeal to his country*.

Let me be forgiven if I cannot speak with temper of such insolence as this: Is a man without title, pension, or place, to suspect the impartiality or the judgment of those who are entrusted with the administration of public affairs? Is he, when the law is not strictly observed in regard to him, to think himself *aggrieved*, to tell his sentiments in print, assert his claim to better usage, and fly for redress to another tribunal?

If such practices are permitted, I will not venture to foretell the effects of them; the ministry may soon be convinced that such sufferers will find compassion, and that it is safer not to bear hard upon them than to allow them to complain.

The power of licensing in general, being firmly established by an Act of Parliament, our poet has not attempted to call in question, but contents himself with censuring the manner in which it has been executed, so that I am not now engaged to assert the licenser's authority, but to defend his conduct.

The poet seems to think himself aggrieved because the licenser kept his tragedy in his hands one and twenty days, whereas the law allows him to detain it only fourteen.

Where will the insolence of the malcontents end? Or how are such unreasonable expectations possibly to be satisfied? Was it ever known that a man exalted into a high station dismissed a suppliant in the time limited by law? Ought not Mr Brooke to think himself happy that his play was not detained longer? If he had been kept a year in suspense, what redress could he have obtained? Let the poets remember when they appear before the licenser, or his deputy, that they stand at the tribunal from which there is no appeal permitted, and where nothing will so well become them as reverence and submission.

Mr Brooke mentions in his preface his knowledge of the laws of his own country; had he extended his enquiries to the civil law, he could have found a full justification of the licenser's conduct, *Boni judicis est ampliare suam auctoritatem.*°

If then it be 'the business of a good judge to enlarge his authority', was it not in the licenser the utmost clemency and forbearance to extend fourteen days only to twenty-one?

I suppose this great man's inclination to perform at least this duty of a good judge is not questioned by any, either of his friends or enemies, I may therefore venture to hope that he will extend his power by proper degrees, and that I shall live to see a malcontent writer earnestly soliciting for the copy of a play which he had delivered to the licenser twenty years before.

'I waited,' says he, 'often on the licenser, and with the utmost importunity entreated an answer.' Let Mr Brooke consider whether that importunity was not a sufficient reason for the disappointment. Let him reflect how much more decent it had been to have waited the leisure of a great man,° than to have pressed upon him with repeated petitions, and to have intruded upon those precious moments which he has dedicated to the service of his country.

Mr Brooke was doubtless led into this improper manner of acting, by an erroneous notion that the grant of a license was not an act of favour but of justice, a mistake into which he could not have fallen, but from a supine inattention to the design of the statute, which was only to bring poets into subjection and dependence, not to encourage good writers, but to discourage all.

There lies no obligation upon the licenser to grant his sanction to a play, however excellent, nor can Mr Brooke demand any reparation, whatever applause his performance may meet with.

Another grievance is that the licenser assigned no reason for his refusal. This is a higher strain of insolence than any of the former. Is it for a poet to demand a licenser's reason for his proceedings? Is he not rather to acquiesce in the decision of authority, and conclude that there are reasons which he cannot comprehend?

Unhappy would it be for men in power, were they always obliged to publish the motives of their conduct. What is power but the liberty of acting without being accountable? The advocates for the licensing act have alleged that the Lord Chamberlain has always had authority to prohibit the representation of a play for just reasons. Why then did we call in all our force to procure an Act of Parliament? Was it to enable him to do what he has always done, to confirm an authority which no man attempted to impair, or pretended to dispute? No, certainly: our intention was to invest him with new privileges, and to empower him to do that *without* reason, which *with* reason he could do before.

We have found by long experience that to lie under a necessity of assigning reasons is very troublesome, and that many an excellent design has miscarried by the loss of time spent unnecessarily in examining reasons.

Always to call for reasons, and always to reject them, shows a strange degree of perverseness; yet such is the daily behaviour of our adversaries, who have never yet been satisfied with any reasons that have been offered by us.

They have made it their practice to demand once a year the reasons for which we maintain a standing army.°

One year we told them that it was necessary, because all the nations round us were involved in war; this had no effect upon them, and therefore resolving to do our utmost for their satisfaction, we told them the next year that it was necessary because all the nations round us were at peace.

This reason finding no better reception than the other, we had recourse to our apprehensions of an invasion from the Pretender, of an insurrection in favour of *gin*,° and of a general disaffection among the people.

But as they continue still impenetrable, and oblige us still to assign our annual reasons, we shall spare no endeavours to procure such as may be more satisfactory than any of the former.

The reason we once gave for building barracks was for fear of the plague, and we intend next year to propose the augmentation of our troops for fear of a famine.

The committee by which the act for licensing the stage was drawn up had too long known the inconvenience of giving reasons, and were too well acquainted with the characters of great men, to lay the Lord Chamberlain, or his deputy, under any such tormenting obligation.

Yet lest Mr Brooke should imagine that a license was refused him without just reasons, I shall condescend to treat him with more regard than he can reasonably expect, and point out such sentiments as not only justly exposed him to that refusal, but would have provoked any ministry less merciful than the present to have inflicted some heavier penalties upon him.

His prologue is filled with such insinuations as no friend of our excellent government can read without indignation and abhorrence, and cannot but be owned to be a proper introduction to such scenes as seem designed to kindle in the audience a flame of opposition, patriotism, public spirit, and independency, that spirit which we have so long endeavoured to suppress, and which cannot be revived without the entire subversion of all our schemes.

This seditious poet, not content with making an open attack upon us by declaring in plain terms that he looks upon freedom as the only source of public happiness and national security, has endeavoured with subtlety, equal to his malice, to make us suspicious of our firmest friends, to infect our consultations with distrust, and to ruin us by disuniting us.

This indeed will not be easily effected; a union founded upon interest and cemented by dependence is naturally lasting. But confederacies which owe their rise to virtue or mere conformity of sentiments are quickly dissolved, since no individual has anything either to hope or fear for himself, and public spirit is generally too weak to combat with private passions.

The poet has, however, attempted to weaken our combination by an artful and sly assertion, which, if suffered to remain unconfuted, may operate by degrees upon our minds in the days of leisure and retirement which are now approaching, and perhaps fill us with such surmises as may at least very much embarrass our affairs.

The law by which the Swedes justified their opposition to the encroachments of the King of Denmark he not only calls

> Great Nature's law, the law within the breast

but proceeds to tell us that it is

> ——Stamped by Heaven upon th' unlettered mind.

By which he evidently intends to insinuate a maxim which is, I hope, as false as it is pernicious, that men are naturally fond of liberty till those unborn ideas and desires are effaced by literature.

The author, if he be not a man mewed up in his solitary study and entirely unacquainted with the conduct of the present ministry, must know that we have hitherto acted upon different principles. We have always regarded *letters* as great obstructions to our scheme of subordination, and have therefore, when we have heard of any man remarkably *unlettered*, carefully noted him down as the most proper person for any employments of trust or honour, and considered him as a man in whom we could safely repose our most important secrets.

From among the uneducated and *unlettered* we have chosen not only our ambassadors° and other negotiators, but even our journalists and pamphleteers, nor have we had any reason to change our measures or to repent of the confidence which we have placed in ignorance.

Are we now therefore to be told that this law is

> Stamped upon th' unlettered mind?

Are we to suspect our place-men, our pensioners, our generals, our lawyers, our best friends in both Houses, all our adherents among the atheists and infidels, and our very gazetteers, clerks, and court-pages, as friends to independency? Doubtless this is the tendency of his assertion, but we have known them too long to be thus imposed upon, the *unlettered* have been our warmest and most constant defenders, nor have we omitted any thing to deserve their favour, but have always endeavoured to raise their reputation, extend their influence, and increase their number.

In his first act he abounds with sentiments very inconsistent with the ends for which the power of licensing was granted; to enumerate them all would be to transcribe a great part of his play, a task which I shall very willingly leave to others, who, though true friends to the government, are not inflamed with zeal so fiery and impatient as mine, and therefore do not feel the same emotions of rage and resentment at the sight of those infamous passages, in which venality and dependence are presented as mean in themselves, and productive of remorse and infelicity.

One line which ought, in my opinion, to be erased from every copy by a special Act of Parliament, is mentioned by Anderson,° as pronounced by the hero in his sleep,

> O Sweden, O my country, yet I'll save thee.

This line I have reason to believe thrown out as a kind of watch-word for the opposing faction, who, when they meet in their seditious assemblies, have been observed to lay their hands upon their breasts, and cry out with great vehemence of accent,

> O B——, O my country, yet I'll save thee.

In the second scene he endeavours to fix epithets of contempt upon those passions and desires which have been always found most useful to the ministry, and most opposite to the spirit of independency.

> Base fear, the laziness of lust, gross appetites,
> These are the ladders and the grov'ling foot-stool
> From whence the tyrant rises——
> Secure and scepter'd in the soul's servility
> He has debauched the genius of our country
> And rides triumphant, while her captive sons
> Await his nod, the silken slaves of pleasure,
> Or fettered in their fears.——

Thus is that decent submission to our superiors, and that proper awe of authority which we are taught in courts, termed *base fear* and the *servility of the soul*. Thus are those gaieties and enjoyments, those elegant amusements, and lulling pleasures which the followers of a court are blessed with, as the just rewards of their attendance and submission, degraded to *lust*, *grossness*, and *debauchery*. The author ought to be told that courts are not to be mentioned with so little ceremony, and that though gallantries and amours are admitted there, it is almost treason to suppose them infected with debauchery or lust.

It is observable that when this hateful writer has conceived any thought of an uncommon malignity, a thought which tends in a more particular manner to excite the love of liberty, animate the heat of patriotism, or degrade the majesty of kings, he takes care to put it in the mouth of his hero, that it may be more forcibly impressed upon his reader. Thus Gustavus, speaking of his tatters, cries out,

> ——Yes, my Arvida,°
> Beyond the sweeping of the proudest train
> That shades a monarch's heel, I prize these weeds,
> For they are sacred to my country's freedom.

Here this abandoned son of liberty makes a full discovery of his execrable principles; the tatters of Gustavus, the usual dress of the assertors of these doctrines, are of more divinity, because they are sacred to freedom than the sumptuous and magnificent robes of regality itself. Such sentiments are truly detestable, nor could any thing be an aggravation of the author's guilt, except his ludicrous manner of mentioning a monarch.

The *heel of a monarch*, or even the print of his *heel*, is a thing too venerable and sacred to be treated with such levity, and placed in contrast with rags and poverty. He that will speak contemptuously of the *heel* of a *monarch* will, whenever he can with security, speak contemptuously of his head.

These are the most glaring passages which have occurred, in the perusal of the first pages; my indignation will not suffer me to proceed farther, and I think much better of the licenser than to believe he went so far.

In the few remarks which I have set down, the reader will easily observe that I have strained no expression beyond its natural import, and have divested myself of all heat, partiality, and prejudice.

So far therefore is Mr Brooke from having received any hard or unwarrantable treatment that the licenser has only acted in pursuance of that law to which he owes his power, a law which every admirer of the administration must own to be very necessary, and to have produced very salutary effects.

I am indeed surprised that this great office is not drawn out into a longer series of deputations, since it might afford a gainful and reputable employment to a great number of the friends of the government; and I should think instead of having immediate recourse to the deputy-licenser himself, it might be sufficient honour for any poet, except the Laureate,° to stand bare-headed in the presence of the deputy of the deputy's deputy in the nineteenth subordination.

Such a number cannot but be thought necessary if we take into consideration the great work of drawing up an *Index Expurgatorius* to all the old plays; which is, I hope, already undertaken, or if it has been hitherto unhappily neglected, I take this opportunity to recommend.

The productions of our old poets are crowded with passages very unfit for the ears of an English audience, and which cannot be pronounced without irritating the minds of the people.

This censure I do not confine to those lines in which liberty, natural equality, wicked ministers, deluded kings, mean arts of negotiation, venal senates, mercenary troops, oppressive officers, servile and exorbitant taxes, universal corruption, the luxuries of a court, the miseries of the people, the decline of trade, or the happiness of independency are directly mentioned. These are such glaring passages as cannot be suffered to pass without the most supine and criminal negligence. I hope the vigilance of the licensers will extend to all such speeches and soliloquies as tend to recommend the pleasures of virtue, the tranquillity of an uncorrupted head, and the satisfactions of conscious innocence; for though such strokes as these do not appear to a common eye to threaten any danger to the government, yet it is well known to more penetrating observers that they have such consequences as cannot be too diligently obviated, or too cautiously avoided.

A man who becomes once enamoured of the charms of virtue is apt to be very little concerned about the acquisition of wealth or titles, and is therefore not easily induced to act in a manner contrary to his real sentiments, or to vote at the word of command; by contracting his desires, and regulating his appetites, he wants much less than other men, and every one versed in the arts of government can tell that men are more easily influenced in proportion as they are more necessitous.

This is not the only reason why virtue should not receive too much countenance from a licensed stage; her admirers and followers are not only naturally independent, but learn such a uniform and consistent manner of speaking and acting that they frequently by the mere force of artless honesty surmount all the obstacles which subtlety and politics can throw in their way, and obtain their ends in spite of the most profound and sagacious ministry.

Such then are the passages to be expunged by the licensers: In many parts indeed the speeches will be imperfect, and the action appear not regularly conducted, but the Poet Laureate may easily supply these vacuities by inserting some of his own verses in praise of wealth, luxury, and venality.

But alas! all those pernicious sentiments which we shall banish from the stage will be vented from the press, and more studiously read because they are prohibited.

I cannot but earnestly implore the friends of the government to leave no art untried by which we may hope to succeed in our design of extending the power of the licenser to the press, and of making it criminal to publish any thing without an *imprimatur*.

How much would this single law lighten the mighty burden of state affairs? With how much security might our ministers enjoy their honours, their places, their reputations, and their admirers, could they once suppress those malicious invectives which are at present so industriously propagated, and so eagerly read, could they hinder any arguments but their own from coming to the ears of the people, and stop effectually the voice of cavil and enquiry.

I cannot but indulge myself a little while by dwelling on this pleasing scene, and imagining those halcyon-days in which no politics shall be read but those of the *Gazetteer*,° nor any poetry but that of the Laureate; when we shall hear of nothing but the successful negotiations of our ministers, and the great actions of ———.°

How much happier would this state be than those perpetual jealousies and contentions which are inseparable from knowledge and liberty, and which have for many years kept this nation in perpetual commotions.

But these are times rather to be wished for than expected, for such is the nature of our unquiet countrymen that if they are not admitted to the knowledge of affairs, they are always suspecting their governors of designs prejudicial to their interest; they have not the least notion of the pleasing tranquillity of ignorance, nor can be brought to imagine that they are kept in the dark, lest too much light should hurt their eyes. They have long claimed a right of directing their superiors, and are exasperated at the least mention of secrets of state.°

This temper makes them very readily encourage any writer or printer who, at the hazard of his life or fortune, will give them any information; and while this humour prevails there never will be wanting some daring adventurer who will write in defence of liberty, and some zealous or avaricious printer who will disperse his papers.

It has never yet been found that any power, however vigilant or despotic, has been able to prevent the publication of seditious journals, ballads, essays and dissertations, *Considerations on the Present State of Affairs*, and *Enquiries into the Conduct of the Administration*.

Yet I must confess that, considering the success with which the present ministry has hitherto proceeded in their attempts to drive out of the world the old prejudices of patriotism and public spirit, I cannot but entertain some hopes that what has been so often attempted by their predecessors is reserved to be accomplished by their superior abilities.

If I might presume to advise them upon this great affair, I should dissuade them from any direct attempt upon the liberty of the press, which is the darling of the common people, and therefore cannot be attacked without immediate danger. They may proceed by a more sure and silent way, and attain the desired end without noise, detraction, or opposition.

There are scattered over this kingdom several little seminaries in which the lower ranks of people, and the younger sons of our nobility and gentry are taught, from their earliest infancy, the pernicious arts of spelling and reading, which they afterwards continue to practise very much to the disturbance of their own quiet, and the interruption of ministerial measures.

These seminaries may, by an Act of Parliament, be at once suppressed, and that our posterity be deprived of all means of reviving this corrupt method of education, it may be made felony to teach to read, without a license from the Lord Chamberlain.

This expedient, which I hope will be carefully concealed from the vulgar, must infallibly answer the great end proposed by it, and set the power of the court not only above the insults of the poets, but in a short time above the necessity of providing against them. The licenser having his authority thus extended will in time enjoy the title and the salary without the trouble of exercising his power, and the nation will rest at length in ignorance and peace.

Annotations to Crousaz, *Commentary* on Pope's *Essay on Man*°

[Crousaz prefers Du Resnel's rendering, 'Sors de l'enchantement, milord, laisse au vulgaire / Le seduisant espoir d'un bien imaginaire,' to Pope's 'Awake, my St John! leave all meaner things / To low ambition, and the pride of Kings' (as given in Silhouette's prose version). 'I cannot however help observing an evident difference between the openings of the two poems: the expressions of Mr Pope are more harsh, and those of Mr Du Resnel more softened.']

Mr Crousaz, who, as he says, understands not English, discovers Du Resnel's variation from Mr Pope by comparing his version with another in prose, on which he writ his Examen, lately translated by an ingenious hand.

The address of one is the exclamation of a freeman, that of the other the murmur of a slave.

It is unnecessary here to remind the reader of Roscommon's° observation upon the English poetry compared with the French,

> One sterling line
> Drawn to French wire will through whole pages shine.

This translator cannot but recall it to his memory giving us 8 lines of 12 or 13 syllables for 2 lines of 10; as for the second couplet,

> Let us, since life can little more supply,
> Than just to look about us, and to die,

he has totally omitted it. . . .

———

[Crousaz: 'Some restraint and modesty of style are decent, especially when great persons are mentioned, whose virtue such numbers conspire to assault that they are more to be admired when they persevere in the right way and more to be lamented when they wander from it.']

May it not be opposed to this soft language that the vices of the great ought to be more severely censured, because they are committed in open day, because they set fashion on the side of wickedness, corrupt whole nations by their influence, and are out of the reach of any other punishment?

———

[Crousaz quotes Du Resnel's version of i. 9–14 of Pope:

> De son coeur tenebreus sondons la profondeur;
> Jusques dans sa bassesse admirons sa grandeur.
> L'un fier de ses talens, enfle de sa science,
> Ne croit rien d'impossible a son intelligence.
> Pour ces dons precieux l'autre plein de mepris,
> De sa propre raison semble ignorer le prix.
> Appellons les tous deux a sa pure lumiere,
> Et cherchons les sentiers ou marche la nature.

Eye Nature's walks—v. 13]

The reader will observe with indignation the dull introduction and common remarks which are interwoven with Mr Pope's animated sentiments. The translator is very injudicious in presuming to add anything of his own, but may perhaps be more easily justified in his omission of these words,

> Shoot Folly as it flies,
> And catch the manners living as they rise.

[Crousaz quotes Du Resnel's 10-line version of i. 15–18 of Pope.]

Of these lines I need not say how distant they are from Mr Pope's sense, and how much inferior to it.

Du Resnel's introduction would be dull in prose, and is very far from giving an idea of Mr Pope's fire and precipitation.

[Crousaz: 'He then goes on to speak of the gradations of the world:

> Ou croissant par degres jusques a l'infini,
> Les etres differens, sans laisser d'intervalle,
> Gradent dans leur progres une justesse egale:
> Si pour remplir ce tout que Dieu forme a son gre,
> Parmi les animaux l'homme occupe un degre,
> Le seul point est de voir, si le ciel equitable
> L'a place dans un rang qui lui soit convenable.

Here then the question is stated, and brought down from general terms to a particular point. God, as Sovereign, and unrestrained, has regulated according to his own pleasure the gradations of the several parts that compose the universe. Our only business is to convince ourselves that man is in possession of that place in this regular gradation which he is best adapted to and which is most agreeable to the justice as well as liberty of his Creator. To this question Mr Resnel answers after his author,

> Dans l'homme, tel qu'il est, ce qui paroit un mal
> Est la source d'un bien dans l'ordre général.
> L'oeil, qui ne voit d'un tout qu'une seule partie,
> Pourra-t-il juger bien ou mal assortie?'

The lines quoted are versions of i. 43–50, 57–60 of Pope.]

Mr Resnel varies here from his author's reasoning, by assuming as one of his premises what in the original is inferred as a conclusion, viz.

> Then in the scale of life and sense 'tis plain,
> There must be somewhere such a rank as Man.

Perhaps it might not be improperly altered thus,

> Il faust que dans ce tout—

Mr Resnel is very far from giving his author's answer. The first of these couplets is indeed as good a translation of the English as perhaps his language will admit, but nothing can excuse his total omission of the seven following lines, which, if not essential to the argument, contain an hypothesis that, if admitted, will contribute very much to illustrate it and must at least be allowed one of the ornaments, if not one of the pillars, of this philosophical structure.

[Crousaz: 'But with regard to man, a frequent reflection upon the certainty of death will very much assist him to conduct his life wisely, and conclude it happily. In this religion and common sense agree; and as man must equally divest himself of both to cry out,

> O blindness to the future, wisely giv'n!

when he adds that it is given to us,

> That each might fill the circle mark'd by Heaven,

he supposes that, if men were informed of their end, and of the circle marked out for them, they might avoid it or deviate from it since it is by means of this ignorance that Heaven conducts every being to the end proposed. But if man cannot employ his powers and direct his actions according to his own will, this consequence is evidently ill-grounded. But the doctrine of fatality is productive of contradictions: and if once we lose sight of it, plain reason carries us away into notions very remote from it. Every page of the writings of the

Stoics is a confirmation of this; the beauty of their morality is founded upon principles that interfere one with another.']

Mr Crousaz, in this reflection, seems to have forgotten either the candour of a moralist, or the sagacity of a commentator; for he either evidently perverts or mistakes his author's expressions and animadverts upon that mistaken sense. Every man perceives how much it contributes to his quiet in the present state to be ignorant of the time and manner of his death. Every man will find, upon the least reflection, that the knowledge of futurity would make such a change in the face of human affairs that we might be accounted almost another order of beings: nor could he, if he had attended to his author, have imagined that he meant to insinuate that a knowledge of its end would enable any being to avoid it, since both the original and the translation include all other animals as well as man in the assertion.

———

[Crousaz: 'Wisdom always tends to some end. As our Maker has bestowed feet upon us, he evidently intends that we should walk upon them and convey ourselves by the help of them to any place where our presence is required: the eye was given us to see with and the organs of voice invite us to conversation. We need only observe ourselves and the objects about us and we may make infinite additions to the knowledge of our end.']

Mr Crousaz seems to impose upon his readers or at least upon himself, by the equivocal and variable import of the word *end* or *destinee*, which signifies either the period of our being, or intentional end for which we are sent into the world. So that his argument against Mr Pope seems to stand thus: *heaven*, says the author, conceals from all earthly beings their *end*, or time of their dissolution. *Heaven*, says the commentator, discovers clearly to man his end, or the intention for which he was created.

———

[Crousaz:

'Regarde l'Indien, dont l'esprit sans culture
N'a point l'art d'alterer les dons de la nature.

I found at verse 23 a great difficulty in annexing a reasonable meaning to the term *nature*. Has Mr Pope given, in this place, a clear explication of it? This nature, whose voice is to be reverenced, and whose steps are to be followed, and whose gifts are not to be changed, is, it seems, that state of the *mind* in which it lies, unimproved, though formed with a capacity of improvement, of endeavouring after perfection, and of acquiring true notions. Are the instructions of nature never to extend beyond the gross informations of the senses? Is this blissful state of nature the condition of a man who, without condescending to call in the assistance of reason, alleviates the troubles of life by giving up himself to the wildest chimeras? And though we should suppose that God looks down with pity upon the poor Indians' darkness, must we judge with equal fervour of their obstinate and voluntary blindness, whom sensuality and pride, and aversion from restraint persuade to shut their eyes against that light which cannot guide them without their own consent?']

Mr Pope, in the original, has not made use of the word *nature* in the passage here referred to, his expression being only

> Lo! the poor Indian, whose untutored mind.

But he has indeed used the word a few lines after,

> Yet simple Nature to his hope has given, &c.

to which, perhaps, all that Mr Crousaz has written may be applied with propriety.

[Crousaz: 'Mr Pope continues to say, in praise of his Indian favourite,

> Que content d'exister, il attend l'heureux jour,
> Ou porte tout a coup dans un autre sejour
> Il ira, jouissant d'une plus douce vie,
> Habiter des humains la commune patrie.

If Mr Pope had intended, by assisting the Indian with his own notions and his poetry to raise his chimeras to an equality with the persuasions of a Christian, could he have spoken in any other terms? Two lines higher he seems to give him the preference,

> Il ne desire point cette celeste flamme,
> Qui des purs Seraphins devore & nourrit l'ame.

Mr Pope, fired by an antithesis, has by the way thrown ridicule upon the happy spirits. The Indian, wiser than they, is content to want a flame which consumes at the same time that it supports.']

Mr Pope only says,

> To be contents his natural desire,
> He asks no angel's wing, no seraph's fire.

Three of these lines, and the latter of the next couplet, are Mr Du Resnel's; who, as he has read Roscommon, ought to have remembered

> That 'tis much safer to leave out than add.

By omitting a just sentiment, we only suppress part of an author's virtues: by adding an improper thought, we charge him with faults of which he is not guilty.

Mr Crousaz is so watchful against impiety that he lets nonsense pass without censure. Can anything consume and nourish at the same time? I take this opportunity of observing, once for all, that he is not sufficiently candid in charging all the errors of this miserable version upon the original author. If he had no way of distinguishing between Mr Pope and his translator, to throw the odium of impiety and the ridicule of nonsense entirely upon the former is at least *stabbing in the dark* and wounding, for aught he knows, an innocent character: but this seems not to be, in reality, the case. He had a prose translation in his hand which he might have compared with Du Resnel's. He has, therefore, done a voluntary wrong to the English poet. What can be the reason of this conduct? Or what can be said in justification of it? Could it be fear of Mr Du Resnel? Mr Pope seems much the more formidable enemy. Could it be friendship for him? The friends of a philosopher and Christian ought to be justice, charity, and truth.

———

[Crousaz: 'I must, by the way, say one word of those peaceful habitations, where

> No Christians thirst for gold.

Can Mr Pope find any fault with those who look with horror upon persecution and inhumanity, which dishonour the Christian religion by a conduct entirely opposite to all its precepts?']

This remark I cannot understand; this persecution and inhumanity are evidently condemned in the English, and no less evidently in the French.

———

[Crousaz: 'Pope has drawn, according to his own imagination, the picture of an Indian temperate and contented. Mr Bayle, in the same manner, has given us pictures of men without any religion, filled with touches that raise esteem, but copied only from his own fancy, and, that he might more easily attain his end, has placed in contrast with them the portrait of a bad Christian.

'The savage lies under a necessity of maintaining himself and of securing his fields and his possessions; he must be a skilful huntsman; he must run the hazard of falling into the hands of his neighbours and being devoured by them, when he is obliged to make incursions into their district to procure slaves by rapine and violence, whom he afterwards obliges to serve him by force.']

Though Mr Pope's picture of the Indian be undoubtedly liable to very just objections, both with regard to the justness of the draught, and the light in which he has placed it, yet perhaps Mr Crousaz's contrast may be no less unjustifiable. India in its most extensive signification comprehends a great part of the globe and includes a multitude of nations, some barbarous and savage to a degree that almost degrades them from the rank of men; some such as the commentator describes, crafty, malicious, provident, and rapacious; some human and civilized almost to politeness, or perhaps to a generosity and good nature far preferable. But I recollect no authentic relation from which it does not appear that civility and religion promote each other. No regulated polity can, I believe, be produced which does not include or presuppose a religious institution; nor is there any people much superior to their dogs in this world that imagine they shall be placed on a level with them in the next.

———

[Crousaz quotes Du Resnel's translation of ii. 31–4 of Pope,

> Des celestes esprits la vive intelligence
> Regarde avec pitie notre foible science.
> Newton, le grand Newton, que nous admirons tous,
> Est peut-etre pour eux ce qu'un singe est pour nous,

and accuses Pope of presenting a Leibnizian view of Newton.]

Mr Pope asserts that the celestial intelligences *admired* the knowledge of Newton, and the translator that they *pitied* it.

Nothing is more remote than this translation from the sense and design of the author, whose meaning in this couplet,

> Could he whose rules the whirling comet find
> Prescribe or fix one movement of the mind,

seems to be this, Could he who has laid down the laws of motion by which the comets and heavenly bodies are directed in their courses explain the operations of the soul? Could he give a physical or mechanical account of our passions or sensations?—Nor does the author cast any reflection upon the knowledge of Newton or upon his studies, which the translator insults without mercy; though, indeed, it is not plain that he refers this paragraph to the former, or makes any connection between them.

———

[Crousaz: 'I know not by what kind of fatality it is that in reading Mr Pope, a man must be always upon his guard against the notion of a physical constitution of things by which moral evil is forced into the world like natural, and is therefore not moral evil.

> De leurs combats divers resultent des accords
> Qui forment l'union & de l'ame & du corps.

This union is beyond my comprehension: every man is not equally subject to passions, but the soul of those who have subdued them is not less united to their bodies than that of those in whom they reign without opposition in their full force.']

Mr Crousaz ought at least, when he met with nonsense, to have consulted Mr Pope in the prose version. To attribute such an uncommon sentiment as *that the passions constitute the union between the soul and body* to a wrong author is such injustice as no man ought either willingly or negligently to be guilty of. What effects might not this wonderful notion produce if carefully inculcated, firmly believed, and diligently pursued? It might perhaps, in time, produce a sect of philosophers who might by continually endeavouring to strengthen this union, and exploding the ancient means of longevity, temperance, and chastity, grow immortal by indulging their passions.

———

[Crousaz, on ii. 131–2 of Pope: 'In this elegant description of that which is called the Ruling Passion, which is not the same in every man, but generally more strong than any other, I shall only remark that it is too general an assertion to say that it is *always opposed*: there are men so far from always opposing it that they live in a state of habitual subjection to it. There are others who sometimes attempt an opposition, but soon remit their efforts, and leave it unmolested, under a plea of weakness, which they are not uneasy at, because it gratifies their laziness and their appetites. There are others who weaken its influence, and there are some who utterly destroy it.']

There seem to me to be many reasonable objections against this system of a Ruling Passion interwoven with the original constitution and perpetually presiding over its motions, invariable, incessant, and insuperable. I have at present no design of entering into an accurate discussion of the question, which is perhaps rather a question of fact and experience than of reason. The author may perhaps be conscious of a Ruling Passion that has influenced all his actions and designs. I am conscious of none but the general desire of happiness, which is not here intended, so that there appears equal evidence on both sides. Men indeed appear very frequently to be influenced a long time by a predominant inclination to fame, money, or power; but perhaps if they review their early years and trace their ideas backwards, they will find that those strong desires were the effects either of example or instruction, the circumstances in which they were placed, the objects which they first received impressions from, the first books they read, or the first company they conversed with. But there are others who do not seem to act in pursuance of any fixed or unvaried principle, but place their highest felicity sometimes in one object, sometimes in another, and these make undoubtedly the gross of mankind. Every observer, however superficial, has remarked that in many men the love of pleasures is the Ruling Passion of their youth, and the love of money that of their advanced years. However this be, it is not proper to dwell too long on the resistless power and despotic authority of this tyrant of the soul, lest the reader should, as it is very natural, take the present inclination, however destructive to society or himself, for the Ruling Passion, and forbear to struggle when he despairs to conquer.

[Crousaz quotes Du Resnel's version of ii. 175-6 of Pope,

> L'eternal artisan qui tira tout de rien,
> Et qui du sein du mal fait eclore le bien:

'The Eternal Artificer. There is a contrast in this expression which has given offence to many persons of understanding, who look upon the word *artificer* as too low a term to be associated with so grand an epithet. It seems likewise to insinuate that the artificer and his work are of equal duration, and the world by consequence eternal.']

It is a great misfortune to have too great an inclination to draw consequences and too strong a desire to search deeper than the rest of mankind. This temper is undoubtedly of a great use in abstruse learning, and on some important occasions; but when carried into the scenes of common life, and exerted without any necessity, only makes the unhappy reasoner suspicious and cautious, shows everything in a false light, and makes his discoveries the sport of the world. What common reader would infer the eternity of the world from the expression of the *Eternal Artificer*? If the word be taken in its common acceptation, the first idea that naturally occurs is that the artificer is prior to his work. If we admit it, as here we certainly must, in a figurative sense, it will imply no more than Creator, which would probably have given no offence. What objections might not such a disposition to cavil have raised against such an expression as Divine Geometrician,° which would have confined the operations of the Supreme Being to this poor despicable spot of earth?

———

[Crousaz quotes Du Resnel's version of ii. 197–200 of Pope: 'At these verses I pause with great satisfaction. A passion may be employed well or ill; for this reason, a wise man considers its nature, all its degrees, and possible effect; and accordingly endeavours to extinguish, preserve or regulate it. Nero needed only to have acted thus, and he had equalled Titus. That magnanimous contempt of death, which was madness in Catiline, who chose rather to perish than not disturb the tranquillity of the public, engages our admiration in Decius and Curtius, who died for no other end than the preservation of their country.']

If the critic acknowledges the truth and beauty of these verses, which only contain an explanation of the foregoing passage, it will be reasonably thought that many of his censures might have been spared, which, though doubtless well intended, are sometimes thrown out with too little reflection. Mr Pope's assertion, in plain prose, seems to be this: there are many different virtues, equally necessary to the happiness of mankind, but which can hardly exist, in the highest degree, in one and the same person; the Supreme Being has, therefore, allotted to every individual a *Ruling Passion*, or strong tendency to some particular end, which generally may be attained by either good or bad means; and by which of the two he will obtain it is left to his choice. The Ruling Passion, the natural bias of the mind, is equally powerful in both cases and will hurry forward to its favourite object with equal rapidity, either through the paths of virtue or of vice. Thus the desire of being distinguished above the rest of mankind, while it was directed by reason, made Nero, in the first years of his reign, an excellent emperor; and afterwards, when he neglected to consult any guide but his appetites, the same passion made him an extravagant debauchee, &c. This system, whether true or not, seems hitherto innocent at least; and besides, as Mr Crousaz might have noticed, contains an evident assertion of free will.

———

[Du Resnel's translation of Pope, ii. 233–6:

> Les fous, les scelerats, dans leur profonde yvresse,
> N'ont-ils pas des lueurs d'honneurs & de sagesse?
> Le sage dont le coeur par l'amour est surpris,
> N'est-il pas pour lui-meme un objet de mepris?
> Aux loix des passions notre ame assujettie
> Du vice a la vertu, de la haine a l'amour.]

Though I shall not mention all the defects in the translation of this passage, I cannot, however, forbear observing in the second couplet the evident marks of a Frenchman's genius, who snatches every opportunity of talking of love,° and misses not the least hint that can serve to guide him to his darling subject. Is the mind of man never disordered by any other passion? Is not a wise man sometimes surprised by envy or cowardice, by ambition or resentment? Is all weakness and folly the consequence of love? But it is the general genius of that airy people; debar them from love, and you debar them from poetry. This prevailing inclination to gallantry has given rise to such numbers of novels, and filled the world with romances, those bulky follies which have served to crowd the closets and imaginations of studious ladies. It had indeed been happy if the infection had stopped here, without extending itself to poetry, and filling the stage with amorous sadness, or refined obscenity. If tragedy be, as it certainly ought to be, a representation of human nature and real life, why is all good or bad fortune made the effect of this single passion? Why does this alone exalt the virtue or inflame the vices of their heroes or princes? It is evident that it is far from operating so powerfully or so universally in the world as it appears to do upon the stage.

———

[Du Resnel:° 'The English is allowed, by all who understand it, to be the most concise language in the world; and this quality it is in which the writers of that country place its beauty, and for which they prefer it to the French, a language which Lord Roscommon, who is acknowledged to have held the first rank among their critics, allows to be copious, florid, pleasing to the ear, and to have more softness than the English; but defies us to produce a single instance of equal strength, closeness and energy: a thought, says he, which we comprehend in a single line, diffused by a French author, would glitter through whole pages.']

I know not what edition of Roscommon has fallen into the hands of Mr Du Resnel, or whence it proceeds that the quotation which he has subjoined in his margin differs from those copies I have seen. The passage, as he has published it, is this:

> 'Tis copious, florid, pleasing to your ear,
> With softness, more, perhaps, than ours can bear.
> But who did ever in French authors, &c.

Which in all the editions that I have read stands thus:

> 'Tis courtly, florid, and abounds in words
> Of softer sound than ours perhaps affords.

How much more poetical and correct this reading is requires no proof, nor is the difference only in elegance but in truth. The genuine reading only admits that the French language is *courtly*, a quality which cannot be denied to a speech consisting wholly of hyperbole: the passage, as cited by Du Resnel, asserts it to be copious, an excellence for which even their own writers have never ventured to commend it.

An Essay on Epitaphs°

Though criticism has been cultivated in every age of learning, by men of great abilities and extensive knowledge, till the rules of writing are become rather burdensome than instructive to the mind; though almost every species of composition has been the subject of particular treatises, and given birth to definitions, distinctions, precepts and illustrations; yet no critic of note that has fallen within my observation has hitherto thought sepulchral inscriptions worthy of a minute examination, or pointed out with proper accuracy their beauties and defects.

The reasons of this neglect it is useless to inquire, and perhaps impossible to discover; it might be justly expected that this kind of writing would have been the favourite topic of criticism, and that self-love might have produced some regard for it, in those authors that have crowded libraries with elaborate dissertations upon Homer; since to afford a subject for heroic poems is the privilege of very few, but every man may expect to be recorded in an epitaph, and, therefore, finds some interest in providing that his memory may not suffer by an unskilful panegyric.

If our prejudices in favour of antiquity deserve to have any part in the regulation of our studies, epitaphs seem entitled to more than common regard, as they are probably of the same age with the art of writing. The most ancient structures in the world, the pyramids, are supposed to be sepulchral monuments, which either pride or gratitude erected, and the same passions which incited men to such laborious and expensive methods of preserving their own memory, or that of their benefactors, would doubtless incline them not to neglect any easier means by which the same ends might be obtained. Nature and reason have dictated to every nation that to preserve good actions from oblivion is both the interest and duty of mankind; and therefore we find no people acquainted with the use of letters that omitted to grace the tombs of their heroes and wise men with panegyrical inscriptions.

To examine, therefore, in what the perfection of epitaphs consists, and what rules are to be observed in composing them, will be at least of as much use as other critical inquiries; and for assigning a few hours to such disquisitions, great examples at least, if not strong reasons, may be pleaded.

An epitaph, as the word itself implies, is an inscription on a tomb, and in its most extensive import may admit indiscriminately satire or praise. But as malice has seldom produced monuments of defamation, and the tombs hitherto raised have been the work of friendship and benevolence, custom has contracted the original latitude of the word, so that it signifies in the general acceptation an inscription engraven on a tomb in honour of the person deceased.

As honours are paid to the dead in order to incite others to the imitation of their excellencies, the principal intention of epitaphs is to perpetuate the examples of virtue, that the tomb of a good man may supply the want of his presence, and veneration for his memory produce the same effect as the observation of his life. Those epitaphs are, therefore, the most perfect which set virtue in the strongest light, and are best adapted to exalt the reader's ideas, and rouse his emulation.

To this end it is not always necessary to recount the actions of a hero, or enumerate the writings of a philosopher; to imagine such informations necessary is to detract from their characters, or to suppose their works mortal, or their achievements in danger of being forgotten. The bare name of such men answers every purpose of a long inscription.

Had only the name of Sir Isaac Newton been subjoined to the design upon his monument, instead of a long detail of his discoveries, which no philosopher can want, and which none but a philosopher can understand, those by whose direction it was raised had done more honour both to him and to themselves.

This, indeed, is a commendation which it requires no genius to bestow, but which can never become vulgar or contemptible, if bestowed with judgment; because no single age produces many men of merit superior to panegyric. None but the first names can stand unassisted against the attacks of time, and if men raised to reputation by accident or caprice have nothing but their names engraved on their tombs, there is danger lest in a few years the inscription require an interpreter. Thus have their expectations been disappointed who honoured Picus of Mirandola with this pompous epitaph:

> Hic situs est PICUS MIRANDOLA, caetera norunt
> Et Tagus et Ganges, forsan et Antipodes.°

His name then celebrated in the remotest corners of the earth is now almost forgotten; and his works, then studied, admired, and applauded, are now mouldering in obscurity.

Next in dignity to the bare name is a short character simple and unadorned, without exaggeration, superlatives, or rhetoric. Such were the inscriptions in use among the Romans, in which the victories gained by their emperors were commemorated by a single epithet; as Caesar Germanicus, Caesar Dacicus, Germanicus, Illyricus. Such would be this epitaph, *Isaacus Newtonus, naturae legibus investigatis, hic quiescit.*°

But to far the greatest part of mankind a longer encomium is necessary for the publication of their virtues, and the preservation of their memories; and, in the composition of these it is that art is principally required, and precepts, therefore, may be useful.

In writing epitaphs, one circumstance is to be considered which affects no other composition; the place in which they are now commonly found restrains them to a particular air of solemnity, and debars them from the admission of all lighter or gayer ornaments. In this, it is that the style of an epitaph necessarily differs from that of an elegy. The customs of burying our dead either in or near our churches, perhaps originally founded on a rational design of fitting the mind for religious exercises, by laying before it the most affecting proofs of the uncertainty of life, makes it proper to exclude from our epitaphs all such allusions as are contrary to the doctrines for the propagation of which the churches are erected, and to the end for which those who peruse the monuments must be supposed to come thither. Nothing is, therefore, more ridiculous than to copy the Roman inscriptions, which were engraven on stones by the highway, and composed by those who generally reflected on mortality only to excite in themselves and others a quicker relish of pleasure, and a more luxurious enjoyment of life, and whose regard for the dead extended no farther than a wish that *the earth might be light upon them.*

All allusions to the heathen mythology are, therefore, absurd, and all regard for the senseless remains of a dead man impertinent and superstitious. One of the first distinctions of the primitive Christians was their neglect of bestowing garlands on the dead, in which they are very rationally defended by their apologist in Minutius Felix.° 'We lavish no flowers nor odours on the dead,' says he, 'because they have no sense of fragrance or of beauty.' We profess to reverence the dead, not for their sake, but for our own. It is therefore always with indignation or contempt that I read the epitaph on Cowley, a man whose learning and poetry were his lowest merits.

> Aurea dum late volitant tua scripta per orbem,
> Et fama eternum vivis, divine poeta,
> Hic placida jaceas requie, custodiat urnam

Cana fides, vigilentque perenni lampade musae!
Sit sacer ille locus, nec quis temerarius ausit
Sacrilega turbare manu venerabile bustum.
Intacti maneant, maneant per saecula dulces
COWLEII cineres, serventque immobile saxum.°

To pray that the ashes of a friend may lie undisturbed, and that the divinities that favoured him in his life may watch for ever round him, to preserve his tomb from violation, and drive sacrilege away, is only rational in him who believes the soul interested in the repose of the body, and the powers which he invokes for its protection able to preserve it. To censure such expressions, as contrary to religion, or as remains of heathen superstition, would be too great a degree of severity. I condemn them only as uninstructive and unaffecting, as too ludicrous for reverence or grief, for Christianity and a temple.

That the designs and decorations of monuments ought, likewise, to be formed with the same regard to the solemnity of the place, cannot be denied; it is an established principle that all ornaments owe their beauty to their propriety. The same glitter of dress that adds graces to gaiety and youth would make age and dignity contemptible. Charon with his boat is far from heightening the awful grandeur of the universal judgment, though drawn by Angelo° himself; nor is it easy to imagine a greater absurdity than that of gracing the walls of a Christian temple with the figure of Mars leading a hero to battle, or Cupids sporting round a virgin. The pope who defaced the statues of the deities at the tomb of Sannazarius° is, in my opinion, more easily to be defended than he that erected them.

It is, for the same reason, improper to address the epitaph to the passenger, a custom which in injudicious veneration for antiquity introduced again at the revival of letters, and which, among many others, Passeratius° suffered to mislead him in his epitaph upon the heart of Henry, king of France, who was stabbed by Clement the monk, which yet deserves to be inserted, for the sake of showing how beautiful even improprieties may become in the hands of a good writer.

Adsta, viator, et dole regum vices.
Cor regis isto conditur sub marmore,
Qui jura Gallis, jura Sarmatis dedit;
Tectus cucullo hunc sustulit sicarius.
Abi, viator, et dole regum vices.°

In the monkish ages, however ignorant and unpolished, the

epitaphs were drawn up with far greater propriety than can be shown in those which more enlightened times have produced.

> Orate pro anima —— miserrimi peccatoris°

was an address to the last degree striking and solemn, as it flowed naturally from the religion then believed, and awakened in the reader sentiments of benevolence for the deceased, and of concern for his own happiness. There was nothing trifling or ludicrous, nothing that did not tend to the noblest end, the propagation of piety, and the increase of devotion.

It may seem very superfluous to lay it down as the first rule for writing epitaphs that the name of the deceased is not to be omitted; nor should I have thought such a precept necessary, had not the practice of the greatest writers shown that it has not been sufficiently regarded. In most of the poetical epitaphs, the names for whom they were composed may be sought to no purpose, being only prefixed on the monument. To expose the absurdity of this omission, it is only necessary to ask how the epitaphs which have outlived the stones on which they were inscribed would have contributed to the information of posterity had they wanted the names of those whom they celebrated.

In drawing the character of the deceased, there are no rules to be observed which do not equally relate to other compositions. The praise ought not to be general, because the mind is lost in the extent of any indefinite idea, and cannot be affected with what it cannot comprehend. When we hear only of a good or great man, we know not in what class to place him, nor have any notion of his character, distinct from that of a thousand others; his example can have no effect upon our conduct, as we have nothing remarkable or eminent to propose to our imitation. The epitaph composed by Ennius for his own tomb has both the faults last mentioned.

> Nemo me decoret lacrumis, nec funera fletu
> Faxit. Cur?—Volito vivu' per ora virum.°

The reader of this epitaph receives scarce any idea from it; he neither conceives any veneration for the man to whom it belongs, nor is instructed by what methods this boasted reputation is to be obtained.

Though a sepulchral inscription is professedly a panegyric, and, therefore, not confined to historical impartiality, yet it ought always to be written with regard to truth. No man ought to be commended for virtues which he never possessed, but whoever is curious to know his faults must inquire after them in other places; the monuments of the dead are not intended to perpetuate the memory of crimes, but to exhibit patterns of virtue. On the tomb of Maecenas his luxury is not to be mentioned with his munificence, nor is the proscription to find a place on the monument of Augustus.

The best subject for epitaphs is private virtue; virtue exerted in the same circumstances in which the bulk of mankind are placed, and which, therefore, may admit of many imitators. He that has delivered his country from oppression, or freed the world from ignorance and error, can excite the emulation of a very small number; but he that has repelled the temptations of poverty, and disdained to free himself from distress at the expense of his virtue, may animate multitudes, by his example, to the same firmness of heart and steadiness of resolution.

Of this kind I cannot forbear the mention of two Greek inscriptions;° one upon a man whose writings are well known, the other upon a person whose memory is preserved only in her epitaph, who both lived in slavery, the most calamitous estate in human life:

Ζωσιμη ἡ πριν ἐουσα μονω τω Σωματι δουλη,
Και τω σωματι νυν εὑρεν ἐλευθεριην.

Zosima, quae solo fuit olim corpore serva,
Corpore nunc etiam libera facta fuit.

Zosima, who, in her life, could only have her body enslaved,
now finds her body, likewise, set at liberty.

It is impossible to read this epitaph without being animated to bear the evils of life with constancy, and to support the dignity of human nature under the most pressing afflictions, both by the example of the heroine, whose grave we behold, and the prospect of that state in which, to use the language of the inspired writers, *The poor cease from their labours, and the weary be at rest.*°

The other is upon Epictetus, the Stoic philosopher:

Δουλος Ἐπικτητος γενομην, και Σωμ' ἀναπηρος,
Και πενιην Ἱρος, και φιλος Ἀθανατοις.

Servus Epictetus, mutilatus corpore, vixi
Pauperieque Irus, curaque prima deum.

Epictetus, who lies here, was a slave and a cripple, poor as
the beggar in the proverb, and the favourite of heaven.

In this distich is comprised the noblest panegyric and the most important instruction. We may learn from it that virtue is impracticable in no condition, since Epictetus could recommend himself to the regard of heaven, amidst the temptations of poverty and slavery; slavery, which has always been found so destructive to virtue that in many languages a slave and a thief are expressed by the same word. And we may be likewise admonished by it not to lay any stress on a man's outward circumstances in making an estimate of his real value, since Epictetus the beggar, the cripple, and the slave, was the favourite of heaven.

Debates in the Senate of Lilliput°

On the 50th day of the last session of the 8th Senate [Parliament] of Gorgenti [George] II [13 February 1741] the Urg; Snadsy [Sandys] stood up and spoke as follows.

Sir,°

The motion which I am about to offer being made necessary by the present state of the nation, its reasonableness is to be evinced, and the approbation of the House to be gained, by a view of our foreign and domestic affairs, by an impartial comparison of our present condition with our past, by an accurate balance of our losses and acquisitions for near twenty years, and an examination to whom we are to impute our sufferings, or ascribe our acquisitions.

A display of our present state, and a view of the measures by which it has been produced, is a task too disagreeable to be undertaken upon any other motives than a conviction of its necessity; for who can be pleased with recounting error after error, with tracing the progress of corruption, with relating the insults of enemies, and the defection of allies, with enumerating fruitless negotiations, expatiating on the idle solemnity of useless treaties, with examining the expense of armies by which no enemy was awed, and of fleets by which our commerce was betrayed? Who can be pleased with making a recital of calamities by which, as he loves his country with greater ardour, he must be more sensibly affected?

. . . .

Such, Sir, has been the conduct of Sir Retrob Walelop [Robert Walpole], with regard to foreign affairs: he has deserted our allies, aggrandized our enemies, betrayed our commerce, and endangered our colonies; and yet this is the least criminal part of his ministry. For what is the loss of allies to the alienation of the people from the government, or the diminution of trade to the destruction of our liberties?

That the people are universally discontented I am under no obligation of endeavouring to prove while an army is supported only to restrain them from rebellion: for no other reason has been given by the annual advocates° for a military establishment. Those indeed who urge the danger of the Rednetrep's [Pretender's] attempts may perhaps make use of other words, but their meaning, if any meaning can be allowed them, is apparently the same, for the Rednetrep can never obtain this throne but by the concurrence of the majority, and that concurrence can only arise from their disapprobation of the present government.

But to what cause, Sir, can be imputed a discontent so general, and a detestation so vehement, to what can we ascribe a desire of an apparent evil, an affection to a prince of a different religion, of a religion which privileges perfidy and sanctifies persecution? How can it be imagined that men should form a wish to be subject to a monarch educated among their enemies, in countries governed by arbitrary power, and who must consequently be infatuated with every wild opinion of the unlimited extent of royal prerogatives, and believe himself entitled to trample upon law, to subvert privilege, and to plunder property?

How miserable must be the condition of that people whom an army is necessary to restrain from a choice like this! What calamities, what oppression must they feel who can fly to such remedies for relief! Were we governed like reasonable beings, that man only ought to be condemned as disaffected to his Majesty who should dare to charge the people with disaffection; for surely no man can more openly or more virulently libel the government than those who declare that the nation would change it for subjection to the Rednetrep.

That there is any such desire among the people, Sir, I am far from affirming or believing, for they are too well instructed in the tendency of the religion which the Rednetrep professes to desire to see it the religion of their king, and too well acquainted with their own rights to think that when they cannot deliver themselves from misery, the Rednetrep will be able to deliver them.

The representations which have been made of their impatience every man knows to be true; every man sees their misery and hears their complaints and their menaces; but their menaces must be feared before their complaints are regarded by those whose hearts corruption has hardened and whose sensibility is extinguished by the luxuries of a court.

To dissipate their own fears they have established an army in opposition to the fundamental laws of the Empire and defend their concurrence in this establishment by alleging the discontent of the people; that discontent which only their measures have produced and which nothing can more increase or confirm than a standing army.

By an army, Sir, distinct from the rest of the community, subjected to particular laws, commanded with absolute authority, and quartered in the country, to fatten in idleness and insult those by whom they are supported, the anger of the nation must be continually inflamed, though the effects of it may for a short time be prevented; and what fatal consequences may be produced by hourly aggravations of distress and new incentives to sedition any man may venture to foretell from a common acquaintance with the conduct of mankind, and a very slight knowledge of the history of former ages.

It may reasonably be expected that the people will not always groan under their burdens in submission; that after having inquired why they were imposed, and from what necessity it arises that they are every day increased, they will at length resolve to shake them off, and resume into their own hands that authority which they have entrusted to their governors, that they will resolve to become judges of their own interest, and regulate those measures of which they must support the expense and in which nothing but their advantage ought to be regarded.

When this important period shall arrive, when justice shall call out for the corrupters of their country, the deserters of their allies, and the enemies of commerce; when Liberty shall publish the crimes of those by whom she has been long ridiculed and oppressed; when the cries of the exasperated people shall be too loud to be repressed and vengeance shall impend over those heads which have so long been lifted up with confidence against truth and virtue, then will be the time in which the army must become the refuge of those who have so long supported it.

Then will the corrupter and his associates, the lacqueys of his train and the slaves of his levee, then will those who have sold their country for opportunities of debauchery and wasted the rewards of perfidy in the pleasures of the stews of the court implore the protection of their military friends and request them to repay those benefits which they have formerly received. What is then to be expected but that either they will be given up to punishment by those whom they have pampered at the expense of the public to secure them from it, which is most ardently to be hoped? or that the people will have recourse to arms in assertion of their demands and that the nation will be laid waste with all the devastations of a civil war? that at length either Lilliputians will be ever deprived of their liberty, that all our rights will be extinct and our constitution at an end? or that victory will declare on the side of justice, that the arms of the people will be successful and that the courtiers and their protectors will perish together?

Such, Sir, are the prospects which the continuance of a standing army sets before our eyes, a species of oppression unknown to any former age, and which must end either in the ruin of the nation or the destruction of those who have introduced it for their own advantage.

.   .   .   .

But, Sir, his most masterly attempt for the establishment of universal slavery, on which he laid out all his interest and all his subtlety, in which he laboured with incessant application and defended with the most tenacious obstinacy was the scheme of extending the laws of excise. By this he would have put a stop to all farther opposition of ministerial power; by this he would have secured himself from the future trouble of corrupting and seducing individuals; he would have crushed the constitution at once, and as the tyrant of old wished to destroy mankind at a blow, our Minister, not less heroically wicked, endeavoured by one fatal vote to oppress liberty for ever.

This, Sir, was indeed a compendious method of oppression, by which he would have diffused his spies and his agents over the nation, by which he would have forced his way into houses, learned the private affairs of families, and be enabled to govern every man in his own dwelling; he would have received every day the homage of the nation in the persons of the excisemen, his representatives, whom he had deputed to exact obedience to his will and to deliver up his enemies to punishment.

To expatiate upon the nature of the excise laws, Sir, and to show how much they infringe our most important privileges, would be to explain what every man has long known and what the whole nation declared in the numberless petitions by which this House was every day solicited while that dreadful question was depending, to have regard to the rights with which it was entrusted and to preserve the people of Lilliput from becoming slaves to the drudges of corruption, from being plundered by the caterpillars of power, and insulted by the slaves of the slaves of the Minister.

With how little compassion their terrors were regarded, Sir, and with how much contempt their remonstrances and arguments were heard by those whom a long dependence on the Minister had hardened equally against reason and compassion, who had been taught by the example of their lord to insult that misery which they had themselves occasioned and to ridicule those arguments which they could not answer is still remembered with resentment proportioned to the crime; nor can it be wondered that the people hold that man in abhorrence who has openly professed to despise and no less openly endeavoured to enslave them, who has attacked their privileges and punished those who refused to resign them.

For to the opposition which the merchants of this Empire raised against the project of extending the excise laws, it is reasonable to impute that settled hatred which the Minister has conceived against them, which he seldom fails to express, however indecently, and which he exerts upon all opportunities without regard to policy or justice. Every motive, every principle has given way to the favourite design of harassing the merchants, whom he considers as the most inflexible enemies of his claims, as situated most remote from his influence, and as the last whom he shall be able to sink into that implicit submission which he has been long accustomed to require.

To his scheme of subjecting this stubborn body of men, no less than to his alliance with the house of Buorbon [Bourbon], is perhaps to be ascribed his connivance at the Iberian [Spanish] depredations; from which, though it is not likely that his influence in foreign courts would have enabled him to prevent them, he might at least have secured many of our ships by convoys. But how little such favours were to be expected from him in time of peace may be discovered from his unwillingness to grant them protection in open war, from his care to conceal their losses and his attempts to vindicate those to whose treachery or negligence they may justly be imputed.

And that no method of ruining his country may remain un-attempted, that he may at least be secure in his designs against the public, he has found means of introducing dependence into the Senate, and of depriving the people of all hope of justice or relief by influencing that assembly to which in all former ages they have appealed, and which has seldom failed to redress their grievances, to drag from behind the throne the oppressors of the nation and to stop up the sources of the public treasure till these men have been punished who were found to have promoted wicked measures and to have favoured any other interest than that of Lilliput.

To what can it be imputed, Sir, that the people have now for many years in vain solicited their representatives for enquiries into the conduct of public offices, that they have annually laid before them their miseries and their fears, without any other effect than the new mortification of seeing themselves neglected by those to whom they have entrusted the care of the commonwealth? What cause can be alleged for the conduct of late Senates so different from that of their predecessors? Why do they now meet only to tax the people and to flatter the court, to offer addresses and to vote supplies? Why is there no regard paid to the remonstrances of our constituents or why have so many years elapsed without one example of justice?

It surely will not be urged on this occasion that this age is uncorrupt beyond the example of former times, since the open wickedness of the present generation has been often represented in this House in terms of the strongest detestation by the vindicators of the ministry; and as it is not to be supposed that virtue is increased by temptations to wickedness or that those posts which have always been imagined dangerous to integrity have now so much changed their nature that they are become preservatives from corruption; as it is not to be conceived that they who dissipate their private fortunes in riot and luxury have been always upright dispensers of the public treasure, the nation cannot but be excited to enquire why the Senate has been content to grant money without any solicitude how it was employed.

This alteration, Sir, of which the consequences are equally obvious and dreadful, can be imputed to no other cause than the endeavours which have been used by the Minister to fill this House with dependents on the court, by scattering lucrative employments amongst them which are to be held by no other tenure than that of an implicit submission to his will and a resignation of all private opinions to his unerring dictates.

When I see in this House, Sir, so great a number of men whose determination I know before the question is proposed, I am in doubt whether the motion which I am about to make will not be a useless effort, an unavailing appeal to a court whose sentence is already passed, yet as the public miseries are too great to be any longer borne without some endeavours to redress them; as in my opinion no redress can be obtained but by depriving the Minister of the power which he has so long and so openly abused, as the obstacles which are most likely to hinder the success of this attempt are every day multiplied, as corruption is continually advanced and virtue hourly more contemned, I take this opportunity of moving, while yet the right of offering any motion against the Minister remains,

That an Address be presented by this House, humbly requesting his Majesty to remove Sir Retrob Walelop from his presence and councils forever.

. . . .

Sir Retrob Walelop then made his defence, to the following effect.

Sir,

Having now heard the charge against me, with all the aggravation which suspicion has been able to form and eloquence to enforce; after the most fruitful inventions have combined to multiply crimes against me, and the most artful rhetoric has been employed to blacken them, I stand up to offer to the House a plain unstudied defence, nor do I solicit any other favour than I shall appear to deserve, or wish to be protected in this storm of accusation by any other shelter than that of innocence.

The gentlemen who have already spoken in my favour have indeed freed me from the necessity of wearying the House with a long defence, since their knowledge and abilities are so great that I can hope to add nothing to their arguments, and their zeal or their friendship so ardent that I shall speak with less warmth in my own cause.

Nor is this, Sir, the only reason for which it is superfluous to dwell long upon my own vindication; for I have not only the assistance of my friends, but the concurrence of the Senate to alleviate my task, since all the public transactions have been approved by the legislature which are now charged upon me as instances of ignorance, negligence, or treachery. Upon the modesty or justice of such accusations it is not my business to remark. The vindication of their own honour is properly the business of the Senate. But I cannot forbear to observe how far backwards the charge has been extended and how many facts have been mentioned which are forgotten by all who do not propose to gratify some passion or promote some private interest by remembering them and which may be therefore misrepresented without fear, since the true state of these affairs are so little known and so difficult to be explained.

In such cases the approbation of the Senate, given at a time when the questions to which it related had been lately discussed, when they were yet the subjects of conversation and were examined with all the acrimony of malice and the sagacity of interest; that approbation which a complete knowledge and exact enquiry produced will surely outweigh a subsequent censure offered by private men at the distance of many years and after a long train of disappointments which may be supposed at least to have vitiated their temper, if it has not perverted their conduct.

But lest it should be thought that an appeal to former Senates proceeded from diffidence in the judgment of this, those to whom my conduct has appeared not to deserve the censure proposed have recollected the arguments which prevailed at those times over discontent, ambition, and resentment, and of which I do not doubt but that they will now produce the same conviction.

The gentlemen by whom the motion has been supported have indeed failed in the most essential part of their accusation. They have not yet attempted to prove that I am the author of those measures which they have so clamorously condemned; but surely they cannot be ignorant that till they have proved the criminal, their declamations upon the crime are empty sounds, that they are arrows shot without a mark, which lose their force in the air, or fall down upon those who discharged them.

It has indeed, Sir, been prudent not to attempt what they are not able to accomplish, for I defy them to show that in any of these transactions I was engaged otherwise than as one among many, as a member of the council in which they were determined on, or of the Senate by which they were approved.

Of the exorbitant power with which I am invested, of the influence which I extend to all parts of the nation, of the tyranny with which I oppress those that oppose, and the liberality with which my followers are rewarded, no instance has been produced, as indeed no effects have been felt. But having first conferred upon me a kind of mock dignity, and styled me Prime Minister, they carry on the fiction which has once heated their imaginations, and impute to me an unpardonable abuse of that chimerical authority which only they have thought it necessary to bestow.

If their dream has really produced in them the terrors which they express, if they are really persuaded that the army is annually established by my authority, that I have the sole disposal of posts and honours, and that I employ this power to the destruction of liberty and the diminution of commerce, compassion would direct us to awaken them from so painful a delusion, to force their eyes open and stimulate them to a clear view of their own condition and that of the public, to show them that the prerogative has made no encroachments, that every supply is granted by the Senate, and every question debated with the utmost freedom, as before that fatal period in which they were seized with this political delirium that has so long harassed them with the loss of trade, the approach of slavery, the power of the crown, and the influence of the Minister.

But I am indeed, Sir, far from believing that they feel in themselves those emotions which they endeavour to communicate to others, I cannot but think so highly of their sagacity as to conclude that even in their own opinion they are complaining of grievances which they do not suffer, and promoting rather their own interest than that of the nation.

Whatever, Sir, is their intention, the House will undoubtedly require that their assertions should be confuted; I shall therefore proceed to some transactions of a more private kind, in which it may be suspected that I was personally engaged.

Among these, Sir, I do not number the affairs of the debentures, with which the gentleman who spoke last has so warmly upbraided me; I have indeed long expected that the fury of the opponents of the government, every day increased by new defeats, would at last hurry them into some wild measures or ridiculous assertions by which their reputation among the people, that reputation which they have with so much labour established, would be totally destroyed.

The day which I have long expected is at last arrived; they must henceforward no longer expect to be reverenced as the great dispensers of political truth, as the guardians of virtue, or the supporters of justice, but must be content to be levelled with those whom they have so long affected to despise, with courtiers, placemen, and adherents to the government: for which of all these, however dependent or corrupt, has attempted to ruin the reputation of another by charging him with a transaction in which he had no part? The debentures of the army were settled before I was advanced to any of the offices which I now enjoy, nor had I any other concern in them than that of promoting and regulating the payment of them; and yet I am charged in this assembly with enriching myself by an illegal traffic on this occasion.

The apparent falsehood of this charge will, Sir, dispose the House to hear more favourably my defence against the rest, since it may be easily imagined that they who advance falsehood will aggravate truth.

With regard to the employments which have been granted to my family, I know not whether any man can accuse me of doing what he would not have done in the same circumstances; nor do I believe that the most abstemious of my accusers, had he been able to obtain the same interest, would not have employed it to the same end. It will not surely be expected that I should obstruct his Majesty's favours when offered to my family, and I hope their advancement cannot be imputed to me as a crime, unless it shall appear that I procured them by false representations of their virtue or abilities.

As to myself, I know not how I have given occasion to any charge of rapacity or avarice, or why I should be suspected of making exorbitant demands upon his Majesty's liberality, since, except the places which I am known to possess, I have obtained no grant from the crown, or fewer at least than perhaps any man who has been supposed to have enjoyed the confidence of his sovereign. All that has been given me is a little house at a small distance from this city, worth about seven hundred sprugs,° which I obtained that I might enjoy the quiet of retirement without remitting my attendance on my office.

The little ornament° upon my shoulder I had indeed forgot, but this surely cannot be mentioned as a proof of avarice; nor though it may be looked on with envy or indignation in another place, can it be supposed to raise any resentment in this House, where many must be pleased to see those honours which their ancestors have worn restored again to the Clinabs.°

Having now, Sir, with due submission offered my defence, I shall wait the decision of the House without any other solicitude than for the honour of their counsels, which cannot but be impaired if passion should precipitate or interest pervert them. For my part, that innocence which has supported me against the clamour of opposition will establish my happiness in obscurity, nor shall I lose by the censure which is now threatened any other pleasure than that of serving my country.

When he had done speaking, the question was put and carried in the negative 290 to 106.°

Review of *Memoirs of the Duchess Dowager of Marlborough*°

Sir,

The *Account of the Conduct of the Duchess of Marlborough* having been so eagerly received, and so attentively considered as to become even at this time of business, contests, wars, and revolutions the most popular topic of conversation, you may perhaps willingly admit into your collection this short essay upon it, which does not appear written with an intention to please or offend any party.

The universal regard which is paid by mankind to such accounts of public transactions as have been written by those who were engaged in them may be with great probability ascribed to that ardent love of truth which nature has kindled in the breast of man, and which remains even where every other laudable passion is extinguished. We cannot but read such narratives with uncommon curiosity, because we consider the writer as indubitably possessed of the ability to give us just representations, and do not always reflect that, very often, proportionate to the opportunities of knowing the truth are the temptations to disguise it.

Authors of this kind have at least an incontestable superiority over those whose passions are the same, and whose knowledge is less. It is evident that those who write in their own defence discover often more impartiality, and less contempt of evidence, than the advocates which faction or interest have raised in their favour.

It is, however, to be remembered that the parent of all memoirs is the ambition of being distinguished from the herd of mankind, and the fear of either infamy or oblivion, passions which cannot but have some degree of influence, and which may at least affect the writer's choice of facts, though they may not prevail upon him to advance known falsehoods. He may aggravate or extenuate particular circumstances, though he preserves the general transaction; as the general likeness may be preserved in painting, though a blemish is hid or a beauty improved.

Every man that is solicitous about the esteem of others is in a greater degree desirous of his own, and makes by consequence his first apology for his conduct to himself, and when he has once deceived his own heart, which is for the greatest part too easy a task, he propagates the deceit in the world, without reluctance or consciousness of falsehood.

But to what purpose, it may be asked, are such reflections, except to make history of no use? The man who knows not the truth *cannot*, and he who knows it, *will not* tell it; what then remains, but to distrust every relation, and live in perpetual negligence of past events; or, what is still more disagreeable, in perpetual suspense?

That by such remarks, some incredulity is indeed produced cannot be denied, but distrust is a necessary qualification of a student in history. Distrust quickens his discernment of different degrees of probability, animates his search after evidence, and perhaps heightens his pleasure at the discovery of truth; for truth, though not always obvious, is generally discoverable, not is it any where more likely to be found than in private memoirs, which are generally published at a time when any gross falsehood may be detected by living witnesses, and which always contain a thousand incidents of which the writer could not but have acquired a certain knowledge, and which he has no reason for disguising.

Such is the account lately published by the Duchess of Marlborough, of her own conduct, by which those who are very little concerned about the character which it is principally intended to preserve or to retrieve may be entertained and instructed. By the perusal of this account, the inquirer into human nature may obtain an intimate acquaintance with the characters of those whose names have crowded the latest histories, and discover the relation between their minds and their actions. The historian may trace the progress of great transactions, and discover the secret causes of important events. And, to mention one use more, the polite writer may learn an unaffected dignity of style, and an artful simplicity of narration.

The method of confirming her relation, by inserting, at length, the letters that every transaction occasioned, has not only set the greatest part of the work above the danger of confutation, but has added to the entertainment of the reader, who has now the satisfaction of forming to himself the characters of the actors, and judging how nearly such as have hitherto been given of them agree with those which they now give of themselves.

Even of those whose letters could not be made public, we have a more exact knowledge than can be expected from general histories, because we see them in their private apartments, in their careless hours, and observe those actions in which they indulged their own inclinations, without any regard to censure or applause.

Thus it is that we are made acquainted with the disposition of King William, of whom it may be collected from various instances that he was arbitrary, insolent, gloomy, rapacious, and brutal, that he was at all times disposed to play the tyrant, *that he had, neither in great things, nor in small, the manners of a gentleman*, that he was capable of gaining money by mean artifices, and that he only regarded his promise when it was his interest to keep it.

There are doubtless great numbers who will be offended with this delineation of the mind of the immortal William, but they whose honesty or sense enables them to consider impartially the events of his reign will now be enabled to discover the reason of the frequent oppositions which he encountered, and of the personal affronts which he was sometimes forced to endure. They will observe that it is not always sufficient to do right, and that it is often necessary to add gracefulness to virtue. They will recollect how vain it is to endeavour to gain men by great qualities, while our cursory behaviour is insolent and offensive, and that those may be disgusted by little things who can scarcely be pleased with great.

Charles the Second, by his affability and politeness, made himself the idol of the nation which he betrayed and sold. William the Third was, for his insolence and brutality, hated by that people which he protected and enriched; had the best part of these two characters been united in one prince, the House of Bourbon had fallen before him.

It is not without pain that the reader observes a shade encroaching upon the light with which the memory of Queen Mary has been hitherto invested. The popular, the beneficent, the pious, the celestial Queen Mary, from whose presence none ever withdrew without an addition to his happiness. What can be charged upon this delight of human kind? Nothing less than that *she wanted bowels*, and was insolent with her power, that she was resentful and pertinacious in her resentment, that she descended to mean acts of revenge, when heavier vengeance was not in her power. That she was desirous of controlling where she had no authority, and backward to forgive, even when she had no real injury to complain of.

This is a character so different from all those that have been hitherto given of this celebrated princess that the reader stands in suspense till he considers the inconsistencies in human conduct, remembers that no virtue is without its weakness, and considers that Queen Mary's character has hitherto had this great advantage, that it has only been compared with those of kings.

The greatest number of the letters inserted in this account were written by Queen Anne, of which it may be truly observed that they will be equally useful for the confutation of those who have exalted or depressed her character. They are written with great purity and correctness, without any forced expressions, affected phrases, or unnatural sentiments, and show uncommon clearness of understanding, tenderness of affection, and rectitude of intention; but discover, at the same time, a temper timorous, anxious, and impatient of misfortune, a tendency to burst into complaints, helpless dependence on the affection of others, and a weak desire of moving compassion. There is indeed nothing insolent or overbearing; but then there is nothing great, or firm, or regal; nothing that enforces obedience and respect, or which does not rather invite opposition and petulance. She seems born for friendship, not for government, and to be unable to regulate the conduct of others otherwise than by her own example.

That this character is just appears from the occurrences in her reign, in which the nation was governed, for many years, by a party whose principles she detested, but whose influence she knew not how to obviate, and to whose schemes she was subservient against her inclination.

The charge of tyrannizing over her, which was made by turns against each party, proves that, in the opinion of both, she was easily to be governed; and though it may be supposed that the letters here published were selected with some regard to respect and ceremony, it appears plainly enough from them that she was what she has been represented, little more than *the slave of the Marlborough family*.

The inferior characters, as they are of less importance, are less accurately delineated; the picture of Harley is at least partially drawn, all the deformities are heightened, and the beauties, for beauties of mind he certainly had, are entirely omitted.

An Account of the Harleian Library°

To solicit a subscription for a catalogue of books exposed to sale is an attempt for which some apology cannot but be necessary; for few would willingly contribute to the expense of volumes by which neither instruction nor entertainment could be afforded, from which only the bookseller could expect advantage, and of which the only use must cease, at the dispersion of the library.

Nor could the reasonableness of an universal rejection of our proposal be denied, if this catalogue were to be compiled with no other view than that of promoting the sale of the books which it enumerates, and drawn up with that inaccuracy and confusion which may be found in those that are daily published.

But our design, like our proposal, is uncommon, and to be prosecuted at a very uncommon expense; it being intended that the books shall be distributed into their distinct classes, and every class ranged with some regard to the age of the writers; that every book shall be accurately described; that the peculiarities of editions shall be remarked, and observations from the authors of literary history occasionally interspersed; that, by this catalogue, we may inform posterity of the excellence and value of this great collection, and promote the knowledge of scarce books, and elegant editions. For this purpose, men of letters are engaged who cannot even be supplied with amanuenses but at an expense above that of a common catalogue.

To show that this collection deserves a particular degree of regard from the learned and the studious, that it excels any library that was ever yet offered to public sale, in the value, as well as number, of the volumes which it contains; and that, therefore, this catalogue will not be of less use to men of letters than those of the Thuanian, Heinsian, or Barberinian libraries,° it may not be improper to exhibit a general account of the different classes, as they are naturally divided by the several sciences.

By this method we can, indeed, exhibit only a general idea, at once magnificent and confused; an idea of the writings of many nations, collected from distant parts of the world, discovered sometimes by chance, and sometimes by curiosity, amidst the rubbish of forsaken monasteries, and the repositories of ancient families, and brought hither from every part, as to the universal receptacle of learning.

It will be no unpleasing effect of this account, if those that shall happen to peruse it should be inclined by it to reflect on the character of the late proprietors, and to pay some tribute of veneration to their ardour for literature, to that generous and exalted curiosity which they gratified with incessant searches and immense expense, and to which they dedicated that time, and that superfluity of fortune, which many others of their rank employ in the pursuit of contemptible amusements, or the gratification of guilty passions. And, surely, every man who considers learning as ornamental and advantageous to the community must allow them the honour of public benefactors who have introduced amongst us authors not hitherto well known, and added to the literary treasures of their native country.

That our catalogue will excite any other man to emulate the collectors of this library, to prefer books and manuscripts to equipage and luxury, and to forsake noise and diversion for the conversation of the learned, and the satisfaction of extensive knowledge, we are very far from presuming to hope, but shall make no scruple to assert that, if any man should happen to be seized with such laudable ambition, he may find in this catalogue hints and informations which are not easily to be met with; he will discover that the boasted Bodleian library is very far from a perfect model, and that even the learned Fabricius° cannot completely instruct him in the early editions of the classic writers.

But the collectors of libraries cannot be numerous, and, therefore, catalogues could not very properly be recommended to the public if they had not a more general and frequent use, a use which every student has experienced, or neglected to his loss. By the means of catalogues only, can it be known what has been written on every part of learning, and the hazard avoided of encountering difficulties which have already been cleared, discussing questions which have already been decided, and digging in mines of literature which former ages have exhausted.

How often this has been the fate of students, every man of letters can declare, and, perhaps, there are very few who have not sometimes valued as new discoveries, made by themselves, those observations, which have long since been published, and of which the world therefore will refuse them the praise; nor can that refusal be censured as any enormous violation of justice; for why should they not forfeit by their ignorance what they might claim by their sagacity?

To illustrate this remark by the mention of obscure names would not much confirm it; and to vilify for this purpose the memory of men truly great would be to deny them the reverence which they may justly claim from those whom their writings have instructed. May the shade at least of one great English critic° rest without disturbance, and may no man presume to insult his memory who wants his learning, his reason, or his wit.

From the vexatious disappointment of meeting reproach where praise is expected, every man will certainly desire to be secured; and therefore that book will have some claim to his regard from which he may receive informations of the labours of his predecessors, such as a catalogue of the Harleian library will copiously afford him.

Nor is the use of catalogues of less importance to those whom curiosity has engaged in the study of literary history, and who think the intellectual revolutions of the world more worthy of their attention than the ravages of tyrants, the desolation of kingdoms, the rout of armies, and the fall of empires. Those who are pleased with observing the first birth of new opinions, their struggles against opposition, their silent progress under persecution, their general reception, and their gradual decline, or sudden extinction; those that amuse themselves with remarking the different periods of human knowledge, and observe how darkness and light succeed each other, by what accident the most gloomy nights of ignorance have given way to the dawn of science, and how learning has languished and decayed, for want of patronage and regard, or been overborne by the prevalence of fashionable ignorance, or lost amidst the tumults of invasion, and the storms of violence. All those who desire any knowledge of the literary transactions of past ages may find in catalogues, like this at least, such an account as is given by annalists, and chronologers of civil history.

Proposals for the *Harleian Miscellany*

AN ACCOUNT OF THIS UNDERTAKING

It has been for a long time a very just complaint, among the learned, that a multitude of valuable productions, published in small pamphlets, or in single sheets, are in a short time, too often by accidents, or negligence, destroyed, and entirely lost; and that those authors, whose reverence for the public has hindered them from swelling their works with repetition, or encumbering them with superfluities, and who, therefore, deserve the praise and gratitude of posterity, are forgotten, for the very reason for which they might expect to be remembered. It has been long lamented that the duration of the monuments of genius and study, as well as of wealth and power, depends in no small measure on their bulk; and that volumes, considerable only for their size, are handed down from one age to another, when compendious treatises, of far greater importance, are suffered to perish, as the compactest bodies sink into the water, while those of which the extension bears a greater proportion to the weight float upon the surface.

This observation hath been so often confirmed by experience, that, in the neighbouring nation, the common appellation of small performances is derived from this unfortunate circumstance; a *flying sheet*, or a *fugitive piece*,° are the terms by which they are distinguished, and distinguished with too great propriety, as they are subject, after having amused mankind for a while, to take their flight, and disappear for ever.

What are the losses which the learned have already sustained, by having neglected to fix those fugitives in some certain residence, it is not easy to say; but there is no doubt that many valuable observations have been repeated, because they were not preserved; and that, therefore, the progress of knowledge has been retarded, by the necessity of doing what had been already done, but was done for those who forgot their benefactor.

The obvious method of preventing these losses, of preserving to every man the reputation he has merited by long assiduity, is to unite these scattered pieces into volumes, that those which are too small to preserve themselves may be secured by their combination with others; to consolidate these atoms of learning into systems, to collect these disunited rays, that their light and their fire may become perceptible.

Of encouraging this useful design, the studious and inquisitive have now an opportunity which, perhaps, was never offered them before, and which, if it should now be lost, there is not any probability that they will ever recover. They may now conceive themselves in possession of the lake into which all those rivulets of science have for many years been flowing; but which, unless its waters are turned into proper channels, will soon burst its banks, or be dispersed in imperceptible exhalations.

In the Harleian library, which I° have purchased, are treasured a greater number of pamphlets and small treatises than were, perhaps, ever yet seen in one place; productions of the writers of all parties, and of every age, from the Reformation; collected with an unbounded and unwearied curiosity, without exclusion of any subject.

So great is the variety that it has been no small labour to peruse the titles, in order to reduce them to a rude division, and range their heaps under general heads; of which the numbers, though not yet increased by the subdivision which an accurate survey will necessarily produce cannot but excite the curiosity of all the studious, as there is scarcely any part of knowledge which some of these articles do not comprehend.

Introduction to the *Harleian Miscellany*

AN ESSAY ON THE ORIGIN AND IMPORTANCE OF SMALL TRACTS AND
FUGITIVE PIECES

Though the scheme of the following miscellany is so obvious that the
title alone is sufficient to explain it; and though several collections
have been formerly attempted upon plans, as to the method, very
little, but, as to the capacity and execution, very different from ours;
we, being possessed of the greatest variety for such a work, hope for a
more general reception than those confined schemes had the fortune
to meet with; and, therefore, think it not wholly unnecessary to
explain our intentions, to display the treasure of materials out of
which this miscellany is to be compiled, and to exhibit a general idea
of the pieces which we intend to insert in it.

There is, perhaps, no nation in which it is so necessary as in our
own to assemble, from time to time, the small tracts and fugitive
pieces which are occasionally published; for, besides the general
subjects of inquiry which are cultivated by us, in common with every
other learned nation, our constitution in church and state naturally
gives birth to a multitude of performances which would either not
have been written, or could not have been made public, in any other
place.

The form of our government, which gives every man that has
leisure, or curiosity, or vanity the right of inquiring into the propriety
of public measures, and, by consequence, obliges those who are
intrusted with the administration of national affairs to give an account
of their conduct to almost every man who demands it, may be
reasonably imagined to have occasioned innumerable pamphlets
which would never have appeared under arbitrary governments,
where every man lulls himself in indolence under calamities of which
he cannot promote the redress, or thinks it prudent to conceal the
uneasiness of which he cannot complain without danger.

The multiplicity of religious sects tolerated among us, of which
every one has found opponents and vindicators, is another source of
unexhaustible publication, almost peculiar to ourselves; for controversies cannot be long continued, nor frequently revived, where an
inquisitor has a right to shut up the disputants in dungeons, or where
silence can be imposed on either party by the refusal of a license.

Not that it should be inferred from hence that political or religious controversies are the only products of the liberty of the British press; the mind once let loose to inquiry, and suffered to operate without restraint, necessarily deviates into peculiar opinions, and wanders in new tracks, where she is indeed sometimes lost in a labyrinth, from which though she cannot return, and scarce knows how to proceed, yet, sometimes, makes useful discoveries, or finds out nearer paths to knowledge.

The boundless liberty with which every man may write his own thoughts, and the opportunity of conveying new sentiments to the public without danger of suffering either ridicule or censure, which every man may enjoy whose vanity does not incite him too hastily to own his performances, naturally invites those who employ themselves in speculation to try how their notions will be received by a nation which exempts caution from fear, and modesty from shame; and it is no wonder that where reputation may be gained, but needs not be lost, multitudes are willing to try their fortune, and thrust their opinions into the light, sometimes with unsuccessful haste, and sometimes with happy temerity.

It is observed that among the natives of England is to be found a greater variety of humour than in any other country; and, doubtless, where every man has a full liberty to propagate his conceptions, variety of humour must produce variety of writers; and, where the number of authors is so great, there cannot but be some worthy of distinction.

All these and many other causes, too tedious to be enumerated, have contributed to make pamphlets and small tracts a very important part of an English library; nor are there any pieces upon which those who aspire to the reputation of judicious collectors of books bestow more attention, or greater expense; because many advantages may be expected from the perusal of these small productions which are scarcely to be found in that of larger works.

If we regard history, it is well known that most political treatises have for a long time appeared in this form, and that the first relations of transactions, while they are yet the subject of conversation, divide the opinions, and employ the conjectures of mankind, are delivered by these petty writers, who have opportunities of collecting the different sentiments of disputants, of inquiring the truth from living witnesses, and of copying their representations from the life; and, therefore, they preserve a multitude of particular incidents, which are forgotten in a short time, or omitted in formal relations, and which are yet to be considered as sparks of truth, which, when united, may afford light in some of the darkest scenes of state, as, we doubt not, will be sufficiently proved in the course of this *Miscellany*; and which it is, therefore, the interest of the public to preserve unextinguished.

The same observation may be extended to subjects of yet more importance. In controversies that relate to the truths of religion, the first essays of reformation are generally timorous; and those who have opinions to offer which they expect to be opposed produce their sentiments by degrees, and, for the most part, in small tracts: by degrees, that they may not shock their readers with too many novelties at once; and in small tracts, that they may be easily dispersed, or privately printed. Almost every controversy, therefore, has been, for a time, carried on in pamphlets, nor has swelled into larger volumes till the first ardour of the disputants has subsided, and they have recollected their notions with coolness enough to digest them into order, consolidate them into systems, and fortify them with authorities.

From pamphlets, consequently, are to be learned the progress of every debate; the various states to which the questions have been changed; the artifices and fallacies which have been used, and the subterfuges by which reason has been eluded. In such writings may be seen how the mind has been opened by degrees, how one truth has led to another, how error has been disentangled, and hints improved to demonstration. Which pleasure, and many others, are lost by him that only reads the larger writers by whom these scattered sentiments are collected, who will see none of the changes of fortune which every opinion has passed through, will have no opportunity of remarking the transient advantages which error may sometimes obtain by the artifices of its patron, or the successful rallies by which truth regains the day, after a repulse; but will be to him who traces the dispute through into particular gradations, as he that hears of a victory to him that sees the battle.

Since the advantages of preserving these small tracts are so numerous, our attempt to unite them in volumes cannot be thought either useless or unseasonable; for there is no other method of securing them from accidents; and they have already been so long neglected that this design cannot be delayed without hazarding the loss of many pieces which deserve to be transmitted to another age.

The practice of publishing pamphlets on the most important subjects has now prevailed more than two centuries among us; and, therefore, it cannot be doubted but that, as no large collections have been yet made, many curious tracts must have perished; but it is too late to lament that loss; nor ought we to reflect upon it with any other view than that of quickening our endeavours for the preservation of those that yet remain; of which we have now a greater number than was, perhaps, ever amassed by any one person.

The first appearance of pamphlets among us is generally thought to be at the new opposition raised against the errors and corruptions of the Church of Rome. Those who were first convinced of the reasonableness of the new learning, as it was then called, propagated their opinions in small pieces, which were cheaply printed, and, what was then of great importance, easily concealed. These treatises were generally printed in foreign countries, and are not, therefore, always very correct. There was not then that opportunity of printing in private; for the number of printers was small, and the presses were easily overlooked by the clergy, who spared no labour or vigilance for the suppression of heresy. There is, however, reason to suspect that some attempts were made to carry on the propagation of truth by a secret press; for one of the first treatises in favour of the Reformation is said, at the end, to be printed *at Greenwich, by the permission of the Lord of Hosts.*

In the time of King Edward the Sixth, the presses were employed in favour of the reformed religion, and small tracts were dispersed over the nation, to reconcile them to the new forms of worship. In this reign, likewise, political pamphlets may be said to have been begun, by the address of the rebels of Devonshire; all which means propagating the sentiments of the people so disturbed the court that no sooner was Queen Mary resolved to reduce her subjects to the Romish superstition but she artfully, by a charter° granted to certain freemen of London, in whose fidelity, no doubt, she confided, entirely prohibited *all* presses but what should be licensed by them; which charter is that by which the Corporation of Stationers in London is, at this time, incorporated.

Under the reign of Queen Elizabeth, when liberty again began to flourish, the practice of writing pamphlets became more general; presses were multiplied, and books more dispersed; and, I believe, it may properly be said that the trade of writing began at this time, and that it has ever since gradually increased in the number, though, perhaps, not in the style of those that followed it.

In this reign was erected the first secret press against the Church, as now established, of which I have found any certain account. It was employed by the Puritans, and conveyed from one part of the nation to another by them, as they found themselves in danger of discovery.

From this press issued most of the pamphlets against Whitgift and his associates in the ecclesiastical government; and, when it was at last seized at Manchester, it was employed upon a pamphlet called *More Work for a Cooper*.

In the peaceable reign of King James, those minds which might, perhaps, with less disturbance of the world, have been engrossed by war were employed in controversy; and writings of all kinds were multiplied among us. The press, however, was not wholly engaged in polemical performances, for more innocent subjects were sometimes treated; and it deserves to be remarked, because it is not generally known, that the treatises of husbandry and agriculture which were published about that time are so numerous that it can scarcely be imagined by whom they were written, or to whom they were sold.

The next reign is too well known to have been a time of confusion and disturbance, and disputes of every kind; and the writings which were produced bear a natural proportion to the number of the questions that were discussed at that time; each party had its authors and its presses, and no endeavours were omitted to gain proselytes to every opinion. I know not whether this may not properly be called *The Age of Pamphlets*; for, though they, perhaps, may not arise to such multitudes as Mr Rawlinson imagined, they were, undoubtedly, more numerous than can be conceived by any who have not had an opportunity of examining them.

After the Restoration, the same differences in religious opinions are well known to have subsisted, and the same political struggles to have been frequently renewed; and, therefore, a great number of pens were employed, on different occasions, till, at length, all other disputes were absorbed in the Popish controversy.

From the pamphlets which these different periods of time produced, it is proposed that this *Miscellany* shall be compiled; for which it cannot be supposed that materials will be wanting, and, therefore, the only difficulty will be in what manner to dispose them.

Those who have gone before us, in undertakings of this kind, have ranged the pamphlets which chance threw into their hands without any regard either to the subject on which they treated, or the time in which they were written; a practice in no wise to be imitated by us, who want for no materials; of which we shall choose those we think best for the particular circumstances of times and things, and most instructing and entertaining to the reader.

Of the different methods which present themselves, upon the first view of the great heaps of pamphlets which the Harleian library exhibits, the two which merit most attention are to distribute the treatises according to their subjects or their dates; but neither of these ways can be conveniently followed. By ranging our collection in order of time, we must necessarily publish those pieces first which least engage the curiosity of the bulk of mankind; and our design must fall to the ground, for want of encouragement, before it can be so far advanced to obtain general regard. By confining ourselves for any long time to any single subject, we shall reduce our readers to one class; and, as we shall lose all the grace of variety, shall disgust all those who read chiefly to be diverted. There is, likewise, one objection of equal force against both these methods, that we shall preclude ourselves from the advantage of any future discoveries, and we cannot hope to assemble at once all the pamphlets which have been written in any age, or on any subject.

It may be added, in vindication of our intended practice, that it is the same with that of Photius,° whose collections are no less miscellaneous than ours, and who declares that he leaves it to his reader to reduce his extracts under their proper heads.

Most of the pieces which shall be offered in this collection to the public will be introduced by short prefaces, in which will be given some account of the reasons for which they are inserted; notes will be sometimes adjoined for the explanation of obscure passages, or obsolete expressions; and care will be taken to mingle use and pleasure through the whole collection. Notwithstanding every subject may not be relished by every reader, yet the buyer may be assured that each number will repay his generous subscription.

An Account of the Life of Mr Richard Savage, Son of the Earl Rivers°

It has been observed in all ages that the advantages of nature or of fortune have contributed very little to the promotion of happiness; and that those whom the splendour of their rank or the extent of their capacity have placed upon the summits of human life have not often given any just occasion to envy in those who look up to them from a lower station; whether it be that apparent superiority incites great designs, and great designs are naturally liable to fatal miscarriages; or that the general lot of mankind is misery, and the misfortunes of those whose eminence drew upon them an universal attention have been more carefully recorded, because they were more generally observed, and have in reality been only more conspicuous than those of others, not more frequent, or more severe.

That affluence and power, advantages extrinsic and adventitious, and therefore easily separable from those by whom they are possessed, should very often flatter the mind with expectation of felicity which they cannot give, raises no astonishment: but it seems rational to hope that intellectual greatness should produce better effects, that minds qualified for great attainments should first endeavour their own benefit, and that they who are most able to teach others the way to happiness should with most certainty follow it themselves.

But this expectation, however plausible, has been very frequently disappointed. The heroes of literary as well as civil history have been very often no less remarkable for what they have suffered than for what they have achieved; and volumes have been written only to enumerate the miseries of the learned, and relate their unhappy lives and untimely deaths.

To these mournful narratives I am about to add the life of Richard Savage, a man whose writings entitle him to an eminent rank in the classes of learning, and whose misfortunes claim a degree of compassion not always due to the unhappy, as they were often the consequences of the crimes of others, rather than his own.

In the year 1697 Anne Countess of Macclesfield, having lived for some time upon very uneasy terms with her husband, thought a public confession of adultery° the most obvious and expeditious method of obtaining her liberty, and therefore declared that the child with which she was then great was begotten by the Earl Rivers. Her husband, being, as may be easily imagined, thus made no less desirous of a separation than herself, prosecuted his design in the most effectual manner; for he applied not to the ecclesiastical courts for a divorce, but to the Parliament for an act by which his marriage might be dissolved, the nuptial contract totally annulled, and the children of his wife illegitimated. This act, after the usual deliberation, he obtained, though without the approbation of some who considered marriage as an affair only cognizable by ecclesiastical judges; and next year on March 3rd was separated from his wife, whose fortune, which was very great, was repaid her, and who having, as well as her husband, the liberty of making another choice, was in a short time married to Colonel Brett.

While the Earl of Macclesfield was prosecuting this affair his wife was, on the 10th of January 1697–8 delivered of a son, and the Earl Rivers, by appearing to consider him as his own, left none any reason to doubt of the sincerity of her declaration; for he was his godfather, and gave him his own name, which was by his direction inserted in the register of St Andrew's parish in Holborn, but unfortunately left him to the care of his mother, whom, as she was now set free from her husband, he probably imagined likely to treat with great tenderness the child that had contributed to so pleasing an event. It is not indeed easy to discover what motives could be found to overbalance that natural affection of a parent, or what interest could be promoted by neglect or cruelty. The dread of shame or of poverty, by which some wretches have been incited to abandon or to murder their children, cannot be supposed to have affected a woman who had proclaimed her crimes and solicited reproach, and on whom the clemency of the legislature had undeservedly bestowed a fortune that would have been very little diminished by the expenses which the care of her child could have brought upon her. It was therefore not likely that she would be wicked without temptation, that she would look upon her son from his birth with a kind of resentment and abhorrence, and, instead of supporting, assisting, and defending him, delight to see him struggling with misery; that she would take every opportunity of aggravating his misfortunes and obstructing his resources, and with an implacable and restless cruelty continue her persecution from the first hour of his life to the last.

But whatever were her motives, no sooner was her son born than she discovered a resolution of disowning him; and in a very short time removed him from her sight, by committing him to the care of a poor woman, whom she directed to educate him as her own, and enjoined never to inform him of his true parents.

Such was the beginning of the life of Richard Savage. Born with a legal claim to honour and to riches he was in two months illegitimated by the Parliament, and disowned by his mother, doomed to poverty and obscurity, and launched upon the ocean of life only that he might be swallowed by its quicksands or dashed upon its rocks.

His mother could not indeed infect others with the same cruelty. As it was impossible to avoid the inquiries which the curiosity or tenderness of her relations made after her child, she was obliged to give some account of the measures that she had taken, and her mother, the Lady Mason, whether in approbation of her design or to prevent more criminal contrivances, engaged to transact with his nurse, pay her for her care, and superintend his education.

In this charitable office she was assisted by his godmother Mrs Lloyd, who while she lived always looked upon him with that tenderness which the barbarity of his mother made peculiarly necessary; but her death, which happened in his tenth year, was another of the misfortunes of his childhood: for though she kindly endeavoured to alleviate his loss by a legacy of three hundred pounds, yet, as he had none to prosecute his claim, or call in law to the assistance of justice, her will was eluded by the executors, and no part of the money was ever paid.

He was however not yet wholly abandoned. The Lady Mason still continued her care, and directed him to be placed at a small grammar school near St Alban's, where he was called by the name of his nurse, without the least intimation that he had a claim to any other.

Here he was initiated in literature, and passed through several of the classes, with what rapidity or what applause cannot now be known. As he always spoke with respect of his master, it is probable that the mean rank in which he then appeared did not hinder his genius from being distinguished, or his industry from being rewarded, and if in so low a state he obtained distinction and rewards, it is not likely that they were gained but by genius and industry.

It is very reasonable to conjecture that his application was equal to his abilities, because his improvement was more than proportioned to the opportunities which he enjoyed; nor can it be doubted that if his early productions had been preserved, like those of happier students, we might in some have found sallies of that sprightly humour which distinguishes *The Author to be Let*, and in others touches of that vigorous imagination which painted the solemn scenes of *The Wanderer*.

While he was thus cultivating his mind, his father the Earl Rivers was seized with a distemper, which in a short time put an end to his life. He had frequently inquired after his son, and had always been amused with fallacious and evasive answers; but being now in his own opinion on his death-bed, he thought it his duty to provide for him among his other natural children, and therefore demanded a positive account of him, with an importunity not to be diverted or denied. His mother, who could no longer refuse an answer, determined at least to give such as should cut him off for ever from that happiness which competence affords, and therefore declared that he was dead; which is perhaps the first instance of a lie invented by a mother to deprive her son of a provision which was designed him by another, and which she could not expect herself, though he should lose it.

This was therefore an act of wickedness which could not be defeated, because it could not be suspected; the Earl did not imagine that there could exist in a human form a mother that would ruin her son without enriching herself, and therefore bestowed upon some other person six thousand pounds, which he had in his will bequeathed to Savage.

The same cruelty which incited his mother to intercept this provision which had been intended him prompted her in a short time to another project, to a project worthy of such a disposition. She endeavoured to rid herself from the danger of being at any time made known to him, by sending him secretly to the American plantations.

By whose kindness this scheme was counteracted, or by what interposition she was induced to lay aside her design, I know not; it is not improbable that the Lady Mason might persuade or compel her to desist, or perhaps she could not easily find accomplices wicked enough to concur in so cruel an action; for it may be conceived that even those who had by a long gradation of guilt hardened their hearts against the sense of common wickedness, would yet be shocked at the design of a mother to expose her son to slavery and want, to expose him without interest, and without provocation; and Savage might on this occasion find protectors and advocates among those who had long traded in crimes, and whom compassion had never touched before.

Being hindered, by whatever means, from banishing him into another country, she formed soon after a scheme for burying him in poverty and obscurity in his own; and that his station of life, if not the place of his residence, might keep him for ever at a distance from her, she ordered him to be placed with a shoemaker in Holborn, that after the usual time of trial, he might become his apprentice.

It is generally reported that this project was for some time successful, and that Savage was employed at the awl longer than he was willing to confess; nor was it perhaps any great advantage to him that an unexpected discovery determined him to quit his occupation.

About this time his nurse, who had always treated him as her own son, died; and it was natural for him to take care of those effects which by her death were, as he imagined, become his own; he therefore went to her house, opened her boxes, and examined her papers, among which he found some letters written to her by the Lady Mason, which informed him of his birth, and the reasons for which it was concealed.

He was now no longer satisfied with the employment which had been allotted him, but thought he had a right to share the affluence of his mother, and therefore without scruple applied to her as her son, and made use of every art to awaken her tenderness, and attract her regard. But neither his letters, nor the interposition of those friends which his merit or his distress procured him, made any impression upon her. She still resolved to neglect, though she could no longer disown him.

It was to no purpose that he frequently solicited her to admit him to see her; she avoided him with the most vigilant precaution, and ordered him to be excluded from her house, by whomsoever he might be introduced and what reason soever he might give for entering it.

Savage was at the same time so touched with the discovery of his real mother that it was his frequent practice to walk in the dark evenings for several hours before her door, in hopes of seeing her as she might come by accident to the window, or cross her apartment with a candle in her hand.

But all his assiduity and tenderness were without effect, for he could neither soften her heart nor open her hand, and was reduced to the utmost miseries of want, while he was endeavouring to awaken the affection of a mother. He was therefore obliged to seek some other means of support, and, having no profession, became, by necessity, an author.

[He publishes a pamphlet on the Bangorian controversy, and writes two comedies, which are produced unsuccessfully. The second brings him the friendship of Steele and the actor Robert Wilks.]

Sir Richard Steele, having declared in his favour with all the ardour of benevolence which constituted his character, promoted his interest with the utmost zeal, related his misfortunes, applauded his merit, took all opportunities of recommending him, and asserted that 'the inhumanity of his mother had given him a right to find every good man his father'.

Nor was Mr Savage admitted to his acquaintance only, but to his confidence, of which he sometimes related an instance too extraordinary to be omitted, as it affords a very just idea of his patron's character.

He was once desired by Sir Richard, with an air of the utmost importance, to come very early to his house the next morning. Mr Savage came as he had promised, found the chariot at the door, and Sir Richard waiting for him, and ready to go out. What was intended, and whither they were to go, Savage could not conjecture, and was not willing to inquire, but immediately seated himself with his friend; the coachman was ordered to drive, and they hurried with the utmost expedition to Hyde-Park Corner, where they stopped at a petty tavern, and retired to a private room. Sir Richard then informed him that he intended to publish a pamphlet, and that he had desired him to come thither that he might write for him. They soon sat down to the work, Sir Richard dictated, and Savage wrote, till the dinner that had been ordered was put upon the table. Savage was surprised at the meanness of the entertainment, and after some hesitation, ventured to ask for wine, which Sir Richard, not without reluctance, ordered to be brought. They then finished their dinner, and proceeded in their pamphlet, which they concluded in the afternoon.

Mr Savage then imagined his task over, and expected that Sir Richard would call for the reckoning, and return home; but his expectations deceived him, for Sir Richard told him that he was without money, and that the pamphlet must be sold before the dinner could be paid for; and Savage was therefore obliged to go and offer their new production to sale for two guineas, which with some difficulty he obtained. Sir Richard then returned home, having retired that day only to avoid his creditors, and composed the pamphlet only to discharge his reckoning.

Mr Savage related another fact equally uncommon, which, though it has no relation to his life, ought to be preserved. Sir Richard Steele having one day invited to his house a great number of persons of the first quality, they were surprised at the number of liveries which surrounded the table; and after dinner, when wine and mirth had set them free from the observation of rigid ceremony, one of them inquired of Sir Richard how such an expensive train of domestics could be consistent with his fortune. He with great frankness confessed that they were fellows of whom he would very willingly be rid. And being then asked why he did not discharge them, declared that they were bailiffs who had introduced themselves with an execution, and whom, since he could not send them away, he had thought it convenient to embellish with liveries that they might do him credit while they stayed.

His friends were diverted with the expedient, and by paying the debt discharged their attendance, having obliged Sir Richard to promise that they should never again find him graced with a retinue of the same kind.

Under such a tutor, Mr Savage was not likely to learn prudence or frugality, and perhaps many of the misfortunes which the want of those virtues brought upon him in the following parts of his life might be justly imputed to so unimproving an example.

Nor did the kindness of Sir Richard end in common favours. He proposed to have established him in some settled scheme of life, and to have contracted a kind of alliance with him, by marrying him to a natural daughter, on whom he intended to bestow a thousand pounds. But though he was always lavish of future bounties, he conducted his affairs in such a manner that he was very seldom able to keep his promises, or execute his own intentions; and as he was never able to raise the sum which he had offered, the marriage was delayed. In the mean time he was officiously informed that Mr Savage had ridiculed him; by which he was so much exasperated that he withdrew the allowance which he had paid him, and never afterwards admitted him to his house.

It is not indeed unlikely that Savage might by his imprudence expose himself to the malice of a tale-bearer; for his patron had many follies, which, as his discernment easily discovered, his imagination might sometimes incite him to mention too ludicrously. A little knowledge of the world is sufficient to discover that such weakness is very common, and that there are few who do not sometimes in the wantonness of thoughtless mirth, or the heat of transient resentment, speak of their friends and benefactors with levity and contempt, though in their cooler moments, they want neither sense of their kindness, nor reverence for their virtue. The fault therefore of Mr Savage was rather negligence than ingratitude; but Sir Richard must likewise be acquitted of severity, for who is there that can patiently bear contempt from one whom he has relieved and supported, whose establishment he has laboured, and whose interest he has promoted?

[Wilks persuades Savage's 'mother' to give him £50. He is befriended by the actress Anne Oldfield, who gives him an annuity which ceases with her death.]

He had sometimes, by the kindness of Mr Wilks, the advantage of a benefit, on which occasions he often received uncommon marks of regard and compassion; and was once told by the Duke of Dorset that it was just to consider him as an injured nobleman, and that in his opinion the nobililty ought to think themselves obliged without solicitation to take every opportunity of supporting him by their countenance and patronage. But he had generally the mortification to hear that the whole interest of his mother was employed to frustrate his applications, and that she never left any expedient untried by which he might be cut off from the possibility of supporting life. The same disposition she endeavoured to diffuse among all those over whom nature or fortune gave her any influence, and indeed succeeded too well in her design; but could not always propagate her effrontery with her cruelty, for some of those whom she incited against him were ashamed of their own conduct, and boasted of that relief which they never gave him.

In this censure I do not indiscriminately involve all his relations; for he has mentioned with gratitude the humanity of one lady, whose name I am now unable to recollect, and to whom therefore I cannot pay the praises which she deserves for having acted well in opposition to influence, precept, and example.

The punishment which our laws inflict upon those parents who murder their infants is well known, nor has its justice ever been contested; but if they deserve death who destroy a child in its birth, what pains can be severe enough for her who forbears to destroy him only to inflict sharper miseries upon him; who prolongs his life only to make it miserable; and who exposes him without care and without pity to the malice of oppression, the caprices of chance, and the temptations of poverty; who rejoices to see him overwhelmed with calamities; and when his own industry or the charity of others has enabled him to rise for a short time above his miseries, plunges him again into his former distress?

[Aaron Hill befriends Savage, and publicizes his 'mother's' mistreatment of him. His tragedy *Sir Thomas Overbury* brings Savage some favourable notice.]

He was now advancing in reputation, and though frequently involved in very distressful perplexities, appeared however to be gaining upon mankind, when both his fame and his life were endangered by an event, of which it is not yet determined whether it ought to be mentioned as a crime or a calamity.

On the 20th of November 1727, Mr Savage came from Richmond,

where he then lodged, that he might pursue his studies with less interruption, with an intent to discharge another lodging which he had in Westminster, and accidentally meeting two gentlemen his acquaintances, whose names were Merchant and Gregory, he went in with them to a neighbouring coffee-house, and sat drinking till it was late, it being in no time of Mr Savage's life any part of his character to be the first of the company that desired to separate. He would willingly have gone to bed in the same house, but there was not room for the whole company, and therefore they agreed to ramble about the streets, and divert themselves with such amusements as should offer themselves till morning.

In their walk they happened unluckily to discover light in Robinson's coffee-house, near Charing-cross, and therefore went in. Merchant, with some rudeness, demanded a room, and was told that there was a good fire in the next parlour, which the company were about to leave, being then paying their reckoning. Merchant, not satisfied with this answer, rushed into the room, and was followed by his companions. He then petulantly placed himself between the company and the fire, and soon after kicked down the table. This produced a quarrel, swords were drawn on both sides, and one Mr James Sinclair was killed. Savage, having wounded likewise a maid that held him, forced his way with Merchant out of the house; but being intimidated and confused, without resolution either to fly or stay, they were taken in a back court by one of the company and some soldiers whom he had called to his assistance.

Being secured and guarded that night, they were in the morning carried before three justices, who committed them to the Gatehouse, from whence, upon the death of Mr Sinclair, which happened the same day, they were removed in the night to Newgate, where they were however treated with some distinction, exempted from the ignominy of chains, and confined, not among the common criminals, but in the Press-Yard.

When the day of trial came the court was crowded in a very unusual manner, and the public appeared to interest itself as in a cause of general concern. The witnesses against Mr Savage and his friends were the woman who kept the house, which was a house of ill fame, and her maid, the men who were in the room with Mr Sinclair, and a woman of the town, who had been drinking with them, and with whom one of them had been seen in bed. They swore in general that Merchant gave the provocation, which Savage and Gregory drew their swords to justify; that Savage drew first, and that he stabbed Sinclair when he was not in a posture of defence, or while Gregory commanded his sword; that after he had given the thrust he turned pale, and would have retired, but that the maid clung round him, and one of the company endeavoured to detain him, from whom he broke by cutting the maid on the head, but was afterwards taken in a court.

There was some difference in their depositions; one did not see Savage give the wound, another saw it given when Sinclair held his point towards the ground; and the woman of the town asserted that she did not see Sinclair's sword at all. This difference however was very far from amounting to inconsistency, but it was sufficient to show that the hurry of the quarrel was such that it was not easy to discover the truth with relation to particular circumstances, and that therefore some deductions were to be made from the credibility of the testimonies.

Sinclair had declared several times before his death that he received his wound from Savage, nor did Savage at his trial deny the fact, but endeavoured partly to extenuate it by urging the suddenness of the whole action, and the impossibility of any ill design, or premeditated malice, and partly to justify it by the necessity of self-defence, and the hazard of his own life if he had lost that opportunity of giving the thrust. He observed that neither reason nor law obliged a man to wait for the blow which was threatened, and which, if he should suffer it, he might never be able to return; that it was always allowable to prevent an assault, and to preserve life by taking away that of the adversary by whom he was endangered.

With regard to the violence with which he endeavoured his escape, he declared that it was not his design to fly from justice, or decline a trial, but to avoid the expenses and severities of a prison, and that he intended to have appeared at the bar without compulsion.

This defence, which took up more than an hour, was heard by the multitude that thronged the court with the most attentive and respectful silence: those who thought he ought not to be acquitted owned that applause could not be refused him; and those who before pitied his misfortunes, now reverenced his abilities.

The witnesses which appeared against him were proved to be persons of characters which did not entitle them to much credit: a common strumpet, a woman by whom strumpets were entertained, and a man by whom they were supported; and the character of Savage was by several persons of distinction asserted to be that of a modest inoffensive man, not inclined to broils, or to insolence, and who had, to that time, been only known for his misfortunes and his wit.

Had his audience been his judges, he had undoubtedly been acquitted; but Mr Page,° who was then upon the bench, treated him with his usual insolence and severity, and when he had summed up the evidence, endeavoured to exasperate the jury, as Mr Savage used to relate it, with this eloquent harangue:

'Gentlemen of the jury, you are to consider that Mr Savage is a very great man, a much greater man than you or I, gentlemen of the jury; that he wears very fine clothes, much finer clothes than you or I, gentlemen of the jury; that he has abundance of money in his pocket, much more money than you or I, gentlemen of the jury; but, gentlemen of the jury, is it not a very hard case, gentlemen of the jury, that Mr Savage should therefore kill you or me, gentlemen of the jury?'

[After Page's hostile summing up, Savage is found guilty of murder and sentenced to death.]

Mr Savage had now no hopes of life but from the mercy of the Crown, which was very earnestly solicited by his friends, and which, with whatever difficulty the story may obtain belief, was obstructed only by his mother.

To prejudice the Queen against him she made use of an incident, which was omitted in the order of time, that it might be mentioned together with the purpose which it was made to serve. Mr Savage, when he had discovered his birth, had an incessant desire to speak to his mother, who always avoided him in public, and refused him admission into her house. One evening walking, as it was his custom, in the street that she inhabited, he saw the door of her house by accident open; he entered it, and finding none in the passage to hinder him, went up stairs to salute her. She discovered him before he could enter her chamber, alarmed the family with the most distressful outcries, and when she had by her screams gathered them about her, ordered them to drive out of the house that villain who had forced himself in upon her, and endeavoured to murder her. Savage, who had attempted with the most submissive tenderness to soften her rage, hearing her utter so detestable an accusation, thought it prudent to retire; and, I believe, never attempted afterwards to speak to her.

But shocked as he was with her falsehood and her cruelty, he imagined that she intended no other use of her lie than to set herself free from his embraces and solicitations, and was very far from suspecting that she would treasure it in her memory as an instrument of future wickedness, or that she would endeavour for this fictitious assault to deprive him of his life.

But when the Queen was solicited for his pardon, and informed of the severe treatment which he had suffered from his judge, she answered that however unjustifiable might be the manner of his trial, or whatever extenuation the action for which he was condemned might admit, she could not think that man a proper object of the King's mercy who had been capable of entering his mother's house in the night with an intent to murder her.

By whom this atrocious calumny had been transmitted to the Queen; whether she that invented had the front to relate it; whether she found any one weak enough to credit it, or corrupt enough to concur with her in her hateful design, I know not: but methods had been taken to persuade the Queen so strongly of the truth of it that she for a long time refused to hear any of those who petitioned for his life.

Thus had Savage perished by the evidence of a bawd, a strumpet, and his mother, had not justice and compassion procured him an advocate of rank too great to be rejected unheard, and of virtue too eminent to be heard without being believed. His merit and his calamities happened to reach the ear of the Countess of Hertford, who engaged in his support with all the tenderness that is excited by pity, and all the zeal which is kindled by generosity; and demanding an audience of the Queen, laid before her the whole series of his mother's cruelty, exposed the improbability of an accusation by which he was charged with an intent to commit a murder that could produce no advantage, and soon convinced her how little his former conduct could deserve to be mentioned as a reason for extraordinary severity.

The interposition of this lady was so successful that he was soon after admitted to bail, and on the 9th of March 1728, pleaded the King's pardon.

It is natural to inquire upon what motives his mother could persecute him in a manner so outrageous and implacable; for what reason she could employ all the arts of malice, and all the snares of calumny, to take away the life of her own son, of a son who never injured her, who was never supported by her expense, nor obstructed any prospect of pleasure or advantage; why she should endeavour to destroy him by a lie; a lie which could not gain credit, but must vanish of itself at the first moment of examination, and of which only this can be said to make it probable, that it may be observed from her conduct that the most execrable crimes are sometimes committed without apparent temptation.

This mother is still alive, and may perhaps even yet, though her malice was so often defeated, enjoy the pleasure of reflecting that the life which she often endeavoured to destroy was at least shortened by her maternal offices; that though she could not transport her son to the plantations, bury him in the shop of a mechanic, or hasten the hand of the public executioner, she has yet had the satisfaction of embittering all his hours, and forcing him into exigencies that hurried on his death.

It is by no means necessary to aggravate the enormity of this woman's conduct by placing it in opposition to that of the Countess of Hertford; no one can fail to observe how much more amiable it is to relieve than to oppress, and to rescue innocence from destruction than to destroy without an injury.

[Savage bore his imprisonment and trial with great fortitude. He compassionately forgave the prostitute who had testified against him.]

He was now indeed at liberty, but was, as before, without any other support than accidental favours and uncertain patronage afforded him; sources by which he was sometimes very liberally supplied, and which at other times were suddenly stopped; so that he spent his life between want and plenty, or what was yet worse, between beggary and extravagance; for as whatever he received was the gift of chance, which might as well favour him at one time as another, he was tempted to squander what he had, because he always hoped to be immediately supplied.

Another cause of his profusion was the absurd kindness of his friends, who at once rewarded and enjoyed his abilities by treating him at taverns and habituating him to pleasures which he could not afford to enjoy, and which he was not able to deny himself, though he purchased the luxury of a single night by the anguish of cold and hunger for a week.

The experience of these inconveniences determined him to endeavour after some settled income, which, having long found submission and entreaties fruitless, he attempted to extort from his mother by rougher methods. He had now, as he acknowledged, lost that tenderness for her which the whole series of her cruelty had not been able wholly to repress, till he found, by the efforts which she made for his destruction, that she was not content with refusing to assist him, and being neutral in his struggles with poverty, but was as ready to snatch every opportunity of adding to his misfortunes, and that she was to be considered as an enemy implacably malicious, whom nothing but his blood could satisfy. He therefore threatened to harass her with lampoons, and to publish a copious narrative of her conduct, unless she consented to purchase an exemption from infamy by allowing him a pension.

This expedient proved successful. Whether shame still survived though virtue was extinct, or whether her relations had more delicacy than herself, and imagined that some of the darts which satire might point at her would glance upon them, Lord Tyrconnel, whatever were his motives, upon his promise to lay aside his design of exposing the cruelty of his mother, received him into his family, treated him as his equal, and engaged to allow him a pension of two hundred pounds a year.

This was the golden part of Mr Savage's life; and for some time he had no reason to complain of fortune; his appearance was splendid, his expenses large, and his acquaintance extensive. He was courted by all who endeavoured to be thought men of genius, and caressed by all who valued themselves upon a refined taste. To admire Mr Savage was a proof of discernment, and to be acquainted with him was a title to poetical reputation. His presence was sufficient to make any place of public entertainment popular; and his approbation and example constituted the fashion. So powerful is genius when it is invested with the glitter of affluence; men willingly pay to fortune that regard which they owe to merit, and are pleased when they have an opportunity at once of gratifying their vanity and practising their duty.

This interval of prosperity furnished him with opportunities of enlarging his knowledge of human nature by contemplating life from its highest gradations to its lowest, and had he afterwards applied to dramatic poetry, he would perhaps not have had many superiors; for as he never suffered any scene to pass before his eyes without notice, he had treasured in his mind all the different combinations of passions, and the innumerable mixtures of vice and virtue which distinguish one character from another; and, as his conception was strong, his expressions were clear, he easily received impressions from objects, and very forcibly transmitted them to others.

[Savage demonstrates these powers in his *An Author To Be Let* (a satire on hack writers), 'a panegyric on Sir Robert Walpole' (his patron Tyrconnel was a political follower of Walpole's), and a 'moral poem', *The Wanderer*.]

This poem was addressed to the Lord Tyrconnel, not only in the first lines, but in a formal dedication filled with the highest strains of panegyric, and the warmest professions of gratitude, but by no means remarkable for delicacy of connection or elegance of style.

These praises in a short time he found himself inclined to retract, being discarded by the man on whom he had bestowed them, and whom he then immediately discovered not to have deserved them. Of this quarrel, which every day made more bitter, Lord Tyrconnel and Mr Savage assigned very different reasons, which might perhaps all in reality concur, though they were not all convenient to be alleged by either party. Lord Tyrconnel affirmed that it was the constant practice of Mr Savage to enter a tavern with any company that proposed it, drink the most expensive wines with great profusion, and when the reckoning was demanded to be without money. If, as it often happened, his companions were willing to defray his part, the affair ended without any ill consequences; but if they were refractory, and expected that the wine should be paid for by him that drank it, his method of composition was to take them with him to his own apartment, assume the government of the house, and order the butler in an imperious manner to set the best wine in the cellar before his company, who often drank till they forgot the respect due to the house in which they were entertained, indulged themselves in the utmost extravagance of merriment, practised the most licentious frolics, and committed all the outrages of drunkenness.

Nor was this the only charge which Lord Tyrconnel brought against him. Having given him a collection of valuable books, stamped with his own arms, he had the mortification to see them in a short time exposed to sale upon the stalls, it being usual with Mr Savage, when he wanted a small sum, to take his books to the pawnbroker.

Whoever was acquainted with Mr Savage easily credited both these accusations: for, having been obliged from his first entrance into the world to subsist upon expedients, affluence was not able to exalt him above them; and so much was he delighted with wine and conversation, and so long had he been accustomed to live by chance, that he would at any time go to the tavern, without scruple, and trust for the reckoning to the liberality of his company, and frequently of company to whom he was very little known. This conduct indeed very seldom drew upon him those inconveniences that might be feared by any other person, for his conversation was so entertaining, and his address so pleasing, that few thought the pleasure which they received from him dearly purchased by paying for his wine. It was his peculiar happiness that he scarcely ever found a stranger whom he did not leave a friend; but it must likewise be added that he had not often a friend long without obliging him to become a stranger.

Mr Savage, on the other hand, declared that Lord Tyrconnel quarrelled with him, because he would not subtract from his own luxury and extravagance what he had promised to allow him, and that his resentment was only a plea for the violation of his promise. He asserted that he had done nothing that ought to exclude him from that subsistence which he thought not so much a favour as a debt, since it was offered him upon conditions which he had never broken; and that his only fault was that he could not be supported with nothing.

He acknowledged that Lord Tyrconnel often exhorted him to regulate his method of life, and not to spend all his nights in taverns, and that he appeared very desirous that he would pass those hours with him which he so freely bestowed upon others. This demand Mr Savage considered as a censure of his conduct, which he could never patiently bear, and which even in the latter and cooler part of his life was so offensive to him that he declared it as his resolution 'to spurn that friend who should presume to dictate to him'; and it is not likely that in his earlier years he received admonitions with more calmness.

He was likewise inclined to resent such expectations as tending to infringe his liberty, of which he was very jealous when it was necessary to the gratification of his passions, and declared that the request was still more unreasonable, as the company to which he was to have been confined was insupportably disagreeable. This assertion affords another instance of that inconsistency of his writings with his conversation which was so often to be observed. He forgot how lavishly he had, in his Dedication to *The Wanderer*, extolled the delicacy and penetration, the humanity and generosity, the candour and politeness of the man whom, when he no longer loved him, he declared to be a wretch without understanding, without good-nature, and without justice; of whose name he thought himself obliged to leave no trace in any future edition of his writings; and accordingly blotted it out of that copy of *The Wanderer* which was in his hands.

[Tyrconnel's patronage enabled Savage to meet and observe persons 'conspicuous at that time for their power or their influence'. He formed a poor opinion of them. After the break with Tyrconnel, Savage published his autobiographical poem *The Bastard*, in which his 'mother's' cruelties are exposed.]

Thus Savage had the satisfaction of finding that though he could not reform his mother, he could punish her, and that he did not always suffer alone.

The pleasure which he received from this increase of his poetical reputation was sufficient for some time to overbalance the miseries of want, which this performance did not much alleviate, for it was sold for a very trivial sum to a bookseller, who, though the success was so uncommon that five impressions were sold, of which many were undoubtedly very numerous, had not generosity sufficient to admit the unhappy writer to any part of the profit.

The sale of this poem was always mentioned by Mr Savage with the utmost elevation of heart, and referred to by him as an incontestable proof of a general acknowledgement of his abilities. It was indeed the only production of which he could justly boast a general reception.

But though he did not lose the opportunity which success gave him of setting a high rate on his abilities, but paid due deference to the suffrages of mankind when they were given in his favour, he did not suffer his esteem of himself to depend upon others, nor found any thing sacred in the voice of the people when they were inclined to censure him; he then readily showed the folly of expecting that the public should judge right, observed how slowly poetical merit had often forced its way into the world; he contented himself with the applause of men of judgement, and was somewhat disposed to exclude all those from the character of men of judgement who did not applaud him.

But he was at other times more favourable to mankind than to think them blind to the beauties of his works, and imputed the slowness of their sale to other causes; either they were published at a time when the town was empty, or when the attention of the public was engrossed by some struggle in the Parliament, or some other object of general concern; or they were by the neglect of the publisher not diligently dispersed, or by his avarice not advertised with sufficient frequency. Address, or industry, or liberality, was always wanting; and the blame was laid rather on any person than the author.

By arts like these, arts which every man practises in some degree, and to which too much of the little tranquillity of life is to be ascribed, Savage was always able to live at peace with himself. Had he indeed only made use of these expedients to alleviate the loss or want of fortune or reputation, or any other advantage which it is not in man's power to bestow upon himself, they might have been justly mentioned as instances of a philosophical mind, and very properly proposed to the imitation of multitudes who, for want of diverting their imaginations with the same dexterity, languish under afflictions which might be easily removed.

It were doubtless to be wished that truth and reason were universally prevalent; that every thing were esteemed according to its real value; and that men would secure themselves from being disappointed in their endeavours after happiness by placing it only in virtue, which is always to be obtained; but if adventitious and foreign pleasures must be pursued, it would be perhaps of some benefit, since that pursuit must frequently be fruitless, if the practice of Savage could be taught, that folly might be an antidote to folly, and one fallacy be obviated by another.

But the danger of this pleasing intoxication must not be concealed; nor indeed can any one, after having observed the life of Savage, need to be cautioned against it. By imputing none of his miseries to himself, he continued to act upon the same principles, and to follow the same path; was never made wiser by his sufferings, nor preserved by one misfortune from falling into another. He proceeded throughout his life to tread the same steps on the same circle; always applauding his past conduct, or at least forgetting it, to amuse himself with phantoms of happiness which were dancing before him; and willingly turned his eyes from the light of reason, when it would have discovered the illusion and shown him, what he never wished to see, his real state.

He is even accused, after having lulled his imagination with those ideal opiates, of having tried the same experiment upon his conscience; and, having accustomed himself to impute all deviations from the right to foreign causes, it is certain that he was upon every occasion too easily reconciled to himself, and that he appeared very little to regret those practices which had impaired his reputation. The reigning error of his life was that he mistook the love for the practice of virtue, and was indeed not so much a good man as the friend of goodness.

This at least must be allowed him, that he always preserved a strong sense of the dignity, the beauty, and the necessity of virtue, and that he never contributed deliberately to spread corruption amongst mankind; his actions, which were generally precipitate, were often blameable, but his writings, being the productions of study, uniformly tended to the exaltation of the mind, and the propagation of morality and piety.

These writings may improve mankind when his failings shall be forgotten, and therefore he must be considered upon the whole as a benefactor to the world; nor can his personal example do any hurt, since whoever hears of his faults will hear of the miseries which they brought upon him, and which would deserve less pity had not his condition been such as made his faults pardonable. He may be considered as a child *exposed* to all the temptations of indigence at an age when resolution was not yet strengthened by conviction, nor virtue confirmed by habit; a circumstance which in his *Bastard* he laments in a very affecting manner:

> ——No Mother's care
> Shielded my infant innocence with prayer:
> No Father's guardian hand my youth maintained,
> Called forth my virtues, or from vice restrained.

[Savage applies for the vacant Poet Laureateship, but it is given to Colley Cibber. Savage then assumes the title of 'Volunteer Laureat' to Queen Caroline, who bestows on him an annual allowance of £50.]

He was still in his usual exigencies, having no certain support but the pension allowed him by the Queen, which, though it might have kept an exact economist from want, was very far from being sufficient for Mr Savage, who had never been accustomed to dismiss any of his appetites without the gratification which they solicited, and whom nothing but want of money withheld from partaking of every pleasure that fell within his view.

His conduct with regard to his pension was very particular. No sooner had he changed the bill than he vanished from the sight of all his acquaintances, and lay for some time out of the reach of all the inquiries that friendship or curiosity could make after him; at length he appeared again penniless as before, but never informed even those whom he seemed to regard most where he had been, nor was his retreat ever discovered.

This was his constant practice during the whole time that he received the pension from the Queen: he regularly disappeared and returned. He indeed affirmed that he retired to study, and that the money supported him in solitude for many months; but his friends declared that the short time in which it was spent sufficiently confuted his own account of his conduct.

[He publishes a poem, *On Public Spirit, in Regard to Public Works*, of which only seventy-two copies are sold.]

It must be however allowed, in justification of the public, that this performance is not the most excellent of Mr Savage's works, and that though it cannot be denied to contain many striking sentiments, majestic lines, and just observations, it is in general not sufficiently polished in the language, or enlivened in the imagery, or digested in the plan.

Thus his poem contributed nothing to the alleviation of his poverty, which was such as very few could have supported with equal patience, but to which it must likewise be confessed that few would have been exposed who received punctually fifty pounds a year; a salary which though by no means equal to the demands of vanity and luxury is yet found sufficient to support families above want, and was undoubtedly more than the necessities of life require.

But no sooner had he received his pension than he withdrew to his darling privacy, from which he returned in a short time to his former distress, and for some part of the year generally lived by chance, eating only when he was invited to the tables of his acquaintances, from which the meanness of his dress often excluded him, when the politeness and variety of his conversation would have been thought a sufficient recompense for his entertainment.

He lodged as much by accident as he dined, and passed the night sometimes in mean houses, which are set open at night to any casual wanderers; sometimes in cellars, among the riot and filth of the meanest and most profligate of the rabble; and sometimes, when he had no money to support even the expenses of these receptacles, walked about the streets till he was weary, and lay down in the summer upon a bulk, or in the winter with his associates in poverty, among the ashes of a glass-house.

In this manner were passed those days and those nights which nature had enabled him to have employed in elevated speculations, useful studies, or pleasing conversation. On a bulk, in a cellar, or in a glass-house among thieves and beggars, was to be found the author of *The Wanderer*, the man of exalted sentiments, extensive views, and curious observations, the man whose remarks on life might have assisted the statesman, whose ideas of virtue might have enlightened the moralist, whose eloquence might have influenced senates, and whose delicacy might have polished courts.

It cannot be imagined but that such necessities might sometimes force him upon disreputable practices, and it is probable that these lines in *The Wanderer* were occasioned by his reflections on his own conduct:

> Though misery leads to fortitude and truth,
> Unequal to the load this languid youth
> (O! let none censure if untried by grief,
> Or amidst woes untempted by relief),
> He stooped, reluctant, to mean acts of shame,
> Which then, ev'n then, he scorned, and blushed to name.

Whoever was acquainted with him was certain to be solicited for small sums, which the frequency of the request made in time considerable, and he was therefore quickly shunned by those who were become familiar enough to be trusted with his necessities; but his rambling manner of life, and constant appearance at houses of public resort, always procured him a new succession of friends, whose kindness had not been exhausted by repeated requests, so that he was seldom absolutely without resources, but had in his utmost exigences this comfort, that he always imagined himself sure of speedy relief.

It was observed that he always asked favours of this kind without the least submission or apparent consciousness of dependence, and that he did not seem to look upon a compliance with his request as an obligation that deserved any extraordinary acknowledgements, but a refusal was resented by him as an affront, or complained of as an injury; nor did he readily reconcile himself to those who either denied to lend, or gave him afterwards any intimation that they expected to be repaid.

He was sometimes so far compassionated by those who knew both his merit and his distresses that they received him into their families, but they soon discovered him to be a very incommodious inmate; for being always accustomed to an irregular manner of life, he could not confine himself to any stated hours, or pay any regard to the rules of a family, but would prolong his conversation till midnight, without considering that business might require his friend's application in the morning; nor, when he had persuaded himself to retire to bed, was he, without equal difficulty, called up to dinner; it was therefore impossible to pay him any distinction without the entire subversion of all economy, a kind of establishment which, wherever he went, he always appeared ambitious to overthrow.

It must therefore be acknowledged, in justification of mankind, that it was not always by the negligence or coldness of his friends that Savage was distressed, but because it was in reality very difficult to preserve him long in a state of ease. To supply him with money was a hopeless attempt, for no sooner did he see himself master of a sum sufficient to set him free from care for a day than he became profuse and luxurious. When once he had entered a tavern, or engaged in a scheme of pleasure he never retired till want of money obliged him to some new expedient. If he was entertained in a family, nothing was any longer to be regarded there but amusements and jollity; wherever Savage entered he immediately expected that order and business should fly before him, that all should thenceforward be left to hazard, and that no dull principle of domestic management should be opposed to his inclination, or intrude upon his gaiety.

His distresses, however afflictive, never dejected him; in his lowest state he wanted not spirit to assert the natural dignity of wit, and was always ready to repress that insolence which superiority of fortune incited, and to trample the reputation which rose upon any other basis than that of merit. He never admitted any gross familiarities, or submitted to be treated otherwise than as an equal. Once when he was without lodging, meat, or clothes, one of his friends, a man not indeed remarkable for moderation in his prosperity, left a message that he desired to see him about nine in the morning. Savage knew that his intention was to assist him, but was very much disgusted that he should presume to prescribe the hour of his attendance, and, I believe, refused to visit him, and rejected his kindness.

[Savage continues to alienate his would-be helpers, and 'spent his time in mean expedients and tormenting suspense', in fear of his creditors. Queen Caroline dies, and his allowance from her ceases.]

So peculiar were the misfortunes of this man; deprived of an estate and title by a particular law, exposed and abandoned by a mother, defrauded by a mother of a fortune which his father had allotted him, he entered the world without a friend; and though his abilities forced themselves into esteem and reputation, he was never able to obtain any real advantage, and whatever prospects arose were always intercepted as he began to approach them. The King's intentions in his favour were frustrated; his dedication to the Prince, whose generosity on every other occasion was eminent, procured him no reward; Sir Robert Walpole, who valued himself upon keeping his promise to others, broke it to him without regret; and the bounty of the Queen was after her death withdrawn from him, and from him only.

Such were his misfortunes, which yet he bore not only with decency, but with cheerfulness, nor was his gaiety clouded even by his last disappointment, though he was in a short time reduced to the lowest degree of distress, and often wanted both lodging and food. At this time he gave another instance of the insurmountable obstinacy of his spirit; his clothes were worn out, and he received notice that at a coffee-house some clothes and linen were left for him; the person who sent them did not, I believe, inform him to whom he was to be obliged, that he might spare the perplexity of acknowledging the benefit; but though the offer was so far generous it was made with some neglect of ceremonies, which Mr Savage so much resented that he refused the present, and declined to enter the house till the clothes that had been designed for him were taken away.

His distress was now publicly known, and his friends, therefore, thought it proper to concert some measures for his relief; and one of them wrote a letter to him, in which he expressed his concern 'for the miserable withdrawing of his pension'; and gave him hopes that in a short time he should find himself supplied with a competence, 'without any dependence on those little creatures which we are pleased to call the Great'.

The scheme proposed for this happy and independent subsistence was that he should retire into Wales, and receive an allowance of fifty pounds a year, to be raised by a subscription, on which he was to live privately in a cheap place, without aspiring any more to affluence, or having any farther care of reputation. ·

This offer Mr Savage gladly accepted, though with intentions very different from those of his friends; for they proposed that he should continue an exile from London for ever, and spend all the remaining part of his life at Swansea; but he designed only to take the opportunity which their scheme offered him of retreating for a short time, that he might prepare his play for the stage, and his other works for the press, and then to return to London to exhibit his tragedy, and live upon the profits of his own labour.

With regard to his works, he proposed very great improvements, which would have required much time, or great application; and when he had finished them, he designed to do justice to his subscribers by publishing them according to his proposals.

As he was ready to entertain himself with future pleasures, he had planned out a scheme of life for the country, of which he had no knowledge but from pastorals and songs. He imagined that he should be transported to scenes of flowery felicity, like those which one poet has reflected to another, and had projected a perpetual round of innocent pleasures, of which he suspected no interruption from pride, or ignorance, or brutality.

With these expectations he was so enchanted that when he was once gently reproached by a friend for submitting to live upon a subscription, and advised rather by a resolute exertion of his abilities to support himself, he could not bear to debar himself from the happiness which was to be found in the calm of a cottage, or lose the opportunity of listening without intermission to the melody of the nightingale, which he believed was to be heard from every bramble, and which he did not fail to mention as a very important part of the happiness of country life.

While this scheme was ripening, his friends directed him to take a lodging in the liberties of the Fleet, that he might be secure from his creditors, and sent him every Monday a guinea, which he commonly spent before the next morning, and trusted, after his usual manner, the remaining part of the week to the bounty of fortune.

He now began very sensibly to feel the miseries of dependence. Those by whom he was to be supported began to prescribe to him with an air of authority, which he knew not how decently to resent nor patiently to bear; and he soon discovered from the conduct of most of his subscribers that he was yet in the hands of 'little creatures'.

Of the insolence that he was obliged to suffer he gave many instances, of which none appeared to raise his indignation to a greater height than the method which was taken of furnishing him with clothes. Instead of consulting him, and allowing him to send to a tailor his orders for what they thought proper to allow him, they proposed to send for a tailor to take his measure, and then to consult how they should equip him.

This treatment was not very delicate, nor was it such as Savage's humanity would have suggested to him on a like occasion; but it had scarcely deserved mention had it not, by affecting him in an uncommon degree, shown the peculiarity of his character. Upon hearing the design that was formed he came to the lodging of a friend with the most violent agonies of rage; and being asked what it could be that gave him such disturbance, he replied with the utmost vehemence of indignation, 'That they had sent for a tailor to measure him.'

[Pope (the 'gentleman' mentioned immediately below) drafts a letter asking a friend to intercede with Tyrconnel for a reconciliation with Savage. Savage indignantly refuses to send it.]

After many alterations and delays, a subscription was at length raised which did not amount to fifty pounds a year, though twenty were paid by one gentleman; such was the generosity of mankind that what had been done by a player without solicitation could not now be effected by application and interest; and Savage had a great number to court and to obey for a pension less than that which Mrs Oldfield paid him without exacting any servilities.

Mr Savage however was satisfied and willing to retire, and was convinced that the allowance, though scanty, would be more than sufficient for him, being now determined to commence a rigid economist, and to live according to the exactest rules of frugality; for nothing was in his opinion more contemptible than a man who, when he knew his income, exceeded it, and yet he confessed that instances of such folly were too common, and lamented that some men were not to be trusted with their own money.

Full of these salutary resolutions, he left London in July 1739, having taken leave with great tenderness of his friends, and parted from the author of this narrative with tears in his eyes. He was furnished with fifteen guineas, and informed that they would be sufficient not only for the expense of his journey, but for his support in Wales for some time; and that there remained but little more of the first collection. He promised a strict adherence to his maxims of parsimony, and went away in the stage coach; nor did his friends expect to hear from him till he informed them of his arrival at Swansea.

But when they least expected, arrived a letter dated the fourteenth day after his departure, in which he sent them word that he was yet upon the road, and without money; and that he therefore could not proceed without a remittance. They then sent him the money that was in their hands, with which he was enabled to reach Bristol, from whence he was to go to Swansea by water.

At Bristol he found an embargo laid upon the shipping, so that he could not immediately obtain a passage; and being therefore obliged to stay there some time, he, with his usual felicity, ingratiated himself with many of the principal inhabitants, was invited to their houses, distinguished at their public feasts, and treated with a regard that gratified his vanity, and therefore easily engaged his affection.

He began very early after his retirement to complain of the conduct of his friends in London, and irritated many of them so much by his letters that they withdrew, however honourably, their contributions; and it is believed that little more was paid him than the twenty pounds a year which were allowed him by the gentleman who proposed the subscription.

After some stay at Bristol, he retired to Swansea, the place *originally* proposed for his residence, where he lived about a year, very much dissatisfied with the diminution of his salary; but contracted, as in other places, acquaintance with those who were most distinguished in that country, among whom he has celebrated Mr Powel and Mrs Jones, by some verses which he inserted in the *Gentleman's Magazine*.

Here he completed his tragedy, of which two acts were wanting when he left London, and was desirous of coming to town to bring it upon the stage. This design was very warmly opposed, and he was advised by his chief benefactor to put it into the hands of Mr Thomson and Mr Mallet, that it might be fitted for the stage, and to allow his friends to receive the profits, out of which an annual pension should be paid him.

This proposal he rejected with the utmost contempt. He was by no means convinced that the judgement of those to whom he was required to submit was superior to his own. He was now determined, as he expressed it, to be 'no longer kept in leading-strings', and had no elevated idea of 'his bounty who proposed to pension him out of the profits of his own labours'.

He attempted in Wales to promote a subscription for his works, and had once hopes of success; but in a short time afterwards, formed a resolution of leaving that part of the country, to which he thought it not reasonable to be confined for the gratification of those who, having promised him a liberal income, had no sooner banished him to a remote corner than they reduced his allowance to a salary scarcely equal to the necessities of life.

His resentment of this treatment, which, in his own opinion at least, he had not deserved, was such that he broke off all correspondence with most of his contributors, and appeared to consider them as persecutors and oppressors, and in the latter part of his life declared that their conduct toward him, since his departure from London, 'had been perfidiousness improving on perfidiousness, and inhumanity on inhumanity'.

It is not to be supposed that the necessities of Mr Savage did not sometimes incite him to satirical exaggerations of the behaviour of those by whom he thought himself reduced to them. But it must be granted that the diminution of his allowance was a great hardship, and that those who withdrew their subscription from a man who, upon the faith of their promise, had gone into a kind of banishment, and abandoned all those by whom he had been before relieved in his distresses, will find it no easy task to vindicate their conduct.

It may be alleged, and perhaps justly, that he was petulant and contemptuous, that he more frequently reproached his subscribers for not giving him more than thanked them for what he received; but it is to be remembered that his conduct, and this is the worst charge that can be drawn up against him, did them no real injury; and that it, therefore, ought rather to have been pitied than resented; at least, the resentment it might provoke ought to have been generous and manly; epithets which his conduct will hardly deserve that starves the man whom he has persuaded to put himself into his power.

It might have been reasonably demanded by Savage that they should, before they had taken away what they promised, have replaced him in his former state, that they should have taken no advantages from the situation to which the appearance of their kindness had reduced him, and that he should have been recalled to London before he was abandoned. He might justly represent that he ought to have been considered as a lion in the toils, and demand to be released before the dogs should be loosed upon him.

He endeavoured, indeed, to release himself, and, with an intent to return to London, went to Bristol, where a repetition of the kindness which he had formerly found invited him to stay. He was not only caressed and treated, but had a collection made for him of about thirty pounds, with which it had been happy if he had immediately departed for London; but his negligence did not suffer him to consider that such proofs of kindness were not often to be expected, and that this ardour of benevolence was in a great degree the effect of novelty, and might, probably, be every day less; and, therefore, he took no care to improve the happy time, but was encouraged by one favour to hope for another, till at length generosity was exhausted, and officiousness wearied.

Another part of his misconduct was the practice of prolonging his visits to unseasonable hours, and disconcerting all the families into which he was admitted. This was an error in a place of commerce which all the charms of his conversation could not compensate; for what trader would purchase such airy satisfaction by the loss of solid gain, which must be the consequence of midnight merriment, as those hours which were gained at night were generally lost in the morning?

Thus Mr Savage, after the curiosity of the inhabitants was gratified, found the number of his friends daily decreasing, perhaps without suspecting for what reason their conduct was altered, for he still continued to harass with his nocturnal intrusions those that yet countenanced him, and admitted him to their houses.

But he did not spend all the time of his residence at Bristol in visits or at taverns, for he sometimes returned to his studies, and began several considerable designs. When he felt an inclination to write, he always retired from the knowledge of his friends, and lay hid in an obscure part of the suburbs till he found himself again desirous of company, to which it is likely that intervals of absence made him more welcome.

He was always full of his design of returning to London to bring his tragedy upon the stage; but having neglected to depart with the money that was raised for him, he could not afterwards procure a sum sufficient to defray the expenses of his journey; nor perhaps would a fresh supply have had any other effect than, by putting immediate pleasures in his power, to have driven the thoughts of his journey out of his mind.

While he was thus spending the day in contriving a scheme for the morrow, distress stole upon him by imperceptible degrees. His conduct had already wearied some of those who were at first enamoured of his conversation; but he might, perhaps, still have devolved to others, whom he might have entertained with equal success, had not the decay of his clothes made it no longer consistent with their vanity to admit him to their tables, or to associate with him in public places. He now began to find every man from home at whose house he called; and was, therefore, no longer able to procure the necessaries of life, but wandered about the town slighted and neglected, in quest of a dinner, which he did not always obtain.

To complete his misery, he was pursued by the officers for small debts which he had contracted; and was, therefore, obliged to withdraw from the small number of friends from whom he had still reason to hope for favours. His custom was to lie in bed the greatest part of the day, and to go out in the dark with the utmost privacy, and after having paid his visit, return again before morning to his lodging, which was in the garret of an obscure inn.

Being thus excluded on one hand, and confined on the other, he suffered the utmost extremities of poverty, and often fasted so long that he was seized with faintness, and had lost his appetite, not being able to bear the smell of meat till the action of his stomach was restored by a cordial.

In this distress he received a remittance of five pounds from London, with which he provided himself a decent coat, and determined to go to London, but unhappily spent his money at a favourite tavern. Thus was he again confined to Bristol, where he was every day hunted by bailiffs. In this exigence he once more found a friend, who sheltered him in his house, though at the usual inconveniences with which his company was attended; for he could neither be persuaded to go to bed in the night, nor to rise in the day.

It is observable that in these various scenes of misery, he was always disengaged and cheerful; he at some times pursued his studies, and at others continued or enlarged his epistolary correspondence, nor was he ever so far dejected as to endeavour to procure an increase of his allowance by any other methods than accusations and reproaches.

He had now no longer any hopes of assistance from his friends at Bristol, who as merchants, and by consequence sufficiently studious of profit, cannot be supposed to have looked with much compassion upon negligence and extravagance, or to think any excellence equivalent to a fault of such consequence as neglect of economy. It is natural to imagine that many of those who would have relieved his real wants were discouraged from the exertion of their benevolence by observation of the use which was made of their favours, and conviction that relief would only be momentary, and that the same necessity would quickly return.

At last he quitted the house of his friend, and returned to his lodging at the inn, still intending to set out in a few days for London, but on the 10th of January 1742–3, having been at supper with two of his friends, he was at his return to his lodgings arrested for a debt of about eight pounds, which he owed at a coffee-house, and conducted to the house of a sheriff's officer.

[Two self-pitying letters of Savage's are quoted.]

When his friends, who had hitherto caressed and applauded, found that to give bail and pay the debt was the same, they all refused to preserve him from a prison at the expense of eight pounds; and therefore after having been for some time at the officer's house, 'at an immense expense', as he observes in his letter, he was at length removed to Newgate.

This expense he was enabled to support by the generosity of Mr Nash at Bath, who, upon receiving from him an account of his condition, immediately sent him five guineas, and promised to promote his subscription at Bath with all his interest.

By his removal to Newgate, he obtained at least a freedom from suspense, and rest from the disturbing vicissitudes of hope and disappointment; he now found that his friends were only companions, who were willing to share his gaiety, but not to partake of his misfortunes; and therefore he no longer expected any assistance from them.

It must however be observed of one gentleman that he offered to release him by paying the debt; but that Mr Savage would not consent, I suppose, because he thought he had been before too burdensome to him.

He was offered by some of his friends that a collection should be made for his enlargement; but he 'treated the proposal', and declared 'that he should again treat it, with disdain. As to writing any mendicant letters, he had too high a spirit, and determined only to write to some ministers of state, to try to regain his pension.'

He continued to complain of those that had sent him into the country, and objected to them that he had 'lost the profits of his play, which had been finished three years', and in another letter declares his resolution to publish a pamphlet, that the world might know how 'he had been used'.

This pamphlet was never written, for he in a very short time recovered his usual tranquillity, and cheerfully applied himself to more inoffensive studies. He indeed steadily declared that he was promised a yearly allowance of fifty pounds, and never received half the sum, but he seemed to resign himself to that as well as to other misfortunes, and lose the remembrance of it in his amusements and employments.

The cheerfulness with which he bore his confinement appears from the following letter, which he wrote, January 30th, to one of his friends in London:

I now write to you from my confinement in Newgate, where I have been ever since Monday last was sev'n-night; and where I enjoy myself with much more tranquillity than I have known for upwards of a twelvemonth past; having a room entirely to myself, and pursuing the amusement of my poetical studies uninterrupted and agreeable to my mind. I thank the Almighty, I am now all collected in myself; and though my person is in confinement, my mind can expatiate on ample and useful subjects with all the freedom imaginable. I am now more conversant with the Nine than ever; and if, instead of a Newgate bird, I may be allowed to be a bird of the Muses, I assure you, Sir, I sing very freely in my cage; sometimes indeed in the plaintive notes of the nightingale, but, at others, in the cheerful strains of the lark.

In another letter he observes that he ranges from one subject to another without confining himself to any particular task, and that he was employed one week upon one attempt, and the next upon another.

Surely the fortitude of this man deserves, at least, to be mentioned with applause, and whatever faults may be imputed to him, the virtue of 'suffering well' cannot be denied him. The two powers which, in the opinion of Epictetus, constituted a wise man are those of 'bearing' and 'forbearing', which cannot indeed be affirmed to have been equally possessed by Savage, but it was too manifest that the want of one obliged him very *frequently* to practise the other.

He was treated by Mr Dagg, the keeper of the prison, with great humanity; was supported by him at his own table without any certainty of recompense, had a room to himself, to which he could at any time retire from all disturbance, was allowed to stand at the door of the prison, and sometimes taken out into the fields; so that he suffered fewer hardships in prison that he had been accustomed to undergo in the greatest part of his life.

The keeper did not confine his benevolence to a gentle execution of his office, but made some overtures to the creditor for his release, though without effect; and continued, during the whole time of his imprisonment, to treat him with the utmost tenderness and civility.

Virtue is undoubtedly most laudable in that state which makes it most difficult; and therefore the humanity of a gaoler certainly deserves this public attestation; and the man whose heart has not been hardened by such an employment may be justly proposed as a pattern of benevolence. If an inscription was once engraved 'to the honest toll-gatherer', less honours ought not to be paid 'to the tender gaoler'.

Mr Savage very frequently received visits, and sometimes presents, from his acquaintances, but they did not amount to a subsistence, for the greater part of which he was indebted to the generosity of this keeper; but these favours, however they might endear to him the particular persons from whom he received them, were very far from impressing upon his mind any advantageous ideas of the people of Bristol, and therefore he thought he could not more properly employ himself in prison than in writing the following poem.

[The incomplete *London and Bristol Delineated*, which bitterly satirizes the citizens of Bristol. Savage vehemently rejects the advice of a friend not to publish it.]

Such was his imprudence, and such his obstinate adherence to his own resolutions, however absurd. A prisoner! supported by charity! and, whatever insults he might have received during the latter part of his stay at Bristol, once caressed, esteemed, and presented with a liberal collection, he could forget on a sudden his danger and his obligations, to gratify the petulance of his wit, or the eagerness of his resentment, and publish a satire by which he might reasonably expect that he should alienate those who then supported him, and provoke those whom he could neither resist nor escape.

This resolution, from the execution of which it is probable that only his death could have hindered him, is sufficient to show how much he disregarded all considerations that opposed his present passions, and how readily he hazarded all future advantages for any immediate gratifications. Whatever was his predominant inclination, neither hope nor fear hindered him from complying with it, nor had opposition any other effect than to heighten his ardour and irritate his vehemence.

This performance was however laid aside while he was employed in soliciting assistance from several great persons, and one interruption succeeding another hindered him from supplying the chasm, and perhaps from retouching the other parts, which he can hardly be imagined to have finished, in his own opinion; for it is very unequal, and some of the lines are rather inserted to rhyme to others than to support or improve the sense; but the first and last parts are worked up with great spirit and elegance.

His time was spent in the prison for the most part in study, or in receiving visits; but sometimes he descended to lower amusements, and diverted himself in the kitchen with the conversation of the criminals; for it was not pleasing to him to be much without company, and though he was very capable of a judicious choice, he was often contented with the first that offered; for this he was sometimes reproved by his friends who found him surrounded with felons; but the reproof was on that as on other occasions thrown away; he continued to gratify himself, and to set very little value on the opinion of others.

But here, as in every other scene of his life, he made use of such opportunities as occurred of benefiting those who were more miserable than himself, and was always ready to perform any offices of humanity to his fellow-prisoners.

He had now ceased from corresponding with any of his subscribers except one, who yet continued to remit him the twenty pounds a year which he had promised him, and by whom it was expected that he would have been in a very short time enlarged, because he had directed the keeper to inquire after the state of his debts.

However, he took care to enter his name according to the forms of the court, that the creditor might be obliged to make him some allowance, if he was continued a prisoner, and when on that occasion he appeared in the hall was treated with very unusual respect.

But the resentment of the city was afterwards raised by some accounts that had been spread of the satire, and he was informed that some of the merchants intended to pay the allowance which the law required, and to detain him a prisoner at their own expense. This he treated as an empty menace, and perhaps might have hastened the publication, only to show how much he was superior to their insults, had not all his schemes been suddenly destroyed.

When he had been six months in prison he received from one of his friends, in whose kindness he had the greatest confidence, and on whose assistance he chiefly depended, a letter that contained a charge of very atrocious ingratitude, drawn up in such terms as sudden resentment dictated. Henley, in one of his advertisements, had mentioned 'Pope's treatment of Savage'. This was supposed by Pope to be the consequence of a complaint made by Savage to Henley, and was therefore mentioned by him with much resentment. Mr Savage returned a very solemn protestation of his innocence, but however appeared much disturbed at the accusation. Some days afterwards he was seized with a pain in his back and side, which, as it was not violent, was not suspected to be dangerous; but growing daily more languid and dejected on the 25th of July he confined himself to his room, and a fever seized his spirits. The symptoms grew every day more formidable, but his condition did not enable him to procure any assistance. The last time that the keeper saw him was on July the 31st, 1743; when Savage, seeing him at his bed-side, said, with an uncommon earnestness, 'I have something to say to you, Sir'; but after a pause, moved his hand in a melancholy manner, and finding himself unable to recollect what he was going to communicate, said, ''Tis gone!' The keeper soon after left him, and the next morning he died. He was buried in the churchyard of St Peter, at the expense of the keeper.

Such were the life and death of Richard Savage, a man equally distinguished by his virtues and vices, and at once remarkable for his weaknesses and abilities.

He was of a middle stature, of a thin habit of body, a long visage, coarse features, and melancholy aspect; of a grave and manly deportment, a solemn dignity of mien, but which upon a nearer acquaintance softened into an engaging easiness of manners. His walk was slow, and his voice tremulous and mournful. He was easily excited to smiles, but very seldom provoked to laughter.

His mind was in an uncommon degree vigorous and active. His judgement was accurate, his apprehension quick, and his memory so tenacious that he was frequently observed to know what he had learned from others in a short time better than those by whom he was informed, and could frequently recollect incidents with all their combination of circumstances, which few would have regarded at the present time, but which the quickness of his apprehension impressed upon him. He had the peculiar felicity that his attention never deserted him; he was present to every object, and regardful of the most trifling occurrences. He had the art of escaping from his own reflections, and accommodating himself to every new scene.

To this quality is to be imputed the extent of his knowledge, compared with the small time which he spent in visible endeavours to acquire it. He mingled in cursory conversation with the same steadiness of attention as others apply to a lecture, and, amidst the appearance of thoughtless gaiety, lost no new idea that was started, nor any hint that could be improved. He had therefore made in coffee-houses the same proficiency as others in their closets; and it is remarkable that the writings of a man of little education and little reading have an air of learning scarcely to be found in any other performances, but which perhaps as often obscures as embellishes them.

His judgement was eminently exact both with regard to writings and to men. The knowledge of life was indeed his chief attainment, and it is not without some satisfaction that I can produce the suffrage of Savage in favour of human nature, of which he never appeared to entertain such odious ideas as some who perhaps had neither his judgement nor experience have published, either in ostentation of their sagacity, vindication of their crimes, or gratification of their malice.

His method of life particularly qualified him for conversation, of which he knew how to practise all the graces. He was never vehement or loud, but at once modest and easy, open and respectful, his language was vivacious and elegant, and equally happy upon grave or humorous subjects. He was generally censured for not knowing when to retire, but that was not the defect of his judgement, but of his fortune; when he left his company he was frequently to spend the remaining part of the night in the street, or at least was abandoned to gloomy reflections, which it is not strange that he delayed as long as he could, and sometimes forgot that he gave others pain to avoid it himself.

It cannot be said that he made use of his abilities for the direction of his own conduct; an irregular and dissipated manner of life had made him the slave of every passion that happened to be excited by the presence of its object, and that slavery to his passions reciprocally produced a life irregular and dissipated. He was not master of his own motions, nor could promise any thing for the next day.

With regard to his economy nothing can be added to the relation of his life: he appeared to think himself born to be supported by others, and dispensed from all necessity of providing for himself; he therefore never prosecuted any scheme of advantage, nor endeavoured even to secure the profits which his writings might have afforded him.

His temper was in consequence of the dominion of his passions uncertain and capricious; he was easily engaged, and easily disgusted; but he is accused of retaining his hatred more tenaciously than his benevolence.

He was compassionate both by nature and principle and always ready to perform offices of humanity, but when he was provoked, and very small offences were sufficient to provoke him, he would prosecute his revenge with the utmost acrimony till his passion had subsided.

His friendship was therefore of little value; for though he was zealous in the support or vindication of those whom he loved, yet it was always dangerous to trust him, because he considered himself as discharged by the first quarrel from all ties of honour or gratitude; and would betray those secrets which in the warmth of confidence had been imparted to him. This practice drew upon him an universal accusation of ingratitude; nor can it be denied that he was very ready to set himself free from the load of an obligation; for he could not bear to conceive himself in a state of dependence, his pride being equally powerful with his other passions, and appearing in the form of insolence at one time and of vanity at another. Vanity, the most innocent species of pride, was most frequently predominant: he could not easily leave off when he had once begun to mention himself or his works, nor ever read his verses without stealing his eyes from the page, to discover in the faces of his audience how they were affected with any favourite passage.

A kinder name than that of vanity ought to be given to the delicacy with which he was always careful to separate his own merit from every other man's; and to reject that praise to which he had no claim. He did not forget, in mentioning his performances, to mark every line that had been suggested or amended, and was so accurate as to relate that he owed *three words* in *The Wanderer* to the advice of his friends.

His veracity was questioned, but with little reason; his accounts, though not indeed always the same, were generally consistent. When he loved any man, he suppressed all his faults, and when he had been offended by him, concealed all his virtues: but his characters were generally true, so far as he proceeded; though it cannot be denied that his partiality might have sometimes the effect of falsehood.

In cases indifferent he was zealous for virtue, truth, and justice; he knew very well the necessity of goodness to the present and future happiness of mankind; nor is there perhaps any writer who has less endeavoured to please by flattering the appetites or perverting the judgement.

As an author therefore, and he now ceases to influence mankind in any other character, if one piece which he had resolved to suppress be excepted, he has very little to fear from the strictest moral or religious censure. And though he may not be altogether secure against the objections of the critic, it must however be acknowledged that his works are the productions of a genius truly poetical; and, what many writers who have been more lavishly applauded cannot boast, that they have an original air, which has no resemblance of any foregoing work; that the versification and sentiments have a cast peculiar to themselves, which no man can imitate with success, because what was nature in Savage would in another be affectation. It must be confessed that his descriptions are striking, his images animated, his fictions justly imagined, and his allegories artfully pursued; that his diction is elevated, though sometimes forced, and his numbers sonorous and majestic, though frequently sluggish and encumbered. Of his style the general fault is harshness, and its general excellence is dignity; of his sentiments, the prevailing beauty is sublimity, and uniformity the prevailing defect.

For his life, or for his writings, none who candidly consider his fortune will think an apology either necessary or difficult. If he was not always sufficiently instructed in his subject, his knowledge was at least greater than could have been attained by others in the same state. If his works were sometimes unfinished, accuracy cannot reasonably be exacted from a man oppressed with want, which he has no hope of relieving but by a speedy publication. The insolence and resentment of which he is accused were not easily to be avoided by a great mind irritated by perpetual hardships, and constrained hourly to return the spurns of contempt and repress the insolence of prosperity; and vanity may surely readily be pardoned in him to whom life afforded no other comforts than barren praises, and the consciousness of deserving them.

Those are no proper judges of his conduct who have slumbered away their time on the down of plenty, nor will a wise man presume to say, 'Had I been in Savage's condition, I should have lived, or written, better than Savage.'

This relation will not be wholly without its use if those who languish under any part of his sufferings shall be enabled to fortify their patience by reflecting that they feel only those afflictions from which the abilities of Savage did not exempt him; or those who in confidence of superior capacities or attainments disregard the common maxims of life shall be reminded that nothing will supply the want of prudence, and that negligence and irregularity long continued will make knowledge useless, wit ridiculous, and genius contemptible.

The Vision of Theodore, the Hermit of Teneriffe, found in his cell°

Son of Perseverance, whoever thou art, whose curiosity has led thee hither, read and be wise. He that now calls upon thee is Theodore, the Hermit of Teneriffe, who in the fifty-seventh year of his retreat left this instruction to mankind, lest his solitary hours should be spent in vain.

I was once what thou art now, a groveller on the earth, and a gazer at the sky; I trafficked and heaped wealth together, I loved and was favoured, I wore the robe of honour and heard the music of adulation; I was ambitious, and rose to greatness; I was unhappy, and retired. I sought for some time what I at length found here, a place where all real wants might be easily supplied, and where I might not be under the necessity of purchasing the assistance of men by the toleration of their follies. Here I saw fruits and herbs and water, and here determined to wait the hand of death, which I hope, when at last it comes, will fall lightly upon me.

Forty-eight years had I now passed in forgetfulness of all mortal cares, and without any inclination to wander farther than the necessity of procuring sustenance required; but as I stood one day beholding the rock that overhangs my cell, I found in myself a desire to climb it; and when I was on its top, was in the same manner determined to scale the next, till by degrees I conceived a wish to view the summit of the mountain, at the foot of which I had so long resided. This motion of my thoughts I endeavoured to suppress, not because it appeared criminal, but because it was new; and all change not evidently for the better alarms a mind taught by experience to distrust itself. I was often afraid that my heart was deceiving me, that my impatience of confinement arose from some earthly passion, and that my ardour to survey the works of nature was only a hidden longing to mingle once again in the scenes of life. I therefore endeavoured to settle my thoughts into their former state, but found their distraction every day greater. I was always reproaching myself with the want of happiness within my reach, and at last began to question whether it was not laziness rather than caution that restrained me from climbing to the summit of Teneriffe.

I rose therefore before the day, and began my journey up the steep of the mountain; but I had not advanced far, old as I was and burdened with provisions, when the day began to shine upon me; the declivities grew more precipitous, and the sand slided from beneath my feet; at last, fainting with labour, I arrived at a small plain almost inclosed by rocks, and open only to the east. I sat down to rest awhile, in full persuasion that when I had recovered my strength I should proceed on my design; but when once I had tasted ease, I found many reasons against disturbing it. The branches spread a shade over my head, and the gales of spring wafted odours to my bosom.

As I sat thus, forming alternately excuses for delay, and resolutions to go forward, an irresistible heaviness suddenly surprised me; I laid my head upon the bank, and resigned myself to sleep: when methought I heard the sound as of the flight of eagles, and a being of more than human dignity stood before me. While I was deliberating how to address him, he took me by the hand with an air of kindness, and asked me solemnly but without severity, 'Theodore, whither art thou going?'

'I am climbing,' answered I, 'to the top of the mountain, to enjoy a more extensive prospect of the works of nature'. 'Attend first', said he, 'to the prospect which this place affords, and what thou dost not understand I will explain. I am one of the benevolent beings who watch over the children of the dust, to preserve them from those evils which will not ultimately terminate in good, and which they do not, by their own faults, bring upon themselves. Look round therefore without fear: observe, contemplate, and be instructed.'

Encouraged by this assurance, I looked and beheld a mountain higher than Teneriffe, to the summit of which the human eye could never reach; when I had tired myself with gazing upon its height, I turned my eyes towards its foot, which I could easily discover, but was amazed to find it without foundation, and placed inconceivably in emptiness and darkness. Thus I stood terrified and confused; above were tracks inscrutable, and below was total vacuity. But my protector, with a voice of admonition, cried out, 'Theodore, be not affrighted, but raise thy eyes again; the Mountain of Existence is before thee, survey it and be wise.'

I then looked with more deliberate attention, and observed the bottom of the mountain to be of gentle rise, and overspread with flowers; the middle to be more steep, embarrassed with crags, and interrupted by precipices, over which hung branches loaded with fruits, and among which were scattered palaces and bowers. The tracts which my eye could reach nearest the top were generally barren; but there were among the clefts of the rocks a few hardy ever-greens, which, though they did not give much pleasure to the sight or smell, yet seemed to cheer the labour and facilitate the steps of those who were clambering among them.

Then, beginning to examine more minutely the different parts, I observed at a great distance a multitude of both sexes issuing into view from the bottom of the mountain. Their first actions I could not accurately discern; but, as they every moment approached nearer, I found that they amused themselves with gathering flowers under the superintendence of a modest virgin in a white robe, who seemed not over-solicitous to confine them to any settled pace or certain track; for she knew that the whole ground was smooth and solid, and that they could not easily be hurt or bewildered. When, as it often happened, they plucked a thistle for a flower, Innocence, so was she called, would smile at the mistake. 'Happy', said I, 'are they who are under so gentle a government, and yet are safe.' But I had no opportunity to dwell long on the consideration of their felicity; for I found that Innocence continued her attendance but a little way, and seemed to consider only the flowery bottom of the mountain as her proper province. Those whom she abandoned scarcely knew that they were left, before they perceived themselves in the hands of Education, a nymph more severe in her aspect and imperious in her commands, who confined them to certain paths, in their opinion too narrow and too rough. These they were continually solicited to leave, by Appetite, whom Education could never fright away, though she sometimes awed her to such timidity that the effects of her presence were scarcely perceptible. Some went back to the first part of the mountain, and seemed desirous of continuing busied in plucking flowers, but were no longer guarded by Innocence; and such as Education could not force back proceeded up the mountain by some miry road, in which they were seldom seen, and scarcely ever regarded.

As Education led her troop up the mountain, nothing was more observable than that she was frequently giving them cautions to beware of Habits; and was calling out to one or another at every step that a Habit was ensnaring them; that they would be under the dominion of Habit before they perceived their danger; and that those whom Habit should once subdue had little hope of regaining their liberty.

Of this caution, so frequently repeated, I was very solicitous to know the reason, when my protector directed my regard to a troop of pygmies, which appeared to walk silently before those that were climbing the mountain, and each to smooth the way before her follower. I found that I had missed the notice of them before, both because they were so minute as not easily to be discerned, and because they grew every moment nearer in their colour to the objects with which they were surrounded. As the followers of Education did not appear to be sensible of the presence of these dangerous associates, or, ridiculing their diminutive size, did not think it possible that human beings should ever be brought into subjection by such feeble enemies, they generally heard her precepts of vigilance with wonder: and, when they thought her eye withdrawn, treated them with contempt. Nor could I myself think her cautions so necessary as her frequent inculcations seemed to suppose, till I observed that each of these petty beings held secretly a chain in her hand, with which she prepared to bind those whom she found within her power. Yet these Habits under the eye of Education went quietly forward, and seemed very little to increase in bulk or strength; for though they were always willing to join with Appetite, yet when Education kept them apart from her, they would very punctually obey command, and make the narrow roads in which they were confined easier and smoother.

It was observable that their stature was never at a stand, but continually growing or decreasing, yet not always in the same proportions: not could I forbear to express my admiration, when I saw in how much less time they generally gained than lost bulk. Though they grew slowly in the road of Education, it might however be perceived that they grew; but if they once deviated at the call of Appetite, their stature soon became gigantic; and their strength was such that Education pointed out to her tribe many that were led in chains by them, whom she could never more rescue from their slavery. She pointed them out, but with little effect; for all her pupils appeared confident of their own superiority to the strongest Habit, and some seemed in secret to regret that they were hindered from following the triumph of Appetite.

It was the peculiar artifice of Habit not to suffer her power to be felt at first. Those whom she led, she had the address of appearing only to attend, but was continually doubling her chains upon her companions; which were so slender in themselves, and so silently fastened, that while the attention was engaged by other objects, they were not easily perceived. Each link grew tighter as it had been longer worn; and when by continual additions they became so heavy as to be felt, they were very frequently too strong to be broken.

When Education had proceeded in this manner to the part of the mountain where the declivity began to grow craggy, she resigned her charge to two powers of superior aspect. The meaner of them appeared capable of presiding in senates, or governing nations, and yet watched the steps of the other with the most anxious attention, and was visibly confounded and perplexed if ever she suffered her regard to be drawn away. The other seemed to approve her submission as pleasing, but with such a condescension as plainly showed that she claimed it as due; and indeed so great was her dignity and sweetness, that he who would not reverence, must not behold her.

'Theodore,' said my protector, 'be fearless, and be wise; approach these powers, whose dominion extends to all the remaining part of the Mountain of Existence.' I trembled, and ventured to address the inferior nymph, whose eyes, though piercing and awful, I was not able to sustain. 'Bright Power,' said I, 'by whatever name it is lawful to address thee, tell me, thou who presidest here, on what condition thy protection will be granted?' 'It will be granted,' said she, 'only to obedience. I am Reason, of all subordinate beings the noblest and the greatest; who, if thou wilt receive my laws, will reward thee like the rest of my votaries, by conducting thee to Religion.'

Charmed by her voice and aspect, I professed my readiness to follow her. She then presented me to her mistress, who looked upon me with tenderness. I bowed before her, and she smiled.

When Education delivered up those for whose happiness she had been so long solicitous, she seemed to expect that they should express some gratitude for her care, or some regret at the loss of that protection which she had hitherto afforded them. But it was easy to discover, by the alacrity which broke out at her departure, that her presence had been long displeasing, and that she had been teaching those who felt in themselves no want of instruction. They all agreed in rejoicing that they should no longer be subject to her caprices, or disturbed by her dictates,° but should be now under the direction only of Reason, to whom they made no doubt of being able to recommend themselves by a steady adherence to all her precepts. Reason counselled them, at their first entrance upon her province, to enlist themselves among the votaries of Religion; and informed them that if they trusted to her alone, they would find the same fate with her other admirers, whom she had not been able to secure against Appetites and Passions, and who, having been seized by Habits in the regions of Desire, had been dragged away to the caverns of Despair. Her admonition was vain, the greater number declared against any other direction, and doubted not but by her superintendency they should climb with safety up the Mountain of Existence. 'My power,' said Reason, 'is to advise, not to compel; I have already told you the

danger of your choice. The path seems now plain and even, but there
are asperities and pitfalls, over which Religion only can conduct you.
Look upwards, and you perceive a mist before you settled upon the
highest visible part of the mountain; a mist by which my prospect is
terminated, and which is pierced only by the eyes of Religion. Beyond
it are the temples of Happiness, in which those who climb the
precipice by her direction, after the toil of their pilgrimage, repose for
ever. I know not the way, and therefore can only conduct you to a
better guide. Pride has sometimes reproached me with the narrowness
of my view, but, when she endeavoured to extend it, could only show
me, below the mist, the bowers of Content; even they vanished as I
fixed my eyes upon them; and those whom she persuaded to travel
towards them were enchained by Habits and engulfed by Despair, a
cruel tyrant, whose caverns are beyond the darkness on the right side
and on the left, from whose prisons none can escape, and whom I
cannot teach you to avoid.'

Such was the declaration of Reason to those who demanded her
protection. Some that recollected the dictates of Education, finding
them now seconded by another authority, submitted with reluctance
to the strict decree, and engaged themselves among the followers of
Religion, who were distinguished by the uniformity of their march,
though many of them were women, and by their continual endeavours
to move upwards without appearing to regard the prospects which at
every step courted their attention.

All those who determined to follow either Reason or Religion were
continually importuned to forsake the road, sometimes by Passions,
and sometimes by Appetites, of whom both had reason to boast the
success of their artifices; for so many were drawn into by-paths that
any way was more populous than the right. The attacks of the
Appetites were more impetuous, those of the Passions longer
continued. The Appetites turned their followers directly from the true
way, but the Passions marched at first in a path nearly in the same
direction with that of Reason and Religion; but deviated by slow
degrees, till at last they entirely changed their course. Appetite drew
aside the dull, and Passion the sprightly. Of the Appetites, Lust was
the strongest; and of the Passions, Vanity. The most powerful assault
was to be feared when a Passion and an Appetite joined their
enticements; and the path of Reason was best followed when a Passion
called to one side, and an Appetite to the other.

These seducers had the greatest success upon the followers of
Reason, over whom they scarcely ever failed to prevail, except when

they counteracted one another. They had not the same triumphs over the votaries of Religion; for though they were often led aside for a time, Religion commonly recalled them by her emissary Conscience, before Habit had time to enchain them. But they that professed to obey Reason, if once they forsook her, seldom returned; for she had no messenger to summon them but Pride, who generally betrayed her confidence, and employed all her skill to support Passion; and if ever she did her duty, was found unable to prevail, if Habit had interposed.

I soon found that the great danger to the followers of Religion was only from Habit; every other power was easily resisted, nor did they find any difficulty, when they inadvertently quitted her, to find her again by the direction of Conscience, unless they had given time to Habit to draw her chain behind them, and bar up the way by which they had wandered. Of some of those, the condition was justly to be pitied, who turned at every call of Conscience, and tried, but without effect, to burst the chains of Habit: saw Religion walking forward at a distance, saw her with reverence, and longed to join her; but were, whenever they approached her, withheld by Habit, and languished in sordid bondage, which they could not escape, though they scorned and hated it.

It was evident that the Habits were so far from growing weaker by these repeated contests that if they were not totally overcome, every struggle enlarged their bulk and increased their strength; and a Habit opposed and victorious was more than twice as strong as before the contest. The manner in which those who were weary of their tyranny endeavoured to escape from them appeared by the event to be generally wrong; they tried to loose their chains one by one, and to retreat by the same degrees as they advanced; but before the deliverance was completed, Habit always threw new chains upon her fugitive; nor did any escape her but those who, by an effort sudden and violent, burst their shackles at once, and left her at a distance; and even of these, many, rushing too precipitately forward, and hindered by their terrors from stopping where they were safe, were fatigued with their own vehemence, and resigned themselves again to that power from whom an escape must be so dearly bought, and whose tyranny was little felt, except when it was resisted.

Some however there always were, who, when they found Habit prevailing over them, called upon Reason or Religion for assistance; each of them willingly came to the succour of her suppliant, but neither with the same strength, nor the same success. Habit, insolent with her power, would often presume to parley with Reason, and offer to loose some of her chains if the rest might remain. To this Reason, who was never certain of victory, frequently consented, but always found her concession destructive, and saw the captive led away by Habit to his former slavery. Religion never submitted to treaty, but held out her hand with certainty of conquest; and if the captive to whom she gave it did not quit his hold, always led him away in triumph, and placed him in the direct path to the Temple of Happiness, where Reason never failed to congratulate his deliverance, and encourage his adherence to that power to whose timely succour he was indebted for it.

When the traveller was again placed in the road of Happiness, I saw Habit again gliding before him, but reduced to the stature of a dwarf, without strength and without activity; but when the Passions or Appetites which had before seduced him made their approach, Habit would on a sudden start into size, and with unexpected violence push him towards them. The wretch, thus impelled on one side, and allured on the other, too frequently quitted the road of Happiness, to which, after his second deviation from it, he rarely returned. But, by a timely call upon Religion, the force of Habit was eluded, her attacks grew fainter, and at last her correspondence with the enemy was entirely destroyed. She then began to employ those restless faculties in compliance with the power which she could not overcome; and as she grew again in stature and in strength, cleared away the asperities of the road to Happiness.

From this road I could not easily withdraw my attention, because all who travelled it appeared cheerful and satisfied; and the farther they proceeded, the greater appeared their alacrity, and the stronger their conviction of the wisdom of their guide. Some who had never deviated but by short excursions had Habit in the middle of their passage vigorously supporting them, and driving off their Appetites and Passions which attempted to interrupt their progress. Others, who had entered this road late, or had long forsaken it, were toiling on without her help at least, and commonly against her endeavours. But I observed, when they approached to the barren top, that few were able to proceed without some support from Habit; and that they whose Habits were strong advanced towards the mists with little emotion, and entered them at last with calmness and confidence; after which, they were seen only by the eye of Religion; and though Reason looked after them with the most earnest curiosity, she could only obtain a faint glimpse, when her mistress, to enlarge her prospect, raised her from the ground. Reason, however, discerned that they were safe, but Religion saw that they were happy.

'Now, Theodore,' said my Protector, 'withdraw thy view from the regions of obscurity, and see the fate of those who, when they were dismissed by Education, would admit no direction but that of Reason. Survey their wanderings, and be wise.'

I looked then upon the road of Reason, which was indeed, so far as it reached, the same with that of Religion, nor had Reason discovered it but by her instruction. Yet when she had once been taught it, she clearly saw that it was right; and Pride had sometimes incited her to declare that she discovered it herself, and persuaded her to offer herself as a guide to Religion; whom after many vain experiments she found it her highest privilege to follow. Reason was however at last well instructed in part of the way, and appeared to teach it with some success, when her precepts were not misrepresented by Passion, or her influence overborne by Appetite. But neither of these enemies was she able to resist. When Passion seized upon her votaries, she seldom attempted opposition: she seemed indeed to contend with more vigour against Appetite, but was generally overwearied in the contest; and if either of her opponents had confederated with Habit, her authority was wholly at an end. When Habit endeavoured to captivate the votaries of Religion, she grew by slow degrees, and gave time to escape; but in seizing the unhappy followers of Reason, she proceeded as one that had nothing to fear, and enlarged her size, and doubled her chains without intermission, and without reserve.

Of those who forsook the directions of Reason, some were led aside by the whispers of Ambition, who was perpetually pointing to stately palaces, situated on eminences on either side, recounting the delights of affluence, and boasting the security of power. They were easily persuaded to follow her, and Habit quickly threw her chains upon them; they were soon convinced of the folly of their choice, but few of them attempted to return. Ambition led them forward from precipice to precipice, where many fell and were seen no more. Those that escaped were, after a long series of hazards, generally delivered over to Avarice, and enlisted by her in the service of Tyranny, where they continued to heap up gold till their patrons or their heirs pushed them headlong at last into the caverns of Despair.

Others were enticed by Intemperance to ramble in search of those fruits that hung over the rocks, and filled the air with their fragrance. I observed that the Habits which hovered about these soon grew to an enormous size, nor were there any who less attempted to return to

Reason, or sooner sunk into the gulfs that lay before them. When these first quitted the road, Reason looked after them with a frown of contempt, but had little expectations of being able to reclaim them; for the bowl of intoxication was of such qualities as to make them lose all regard but for the present moment; neither Hope nor Fear could enter their retreats; and Habit had so absolute a power that even Conscience, if Religion had employed her in their favour, would not have been able to force an entrance.

There were others whose crime it was rather to neglect Reason than to disobey her; and who retreated from the heat and tumult of the way, not to the bowers of Intemperance, but to the maze of Indolence. They had this peculiarity in their condition, that they were always in sight of the road of Reason, always wishing for her presence, and always resolving to return tomorrow. In these was most eminently conspicuous the subtlety of Habit, who hung imperceptible shackles upon them, and was every moment leading them farther from the road, which they always imagined that they had the power of reaching. They wandered on from one double of the labyrinth to another with the chains of Habit hanging secretly upon them, till, as they advanced, the flowers grew paler, and the scents fainter; they proceeded in their dreary march without pleasure in their progress, yet without power to return; and had this aggravation above all others, that they were criminal but not delighted. The drunkard for a time laughed over his wine; the ambitious man triumphed in the miscarriage of his rival; but the captives of Indolence had neither superiority nor merriment. Discontent lowered in their looks, and Sadness hovered round their shades; yet they crawled on reluctant and gloomy, till they arrived at the depth of the recess, varied only with poppies and nightshade, where the dominion of Indolence terminates, and the hopeless wanderer is delivered up to Melancholy: the chains of Habit are riveted for ever; and Melancholy, having tortured her prisoner for a time, consigns him at last to the cruelty of Despair.

While I was musing on this miserable scene, my Protector called out to me, 'Remember, Theodore, and be wise, and let not Habit prevail against thee.' I started, and beheld myself surrounded by the rocks of Teneriffe; the birds of light were singing in the trees, and the glances of the morning darted upon me.

The Rambler,° No. 4

SATURDAY, MARCH 31, 1750

[The New Realistic Novel]

The works of fiction with which the present generation seems more particularly delighted are such as exhibit life in its true state, diversified only by accidents that daily happen in the world, and influenced by passions and qualities which are really to be found in conversing with mankind.

This kind of writing may be termed not improperly the comedy of romance, and is to be conducted nearly by the rules of comic poetry. Its province is to bring about natural events by easy means, and to keep up curiosity without the help of wonder: it is therefore precluded from the machines and expedients of the heroic romance, and can neither employ giants to snatch away a lady from the nuptial rites, nor knights to bring her back from captivity: it can neither bewilder its personages in deserts nor lodge them in imaginary castles.

I remember a remark made by Scaliger upon Pontanus, that all his writings are filled with the same images; and that if you take from him his lilies and his roses, his satyrs and his dryads, he will have nothing left that can be called poetry. In like manner, almost all the fictions of the last age will vanish if you deprive them of a hermit and a wood, a battle and a shipwreck.

Why this wild strain of imagination found reception so long in polite and learned ages, it is not easy to conceive; but we cannot wonder that, while readers could be procured, the authors were willing to continue it: for when a man had by practice gained some fluency of language, he had no further care than to retire to his closet, let loose his invention, and heat his mind with incredibilities; a book was thus produced without fear of criticism, without the toil of study, without knowledge of nature, or acquaintance with life.

The task of our present writers is very different; it requires, together with that learning which is to be gained from books, that experience which can never be attained by solitary diligence, but must arise from general converse, and accurate observation of the living world. Their performances have, as Horace expresses it, *plus oneris quantum veniae minus*, little indulgence, and therefore more difficulty. They are engaged in portraits of which every one knows the original, and can detect any deviation from exactness of resemblance. Other writings are safe, except from the malice of learning, but these are in danger from every common reader; as the slipper ill executed was censured by a shoemaker who happened to stop in his way at the Venus of Apelles.

But the fear of not being approved as just copiers of human manners is not the most important concern that an author of this sort ought to have before him. These books are written chiefly to the young, the ignorant, and the idle, to whom they serve as lectures of conduct, and introductions into life. They are the entertainment of minds unfurnished with ideas, and therefore easily susceptible of impressions; not fixed by principles, and therefore easily following the current of fancy; not informed by experience, and consequently open to every false suggestion and partial account.

That the highest degree of reverence should be paid to youth, and that nothing indecent should be suffered to approach their eyes or ears, are precepts extorted by sense and virtue from an ancient writer, by no means eminent for chastity of thought. The same kind, though not the same degree, of caution, is required in every thing which is laid before them, to secure them from unjust prejudices, perverse opinions, and incongruous combinations of images.

In the romances formerly written, every transaction and sentiment was so remote from all that passes among men that the reader was in very little danger of making any applications to himself; the virtues and crimes were equally beyond his sphere of activity; and he amused himself with heroes and with traitors, deliverers and persecutors, as with beings of another species, whose actions were regulated upon motives of their own, and who had neither faults nor excellencies in common with himself.

But when an adventurer is levelled with the rest of the world, and acts in such scenes of the universal drama as may be the lot of any other man, young spectators fix their eyes upon him with closer attention, and hope by observing his behaviour and success to regulate their own practices, when they shall be engaged in the like part.

For this reason these familiar histories may perhaps be made of greater use than the solemnities of professed morality, and convey the knowledge of vice and virtue with more efficacy than axioms and definitions. But if the power of example is so great as to take possession of the memory by a kind of violence, and produce effects almost without the intervention of the will, care ought to be taken that, when the choice is unrestrained, the best examples only should be exhibited; and that which is likely to operate so strongly should not be mischievous or uncertain in its effects.

The chief advantage which these fictions have over real life is that their authors are at liberty, though not to invent, yet to select objects, and to cull from the mass of mankind those individuals upon which the attention ought most to be employed, as a diamond, though it cannot be made, may be polished by art, and placed in such a situation as to display that lustre which before was buried among common stones.

It is justly considered as the greatest excellency of art to imitate nature; but it is necessary to distinguish those parts of nature which are most proper for imitation: greater care is still required in representing life, which is so often discoloured by passion, or deformed by wickedness. If the world be promiscuously described, I cannot see of what use it can be to read the account; or why it may not be as safe to turn the eye immediately upon mankind, as upon a mirror which shows all that presents itself without discrimination.

It is therefore not a sufficient vindication of a character that it is drawn as it appears, for many characters ought never to be drawn; nor of a narrative that the train of events is agreeable to observation and experience, for that observation which is called knowledge of the world will be found much more frequently to make men cunning than good. The purpose of these writings is surely not only to show mankind, but to provide that they may be seen hereafter with less hazard; to teach the means of avoiding the snares which are laid by Treachery for Innocence without infusing any wish for that superiority with which the betrayer flatters his vanity; to give the power of counteracting fraud without the temptation to practise it; to initiate youth by mock encounters in the art of necessary defence, and to increase prudence without impairing virtue.

Many writers, for the sake of following nature, so mingle good and bad qualities in their principal personages that they are both equally conspicuous; and as we accompany them through their adventures with delight, and are led by degrees to interest ourselves in their favour, we lose the abhorrence of their faults, because they do not hinder our pleasure, or perhaps, regard them with some kindness for being united with so much merit.

There have been men indeed splendidly wicked, whose endowments threw a brightness on their crimes, and whom scarce any villainy made perfectly detestable, because they never could be wholly divested of their excellencies; but such have been in all ages the great corrupters of the world, and their resemblance ought no more to be preserved than the art of murdering without pain.

Some have advanced, without due attention to the consequences of this notion, that certain virtues have their correspondent faults, and therefore that to exhibit either apart is to deviate from probability. Thus men are observed by Swift to be 'grateful in the same degree as they are resentful'. This principle, with others of the same kind, supposes man to act from a brute impulse, and pursue a certain degree of inclination without any choice of the object; for, otherwise, though it should be allowed that gratitude and resentment arise from the same constitution of the passions, it follows not that they will be equally indulged when reason is consulted; yet unless that consequence be admitted, this sagacious maxim becomes an empty sound, without any relation to practice or to life.

Nor is it evident that even the first motions to these effects are always in the same proportion. For pride, which produces quickness of resentment, will obstruct gratitude, by unwillingness to admit that inferiority which obligation implies; and it is very unlikely that he who cannot think he receives a favour will acknowledge or repay it.

It is of the utmost importance to mankind that positions of this tendency should be laid open and confuted; for while men consider good and evil as springing from the same root, they will spare the one for the sake of the other, and in judging, if not of others at least of themselves, will be apt to estimate their virtues by their vices. To this fatal error all those will contribute who confound the colours of right and wrong, and instead of helping to settle their boundaries, mix them with so much art that no common mind is able to disunite them.

In narratives where historical veracity has no place, I cannot discover why there should not be exhibited the most perfect idea of virtue; of virtue not angelical, nor above probability, for what we cannot credit we shall never imitate, but the highest and purest that humanity can reach, which, exercised in such trials as the various revolutions of things shall bring upon it, may, by conquering some calamities, and enduring others, teach us what we may hope, and what we can perform. Vice, for vice is necessary to be shown, should always disgust; nor should the graces of gaiety, or the dignity of courage, be so united with it as to reconcile it to the mind. Wherever it appears, it should raise hatred by the malignity of its practices, and contempt by the meanness of its stratagems; for while it is supported by either parts or spirit, it will be seldom heartily abhorred. The Roman tyrant° was content to be hated, if he was but feared; and there are thousands of the readers of romances willing to be thought wicked if they may be allowed to be wits. It is therefore to be steadily inculcated that virtue is the highest proof of understanding, and the only solid basis of greatness; and that vice is the natural consequence of narrow thoughts, that it begins in mistake, and ends in ignominy.

The Rambler, No. 18

SATURDAY, MAY 19, 1750

[Marriage (1)]

There is no observation more frequently made by such as employ themselves in surveying the conduct of mankind than that marriage, though the dictate of Nature, and the institution of Providence, is yet very often the cause of misery, and that those who enter into that state can seldom forbear to express their repentance, and their envy of those whom either chance or caution has withheld from it.

This general unhappiness has given occasion to many sage maxims among the serious and smart remarks among the gay; the moralist and the writer of epigrams have equally shown their abilities upon it; some have lamented, and some have ridiculed it; but as the faculty of writing has been chiefly a masculine endowment, the reproach of making the world miserable has been always thrown upon the women, and the grave and the merry have equally thought themselves at liberty to conclude either with declamatory complaints, or satirical censures, of female folly or fickleness, ambition or cruelty, extravagance or lust.

Led by such a number of examples, and incited by my share in the common interest, I sometimes venture to consider this universal grievance, having endeavoured to divest my heart of all partiality, and place myself as a kind of neutral being between the sexes, whose clamours, being equally vented on both sides with all the vehemence of distress, all the apparent confidence of justice, and all the indignation of injured virtue, seem entitled to equal regard. The men have, indeed, by their superiority of writing, been able to collect the evidence of many ages, and raise prejudices in their favour by the venerable testimonies of philosophers, historians and poets; but the pleas of the ladies appeal to passions of more forcible operation than the reverence of antiquity. If they have not so great names on their side, they have stronger arguments; it is to little purpose that Socrates, or Euripides, are produced against the sighs of softness and the tears of beauty. The most frigid and inexorable judge would, at least, stand suspended between equal powers, as Lucan was perplexed in the determination of the cause, where the deities were on one side, and Cato on the other.

But I, who have long studied the severest and most abstracted philosophy, have now, in the cool maturity of life, arrived to such command over my passions that I can hear the vociferations of either sex without catching any of the fire from those that utter them. For I have found, by long experience, that a man will sometimes rage at his wife, when in reality his mistress has offended him; and a lady complain of the cruelty of her husband, when she has no other enemy than bad cards. I do not suffer myself to be any longer imposed upon by oaths on one side, or fits on the other; nor when the husband hastens to the tavern, and the lady retires to her closet, am I always confident that they are driven by their miseries; since I have sometimes reason to believe that they purpose not so much to soothe their sorrows as to animate their fury. But how little credit soever may be given to particular accusations, the general accumulation of the charge shows, with too much evidence, that married persons are not very often advanced in felicity; and, therefore, it may be proper to examine at what avenues so many evils have made their way into the world. With this purpose, I have reviewed the lives of my friends who have been least successful in connubial contracts, and attentively considered by what motives they were incited to marry, and by what principles they regulated their choice.

One of the first of my acquaintances that resolved to quit the unsettled thoughtless condition of a bachelor was Prudentius, a man of slow parts, but not without knowledge or judgment in things which he had leisure to consider gradually before he determined them. Whenever we met at a tavern, it was his province to settle the scheme of our entertainment, contract with the cook, and inform us when we had called for wine to the sum originally proposed. This grave considerer found by deep meditation that a man was no loser by marrying early, even though he contented himself with a less fortune; for estimating the exact worth of annuities, he found that, considering the constant diminution of the value of life, with the probable fall of the interest of money, it was not worse to have ten thousand pounds at the age of two and twenty years than a much larger fortune at thirty; for many opportunities, says he, occur of improving money, which if a man misses, he may not afterwards recover.

Full of these reflections, he threw his eyes about him, not in search of beauty or elegance, dignity or understanding, but of a woman with ten thousand pounds. Such a woman, in a wealthy part of the kingdom, it was not very difficult to find; and by artful management with her father, whose ambition was to make his daughter a gentle-woman, my friend got her, as he boasted to us in confidence two days after his marriage, for a settlement of seventy-three pounds a year less than her fortune might have claimed, and less than he would himself have given, if the fools had been but wise enough to delay the bargain.

Thus, at once delighted with the superiority of his parts, and the augmentation of his fortune, he carried Furia to his own house, in which he never afterwards enjoyed one hour of happiness. For Furia was a wretch of mean intellects, violent passions, a strong voice, and low education, without any sense of happiness but that which consisted in eating and counting money. Furia was a scold. They agreed in the desire of wealth, but with this difference, that Prudentius was for growing rich by gain, Furia by parsimony. Prudentius would venture his money with chances very much in his favour; but Furia very wisely observing that what they had was, while they had it, *their own*, thought all traffic too great a hazard, and was for putting it out at low interest, upon good security. Prudentius ventured, however, to insure a ship, at a very unreasonable price, but happening to lose his money, was so tormented with the clamours of his wife, that he never durst try a second experiment. He has now grovelled seven and forty years under Furia's direction, who never once mentioned him, since his bad luck, by any other name than that of *the insurer*.

The next that married from our society was Florentius. He happened to see Zephyretta in a chariot at a horse-race, danced with her at night, was confirmed in his first ardour, waited on her next morning, and declared himself her lover. Florentius had not know-ledge enough of the world to distinguish between the flutter of coquetry and the sprightliness of wit, or between the smile of allurement and that of cheerfulness. He was soon waked from his rapture by conviction that his pleasure was but the pleasure of a day. Zephyretta had in four and twenty hours spent her stock of repartee, gone round the circle of her airs, and had nothing remaining for him but childish insipidity, or for herself but the practice of the same artifices upon new men.

Melissus was a man of parts, capable of enjoying and of improving life. He had passed through the various scenes of gaiety with that indifference and possession of himself natural to men who have something higher and nobler in their prospect. Retiring to spend the summer in a village little frequented, he happened to lodge in the same house with Ianthe, and was unavoidably drawn to some acquaintance, which her wit and politeness soon invited him to improve. Having no opportunity of any other company, they were always together; and, as they owed their pleasures to each other, they began to forget that any pleasure was enjoyed before their meeting. Melissus, from being delighted with her company, quickly began to be uneasy in her absence, and being sufficiently convinced of the force of her understanding, and finding, as he imagined, such a conformity of temper as declared them formed for each other, addressed her as a lover, after no very long courtship obtained her for his wife, and brought her next winter to town in triumph.

Now began their infelicity. Melissus had only seen her in one scene, where there was no variety of objects to produce the proper excitements to contrary desires. They had both loved solitude and reflection, where there was nothing but solitude and reflection to be loved, but when they came into public life, Ianthe discovered those passions which accident rather than hypocrisy had hitherto concealed. She was, indeed, not without the power of thinking, but was wholly without the exertion of that power, when either gaiety or splendour played on her imagination. She was expensive in her diversions, vehement in her passions, insatiate of pleasure however dangerous to her reputation, and eager of applause by whomsoever it might be given. This was the wife which Melissus the philosopher found in his retirement, and from whom he expected an associate in his studies, and an assistant to his virtues.

Prosapius, upon the death of his younger brother, that the family might not be extinct, married his housekeeper, and has ever since been complaining to his friends that mean notions are instilled into his children, that he is ashamed to sit at his own table, and that his house is uneasy to him for want of suitable companions.

Avaro, master of a very large estate, took a woman of bad reputation, recommended to him by a rich uncle, who made that marriage the condition on which he should be his heir. Avaro now wonders to perceive his own fortune, his wife's, and his uncle's insufficient to give him that happiness which is to be found only with a woman of virtue.

I intend to treat in more papers on this important article of life, and shall, therefore, make no reflexion upon these histories, except that all whom I have mentioned failed to obtain happiness, for want of considering that marriage is the strictest tie of perpetual friendship; that there can be no friendship without confidence, and no confidence without integrity; and that he must expect to be wretched who pays to beauty, riches, or politeness that regard which only virtue and piety can claim.

The Rambler, No. 23

TUESDAY, JUNE 5, 1750

[The Rambler and His Critics]

That every man should regulate his actions by his own conscience, without any regard to the opinions of the rest of the world, is one of the first precepts of moral prudence; justified not only by the suffrage of reason, which declares that none of the gifts of heaven are to lie useless, but by the voice likewise of experience, which will soon inform us that, if we make the praise or blame of others the rule of our conduct, we shall be distracted by a boundless variety of irreconcilable judgments, be held in perpetual suspense between contrary impulses, and consult for ever without determination.

I know not whether, for the same reason, it is not necessary for an author to place some confidence in his own skill, and to satisfy himself in the knowledge that he has not deviated from the established law of composition, without submitting his works to frequent examinations before he gives them to the public, or endeavouring to secure success by a solicitous conformity to advice and criticism.

It is, indeed, quickly discoverable that consultation and compliance can conduce little to the perfection of any literary performance; for whoever is so doubtful of his own abilities as to encourage the remarks of others will find himself every day embarrassed with new difficulties, and will harass his mind, in vain, with the hopeless labour of uniting heterogeneous ideas, digesting independent hints, and collecting into one point the several rays of borrowed light, emitted often with contrary directions.

Of all authors, those who retail their labours in periodical sheets would be most unhappy, if they were much to regard the censures or the admonitions of their readers; for, as their works are not sent into the world at once, but by small parts in gradual succession, it is always imagined, by those who think themselves qualified to give instructions, that they may yet redeem their former failings by hearkening to better judges, and supply the deficiencies of their plan by the help of the criticisms which are so liberally afforded.

I have had occasion to observe, sometimes with vexation, and sometimes with merriment, the different temper with which the same man reads a printed and manuscript performance. When a book is once in the hands of the public, it is considered as permanent and unalterable; and the reader, if he be free from personal prejudices, takes it up with no other intention than of pleasing or instructing himself; he accommodates his mind to the author's design; and, having no interest in refusing the amusement that is offered him, never interrupts his own tranquillity by studied cavils, or destroys his satisfaction in that which is already well, by an anxious enquiry how it might be better; but is often contented without pleasure, and pleased without perfection.

But if the same man be called to consider the merit of a production yet unpublished, he brings an imagination heated with objections to passages which he has yet never heard; he invokes all the powers of criticism, and stores his memory with Taste and Grace, Purity and Delicacy, Manners and Unities, sounds which, having been once uttered by those that understood them, have been since re-echoed without meaning, and kept up to the disturbance of the world, by a constant repercussion from one coxcomb to another. He considers himself as obliged to show, by some proof of his abilities, that he is not consulted to no purpose, and, therefore, watches every opening for objection, and looks round for every opportunity to propose some specious alteration. Such opportunities a very small degree of sagacity will enable him to find; for, in every work of imagination, the disposition of parts, the insertion of incidents, and use of decorations, may be varied a thousand ways with equal propriety; and as, in things nearly equal, that will always seem best to every man which he himself produces, the critic whose business is only to propose without the care of execution can never want the satisfaction of believing that he has suggested very important improvements, nor the power of enforcing his advice by arguments which, as they appear convincing to himself, either his kindness, or his vanity, will press obstinately and importunately, without suspicion that he may possibly judge too hastily in favour of his own advice, or enquiry whether the advantage of the new scheme be proportionate to the labour.

It is observed by the younger Pliny that an orator ought not so much to select the strongest arguments which his cause admits, as to employ all which his imagination can afford; for, in pleading, those reasons are of most value which will most affect the judges; and the judges, says he, will be always most touched with that which they had before conceived. Every man who is called to give his opinion of a performance decides upon the same principle; he first suffers himself to form expectations, and then is angry at his disappointment. He lets his imagination rove at large, and wonders that another, equally unconfined in the boundless ocean of possibility, takes a different course.

But, though the rule of Pliny be judiciously laid down, it is not applicable to the writer's cause, because there always lies an appeal from domestic criticism to a higher judicature, and the public, which is never corrupted, nor often deceived, is to pass the last sentence upon literary claims.

Of the great force of preconceived opinions I had many proofs, when I first entered upon this weekly labour. My readers having, from the performances of my predecessors, established an idea of unconnected essays, to which they believed all future authors under a necessity of conforming, were impatient of the least deviation from their system, and numerous remonstrances were accordingly made by each, as he found his favourite subject omitted or delayed. Some were angry that the Rambler did not, like the Spectator, introduce himself to the acquaintance of the public by an account of his own birth and studies, and enumeration of his adventures, and a description of his physiognomy. Others soon began to remark that he was a solemn, serious, dictatorial writer, without sprightliness or gaiety, and called out with vehemence for mirth and humour. Another admonished him to have a special eye upon the various clubs of this great city, and informed him that much of the Spectator's vivacity was laid out upon such assemblies. He has been censured for not imitating the politeness of his predecessors, having hitherto neglected to take the ladies under his protection, and give them rules for the just opposition of colours, and the proper dimensions of ruffles and pinners. He has been required by one to fix a particular censure upon those matrons who play at cards with spectacles. And another is very much offended whenever he meets with a speculation in which naked precepts are comprised, without the illustration of examples and characters.

I make not the least question that all these monitors intend the promotion of my design, and the instruction of my readers; but they do not know, or do not reflect that an author has a rule of choice peculiar to himself; and selects those subjects which he is best qualified to treat by the course of his studies, or the accidents of his life; that some topics of amusement have been already treated with too much success to invite a competition; and that he who endeavours to gain many readers must try various arts of invitation, essay every avenue of pleasure, and make frequent changes in his methods of approach.

I cannot but consider myself amidst this tumult of criticism as a ship in a poetical tempest, impelled at the same time by opposite winds, and dashed by the waves from every quarter, but held upright by the contrariety of the assailants, and secured, in some measure, by multiplicity of distress. Had the opinion of my censurers been unanimous, it might, perhaps, have overset my resolution; but since I find them at variance with each other, I can, without scruple, neglect them, and endeavour to gain the favour of the public by following the direction of my own reason, and indulging the sallies of my own imagination.

The Rambler, No. 32

SATURDAY, JULY 7, 1750

[Stoicism]

So large a part of human life passes in a state contrary to our natural desires that one of the principal topics of moral instruction is the art of bearing calamities. And such is the certainty of evil that it is the duty of every man to furnish his mind with those principles that may enable him to act under it with decency and propriety.

The sect of ancient philosophers that boasted to have carried this necessary science to the highest perfection were the Stoics, or scholars of Zeno, whose wild enthusiastic virtue pretended to an exemption from the sensibilities of unenlightened mortals, and who proclaimed themselves exalted, by the doctrines of their sect, above the reach of those miseries which embitter life to the rest of the world. They therefore removed pain, poverty, loss of friends, exile, and violent death from the catalogue of evils; and passed, in their haughty style, a kind of irreversible decree, by which they forbade them to be counted any longer among the objects of terror or anxiety, or to give any disturbance to the tranquillity of a wise man.

This edict was, I think, not universally observed, for though one of the more resolute, when he was tortured by a violent disease, cried out that let pain harass him to its utmost power, it should never force him to consider it as other than indifferent and neutral; yet all had not stubbornness to hold out against their senses: for a weaker pupil of Zeno is recorded to have confessed in the anguish of the gout that 'he now found pain to be an evil'.

It may however be questioned whether these philosophers can be very properly numbered among the teachers of patience; for if pain be not an evil, there seems no instruction requisite how it may be borne; and therefore when they endeavour to arm their followers with arguments against it, they may be thought to have given up their first position. But such inconsistencies are to be expected from the greatest understandings when they endeavour to grow eminent by singularity, and employ their strength in establishing opinions opposite to nature.

The controversy about the reality of external evils is now at an end. That life has many miseries, and that those miseries are, sometimes at least, equal to all the powers of fortitude, is now universally confessed; and therefore it is useful to consider not only how we may escape them, but by what means those which either the accidents of affairs or the infirmities of nature must bring upon us may be mitigated and lightened; and how we may make those hours less wretched which the condition of our present existence will not allow to be very happy.

The cure for the greatest part of human miseries is not radical, but palliative. Infelicity is involved in corporeal nature, and interwoven with our being; all attempts therefore to decline it wholly are useless and vain: the armies of pain send their arrows against us on every side, the choice is only between those which are more or less sharp, or tinged with poison of greater or less malignity, and the strongest armour which reason can supply will only blunt their points, but cannot repel them.

The great remedy which heaven has put in our hands is patience, by which, though we cannot lessen the torments of the body, we can in a great measure preserve the peace of the mind, and shall suffer only the natural and genuine force of an evil, without heightening its acrimony, or prolonging its effects.

There is indeed nothing more unsuitable to the nature of man in any calamity than rage and turbulence, which, without examining whether they are not sometimes impious, are at least always offensive, and incline others rather to hate and despise than to pity and assist us. If what we suffer has been brought upon us by ourselves, it is observed by an ancient poet that patience is eminently our duty, since no one should be angry at feeling that which he has deserved.

> *Leniter ex merito quicquid patiare ferendum est.*
> Ovid, *Heroides*, v. 7.
> Let pain deserved without complaint be borne.

And surely, if we are conscious that we have not contributed to our own sufferings, if punishment fall upon innocence, or disappointment happens to industry and prudence, patience, whether more necessary or not, is much easier, since our pain is then without aggravation, and we have not the bitterness of remorse to add to the asperity of misfortune.

In those·evils which are allotted to us by Providence, such as deformity, privation of any of the senses, or old age, it is always to be remembered that impatience can have no present effect but to deprive us of the consolations which our condition admits, by driving away from us those by whose conversation or advice we might be amused or helped; and that with regard to futurity it is yet less to be justified, since, without lessening the pain, it cuts off the hope of that reward which he by whom it is inflicted will confer upon them that bear it well.

In all evils which admit a remedy, impatience is to be avoided, because it wastes that time and attention in complaints that, if properly applied, might remove the cause. Turenne, among the acknowledgments which he used to pay in conversation to the memory of those by whom he had been instructed in the art of war, mentioned one with honour who taught him not to spend his time in regretting any mistake which he had made, but to set himself immediately and vigorously to repair it.

Patience and submission are very carefully to be distinguished from cowardice and indolence. We are not to repine, but we may lawfully struggle; for the calamities of life, like the necessities of nature, are calls to labour, and exercises of diligence. When we feel any pressure of distress, we are not to conclude that we can only obey the will of heaven by languishing under it, any more than when we perceive the pain of thirst we are to imagine that water is prohibited. Of misfortune it never can be certainly known whether, as proceeding from the hand of God, it is an act of favour, or of punishment: but since all the ordinary dispensations of providence are to be interpreted according to the general analogy of things, we may conclude that we have a right to remove one inconvenience as well as another; that we are only to take care lest we purchase ease with guilt; and that our Maker's purpose, whether of reward or severity, will be answered by the labours which he lays us under the necessity of performing.

This duty is not more difficult in any state than in diseases intensely painful, which may indeed suffer such exacerbations as seem to strain the powers of life to their utmost stretch, and leave very little of the attention vacant to precept or reproof. In this state the nature of man requires some indulgence, and every extravagance but impiety may be easily forgiven him. Yet, lest we should think ourselves too soon entitled to the mournful privileges of irresistible misery, it is proper to reflect that the utmost anguish which human wit can contrive, or human malice can inflict, has been borne with constancy; and that if the pains of disease be, as I believe they are, sometimes greater than those of artificial torture, they are therefore in their own nature shorter, the vital frame is quickly broken, or the union between soul and body is for a time suspended by insensibility, and we soon cease to feel our maladies when they once become too violent to be borne. I think there is some reason for questioning whether the body and mind are not so proportioned that the one can bear all which can be inflicted on the other, whether virtue cannot stand its ground as long as life, and whether a soul well-principled will not be separated sooner than subdued.

In calamities which operate chiefly on our passions, such as diminution of fortune, loss of friends, or declension of character, the chief danger of impatience is upon the first attack, and many expedients have been contrived by which the blow may be broken. Of these the most general precept is not to take pleasure in any thing of which it is not in our power to secure the possession to ourselves. This counsel, when we consider the enjoyment of any terrestrial advantage as opposite to a constant and habitual solicitude for future felicity, is undoubtedly just, and delivered by that authority which cannot be disputed; but in any other sense, is it not like advice not to walk lest we should stumble, or not to see lest our eyes should light upon deformity? It seems to me reasonable to enjoy blessings with confidence as well as to resign them with submission, and to hope for the continuance of good which we possess without insolence or voluptuousness as for the restitution of that which we lose without despondency or murmurs.

The chief security against the fruitless anguish of impatience must arise from frequent reflection on the wisdom and goodness of the God of nature, in whose hands are riches and poverty, honour and disgrace, pleasure and pain, and life and death. A settled conviction of the tendency of every thing to our good, and of the possibility of turning miseries into happiness, by receiving them rightly, will incline us to *bless the name of the Lord, whether he gives or takes away.*°

The Rambler, No. 36

SATURDAY, JULY 21, 1750

[Pastoral Poetry (1)]

There is scarcely any species of poetry that has allured more readers or excited more writers than the pastoral. It is generally pleasing because it entertains the mind with representations of scenes familiar to almost every imagination, and of which all can equally judge whether they are well described. It exhibits a life to which we have been always accustomed to associate peace and leisure and innocence: and therefore we readily set open the heart for the admission of its images, which contribute to drive away cares and perturbations, and suffer ourselves without resistance to be transported to Elysian regions, where we are to meet with nothing but joy and plenty and contentment; where every gale whispers pleasure, and every shade promises repose.

It has been maintained by some who love to talk of what they do not know that pastoral is the most ancient poetry; and, indeed, since it is probable that poetry is nearly of the same antiquity with rational nature, and since the life of the first men was certainly rural, we may reasonably conjecture that, as their ideas would necessarily be borrowed from those objects with which they were acquainted, their composures, being filled chiefly with such thoughts on the visible creation as must occur to the first observers, were pastoral hymns like those which Milton introduces the original pair singing, in the day of innocence, to the praise of their Maker.

For the same reason that pastoral poetry was the first employment of the human imagination, it is generally the first literary amusement of our minds. We have seen fields and meadows and groves from the time that our eyes opened upon life; and are pleased with birds and brooks and breezes much earlier than we engage among the actions and passions of mankind. We are therefore delighted with rural pictures, because we know the original at an age when our curiosity can be very little awakened by descriptions of courts which we never beheld, or representations of passion which we never felt.

The satisfaction received from this kind of writing not only begins early, but lasts long; we do not, as we advance into the intellectual world, throw it away among other childish amusements and pastimes, but willingly return to it in any hour of indolence and relaxation. The images of true pastoral have always the power of exciting delight, because the works of nature from which they are drawn have always the same order and beauty, and continue to force themselves upon our thoughts, being at once obvious to the most careless regard, and more than adequate to the strongest reason and severest contemplation. Our inclination to stillness and tranquillity is seldom much lessened by long knowledge of the busy and tumultuary part of the world. In childhood we turn our thoughts to the country, as to the region of pleasure; we recur to it in old age as a port of rest, and perhaps with that secondary and adventitious gladness which every man feels on reviewing those places, or recollecting those occurrences, that contributed to his youthful enjoyments, and bring him back to the prime of life, when the world was gay with the bloom of novelty, when mirth wantoned at his side, and hope sparkled before him.

The sense of this universal pleasure has invited *numbers without number* to try their skill in pastoral performances, in which they have generally succeeded after the manner of other imitators, transmitting the same images in the same combination from one to another, till he that reads the title of a poem may guess at the whole series of the composition; nor will a man, after the perusal of thousands of these performances, find his knowledge enlarged with a single view of nature not produced before, or his imagination amused with any new application of those views to moral purposes.

The range of pastoral is indeed narrow, for though nature itself, philosophically considered, be inexhaustible, yet its general effects on the eye and on the ear are uniform, and incapable of much variety of description. Poetry cannot dwell upon the minuter distinctions by which one species differs from another without departing from that simplicity of grandeur which fills the imagination; nor dissect the latent qualities of things without losing its general power of gratifying every mind by recalling its conceptions. However, as each age makes some discoveries, and those discoveries are by degrees generally known, as new plants or modes of culture are introduced, and by little and little become common, pastoral might receive, from time to time, small augmentations, and exhibit once in a century a scene somewhat varied.

But pastoral subjects have been often, like others, taken into the hands of those that were not qualified to adorn them, men to whom the face of nature was so little known that they have drawn it only after their own imagination, and changed or distorted her features, that their portraits might appear something more than servile copies from their predecessors.

Not only the images of rural life, but the occasions on which they can be properly produced, are few and general. The state of a man confined to the employments and pleasures of the country is so little diversified, and exposed to so few of those accidents which produce perplexities, terrors and surprises in more complicated transactions that he can be shown but seldom in such circumstances as attract curiosity. His ambition is without policy, and his love without intrigue. He has no complaints to make of his rival but that he is richer than himself; nor any disasters to lament but a cruel mistress or a bad harvest.

The conviction of the necessity of some new source of pleasure induced Sannazarius to remove the scene from the fields to the sea, to substitute fishermen for shepherds, and derive his sentiments from the piscatory life; for which he has been censured by succeeding critics, because the sea is an object of terror, and by no means proper to amuse the mind and lay the passions asleep. Against this objection he might be defended by the established maxim that the poet has a right to select his images, and is no more obliged to show the sea in a storm than the land under an inundation; but may display all the pleasures, and conceal the dangers of the water, as he may lay his shepherd under a shady beech without giving him an ague, or letting a wild beast loose upon him.

There are however two defects in the piscatory eclogue which perhaps cannot be supplied. The sea, though in hot countries it is considered by those who live, like Sannazarius, upon the coast as a place of pleasure and diversion, has notwithstanding much less variety than the land, and therefore will be sooner exhausted by a descriptive writer. When he has once shown the sun rising or setting upon it, curled its waters with the vernal breeze, rolled the waves in gentle succession to the shore, and enumerated the fish sporting in the shallows, he has nothing remaining but what is common to all other poetry, the complaint of a nymph for a drowned lover, or the indignation of a fisher that his oysters are refused, and Mycon's accepted.

Another obstacle to the general reception of this kind of poetry is the ignorance of maritime pleasures, in which the greater part of mankind must always live. To all the inland inhabitants of every region, the sea is only known as an immense diffusion of waters, over which men pass from one country to another, and in which life is frequently lost. They have, therefore, no opportunity of tracing, in their own thoughts, the descriptions of winding shores and calm bays, nor can look on the poem in which they are mentioned with other sensations than on a sea chart, or the metrical geography of Dionysius.

This defect Sannazarius was hindered from perceiving by writing in a learned language to readers generally acquainted with the works of nature; but if he had made his attempt in any vulgar tongue, he would soon have discovered how vainly he had endeavoured to make that loved which was not understood.

I am afraid it will not be found easy to improve the pastorals of antiquity by any great additions or diversifications. Our descriptions may indeed differ from those of Virgil, as an English from an Italian summer, and, in some respects, as modern from ancient life; but as nature is in both countries nearly the same, and as poetry has to do rather with the passions of men, which are uniform, than their customs, which are changeable, the varieties which time or place can furnish will be inconsiderable: and I shall endeavour to show, in the next paper, how little the latter ages have contributed to the improvement of the rustic muse.

The Rambler, No. 37

TUESDAY, JULY 24, 1750

[Pastoral Poetry (2)]

In writing or judging of pastoral poetry, neither the authors nor critics of latter times seem to have paid sufficient regard to the originals left us by antiquity, but have entangled themselves with unnecessary difficulties, by advancing principles which, having no foundation in the nature of things, are wholly to be rejected from a species of composition in which, above all others, mere nature is to be regarded.

It is, therefore, necessary to enquire after some more distinct and exact idea of this kind of writing. This may, I think, be easily found in the pastorals of Virgil, from whose opinion it will not appear very safe to depart if we consider that every advantage of nature, and of fortune, concurred to complete his productions; that he was born with great accuracy and severity of judgment, enlightened with all the learning of one of the brightest ages, and embellished with the elegance of the Roman court; that he employed his powers rather in improving, than inventing, and therefore must have endeavoured to recompense the want of novelty by exactness; that taking Theocritus for his original, he found pastoral far advanced towards perfection, and that having so great a rival, he must have proceeded with uncommon caution.

If we search the writings of Virgil for the true definition of a pastoral, it will be found 'a poem in which any action or passion is represented by its effects upon a country life'. Whatsoever therefore may, according to the common course of things, happen in the country may afford a subject for a pastoral poet.

In this definition, it will immediately occur to those who are versed in the writings of the modern critics that there is no mention of the Golden Age. I cannot indeed easily discover why it is thought necessary to refer descriptions of a rural state to remote times, nor can I perceive that any writer has consistently preserved the Arcadian manners and sentiments. The only reason that I have read on which this rule has been founded is that, according to the customs of modern life, it is improbable that shepherds should be capable of harmonious numbers, or delicate sentiments; and therefore the reader must exalt his ideas of the pastoral character by carrying his thoughts back to the age in which the care of herds and flocks was the employment of the wisest and greatest men.

These reasoners seem to have been led into their hypothesis by considering pastoral, not in general, as a representation of rural nature, and consequently as exhibiting the ideas and sentiments of those, whoever they are, to whom the country affords pleasure or employment, but simply as a dialogue or narrative of men actually tending sheep, and busied in the lowest and most laborious offices; from whence they very readily concluded, since characters must necessarily be preserved, that either the sentiments must sink to the level of the speakers, or the speakers must be raised to the height of the sentiments.

In consequence of these original errors, a thousand precepts have been given which have only contributed to perplex and to confound. Some have thought it necessary that the imaginary manners of the Golden Age should be universally preserved, and have therefore believed that nothing more could be admitted in pastoral than lilies and roses, and rocks and streams, among which are heard the gentle whispers of chaste fondness, or the soft complaints of amorous impatience. In pastoral, as in other writings, chastity of sentiment ought doubtless to be observed, and purity of manners to be represented; not because the poet is confined to the images of the Golden Age, but because, having the subject in his own choice, he ought always to consult the interest of virtue.

These advocates for the Golden Age lay down other principles, not very consistent with their general plan; for they tell us that, to support the character of the shepherd, it is proper that all refinement should be avoided, and that some slight instances of ignorance should be interspersed. Thus the shepherd in Virgil is supposed to have forgot the name of Anaximander, and in Pope the term *Zodiac* is too hard for a rustic apprehension. But if we place our shepherds in their primitive condition, we may give them learning among their other qualifications; and if we suffer them to allude at all to things of later existence, which, perhaps, cannot with any great propriety be allowed, there can be no danger of making them speak with too much accuracy, since they conversed with divinities, and transmitted to succeeding ages the arts of life.

Other writers, having the mean and despicable condition of a shepherd always before them, conceive it necessary to degrade the language of pastoral by obsolete terms and words, which they very learnedly call Doric, without reflecting that they thus become authors of a mingled dialect which no human being ever could have spoken, that they may as well refine the speech as the sentiments of their personages, and that none of the inconsistencies which they endeavour to avoid is greater than that of joining elegance of thought with coarseness of diction. Spenser begins one of his pastorals with studied barbarity:

> Diggon Davie, I bid her good day:
> Or, Diggon her is, or I missay.
> *Dig.* Her was her while it was daylight,
> But now her is a most wretched wight.
>
> *Shepherd's Calendar*, 'September',
> ll. 1–4

What will the reader imagine to be the subject on which speakers like these exercise their eloquence? Will he not be somewhat disappointed when he finds them met together to condemn the corruptions of the church of Rome? Surely, at the same time that a shepherd learns theology, he may gain some acquaintance with his native language.

Pastoral admits of all ranks of persons, because persons of all ranks inhabit the country. It excludes not, therefore, on account of the characters necessary to be introduced, any elevation or delicacy of sentiment; those ideas only are improper which, not owing their original to rural objects, are not pastoral. Such is the exclamation in Virgil:

Nunc scio quid sit Amor, duris in cautibus illum
Ismarus, aut Rhodope, aut extremi Garamantes,
Nec generis nostri puerum nec sanguinis, edunt.
                                   Eclogues, viii. 43–5

I know thee, Love, in deserts thou wert bred,
And at the dugs of savage tigers fed:
Alien of birth, usurper of the plains,
                                             Dryden.

which Pope endeavouring to copy was carried to still greater
impropriety,

I know thee, Love, wild as the raging main,
More fierce than tigers on the Libyan plain;
Thou wert from Etna's burning entrails torn,
Begot in tempests, and in thunders born!
                                   'Autumn', ll. 89–92

Sentiments like these, as they have no ground in nature, are indeed of
little value in any poem, but in pastoral they are particularly liable to
censure, because it wants that exaltation above common life which in
tragic or heroic writings often reconciles us to bold flights and daring
figures.

Pastoral, being the *representation of an action or passion by its effects
upon a country life*, has nothing peculiar but its confinement to rural
imagery, without which it ceases to be pastoral. This is its true
characteristic, and this it cannot lose by any dignity of sentiment, or
beauty of diction. The Pollio of Virgil, with all its elevation, is a
composition truly bucolic, though rejected by the critics; for all the
images are either taken from the country, or from the religion of the
age common to all parts of the empire.

The Silenus is indeed of a more disputable kind, because though
the scene lies in the country, the song being religious and historical
had been no less adapted to any other audience or place. Neither can it
well be defended as a fiction, for the introduction of a god seems to
imply the Golden Age, and yet he alludes to many subsequent
transactions, and mentions Gallus, the poet's contemporary.

It seems necessary to the perfection of this poem that the occasion
which is supposed to produce it be at least not inconsistent with a
country life, or less likely to interest those who have retired into places
of solitude and quiet than the more busy part of mankind. It is
therefore improper to give the title of a pastoral to verses in which the
speakers, after the slight mention of their flocks, fall to complaints of

errors in the church and corruptions in the government, or to lamentations of the death of some illustrious person, whom when once the poet has called a shepherd, he has no longer any labour upon his hands, but can make the clouds weep, and lilies wither, and the sheep hang their heads, without art or learning, genius, or study.

It is part of Claudian's character of his rustic that he computes his time not by the succession of consuls, but of harvests. Those who pass their days in retreats distant from the theatres of business are always least likely to hurry their imagination with public affairs.

The facility of treating actions or events in the pastoral style has incited many writers from whom more judgment might have been expected to put the sorrow or the joy which the occasion required into the mouth of Daphne or of Thyrsis, and as one absurdity must naturally be expected to make way for another, they have written with an utter disregard both of life and nature, and filled their productions with mythological allusions, with incredible fictions, and with sentiments which neither passion nor reason could have dictated since the change which religion has made in the whole system of the world.

The Rambler, No. 39

TUESDAY, JULY 31, 1750

[Marriage (2)]

The condition of the female sex has been frequently the subject of compassion to medical writers, because their constitution of body is such that every state of life brings its peculiar diseases: they are placed, according to the proverb, between Scylla and Charybdis, with no other choice than of dangers equally formidable; and whether they embrace marriage, or determine upon a single life, are exposed, in consequence of their choice, to sickness, misery, and death.

It were to be wished that so great a degree of natural infelicity might not be increased by adventitious and artificial miseries; and that beings whose beauty we cannot behold without admiration, and whose delicacy we cannot contemplate without tenderness, might be suffered to enjoy every alleviation of their sorrows. But, however it has happened, the custom of the world seems to have been formed in a kind of conspiracy against them, though it does not appear but they had themselves an equal share in its establishment; and prescriptions which, by whomsoever they were begun, are now of long continuance, and by consequence of great authority, seem to have almost excluded them from content, in whatsoever condition they shall pass their lives.

If they refuse the society of men, and continue in that state which is reasonably supposed to place happiness most in their own power, they seldom give those that frequent their conversation any exalted notions of the blessing of liberty; for whether it be that they are angry to see with what inconsiderate eagerness other heedless females rush into slavery, or with what absurd vanity the married ladies boast the change of their condition, and condemn the heroines who endeavour to assert the natural dignity of their sex; whether they are conscious that like barren countries they are free only because they were never thought to deserve the trouble of a conquest, or imagine that their sincerity is not always unsuspected, when they declare their contempt of men; it is certain that they generally appear to have some great and incessant cause of uneasiness, and that many of them have at last been persuaded, by powerful rhetoricians, to try the life which they had so long contemned, and put on the bridal ornaments at a time when they least became them.

What are the real causes of the impatience which the ladies discover in a virgin state, I shall perhaps take some other occasion to examine. That it is not to be envied for its happiness appears from the solicitude with which it is avoided; from the opinion universally prevalent among the sex that no woman continues long in it but because she is not invited to forsake it; from the disposition always shown to treat old maids as the refuse of the world; and from the willingness with which it is often quitted at last, by those whose experience has enabled them to judge at leisure, and decide with authority.

Yet such is life that whatever is proposed, it is much easier to find reasons for rejecting than embracing. Marriage, though a certain security from the reproach and solitude of antiquated virginity, has yet, as it is usually conducted, many disadvantages, that take away much from the pleasure which society promises, and might afford, if pleasures and pains were honestly shared, and mutual confidence inviolably preserved.

The miseries, indeed, which many ladies suffer under conjugal vexations, are to be considered with great pity, because their husbands are often not taken by them as objects of affection, but forced upon them by authority and violence, or by persuasion and importunity, equally resistless when urged by those whom they have been always accustomed to reverence and obey; and it very seldom appears that those who are thus despotic in the disposal of their children pay any regard to their domestic and personal felicity, or think it so much to be enquired whether they will be happy, as whether they will be rich.

It may be urged, in extenuation of this crime, which parents, not in any other respect to be numbered with robbers and assassins, frequently commit, that, in their estimation, riches and happiness are equivalent terms. They have passed their lives with no other wish than that of adding acre to acre, and filling one bag after another, and imagine the advantage of a daughter sufficiently considered when they have secured her a large jointure, and given her reasonable expectations of living in the midst of those pleasures with which she had seen her father and mother solacing their age.

There is an economical oracle received among the prudential part of the world, which advises fathers *to marry their daughters lest they should marry themselves*; by which I suppose it is implied that women left to their own conduct generally unite themselves with such partners as can contribute very little to their felicity. Who was the author of this maxim, or with what intention it was originally uttered, I have not yet discovered; but imagine that however solemnly it may be transmitted, or however implicitly received, it can confer no authority which nature has denied; it cannot license Titius to be unjust, lest Caia should be imprudent; nor give right to imprison for life, lest liberty should be ill employed.

That the ladies have sometimes incurred imputations which might naturally produce edicts not much in their favour must be confessed by their warmest advocates; and I have indeed seldom observed that when the tenderness or virtue of their parents has preserved them from forced marriage, and left them at large to choose their own path in the labyrinth of life, they have made any great advantage of their liberty. They commonly take the opportunity of independence to trifle away youth and lose their bloom in a hurry of diversions, recurring in a succession too quick to leave room for any settled reflection; they see the world without gaining experience, and at last regulate their choice by motives trifling as those of a girl, or mercenary as those of a miser.

Melanthia came to town upon the death of her father, with a very large fortune, and with the reputation of a much larger; she was therefore followed and caressed by many men of rank, and by some of understanding; but having an insatiable desire of pleasure, she was not at leisure, from the park, the gardens, the theatres, visits, assemblies, and masquerades, to attend seriously to any proposal, but was still impatient for a new flatterer, and neglected marriage as always in her power; till in time her admirers fell away, wearied with expense, disgusted at her folly, or offended by her inconstancy; she heard of concerts to which she was not invited, and was more than once forced to sit still at an assembly, for want of a partner. In this distress, chance threw in her way Philotryphus, a man vain, glittering, and thoughtless as herself, who had spent a small fortune in equipage and dress, and was shining in the last suit for which his tailor would give him credit. He had been long endeavouring to retrieve his extravagance by marriage, and therefore soon paid his court to Melanthia, who after some weeks of insensibility saw him at a ball, and was wholly overcome by his performance in a minuet. They married; but a man cannot always dance, and Philotryphus had no other method of pleasing: however, as neither was in any great degree vicious, they live together with no other unhappiness than vacuity of mind, and that tastelessness of life which proceeds from a satiety of juvenile pleasures, and an utter inability to fill their place by nobler employments. As they have known the fashionable world at the same time, they agree in their notions of all those subjects on which they ever speak, and being able to add nothing to the ideas of each other, are not much inclined to conversation, but very often join in one wish, *That they could sleep more, and think less.*

Argyris, after having refused a thousand offers, at last consented to marry Cotylus, the younger brother of a duke, a man without elegance of mien, beauty of person, or force of understanding; who, while he courted her, could not always forbear allusions to her birth, and hints how cheaply she would purchase an alliance to so illustrious a family. His conduct from the hour of his marriage has been insufferably tyrannical, nor has he any other regard to her than what arises from his desire that her appearance may not disgrace him. Upon this principle, however, he always orders that she should be gaily dressed, and splendidly attended; and she has, among all her mortifications, the happiness to take place of her eldest sister.

The Rambler, No. 47

TUESDAY, AUGUST 28, 1750

[Sorrow]

Of the passions with which the mind of man is agitated, it may be observed that they naturally hasten towards their own extinction by inciting and quickening the attainment of their objects. Thus fear urges our flight, and desire animates our progress; and if there are some which perhaps may be indulged till they outgrow the good appropriated to their satisfaction, as is frequently observed of avarice and ambition, yet their immediate tendency is to some means of happiness really existing, and generally within the prospect. The miser always imagines that there is a certain sum that will fill his heart to the brim; and every ambitious man, like king Pyrrhus, has an acquisition in his thoughts that is to terminate his labours, after which he shall pass the rest of his life in ease or gaiety, in repose or devotion.

Sorrow is perhaps the only affection of the breast that can be excepted from this general remark, and it therefore deserves the particular attention of those who have assumed the arduous province of preserving the balance of the mental constitution. The other passions are diseases indeed, but they necessarily direct us to their proper cure. A man at once feels the pain and knows the medicine, to which he is carried with greater haste as the evil which requires it is more excruciating, and cures himself by unerring instinct, as the wounded stags of Crete are related by Ælian to have recourse to vulnerary herbs. But for sorrow there is no remedy provided by nature; it is often occasioned by accidents irreparable, and dwells upon objects that have lost or changed their existence; it requires what it cannot hope, that the laws of the universe should be repealed; that the dead should return, or the past should be recalled.

Sorrow is not that regret for negligence or error which may animate us to future care or activity, or that repentance of crimes for which, however irrevocable, our Creator has promised to accept it as an atonement; the pain which arises from these causes has very salutary effects, and is every hour extenuating itself by the reparation of those miscarriages that produce it. Sorrow is properly that state of the mind in which our desires are fixed upon the past, without looking forward to the future, an incessant wish that something were otherwise than it has been, a tormenting and harassing want of some enjoyment or possession which we have lost, and which no endeavours can possibly regain. Into such anguish many have sunk upon some sudden diminution of their fortune, an unexpected blast of their reputation, or the loss of children or of friends. They have suffered all sensibility of pleasure to be destroyed by a single blow, have given up for ever the hopes of substituting any other object in the room of that which they lament, resigned their lives to gloom and despondency, and worn themselves out in unavailing misery.

Yet so much is this passion the natural consequence of tenderness and endearment that, however painful and however useless, it is justly reproachful not to feel it on some occasions; and so widely and constantly has it always prevailed that the laws of some nations, and the customs of others, have limited a time for the external appearances of grief caused by the dissolution of close alliances, and the breach of domestic union.

It seems determined, by the general suffrage of mankind, that sorrow is to a certain point laudable, as the offspring of love, or at least pardonable as the effect of weakness; but that it ought not to be suffered to increase by indulgence, but must give way, after a stated time, to social duties, and the common avocations of life. It is at first unavoidable, and therefore must be allowed, whether with or without our choice; it may afterwards be admitted as a decent and affectionate testimony of kindness and esteem; something will be extorted by nature, and something may be given to the world. But all beyond the bursts of passion, or the forms of solemnity, is not only useless, but culpable; for we have no right to sacrifice, to the vain longings of affection, that time which providence allows us for the task of our station.

Yet it too often happens that sorrow, thus lawfully entering, gains such a firm possession of the mind that it is not afterwards to be ejected; the mournful ideas, first violently impressed, and afterwards willingly received, so much engross the attention as to predominate in every thought, to darken gaiety, and perplex ratiocination. An habitual sadness seizes upon the soul, and the faculties are chained to a single object, which can never be contemplated but with hopeless uneasiness.

From this state of dejection it is very difficult to rise to cheerfulness and alacrity, and therefore many who have laid down rules of intellectual health think preservatives easier than remedies, and teach us not to trust ourselves with favourite enjoyments, not to indulge the luxury of fondness, but to keep our minds always suspended in such indifference that we may change the objects about us without emotion.

An exact compliance with this rule might, perhaps, contribute to tranquillity, but surely it would never produce happiness. He that regards none so much as to be afraid of losing them must live for ever without the gentle pleasures of sympathy and confidence; he must feel no melting fondness, no warmth of benevolence, nor any of those honest joys which nature annexes to the power of pleasing. And as no man can justly claim more tenderness than he pays, he must forfeit his share in that officious and watchful kindness which love only can dictate, and those lenient endearments by which love only can soften life. He may justly be overlooked and neglected by such as have more warmth in their heart; for who would be the friend of him whom, with whatever assiduity he may be courted, and with whatever services obliged, his principles will not suffer to make equal returns, and who, when you have exhausted all the instances of good will, can only be prevailed on not to be an enemy?

An attempt to preserve life in a state of neutrality and indifference is unreasonable and vain. If by excluding joy we could shut out grief, the scheme would deserve very serious attention; but since, however we may debar ourselves from happiness, misery will find its way at many inlets, and the assaults of pain will force our regard, though we may withhold it from the invitations of pleasure, we may surely endeavour to raise life above the middle point of apathy at one time, since it will necessarily sink below it at another.

But though it cannot be reasonable not to gain happiness for fear of losing it, yet it must be confessed that in proportion to the pleasure of possession will be for some time our sorrow for the loss; it is therefore the province of the moralist to enquire whether such pains may not quickly give way to mitigation. Some have thought that the most certain way to clear the heart from its embarrassment is to drag it by force into scenes of merriment. Others imagine that such a transition is too violent, and recommend rather to soothe it into tranquillity, by making it acquainted with miseries more dreadful and afflictive, and diverting to the calamities of others the regard which we are inclined to fix too closely upon our own misfortunes.

It may be doubted whether either of those remedies will be sufficiently powerful. The efficacy of mirth it is not always easy to try, and the indulgence of melancholy may be suspected to be one of those medicines which will destroy, if it happens not to cure.

The safe and general antidote against sorrow is employment. It is commonly observed that among soldiers and seamen, though there is much kindness, there is little grief; they see their friend fall without any of that lamentation which is indulged in security and idleness, because they have no leisure to spare from the care of themselves; and whoever shall keep his thoughts equally busy will find himself equally unaffected with irretrievable losses.

Time is observed generally to wear out sorrow, and its effects might doubtless be accelerated by quickening the succession, and enlarging the variety of objects. . . .°

Sorrow is a kind of rust of the soul, which every new idea contributes in its passage to scour away. It is the putrefaction of stagnant life, and is remedied by exercise and motion.

The Rambler, No. 60

SATURDAY, OCTOBER 13, 1750

[Biography]

All joy or sorrow for the happiness or calamities of others is produced by an act of the imagination that realizes the event however fictitious, or approximates it however remote, by placing us, for a time, in the condition of him whose fortune we contemplate; so that we feel, while the deception lasts, whatever motions would be excited by the same good or evil happening to ourselves.

Our passions are therefore more strongly moved, in proportion as we can more readily adopt the pains or pleasures proposed to our minds, by recognizing them as once our own, or considering them as naturally incident to our state of life. It is not easy for the most artful writer to give us an interest in happiness or misery which we think ourselves never likely to feel, and with which we have never yet been made acquainted. Histories of the downfall of kingdoms, and revolutions of empires, are read with great tranquillity; the imperial tragedy pleases common auditors only by its pomp of ornament, and grandeur of ideas; and the man whose faculties have been engrossed by business, and whose heart never fluttered but at the rise or fall of stocks, wonders how the attention can be seized, or the affections agitated by a tale of love.

Those parallel circumstances, and kindred images, to which we readily conform our minds, are, above all other writings, to be found in narratives of the lives of particular persons; and therefore no species of writing seems more worthy of cultivation than biography, since none can be more delightful or more useful, none can more certainly enchain the heart by irresistible interest, or more widely diffuse instruction to every diversity of condition.

The general and rapid narratives of history, which involve a thousand fortunes in the business of a day, and complicate innumerable incidents in one great transaction, afford few lessons applicable to private life, which derives its comforts and its wretchedness from the right or wrong management of things which nothing but their frequency makes considerable, *Parva, si non fiant quotidie*, says Pliny, and which can have no place in those relations which never descend below the consultation of senates, the motions of armies, and the schemes of conspirators.

I have often thought that there has rarely passed a life of which a judicious and faithful narrative would not be useful. For, not only every man has, in the mighty mass of the world, great numbers in the same condition with himself, to whom his mistakes and miscarriages, escapes and expedients, would be of immediate and apparent use; but there is such an uniformity in the state of man, considered apart from adventitious and separable decorations and disguises, that there is scarce any possibility of good or ill, but is common to human kind. A great part of the time of those who are placed at the greatest distance by fortune, or by temper, must unavoidably pass in the same manner; and though, when the claims of nature are satisfied, caprice, and vanity, and accident begin to produce discriminations and peculiarities, yet the eye is not very heedful, or quick, which cannot discover the same causes still terminating their influence in the same effects, though sometimes accelerated, sometimes retarded, or perplexed by multiplied combinations. We are all prompted by the same motives, all deceived by the same fallacies, all animated by hope, obstructed by danger, entangled by desire, and seduced by pleasure.

It is frequently objected to relations of particular lives that they are not distinguished by any striking or wonderful vicissitudes. The scholar who passed his life among his books, the merchant who conducted only his own affairs, the priest whose sphere of action was not extended beyond that of his duty, are considered as no proper objects of public regard, however they might have excelled in their several stations, whatever might have been their learning, integrity, and piety. But this notion arises from false measures of excellence and dignity, and must be eradicated by considering that, in the esteem of uncorrupted reason, what is of most use is of most value.

It is, indeed, not improper to take honest advantages of prejudice, and to gain attention by a celebrated name; but the business of the biographer is often to pass slightly over those performances and incidents which produce vulgar greatness, to lead the thoughts into domestic privacies, and display the minute details of daily life, where exterior appendages are cast aside, and men excel each other only by prudence and by virtue. The account of Thuanus is, with great propriety, said by its author to have been written that it might lay open to posterity the private and familiar character of that man *cujus ingenium et candorem ex ipsius scriptis sunt olim semper miraturi*, whose candour and genius will to the end of time be by his writings preserved in admiration.

There are many invisible circumstances which, whether we read as enquirers after natural or moral knowledge, whether we intend to enlarge our science, or increase our virtue, are more important than public occurrences. Thus Sallust, the great master of nature, has not forgot, in his account of Catiline, to remark that 'his walk was now quick, and again slow', as an indication of a mind revolving something with violent commotion. Thus the story of Melancthon affords a striking lecture on the value of time, by informing us that when he made an appointment, he expected not only the hour, but the minute to be fixed, that the day might not run out in the idleness of suspense; and all the plans and enterprises of De Witt are now of less importance to the world than that part of his personal character which represents him as 'careful of his health, and negligent of his life'.

But biography has often been allotted to writers who seem very little acquainted with the nature of their task, or very negligent about the performance. They rarely afford any other account than might be collected from public papers, but imagine themselves writing a life when they exhibit a chronological series of actions or preferments; and so little regard the manners or behaviour of their heroes that more knowledge may be gained of a man's real character by a short conversation with one of his servants, than from a formal and studied narrative, begun with his pedigree and ended with his funeral.

If now and then they condescend to inform the world of particular facts, they are not always so happy as to select the most important. I know not well what advantage posterity can receive from the only circumstance by which Tickell has distinguished Addison from the rest of mankind, 'the irregularity of his pulse': nor can I think myself overpaid for the time spent in reading the life of Malherbe by being enabled to relate, after the learned biographer, that Malherbe had two predominant opinions; one, that the looseness of a single woman might destroy all the boast of ancient descent; the other, that the French beggars made use very improperly and barbarously of the phrase, 'noble gentleman', because either word included the sense of both.

There are, indeed, some natural reasons why these narratives are often written by such as were not likely to give much instruction or delight, and why most accounts of particular persons are barren and useless. If a life be delayed till interest and envy are at an end, we may hope for impartiality, but must expect little intelligence; for the incidents which give excellence to biography are of a volatile and evanescent kind, such as soon escape the memory, and are rarely transmitted by tradition. We know how few can portray a living acquaintance except by his most prominent and observable particularities, and the grosser features of his mind; and it may be easily imagined how much of this little knowledge may be lost in imparting it, and how soon a succession of copies will lose all resemblance of the original.

If the biographer writes from personal knowledge, and makes haste to gratify the public curiosity, there is danger lest his interest, his fear, his gratitude, or his tenderness, overpower his fidelity, and tempt him to conceal, if not to invent. There are many who think it an act of piety to hide the faults or failings of their friends, even when they can no longer suffer by their detection; we therefore see whole ranks of characters adorned with uniform panegyric, and not to be known from one another, but by extrinsic and casual circumstances. 'Let me remember,' says Hale,° 'when I find myself inclined to pity a criminal, that there is likewise a pity due to the country.' If we owe regard to the memory of the dead, there is yet more respect to be paid to knowledge, to virtue, and to truth.

The Rambler, No. 113

TUESDAY, APRIL 16, 1751

[Marriage (3)]

TO THE RAMBLER.

SIR,

I know not whether it is always a proof of innocence to treat censure with contempt. We owe so much reverence to the wisdom of mankind as justly to wish that our own opinion of our merit may be ratified by the concurrence of other suffrages; and since guilt and infamy must have the same effect upon intelligences unable to pierce beyond external appearance, and influenced often rather by example than precept, we are obliged to refute a false charge, lest we should countenance the crime which we have never committed. To turn away from an accusation with supercilious silence is equally in the power of him that is hardened by villainy, and inspirited by innocence. The wall of brass which Horace erects upon a clear conscience may be sometimes raised by impudence or power; and we should always wish to preserve the dignity of virtue by adorning her with graces which wickedness cannot assume.

For this reason I have determined no longer to endure, with either patient or sullen resignation, a reproach which is, at least in my opinion, unjust; but will lay my case honestly before you, that you or your readers may at length decide it.

Whether you will be able to preserve your boasted impartiality when you hear that I am considered as an adversary by half the female world, you may surely pardon me for doubting, notwithstanding the veneration to which you may imagine yourself entitled by your age, your learning, your abstraction, or your virtue. Beauty, Mr Rambler, has often overpowered the resolutions of the firm, and the reasonings of the wise, roused the old to sensibility, and subdued the rigorous to softness.

I am one of those unhappy beings who have been marked out as husbands for many different women, and deliberated a hundred times on the brink of matrimony. I have discussed all the nuptial preliminaries so often that I can repeat the forms in which jointures are settled, pin-money secured, and provisions for younger children ascertained; but am at last doomed by general consent to everlasting solitude, and excluded by an irreversible decree from all hopes of connubial felicity. I am pointed out by every mother as a man whose visits cannot be admitted without reproach; who raises hopes only to embitter disappointment, and makes offers only to seduce girls into a waste of that part of life in which they might gain advantageous matches, and become mistresses and mothers.

I hope you will think that some part of this penal severity may justly be remitted when I inform you that I never yet professed love to a woman without sincere intentions of marriage; that I have never continued an appearance of intimacy from the hour that my inclination changed, but to preserve her whom I was leaving from the shock of abruptness, or the ignominy of contempt; that I always endeavoured to give the ladies an opportunity of seeming to discard me; and that I never forsook a mistress for larger fortune, or brighter beauty, but because I discovered some irregularity in her conduct, or some depravity in her mind; not because I was charmed by another, but because I was offended by herself.

I was very early tired of that succession of amusements by which the thoughts of most young men are dissipated, and had not long glittered in the splendour of an ample patrimony before I wished for the calm of domestic happiness. Youth is naturally delighted with sprightliness and ardour, and therefore I breathed out the sighs of my first affection at the feet of the gay, the sparkling, the vivacious Ferocula. I fancied to myself a perpetual source of happiness in wit never exhausted, and spirit never depressed; looked with veneration on her readiness of expedients, contempt of difficulty, assurance of address, and promptitude of reply; considered her as exempt by some prerogative of nature from the weakness and timidity of female minds; and congratulated myself upon a companion superior to all common troubles and embarrassments. I was, indeed, somewhat disturbed by the unshaken perseverance with which she enforced her demands of an unreasonable settlement; yet I should have consented to pass my life in union with her, had not my curiosity led me to a crowd gathered in the street, where I found Ferocula, in the presence of hundreds, disputing for six pence with a chairman. I saw her in so little need of assistance that it was no breach of the laws of chivalry to forbear interposition, and I spared myself the shame of owning her acquaintance. I forgot some point of ceremony at our next interview, and soon provoked her to forbid me her presence.

My next attempt was upon a lady of great eminence for learning and philosophy. I had frequently observed the barrenness and uniformity of connubial conversation, and therefore thought highly of my own prudence and discernment when I selected from a multitude of wealthy beauties the deep-read Misothea,° who declared herself the inexorable enemy of ignorant pertness, and puerile levity; and scarcely condescended to make tea, but for the linguist, the geometrician, the astronomer, or the poet. The queen of the Amazons was only to be gained by the hero who could conquer her in single combat; and Misothea's heart was only to bless the scholar who could overpower her by disputation. Amidst the fondest transports of courtship she could call for a definition of terms, and treated every argument with contempt that could not be reduced to regular syllogism. You may easily imagine that I wished this courtship at an end; but when I desired her to shorten my torments, and fix the day of my felicity, we were led into a long conversation, in which Misothea endeavoured to demonstrate the folly of attributing choice and self-direction to any human being. It was not difficult to discover the danger of committing myself for ever to the arms of one who might at any time mistake the dictates of passion, or the calls of appetite, for the decree of fate; or consider cuckoldom as necessary to the general system, as a link in the everlasting chain of successive causes. I therefore told her that destiny had ordained us to part; and that nothing should have torn me from her but the talons of necessity.

I then solicited the regard of the calm, the prudent, the economical Sophronia, a lady who considered wit as dangerous, and learning as superfluous; and thought that the woman who kept her house clean, and her accounts exact, took receipts for every payment, and could find them at a sudden call, enquired nicely after the condition of the tenants, read the price of stocks once a week, and purchased every thing at the best market, could want no accomplishments necessary to the happiness of a wise man. She discoursed with great solemnity on the care and vigilance which the superintendence of a family demands; observed how many were ruined by confidence in servants; and told me that she never expected honesty but from a strong chest, and that the best storekeeper was the mistress's eye. Many such oracles of generosity she uttered, and made every day new improvements in her schemes for the regulation of her servants, and the distribution of her time. I was convinced that whatever I might suffer from Sophronia, I should escape poverty; and we therefore proceeded to adjust the settlements according to her own rule, *fair and softly*. But one morning her maid came to me in tears to intreat my interest for a reconciliation to her mistress, who had turned her out at night for breaking six teeth in a tortoise-shell comb: she had attended her lady from a distant province, and having not lived long enough to save much money, was destitute among strangers, and though of a good family, in danger of perishing in the streets, or of being compelled by hunger to prostitution. I made no scruple of promising to restore her; but upon my first application to Sophronia was answered with an air which called for approbation that if she neglected her own affairs, I might suspect her of neglecting mine; that the comb stood her in three half-crowns; that no servant should wrong her twice; and that indeed, she took the first opportunity of parting with Phyllida, because, though she was honest, her constitution was bad, and she thought her very likely to fall sick. Of our conference I need not tell you the effect; it surely may be forgiven me, if on this occasion I forgot the decency of common forms.

From two more ladies I was disengaged by finding that they entertained my rivals at the same time, and determined their choice by the liberality of our settlements. Another I thought myself justified in forsaking, because she gave my attorney a bribe to favour her in the bargain; another, because I could never soften her to tenderness, till she heard that most of my family had died young; and another, because to increase her fortune by expectations, she represented her sister as languishing and consumptive.

I shall in another letter give the remaining part of my history of courtship. I presume that I should hitherto have injured the majesty of female virtue, had I not hoped to transfer my affection to higher merit.

I am, &c.
HYMENAEUS.°

The Rambler, No. 114

SATURDAY, APRIL 20, 1751

[Capital Punishment]

Power and superiority are so flattering and delightful that, fraught with temptation and exposed to danger as they are, scarcely any virtue is so cautious, or any prudence so timorous, as to decline them. Even those that have most reverence for the laws of right are pleased with showing that not fear, but choice, regulates their behaviour; and would be thought to comply, rather than obey. We love to overlook the boundaries which we do not wish to pass; and, as the Roman satirist remarks, he that has no design to take the life of another is yet glad to have it in his hands.

From the same principle, tending yet more to degeneracy and corruption, proceeds the desire of investing lawful authority with terror, and governing by force rather than persuasion. Pride is unwilling to believe the necessity of assigning any other reason than her own will; and would rather maintain the most equitable claims by violence and penalties, than descend from the dignity of command to dispute and expostulation.

It may, I think, be suspected that this political arrogance has sometimes found its way into legislative assemblies, and mingled with deliberations upon property and life. A slight perusal of the laws by which the measures of vindictive and coercive justice are established will discover so many disproportions between crimes and punishments, such capricious distinctions of guilt, and such confusion of remissness and severity, as can scarcely be believed to have been produced by public wisdom sincerely and calmly studious of public happiness.

The learned, the judicious, the pious Boerhaave relates that he never saw a criminal dragged to execution without asking himself,

'Who knows whether this man is not less culpable than me?' On the days when the prisons of this city are emptied into the grave, let every spectator of the dreadful procession put the same question to his own heart. Few among those that crowd in thousands to the legal massacre, and look with carelessness, perhaps with triumph, on the utmost exacerbations of human misery, would then be able to return without horror and dejection. For who can congratulate himself upon a life passed without some act more mischievous to the peace or prosperity of others than the theft of a piece of money?

It has been always the practice, when any particular species of robbery becomes prevalent and common, to endeavour its suppression by capital denunciations. Thus, one generation of malefactors is commonly cut off, and their successors are frighted into new expedients; the art of thievery is augmented with greater variety of fraud, and subtilized to higher degrees of dexterity, and more occult methods of conveyance. The law then renews the pursuit in the heat of anger, and overtakes the offender again with death. By this practice, capital inflictions are multiplied, and crimes very different in their degrees of enormity are equally subjected to the severest punishment that man has the power of exercising upon man.

The lawgiver is undoubtedly allowed to estimate the malignity of an offence, not merely by the loss or pain which single acts may produce, but by the general alarm and anxiety arising from the fear of mischief, and insecurity of possession: he therefore exercises the right which societies are supposed to have over the lives of those that compose them, not simply to punish a transgression, but to maintain order, and preserve quiet; he enforces those laws with severity that are most in danger of violation, as the commander of a garrison doubles the guard on that side which is threatened by the enemy.

This method has been long tried, but tried with so little success that rapine and violence are hourly increasing; yet few seem willing to despair of its efficacy, and of those who employ their speculations upon the present corruption of the people, some propose the introduction of more horrid, lingering and terrific punishments; some are inclined to accelerate the executions; some to discourage pardons; and all seem to think that lenity has given confidence to wickedness, and that we can only be rescued from the talons of robbery by inflexible rigour, and sanguinary justice.

Yet since the right of setting an uncertain and arbitrary value upon life has been disputed, and since experience of past times gives us little reason to hope that any reformation will be effected by a periodical havoc of our fellow-beings, perhaps it will not be useless to consider what consequences might arise from relaxations of the law, and a more rational and equitable adaptation of penalties to offences.

Death is, as one of the ancients observes, τὸ τῶν φοβερῶν φοβερώτατον, 'of dreadful things the most dreadful'; an evil beyond which nothing can be threatened by sublunary power, or feared from human enmity or vengeance. This terror should, therefore, be reserved as the last resort of authority, as the strongest and most operative of prohibitory sanctions, and placed before the treasure of life, to guard from invasion what cannot be restored. To equal robbery with murder is to reduce murder to robbery, to confound in common minds the gradations of iniquity, and incite the commission of a greater crime to prevent the detection of a less. If only murder were punished with death, very few robbers would stain their hands in blood; but when by the last act of cruelty no new danger is incurred, and greater security may be obtained, upon what principle shall we bid them forbear?

It may be urged that the sentence is often mitigated to simple robbery; but surely this is to confess that our laws are unreasonable in our own opinion; and indeed, it may be observed that all but murderers have, at their last hour, the common sensations of mankind pleading in their favour.

From this conviction of the inequality of the punishment to the offence proceeds the frequent solicitation of pardons. They who would rejoice at the correction of a thief are yet shocked at the thought of destroying him. His crime shrinks to nothing, compared with his misery; and severity defeats itself by exciting pity.

The gibbet, indeed, certainly disables those who die upon it from infesting the community; but their death seems not to contribute more to the reformation of their associates than any other method of separation. A thief seldom passes much of his time in recollection or anticipation, but from robbery hastens to riot, and from riot to robbery; nor, when the grave closes upon his companion, has any other care than to find another.

The frequency of capital punishments therefore rarely hinders the commission of a crime, but naturally and commonly prevents its detection, and is, if we proceed only upon prudential principles, chiefly for that reason to be avoided. Whatever may be urged by casuists or politicians, the greater part of mankind, as they can never think that to pick the pocket and to pierce the heart is equally criminal, will scarcely believe that two malefactors so different in guilt can be justly doomed to the same punishment; nor is the necessity of submitting the conscience to human laws so plainly evinced, so clearly stated, or so generally allowed, but that the pious, the tender, and the just will always scruple to concur with the community in an act which their private judgment cannot approve.

He who knows not how often rigorous laws produce total impunity, and how many crimes are concealed and forgotten for fear of hurrying the offender to that state in which there is no repentance, has conversed very little with mankind. And whatever epithets of reproach or contempt this compassion may incur from those who confound cruelty with firmness, I know not whether any wise man would wish it less powerful, or less extensive.

If those whom the wisdom of our laws has condemned to die had been detected in their rudiments of robbery, they might by proper discipline and useful labour have been disentangled from their habits, they might have escaped all the temptations to subsequent crimes, and passed their days in reparation and penitence; and detected they might all have been, had the prosecutors been certain that their lives would have been spared. I believe every thief will confess that he has been more than once seized and dismissed; and that he has sometimes ventured upon capital crimes because he knew that those whom he injured would rather connive at his escape than cloud their minds with the horrors of his death.

All laws against wickedness are ineffectual unless some will inform, and some will prosecute; but till we mitigate the penalties for mere violations of property, information will always be hated, and prosecution dreaded. The heart of a good man cannot but recoil at the thought of punishing a slight injury with death; especially when he remembers that the thief might have procured safety by another crime, from which he was restrained only by his remaining virtue.

The obligations to assist the exercise of public justice are indeed strong; but they will certainly be overpowered by tenderness for life. What is punished with severity contrary to our ideas of adequate retribution will be seldom discovered; and multitudes will be suffered to advance from crime to crime till they deserve death, because if they had been sooner prosecuted, they would have suffered death before they deserved it.

This scheme of invigorating the laws by relaxation, and extirpating wickedness by lenity, is so remote from common practice that I might reasonably fear to expose it to the public, could it be supported only by my own observations: I shall, therefore, by ascribing it to its author, Sir Thomas More,° endeavour to procure it that attention which I wish always paid to prudence, to justice, and to mercy.

The Rambler, No. 121

TUESDAY, MAY 14, 1751

[Literary Imitation]

I have been informed by a letter from one of the universities that among the youth from whom the next swarm of reasoners is to learn philosophy, and the next flight of beauties to hear elegies and sonnets,° there are many who, instead of endeavouring by books and meditation to form their own opinions, content themselves with the secondary knowledge which a convenient bench in a coffee-house can supply; and, without any examination or distinction, adopt the criticisms and remarks which happen to drop from those who have risen, by merit or fortune, to reputation and authority.

These humble retailers of knowledge my correspondent stigmatizes with the name of Echoes; and seems desirous that they should be made ashamed of lazy submission, and animated to attempts after new discoveries, and original sentiments.

It is very natural for young men to be vehement, acrimonious, and severe. For, as they seldom comprehend at once all the consequences of a position, or perceive the difficulties by which cooler and more experienced reasoners are restrained from confidence, they form their conclusions with great precipitance. Seeing nothing that can darken or embarrass the question, they expect to find their own opinion universally prevalent, and are inclined to impute uncertainty and hesitation to want of honesty, rather than of knowledge. I may, perhaps, therefore be reproached by my lively correspondent, when it shall be found that I have no inclination to persecute these collectors of fortuitous knowledge with the severity required; yet, as I am now too old to be much pained by hasty censure, I shall not be afraid of taking into protection those whom I think condemned without a sufficient knowledge of their cause.

He that adopts the sentiments of another whom he has reason to believe wiser than himself is only to be blamed when he claims the honours which are not due but to the author, and endeavours to deceive the world into praise and veneration; for to learn is the proper business of youth; and whether we increase our knowledge by books, or by conversation, we are equally indebted to foreign assistance.

The greater part of students are not born with abilities to construct systems, or advance knowledge; nor can have any hope beyond that of becoming intelligent hearers in the schools of art, of being able to comprehend what others discover, and to remember what others teach. Even those to whom Providence has allotted greater strength of understanding can expect only to improve a single science. In every other part of learning, they must be content to follow opinions which they are not able to examine; and even in that which they claim as peculiarly their own can seldom add more than some small particle of knowledge to the hereditary stock devolved to them from ancient times, the collective labour of a thousand intellects.

In science, which, being fixed and limited, admits of no other variety than such as arises from new methods of distribution, or new arts of illustration, the necessity of following the traces of our predecessors is indisputably evident; but there appears no reason why imagination should be subject to the same restraint. It might be conceived that of those who profess to forsake the narrow paths of truth every one may deviate towards a different point, since though rectitude is uniform and fixed, obliquity may be infinitely diversified. The roads of science are narrow, so that they who travel them must either follow or meet one another; but in the boundless regions of possibility which fiction claims for her dominion, there are surely a thousand recesses unexplored, a thousand flowers unplucked, a thousand fountains unexhausted, combinations of imagery yet unobserved, and races of ideal inhabitants not hitherto described.

Yet, whatever hope may persuade, or reason evince, experience can boast of very few additions to ancient fable. The wars of Troy, and the travels of Ulysses, have furnished almost all succeeding poets with incidents, characters, and sentiments. The Romans are confessed to have attempted little more than to display in their own tongue the inventions of the Greeks. There is, in all their writings, such a perpetual recurrence of allusions to the tales of the fabulous age that they must be confessed often to want that power of giving pleasure which novelty supplies; nor can we wonder that they excelled so much in the graces of diction, when we consider how rarely they were employed in search of new thoughts.

The warmest admirers of the great Mantuan poet° can extol him for little more than the skill with which he has, by making his hero both a traveller and a warrior, united the beauties of the *Iliad* and *Odyssey* in one composition: yet his judgment was perhaps sometimes overborne by his avarice of the Homeric treasures; and, for fear of suffering a sparkling ornament to be lost, he has inserted it where it cannot shine with its original splendor.

When Ulysses visited the infernal regions, he found, among the heroes that perished at Troy, his competitor Ajax, who, when the arms of Achilles were adjudged to Ulysses, died by his own hand in the madness of disappointment. He still appeared to resent, as on earth, his loss and disgrace. Ulysses endeavoured to pacify him with praises and submission; but Ajax walked away without reply. This passage has always been considered as eminently beautiful; because Ajax, the haughty chief, the unlettered soldier, of unshaken courage, of immovable constancy, but without the power of recommending his own virtues by eloquence, or enforcing his assertions by any other argument than the sword, had no way of making his anger known but by gloomy sullenness, and dumb ferocity. His hatred of a man whom he conceived to have defeated him only by volubility of tongue was therefore naturally shown by silence more contemptuous and piercing than any words that so rude an orator could have found, and by which he gave his enemy no opportunity of exerting the only power in which he was superior.

When Æneas is sent by Virgil to the shades, he meets Dido the queen of Carthage, whom his perfidy had hurried to the grave; he accosts her with tenderness and excuses; but the lady turns away like Ajax in mute disdain. She turns away like Ajax, but she resembles him in none of those qualities which give either dignity or propriety to silence. She might, without any departure from the tenor of her conduct, have burst out like other injured women into clamour, reproach, and denunciation; but Virgil had his imagination full of Ajax, and therefore could not prevail on himself to teach Dido any other mode of resentment.

If Virgil could be thus seduced by imitation, there will be little hope that common wits should escape; and accordingly we find that besides the universal and acknowledged practice of copying the ancients, there has prevailed in every age a particular species of fiction. At one time all truth was conveyed in allegory; at another, nothing was seen but in a vision; at one period, all the poets followed sheep, and every event produced a pastoral; at another they busied themselves wholly in giving directions to a painter.

It is indeed easy to conceive why any fashion should become popular by which idleness is favoured, and imbecility assisted; but surely no man of genius can much applaud himself for repeating a tale with which the audience is already tired, and which could bring no honour to any but its inventor.

There are, I think, two schemes of writing on which the laborious wits of the present time employ their faculties. One is the adaptation of sense to all the rhymes which our language can supply to some word that makes the burden of the stanza; but this, as it has been only used in a kind of amorous burlesque, can scarcely be censured with much acrimony. The other is the imitation of Spenser,° which, by the influence of some men of learning and genius, seems likely to gain upon the age, and therefore deserves to be more attentively considered.

To imitate the fictions and sentiments of Spenser can incur no reproach, for allegory is perhaps one of the most pleasing vehicles of instruction. But I am very far from extending the same respect to his diction or his stanza. His style was in his own time allowed to be vicious, so darkened with old words and peculiarities of phrase, and so remote from common use, that Jonson boldly pronounces him 'to have written no language'. His stanza is at once difficult and unpleasing; tiresome to the ear by its uniformity, and to the attention by its length. It was at first formed in imitation of the Italian poets, without due regard to the genius of our language. The Italians have little variety of termination, and were forced to contrive such a stanza as might admit the greatest number of similar rhymes; but our words end with so much diversity that it is seldom convenient for us to bring more than two of the same sound together. If it be justly observed by Milton that rhyme obliges poets to express their thoughts in improper terms, these improprieties must always be multiplied as the difficulty of rhyme is increased by long concatenations.

The imitators of Spenser are indeed not very rigid censors of themselves, for they seem to conclude that when they have disfigured their lines with a few obsolete syllables, they have accomplished their design, without considering that they ought not only to admit old words, but to avoid new. The laws of imitation are broken by every word introduced since the time of Spenser, as the character of Hector is violated by quoting Aristotle in the play.° It would indeed be difficult to exclude from a long poem all modern phrases, though it is easy to sprinkle it with gleanings of antiquity. Perhaps, however, the style of Spenser might by long labour be justly copied; but life is surely given us for higher purposes than to gather what our ancestors have wisely thrown away, and to learn what is of no value but because it has been forgotten.

The Rambler, No. 129

TUESDAY, JUNE 11, 1751

[The Need for Enterprise]

Moralists, like other writers, instead of casting their eyes abroad in the living world, and endeavouring to form maxims of practice and new hints of theory, content their curiosity with that secondary knowledge which books afford, and think themselves entitled to reverence by a new arrangement of an ancient system, or new illustration of established principles. The sage precepts of the first instructors of the world are transmitted from age to age with little variation, and echoed from one author to another, not perhaps without some loss of their original force at every repercussion.

I know not whether any other reason than this idleness of imitation can be assigned for that uniform and constant partiality by which some vices have hitherto escaped censure, and some virtues wanted recommendation; nor can I discover why else we have been warned only against part of our enemies, while the rest have been suffered to steal upon us without notice; why the heart has on one side been doubly fortified, and laid open on the other to the incursions of error, and the ravages of vice.

Among the favourite topics of moral declamation may be numbered the miscarriages of imprudent boldness, and the folly of attempts beyond our power. Every page of every philosopher is crowded with examples of temerity that sunk under burdens which she laid upon herself, and called out enemies to battle by whom she was destroyed.

Their remarks are too just to be disputed, and too salutary to be rejected; but there is likewise some danger lest timorous prudence should be inculcated till courage and enterprise are wholly repressed, and the mind congealed in perpetual inactivity by the fatal influence of frigorific wisdom.

Every man should, indeed, carefully compare his force with his undertaking; for though we ought not to live only for our own sakes, and though therefore danger or difficulty should not be avoided merely because we may expose ourselves to misery or disgrace; yet it may be justly required of us not to throw away our lives upon inadequate and hopeless designs, since we might by a just estimate of our abilities become more useful to mankind.

There is an irrational contempt of danger which approaches nearly to the folly, if not the guilt, of suicide; there is a ridiculous perseverance in impracticable schemes which is justly punished with ignominy and reproach. But in the wide regions of probability which are the proper province of prudence and election, there is always room to deviate on either side of rectitude without rushing against apparent absurdity; and according to the inclinations of nature, or the impressions of precept, the daring and the cautious may move in different directions without touching upon rashness or cowardice.

That there is a middle path which it is every man's duty to find and to keep is unanimously confessed; but it is likewise acknowledged that this middle path is so narrow that it cannot easily be discovered, and so little beaten that there are no certain marks by which it can be followed; the care therefore of all those who conduct others has been that whenever they decline into obliquities, they should tend towards the side of safety.

It can, indeed, raise no wonder that temerity has been generally censured; for it is one of the vices with which few can be charged, and which therefore great numbers are ready to condemn. It is the vice of noble and generous minds, the exuberance of magnanimity, and the ebullition of genius; and is therefore not regarded with much tenderness, because it never flatters us by that appearance of softness and imbecility which is commonly necessary to conciliate compassion. But if the same attention had been applied to the search of arguments against the folly of presupposing impossibilities, and anticipating frustration, I know not whether many would not have been roused to usefulness who, having been taught to confound prudence with timidity, never ventured to excel, lest they should unfortunately fail.

It is necessary to distinguish our own interest from that of others, and that distinction will perhaps assist us in fixing the just limits of caution and adventurousness. In an undertaking that involves the happiness, or the safety of many, we have certainly no right to hazard more than is allowed by those who partake the danger; but where only ourselves can suffer by miscarriage, we are not confined within such narrow limits; and still less is the reproach of temerity when numbers will receive advantage by success, and only one be incommoded by failure.

Men are generally willing to hear precepts by which ease is favoured; and as no resentment is raised by general representations of human folly, even in those who are most eminently jealous of comparative reputation, we confess, without reluctance, that vain man is ignorant of his own weakness, and therefore frequently presumes to attempt what he can never accomplish; but it ought likewise to be remembered that man is no less ignorant of his own powers, and might perhaps have accomplished a thousand designs which the prejudices of cowardice restrained him from attempting.

It is observed in the golden verses of Pythagoras that 'Power is never far from necessity'. The vigour of the human mind quickly appears when there is no longer any place for doubt and hesitation, when diffidence is absorbed in the sense of danger, or overwhelmed by some resistless passion. We then soon discover that difficulty is, for the most part, the daughter of idleness, that the obstacles with which our way seemed to be obstructed were only phantoms which we believed real because we durst not advance to a close examination; and we learn that it is impossible to determine without experience how much constancy may endure, or perseverance perform.

But whatever pleasure may be found in the review of distresses when art or courage has surmounted them, few will be persuaded to wish that they may be awakened by want or terror to the conviction of their own abilities. Every one should therefore endeavour to invigorate himself by reason and reflection, and determine to exert the latent force that nature may have reposited in him before the hour of exigence comes upon him, and compulsion shall torture him to diligence. It is below the dignity of a reasonable being to owe that strength to necessity which ought always to act at the call of choice, or to need any other motive to industry than the desire of performing his duty.

Reflections that may drive away despair cannot be wanting to him who considers how much life is now advanced beyond the state of naked, undisciplined, uninstructed nature. Whatever has been effected for convenience or elegance, while it was yet unknown, was believed impossible; and therefore would never have been attempted, had not some, more daring than the rest, adventured to bid defiance to prejudice and censure. Nor is there yet any reason to doubt that the same labour would be rewarded with the same success. There are qualities in the products of nature yet undiscovered, and combinations in the powers of art yet untried. It is the duty of every man to endeavour that something may be added by his industry to the hereditary aggregate of knowledge and happiness. To add much can indeed be the lot of few, but to add something, however little, every one may hope; and of every honest endeavour it is certain that, however unsuccessful, it will be at last rewarded.

[The Need for General Knowledge]

That wonder is the effect of ignorance has been often observed. The awful stillness of attention with which the mind is overspread at the first view of an unexpected effect ceases when we have leisure to disentangle complications and investigate causes. Wonder is a pause of reason, a sudden cessation of the mental progress, which lasts only while the understanding is fixed upon some single idea, and is at an end when it recovers force enough to divide the object into its parts, or mark the intermediate gradations from the first agent to the last consequence.

It may be remarked with equal truth that ignorance is often the effect of wonder. It is common for those who have never accustomed themselves to the labour of enquiry, nor invigorated their confidence by conquests over difficulty, to sleep in the gloomy quiescence of astonishment, without any effort to animate enquiry or dispel obscurity. What they cannot immediately conceive, they consider as too high to be reached, or too extensive to be comprehended; they therefore content themselves with the gaze of folly, forbear to attempt what they have no hopes of performing, and resign the pleasure of rational contemplation to more pertinacious study or more active faculties.

Among the productions of mechanic art, many are of a form so different from that of their first materials, and many consist of parts so numerous and so nicely adapted to each other, that it is not possible to view them without amazement. But when we enter the shops of artificers, observe the various tools by which every operation is facilitated, and trace the progress of a manufacture through the different hands that, in succession to each other, contribute to its perfection, we soon discover that every single man has an easy task, and that the extremes however remote of natural rudeness and artificial elegance are joined by a regular concatenation of effects, of which every one is introduced by that which precedes it, and equally introduces that which is to follow.

The same is the state of intellectual and manual performances. Long calculations or complex diagrams affright the timorous and unexperienced from a second view; but if we have skill sufficient to analyse them into simple principles, it will be discovered that our fear was groundless. *Divide and conquer* is a principle equally just in science as in policy. Complication is a species of confederacy, which, while it continues united, bids defiance to the most active and vigorous intellect; but of which every member is separately weak, and which may therefore be quickly subdued if it can once be broken.

The chief art of learning, as Locke has observed, is to attempt but little at a time. The widest excursions of the mind are made by short flights frequently repeated; the most lofty fabrics of science are formed by the continued accumulation of single propositions.

It often happens, whatever be the cause, that impatience of labour or dread of miscarriage seizes those who are most distinguished for quickness of apprehension; and that they who might with greatest reason promise themselves victory are least willing to hazard the encounter. This diffidence, where the attention is not laid asleep by laziness or dissipated by pleasures, can arise only from confused and general views, such as negligence snatches in haste, or from the disappointment of the first hopes formed by arrogance without reflection. To expect that the intricacies of science will be pierced by a careless glance, or the eminences of fame ascended without labour, is to expect a peculiar privilege, a power denied to the rest of mankind; but to suppose that the maze is inscrutable to diligence, or the heights inaccessible to perseverance, is to submit tamely to the tyranny of fancy, and enchain the mind in voluntary shackles.

It is the proper ambition of the heroes in literature to enlarge the boundaries of knowledge by discovering and conquering new regions of the intellectual world. To the success of such undertakings perhaps some degree of fortuitous happiness is necessary, which no man can promise or procure to himself; and therefore doubt and irresolution may be forgiven in him that ventures into the unexplored abysses of truth, and attempts to find his way through the fluctuations of uncertainty, and the conflicts of contradiction. But when nothing more is required than to pursue a path already beaten, and to trample obstacles which others have demolished, why should any man so much distrust his own intellect as to imagine himself unequal to the attempt?

It were to be wished that they who devote their lives to study would at once believe nothing too great for their attainment, and consider nothing as too little for their regard; that they would extend their notice alike to science and to life, and unite some knowledge of the present world to their acquaintance with past ages and remote events.

Nothing has so much exposed men of learning to contempt and ridicule as their ignorance of things which are known to all but themselves. Those who have been taught to consider the institutions of the schools as giving the last perfection to human abilities are surprised to see men wrinkled with study yet wanting to be instructed in the minute circumstances of propriety, or the necessary forms of daily transaction; and quickly shake off their reverence for modes of education which they find to produce no ability above the rest of mankind.

'Books,' says Bacon, 'can never teach the use of books.' The student must learn by commerce with mankind to reduce his speculations to practice, and accommodate his knowledge to the purposes of life.

It is too common for those who have been bred to scholastic professions, and passed much of their time in academies where nothing but learning confers honours, to disregard every other qualification, and to imagine that they shall find mankind ready to pay homage to their knowledge, and to crowd about them for instruction. They, therefore, step out from their cells into the open world with all the confidence of authority and dignity of importance; they look round about them at once with ignorance and scorn on a race of beings to whom they are equally unknown and equally contemptible, but whose manners they must imitate, and with whose opinions they must comply, if they desire to pass their time happily among them.

To lessen that disdain with which scholars are inclined to look on the common business of the world, and the unwillingness with which they condescend to learn what is not to be found in any system of philosophy, it may be necessary to consider that though admiration is excited by abstruse researches and remote discoveries, yet pleasure is not given, nor affection conciliated, but by softer accomplishments, and qualities more easily communicable to those about us. He that can only converse upon questions about which only a small part of mankind has knowledge sufficient to make them curious must lose his days in unsocial silence, and live in the crowd of life without a companion. He that can only be useful in great occasions may die without exerting his abilities, and stand a helpless spectator of a thousand vexations which fret away happiness, and which nothing is required to remove but a little dexterity of conduct and readiness of expedients.

No degree of knowledge attainable by man is able to set him above the want of hourly assistance, or to extinguish the desire of fond endearments, and tender officiousness; and therefore no one should think it unnecessary to learn those arts by which friendship may be gained. Kindness is preserved by a constant reciprocation of benefits or interchange of pleasures; but such benefits only can be bestowed as others are capable to receive, and such pleasures only imparted as others are qualified to enjoy.

By this descent from the pinnacles of art no honour will be lost; for the condescensions of learning are always overpaid by gratitude. An elevated genius employed in little things appears, to use the simile of Longinus, like the sun in his evening declination; he remits his splendour but retains his magnitude, and pleases more, though he dazzles less.

The Rambler, No. 142

SATURDAY, JULY 27, 1751

[A Rural Tyrant]

TO THE RAMBLER

SIR,

Having been accustomed to retire annually from the town, I lately accepted the invitation of Eugenio, who has an estate and seat in a distant county. As we were unwilling to travel without improvement, we turned often from the direct road to please ourselves with the view of nature or of art; we examined every wild mountain and medicinal spring, criticised every edifice, contemplated every ruin, and compared every scene of action with the narratives of historians. By this succession of amusements we enjoyed the exercise of a journey without suffering the fatigue, and had nothing to regret but that by a progress so leisurely and gentle, we missed the adventures of a post chaise, and the pleasure of alarming villages with the tumult of our passage, and of disguising our insignificance by the dignity of hurry.

The first week after our arrival at Eugenio's house was passed in receiving visits from his neighbours, who crowded about him with all the eagerness of benevolence; some impatient to learn the news of the court and town, that they might be qualified by authentic information to dictate to the rural politicians on the next bowling day; others desirous of his interest to accommodate disputes, or of his advice in the settlement of their fortunes and the marriage of their children.

The civilities which we had received were soon to be returned; and

I passed some time with great satisfaction in roving through the country, and viewing the seats, gardens and plantations which are scattered over it. My pleasure would indeed have been greater had I been sometimes allowed to wander in a park or wilderness alone, but to appear as the friend of Eugenio was an honour not to be enjoyed without some inconveniences; so much was every one solicitous for my regard that I could seldom escape to solitude, or steal a moment from the emulation of complaisance, and the vigilance of officiousness.

In these rambles of good neighbourhood, we frequently passed by a house of unusual magnificence. While I had my curiosity yet distracted among many novelties, it did not much attract my observation; but in a short time I could not forbear surveying it with particular notice; for the length of the wall which enclosed the gardens, the disposition of the shades that waved over it, and the canals of which I could obtain some glimpses through the trees from our own windows gave me reason to expect more grandeur and beauty than I had yet seen in that province. I therefore enquired, as we rode by it, why we never amongst our excursions spent an hour where there was such appearance of splendor and affluence. Eugenio told me that the seat which I so much admired was commonly called in the country the 'haunted house', and that no visits were paid there by any of the gentlemen whom I had yet seen. As the haunts of incorporeal beings are generally ruinous, neglected and desolate, I easily conceived that there was something to be explained, and told him that I supposed it only fairy ground, on which we might venture by day light without danger. The danger, says he, is indeed only that of appearing to solicit the acquaintance of a man with whom it is not possible to converse without infamy, and who has driven from him, by his insolence or malignity, every human being who can live without him.

Our conversation was then accidentally interrupted; but my inquisitive humour, being now in motion, could not rest without a full account of this newly discovered prodigy. I was soon informed that the fine house and spacious gardens were haunted by Squire Bluster,° of whom it was very easy to learn the character, since nobody had regard for him sufficient to hinder them from telling whatever they could discover.

Squire Bluster is descended of an ancient family. The estate which his ancestors had immemorially possessed was much augmented by Captain Bluster, who served under Drake in the reign of Elizabeth; and the Blusters, who were before only petty gentlemen, have from that time frequently represented the shire in parliament, been chosen to present addresses, and given laws at hunting-matches and races. They were eminently hospitable and popular, till the father of this gentleman died of a fever which he caught in the crowd of an election. His lady went to the grave soon after him, and left the heir, then only ten years old, to the care of his grandmother, who would not suffer him to be controlled, because she could not bear to hear him cry; and never sent him to school, because she was not able to live without his company. She taught him however very early to inspect the steward's accounts, to dog the butler from the cellar, and to catch the servants at a junket; so that he was at the age of eighteen a complete master of all the lower arts of domestic policy, had often on the road detected combinations between the coachman and the ostler, and procured the discharge of nineteen maids for illicit correspondence with cottagers and charwomen.

By the opportunities of parsimony which minority affords, and which the probity of his guardians had diligently improved, a very large sum of money was accumulated, and he found himself, when he took his affairs into his own hands, the richest man in the county. It has been long the custom of this family to celebrate the heir's completion of his twenty-first year by an entertainment at which the house is thrown open to all that are inclined to enter it, and the whole province flocks together as to a general festivity. On this occasion young Bluster exhibited the first tokens of his future eminence by shaking his purse at an old gentleman, who had been the intimate friend of his father, and offering to wager a greater sum than he could afford to venture; a practice with which he has at one time or other insulted every freeholder within ten miles round him.

His next acts of offence were committed in a contentious and spiteful vindication of the privileges of his manors, and a rigorous and relentless prosecution of every man that presumed to violate his game. As he happens to have no estate adjoining equal to his own, his oppressions are often borne without resistance for fear of a long suit, of which he delights to count the expenses without the least solicitude about the event; for he knows that where nothing but an honorary right is contested, the poorer antagonist must always suffer, whatever shall be the last decision of the law.

By the success of some of these disputes, he has so elated his insolence, and by reflection upon the general hatred which they have brought upon him, so irritated his virulence that his whole life is spent in meditating or executing mischief. It is his common practice to procure his hedges to be broken in the night, and then to demand satisfaction for damages which his grounds have suffered from his neighbour's cattle. An old widow was yesterday soliciting Eugenio to enable her to replevin her only cow then in the pound by Squire Bluster's order, who had sent one of his agents to take advantage of her calamity, and persuade her to sell the cow at an under rate. He has driven a day-labourer from his cottage for gathering blackberries in a hedge for his children; and has now an old woman in the county-jail for a trespass which she committed by coming into his grounds to pick up acorns for her hog.

Money, in whatever hands, will confer power. Distress will fly to immediate refuge, without much consideration of remote consequences. Bluster has therefore a despotic authority in many families whom he has assisted, on pressing occasions, with larger sums than they can easily repay. The only visits that he makes are to these houses of misfortune, where he enters with the insolence of absolute command, enjoys the terrors of the family, exacts their obedience, riots at their charge, and in the height of his joy insults the father with menaces, and the daughters with obscenity.

He is of late somewhat less offensive; for one of his debtors, after gentle expostulations, by which he was only irritated to grosser outrage, seized him by the sleeve, led him trembling into the court-yard, and closed the door upon him in a stormy night. He took his usual revenge next morning by a writ, but the debt was discharged by the assistance of Eugenio.

It is his rule to suffer his tenants to owe him rent, because by this indulgence, he secures to himself the power of seizure whenever he has an inclination to amuse himself with calamity, and feast his ears with entreaties and lamentations. Yet as he is sometimes capriciously liberal to those whom he happens to adopt as favourites, and lets his lands at a cheap rate, his farms are never long unoccupied; and when one is ruined by oppression, the possibility of better fortune quickly lures another to supply his place.

Such is the life of Squire Bluster; a man in whose power fortune has liberally placed the means of happiness, but who has defeated all her gifts of their end by the depravity of his mind. He is wealthy without followers; he is magnificent without witnesses; he has birth without alliance, and influence without dignity. His neighbours scorn him as a brute; his dependents dread him as an oppressor; and he has only the gloomy comfort of reflecting that if he is hated, he is likewise feared.°

I am, Sir, &c.
VAGULUS.

[Journalists]°

It is allowed that vocations and employments of least dignity are of the most apparent use; that the meanest artisan or manufacturer contributes more to the accommodation of life than the profound scholar and argumentative theorist; and that the public would suffer less present inconvenience from the banishment of philosophers than from the extinction of any common trade.

Some have been so forcibly struck with this observation that they have, in the first warmth of their discovery, thought it reasonable to alter the common distribution of dignity, and ventured to condemn mankind of universal ingratitude. For justice exacts that those by whom we are most benefited should be most honoured. And what labour can be more useful than that which procures to families and communities those necessaries which supply the wants of nature, or those conveniences by which ease, security, and elegance are conferred?

This is one of the innumerable theories which the first attempt to reduce them into practice certainly destroys. If we estimate dignity by immediate usefulness, agriculture is undoubtedly the first and noblest science; yet we see the plow driven, the clod broken, the manure spread, the seeds scattered, and the harvest reaped by men whom those that feed upon their industry will never be persuaded to admit into the same rank with heroes, or with sages; and who, after all the confessions which truth may extort in favour of their occupation, must be content to fill up the lowest class of the commonwealth, to form the base of the pyramid of subordination, and lie buried in obscurity themselves, while they support all that is splendid, conspicuous, or exalted.

It will be found, upon a closer inspection, that this part of the conduct of mankind is by no means contrary to reason or equity. Remuneratory honours are proportioned at once to the usefulness and difficulty of performances, and are properly adjusted by comparison of the mental and corporeal abilities which they appear to employ. That work, however necessary, which is carried on only by muscular strength and manual dexterity, is not of equal esteem, in the consideration of rational beings, with the tasks that exercise the intellectual powers, and require the active vigour of imagination, or the gradual and laborious investigations of reason.

The merit of all manual occupations seems to terminate in the inventor; and surely the first ages cannot be charged with ingratitude; since those who civilized barbarians, and taught them how to secure themselves from cold and hunger were numbered amongst their deities. But these arts once discovered by philosophy, and facilitated by experience, are afterwards practised with very little assistance from the faculties of the soul; nor is any thing necessary to the regular discharge of these inferior duties beyond that rude observation which the most sluggish intellect may practise, and that industry which the stimulations of necessity naturally enforce.

Yet, though the refusal of statues and panegyrics to those who employ only their hands and feet in the service of mankind may be easily justified, I am far from intending to incite the petulance of pride to justify the superciliousness of grandeur, or to intercept any part of that tenderness and benevolence which by the privilege of their common nature one man may claim from another.

That it would be neither wise nor equitable to discourage the husbandman, the labourer, the miner, or the smith, is generally granted; but there is another race of beings equally obscure and equally indigent, who because their usefulness is less obvious to vulgar apprehensions, live unrewarded and die unpitied, and who have been long exposed to insult without a defender, and to censure without an apologist.

The authors of London were formerly computed by Swift at several thousands, and there is not any reason for suspecting that their number has decreased. Of these only a very few can be said to produce, or endeavour to produce new ideas, to extend any principle of science, or gratify the imagination with any uncommon train of images or contexture of events; the rest, however laborious, however arrogant, can only be considered as the drudges of the pen, the manufacturers of literature, who have set up for authors, either with or without a regular initiation, and like other artificers, have no other care than to deliver their tale of wares at the stated time.

It has been formerly imagined that he who intends the entertainment or instruction of others must feel in himself some peculiar impulse of genius; that he must watch the happy minute in which his natural fire is excited, in which his mind is elevated with nobler sentiments, enlightened with clearer views, and invigorated with stronger comprehension; that he must carefully select his thoughts and polish his expressions; and animate his efforts with the hope of raising a monument of learning which neither time nor envy shall be able to destroy.

But the authors whom I am now endeavouring to recommend have been too long *hackneyed in the ways of men*° to indulge the chimerical ambition of immortality; they have seldom any claim to the trade of writing but that they have tried some other without success; they perceive no particular summons to composition except the sound of the clock; they have no other rule than the law or the fashion for admitting their thoughts or rejecting them; and about the opinion of posterity they have little solicitude, for their productions are seldom intended to remain in the world longer than a week.

That such authors are not to be rewarded with praise is evident, since nothing can be admired when it ceases to exist; but surely though they cannot aspire to honour, they may be exempted from ignominy, and adopted into that order of men which deserves our kindness though not our reverence. These papers of the day, the *Ephemerae* of learning, have uses more adequate to the purposes of common life than more pompous and durable volumes. If it is necessary for every man to be more acquainted with his contemporaries than with past generations, and to rather know the events which may immediately affect his fortune or quiet than the revolutions of ancient kingdoms, in which he has neither possessions nor expectations; if it be pleasing to hear of the preferment and dismission of statesmen, the birth of heirs, and the marriage of beauties, the humble author of journals and gazettes must be considered as a liberal dispenser of beneficial knowledge.

Even the abridger, compiler and translator, though their labours cannot be ranked with those of the diurnal historiographer, yet must not be rashly doomed to annihilation. Every size of readers requires a genius of correspondent capacity; some delight in abstracts and epitomes because they want room in their memory for long details, and content themselves with effects, without enquiry after causes; some minds are overpowered by splendor of sentiment, as some eyes are offended by a glaring light; such will gladly contemplate an author in an humble imitation, as we look without pain upon the sun in the water.

As every writer has his use, every writer ought to have his patrons; and since no man, however high he may now stand, can be certain that he shall not be soon thrown down from his elevation by criticism or caprice, the common interest of learning requires that her sons should cease from intestine hostilities, and instead of sacrificing each other to malice and contempt, endeavour to avert persecution from the meanest of their fraternity.

The Rambler, No. 148

SATURDAY, AUGUST 17, 1751

[Parental Tyranny]

Politicians° remark that no oppression is so heavy or lasting as that which is inflicted by the perversion and exorbitance of legal authority. The robber may be seized, and the invader repelled whenever they are found; they who pretend no right but that of force may by force be punished or suppressed. But when plunder bears the name of impost, and murder is perpetrated by a judicial sentence, fortitude is intimidated and wisdom confounded; resistance shrinks from an alliance with rebellion, and the villain remains secure in the robes of the magistrate.

Equally dangerous and equally detestable are the cruelties often exercised in private families, under the venerable sanction of parental authority: the power which we are taught to honour from the first moments of reason; which is guarded from insult and violation by all that can impress awe upon the mind of man; and which therefore may wanton in cruelty without control, and trample the bounds of right with innumerable transgressions, before duty and piety will dare to seek redress, or think themselves at liberty to recur to any other means of deliverance than supplications by which insolence is elated, and tears by which cruelty is gratified.

It was for a long time imagined by the Romans that no son could be the murderer of his father, and they had therefore no punishment appropriated to parricide. They seem likewise to have believed with equal confidence that no father could be cruel to his child, and therefore they allowed every man the supreme judicature in his own house, and put the lives of his offspring into his hands. But experience informed them by degrees that they had determined too hastily in favour of human nature; they found that instinct and habit were not able to contend with avarice or malice; that the nearest relation might be violated; and that power, to whomsoever entrusted, might be ill employed. They were therefore obliged to supply and to change their institutions; to deter the parricide by a new law, and to transfer capital punishments from the parent to the magistrate.

There are indeed many houses which it is impossible to enter familiarly without discovering that parents are by no means exempt from the intoxications of dominion; and that he who is in no danger of hearing remonstrances but from his own conscience will seldom be long without the art of controlling his convictions, and modifying justice by his own will.

If in any situation the heart were inaccessible to malignity, it might be supposed to be sufficiently secured by parental relation. To have voluntarily become to any being the occasion of its existence produces an obligation to make that existence happy. To see helpless infancy stretching out her hands and pouring out her cries in testimony of dependance, without any powers to alarm jealousy, or any guilt to alienate affection, must surely awaken tenderness in every human mind; and tenderness once excited will be hourly increased by the natural contagion of felicity, by the repercussion of communicated pleasure, and the consciousness of the dignity of benefaction. I believe no generous or benevolent man can see the vilest animal courting his regard, and shrinking at his anger, playing his gambols of delight before him, calling on him in distress, and flying to him in danger, without more kindness than he can persuade himself to feel for the wild and unsocial inhabitants of the air and water. We naturally endear to ourselves those to whom we impart any kind of pleasure, because we imagine their affection and esteem secured to us by the benefits which they receive.

There is indeed another method by which the pride of superiority may be likewise gratified. He that has extinguished all the sensations of humanity, and has no longer any satisfaction in the reflection that he is loved as the distributor of happiness, may please himself with exciting terror as the inflicter of pain; he may delight his solitude with contemplating the extent of his power and the force of his commands, in imagining the desires that flutter on the tongue which is forbidden to utter them, or the discontent which preys on the heart in which fear confines it; he may amuse himself with new contrivances of detection, multiplications of prohibition, and varieties of punishment; and swell with exultation when he considers how little of the homage that he receives he owes to choice.

That princes of this character have been known, the history of all absolute kingdoms will inform us; and since, as Aristotle observes, ἡ οἰκονομικὴ μοναρχία, 'the government of a family is naturally monarchical,' it is like other monarchies too often arbitrarily administered. The regal and parental tyrant differ only in the extent of their dominions, and the number of their slaves. The same passions cause the same miseries; except that seldom any prince, however despotic, has so far shaken off all awe of the public eye as to venture upon those freaks of injustice which are sometimes indulged under the secrecy of a private dwelling. Capricious injunctions, partial decisions, unequal allotments, distributions of reward not by merit but by fancy, and punishments regulated not by the degree of the offence, but by the humour of the judge, are too frequent where no power is known but that of a father.

That he delights in the misery of others no man will confess, and yet what other motive can make a father cruel? The king may be instigated by one man to the destruction of another; he may sometimes think himself endangered by the virtues of a subject; he may dread the successful general or the popular orator; his avarice may point out golden confiscations; and his guilt may whisper that he can only be secure by cutting off all power of revenge.

But what can a parent hope from the oppression of those who were born to his protection, of those who can disturb him with no competition, who can enrich him with no spoils? Why cowards are cruel may be easily discovered; but for what reason not more infamous than cowardice can that man delight in oppression who has nothing to fear?

The unjustifiable severity of a parent is loaded with this aggravation, that those whom he injures are always in his sight. The injustice of a prince is often exercised upon those of whom he never had any personal or particular knowledge; and the sentence which he pronounces, whether of banishment, imprisonment, or death, removes from his view the man whom he condemns. But the domestic oppressor dooms himself to gaze upon those faces which he clouds with terror and with sorrow; and beholds every moment the effects of his own barbarities. He that can bear to give continual pain to those who surround him, and can walk with satisfaction in the gloom of his own presence; he that can see submissive misery without relenting, and meet without emotion the eye that implores mercy, or demands justice, will scarcely be amended by remonstrance or admonition; he has found means of stopping the avenues of tenderness, and arming his heart against the force of reason.

Even though no consideration should be paid to the great law of social beings,° by which every individual is commanded to consult the happiness of others, yet the harsh parent is less to be vindicated than any other criminal, because he less provides for the happiness of himself. Every man, however little he loves others, would willingly be loved; every man hopes to live long, and therefore hopes for that time at which he shall sink back to imbecility, and must depend for ease and cheerfulness upon the officiousness° of others. But how has he obviated the inconveniences of old age who alienates from him the assistance of his children, and whose bed must be surrounded in his last hours, in the hours of languor and dejection, of impatience and of pain, by strangers to whom his life is indifferent, or by enemies to whom his death is desirable?

Piety will indeed in good minds overcome provocation, and those who have been harassed by brutality will forget the injuries which they have suffered so far as to perform the last duties with alacrity and zeal. But surely no resentment can be equally painful with kindness thus undeserved, nor can severer punishment be imprecated upon a man not wholly lost in meanness and stupidity than through the tediousness of decrepitude to be reproached by the kindness of his own children, to receive not the tribute but the alms of attendance, and to owe every relief of his miseries not to gratitude but to mercy.

The Rambler, No. 156

SATURDAY, SEPTEMBER 14, 1751

['Rules' of Writing]°

Every government, say the politicians, is perpetually degenerating towards corruption, from which it must be rescued at certain periods by the resuscitation of its first principles, and the re-establishment of its original constitution. Every animal body, according to the methodic physicians, is, by the predominance of some exuberant quality, continually declining towards disease and death, which must be obviated by a seasonable reduction of the peccant humour to the just equipoise which health requires.

In the same manner the studies of mankind, all at least which, not being subject to rigorous demonstration, admit the influence of fancy and caprice, are perpetually tending to error and confusion. Of the great principles of truth which the first speculatists discovered, the simplicity is embarrassed by ambitious additions, or the evidence obscured by inaccurate argumentation; and as they descend from one succession of writers to another, like light transmitted from room to room, they lose their strength and splendour, and fade at last in total evanescence.

The systems of learning therefore must be sometimes reviewed, complications analysed into principles, and knowledge disentangled from opinion. It is not always possible, without a close inspection, to separate the genuine shoots of consequential reasoning, which grow out of some radical postulate, from the branches which art has engrafted on it. The accidental prescriptions of authority, when time has procured them veneration, are often confounded with the laws of nature, and those rules are supposed coeval with reason of which the first rise cannot be discovered.

Criticism has sometimes permitted fancy to dictate the laws by which fancy ought to be restrained, and fallacy to perplex the principles by which fallacy is to be detected; her superintendence of others has betrayed her to negligence of herself; and, like the ancient Scythians, by extending her conquests over distant regions, she has left her throne vacant to her slaves.

Among the laws of which the desire of extending authority, or ardour of promoting knowledge, has prompted the prescription, all which writers have received had not the same original right to our regard. Some are to be considered as fundamental and indispensable, others only as useful and convenient; some as dictated by reason and necessity, others as enacted by despotic antiquity; some as invincibly supported by their conformity to the order of nature and operations of the intellect; others as formed by accident, or instituted by example, and therefore always liable to dispute and alteration.

That many rules have been advanced without consulting nature or reason, we cannot but suspect, when we find it peremptorily decreed by the ancient masters that 'only three speaking personages should appear at once upon the stage'; a law which, as the variety and intricacy of modern plays has made it impossible to be observed, we now violate without scruple, and, as experience proves, without inconvenience.

The original of this precept was merely accidental. Tragedy was a monody or solitary song in honour of Bacchus, improved afterwards into a dialogue by the addition of another speaker; but the ancients, remembering that the tragedy was at first pronounced only by one, durst not for some time venture beyond two; at last when custom and impunity had made them daring, they extended their liberty to the admission of three, but restrained themselves by a critical edict from further exorbitance.

By what accident the number of acts was limited to five, I know not that any author has informed us; but certainly it is not determined by any necessity arising either from the nature of action or propriety of exhibition. An act is only the representation of such a part of the business of the play as proceeds in an unbroken tenor, or without any intermediate pause. Nothing is more evident than that of every real, and by consequence of every dramatic, action, the intervals may be more or fewer than five; and indeed the rule is upon the English stage every day broken in effect, without any other mischief than that which arises from an absurd endeavour to observe it in appearance. Whenever the scene is shifted the act ceases, since some time is necessarily supposed to elapse while the personages of the drama change their place.

With no greater right to our obedience have the critics confined the dramatic action to a certain number of hours. Probability requires that the time of action should approach somewhat nearly to that of exhibition, and those plays will always be thought most happily conducted which crowd the greatest variety into the least space. But since it will frequently happen that some delusion must be admitted, I know not where the limits of imagination can be fixed. It is rarely observed that minds not prepossessed by mechanical criticism feel any offence from the extension of the intervals between the acts; nor can I conceive it absurd or impossible that he who can multiply three hours into twelve or twenty-four might image with equal ease a greater number.

I know not whether he that professes to regard no other laws than those of nature will not be inclined to receive tragi-comedy to his protection whom, however generally condemned, her own laurels have hitherto shaded from the fulminations of criticism. For what is there in the mingled drama which impartial reason can condemn? The connexion of important with trivial incidents, since it is not only common but perpetual in the world, may surely be allowed upon the stage, which pretends only to be the mirror of life. The impropriety of suppressing passions before we have raised them to the intended agitation, and of diverting the expectation from an event which we keep suspended only to raise it, may be speciously urged. But will not experience show this objection to be rather subtle than just? Is it not certain that the tragic and comic affections have been moved alternately with equal force, and that no plays have oftener filled the eye with tears, and the breast with palpitation than those which are variegated with interludes of mirth?

I do not however think it safe to judge of works of genius merely by the event. These resistless vicissitudes of the heart, this alternate prevalence of merriment and solemnity, may sometimes be more properly ascribed to the vigour of the writer than the justness of the design: and instead of vindicating tragi-comedy by the success of Shakespeare, we ought perhaps to pay new honours to that transcendent and unbounded genius that could preside over the passions in sport; who, to actuate the affections, needed not the slow gradation of common means, but could fill the heart with instantaneous jollity or sorrow, and vary our disposition as he changed his scenes. Perhaps the effects even of Shakespeare's poetry might have been yet greater had he not counteracted himself; and we might have been more interested in the distresses of his heroes had we not been so frequently diverted by the jokes of his buffoons.

There are other rules more fixed and obligatory. It is necessary that of every play the chief action should be single; for since a play represents some transaction, through its regular maturation to its final event, two actions equally important must evidently constitute two plays.

As the design of tragedy is to instruct by moving the passions, it must always have a hero, a personage apparently and incontestably superior to the rest, upon whom the attention may be fixed, and the anxiety suspended. For though of two persons opposing each other with equal abilities and equal virtue, the auditor will inevitably in time choose his favourite, yet as that choice must be without any cogency of conviction, the hopes or fears which it raises will be faint and languid. Of two heroes acting in confederacy against a common enemy, the virtues or dangers will give little emotion, because each claims our concern with the same right, and the heart lies at rest between equal motives.

It ought to be the first endeavour of a writer to distinguish nature from custom, or that which is established because it is right from that which is right only because it is established; that he may neither violate essential principles by a desire of novelty, nor debar himself from the attainment of beauties within his view by a needless fear of breaking rules which no literary dictator had authority to enact.

The Rambler, No. 161

TUESDAY, OCTOBER 1, 1751

[A Rooming-House Chronicle]

MR RAMBLER,

SIR,

You have formerly observed that curiosity often terminates in barren knowledge, and that the mind is prompted to study and enquiry rather by the uneasiness of ignorance than the hope of profit. Nothing can be of less importance to any present interest than the fortune of those who have been long lost in the grave, and from whom nothing now can be hoped or feared. Yet to rouse the zeal of a true antiquary little more is necessary than to mention a name which mankind have conspired to forget; he will make his way to remote scenes of action through obscurity and contradiction, as Tully sought amidst bushes and brambles the tomb of Archimedes.

It is not easy to discover how it concerns him that gathers the produce or receives the rent of an estate to know through what families the land has passed, who is registered in the Conqueror's survey as its possessor, how often it has been forfeited by treason, or how often sold by prodigality. The power or wealth of the present inhabitants of a country cannot be much increased by an enquiry after the names of those barbarians who destroyed one another twenty centuries ago, in contests for the shelter of woods or convenience of pasturage. Yet we see that no man can be at rest in the enjoyment of a new purchase till he has learned the history of his grounds from the ancient inhabitants of the parish, and that no nation omits to record the actions of their ancestors, however bloody, savage and rapacious.

The same disposition, as different opportunities call it forth, discovers itself in great or little things. I have always thought it unworthy of a wise man to slumber in total inactivity only because he happens to have no employment equal to his ambition or genius; it is therefore my custom to apply my attention to the objects before me, and as I cannot think any place wholly unworthy of notice that affords a habitation to a man of letters, I have collected the history and antiquities of the several garrets in which I have resided.

Quantulacunque estis, vos ego magna voco.

Ovid, *Amores*, III. xv. 14.

How small to others, but how great to me!

Many of these narratives my industry has been able to extend to a considerable length; but the woman with whom I now lodge has lived only eighteen months in the house, and can give no account of its ancient revolutions; the plasterer, having, at her entrance, obliterated by his white wash all the smoky memorials which former tenants had left upon the ceiling, and perhaps drawn the veil of oblivion over politicians, philosophers, and poets.

When I first cheapened° my lodgings, the landlady told me that she hoped I was not an author, for the lodgers on the first floor had stipulated that the upper rooms should not be occupied by a noisy trade. I very readily promised to give no disturbance to her family, and soon dispatched a bargain on the usual terms.

I had not slept many nights in my new apartment before I began to enquire after my predecessors, and found my landlady, whose imagination is filled chiefly with her own affairs, very ready to give me information.

Curiosity, like all other desires, produces pain as well as pleasure. Before she began her narrative, I had heated my head with expectations of adventures and discoveries, of elegance in disguise, and learning in distress; and was somewhat mortified when I heard that the first tenant was a tailor, of whom nothing was remembered but that he complained of his room for want of light; and, after having lodged in it a month, and paid only a week's rent, pawned a piece of cloth which he was trusted to cut out, and was forced to make a precipitate retreat from this quarter of the town.

The next was a young woman newly arrived from the country, who lived for five weeks with great regularity, and became by frequent treats very much the favourite of the family, but at last received visits so frequently from a cousin in Cheapside that she brought the reputation of the house into danger, and was therefore dismissed with good advice.

The room then stood empty for a fortnight; my landlady began to think that she had judged hardly, and often wished for such another lodger. At last an elderly man of a grave aspect read the bill, and bargained for the room at the very first price that was asked. He lived in close retirement, seldom went out till evening, and then returned early, sometimes cheerful, and at other times dejected. It was remarkable that whatever he purchased, he never had small money in his pocket, and though cool and temperate on other occasions, was always vehement and stormy till he received his change. He paid his rent with great exactness, and seldom failed once a week to requite my landlady's civility with a supper. At last, such is the fate of human felicity, the house was alarmed at midnight by the constable, who demanded to search the garrets. My landlady assuring him that he had mistaken the door, conducted him up stairs, where he found the tools of a coiner; but the tenant had crawled along the roof to an empty house, and escaped; much to the joy of my landlady, who declares him a very honest man, and wonders why anybody should be hanged for making money when such numbers are in want of it. She however confesses that she shall for the future always question the character of those who take her garret without beating down the price.

The bill was then placed again in the window, and the poor woman was teased for seven weeks by innumerable passengers, who obliged her to climb with them every hour up five stories, and then disliked the prospect, hated the noise of a public street, thought the stairs narrow, objected to a low ceiling, required the walls to be hung with fresher paper, asked questions about the neighbourhood, could not think of living so far from their acquaintance, wished the window had looked to the south rather than the west, told how the door and chimney might have been better disposed, bid her half the price that she asked, or promised to give her earnest the next day, and came no more.

At last, a short meagre man, in a tarnished waistcoat, desired to see the garret, and when he had stipulated for two long shelves and a larger table, hired it at a low rate. When the affair was completed, he looked round him with great satisfaction, and repeated some words which the woman did not understand. In two days he brought a great box of books, took possession of his room, and lived very inoffensively, except that he frequently disturbed the inhabitants of the next floor by unseasonable noises. He was generally in bed at noon, but from evening to midnight he sometimes talked aloud with great vehemence, sometimes stamped as in rage, sometimes threw down his poker, then clattered his chairs, then sat down in deep thought, and again burst out into loud vociferations; sometimes he would sigh as oppressed with misery, and sometimes shake with convulsive laughter. When he encountered any of the family he gave way or bowed, but rarely spoke, except that as he went up stairs he often repeated,

——Ὅς ὑπέρτατα δώματα ναίει.

Hesiod, *Works and Days*, l. 8.

This habitant th' aerial regions boast,

hard words, to which his neighbours listened so often that they learned them without understanding them. What was his employment she did not venture to ask him, but at last heard a printer's boy enquire for the author.

My landlady was very often advised to beware of this strange man, who, though he was quiet for the present, might perhaps become outrageous in the hot months; but as she was punctually paid, she could not find any sufficient reason for dismissing him, till one night he convinced her by setting fire to his curtains that it was not safe to have an author for her inmate.

She had then for six weeks a succession of tenants who left the house on Saturday, and instead of paying their rent, stormed at their landlady. At last she took in two sisters, one of whom had spent her little fortune in procuring remedies for a lingering disease, and was now supported and attended by the other: she climbed with difficulty to the apartment, where she languished eight weeks, without impatience or lamentation, except for the expense and fatigue which her sister suffered, and then calmly and contentedly expired. The sister followed her to the grave, paid the few debts which they had contracted, wiped away the tears of useless sorrow, and returning to the business of common life, resigned to me the vacant habitation.

Such, Mr Rambler, are the changes which have happened in the narrow space where my present fortune has fixed my residence. So true is it that amusement and instruction are always at hand for those who have skill and willingness to find them; and so just is the observation of Juvenal, that a single house will show whatever is done or suffered in the world.

I am, Sir, &c.

The Rambler, No. 167

TUESDAY, OCTOBER 22, 1751

[Marriage (4)]°

SIR,

It is not common to envy those with whom we cannot easily be placed in comparison. Every man sees without malevolence the progress of another in the tracks of life which he has himself no desire to tread, and hears without inclination to cavils or contradiction the renown of those whose distance will not suffer them to draw the attention of mankind from his own merit. The sailor never thinks it necessary to contest the lawyer's abilities; nor would the Rambler, however jealous of his reputation, be much disturbed by the success of rival wits at Agra or Ispahan.

We do not therefore ascribe to you any superlative degree of virtue, when we believe that we may inform you of our change of condition without danger of malignant fascination; and that when you read of the marriage of your correspondents Hymenaeus and Tranquilla, you will join your wishes to those of their other friends for the happy event of an union in which caprice and selfishness had so little part.

There is at least this reason why we should be less deceived in our connubial hopes than many who enter into the same state, that we have allowed our minds to form no unreasonable expectations, nor vitiated our fancies in the soft hours of courtship with visions of felicity which human power cannot bestow, or of perfection which human virtue cannot attain. That impartiality with which we endeavoured to inspect the manners of all whom we have known was never so much overpowered by our passion but that we discovered some faults and weaknesses in each other; and joined our hands in conviction that as there are advantages to be enjoyed in marriage, there are inconveniences likewise to be endured; and that, together with confederate intellects and auxiliar virtues, we must find different opinions and opposite inclinations.

We however flatter ourselves, for who is not flattered by himself as well as by others on the day of marriage, that we are eminently qualified to give mutual pleasure. Our birth is without any such remarkable disparity as can give either an opportunity of insulting the other with pompous names and splendid alliances, or of calling in upon any domestic controversy the overbearing assistance of powerful relations. Our fortune was equally suitable, so that we meet without any of those obligations which always produce reproach or suspicion of reproach, which, though they may be forgotten in the gaieties of the first month, no delicacy will always suppress, or of which the suppression must be considered as a new favour, to be repaid by tameness and submission, till gratitude takes the place of love, and the desire of pleasing degenerates by degrees into the fear of offending.

The settlements caused no delay; for we did not trust our affairs to the negotiation of wretches who would have paid their court by multiplying stipulations. Tranquilla scorned to detain any part of her fortune from him into whose hands she delivered up her person; and Hymenaeus thought no act of baseness more criminal than his who enslaves his wife by her own generosity, who by marrying without a jointure condemns her to all the dangers of accident and caprice, and at last boasts his liberality by granting what only the indiscretion of her kindness enabled him to withhold. He therefore received on the common terms the portion which any other woman might have brought him, and reserved all the exuberance of acknowledgment for those excellencies which he has yet been able to discover only in Tranquilla.

We did not pass the weeks of courtship like those who consider themselves as taking the last draught of pleasure, and resolve not to quit the bowl without a surfeit, or who know themselves about to set happiness to hazard, and endeavour to lose their sense of danger in the ebriety of perpetual amusement, and whirl round the gulf before they sink. Hymenaeus often repeated a medical axiom, that *the succours of sickness ought not to be wasted in health*. We know that however our eyes may yet sparkle, and our hearts bound at the presence of each other, the time of listlessness and satiety, of peevishness and discontent must come at last, in which we shall be driven for relief to shows and recreations; that the uniformity of life must be sometimes diversified, and the vacuities of conversation sometimes supplied. We rejoice in the reflection that we have stores of novelty yet unexhausted, which may be opened when repletion shall call for change, and gratifications yet untasted, by which life when it shall become vapid or bitter may be restored to its former sweetness and sprightliness, and again irritate the appetite, and again sparkle in the cup.

Our time will probably be less tasteless than that of those whom the authority and avarice of parents unites almost without their consent in their early years, before they have accumulated any fund of reflection, or collected materials for mutual entertainment. Such we have often seen rising in the morning to cards, and retiring in the afternoon to doze, whose happiness was celebrated by their neighbours, because they happened to grow rich by parsimony, and to be kept quiet by insensibility, and agreed to eat and to sleep together.

We have both mingled with the world, and are therefore no strangers to the faults and virtues, the designs and competitions, the hopes and fears of our contemporaries. We have both amused our leisure with books, and can therefore recount the events of former times, or cite the dictates of ancient wisdom. Every occurrence furnishes us with some hint which one or the other can improve, and if it should happen that memory or imagination fail us, we can retire to no idle or unimproving solitude.

Though our characters, beheld at a distance, exhibit this general resemblance, yet a nearer inspection discovers such a dissimilitude of our habitudes and sentiments as leaves each some peculiar advantages, and affords that *concordia discors*,° that suitable disagreement which is always necessary to intellectual harmony. There may be a total diversity of ideas which admits no participation of the same delight, and there may likewise be such a conformity of notions as leaves neither any thing to add to the decisions of the other. With such contrariety there can be no peace, with such similarity there can be no pleasure. Our reasonings, though often formed upon different views, terminate generally in the same conclusion. Our thoughts, like rivulets issuing from distant springs, are each impregnated in its course with various mixtures, and tinged by infusions unknown to the other, yet at last easily unite into one stream, and purify themselves by the gentle effervescence of contrary qualities.

These benefits we receive in a greater degree as we converse without reserve, because we have nothing to conceal. We have no debts to be paid by imperceptible deductions from avowed expenses, no habits to be indulged by the private subserviency of a favoured servant, no private interviews with needy relations, no intelligence with spies placed upon each other. We considered marriage as the most solemn league of perpetual friendship, a state from which artifice and concealment are to be banished for ever, and in which every act of dissimulation is a breach of faith.

The impetuous vivacity of youth, and that ardour of desire which the first sight of pleasure naturally produces have long ceased to hurry us into irregularity and vehemence; and experience has shown us that few gratifications are too valuable to be sacrificed to complaisance. We have thought it convenient to rest from the fatigue of pleasure, and now only continue that course of life into which we had before entered, confirmed in our choice by mutual approbation, supported in our resolution by mutual encouragement, and assisted in our efforts by mutual exhortation.

Such, Mr Rambler, is our prospect of life, a prospect which as it is beheld with more attention, seems to open more extensive happiness, and spreads by degrees into the boundless regions of eternity. But if all our prudence has been in vain, and we are doomed to give one instance more of the uncertainty of human discernment, we shall comfort ourselves, amidst our disappointments, that we were not betrayed but by such delusions as caution could not escape, since we sought happiness only in the arms of virtue. We are,

Sir,
Your humble servants,
HYMENAEUS,
TRANQUILLA.

The Rambler, No. 168

SATURDAY, OCTOBER 26, 1751

[Congruent Diction]

It has been observed by Boileau° that 'a mean or common thought expressed in pompous diction generally pleases more than a new or noble sentiment delivered in low and vulgar language; because the number is greater of those whom custom has enabled to judge of words than whom study has qualified to examine things.'

This solution might satisfy, if such only were offended with meanness of expression as are unable to distinguish propriety of thought, and to separate propositions or images from the vehicles by which they are conveyed to the understanding. But this kind of disgust is by no means confined to the ignorant or superficial; it operates uniformly and universally upon readers of all classes; every man, however profound or abstracted, perceives himself irresistibly alienated by low terms; they who profess the most zealous adherence to truth are forced to admit that she owes part of her charms to her ornaments, and loses much of her power over the soul when she appears disgraced by a dress uncouth or ill-adjusted.

We are all offended by low terms, but are not disgusted alike by the same compositions, because we do not all agree to censure the same terms as low. No word is naturally or intrinsically meaner than another; our opinion therefore of words, as of other things arbitrarily and capriciously established, depends wholly upon accident and custom. The cottager thinks those apartments splendid and spacious which an inhabitant of palaces will despise for their inelegance; and to him who has passed most of his hours with the delicate and polite, many expressions will seem sordid which another, equally acute, may hear without offence; but a mean term never fails to displease him to whom it appears mean, as poverty is certainly and invariably despised, though he who is poor in the eyes of some may by others be envied for his wealth.

Words become low by the occasions to which they are applied, or the general character of them who use them; and the disgust which they produce arises from the revival of those images with which they are commonly united. Thus if, in the most solemn discourse, a phrase happens to occur which has been successfully employed in some ludicrous narrative, the gravest auditor finds it difficult to refrain from laughter, when they who are not prepossessed by the same accidental association are utterly unable to guess the reason of his merriment. Words which convey ideas of dignity in one age are banished from elegant writing or conversation in another, because they are in time debased by vulgar mouths, and can be no longer heard without the involuntary recollection of unpleasing images.

When Macbeth° is confirming himself in the horrid purpose of stabbing his king, he breaks out amidst his emotions into a wish natural to a murderer,

> ———— Come, thick night!
> And pall thee in the dunnest smoke of hell,
> That my keen knife see not the wound it makes;
> Nor heav'n peep through the blanket of the dark,
> To cry, hold, hold!————

In this passage is exerted all the force of poetry, that force which calls new powers into being, which embodies sentiment, and animates matter; yet perhaps scarce any man now peruses it without some disturbance of his attention from the counteraction of the words to the ideas. What can be more dreadful than to implore the presence of night, invested not in common obscurity, but in the smoke of hell? Yet the efficacy of this invocation is destroyed by the insertion of an epithet now seldom heard but in the stable, and *dun*° night may come or go without any other notice than contempt.

If we start into raptures when some hero of the *Iliad* tells us that δόρυ μάινεται, his lance rages with eagerness to destroy; if we are alarmed at the terror of the soldiers commanded by Caesar to hew down the sacred grove, who dreaded, says Lucan, lest the axe aimed at the oak should fly back upon the striker,

> ———— *Si robora sacra ferirent,*
> *In sua credebant redituras membra secures,*
>
> *Pharsalia,* iii. 430–1.

> None dares with impious steel the grove to rend,
> Lest on himself the destin'd stroke descend,

we cannot surely but sympathise with the horrors of a wretch about to murder his master, his friend, his benefactor, who suspects that the weapon will refuse its office, and start back from the breast which he is preparing to violate. Yet this sentiment is weakened by the name of an instrument used by butchers and cooks in the meanest employments; we do not immediately conceive that any crime of importance is to be committed with a *knife*; or who does not, at last, from the long habit of connecting a knife with sordid offices, feel aversion rather than terror?

Macbeth proceeds to wish, in the madness of guilt, that the inspection of heaven may be intercepted, and that he may in the involutions of infernal darkness escape the eye of Providence. This is the utmost extravagance of determined wickedness; yet this is so debased by two unfortunate words that while I endeavour to impress on my reader the energy of the sentiment, I can scarce check my risibility when the expression forces itself upon my mind; for who, without some relaxation of his gravity, can hear of the avengers of guilt 'peeping through a blanket'?

These imperfections of diction are less obvious to the reader as he is less acquainted with common usages; they are therefore wholly imperceptible to a foreigner who learns our language from books, and will strike a solitary academic less forcibly than a modish lady.

Among the numerous requisites that must concur to complete an author, few are of more importance than an early entrance into the living world. The seeds of knowledge may be planted in solitude, but must be cultivated in public. Argumentation may be taught in colleges, and theories formed in retirement, but the artifice of embellishment, and the powers of attraction, can be gained only by general converse.

An acquaintance with prevailing customs and fashionable elegance is necessary likewise for other purposes. The injury that grand imagery suffers from unsuitable language, personal merit may fear from rudeness and indelicacy. When the success of Æneas depended on the favour of the queen upon whose coasts he was driven, his celestial protectress thought him not sufficiently secured against rejection by his piety or bravery, but decorated him for the interview with preternatural beauty. Whoever desires, for his writings or himself, what none can reasonably contemn, the favour of mankind, must add grace to strength, and make his thoughts agreeable as well as useful. Many complain of neglect who never tried to attract regard. It cannot be expected that the patrons of science or virtue should be solicitous to discover excellencies which they who possess them shade and disguise. Few have abilities so much needed by the rest of the world as to be caressed on their own terms and he that will not condescend to recommend himself by external embellishments must submit to the fate of just sentiments meanly expressed, and be ridiculed and forgotten before he is understood.

The Rambler, No. 170

SATURDAY, NOVEMBER 2, 1751

[A Prostitute's Story (1)]

TO THE RAMBLER.

SIR,

I am one of those beings from whom many that melt at the sight of all other misery think it meritorious to withhold relief; one whom the rigour of virtuous indignation dooms to suffer without complaint, and perish without regard; and whom I myself have formerly insulted in the pride of reputation and security of innocence.

I am of a good family, but my father was burdened with more children than he could decently support. A wealthy relation, as he travelled from London to his country seat, condescending to make him a visit, was touched with compassion of his narrow fortune, and resolved to ease him of part of his charge by taking the care of a child upon himself. Distress on one side and ambition on the other were too powerful for parental fondness, and the little family passed in review before him, that he might make his choice. I was then ten years old, and without knowing for what purpose, I was called to my great cousin, endeavoured to recommend myself by my best courtesy, sung him my prettiest song, told the last story that I had read, and so much endeared myself by my innocence that he declared his resolution to adopt me, and to educate me with his own daughters.

My parents felt the common struggles at the thought of parting, and 'some natural tears they dropped, but wiped them soon'.° They considered, not without that false estimation of the value of wealth which poverty long continued always produces, that I was raised to higher rank than they could give me, and to hopes of more ample fortune than they could bequeath. My mother sold some of her ornaments to dress me in such a manner as might secure me from contempt at my first arrival; and when she dismissed me, pressed me to her bosom with an embrace that I still feel, gave me some precepts of piety which, however neglected, I have not forgotten, and uttered prayers for my final happiness, of which I have not yet ceased to hope that they will at last be granted.

My sisters envied my new finery, and seemed not much to regret our separation; my father conducted me to the stage coach with a kind of cheerful tenderness; and in a very short time, I was transported to splendid apartments, and a luxurious table, and grew familiar to show, noise and gaiety.

In three years my mother died, having implored a blessing on her family with her last breath. I had little opportunity to indulge a sorrow which there was none to partake with me, and therefore soon ceased to reflect much upon my loss. My father turned all his care upon his other children, whom some fortunate adventures and unexpected legacies enabled him, when he died four years after my mother, to leave in a condition above their expectations.

I should have shared the increase of his fortune, and had once a portion assigned me in his will; but my cousin assuring him that all care for me was needless, since he had resolved to place me happily in the world, directed him to divide my part amongst my sisters.

Thus I was thrown upon dependence without resource. Being now at an age in which young women are initiated in company, I was no longer to be supported in my former character but at considerable expense; so that partly lest I should waste money, and partly lest my appearance might draw too many compliments and assiduities, I was insensibly degraded from my equality, and enjoyed few privileges above the head servant but that of receiving no wages.

I felt every indignity, but knew that resentment would precipitate my fall. I therefore endeavoured to continue my importance by little services and active officiousness, and for a time preserved myself from neglect by withdrawing all pretences to competition, and studying to please rather than to shine. But my interest, notwithstanding this expedient, hourly declined, and my cousin's favourite maid began to exchange repartees with me, and consult me about the alterations of a cast gown.

I was now completely depressed, and though I had seen mankind enough to know the necessity of outward cheerfulness, I often withdrew to my chamber to vent my grief, or turn my condition in my mind, and examine by what means I might escape from perpetual mortification. At last, my schemes and sorrows were interrupted by a sudden change of my relation's behaviour, who one day took an occasion when we were left together in a room to bid me suffer myself no longer to be insulted, but assume the place which he always intended me to hold in the family. He assured me that his wife's preference of her own daughters should never hurt me; and, accompanying his professions with a purse of gold, ordered me to bespeak a rich suit at the mercer's, and to apply privately to him for money when I wanted it, and insinuate that my other friends supplied me, which he would take care to confirm.

By this stratagem, which I did not then understand, he filled me with tenderness and gratitude, compelled me to repose on him as my only support, and produced a necessity of private conversation. He often appointed interviews at the house of an acquaintance, and sometimes called on me with a coach, and carried me abroad. My sense of his favour, and the desire of retaining it, disposed me to unlimited complaisance, and though I saw his kindness grow every day more fond, I did not suffer any suspicion to enter my thoughts. At last the wretch took advantage of the familiarity which he enjoyed as my relation, and the submission which he exacted as my benefactor, to complete the ruin of an orphan whom his own promises had made indigent, whom his indulgence had melted, and his authority subdued.

I know not why it should afford subject of exultation to overpower on any terms the resolution, or surprise the caution of a girl; but of all the boasters that deck themselves in the spoils of innocence and

beauty, they surely have the least pretensions to triumph who submit
to owe their success to some casual influence. They neither employ
the graces of fancy, nor the force of understanding, in their attempts;
they cannot please their vanity with the art of their approaches, the
delicacy of their adulations, the elegance of their address, or the
efficacy of their eloquence; nor applaud themselves as possessed of
any qualities by which affection is attracted. They surmount no
obstacles, they defeat no rivals, but attack only those who cannot
resist, and are often content to possess the body without any solicitude
to gain the heart.

Many of these despicable wretches does my present acquaintance
with infamy and wickedness enable me to number among the heroes
of debauchery. Reptiles whom their own servants would have
despised, had they not been their servants, and with whom beggary
would have disdained intercourse, had she not been allured by hopes of
relief. Many of the beings which are now rioting in taverns, or
shivering in the streets, have been corrupted not by arts of gallantry
which stole gradually upon the affections and laid prudence asleep,
but by the fear of losing benefits which were never intended, or of
incurring resentment which they could not escape; some have been
frighted by masters, and some awed by guardians into ruin.

Our crime had its usual consequence, and he soon perceived that I
could not long continue in his family. I was distracted at the thought
of the reproach which I now believed inevitable. He comforted me
with hopes of eluding all discovery, and often upbraided me with the
anxiety which perhaps none but himself saw in my countenance; but
at last mingled his assurances of protection and maintenance with
menaces of total desertion, if in the moments of perturbation I should
suffer his secret to escape, or endeavour to throw on him any part of
my infamy.

Thus passed the dismal hours till my retreat could no longer be
delayed. It was pretended that my relations had sent for me to a
distant county, and I entered upon a state which shall be described in
my next letter.

I am, Sir, &c.
MISELLA.°

[A Prostitute's Story (2)]

TO THE RAMBLER.

SIR,

Misella now sits down to continue her narrative. I am convinced that nothing would more powerfully preserve youth from irregularity, or guard inexperience from seduction, than a just description of the condition into which the wanton plunges herself, and therefore hope that my letter may be a sufficient antidote to my example.

After the distraction, hesitation and delays which the timidity of guilt naturally produces, I was removed to lodgings in a distant part of the town, under one of the characters commonly assumed upon such occasions. Here being, by my circumstances, condemned to solitude, I passed most of my hours in bitterness and anguish. The conversation of the people with whom I was placed was not at all capable of engaging my attention or dispossessing the reigning ideas. The books which I carried to my retreat were such as heightened my abhorrence of myself; for I was not so far abandoned as to sink voluntarily into corruption, or endeavour to conceal from my own mind the enormity of my crime.

My relation remitted none of his fondness, but visited me so often that I was sometimes afraid lest his assiduity should expose him to suspicion. Whenever he came he found me weeping, and was therefore less delightfully entertained than he expected. After frequent expostulations upon the unreasonableness of my sorrow, and innumerable protestations of everlasting regard, he at last found that I was more affected with the loss of my innocence than the danger of my fame, and that he might not be disturbed by my remorse, began to lull my conscience with the opiates of irreligion. His arguments were such as my course of life has since exposed me often to the necessity of hearing, vulgar, empty and fallacious; yet they at first confounded me by their novelty, filled me with doubt and perplexity, and interrupted that peace which I began to feel from the sincerity of my repentance, without substituting any other support. I listened a while to his impious gabble, but influence was soon overpowered by natural reason and early education, and the convictions which this new attempt gave me of his baseness completed my abhorrence. I have heard of barbarians, who, when tempests drive ships upon their coast, decoy them to the rocks that they may plunder their lading, and have always thought that wretches thus merciless in their depredations ought to be destroyed by a general insurrection of all social beings; yet how light is this guilt to the crime of him who in the agitations of remorse cuts away the anchor of piety, and when he has drawn aside credulity from the paths of virtue, hides the light of heaven which would direct her to return. I had hitherto considered him as a man equally betrayed with myself by the concurrence of appetite and opportunity; but I now saw with horror that he was contriving to perpetuate his gratification, and was desirous to fit me to his purpose by complete and radical corruption.

To escape, however, was not yet in my power. I could support the expenses of my condition only by the continuance of his favour. He provided all that was necessary, and in a few weeks, congratulated me upon my escape from the danger which we had both expected with so much anxiety. I then began to remind him of his promise to restore me with my fame uninjured to the world. He promised me in general terms that nothing should be wanting which his power could add to my happiness, but forbore to release me from my confinement. I knew how much my reception in the world depended upon my speedy return, and was therefore outrageously impatient of his delays, which I now perceived to be only artifices of lewdness. He told me, at last, with an appearance of sorrow, that all hopes of restoration to my former state were for ever precluded; that chance had discovered my secret, and malice divulged it; and that nothing now remained but to seek a retreat more private, where curiosity or hatred could never find us.

The rage, anguish, and resentment which I felt at this account are not to be expressed. I was in so much dread of reproach and infamy, which he represented as pursuing me with full cry, that I yielded myself implicitly to his disposal, and was removed with a thousand studied precautions through by-ways and dark passages to another house, where I harassed him with perpetual solicitations for a small annuity that might enable me to live in the country with obscurity and innocence.

This demand he at first evaded with ardent professions, but in time appeared offended at my importunity and distrust; and having one day endeavoured to soothe me with uncommon expressions of tenderness, when he found my discontent immovable, left me with some inarticulate murmurs of anger. I was pleased that he was at last roused to sensibility, and expecting that at his next visit he would comply with my request, lived with great tranquility upon the money in my hands, and was so much pleased with this pause of persecution that I did not reflect how much his absence had exceeded the usual intervals, till I was alarmed with the danger of wanting subsistence. I then suddenly contracted my expenses, but was unwilling to supplicate for assistance. Necessity, however, soon overcame my modesty or my pride, and I applied to him by a letter, but had no answer. I writ in terms more pressing, but without effect. I then sent an agent to enquire after him, who informed me that he had quitted his house, and was gone with his family to reside for some time upon his estate in Ireland.

However shocked at this abrupt departure, I was yet unwilling to believe that he could wholly abandon me, and therefore by the sale of my clothes I supported myself, expecting that every post would bring me relief. Thus I passed seven months between hope and dejection, in a gradual approach to poverty and distress, emaciated with discontent and bewildered with uncertainty. At last, my landlady, after many hints of the necessity of a new lover, took the opportunity of my absence to search my boxes, and missing some of my apparel, seized the remainder for rent, and led me to the door.

To remonstrate against legal cruelty was vain; to supplicate obdurate brutality was hopeless. I went away I knew not whither, and wandered about without any settled purpose, unacquainted with the usual expedients of misery, unqualified for laborious offices, afraid to meet an eye that had seen me before, and hopeless of relief from those who were strangers to my former condition. Night came on in the midst of my distraction, and I still continued to wander till the menaces of the watch obliged me to shelter myself in a covered passage.

Next day, I procured a lodging in the backward garret of a mean house, and employed my landlady to enquire for a service. My applications were generally rejected for want of a character. At length, I was received at a draper's; but when it was known to my mistress that I had only one gown, and that of silk, she was of opinion that I looked like a thief, and without warning, hurried me away. I then tried to support myself by my needle, and by my landlady's recommendation, obtained a little work from a shop, and for three weeks lived without repining; but when my punctuality had gained me so much reputation that I was trusted to make up a head of some value, one of my fellow-lodgers stole the lace, and I was obliged to fly from a prosecution.

Thus driven again into the streets, I lived upon the least that could support me, and at night accommodated myself under penthouses as well as I could. At length I became absolutely penniless; and having strolled all day without sustenance, was at the close of evening accosted by an elderly man, with an invitation to a tavern. I refused him with hesitation; he seized me by the hand, and drew me into a neighbouring house, where when he saw my face pale with hunger, and my eyes swelling with tears, he spurned me from him, and bade me cant and whine in some other place; he for his part would take care of his pockets.

I still continued to stand in the way, having scarcely strength to walk farther, when another soon addressed me in the same manner. When he saw the same tokens of calamity, he considered that I might be obtained at a cheap rate, and therefore quickly made overtures, which I had no longer firmness to reject. By this man I was maintained four months in penurious wickedness, and then abandoned to my former condition, from which I was delivered by another keeper.

In this abject state I have now passed four years, the drudge of extortion and the sport of drunkenness; sometimes the property of one man, and sometimes the common prey of accidental lewdness; at one time tricked up for sale by the mistress of a brothel, at another begging in the streets to be relieved from hunger by wickedness; without any hope in the day but of finding some whom folly or excess may expose to my allurements, and without any reflections at night but such as guilt and terror impress upon me.

If those who pass their days in plenty and security could visit for an hour the dismal receptacles to which the prostitute retires from her nocturnal excursions, and see the wretches that lie crowded together, mad with intemperance, ghastly with famine, nauseous with filth, and noisome with disease; it would not be easy for any degree of abhorrence to harden them against compassion, or to repress the desire which they must immediately feel to rescue such numbers of human beings from a state so dreadful.

It is said that in France they annually evacuate their streets, and ship their prostitutes and vagabonds to their colonies. If the women that infest this city had the same opportunity of escaping from their miseries, I believe very little force would be necessary; for who among them can dread any change? Many of us indeed are wholly unqualified for any but the most servile employments, and those perhaps would require the care of a magistrate to hinder them from following the same practices in another country; but others are only precluded by infamy from reformation, and would gladly be delivered on any terms from the necessity of guilt and the tyranny of chance. No place but a populous city can afford opportunities for open prostitution, and where the eye of justice can attend to individuals, those who cannot be made good may be restrained from mischief. For my part I should exult at the privilege of banishment, and think myself happy in any region that should restore me once again to honesty and peace.

I am, Sir, &c.
MISELLA.

The Rambler, No. 191

TUESDAY, JANUARY 14, 1752

[An Astute Young Lady]

TO THE RAMBLER.

Dear Mr Rambler,

I have been four days confined to my chamber by a cold, which has already kept me from three plays, nine sales, five shows, and six card-tables, and put me seventeen visits behind hand; and the doctor tells my mamma that if I fret and cry it will settle in my head, and I shall not be fit to be seen these six weeks. But, dear Mr Rambler, how can I help it? At this very time Melissa is dancing with the prettiest gentleman;—she will breakfast with him tomorrow and then run to two auctions and hear compliments and have presents; then she will be dressed and visit and get a ticket to the play; then go to cards and win and come home with two flambeaus before her chair. Dear Mr Rambler, who can bear it?

My aunt has just brought me a bundle of your papers for my amusement. She says you are a philosopher, and will teach me to moderate my desires and look upon the world with indifference. But, dear sir, I do not wish nor intend to moderate my desires, nor can I think it proper to look upon the world with indifference till the world looks with indifference on me. I have been forced, however, to sit this morning a whole quarter of an hour with your paper before my face;

but just as my aunt came in, Phyllida had brought me a letter from Mr Trip, which I put within the leaves, and read about *absence* and *inconsolableness*, and *ardour* and *irresistible passion* and *eternal constancy*, while my aunt imagined that I was puzzling myself with your philosophy, and often cried out, when she saw me look confused, 'If there is any word that you do not understand, child, I will explain it.'

Dear soul! How old people that think themselves wise may be imposed upon! But it is fit that they should take their turn, for I am sure while they can keep poor girls close in the nursery they tyrannize over us in a very shameful manner, and fill our imaginations with tales of terror only to make us live in quiet subjection, and fancy that we can never be safe but by their protection.

I have a mamma and two aunts, who have all been formerly celebrated for wit and beauty, and are still generally admired by those that value themselves upon their understanding, and love to talk of vice and virtue, nature and simplicity, and beauty, and propriety; but if there was not some hope of meeting me, scarcely a creature would come near them that wears a fashionable coat. These ladies, Mr Rambler, have had me under their government fifteen years and a half, and have all that time been endeavouring to deceive me by such representations of life as I now find not to be true; but I knew not whether I ought to impute them to ignorance or malice, as it is possible the world may be much changed since they mingled in general conversation.

Being desirous that I should love books, they told me that nothing but knowledge could make me an agreeable companion to men of sense, or qualify me to distinguish the superficial glitter of vanity from the solid merit of understanding; and that a habit of reading would enable me to fill up the vacuities of life without the help of silly or dangerous amusements, and preserve me from the snares of idleness and the inroads of temptation.

But their principal intention was to make me afraid of men, in which they succeeded so well for a time that I durst not look in their faces, or be left alone with them in a parlour; for they made me fancy that no man ever spoke but to deceive or looked but to allure; that the girl who suffered him that had once squeezed her hand to approach her a second time was on the brink of ruin; and that she who answered a billet without consulting her relations gave love such power over her that she would certainly become either poor or infamous.

From the time that my leading-strings were taken off, I scarce heard any mention of my beauty but from the milliner, the mantua-maker, and my own maid; for my mamma never said more when she heard me commended but 'The girl is very well,' and then endeavoured to divert my attention by some inquiry after my needle or my book.

It is now three months since I have been suffered to pay and receive visits, to dance at public assemblies, to have a place kept for me in the boxes, and to play at Lady Racket's rout, and you may easily imagine what I think of those who have so long cheated me with false expectations, disturbed me with fictitious terrors, and concealed from me all that I have found to make the happiness of woman.

I am so far from perceiving the usefulness or necessity of books that if I had not dropped all pretensions to learning I should have lost Mr Trip, whom I once frighted into another box by retailing some of Dryden's remarks upon a tragedy; for Mr Trip declares that he hates nothing like hard words, and I am sure there is not a better partner to be found; his very walk is a dance. I have talked once or twice among ladies about principles and ideas, but they put their fans before their faces and told me I was too wise for them, who for their part never pretended to read anything but the playbill, and asked me the price of my best head.

Those vacancies of time which are to be filled up with books I have never yet obtained; for, consider, Mr Rambler, I go to bed late and therefore cannot rise early; as soon as I am up I dress for the gardens; then walk in the park; then always go to some sale or show or entertainment at the Little Theatre, then must be dressed for dinner; then must pay my visits; then walk in the park; then hurry to the play; and from thence to the card-table. This is the general course of the day when there happens nothing extraordinary; but sometimes I ramble into the country and come back again to a ball; sometimes I am engaged for a whole day and part of the night. If, at any time, I can gain an hour by not being at home, I have so many things to do, so many orders to give to the milliner, so many alterations to make in my clothes, so many visitants' names to read over, so many invitations to accept or refuse, so many cards to write, and so many fashions to consider, that I am lost in confusion, forced at last to let in company or step into my chair, and leave half my affairs to the direction of my maid.

This is the round of my day; and when shall I either stop my course or so change it as to want a book? I suppose it cannot be imagined that any of these diversions will be soon at an end. There will always be gardens and a park and auctions and shows and playhouses and cards;

visits will always be paid and clothes always be worn; and how can I have time unemployed upon my hands?

But I am most at a loss to guess for what purpose they related such tragic stories of the cruelty, perfidy, and artifices of men, who, if they ever were so malicious and destructive, have certainly now reformed their manners. I have not since my entrance into the world found one who does not profess himself devoted to my service, and ready to live or die as I shall command him. They are so far from intending to hurt me that their only contention is who shall be allowed most closely to attend and most frequently to treat me; when different places of entertainment or schemes of pleasure are mentioned, I can see the eyes sparkle and the cheeks glow of him whose proposals obtain my approbation; he then leads me off in triumph, adores my condescension, and congratulates himself that he has lived to the hour of felicity. Are these, Mr Rambler, creatures to be feared? Is it likely that any injury will be done me by those who can enjoy life only while I favour them with my presence?

As little reason can I yet find to suspect them of stratagems and fraud. When I play at cards, they never take advantage of my mistakes nor exact from me a rigorous observation of the game. Even Mr Shuffle, a grave gentleman who has daughters older than myself, plays with me so negligently that I am sometimes inclined to believe he loses his money by design, and yet he is so fond of play that he says he will one day take me to his house in the country that we may try by ourselves who can conquer. I have not yet promised him; but when the town grows a little empty I shall think upon it, for I want some trinkets like Letitia's to my watch. I do not doubt my luck, but must study some means of amusing my relations.

For all these distinctions I find myself indebted to that beauty which I was never suffered to hear praised, and of which therefore I did not before know the full value. This concealment was certainly an intentional fraud, for my aunts have eyes like other people, and I am every day told that nothing but blindness can escape the influence of my charms. Their whole account of that world which they pretend to know so well has been only one fiction entangled with another; and though the modes of life oblige me to continue some appearances of respect, I cannot think that they who have been so clearly detected in ignorance or imposture have any right to the esteem, veneration, or obedience of,

Sir, Yours,
BELLARIA.

The Adventurer, No. 67

TUESDAY, JUNE 26, 1753

[The Benefits of Human Society]

That familiarity produces neglect has been long observed. The effect of all external objects, however great or splendid, ceases with their novelty: the courtier stands without emotion in the royal presence; the rustic tramples under his foot the beauties of the spring, with little attention to their colour or their fragrance; and the inhabitant of the coast darts his eye upon the immense diffusion of waters, without awe, wonder, or terror.

Those who have passed much of their lives in this great city look upon its opulence and its multitudes, its extent and variety, with cold indifference; but an inhabitant of the remoter parts of the kingdom is immediately distinguished by a kind of dissipated curiosity, a busy endeavour to divide his attention amongst a thousand objects, and a wild confusion of astonishment and alarm.

The attention of a newcomer is generally first struck by the multiplicity of cries that stun him in the streets, and the variety of merchandise and manufactures which the shopkeepers expose on every hand; and he is apt, by unwary bursts of admiration, to excite the merriment and contempt of those who mistake the use of their eyes for effects of their understanding, and confound accidental knowledge with just reasoning.

But, surely, these are subjects on which any man may without reproach employ his meditations: the innumerable occupations among which the thousands that swarm in the streets of London are distributed may furnish employment to minds of every cast, and capacities of every degree. He that contemplates the extent of this wonderful city finds it difficult to conceive by what method plenty is maintained in our markets, and how the inhabitants are regularly supplied with the necessaries of life; but when he examines the shops and warehouses, sees the immense stores of every kind of merchandise piled up for sale, and runs over all the manufactures of art and products of nature, which are every where attracting his eye and soliciting his purse, he will be inclined to conclude that such quantities cannot easily be exhausted, and that part of mankind must soon stand still for want of employment till the wares already provided shall be worn out and destroyed.

As Socrates was passing through the fair at Athens, and casting his eyes over the shops and customers, 'How many things are here,' says he, 'that I do not want!' The same sentiment is every moment rising in the mind of him that walks the streets of London, however inferior in philosophy to Socrates: he beholds a thousand shops crowded with goods of which he can scarcely tell the use, and which, therefore, he is apt to consider as of no value; and, indeed, many of the arts by which families are supported, and wealth is heaped together, are of that minute and superfluous kind which nothing but experience could evince possible to be prosecuted with advantage, and which, as the world might easily want, it could scarcely be expected to encourage.

But so it is, that custom, curiosity, or wantonness supplies every art with patrons, and finds purchasers for every manufacture; the world is so adjusted that not only bread but riches may be obtained without great abilities, or arduous performances: the most unskilful hand and unenlightened mind have sufficient incitements to industry; for he that is resolutely busy can scarcely be in want. There is, indeed, no employment, however despicable, from which a man may not promise himself more than competence, when he sees thousands and myriads raised to dignity, by no other merit than that of contributing to supply their neighbours with the means of sucking smoke through a tube of clay; and others raising contributions upon those whose elegance disdains the grossness of smoky luxury by grinding the same materials into a powder that may at once gratify and impair the smell.

Not only by these popular and modish trifles, but by a thousand unheeded and evanescent kinds of business, are the multitudes of this city preserved from idleness, and consequently from want. In the endless variety of tastes and circumstances that diversify mankind, nothing is so superfluous but that some one desires it; or so common but that some one is compelled to buy it. As nothing is useless but because it is in improper hands, what is thrown away by one is gathered up by another; and the refuse of part of mankind furnishes a subordinate class with the materials necessary to their support.

When I look round upon those who are thus variously exerting their qualifications, I cannot but admire the secret concatenation of society that links together the great and the mean, the illustrious and the obscure; and consider with benevolent satisfaction that no man, unless his body or mind be totally disabled, has need to suffer the mortification of seeing himself useless or burdensome to the community: he that will diligently labour, in whatever occupation, will deserve the sustenance which he obtains, and the protection which he enjoys; and may lie down every night with the pleasing consciousness of having contributed something to the happiness of life.

Contempt and admiration are equally incident to narrow minds: he whose comprehension can take in the whole subordination of mankind, and whose perspicacity can pierce to the real state of things through the thin veils of fortune or of fashion, will discover meanness in the highest stations, and dignity in the meanest; and find that no man can become venerable but by virtue, or contemptible but by wickedness.

In the midst of this universal hurry, no man ought to be so little influenced by example, or so void of honest emulation, as to stand a lazy spectator of incessant labour; or please himself with the mean happiness of a drone, while the active swarms are buzzing about him: no man is without some quality by the due application of which he might deserve well of the world; and whoever he be that has but little in his power should be in haste to do that little, lest he be confounded with him that can do nothing.

By this general concurrence of endeavours, arts of every kind have been so long cultivated that all the wants of man may be immediately supplied; Idleness can scarcely form a wish which she may not gratify by the toil of others, or Curiosity dream of a toy which the shops are not ready to afford her.

Happiness is enjoyed only in proportion as it is known; and such is the state or folly of man that it is known only by experience of its contrary: we who have long lived amidst the conveniences of a town immensely populous have scarce an idea of a place where desire cannot be gratified by money. In order to have a just sense of this artificial plenty, it is necessary to have passed some time in a distant colony, or those parts of our island which are thinly inhabited: he that has once known how many trades every man in such situations is compelled to exercise, with how much labour the products of nature must be accommodated to human use, how long the loss or defect of any common utensil must be endured, or by what awkward expedients it must be supplied, how far men may wander with money in their hands before any can sell them what they wish to buy, will know how to rate at its proper value the plenty and ease of a great city.

But that the happiness of man may still remain imperfect, as wants in this place are easily supplied, new wants likewise are easily created: every man, in surveying the shops of London, sees numberless instruments and conveniences of which, while he did not known them, he never felt the need; and yet, when use has made them familiar, wonders how life could be supported without them. Thus it comes to pass that our desires always increase with our possessions; the knowledge that something remains yet unenjoyed impairs our enjoyment of the good before us.

They who have been accustomed to the refinements of science, and multiplications of contrivance, soon lose their confidence in the unassisted powers of nature, forget the paucity of our real necessities, and overlook the easy methods by which they may be supplied. It were a speculation worthy of a philosophical mind to examine how much is taken away from our native abilities, as well as added to them, by artificial expedients. We are so accustomed to give and receive assistance that each of us singly can do little for himself; and there is scarce any one amongst us, however contracted may be his form of life, who does not enjoy the labour of a thousand artists.

But a survey of the various nations that inhabit the earth will inform us that life may be supported with less assistance, and that the dexterity which practice enforced by necessity produces is able to effect much by very scanty means. The nations of Mexico and Peru erected cities and temples without the use of iron; and at this day the rude Indian supplies himself with all the necessities of life: sent like the rest of mankind naked into the world, as soon as his parents have nursed him up to strength, he is to provide by his own labour for his own support. His first care is to find a sharp flint among the rocks; with this he undertakes to fell the trees of the forest; he shapes his bow, heads his arrows, builds his cottage, and hollows his canoe, and from that time lives in a state of plenty and prosperity; he is sheltered from the storms, he is fortified against beasts of prey, he is enabled to pursue the fish of the sea, and the deer of the mountains; and as he does not know, does not envy the happiness of polished nations, where gold can supply the want of fortitude and skill, and he whose laborious ancestors have made him rich may lie stretched upon a couch, and see all the treasures of all the elements poured down before him.

This picture of a savage life, if it shows how much individuals may perform, shows likewise how much society is to be desired. Though the perseverance and address of the Indian excite our admiration, they nevertheless cannot procure him the conveniences which are enjoyed by the vagrant beggar of a civilized country: he hunts like a wild beast to satisfy his hunger; and when he lies down to rest after a successful chase, cannot pronounce himself secure against the danger of perishing in a few days; he is, perhaps, content with his condition, because he knows not that a better is attainable by man; as he that is born blind does not long for the perception of light, because he cannot conceive the advantages which light would afford him: but hunger, wounds, and weariness are real evils, though he believes them equally incident to all his fellow creatures; and when a tempest compels him to lie starving in his hut, he cannot justly be concluded equally happy with those whom art has exempted from the power of chance, and who make the foregoing year provide for the following.

To receive and to communicate assistance constitutes the happiness of human life: man may indeed preserve his existence in solitude, but can enjoy it only in society: the greatest understanding of an individual doomed to procure food and clothing for himself will barely supply him with expedients to keep off death from day to day; but as one of a large community performing only his share of the common business, he gains leisure for intellectual pleasures, and enjoys the happiness of reason and reflection.

The Adventurer, No. 84

SATURDAY, AUGUST 23, 1753

[Vanity in a Stage Coach]

TO THE ADVENTURER.

SIR,

It has been observed, I think, by Sir William Temple, and after him by almost every other writer, that England affords a greater variety of characters than the rest of the world. This is ascribed to the liberty prevailing amongst us, which gives every man the privilege of being wise or foolish his own way, and preserves him from the necessity of hypocrisy, or the servility of imitation.

That the position itself is true, I am not completely satisfied. To be nearly acquainted with the people of different countries can happen to very few; and in life, as in every thing else beheld at a distance, there appears an even uniformity; the petty discriminations which diversify the natural character are not discoverable but by a close inspection; we therefore find them most at home, because there we have most opportunities of remarking them. Much less am I convinced that this peculiar diversification, if it be real, is the consequence of peculiar liberty: for where is the government to be found that superintends individuals with so much vigilance as not to leave their private conduct without restraint? Can it enter into a reasonable mind to imagine that men of every other nation are not equally masters of their own time or houses with ourselves, and equally at liberty to be parsimonious or profuse, frolic or sullen, abstinent or luxurious? Liberty is certainly necessary to the full play of predominant humours; but such liberty is to be found alike under the government of the many or the few; in monarchies or in commonwealths.

How readily the predominant passion snatches an interval of liberty, and how fast it expands itself when the weight of restraint is taken away, I had lately an opportunity to discover, as I took a journey into the country in a stage coach; which, as every journey is a kind of adventure, may be very properly related to you, though I can display no such extraordinary assembly as Cervantes has collected at Don Quixote's inn.

In a stage coach the passengers are for the most part wholly unknown to one another, and without expectation of ever meeting again when their journey is at an end; one should therefore imagine that it was of little importance to any of them what conjectures the rest should form concerning him. Yet so it is, that as all think themselves secure from detection, all assume that character of which they are most desirous, and on no occasion is the general ambition of superiority more apparently indulged.

On the day of our departure, in the twilight of the morning, I ascended the vehicle, with three men and two women my fellow travellers. It was easy to observe the affected elevation of mien with which every one entered, and the supercilious civility with which they paid their compliments to each other. When the first ceremony was dispatched, we sat silent for a long time, all employed in collecting importance into our faces, and endeavouring to strike reverence and submission into our companions.

It is always observable that silence propagates itself, and that the longer talk has been suspended, the more difficult it is to find anything to say. We began now to wish for conversation; but no one seemed inclined to descend from his dignity, or first to propose a topic of discourse. At last a corpulent gentlemen, who had equipped himself for this expedition with a scarlet surtout, and a large hat with a broad lace, drew out his watch, looked on it in silence, and then held it dangling at his finger. This was, I suppose, understood by all the company as an invitation to ask the time of the day; but nobody appeared to heed his overture: and his desire to be talking so far overcame his resentment that he let us know of his own accord that it was past five, and that in two hours we should be at breakfast.

His condescension was thrown away; we continued all obdurate: the ladies held up their heads: I amused myself with watching their behaviour; and of the other two, one seemed to employ himself in counting the trees as we drove by them, the other drew his hat over his eyes, and counterfeited a slumber. The man of benevolence, to show that he was not depressed by our neglect, hummed a tune and beat time upon his snuff-box.

Thus universally displeased with one another, and not much delighted with ourselves, we came at last to the little inn appointed for our repast, and all began at once to recompense themselves for the constraint of silence by innumerable questions and orders to the people that attended us. At last, what every one had called for was got, or declared impossible to be got at that time, and we were persuaded to sit round the same table; when the gentleman in the red surtout looked again upon his watch, and told us that we had half an hour to spare, but he was sorry to see so little merriment among us; that all fellow travellers were for the time upon the level, and that it was always his way to make himself one of the company. 'I remember,' says he, 'it was on just such a morning as this that I and my lord Mumble and the duke of Tenterden were out upon a ramble; we called at a little house as it might be this; and my landlady, I warrant you, not suspecting to whom she was talking, was so jocular and facetious, and made so many merry answers to our questions, that we were all ready to burst with laughter. At last the good woman, happening to overhear me whisper the duke and call him by his title, was so surprised and confounded that we could scarcely get a word from her: and the duke never met me from that day to this, but he talks of the little house, and quarrels with me for terrifying the landlady.'

He had scarcely had time to congratulate himself on the veneration which this narrative must have procured him from the company, when one of the ladies having reached out for a plate on a distant part of the table, began to remark 'the inconveniences of travelling, and the difficulty which they who never sat at home without a great number of attendants found in performing for themselves such offices as the road required; but that people of quality often travelled in disguise, and might be generally known from the vulgar by their condescension to poor inn-keepers, and the allowance which they made for any defect in their entertainment: that for her part, while people were civil and meant well, it was never her custom to find fault; for one was not to expect upon a journey all that one enjoyed at one's own house.'

A general emulation seemed now to be excited. One of the men, who had hitherto said nothing, called for the last newspaper; and having perused it a while with deep pensiveness, 'It is impossible,' says he, 'for any man to guess how to act with regard to the stocks; last week it was the general opinion that they would fall; and I sold out twenty thousand pounds in order to a purchase: they have now risen unexpectedly; and I make no doubt but at my return to London I shall risk thirty thousand pounds amongst them again.'

A young man, who had hitherto distinguished himself only by the vivacity of his look, and a frequent diversion of his eyes from one object to another, upon this closed his snuff-box, and told us that 'he had a hundred times talked with the Chancellor and the judges on the subject of the stocks; that for his part he did not pretend to be well acquainted with the principles on which they were established, but had always heard them reckoned pernicious to trade, uncertain in their produce, and unsolid in their foundation; and that he had been advised by three judges, his most intimate friends, never to venture his money in the funds, but to put it out upon land security, till he could light upon an estate in his own country.'

It might be expected that, upon these glimpses of latent dignity, we should all have began to look around us with veneration, and have behaved like the princes of romance, when the enchantment that disguises them is dissolved, and they discover the dignity of each other: yet it happened that none of these hints made much impression on the company; every one was apparently suspected of endeavouring to impose false appearances upon the rest; all continued their haughtiness, in hopes to enforce their claims; and all grew every hour more sullen, because they found their representations of themselves without effect.

Thus we travelled on four days with malevolence perpetually increasing, and without any endeavour but to outvie each other in superciliousness and neglect; and when any two of us could separate ourselves for a moment, we vented our indignation at the sauciness of the rest.

At length the journey was at an end, and time and chance, that strip off all disguises, have discovered that the intimate of lords and dukes is a nobleman's butler, who has furnished a shop with the money he has saved; the man who deals so largely in the funds is the clerk of a broker in Change-alley; the lady who so carefully concealed her quality keeps a cook-shop behind the Exchange; and the young man who is so happy in the friendship of the judges engrosses and transcribes for bread in a garret of the Temple. Of one of the women only I could make no disadvantageous detection, because she had assumed no character, but accommodated herself to the scene before her, without any struggle for distinction or superiority.

I could not forbear to reflect on the folly of practising a fraud which, as the event showed, had been already practised too often to succeed, and by the success of which no advantage could have been obtained; of assuming a character which was to end with the day; and of claiming upon false pretences honours which must perish with the breath that paid them.

But, Mr Adventurer, let not those who laugh at me and my companions think this folly confined to a stage coach. Every man in the journey of life takes the same advantage of the ignorance of his fellow travellers, disguises himself in counterfeited merit, and hears those praises with complacency which his conscience reproaches him for accepting. Every man deceives himself while he thinks he is deceiving others; and forgets that the time is at hand when every illusion shall cease; when fictitious excellence shall be torn away; and All must be shown to All in their real state.

> I am, Sir,
> Your humble Servant,
> VIATOR.

The Adventurer, No. 85

TUESDAY, AUGUST 28, 1753

[The Role of the Scholar]

It is observed by Bacon, that 'reading makes a full man, conversation a ready man, and writing an exact man'.

As Bacon attained to degrees of knowledge scarcely ever reached by any other man, the directions which he gives for study have certainly a just claim to our regard; for who can teach an art with so great authority as he that has practised it with undisputed success?

Under the protection of so great a name, I shall, therefore, venture to inculcate to my ingenious contemporaries the necessity of reading, the fitness of consulting other understandings than their own, and of considering the sentiments and opinions of those who, however neglected in the present age, had in their own times, and many of them a long time afterwards, such reputation for knowledge and acuteness as will scarcely ever be attained by those that despise them.

An opinion has of late been, I know not how, propagated among us, that libraries are filled only with useless lumber; that men of parts stand in need of no assistance; and that to spend life in poring upon books is only to imbibe prejudices, to obstruct and embarrass the powers of nature, to cultivate memory at the expense of judgement, and to bury reason under a chaos of indigested learning.

Such is the talk of many who think themselves wise, and of some who are thought wise by others; of whom part probably believe their own tenets, and part may be justly suspected of endeavouring to shelter their ignorance in multitudes, and of wishing to destroy that reputation which they have no hopes to share. It will, I believe, be found invariably true that learning was never decried by any learned man; and what credit can be given to those who venture to condemn that which they do not know?

If reason has the power ascribed to it by its advocates, if so much is to be discovered by attention and meditation, it is hard to believe that so many millions, equally participating of the bounties of nature with ourselves, have been for ages upon ages meditating in vain: if the wits of the present time expect the regard of posterity, which will then inherit the reason which is now thought superior to instruction, surely they may allow themselves to be instructed by the reason of former generations. When, therefore, an author declares that he has been able to learn nothing from the writings of his predecessors, and such a declaration has been lately made, nothing but a degree of arrogance unpardonable in the greatest human understanding can hinder him from perceiving that he is raising prejudices against his own performance; for with what hopes of success can he attempt that in which greater abilities have hitherto miscarried? Or with what peculiar force does he suppose himself invigorated, that difficulties hitherto invincible should give way before him?

Of those whom Providence has qualified to make any additions to human knowledge, the number is extremely small; and what can be added by each single mind even of this superior class is very little: the greatest part of mankind must owe all their knowledge, and all must owe far the larger part of it, to the information of others. To understand the works of celebrated authors, to comprehend their systems, and retain their reasonings is a task more than equal to common intellects; and he is by no means to be accounted useless or idle who has stored his mind with acquired knowledge, and can detail it occasionally to others who have less leisure or weaker abilities.

Persius has justly observed that knowledge is nothing to him who is not known by others to possess it: to the scholar himself it is nothing with respect either to honour or advantage, for the world cannot reward those qualities which are concealed from it; with respect to others it is nothing, because it affords no help to ignorance or error.

It is with justice, therefore, that in an accomplished character, Horace unites just sentiments with the power of expressing them; and he that has once accumulated learning is next to consider how he shall most widely diffuse and most agreeably impart it.

A ready man is made by conversation. He that buries himself among his manuscripts *besprent*, as Pope° expresses it, *with learned dust*, and wears out his days and nights in perpetual research and solitary meditation, is too apt to lose in his elocution what he adds to his wisdom, and when he comes into the world, to appear overloaded with his own notions, like a man armed with weapons which he cannot wield. He has no facility of inculcating his speculations, of adapting himself to the various degrees of intellect which the accidents of conversation will present; but will talk to most unintelligibly, and to all unpleasantly.

I was once present at the lectures of a profound philosopher, a man really skilled in the science which he professed, who having occasion to explain the terms *opacum* and *pellucidum*, told us, after some hesitation, that *opacum* was as one might say *opaque*, and that *pellucidum* signified *pellucid*. Such was the dexterity with which this learned reader facilitated to his auditors the intricacies of science; and so true is it that a man may know what he cannot teach.

Boerhaave complains that the writers who have treated of chemistry before him are useless to the greater part of students; because they presuppose their readers to have such degrees of skill as are not often to be found. Into the same error are all men apt to fall who have familiarized any subject to themselves in solitude: they discourse as if they thought every other man had been employed in the same inquiries; and expect that short hints and obscure allusions will produce in others the same train of ideas which they excite in themselves.

Nor is this the only inconvenience which the man of study suffers from a recluse life. When he meets with an opinion that pleases him, he catches it up with eagerness; looks only after such arguments as tend to his confirmation; or spares himself the trouble of discussion, and adopts it with very little proof; indulges it long without suspicion, and in time unites it to the general body of his knowledge, and treasures it up among incontestible truths: but when he comes into the world among men who, arguing upon dissimilar principles, have been led to different conclusions, and being placed in various situations view the same object on many sides, he finds his darling position attacked, and himself in no condition to defend it: having thought always in one train, he is in the state of a man who having fenced always with the same master is perplexed and amazed by a new posture of his antagonist; he is entangled in unexpected difficulties, he is harassed by sudden objections, he is unprovided with solutions or replies, his surprise impedes his natural powers of reasoning, his thoughts are scattered and confounded, and he gratifies the pride of airy petulance with an easy victory.

It is difficult to imagine with what obstinacy truths which one mind perceives almost by intuition will be rejected by another; and how many artifices must be practised to procure admission for the most evident propositions into understandings frighted by their novelty, or hardened against them by accidental prejudice: it can scarcely be conceived how frequently in these extemporaneous controversies the dull will be subtle, and the acute absurd; how often stupidity will elude the force of argument, by involving itself in its own gloom; and mistaken ingenuity will weave artful fallacies, which reason can scarcely find means to disentangle.

In these encounters the learning of the recluse usually fails him: nothing but long habit and frequent experiments can confer the power of changing a position into various forms, presenting it in different points of view, connecting it with known and granted truths, fortifying it with intelligible arguments, and illustrating it by apt similitudes; and he, therefore, that has collected his knowledge in solitude must learn its application by mixing with mankind.

But while the various opportunities of conversation invite us to try every mode of argument, and every art of recommending our sentiments, we are frequently betrayed to the use of such as are not in themselves strictly defensible: a man heated in talk, and eager of victory, takes advantage of the mistakes or ignorance of his adversary, lays hold of concessions to which he knows he has no right, and urges proofs likely to prevail on his opponent, though he knows himself that they have no force: thus the severity of reason is relaxed; many topics are accumulated, but without just arrangement or distinction; we learn to satisfy ourselves with such ratiocination as silences others, and seldom recall to a close examination that discourse which has gratified our vanity with victory and applause.

Some caution, therefore, must be used, lest copiousness and facility be made less valuable by inaccuracy and confusion. To fix the thoughts by writing, and subject them to frequent examinations and reviews, is the best method of enabling the mind to detect its own sophisms, and keep it on guard against the fallacies which it practises on others: in conversation we naturally diffuse our thoughts, and in writing we contract them; method is the excellence of writing, and unconstraint the grace of conversation.

To read, write, and converse in due proportions is, therefore, the business of a man of letters. For all these there is not often equal opportunity; excellence, therefore, is not often attainable: and most men fail in one or other of the ends proposed, and are full without readiness, or ready without exactness. Some deficiency must be forgiven all, because all are men; and more must be allowed to pass uncensured in the greater part of the world, because none can confer upon himself abilities, and few have the choice of situations proper for the improvement of those which nature has bestowed: it is, however, reasonable to have perfection in our eye; that we may always advance towards it, though we know it never can be reached.

The Adventurer, No. 99

TUESDAY, OCTOBER 16, 1753

['Projectors', Successful and Unsuccessful]

It has always been the practice of mankind to judge of actions by the event. The same attempts, conducted in the same manner, but terminated by different success, produce different judgements: they who attain their wishes never want celebrators of their wisdom and their virtue; and they that miscarry are quickly discovered to have been defective not only in mental but in moral qualities. The world will never be long without some good reason to hate the unhappy; their real faults are immediately detected, and if those are not sufficient to sink them into infamy, an additional weight of calumny will be superadded: he that fails in his endeavours after wealth or power will not long retain either honesty or courage.

This species of injustice has so long prevailed in universal practice that it seems likewise to have infected speculation: so few minds are able to separate the ideas of greatness and prosperity that even Sir William Temple has determined that 'he who can deserve the name of a hero must not only be virtuous but fortunate'.

By this unreasonable distribution of praise and blame, none have suffered oftener than projectors, whose rapidity of imagination and vastness of design raise such envy in their fellow mortals that every eye watches for their fall, and every heart exults at their distresses: yet even a projector may gain favour by success; and the tongue that was prepared to hiss then endeavours to excel others in loudness of applause.

When Coriolanus, in Shakespeare, deserted to Aufidius, the Volscian servants at first insulted him, even while he stood under the protection of the household gods: but when they saw that the project took effect, and the stranger was seated at the head of the table, one of them very judiciously observes, 'that he always thought there was more in him than he could think'.

Machiavel has justly animadverted on the different notice taken by all succeeding times of the two great projectors Catiline and Caesar. Both formed the same project, and intended to raise themselves to power by subverting the commonwealth: they pursued their design, perhaps, with equal abilities, and with equal virtue; but Catiline perished in the field, and Caesar returned from Pharsalia with unlimited authority: and from that time, every monarch of the earth has thought himself honoured by a comparison with Caesar; and Catiline has been never mentioned but that his name might be applied to traitors and incendiaries.

In an age more remote, Xerxes projected the conquest of Greece, and brought down the power of Asia against it: but after the world had been filled with expectation and terror, his army was beaten, his fleet was destroyed, and Xerxes has been never mentioned without contempt.

A few years afterwards, Greece likewise had her turn of giving birth to a projector; who invading Asia with a small army, went forward in search of adventures, and by his escape from one danger gained only more rashness to rush into another: he stormed city after city, overran kingdom after kingdom, fought battles only for barren victory, and invaded nations only that he might make his way through them to new invasions: but having been fortunate in the execution of his projects, he died with the name of Alexander the Great.

These are, indeed, events of ancient time; but human nature is always the same, and every age will afford us instances of public censures influenced by events. The great business of the middle centuries was the holy war; which undoubtedly was a noble project, and was for a long time prosecuted with a spirit equal to that with which it had been contrived: but the ardour of the European heroes only hurried them to destruction; for a long time they could not gain the territories for which they fought, and, when at last gained, they could not keep them: their expeditions, therefore, have been the scoff of idleness and ignorance, their understanding and their virtue have been equally vilified, their conduct has been ridiculed, and their cause has been defamed.

When Columbus had engaged King Ferdinand in the discovery of the other hemisphere, the sailors with whom he embarked in the expedition had so little confidence in their commander that after having been long at sea looking for coasts which they expected never to find, they raised a general mutiny, and demanded to return. He found means to soothe them into a permission to continue the same course three days longer, and on the evening of the third day descried land. Had the impatience of his crew denied him a few hours of the time requested, what had been his fate but to have come back with the infamy of a vain projector, who had betrayed the king's credulity to useless expenses, and risked his life in seeking countries that had no existence: how would those that had rejected his proposals have triumphed in their acuteness? and when would his name have been mentioned, but with the makers of potable gold and malleable glass?

The last royal projectors with whom the world has been troubled were Charles of Sweden and the Czar of Muscovy. Charles, if any judgement may be formed of his designs by his measures and his enquiries, had purposed first to dethrone the Czar, then to lead his army through pathless deserts into China, thence to make his way by the sword through the whole circuit of Asia, and by the conquest of Turkey to unite Sweden with his new dominions: but this mighty project was crushed at Pultowa, and Charles has since been considered as a madman by those powers who sent their ambassadors to solicit his friendship, and their generals 'to learn under him the art of war'.

The Czar found employment sufficient in his own dominions, and amused himself in digging canals, and building cities; murdering his subjects with insufferable fatigues, and transplanting nations from one corner of his dominions to another, without regretting the thousands that perished on the way: but he attained his end, he made his people formidable, and is numbered by fame among the demigods.

I am far from intending to vindicate the sanguinary projects of heroes and conquerors, and would wish rather to diminish the reputation of their success than the infamy of their miscarriages: for I cannot conceive why he that has burnt cities, and wasted nations, and filled the world with horror and desolation should be more kindly regarded by mankind than he that died in the rudiments of wickedness; why he that accomplished mischief should be glorious, and he that only endeavoured it should be criminal: I would wish Caesar and Catiline, Xerxes and Alexander, Charles and Peter huddled together in obscurity or detestation.

But there is another species of projectors, to whom I would willingly conciliate mankind; whose ends are generally laudable, and whose labours are innocent; who are searching out new powers of nature, or contriving new works of art; but who are yet persecuted with incessant obloquy, and whom the universal contempt with which they are treated often debars from that success which their industry would obtain if it were permitted to act without opposition.

They who find themselves inclined to censure new undertakings, only because they are new, should consider that the folly of projection is very seldom the folly of a fool; it is commonly the ebullition of a capacious mind, crowded with variety of knowledge, and heated with intenseness of thought; it proceeds often from the consciousness of uncommon powers, from the confidence of those who, having already done much, are easily persuaded that they can do more: when Rowley had completed the Orrery, he attempted the perpetual motion; when Boyle had exhausted the secrets of vulgar chemistry, he turned his thoughts to the work of transmutation.

A projector generally unites those qualities which have the fairest claim to veneration, extent of knowledge and greatness of design: it was said of Catiline, 'immoderata, incredibilia, nimis alta semper cupiebat'. Projectors of all kinds agree in their intellects, though they differ in their morals; they all fail by attempting things beyond their power, by despising vulgar attainments, and aspiring to performances to which, perhaps, nature has not proportioned the force of man: when they fail, therefore, they fail not by idleness or timidity, but by rash adventure and fruitless diligence.

That the attempts of such men will often miscarry, we may reasonably expect; yet from such men, and such only, are we to hope for the cultivation of those parts of nature which lie yet waste, and the invention of those arts which are yet wanting to the felicity of life. If they are, therefore, universally discouraged, art and discovery can make no advances. Whatever is attempted without previous certainty of success may be considered as a project, and amongst narrow minds may, therefore, expose its author to censure and contempt; and if the liberty of laughing be once indulged, every man will laugh at what he does not understand, every project will be considered as madness, and every great or new design will be censured as a project. Men unaccustomed to reason and researches think every enterprise impracticable which is extended beyond common effects, or comprises many intermediate operations. Many that presume to laugh at projectors would consider a flight through the air in a winged chariot, and the movement of a mighty engine by the steam of water, as equally the dreams of mechanic lunacy; and would hear, with equal negligence, of the union of the Thames and Severn by a canal,° and the scheme of Albuquerque the viceroy of the Indies, who in the rage of hostility had contrived to make Egypt a barren desert by turning the Nile into the Red Sea.

Those who have attempted much have seldom failed to perform more than those who never deviate from the common roads of action: many valuable preparations of chemistry are supposed to have risen from unsuccessful enquiries after the grand elixir: it is, therefore, just to encourage those who endeavour to enlarge the power of art, since they often succeed beyond expectation; and when they fail, may sometimes benefit the world even by their miscarriages.

The Idler, No. 5

SATURDAY, MAY 13, 1758

[A Female Army]

Our military operations° are at last begun; our troops are marching in all the pomp of war, and a camp is marked out on the Isle of Wight; the heart of every Englishman now swells with confidence, though somewhat softened by generous compassion for the consternation and distresses of our enemies.

This formidable armament and splendid march produce different effects upon different minds, according to the boundless diversities of temper, occupation, and habits of thought.

Many a tender maiden considers her lover as already lost, because he cannot reach the camp but by crossing the sea; men, of a more political understanding, are persuaded that we shall now see, in a few days, the ambassadors of France supplicating for pity. Some are hoping for a bloody battle, because a bloody battle makes a vendible narrative; some are composing songs of victory; some planning arches of triumph; and some are mixing fireworks for the celebration of a peace.

Of all extensive and complicated objects different parts are selected by different eyes; and minds are variously affected, as they vary their attention. The care of the public is now fixed upon our soldiers, who are leaving their native country to wander, none can tell how long, in the pathless deserts of the Isle of Wight. The tender sigh for their sufferings, and the gay drink to their success. I, who look, or believe myself to look, with more philosophic eyes on human affairs, must confess that I saw the troops march with little emotion; my thoughts were fixed upon other scenes, and the tear stole into my eyes, not for those who were going away, but for those who were left behind.

We have no reason to doubt but our troops will proceed with proper caution; there are men among them who can take care of themselves. But how shall the ladies endure without them? By what arts can they, who have long had no joy but from the civilities of a soldier, now amuse their hours, and solace their separation?

Of fifty thousand men now destined to different stations, if we allow each to have been occasionally necessary only to four women, a short computation will inform us that two hundred thousand ladies are left to languish in distress; two hundred thousand ladies, who must run to sales and auctions without an attendant; sit at the play, without a critic to direct their opinion; buy their fans by their own judgment; dispose shells by their own invention; walk in the Mall without a gallant; go to the Gardens without a protector; and shuffle cards with vain impatience for want of a fourth to complete the party.

Of these ladies, some, I hope, have lapdogs, and some monkeys, but they are unsatisfactory companions. Many useful offices are performed by men of scarlet to which neither dog nor monkey has adequate abilities: a parrot, indeed, is as fine as a colonel, and if he has been much used to good company, is not wholly without conversation; but a parrot, after all, is a poor little creature, and has neither sword nor shoulder-knot, can neither dance nor play at cards.

Since the soldiers must obey the call of their duty, and go to that side of the kingdom which faces France, I know not why the ladies, who cannot live without them, should not follow them. The prejudices and pride of man have long presumed the sword and spindle made for different hands, and denied the other sex to partake the grandeur of military glory. This notion may be consistently enough received in France, where the Salic law excludes females from the throne; but we, who allow them to be sovereigns, may surely suppose them capable to be soldiers.

It were to be wished that some man whose experience and authority might enforce regard would propose that our encampments for the present year should comprise an equal number of men and women, who should march and fight in mingled bodies. If proper colonels were once appointed, and the drums ordered to beat for female volunteers, our regiments would soon be filled without the reproach or cruelty of an impress.

Of these heroines, some might serve on foot, under the denomination of the *Female Buffs*, and some on horseback, with the title of *Lady Hussars*.

What objections can be made to this scheme I have endeavoured maturely to consider; and cannot find that a modern soldier has any duties, except that of obedience, which a lady cannot perform. If the hair has lost its powder, a lady has a puff. If a coat be spotted, a lady has a brush. Strength is of less importance since fire-arms have been used; blows of the hand are now seldom exchanged; and what is there to be done in the charge or the retreat beyond the powers of a sprightly maiden?

Our masculine squadrons will not suppose themselves disgraced by their auxiliaries till they have done something which women could not have done. The troops of Braddock° never saw their enemies, and perhaps were defeated by women. If our American general had headed an army of girls, he might still have built a fort, and taken it. Had Minorca been defended by a female garrison, it might have been surrendered, as it was, without a breach; and I cannot but think that seven thousand women might have ventured to look at Rochfort, sack a village, rob a vineyard, and return in safety.

The Idler, No. 10

SATURDAY, JUNE 17, 1758

[Political Partisanship]

Credulity, or confidence of opinion too great for the evidence from which opinion is derived, we find to be a general weakness imputed by every sect and party to all others, and indeed by every man to every other man.

Of all kinds of credulity, the most obstinate and wonderful is that of political zealots; of men, who, being numbered, they know not how nor why, in any of the parties that divide a state, resign the use of their own eyes and ears, and resolve to believe nothing that does not favour those whom they profess to follow.

The bigot of philosophy is seduced by authorities which he has not always opportunities to examine, is entangled in systems by which truth and falsehood are inextricably complicated, or undertakes to talk on subjects which nature did not form him able to comprehend.

The Cartesian,° who denies that his horse feels the spur, or that the hare is afraid when the hounds approach her; the disciple of Malebranche, who maintains that the man was not hurt by the bullet which, according to vulgar apprehensions, swept away his legs; the follower of Berkeley,° who, while he sits writing at his table, declares that he has neither table, paper, nor fingers, have all the honour at least of being deceived by fallacies not easily detected, and may plead that they did not forsake truth but for appearances which they were not able to distinguish from it.

But the man who engages in a party has seldom to do with anything remote or abstruse. The present state of things is before his eyes; and, if he cannot be satisfied without retrospection, yet he seldom extends his views beyond the historical events of the last century. All the knowledge that he can want is within his attainment, and most of the arguments which he can hear are within his capacity.

Yet so it is that an Idler meets every hour of his life with men who have different opinions upon every thing past, present, and future; who deny the most notorious facts, contradict the most cogent truths, and persist in asserting today what they asserted yesterday, in defiance of evidence, and contempt of confutation.

Two of my companions, who are grown old in idleness, are Tom Tempest and Jack Sneaker. Both of them consider themselves as neglected by their parties, and therefore entitled to credit, for why should they favour ingratitude? They are both men of integrity where no factious interest is to be promoted, and both lovers of truth when they are not heated with political debate.

Tom Tempest is a steady friend to the House of Stuart. He can recount the prodigies that have appeared in the sky, and the calamities that have afflicted the nation every year from the Revolution, and is of opinion that if the exiled family had continued to reign, there would have neither been worms in our ships nor caterpillars on our trees. He wonders that the nation was not awakened by the hard frost to a revocation of the true king, and is hourly afraid that the whole island will be lost in the sea. He believes that King William burned Whitehall° that he might steal the furniture, and that Tillotson° died an atheist. Of Queen Anne he speaks with more tenderness, owns that she meant well, and can tell by whom and why she was poisoned. In the succeeding reigns all has been corruption, malice, and design. He believes that nothing ill has ever happened for these forty years by chance or error; he holds that the battle of Dettingen was won by mistake, and that of Fontenoy lost by contract; that the *Victory* was sunk by a private order; that Cornhill was fired by emissaries from the Council; and the arch of Westminster Bridge was so contrived as to sink on purpose that the nation might be put to charge. He considers the new road to Islington as an encroachment on liberty, and often asserts that *broad wheels*° will be the ruin of England.

Tom is generally vehement and noisy, but nevertheless has some secrets which he always communicates in a whisper. Many and many a time has Tom told me, in a corner, that our miseries were almost at an end, and that we should see, in a month, another monarch on the throne; the time elapses without a revolution; Tom meets me again with new intelligence, the whole scheme is now settled, and we shall see great events in another month.

Jack Sneaker° is a hearty adherent to the present establishment; he has known those who saw the bed into which the Pretender was conveyed in a warming-pan. He often rejoices that the nation was not enslaved by the Irish. He believes that King William never lost a battle, and that if he had lived one year longer he would have conquered France. He holds that Charles the First was a Papist. He allows there were some good men in the reign of Queen Anne, but the Peace of Utrecht brought a blast upon the nation, and has been the cause of all the evil that we have suffered to the present hour. He believes that the scheme of the South Sea was well intended, but that it miscarried by the influence of France. He considers a standing army as the bulwark of liberty, thinks us secured from corruption by septennial parliaments, relates how we are enriched and strengthened by the electoral dominions,° and declares that the public debt is a blessing to the nation.

Yet amidst all this prosperity, poor Jack is hourly disturbed by the dread of Popery. He wonders that some stricter laws are not made against Papists, and is sometimes afraid that they are busy with French gold among the bishops and judges.

He cannot believe that the nonjurors° are so quiet for nothing, they must certainly be forming some plot for the establishment of Popery; he does not think the present oaths sufficiently binding, and wishes that some better security could be found for the succession of Hanover. He is zealous for the naturalization of foreign Protestants, and rejoiced at the admission of the Jews° to the English privileges, because he thought a Jew would never be a Papist.

The Idler, No. 22 [original numbering]°

SEPTEMBER 9, 1758

[The Vultures' View of Man]

Many naturalists are of opinion that the animals which we commonly consider as mute have the power of imparting their thoughts to one another. That they can express general sensations is very certain; every being that can utter sounds has a different voice for pleasure and for pain. The hound informs his fellows when he scents his game; the hen calls her chickens to their food by her cluck, and drives them from danger by her scream.

Birds have the greatest variety of notes; they have indeed a variety which seems almost sufficient to make a speech adequate to the purposes of a life which is regulated by instinct, and can admit little change or improvement. To the cries of birds, curiosity or superstition has been always attentive; many have studied the language of the feathered tribes, and some have boasted that they understood it.

The most skilful or most confident interpreters of the silvan dialogues have been commonly found among the philosophers of the East, in a country where the calmness of the air, and the mildness of the seasons, allow the student to pass a great part of the year in groves and bowers. But what may be done in one place by peculiar opportunities may be performed in another by peculiar diligence. A shepherd of Bohemia has, by long abode in the forests, enabled himself to understand the voice of birds; at least he relates with great confidence a story of which the credibility may be considered by the learned.

'As I was sitting,' said he, 'within a hollow rock, and watching my sheep that fed in the valley, I heard two vultures interchangeably crying on the summit of the cliff. Both voices were earnest and deliberate. My curiosity prevailed over my care of the flock; I climbed slowly and silently from crag to crag, concealed among the shrubs, till I found a cavity where I might sit and listen without suffering, or giving disturbance.

'I soon perceived that my labour would be well repaid; for an old vulture was sitting on a naked prominence, with her young about her, whom she was instructing in the arts of a vulture's life, and preparing, by the last lecture, for their final dismission to the mountains and the skies.

'"My children," said the old vulture, "you will the less want my instructions because you have had my practice before your eyes; you have seen me snatch from the farm the household fowl, you have seen me seize the leveret in the bush, and the kid in the pasture, you know how to fix your talons, and how to balance your flight when you are laden with your prey. But you remember the taste of more delicious food; I have often regaled you with the flesh of man."

'"Tell us," said the young vultures, "where man may be found, and how he may be known; his flesh is surely the natural food of a vulture. Why have you never brought a man in your talons to the nest?"

'"He is too bulky," said the mother; "when we find a man, we can only tear away his flesh, and leave his bones upon the ground."

'"Since man is so big," said the young ones, "how do you kill him? You are afraid of the wolf and of the bear; by what power are vultures superior to man; is man more defenceless than a sheep?"

'"We have not the strength of man," returned the mother, "and I am sometimes in doubt whether we have the subtlety; and the vultures would seldom feast upon his flesh, had not Nature, that devoted him to our uses, infused into him a strange ferocity, which I have never observed in any other being that feeds upon the earth. Two herds of men will often meet and shake his earth with noise, and fill the air with fire. When you hear noise and see fire which flashes along the ground, hasten to the place with your swiftest wing, for men are surely destroying one another; you will then find the ground smoking with blood and covered with carcasses, of which many are dis-membered and mangled for the convenience of the vulture."

'"But when men have killed their prey," said the pupil, "why do they not eat it? When the wolf has killed a sheep, he suffers not the vulture to touch it till he has satisfied himself. Is not man another kind of wolf?"

"'Man,' said the mother, "is the only beast who kills that which he does not devour, and this quality makes him so much a benefactor to our species."

"'If men kill our prey and lay it in our way,' said the young one, "what need shall we have of labouring for ourselves?"

"'Because man will, sometimes,' replied the mother, "remain for a long time quiet in his den. The old vultures will tell you when you are to watch his motions. When you see men in great numbers moving close together, like a flight of storks, you may conclude that they are hunting, and that you will soon revel in human blood."

"'But still,' said the young one, "I would gladly know the reason of this mutual slaughter. I could never kill what I could not eat."

"'My child,' said the mother, "this is a question which I cannot answer, though I am reckoned the most subtle bird of the mountain. When I was young I used frequently to visit the eyrie of an old vulture who dwelt upon the Carpathian rocks; he had made many observations; he knew the places that afforded prey round his habitation, as far in every direction as the strongest wing can fly between the rising and setting of the summer sun; he had fed year after year on the entrails of men. His opinion was that men had only the appearance of animal life,° being really vegetables with a power of motion; and that as the boughs of an oak are dashed together by the storm, that swine may fatten upon the falling acorns, so men are by some unaccountable power driven one against another, till they lose their motion, that vultures may be fed. Others think they have observed something of contrivance and policy among these mischievous beings, and those that hover more closely round them pretend that there is, in every herd, one that gives directions to the rest, and seems to be more eminently delighted with a wide carnage. What it is that entitles him to such pre-eminence we know not; he is seldom the biggest or the swiftest, but he shows by his eagerness and diligence that he is, more than any of the others, a friend to vultures.'"

The Idler, No. 22 [23]

SATURDAY, SEPTEMBER 16, 1758

[Debtors' Prisons (1)]

TO THE IDLER.

SIR,

As I was passing lately under one of the gates of this city, I was struck with horror by a rueful cry, which summoned me 'to remember the poor debtors'.

The wisdom and justice of the English laws are, by Englishmen at least, loudly celebrated; but scarcely the most zealous admirers of our institutions can think that law wise which, when men are capable of work, obliges them to beg; or just which exposes the liberty of one to the passions of another.

The prosperity of a people is proportionate to the number of hands and minds usefully employed. To the community sedition is a fever, corruption is a gangrene, and idleness an atrophy. Whatever body, and whatever society, wastes more than it acquires must gradually decay; and every being that continues to be fed, and ceases to labour, takes away something from the public stock.

The confinement, therefore, of any man in the sloth and darkness of a prison is a loss to the nation, and no gain to the creditor. For of the multitudes who are pining in those cells of misery, a very small part is suspected of any fraudulent act by which they retain what belongs to others. The rest are imprisoned by the wantonness of pride, the malignity of revenge, or the acrimony of disappointed expectation.

If those who thus rigorously exercise the power which the law has put into their hands be asked why they continue to imprison those whom they know to be unable to pay them, one will answer that his debtor once lived better than himself; another, that his wife looked above her neighbours, and his children went in silk clothes to the dancing school; and another, that he pretended to be a joker and a wit. Some will reply that if they were in debt they should meet with the same treatment; some, that they owe no more than they can pay, and need therefore give no account of their actions. Some will confess their resolution that their debtors shall rot in jail; and some will discover that they hope, by cruelty, to wring the payment from their friends.

The end of all civil regulations is to secure private happiness from private malignity; to keep individuals from the power of one another; but this end is apparently neglected when a man, irritated with loss, is allowed to be the judge of his own cause, and to assign the punishment of his own pain; when the distinction between guilt and unhappiness, between casualty and design, is entrusted to eyes blind with interest, to understandings depraved by resentment.

Since poverty is punished among us as a crime, it ought at least to be treated with the same lenity as other crimes; the offender ought not to languish at the will of him whom he has offended, but to be allowed some appeal to the justice of his country. There can be no reason why any debtor should be imprisoned, but that he may be compelled to payment; and a term should therefore be fixed in which the creditor should exhibit his accusation of concealed property. If such property can be discovered, let it be given to the creditor; if the charge is not offered, or cannot be proved, let the prisoner be dismissed.

Those who made the laws have apparently supposed that every deficiency of payment is the crime of the debtor. But the truth is that the creditor always shares the act, and often more than shares the guilt of improper trust. It seldom happens that any man imprisons another but for debts which he suffered to be contracted in hope of advantage to himself, and for bargains in which he proportioned his profit to his own opinion of the hazard; and there is no reason why one should punish the other for a contract in which both concurred.

Many of the inhabitants of prisons may justly complain of harder treatment. He that once owes more than he can pay is often obliged to bribe his creditor to patience, by increasing his debt. Worse and worse commodities, at a higher and higher price, are forced upon him; he is impoverished by compulsive traffic, and at last overwhelmed, in the common receptacles of misery, by debts which, without his own consent, were accumulated on his head. To the relief of this distress, no other objection can be made but that by an easy dissolution of debts, fraud will be left without punishment, and imprudence without awe, and that when insolvency shall be no longer punishable, credit will cease.

The motive to credit is the hope of advantage. Commerce can never be at a stop while one man wants what another can supply; and credit will never be denied while it is likely to be repaid with profit. He that trusts one whom he designs to sue is criminal by the act of trust; the cessation of such insidious traffic is to be desired, and no reason can be given why a change of the law should impair any other.

We see nation trade with nation, where no payment can be compelled. Mutual convenience produces mutual confidence, and the merchants continue to satisfy the demands of each other, though they have nothing to dread but the loss of trade.

It is vain to continue an institution which experience shows to be ineffectual. We have now imprisoned one generation of debtors after another, but we do not find that their numbers lessen. We have now learned that rashness and imprudence will not be deterred from taking credit; let us try whether fraud and avarice may be more easily restrained from giving it.

I am, Sir, &c.

The Idler, No. 38 [39]

SATURDAY, JANUARY 6, 1759

[Debtors' Prisons (2)]

Since the publication of the letter concerning the condition of those who are confined in gaols by their creditors, an enquiry is said to have been made by which it appears that more than twenty thousand are at this time prisoners for debt.

We often look with indifference on the successive parts of that which, if the whole were seen together, would shake us with emotion. A debtor is dragged to prison, pitied for a moment, and then forgotten; another follows him, and is lost alike in the caverns of oblivion; but when the whole mass of calamity rises up at once, when twenty thousand reasonable beings are heard all groaning in un- necessary misery, not by the infirmity of nature, but the mistake or negligence of policy, who can forbear to pity and lament, to wonder and abhor?

There is here no need of declamatory vehemence; we live in an age of commerce and computation; let us therefore coolly enquire what is the sum of evil which the imprisonment of debtors brings upon our country.

It seems to be the opinion of the later computists that the inhabitants of England do not exceed six millions, of which twenty thousand is the three-hundredth part. What shall we say of the humanity or the wisdom of a nation that voluntarily sacrifices one in every three hundred to lingering destruction!

The misfortunes of an individual do not extend their influence to many; yet, if we consider the effects of consanguinity and friendship, and the general reciprocation of wants and benefits, which make one man dear or necessary to another, it may reasonably be supposed that every man languishing in prison gives trouble of some kind to two others who love or need him. By this multiplication of misery we see distress extended to the hundredth part of the whole society.

If we estimate at a shilling a day what is lost by the inaction and consumed in the support of each man thus chained down to involuntary idleness, the public loss will rise in one year to three hundred thousand pounds; in ten years to more than a sixth part of our circulating coin.

I am afraid that those who are best acquainted with the state of our prisons will confess that my conjecture is too near the truth when I suppose that the corrosion of resentment, the heaviness of sorrow, the corruption of confined air, the want of exercise, and sometimes of food, the contagion of diseases from which there is no retreat, and the severity of tyrants against whom there can be no resistance, and all the complicated horrors of a prison put an end every year to the life of one in four of those that are shut up from the common comforts of human life.

Thus perish yearly five thousand men, overborne with sorrow, consumed by famine, or putrified by filth; many of them in the most vigorous and useful part of life; for the thoughtless and imprudent are commonly young, and the active and busy are seldom old.

According to the rule generally received, which supposes that one in thirty dies yearly, the race of man may be said to be renewed at the end of thirty years. Who would have believed till now that of every English generation a hundred and fifty thousand perish in our gaols! That in every century, a nation eminent for science, studious of commerce, ambitious of empire, should willingly lose, in noisome dungeons, five hundred thousand of its inhabitants: a number greater than has ever been destroyed in the same time by the pestilence and sword!

A very late occurrence may show us the value of the number which we thus condemn to be useless; in the re-establishment of the trained bands,° thirty thousand are considered as a force sufficient against all exigencies: while, therefore, we detain twenty thousand in prison, we shut up in darkness and uselessness two thirds of an army which ourselves judge equal to the defence of our country.

The monastic institutions have been often blamed as tending to retard the increase of mankind. And perhaps retirement ought rarely to be permitted, except to those whose employment is consistent with abstraction, and who, though solitary, will not be idle; to those whom infirmity makes useless to the commonwealth, or to those who have paid their due proportion to society, and who, having lived for others, may be honourably dismissed to live for themselves. But whatever be the evil or the folly of these retreats, those have no right to censure them whose prisons contain greater numbers than the monasteries of other countries. It is, surely, less foolish and less criminal to permit inaction than compel it; to comply with doubtful opinions of happiness than condemn to certain and apparent misery; to indulge the extravagancies of erroneous piety than to multiply and enforce temptations to wickedness.

The misery of gaols is not half their evil; they are filled with every corruption which poverty and wickedness can generate between them; with all the shameless and profligate enormities that can be produced by the impudence of ignominy, the rage of want, and the malignity of despair. In a prison the awe of the public eye is lost, and the power of the law is spent; there are few fears, there are no blushes. The lewd inflame the lewd, the audacious harden the audacious. Every one fortifies himself as he can against his own sensibility, endeavours to practise on others the arts which are practised on himself; and gains the kindness of his associates by similitude of manners.

Thus some sink amidst their misery, and others survive only to propagate villainy. It may be hoped that our lawgivers will at length take away from us this power of starving and depraving one another: but, if there be any reason why this inveterate evil should not be removed in our age, which true policy has enlightened beyond any former time, let those whose writings form the opinions and the practices of their contemporaries endeavour to transfer the reproach of such imprisonment from the debtor to the creditor, till universal infamy shall pursue the wretch whose wantonness of power, or revenge of disappointment, condemns another to torture and to ruin; till he shall be hunted through the world as an enemy to man, and find in riches no shelter from contempt.

Surely, he whose debtor has perished in prison, though he may acquit himself of deliberate murder, must at least have his mind clouded with discontent when he considers how much another has suffered from him; when he thinks on the wife bewailing her husband, or the children begging the bread which their father would have earned. If there are any made so obdurate by avarice or cruelty as to revolve these consequences without dread or pity, I must leave them to be awakened by some other power, for I write only to human beings.

The Idler, No. 60 [61]

SATURDAY, JUNE 9, 1759

[How to Become a Critic (1)]

Criticism is a study by which men grow important and formidable at very small expense. The power of invention has been conferred by nature upon few, and the labour of learning those sciences which may, by mere labour, be obtained is too great to be willingly endured; but every man can exert such judgment as he has upon the works of others; and he whom nature has made weak, and idleness keeps ignorant, may yet support his vanity by the name of a critic.

I hope it will give comfort to great numbers who are passing through the world in obscurity when I inform them how easily distinction may be obtained. All the other powers of literature are coy and haughty, they must be long courted, and at last are not always gained; but criticism is a goddess easy of access and forward of advance, who will meet the slow and encourage the timorous; the want of meaning she supplies with words, and the want of spirit she recompenses with malignity.

This profession has one recommendation peculiar to itself, that it gives vent to malignity without real mischief. No genius was ever blasted by the breath of critics. The poison which, if confined, would have burst the heart, fumes away in empty hisses, and malice is set at ease with very little danger to merit. The critic is the only man whose triumph is without another's pain, and whose greatness does not rise upon another's ruin.

To a study at once so easy and so reputable, so malicious and so harmless, it cannot be necessary to invite my readers by a long or laboured exhortation; it is sufficient, since all would be critics if they could, to show by one eminent example that all can be critics if they will.

Dick Minim,° after the common course of puerile studies, in which he was no great proficient, was put apprentice to a brewer, with whom he had lived two years, when his uncle died in the City, and left him a large fortune in the stocks. Dick had for six months before used the company of the lower players, of whom he had learned to scorn a trade, and being now at liberty to follow his genius, he resolved to be a man of wit and humour. That he might be properly initiated in his new character, he frequented the coffee-houses near the theatres, where he listened very diligently day after day to those who talked of language and sentiments, and unities and catastrophes, till by slow degrees he began to think that he understood something of the stage, and hoped in time to talk himself.

But he did not trust so much to natural sagacity as wholly to neglect the help of books. When the theatres were shut, he retired to Richmond with a few select writers, whose opinions he impressed upon his memory by unwearied diligence; and when he returned with other wits to the town, was able to tell, in very proper phrases, that the chief business of art is to copy nature; that a perfect writer is not to be expected, because genius decays as judgment increases; that the great art is the art of blotting, and that according to the rule of Horace every piece should be kept nine years.

Of the great authors he now began to display the characters, laying down as an universal position that all had beauties and defects. His opinion was that Shakespeare, committing himself wholly to the impulse of nature, wanted that correctness which learning would have given him; and that Jonson, trusting to learning, did not sufficiently cast his eye on nature. He blamed the stanza of Spenser, and could not bear the hexameters of Sidney. Denham and Waller he held the first reformers of English numbers, and thought that if Waller could have obtained the strength of Denham, or Denham the sweetness of Waller, there had been nothing wanting to complete a poet. He often expressed his commiseration of Dryden's poverty, and his indignation at the age which suffered him to write for bread; he repeated with rapture the first lines of *All for Love*, but wondered at the corruption of taste which could bear any thing so unnatural as rhyming tragedies. In Otway he found uncommon powers of moving the passions, but was disgusted by his general negligence, and blamed him for making a conspirator his hero; and never concluded his disquisition without remarking how happily the sound of the clock is made to alarm the audience. Southern would have been his favourite, but that he mixes comic with tragic scenes, intercepts the natural course of the passions, and fills the mind with a wild confusion of mirth and melancholy. The versification of Rowe he thought too melodious for the stage, and too little varied in different passions. He made it the great fault of

Congreve that all his persons were wits, and that he always wrote with
more art than nature. He considered *Cato* rather as a poem than a
play, and allowed Addison to be the complete master of allegory and
grave humour, but paid no great deference to him as a critic. He
thought the chief merit of Prior was in his easy tales and lighter
poems, though he allowed that his *Solomon* had many noble
sentiments elegantly expressed. In Swift he discovered an inimitable
vein of irony, and an easiness which all would hope and few would
attain. Pope he was inclined to degrade from a poet to a versifier, and
thought his numbers rather luscious than sweet. He often lamented
the neglect of *Phaedra and Hippolitus*, and wished to see the stage
under better regulations.

These assertions passed commonly uncontradicted; and if now and
then an opponent started up, he was quickly repressed by the suffrages
of the company, and Minim went away from every dispute with
elation of heart and increase of confidence.

He now grew conscious of his abilities, and began to talk of the
present state of dramatic poetry; wondered what was become of the
comic genius which supplied our ancestors with wit and pleasantry,
and why no writer could be found that durst now venture beyond a
farce. He saw no reason for thinking that the vein of humour was
exhausted, since we live in a country where liberty suffers every
character to spread itself to its utmost bulk, and which therefore
produces more originals than all the rest of the world together. Of
tragedy he concluded business to be the soul, and yet often hinted that
love predominates too much upon the modern stage.

He was now an acknowledged critic and had his own seat in the
coffee-house, and headed a party in the pit. Minim has more vanity
than ill-nature, and seldom desires to do much mischief; he will
perhaps murmur a little in the ear of him that sits next him, but
endeavours to influence the audience to favour by clapping when an
actor exclaims 'ye Gods', or laments the misery of his country.

By degrees he was admitted to rehearsals, and many of his friends
are of opinion that our present poets are indebted to him for their
happiest thoughts; by his contrivance the bell was rung twice in
Barbarossa,° and by his persuasion the author of *Cleone* concluded his
play without a couplet; for what can be more absurd, said Minim,
than that part of a play should be rhymed, and part written in blank
verse? and by what acquisition of faculties is the speaker who never
could find rhymes before enabled to rhyme at the conclusion of an act!

He is the great investigator of hidden beauties, and is particularly delighted when he finds 'the sound an echo to the sense'.° He has read all our poets with particular attention to this delicacy of versification, and wonders at the supineness with which their works have been hitherto perused, so that no man has found the sound of a drum in this distich,

> When pulpit, drum ecclesiastic,
> Was beat with fist instead of a stick;

and that the wonderful lines upon honour and a bubble have hitherto passed without notice,

> Honour is like the glassy bubble,
> Which costs philosophers such trouble,
> Where one part cracked, the whole does fly,
> And wits are cracked to find out why.

In these verses, says Minim, we have two striking accommodations of the sound to the sense. It is impossible to utter the two lines emphatically without an act like that which they describe; *bubble* and *trouble* causing a momentary inflation of the cheeks by the retention of the breath, which is afterwards forcibly emitted, as in the practice of *blowing bubbles*. But the greatest excellence is in the third line, which is *cracked* in the middle to express a crack, and then shivers into monosyllables. Yet has this diamond lain neglected with common stones, and among the innumerable admirers of *Hudibras* the observation of this superlative passage has been reserved for the sagacity of Minim.

The Idler, No. 61 [62]

SATURDAY, JUNE 16, 1759

[How to Become a Critic (2)]

Mr Minim had now advanced himself to the zenith of critical reputation; when he was in the pit, every eye in the boxes was fixed upon him, when he entered his coffee-house, he was surrounded by circles of candidates, who passed their novitiate of literature under his tuition; his opinion was asked by all who had no opinion of their own, and yet loved to debate and decide; and no composition was supposed to pass in safety to posterity till it had been secured by Minim's approbation.

Minim professes great admiration of the wisdom and munificence by which the academies of the continent were raised, and often wishes for some standard of taste, for some tribunal, to which merit may appeal from caprice, prejudice, and malignity. He has formed a plan for an academy of criticism, where every work of imagination may be read before it is printed, and which shall authoritatively direct the theatres what pieces to receive or reject, to exclude or to revive.

Such an institution would, in Dick's opinion, spread the fame of English literature over Europe, and make London the metropolis of elegance and politeness, the place to which the learned and ingenious of all countries would repair for instruction and improvement, and where nothing would any longer be applauded or endured that was not conformed to the nicest rules, and finished with the highest elegance.

Till some happy conjunction of the planets shall dispose our princes or ministers to make themselves immortal by such an academy, Minim contents himself to preside four nights in a week in a critical society selected by himself, where he is heard without contradiction, and whence his judgment is disseminated through the great vulgar and the small.

When he is placed in the chair of criticism, he declares loudly for the noble simplicity of our ancestors, in opposition to the petty refinements, and ornamental luxuriance. Sometimes he is sunk in despair, and perceives false delicacy daily gaining ground, and sometimes brightens his countenance with a gleam of hope, and predicts the revival of the true sublime. He then fulminates his loudest censures against the monkish barbarity of rhyme; wonders how beings that pretend to reason can be pleased with one line always ending like another; tells how unjustly and unnaturally sense is sacrificed to sound; how often the best thoughts are mangled by the necessity of confining or extending them to the dimensions of a couplet; and rejoices that genius has, in our days, shaken off the shackles which had encumbered it so long. Yet he allows that rhyme may sometimes be borne, if the lines be often broken, and the pauses judiciously diversified.

From blank verse he makes an easy transition to Milton, whom he produces as an example of the slow advance of lasting reputation. Milton is the only writer whose books Minim can read for ever without weariness. What cause it is that exempts this pleasure from satiety he has long and diligently enquired, and believes it to consist in the perpetual variation of the numbers, by which the ear is gratified and the attention awakened. The lines that are commonly thought rugged and unmusical, he conceives to have been written to temper the melodious luxury of the rest, or to express things by a proper cadence: for he scarcely finds a verse that has not this favourite beauty; he declares that he could shiver in a hot-house when he reads that

> the ground
> Burns frore, and cold performs th' effect of fire.

And that when Milton bewails his blindness, the verse

> So thick a drop serene has quenched these orbs

has, he knows not how, something that strikes him with an obscure sensation like that which he fancies would be felt from the sound of darkness.

Minim is not so confident of his rules of judgment as not very eagerly to catch new light from the name of the author. He is commonly so prudent as to spare those whom he cannot resist, unless, as will sometimes happen, he finds the public combined against them. But a fresh pretender to fame he is strongly inclined to censure, till his own honour requires that he commend him. Till he knows the success of a composition, he intrenches himself in general terms; there are some new thoughts and beautiful passages, but there is likewise much which he would have advised the author to expunge. He has several favourite epithets, of which he has never settled the meaning, but which are very commodiously applied to books which he has not read, or cannot understand. One is *manly*, another is *dry*, another *stiff*, and another *flimsy*; sometimes he discovers delicacy of style, and sometimes meets with *strange expressions*.

He is never so great, or so happy, as when a youth of promising parts is brought to receive his directions for the prosecution of his studies. He then puts on a very serious air; he advises the pupil to read none but the best authors, and, when he finds one congenial to his own mind, to study his beauties, but avoid his faults, and, when he sits down to write, to consider how his favourite author would think at the present time on the present occasion. He exhorts him to catch those moments when he finds his thoughts expanded and his genius exalted, but to take care lest imagination hurry him beyond the bounds of nature. He holds diligence the mother of success, yet enjoins him, with great earnestness, not to read more than he can digest, and not to confuse his mind by pursuing studies of contrary tendencies. He tells him that every man has his genius, and that Cicero could never be a poet. The boy retires illuminated, resolves to follow his genius, and to think how Milton would have thought; and Minim feasts upon his own beneficence till another day brings another pupil.

The Idler, No. 81 [82]°

SATURDAY, NOVEMBER 3, 1759

[European Oppression in America]

As the English army was passing towards Quebec along a soft savanna between a mountain and a lake, one of the petty chiefs of the inland regions stood upon a rock surrounded by his clan, and from behind the shelter of the bushes contemplated the art and regularity of European war. It was evening, the tents were pitched, he observed the security with which the troops rested in the night, and the order with which the march was renewed in the morning. He continued to pursue them with his eye till they could be seen no longer, and then stood for some time silent and pensive.

Then turning to his followers, 'My children,' said he, 'I have often heard from men hoary with long life that there was a time when our ancestors were absolute lords of the woods, the meadows, and the lakes, wherever the eye can reach or the foot can pass. They fished and hunted, feasted and danced, and when they were weary lay down under the first thicket, without danger and without fear. They changed their habitations as the seasons required, convenience prompted, or curiosity allured them, and sometimes gathered the fruits of the mountain, and sometimes sported in canoes along the coast.

'Many years and ages are supposed to have been thus passed in plenty and security; when at last, a new race of men entered our country from the great ocean. They enclosed themselves in habitations of stone, which our ancestors could neither enter by violence, nor destroy by fire. They issued from those fastnesses, sometimes covered like the armadillo with shells, from which the lance rebounded on the striker, and sometimes carried by mighty beasts which had never been seen in our vales or forests, of such strength and swiftness that flight and opposition were vain alike. Those invaders ranged over the continent, slaughtering in their rage those that resisted, and those that submitted in their mirth. Of those that remained, some were buried in caverns, and condemned to dig metals° for their masters; some were employed in tilling the ground, of which foreign tyrants devour the produce; and when the sword and the mines have destroyed the natives, they supply their place by human beings of another colour,° brought from some distant country to perish here under toil and torture.

'Some there are who boast their humanity, and content themselves to seize our chases and fisheries, who drive us from every tract of ground where fertility and pleasantness invite them to settle, and make no war upon us except when we intrude upon our own lands.

'Others pretend to have purchased a right of residence and tyranny; but surely the insolence of such bargains is more offensive than the avowed and open dominion of force. What reward can induce the possessor of a country to admit a stranger more powerful than himself? Fraud or terror must operate in such contracts;° either they promised protection which they never have afforded, or instruction which they never imparted. We hoped to be secured by their favour from some other evil, or to learn the arts of Europe, by which we might be able to secure ourselves. Their power they have never exerted in our defence, and their arts they have studiously concealed from us. Their treaties are only to deceive, and their traffic only to defraud us. They have a written law° among them, of which they boast as derived from him who made the earth and sea, and by which they profess to believe that man will be made happy when life shall forsake him. Why is not this law communicated to us? It is concealed because it is violated. For how can they preach it to an Indian nation, when I am told that one of its first precepts forbids them to do to others what they would not that others should do to them.

'But the time perhaps is now approaching when the pride of usurpation shall be crushed, and the cruelties of invasion shall be revenged. The sons of rapacity have now drawn their swords upon each other, and referred their claims to the decision of war; let us look unconcerned upon the slaughter, and remember that the death of every European delivers the country from a tyrant and a robber; for what is the claim of either nation, but the claim of the vulture to the leveret, of the tiger to the fawn? Let them then continue to dispute their title to regions which they cannot people, to purchase by danger and blood the empty dignity of dominion over mountains which they will never climb, and rivers which they will never pass. Let us endeavour, in the mean time, to learn their discipline, and to forge their weapons; and when they shall be weakened with mutual slaughter, let us rush down upon them, force their remains to take shelter in their ships, and reign once more in our native country.'

The Idler, No. 84 [85]°

SATURDAY, NOVEMBER 24, 1759

[Autobiography]

Biography is, of the various kinds of narrative writing, that which is most eagerly read, and most easily applied to the purposes of life.

In romances, when the wild field of possibility lies open to invention, the incidents may easily be made more numerous, the vicissitudes more sudden, and the events more wonderful; but from the time of life when fancy begins to be overruled by reason and corrected by experience, the most artful tale raises little curiosity when it is known to be false; though it may, perhaps, be sometimes read as a model of a neat or elegant style, not for the sake of knowing what it contains, but how it is written; or those that are weary of themselves may have recourse to it as a pleasing dream, of which, when they awake, they voluntarily dismiss the images from their minds.

The examples and events of history press, indeed, upon the mind with the weight of truth; but when they are reposited in the memory, they are oftener employed for show than use, and rather diversify conversation than regulate life. Few are engaged in such scenes as give them opportunities of growing wiser by the downfall of statesmen or the defeat of generals. The stratagems of war, and the intrigues of courts, are read by far the greater part of mankind with the same indifference as the adventures of fabled heroes, or the revolutions of a fairy region. Between falsehood and useless truth there is little difference. As gold which he cannot spend will make no man rich, so knowledge which he cannot apply will make no man wise.

The mischievous consequences of vice and folly, of irregular desires and predominant passions, are best discovered by those relations which are levelled with the general surface of life, which tell not how any man became great, but how he was made happy; not how he lost the favour of his prince, but how he became discontented with himself.

Those relations are therefore commonly of most value in which the writer tells his own story. He that recounts the life of another commonly dwells most upon conspicuous events, lessens the familiarity of his tale to increase its dignity, shows his favourite at a distance decorated and magnified like the ancient actors in their tragic dress, and endeavours to hide the man that he may produce a hero.

But if it be true which was said by a French prince,° 'that no man was a hero to the servants of his chamber', it is equally true that every man is yet less a hero to himself. He that is most elevated above the crowd by the importance of his employments or the reputation of his genius feels himself affected by fame or business but as they influence his domestic life. The high and low, as they have the same faculties and the same senses, have no less similitude in their pains and pleasures. The sensations are the same in all, though produced by very different occasions. The prince feels the same pain when an invader seizes a province as the farmer when a thief drives away his cow. Men thus equal in themselves will appear equal in honest and impartial biography; and those whom fortune or nature place at the greatest distance may afford instruction to each other.

The writer of his own life has at least the first qualification of an historian, the knowledge of the truth; and though it may be plausibly objected that his temptations to disguise it are equal to his opportunities of knowing it, yet I cannot but think that impartiality may be expected with equal confidence from him that relates the passages of his own life, as from him that delivers the transactions of another.

Certainty of knowledge not only excludes mistake but fortifies veracity. What we collect by conjecture, and by conjecture only can one man judge of another's motives or sentiments, is easily modified by fancy or by desire; as objects imperfectly discerned take forms from the hope or fear of the beholder. But that which is fully known cannot be falsified but with reluctance of understanding, and alarm of conscience; of understanding, the lover of truth; of conscience, the sentinel of virtue.

He that writes the life of another is either his friend or his enemy, and wishes either to exalt his praise or aggravate his infamy; many temptations to falsehood will occur in the disguise of passions too specious to fear much resistance. Love of virtue will animate panegyric, and hatred of wickedness embitter censure. The zeal of gratitude, the ardour of patriotism, fondness for an opinion, or fidelity to a party may easily overpower the vigilance of a mind habitually well disposed, and prevail over unassisted and unfriended veracity.

But he that speaks of himself has no motive to falsehood or partiality except self-love, by which all have so often been betrayed that all are on the watch against its artifices. He that writes an apology for a single action, to confute an accusation, or recommend himself to favour, is indeed always to be suspected of favouring his own cause; but he that sits down calmly and voluntarily to review his life for the admonition of posterity, or to amuse himself, and leaves this account unpublished, may be commonly presumed to tell the truth, since falsehood cannot appease his own mind, and fame will not be heard beneath the tomb.

The Idler, No. 88 [89]

SATURDAY, DECEMBER 22, 1759

[Limitations of Human Achievement]

When the philosophers of the last age were first congregated into the Royal Society, great expectations were raised of the sudden progress of useful arts; the time was supposed to be near when engines should turn by a perpetual motion, and health be secured by the universal medicine; when learning should be facilitated by a real character,° and commerce extended by ships which could reach their ports in defiance of the tempest.

But improvement is naturally slow. The society met and parted without any visible diminution of the miseries of life. The gout and stone were still painful, the ground that was not ploughed brought no harvest, and neither oranges nor grapes would grow upon the hawthorn. At last, those who were disappointed began to be angry; those likewise who hated innovation were glad to gain an opportunity of ridiculing men who had depreciated, perhaps with too much arrogance, the knowledge of antiquity. And it appears from some of their earliest apologies that the philosophers felt with great sensibility the unwelcome importunities of those who were daily asking, 'What have ye done?'°

The truth is that little had been done compared with what fame had been suffered to promise; and the question could only be answered by general apologies and by new hopes, which, when they were frustrated, gave a new occasion to the same vexatious enquiry.

This fatal question has disturbed the quiet of many other minds. He that in the latter part of his life too strictly enquires what he has done can very seldom receive from his own heart such an account as will give him satisfaction.

We do not indeed so often disappoint others as ourselves. We not only think more highly than others of our own abilities, but allow ourselves to form hopes which we never communicate, and please our thoughts with employments which none ever will allot us, and with elevations to which we are never expected to rise; and when our days and years have passed away in common business or common amusements, and we find at last that we have suffered our purposes to sleep till the time of action is past, we are reproached only by our own reflections; neither our friends nor our enemies wonder that we live and die like the rest of mankind, that we live without notice and die without memorial; they know not what task we had proposed, and therefore cannot discern whether it is finished.

He that compares what he has done with what he has left undone will feel the effect which must always follow the comparison of imagination with reality; he will look with contempt on his own unimportance, and wonder to what purpose he came into the world; he will repine that he shall leave behind him no evidence of his having been, that he has added nothing to the system of life, but has glided from youth to age among the crowd, without any effort for distinction.

Man is seldom willing to let fall the opinion of his own dignity, or to believe that he does little only because every individual is a very little being. He is better content to want diligence than power, and sooner confesses the depravity of his will than the imbecility of his nature.

From this mistaken notion of human greatness it proceeds that many who pretend to have made great advances in wisdom so loudly declare that they despise themselves. If I had ever found any of the self-contemners much irritated or pained by the consciousness of their meanness, I should have given them consolation by observing that a little more than nothing is as much as can be expected from a being who with respect to the multitudes about him is himself little more than nothing. Every man is obliged by the supreme master of the universe to improve all the opportunities of good which are afforded him, and to keep in continual activity such abilities as are bestowed upon him. But he has no reason to repine though his abilities are small and his opportunities few. He that has improved the virtue or advanced the happiness of one fellow-creature, he that has ascertained a single moral proposition, or added one useful experiment to natural knowledge, may be contented with his own performance, and, with respect to mortals like himself, may demand, like Augustus,° to be dismissed at his departure with applause.

The Idler, No. 100 [101]

SATURDAY, MARCH 15, 1760

[A Good Sort of Woman]

TO THE IDLER.

SIR,

The uncertainty and defects of language have produced very frequent complaints among the learned; yet there still remain many words among us undefined, which are very necessary to be rightly understood, and which produce very mischievous mistakes when they are erroneously interpreted.

I lived in a state of celibacy beyond the usual time. In the hurry first of pleasure and afterwards of business, I felt no want of a domestic companion; but becoming weary of labour I soon grew more weary of idleness, and thought it reasonable to follow the custom of life, and to seek some solace of my cares in female tenderness, and some amusement of my leisure in female cheerfulness.

The choice which has been long delayed is commonly made at last with great caution. My resolution was to keep my passions neutral, and to marry only in compliance with my reason. I drew upon a page of my pocket book a scheme of all female virtues and vices, with the vices which border upon every virtue, and the virtues which are allied to every vice. I considered that wit was sarcastic, and magnanimity imperious; that avarice was economical, and ignorance obsequious; and having estimated the good and evil of every quality, employed my own diligence and that of my friends to find the lady in whom nature and reason had reached that happy mediocrity which is equally remote from exuberance and deficience.

Every woman had her admirers and her censurers, and the expectations which one raised were by another quickly depressed: yet there was one in whose favour almost all suffrages concurred. Miss Gentle was universally allowed to be a good sort of woman. Her fortune was not large, but so prudently managed that she wore finer clothes and saw more company than many who were known to be twice as rich. Miss Gentle's visits were everywhere welcome, and whatever family she favoured with her company, she always left behind her such a degree of kindness as recommended her to others; every day extended her acquaintance, and all who knew her declared that they never met with a better sort of woman.

To Miss Gentle I made my addresses, and was received with great equality of temper. She did not in the days of courtship assume the privilege of imposing rigorous commands, or resenting slight offences. If I forgot any of her injunctions I was gently reminded, if I missed the minute of appointment I was easily forgiven. I foresaw nothing in marriage but a halcyon calm, and longed for the happiness which was to be found in the inseparable society of a good sort of woman.

The jointure was soon settled by the intervention of friends, and the day came in which Miss Gentle was made mine for ever. The first month was passed easily enough in receiving and repaying the civilities of our friends. The bride practised with great exactness all the niceties of ceremony, and distributed her notice in the most punctilious proportions to the friends who surrounded us with their happy auguries.

But the time soon came when we were left to ourselves, and were to receive our pleasures from each other, and I then began to perceive that I was not formed to be much delighted by a good sort of woman. Her great principle is that the orders of a family must not be broken. Every hour of the day has its employment inviolably appropriated, nor will any importunity persuade her to walk in the garden at the time which she has devoted to her needlework, or to sit upstairs in that part of the forenoon which she has accustomed herself to spend in the back parlour. She allows herself to sit half an hour after breakfast, and an hour after dinner; while I am talking or reading to her, she keeps her eye upon her watch, and when the minute of departure comes, will leave an argument unfinished, or the intrigue of a play unravelled. She once called me to supper when I was watching an eclipse, and summoned me at another time to bed when I was going to give directions at a fire.

Her conversation is so habitually cautious that she never talks to me but in general terms, as to one whom it is dangerous to trust. For discriminations of character she has no names; all whom she mentions are honest men and agreeable women. She smiles not by sensation but by practice. Her laughter is never excited but by a joke, and her notion of a joke is not very delicate. The repetition of a good joke does not weaken its effect; if she has laughed once, she will laugh again.

She is an enemy to nothing but ill nature and pride, but she has frequent reason to lament that they are so frequent in the world. All who are not equally pleased with the good and bad, with the elegant and gross, with the witty and the dull, all who distinguish excellence from defect she considers as ill-natured; and she condemns as proud all who repress impertinence or quell presumption, or expect respect from any other eminence than that of fortune, to which she is always willing to pay homage.

There are none whom she openly hates; for if once she suffers, or believes herself to suffer, any contempt or insult, she never dismisses it from her mind but takes all opportunities to tell how easily she can forgive. There are none whom she loves much better than others; for when any of her acquaintance decline in the opinion of the world she always finds it inconvenient to visit them; her affection continues unaltered but it is impossible to be intimate with the whole town.

She daily exercises her benevolence by pitying every misfortune that happens to every family within her circle of notice; she is in hourly terrors lest one should catch cold in the rain, and another be frighted by the high wind. Her charity she shows by lamenting that so many poor wretches should languish in the streets, and by wondering what the great can think on that they do so little good with such large estates.

Her house is elegant and her table dainty though she has little taste of elegance, and is wholly free from vicious luxury; but she comforts herself that nobody can say that her house is dirty, or that her dishes are not well dressed.

This, Mr Idler, I have found by long experience to be the character of a good sort of woman, which I have sent you for the information of those by whom *a good sort of woman* and *a good woman* may happen to be used as equivalent terms, and who may suffer by the mistake like

Your humble servant,
TIM WARNER.

The Idler, No. 103 [104]

SATURDAY, APRIL 5, 1760

['This Is the Last']

Much of the pain and pleasure of mankind arises from the conjectures which every one makes of the thoughts of others; we all enjoy praise which we do not hear, and resent contempt which we do not see. The Idler may therefore be forgiven, if he suffers his imagination to represent to him what his readers will say or think when they are informed that they have now his last paper in their hands.

Value is more frequently raised by scarcity than by use. That which lay neglected when it was common rises in estimation as its quantity becomes less. We seldom learn the true want of what we have till it is discovered that we can have no more.

This essay will, perhaps, be read with care even by those who have not yet attended to any other; and he that finds this late attention recompensed will not forbear to wish that he had bestowed it sooner.

Though the Idler and his readers have contracted no close friendship they are perhaps both unwilling to part. There are few things not purely evil of which we can say without some emotion of uneasiness 'this is the last'. Those who never could agree together shed tears when mutual discontent has determined them to final separation; of a place which has been frequently visited, though without pleasure, the last look is taken with heaviness of heart; and the Idler, with all his chillness of tranquillity, is not wholly unaffected by the thought that his last essay is now before him.

This secret horror of the last is inseparable from a thinking being whose life is limited, and to whom death is dreadful. We always make a secret comparison between a part and the whole; the termination of any period of life reminds us that life itself has likewise its termination; when we have done any thing for the last time, we involuntarily reflect that a part of the days allotted us is past, and that as more is past there is less remaining.

It is very happily and kindly provided that in every life there are certain pauses and interruptions, which force consideration upon the careless, and seriousness upon the light; points of time where one course of action ends and another begins; and by vicissitude of fortune, or alteration of employment, by change of place, or loss of friendship, we are forced to say of something, 'this is the last'.

An even and unvaried tenor of life always hides from our apprehension the approach of its end. Succession is not perceived but by variation; he that lives today as he lived yesterday, and expects that, as the present day is, such will be the morrow, easily conceives time as running in a circle and returning to itself. The uncertainty of our duration is impressed commonly by dissimilitude of condition; it is only by finding life changeable that we are reminded of its shortness.

This conviction, however forcible at every new impression, is every moment fading from the mind; and partly by the inevitable incursion of new images, and partly by voluntary exclusion of unwelcome thoughts, we are again exposed to the universal fallacy; and we must do another thing for the last time, before we consider that the time is nigh when we shall do no more.

As the last *Idler* is published in that solemn week° which the Christian world has always set apart for the examination of the conscience, the review of life, the extinction of earthly desires and the renovation of holy purposes, I hope that my readers are already disposed to view every incident with seriousness, and improve it by meditation; and that when they see this series of trifles brought to a conclusion, they will consider that by outliving the *Idler*, they have passed weeks, months, and years which are now no longer in their power; that an end must in time be put to every thing great as to every thing little; that to life must come its last hour, and to this system of being its last day, the hour at which probation ceases, and repentance will be vain; the day in which every work of the hand, and imagination of the heart shall be brought to judgment, and an everlasting futurity shall be determined by the past.

A Dictionary of the English Language

IN WHICH THE WORDS ARE DEDUCED FROM THEIR ORIGINALS AND
ILLUSTRATED IN THEIR DIFFERENT SIGNIFICATIONS BY EXAMPLES FROM
THE BEST WRITERS

PREFACE

It is the fate of those who toil at the lower employments of life to be rather driven by the fear of evil than attracted by the prospect of good; to be exposed to censure, without hope of praise; to be disgraced by miscarriage, or punished for neglect, where success would have been without applause, and diligence without reward.

Among these unhappy mortals is the writer of dictionaries; whom mankind have considered, not as the pupil, but the slave of science, the pioneer° of literature, doomed only to remove rubbish and clear obstructions from the paths through which Learning and Genius press forward to conquest and glory, without bestowing a smile on the humble drudge that facilitates their progress. Every other author may aspire to praise; the lexicographer can only hope to escape reproach, and even this negative recompense has been yet granted to very few.

I have, notwithstanding this discouragement, attempted a dictionary of the English language, which, while it was employed in the cultivation of every species of literature, has itself been hitherto neglected; suffered to spread, under the direction of chance, into wild exuberance, resigned to the tyranny of time and fashion, and exposed to the corruptions of ignorance, and caprices of innovation.

When I took the first survey of my undertaking, I found our speech copious without order, and energetic without rules: wherever I turned my view, there was perplexity to be disentangled, and confusion to be regulated; choice was to be made out of boundless variety, without any established principle of selection; adulterations were to be detected, without a settled test of purity, and modes of expression to be rejected or received, without the suffrages of any writers of classical reputation or acknowledged authority.

Having therefore no assistance but from general grammar, I applied myself to the perusal of our writers; and noting whatever might be of use to ascertain or illustrate any word or phrase, accumulated in time the materials of a dictionary, which, by degrees, I reduced to method, establishing to myself, in the progress of the work, such rules as experience and analogy suggested to me; experience, which practice and observation were continually increasing; and analogy, which, though in some words obscure, was evident in others.

In adjusting the ORTHOGRAPHY, which has been to this time unsettled and fortuitous, I found it necessary to distinguish those irregularities that are inherent in our tongue, and perhaps coeval with it, from others which the ignorance or negligence of later writers has produced. Every language has its anomalies, which, though inconvenient, and in themselves once unnecessary, must be tolerated among the imperfections of human things, and which require only to be registered, that they may not be increased, and ascertained, that they may not be confounded: but every language has likewise its improprieties and absurdities, which it is the duty of the lexicographer to correct or proscribe.

As language was at its beginning merely oral, all words of necessary or common use were spoken before they were written; and while they were unfixed by any visible signs, must have been spoken with great diversity, as we now observe those who cannot read to catch sounds imperfectly, and utter them negligently. When this wild and barbarous jargon was first reduced to an alphabet, every penman endeavoured to express, as he could, the sounds which he was accustomed to pronounce or to receive, and vitiated in writing such words as were already vitiated in speech. The powers of the letters, when they were applied to a new language, must have been vague and unsettled, and, therefore, different hands would exhibit the same sound by different combinations.

From this uncertain pronunciation arise, in a great part, the various dialects of the same country, which will always be observed to grow fewer and less different, as books are multiplied; and from this arbitrary representation of sounds by letters proceeds that diversity of spelling, observable in the Saxon remains, and, I suppose, in the first books of every nation, which perplexes or destroys analogy, and produces anomalous formations that being once incorporated can never be afterward dismissed or reformed.

Of this kind are the derivatives *length* from *long*, *strength* from *strong*, *darling* from *dear*, *breadth* from *broad*, from *dry*, *drought*, and from *high*, *height*, which Milton, in zeal for analogy, writes *highth*. *Quid te exempta juvat spinis de pluribus una?*:° to change all would be too much, and to change one is nothing.

This uncertainty is most frequent in the vowels, which are so capriciously pronounced, and so differently modified, by accident or affectation, not only in every province, but in every mouth, that to them, as is well known to etymologists, little regard is to be shown in the deduction of one language from another.

Such defects are not errors in orthography, but spots of barbarity impressed so deep in the English language that criticism can never wash them away; these, therefore, must be permitted to remain untouched: but many words have likewise been altered by accident, or depraved by ignorance, as the pronunciation of the vulgar has been weakly followed; and some still continue to be variously written, as authors differ in their care or skill: of these it was proper to inquire the true orthography, which I have always considered as depending on their derivation, and have therefore referred them to their original languages: thus I write *enchant*, *enchantment*, *enchanter*, after the French, and *incantation* after the Latin; thus *entire* is chosen rather than *intire*, because it passed to us not from the Latin *integer*, but from the French *entier*.

Of many words it is difficult to say whether they were immediately received from the Latin or the French, since at the time when we had dominions in France, we had Latin service in our churches. It is, however, my opinion that the French generally supplied us; for we have few Latin words, among the terms of domestic use, which are not French; but many French, which are very remote from Latin.

Even in words of which the derivation is apparent, I have been often obliged to sacrifice uniformity to custom; thus I write, in compliance with a numberless majority, *convey* and *inveigh*, *deceit* and *receipt*, *fancy* and *phantom*; sometimes the derivative varies from the primitive, as *explain* and *explanation*, *repeat* and *repetition*.

Some combinations of letters having the same power are used indifferently without any discoverable reason of choice, as in *choak*, *choke*; *soap*, *sope*; *fewel*, *fuel*, and many others; which I have sometimes inserted twice, that those who search for them under either form may not search in vain.

In examining the orthography of any doubtful word, the mode of spelling by which it is inserted in the series of the Dictionary is to be considered as that to which I give, perhaps not often rashly, the preference. I have left, in the examples, to every author his own practice unmolested, that the reader may balance suffrages, and judge between us: but this question is not always to be determined by reputed or by real learning; some men, intent upon greater things, have thought little on sounds and derivations; some, knowing in the ancient tongues, have neglected those in which our words are commonly to be sought. Thus Hammond writes *fecibleness* for *feasibleness*, because, I suppose, he imagined it derived immediately from the Latin; and some words, such as *dependant*, *dependent*, *dependance*, *dependence*, vary their final syllable, as one or another language is present to the writer.

In this part of the work, where caprice has long wantoned without control, and vanity sought praise by petty reformation, I have endeavoured to proceed with a scholar's reverence for antiquity, and a grammarian's regard to the genius of our tongue. I have attempted few alterations, and among those few, perhaps, the greater part is from the modern to the ancient practice; and I hope I may be allowed to recommend to those whose thoughts have been, perhaps, employed too anxiously on verbal singularities, not to disturb, upon narrow views, or for minute propriety, the orthography of their fathers. It has been asserted that for the law to be *known* is of more importance than to be *right*. 'Change,' says Hooker,° 'is not made without inconvenience, even from worse to better.' There is in constancy and stability a general and lasting advantage, which will always overbalance the slow improvements of gradual correction. Much less ought our written language to comply with the corruptions of oral utterance, or copy that which every variation of time or place makes different from itself, and imitate those changes which will again be changed, while imitation is employed in observing them.

This recommendation of steadiness and uniformity does not proceed from an opinion that particular combinations of letters have much influence on human happiness; or that truth may not be successfully taught by modes of spelling fanciful and erroneous: I am not yet so lost in lexicography as to forget that *words are the daughters of earth*, *and that things are the sons of heaven*.° Language is only the instrument of science, and words are but the signs of ideas: I wish, however, that the instrument might be less apt to decay, and that signs might be permanent, like the things which they denote.

In settling the orthography, I have not wholly neglected the pronunciation, which I have directed by printing an accent upon the acute or elevated syllable. It will sometimes be found that the accent is placed by the author quoted on a different syllable from that marked in the alphabetical series; it is then to be understood that custom has varied, or that the author has, in my opinion, pronounced wrong. Short directions are sometimes given where the sound of letters is irregular; and if they are sometimes omitted, defect in such minute observations will be more easily excused than superfluity.

In the investigation both of the orthography and signification of words, their ETYMOLOGY was necessarily to be considered, and they were therefore to be divided into primitives and derivatives. A primitive word is that which can be traced no further to any English root; thus *circumspect*, *circumvent*, *circumstance*, *delude*, *concave*, and *complicate*, though compounds in the Latin, are to us primitives. Derivatives are all those that can be referred to any word in English of greater simplicity.

The derivatives I have referred to their primitives, with an accuracy sometimes needless; for who does not see that *remoteness* comes from *remote*, *lovely* from *love*, *concavity* from *concave*, and *demonstrative* from *demonstrate*? But this grammatical exuberance the scheme of my work did not allow me to repress. It is of great importance, in examining the general fabric of a language, to trace one word from another by noting the usual modes of derivation and inflection; and uniformity must be preserved in systematical works, though sometimes at the expense of particular propriety.

Among other derivatives, I have been careful to insert and elucidate the anomalous plurals of nouns and preterites of verbs, which in the Teutonic dialects are very frequent, and, though familiar to those who have always used them, interrupt and embarrass the learners of our language.

The two languages from which our primitives have been derived are the Roman and Teutonic: under the Roman I comprehend the French and provincial tongues; and under the Teutonic range the Saxon, German, and all their kindred dialects. Most of our polysyllables are Roman, and our words of one syllable are very often Teutonic.

In assigning the Roman original, it has perhaps sometimes happened that I have mentioned only the Latin, when the word was borrowed from the French; and considering myself as employed only in the illustration of my own language, I have not been very careful to observe whether the Latin word be pure or barbarous, or the French elegant or obsolete.

For the Teutonic etymologies, I am commonly indebted to Junius and Skinner,° the only names which I have forborne to quote when I copied their books; not that I might appropriate their labours or usurp their honours, but that I might spare a perpetual repetition by one general acknowledgment. Of these, whom I ought not to mention but with the reverence due to instructors and benefactors, Junius appears to have excelled in extent of learning, and Skinner in rectitude of understanding. Junius was accurately skilled in all the northern languages; Skinner probably examined the ancient and remoter dialects only by occasional inspection into dictionaries; but the learning of Junius is often of no other use than to show him a track by which he may deviate from his purpose, to which Skinner always presses forward by the shortest way. Skinner is often ignorant, but never ridiculous: Junius is always full of knowledge; but his variety distracts his judgment, and his learning is very frequently disgraced by his absurdities.

The votaries of the northern muses° will not, perhaps, easily restrain their indignation when they find the name of Junius thus degraded by a disadvantageous comparison; but whatever reverence is due to his diligence, or his attainments, it can be no criminal degree of censoriousness to charge that etymologist with want of judgment who can seriously derive *dream* from *drama*, because *life is a drama, and a drama is a dream*; and who declares with a tone of defiance, that no man can fail to derive *moan* from μόνος, *monos*, *single* or *solitary*, who considers that grief naturally loves to be alone.°

Our knowledge of the northern literature is so scanty that of words undoubtedly Teutonic the original is not always to be found in any ancient language; and I have therefore inserted Dutch or German substitutes, which I consider not as radical, but parallel, not as the parents, but sisters of the English.

The words which are represented as thus related by descent or cognation do not always agree in sense; for it is incident to words, as to their authors, to degenerate from their ancestors, and to change their manners when they change their country. It is sufficient, in etymological inquiries, if the senses of kindred words be found such as may easily pass into each other, or such as may both be referred to one general idea.

The etymology, so far as it is yet known, was easily found in the volumes where it is particularly and professedly delivered; and, by proper attention to the rules of derivation, the orthography was soon adjusted. But to COLLECT the WORDS of our language was a task of greater difficulty: the deficiency of dictionaries was immediately apparent; and when they were exhausted, what was yet wanting must be sought by fortuitous and unguided excursions into books, and gleaned as industry should find, or chance should offer it, in the boundless chaos of a living speech. My search, however, has been either skilful or lucky; for I have much augmented the vocabulary.

As my design was a dictionary common or appellative, I have omitted all words which have relation to proper names; such as *Arian*,

Socinian, Calvinist, Benedictine, Mahometan; but have retained those of a more general nature, as *Heathen, Pagan*.

Of the terms of art I have received such as could be found either in books of science or technical dictionaries; and have often inserted, from philosophical writers, words which are supported perhaps only by a single authority, and which being not admitted into general use, stand yet as candidates or probationers, and must depend for their adoption on the suffrage of futurity.

The words which our authors have introduced by their knowledge of foreign languages, or ignorance of their own, by vanity or wantonness, by compliance with fashion or lust of innovation, I have registered as they occurred, though commonly only to censure them, and warn others against the folly of naturalizing useless foreigners to the injury of the natives.

I have not rejected any by design, merely because they were unnecessary or exuberant; but have received those which by different writers have been differently formed, as *viscid*, and *viscidity*, *viscous*, and *viscosity*.

Compounded or double words I have seldom noted, except when they obtain a signification different from that which the components have in their simple state. Thus *highwayman*, *woodman* and *horse-courser* require an explanation; but of *thieflike* or *coachdriver* no notice was needed, because the primitives contain the meaning of the compounds.

Words arbitrarily formed by a constant and settled analogy, like diminutive adjectives in *ish*, as *greenish*, *bluish*, adverbs in *ly*, as *dully*, *openly*, substantives in *ness*, as *vileness*, *faultiness*, were less diligently sought, and sometimes have been omitted, when I had no authority that invited me to insert them; not that they are not genuine and regular offsprings of English roots, but, because their relation to the primitive being always the same, their signification cannot be mistaken.

The verbal nouns in *ing*, such as the *keeping* of the *castle*, the *leading* of the *army*, are always neglected, or placed only to illustrate the sense of the verb, except when they signify things as well as actions, and have, therefore, a plural number, as *dwelling*, *living*; or have an absolute and abstract signification, as *colouring*, *painting*, *learning*.

The participles are likewise omitted, unless, by signifying rather qualities than action, they take the nature of adjectives; as a *thinking* man, a man of prudence; a *pacing* horse, a horse that can pace: these I have ventured to call *participial adjectives*. But neither are these always inserted, because they are commonly to be understood, without any danger of mistake, by consulting the verb.

Obsolete words are admitted, when they are found in authors not obsolete, or when they have any force or beauty that may deserve revival.

As composition is one of the chief characteristics of a language, I have endeavoured to make some reparation for the universal negligence of my predecessors, by inserting great numbers of compounded words, as may be found under *after*, *fore*, *new*, *night*, and many more. These, numerous as they are, might be multiplied, but that use and curiosity are here satisfied, and the frame of our language and modes of our combination amply discovered.

Of some forms of composition, such as that by which *re* is prefixed to note *repetition*, and *un* to signify *contrariety* or *privation*, all the examples cannot be accumulated, because the use of these particles, if not wholly arbitrary, is so little limited that they are hourly united to new words as occasion requires, or is imagined to require them.

There is another kind of composition more frequent in our language than perhaps in any other, from which arises to foreigners the greatest difficulty. We modify the signification of many verbs by a particle subjoined; as to *come off*, to escape by a fetch; to *fall on*, to attack; to *fall off*, to apostatize; to *break off*, to stop abruptly; to *bear out*, to justify; to *fall in*, to comply; to *give over*, to cease; to *set off*, to embellish; to *set in*, to begin a continual tenor; to *set out*, to begin a course or journey; to *take off*, to copy; with innumerable expressions of the same kind, of which some appear wildly irregular, being so far distant from the sense of the simple words that no sagacity will be able to trace the steps by which they arrived at the present use. These I have noted with great care; and though I cannot flatter myself that the collection is complete, I have perhaps so far assisted the students of our language that this kind of phraseology will be no longer insuperable; and the combinations of verbs and particles by chance omitted will be easily explained by comparison with those that may be found.

Many words yet stand supported only by the name of Bailey, Ainsworth, Philips, or the contracted *Dict.* for *Dictionaries* subjoined; of these I am not always certain that they are seen in any book but the works of lexicographers. Of such I have omitted many, because I had never read them; and many I have inserted, because they may perhaps exist, though they have escaped my notice: they are, however, to be yet considered as resting only upon the credit of former dictionaries.

Others, which I considered as useful, or know to be proper, though I could not at present support them by authorities, I have suffered to stand upon my own attestation, claiming the same privilege with my predecessors, of being sometimes credited without proof.

The words, thus selected and disposed, are grammatically considered; they are referred to the different parts of speech; traced, when they are irregularly inflected, through their various terminations; and illustrated by observations, not indeed of great or striking importance, separately considered, but necessary to the elucidation of our language, and hitherto neglected or forgotten by English grammarians.

That part of my work on which I expect malignity most frequently to fasten is the EXPLANATION, in which I cannot hope to satisfy those who are perhaps not inclined to be pleased, since I have not always been able to satisfy myself. To interpret a language by itself is very difficult; many words cannot be explained by synonyms because the idea signified by them has not more than one appellation; nor by paraphrase, because simple ideas cannot be described. When the nature of things is unknown, or the notion unsettled and indefinite, and various in various minds, the words by which such notions are conveyed, or such things denoted, will be ambiguous and perplexed. And such is the fate of hapless lexicography that not only darkness, but light, impedes and distresses it; things may be not only too little, but too much known, to be happily illustrated. To explain requires the use of terms less abstruse than that which is to be explained, and such terms cannot always be found; for as nothing can be proved but by supposing something intuitively known, and evident without proof, so nothing can be defined but by the use of words too plain to admit a definition.

Other words there are, of which the sense is too subtle and evanescent to be fixed in a paraphrase; such are all those which are by the grammarians termed expletives, and, in dead languages, are suffered to pass for empty sounds, of no other use than to fill a verse, or to modulate a period, but which are easily perceived in living tongues to have power and emphasis, though it be sometimes such as no other form of expression can convey.

My labour has likewise been much increased by a class of verbs too frequent in the English language, of which the signification is so loose and general, the use so vague and indeterminate, and the senses detorted so widely from the first idea, that it is hard to trace them through the maze of variation, to catch them on the brink of utter inanity, to circumscribe them by any limitations, or interpret them by any words of distinct and settled meaning: such are *bear*, *break*, *come*, *cast*, *fall*,° *get*, *give*, *do*, *put*, *set*, *go*, *run*, *make*, *take*, *turn*, *throw*. If of these the whole power is not accurately delivered, it must be remembered that while our language is yet living, and variable by the caprice of every one that speaks it, these words are hourly shifting their relations, and can no more be ascertained in a dictionary than a grove, in the agitation of a storm, can be accurately delineated from its picture in the water.

The particles are among all nations applied with so great latitude that they are not easily reducible under any regular scheme of explication: this difficulty is not less, nor perhaps greater, in English than in other languages. I have laboured them with diligence, I hope with success; such at least as can be expected in a task which no man, however learned or sagacious, has yet been able to perform.

Some words there are which I cannot explain, because I do not understand them; these might have been omitted very often with little inconvenience, but I would not so far indulge my vanity as to decline this confession; for when Tully owns himself ignorant whether *lessus*, in the Twelve Tables, means a *funeral song*, or *mourning garment*; and Aristotle doubts whether οὔρευς in the *Iliad*, signifies a *mule*, or *muleteer*, I may surely, without shame, leave some obscurities to happier industry, or future information.

The rigour of interpretative lexicography requires that *the explanation*, and *the word explained*, *should be always reciprocal*; this I have always endeavoured, but could not always attain. Words are seldom exactly synonymous; a new term was not introduced but because the former was thought inadequate: names, therefore, have often many ideas, but few ideas have many names. It was then necessary to use the proximate word, for the deficiency of single terms can very seldom be supplied by circumlocution; nor is the inconvenience great of such mutilated interpretations, because the sense may easily be collected entire from the examples.

In every word of extensive use, it was requisite to mark the progress of its meaning, and show by what gradations of intermediate sense it has passed from its primitive to its remote and accidental signification; so that every foregoing explanation should tend to that which follows, and the series be regularly concatenated from the first notion to the last.

This is specious, but not always practicable; kindred senses may be so interwoven that the perplexity cannot be disentangled, nor any reason be assigned why one should be ranged before the other. When the radical idea branches out into parallel ramifications, how can a consecutive series be formed of senses in their nature collateral? The shades of meaning sometimes pass imperceptibly into each other, so that though on one side they apparently differ, yet it is impossible to mark the point of contact. Ideas of the same race, though not exactly alike, are sometimes so little different, that no words can express the dissimilitude, though the mind easily perceives it when they are exhibited together; and sometimes there is such a confusion of acceptations that discernment is wearied and distinction puzzled, and perseverance herself hurries to an end by crowding together what she cannot separate.

These complaints of difficulty will, by those that have never considered words beyond their popular use, be thought only the jargon of a man willing to magnify his labours, and procure veneration to his studies by involution and obscurity. But every art is obscure to those that have not learned it: this uncertainty of terms, and commixture of ideas, is well known to those who have joined philosophy with grammar; and, if I have not expressed them very clearly, it must be remembered that I am speaking of that which words are insufficient to explain.

The original sense of words is often driven out of use by their metaphorical acceptations, yet must be inserted for the sake of a regular origination. Thus I know not whether *ardour* is used for *material heat*, or whether *flagrant*, in English, ever signifies the same with *burning*; yet such are the primitive ideas of these words, which are therefore set first, though without examples, that the figurative senses may be commodiously deduced.

Such is the exuberance of signification which many words have obtained that it was scarcely possible to collect all their senses; sometimes the meaning of derivatives must be sought in the mother term, and sometimes deficient explanations of the primitive may be supplied in the train of derivation. In any case of doubt or difficulty, it will be always proper to examine all the words of the same race; for some words are slightly passed over to avoid repetition, some admitted easier and clearer explanation than others, and all will be better understood as they are considered in greater variety of structures and relations.

All the interpretations of words are not written with the same skill, or the same happiness: things equally easy in themselves are not all equally easy to any single mind. Every writer of a long work commits errors where there appears neither ambiguity to mislead, nor obscurity to confound him; and, in a search like this, many felicities of expression will be casually overlooked, many convenient parallels will be forgotten, and many particulars will admit improvement from a mind utterly unequal to the whole performance.

But many seeming faults are to be imputed rather to the nature of the undertaking, than the negligence of the performer. Thus some explanations are unavoidably reciprocal or circular, as *hind*, *the female of the stag*; *stag*, *the male of the hind*: sometimes easier words are changed into harder, as *burial* into *sepulture* or *interment*, *drier* into *desiccative*, *dryness* into *siccity* or *aridity*, *fit* into *paroxysm*; for the easiest word, whatever it be, can never be translated into one more easy. But easiness and difficulty are merely relative; and, if the present prevalence of our language should invite foreigners to this dictionary, many will be assisted by those words which now seem only to increase or produce obscurity. For this reason I have endeavoured frequently to join a Teutonic and Roman interpretation, as to *cheer*, to *gladden* or *exhilarate*, that every learner of English may be assisted by his own tongue.

The solution of all difficulties, and the supply of all defects, must be sought in the examples subjoined to the various senses of each word, and ranged according to the time of their authors.

When first I collected these authorities, I was desirous that every quotation should be useful to some other end than the illustration of a word; I therefore extracted from philosophers principles of science; from historians remarkable facts; from chemists complete processes; from divines striking exhortations; and from poets beautiful descriptions. Such is design, while it is yet at a distance from execution. When the time called upon me to range this accumulation of elegance and wisdom into an alphabetical series, I soon discovered that the bulk of my volumes would fright away the student, and was forced to depart from my scheme of including all that was pleasing or useful in English literature, and reduce my transcripts very often to clusters of words in which scarcely any meaning is retained: thus to the weariness of copying, I was condemned to add the vexation of expunging. Some passages I have yet spared which may relieve the labour of verbal searches, and intersperse with verdure and flowers the dusty deserts of barren philology.

The examples, thus mutilated, are no longer to be considered as conveying the sentiments or doctrine of their authors; the word for the sake of which they are inserted, with all its appendant clauses, has been carefully preserved; but it may sometimes happen, by hasty detruncation, that the general tendency of the sentence may be changed: the divine may desert his tenets, or the philosopher his system.

Some of the examples have been taken from writers who were never mentioned as masters of elegance, or models of style; but words must be sought where they are used; and in what pages eminent for purity can terms of manufacture or agriculture be found? Many quotations serve no other purpose than that of proving the bare existence of words, and are therefore selected with less scrupulousness than those which are to teach their structures and relations.

My purpose was to admit no testimony of living authors, that I might not be misled by partiality, and that none of my contemporaries might have reason to complain; nor have I departed from this resolution but when some performance of uncommon excellence excited my veneration, when my memory supplied me from late books with an example that was wanting, or when my heart, in the tenderness of friendship, solicited admission for a favourite name.°

So far have I been from any care to grace my pages with modern decorations that I have studiously endeavoured to collect examples and authorities from the writers before the Restoration, whose works I regard as *the wells of English undefiled*,° as the pure sources of genuine diction. Our language, for almost a century, has, by the concurrence of many causes, been gradually departing from its original Teutonic character, and deviating towards a Gallic structure and phraseology, from which it ought to be our endeavour to recall it, by making our ancient volumes the ground-work of style, admitting among the additions of later times only such as may supply real deficiencies, such as are readily adopted by the genius of our tongue, and incorporate easily with our native idioms.

But as every language has a time of rudeness antecedent to perfection, as well as of false refinement and declension, I have been cautious lest my zeal for antiquity might drive me into times too remote, and crowd my book with words now no longer understood. I have fixed Sidney's work for the boundary beyond which I make few excursions. From the authors which rose in the time of Elizabeth, a speech might be formed adequate to all the purposes of use and elegance. If the language of theology were extracted from Hooker and the translation of the Bible; the terms of natural knowledge from Bacon; the phrases of policy, war, and navigation from Raleigh; the dialect of poetry and fiction from Spenser and Sidney; and the diction of common life from Shakespeare, few ideas would be lost to mankind for want of English words in which they might be expressed.

It is not sufficient that a word is found, unless it be so combined as that its meaning is apparently determined by the tract and tenor of the sentence; such passages I have therefore chosen, and when it happened that any author gave a definition of a term, or such an explanation as is equivalent to a definition, I have placed his authority as a supplement to my own, without regard to the chronological order that is otherwise observed

Some words, indeed, stand unsupported by any authority, but they are commonly derivative nouns or adverbs, formed from their primitives by regular and constant analogy, or names of things seldom occurring in books, or words of which I have reason to doubt the existence.

There is more danger of censure from the multiplicity than paucity of examples; authorities will sometimes seem to have been accumulated without necessity or use, and perhaps some will be found which might, without loss, have been omitted. But a work of this kind is not hastily to be charged with superfluities: those quotations which to careless or unskilful perusers appear only to repeat the same sense will often exhibit, to a more accurate examiner, diversities of signification or, at least, afford different shades of the same meaning: one will show the word applied to persons, another to things; one will express an ill, another a good, and a third a neutral sense; one will prove the expression genuine from an ancient author; another will show it elegant from a modern: a doubtful authority is corroborated by another of more credit; an ambiguous sentence is ascertained by a passage clear and determinate; the word, how often soever repeated, appears with new associates, and in different combinations, and every quotation contributes something to the stability or enlargement of the language.

When words are used equivocally, I receive them in either sense; when they are metaphorical, I adopt them in their primitive acceptation.

I have sometimes, though rarely, yielded to the temptation of exhibiting a genealogy of sentiments, by showing how one author copied the thoughts and diction of another: such quotations are, indeed, little more than repetitions, which might justly be censured, did they not gratify the mind, by affording a kind of intellectual history.

The various syntactical structures occurring in the examples have been carefully noted; the license or negligence with which many words have been hitherto used has made our style capricious and indeterminate; when the different combinations of the same word are exhibited together, the preference is readily given to propriety, and I have often endeavoured to direct the choice.

Thus have I laboured, by settling the orthography, displaying the analogy, regulating the structures, and ascertaining the signification of English words, to perform all the parts of a faithful lexicographer: but I have not always executed my own scheme, or satisfied my own expectations. The work, whatever proofs of diligence and attention it may exhibit, is yet capable of many improvements: the orthography which I recommend is still controvertible, the etymology which I adopt is uncertain, and, perhaps, frequently erroneous; the explanations are sometimes too much contracted, and sometimes too much diffused, the significations are distinguished rather with subtlety than skill, and the attention is harassed with unnecessary minuteness.

The examples are too often injudiciously truncated, and perhaps sometimes, I hope very rarely, alleged in a mistaken sense; for in making this collection I trusted more to memory than, in a state of disquiet and embarrassment, memory can contain, and purposed to supply at the review what was left incomplete in the first transcription.

Many terms appropriated to particular occupations, though necessary and significant, are undoubtedly omitted; and of the words most studiously considered and exemplified, many senses have escaped observation.

Yet these failures, however frequent, may admit extenuation and apology. To have attempted much is always laudable, even when the enterprise is above the strength that undertakes it. To rest below his own aim is incident to every one whose fancy is active, and whose views are comprehensive; nor is any man satisfied with himself because he has done much, but because he can conceive little. When first I engaged in this work, I resolved to leave neither words nor things unexamined, and pleased myself with a prospect of the hours which I should revel away in feasts of literature, the obscure recesses of northern learning which I should enter and ransack, the treasures with which I expected every search into those neglected mines to reward my labour, and the triumph with which I should display my acquisitions to mankind. When I had thus inquired into the original of words, I resolved to show likewise my attention to things; to pierce deep into every science, to inquire the nature of every substance of which I inserted the name, to limit every idea by a definition strictly logical, and exhibit every production of art or nature in an accurate description, that my book might be in place of all other dictionaries whether appellative or technical. But these were the dreams of a poet doomed at last to wake a lexicographer. I soon found that it is too late to look for instruments when the work calls for execution, and that whatever abilities I had brought to my task, with those I must finally perform it. To deliberate whenever I doubted, to inquire whenever I was ignorant, would have protracted the undertaking without end, and, perhaps, without much improvement; for I did not find by my first experiments that what I had not of my own was easily to be obtained: I saw that one inquiry only gave occasion to another, that book referred to book, that to search was not always to find, and to find was not always to be informed; and that thus to pursue perfection was, like the first inhabitants of Arcadia, to chase the sun, which, when they had reached the hill where he seemed to rest, was still beheld at the same distance from them.

I then contracted my design, determining to confide in myself, and no longer to solicit auxiliaries which produced more encumbrance than assistance; by this I obtained at least one advantage, that I set limits to my work, which would in time be ended, though not completed.

Despondency has never so far prevailed as to depress me to negligence; some faults will at last appear to be the effects of anxious diligence and persevering activity. The nice and subtle ramifications of meaning were not easily avoided by a mind intent upon accuracy, and convinced of the necessity of disentangling combinations, and separating similitudes. Many of the distinctions which to common readers appear useless and idle will be found real and important by men versed in the school philosophy, without which no dictionary ever shall be accurately compiled, or skilfully examined.

Some senses however there are, which, though not the same, are yet so nearly allied that they are often confounded. Most men think indistinctly, and therefore cannot speak with exactness; and consequently some examples might be indifferently put to either signification: this uncertainty is not to be imputed to me, who do not form, but register the language; who do not teach men how they should think, but relate how they have hitherto expressed their thoughts.

The imperfect sense of some examples I lamented, but could not remedy, and hope they will be compensated by innumerable passages selected with propriety, and preserved with exactness; some shining with sparks of imagination, and some replete with treasures of wisdom.

The orthography and etymology, though imperfect, are not imperfect for want of care, but because care will not always be successful, and recollection or information come too late for use.

That many terms of art and manufacture are omitted must be frankly acknowledged; but for this defect I may boldly allege that it was unavoidable: I could not visit caverns to learn the miner's language, nor take a voyage to perfect my skill in the dialect of navigation, nor visit the warehouses of merchants, and shops of artificers, to gain the names of commodities, utensils, tools, and operations of which no mention is found in books; what favourable accident or easy inquiry brought within my reach has not been neglected; but it had been a hopeless labour to glean up words by courting living information, and contesting with the sullenness of one, and the roughness of another.

To furnish the academicians *della Crusca* with words of this kind, a series of comedies called *la Fiera*, or *the Fair*, was professedly written by Buonarotti; but I had no such assistant, and therefore was content to want what they must have wanted likewise, had they not luckily been so supplied.

Nor are all words which are not found in the vocabulary to be lamented as omissions. Of the laborious and mercantile part of the people, the diction is in a great measure casual and mutable; many of their terms are formed for some temporary or local convenience, and though current at certain times and places, are in others utterly unknown. This fugitive cant, which is always in a state of increase or decay, cannot be regarded as any part of the durable materials of a language, and therefore must be suffered to perish with other things unworthy of preservation.

Care will sometimes betray to the appearance of negligence. He that is catching opportunities which seldom occur will suffer those to pass by unregarded which he expects hourly to return; he that is searching for rare and remote things will neglect those that are obvious and familiar: thus many of the most common and cursory words have been inserted with little illustration, because in gathering the authorities, I forbore to copy those which I thought likely to occur whenever they were wanted. It is remarkable that, in reviewing my collection, I found the word SEA unexemplified.

Thus it happens that in things difficult there is danger from ignorance, and in things easy from confidence; the mind, afraid of greatness, and disdainful of littleness, hastily withdraws herself from painful searches, and passes with scornful rapidity over tasks not adequate to her powers, sometimes too secure for caution, and again too anxious for vigorous effort; sometimes idle in a plain path, and sometimes distracted in labyrinths, and dissipated by different intentions.

A large work is difficult because it is large, even though all its parts might singly be performed with facility; where there are many things to be done, each must be allowed its share of time and labour in the proportion only which it bears to the whole; nor can it be expected that the stones which form the dome of a temple should be squared and polished like the diamond of a ring.

Of the event of this work, for which, having laboured it with so much application, I cannot but have some degree of parental fondness, it is natural to form conjectures. Those who have been persuaded to think well of my design will require that it should fix our language, and put a stop to those alterations which time and chance have hitherto been suffered to make in it without opposition. With this consequence I will confess that I flattered myself for a while; but now begin to fear that I have indulged expectation which neither reason nor experience can justify. When we see men grow old and die at a certain time one after another, from century to century, we laugh at the elixir that promises to prolong life to a thousand years; and with equal justice may the lexicographer be derided who being able to produce no example of a nation that has preserved their words and phrases from mutability shall imagine that his dictionary can embalm his language, and secure it from corruption and decay, that it is in his power to change sublunary nature, or clear the world at once from folly, vanity, and affectation.

With this hope, however, academies° have been instituted, to guard the avenues of their languages, to retain fugutives, and repulse intruders; but their vigilance and activity have hitherto been vain; sounds are too volatile and subtle for legal restraints; to enchain syllables, and to lash the wind,° are equally the undertakings of pride, unwilling to measure its desires by its strength. The French language has visibly changed under the inspection of the academy; the style of Amelot's translation of Father Paul is observed by Le Courayer to be *un peu passé*; and no Italian will maintain that the diction of any modern writer is not perceptibly different from that of Boccace, Machiavel, or Caro.

Total and sudden transformations of a language seldom happen;

conquests and migrations are now very rare; but there are other causes of change, which, though slow in their operation, and invisible in their progress, are perhaps as much superior to human resistance as the revolutions of the sky, or intumescence of the tide. Commerce, however necessary, however lucrative, as it depraves the manners, corrupts the language; they that have frequent intercourse with strangers, to whom they endeavour to accommodate themselves, must in time learn a mingled dialect, like the jargon which serves the traffickers on the Mediterranean and Indian coasts. This will not always be confined to the exchange, the warehouse, or the port, but will be communicated by degrees to other ranks of the people, and be at last incorporated with the current speech.

There are likewise internal causes equally forcible. The language most likely to continue long without alteration would be that of a nation raised a little, and but a little, above barbarity, secluded from strangers, and totally employed in procuring the conveniencies of life; either without books, or, like some of the Mahometan countries, with very few: men thus busied and unlearned, having only such words as common use requires, would perhaps long continue to express the same notions by the same signs. But no such constancy can be expected in a people polished by arts, and classed by subordination, where one part of the community is sustained and accommodated by the labour of the other. Those who have much leisure to think will always be enlarging the stock of ideas; and every increase of knowledge, whether real or fancied, will produce new words, or combinations of words. When the mind is unchained from necessity, it will range after convenience; when it is left at large in the fields of speculation, it will shift opinions; as any custom is disused, the words that expressed it must perish with it; as any opinion grows popular, it will innovate speech in the same proportion as it alters practice.

As by the cultivation of various sciences a language is amplified, it will be more furnished with words deflected from their original sense; the geometrician will talk of a courtier's zenith, or the eccentric virtue of a wild hero, and the physician of sanguine expectations and phlegmatic delays. Copiousness of speech will give opportunities to capricious choice, by which some words will be preferred, and others degraded; vicissitudes of fashion will enforce the use of new or extend the signification of known terms. The tropes of poetry will make hourly encroachments, and the metaphorical will become the current sense: pronunciation will be varied by levity or ignorance, and the pen must at length comply with the tongue; illiterate writers will at one time or other, by public infatuation, rise into renown, who, not knowing the original import of words, will use them with colloquial licentiousness, confound distinction, and forget propriety. As politeness increases, some expressions will be considered as too gross and vulgar for the delicate, others as too formal and ceremonious for the gay and airy; new phases are therefore adopted which must, for the same reasons, be in time dismissed. Swift, in his petty treatise° on the English language, allows that new words must sometimes be introduced, but proposes that none should be suffered to become obsolete. But what makes a word obsolete, more than general agreement to forbear it? and how shall it be continued, when it conveys an offensive idea, or recalled again into the mouths of mankind, when it has once become unfamiliar by disuse, and unpleasing by unfamiliarity?

There is another cause of alteration more prevalent than any other, which yet in the present state of the world cannot be obviated. A mixture of two languages will produce a third distinct from both; and they will always be mixed, where the chief part of education, and the most conspicuous accomplishment, is skill in ancient or in foreign tongues. He that has long cultivated another language will find its words and combinations crowd upon his memory; and haste or negligence, refinement or affectation, will obtrude borrowed terms and exotic expressions.

The great pest of speech is frequency of translation. No book was ever turned from one language into another without imparting something of its native idiom; this is the most mischievous and comprehensive innovation; single words may enter by thousands, and the fabric of the tongue continue the same, but new phraseology changes much at once; it alters not the single stones of the building, but the order of the columns. If an academy should be established for the cultivation of our style, which I, who can never wish to see dependence multiplied, hope the spirit of English liberty will hinder or destroy, let them, instead of compiling grammars and dictionaries, endeavour, with all their influence, to stop the licence of translators, whose idleness and ignorance, if it be suffered to proceed, will reduce us to babble a dialect of France.

If the changes we fear be thus irresistible, what remains but to acquiesce with silence, as in the other insurmountable distresses of humanity? It remains that we retard what we cannot repel, that we palliate what we cannot cure. Life may be lengthened by care, though death cannot be ultimately defeated: tongues, like governments, have a natural tendency to degeneration; we have long preserved our constitution, let us make some struggles for our language.

In hope of giving longevity to that which its own nature forbids to be immortal, I have devoted this book, the labour of years, to the honour of my country, that we may no longer yield the palm of philology without a contest to the nations of the continent. The chief glory of every people arises from its authors: whether I shall add any thing by my own writings to the reputation of English literature must be left to time: much of my life has been lost under the pressure of disease; much has been trifled away; and much has always been spent in provision for the day that was passing over me; but I shall not think my employment useless or ignoble, if by my assistance foreign nations, and distant ages, gain access to the propagators of knowledge, and understand the teachers of truth; if my labours afford light to the repositories of science, and add celebrity to Bacon, to Hooker, to Milton, and to Boyle.

When I am animated by this wish, I look with pleasure on my book, however defective, and deliver it to the world with the spirit of a man that has endeavoured well. That it will immediately become popular I have not promised to myself: a few wild blunders, and risible absurdities, from which no work of such multiplicity was ever free, may for a time furnish folly with laughter, and harden ignorance in contempt; but useful diligence will at last prevail, and there never can be wanting some who distinguish desert; who will consider that no dictionary of a living tongue ever can be perfect, since while it is hastening to publication, some words are budding, and some falling away; that a whole life cannot be spent upon syntax and etymology, and that even a whole life would not be sufficient; that he whose design includes whatever language can express must often speak of what he does not understand; that a writer will sometimes be hurried by eagerness to the end, and sometimes faint with weariness under a task which Scaliger compares to the labours of the anvil and the mine; that what is obvious is not always known, and what is known is not always present; that sudden fits of inadvertency will surprise vigilance, slight avocations will seduce attention, and casual eclipses of the mind will darken learning; and that the writer shall often in vain trace his memory at the moment of need for that which yesterday he knew with intuitive readiness, and which will come uncalled into his thoughts tomorrow.

In this work, when it shall be found that much is omitted, let it not be forgotten that much likewise is performed; and though no book was ever spared out of tenderness to the author, and the world is little solicitous to know whence proceeded the faults of that which it condemns; yet it may gratify curiosity to inform it that the *English Dictionary* was written with little assistance of the learned, and without any patronage of the great; not in the soft obscurities of retirement, or under the shelter of academic bowers, but amidst inconvenience and distraction, in sickness and in sorrow: and it may repress the triumph of malignant criticism to observe that if our language is not here fully displayed, I have only failed in an attempt which no human powers have hitherto completed. If the lexicons of ancient tongues, now immutably fixed, and comprised in a few volumes, be yet, after the toil of successive ages, inadequate and delusive; if the aggregated knowledge and co-operating diligence of the Italian academicians did not secure them from the censure of Beni; if the embodied critics of France, when fifty years had been spent upon their work, were obliged to change its economy, and give their second edition another form, I may surely be contented without the praise of perfection, which, if I could obtain, in this gloom of solitude, what would it avail me? I have protracted my work till most of those whom I wished to please have sunk into the grave, and success and miscarriage are empty sounds: I therefore dismiss it with frigid tranquillity, having little to fear or hope from censure or from praise.

From *A Dictionary of the English Language*°

FA´IRLY. *adv.* [from *fair.*]

1. Beautifully ; as, *a city fairly situated.*

2. Commodiously ; conveniently ; suitably to any purpose or design,
> 'Waiting 'till willing winds their sails supply'd,
> Within a trading town they long abide,
> Full *fairly* situate on a haven's side. *Dryden.*

3. Honestly ; justly ; without shift ; without fraud ; not foully.
> There is due from the judge to the advocate.some commendation and gracing where causes are fairly pleaded. *Bacon.*
> To the first advantages we may *fairly* lay claim ; I wish we had as good a title to the latter. *Atterbury.*
> It is a church of England-man's opinion, that the freedom of a nation consists in an absolute unlimited legislative power, wherein the whole body of the people are *fairly* represented in an executive duly limited. *Swift.*

4. Ingeniously ; plainly ; openly.
> The stage how loosely does Astrea tread,
> Who *fairly* puts all characters to bed ! *Pope.*

5. Candidly ; without sinistrous interpretations.
> As I interpret *fairly* your design,
> So look not with severer eyes on mine. *Dryden.*

6. Without violence to right reason.
> Where I have enlarged them, I desire the false criticks would not always think that those thoughts are wholly mine ; but that either they are secretly in the poet, or may be *fairly* deduced from him. *Dryden.*
> This nutritious juice, being a subtile liquor, scarce obtainable by a human body, is the serum of the blood is *fairly* substituted in its place. *Arbuthnot on Alim.*

7. Without blots.
> Here is th' indictment of the good lord Hastings, Which in a set hand *fairly* is engross'd. *Shakspeare.*

8. Completely ; without any deficience.
> All this they *fairly* overcame, by reason of the continual presence of their king. *Spens. State of Ireland.*
> Let them say, 'tis grossly done ; so it be *fairly* done, no matter. *Shakspeare's Merry Wives of Windsor.*
> Our love is not so great, Hortensio, but we may blow our nails together, and fast it *fairly* out. *Shakspeare's Taming of the Shrew.*

FA´IRNESS. *n. s.* [from *fair.*]

1. Beauty ; elegance of form.
> That which made her *fairness* much the fairer, was that it was but a fair embassador of a most fair mind full of wit, and a wit which delighted more to judge itself than to show itself. *Sidney.*

2. Honesty ; candour ; ingenuity.
> There may be somewhat of wisdom, but little of goodness or *fairness* in this conduct. *Atterbury.*

FA´IRSPOKEN. *adj.* [from *fair* and *speak.*] Bland and civil in language and address.
> Arius, a priest in the church of Alexandria, a subtlewitted and a marvellous *fairspoken* man, but discontented that we should be placed before him in honour, whose superior he thought himself in desert ; because through envy and stomach prone unto contradiction. *Hooker.*

FA´IRY. *n. s.* [ƿenhð, Sax. *fee,* Fr. Ab. εϱα, terra, fit et Φιϱα Macedonum dialecto ; unde ενεϱοι ινϑεϱοι, et Romanis inferi, qui Scoto-Saxonibus dicuntur *feries,* nostratiq ; vulgo corruptius *fairies,* ϰαταχϑονιοι δαιμονες, sive dii manes. *Baxter's Glossary.*]

1. A kind of fabled beings supposed to appear in a diminutive human form, and to dance in the meadows, and reward cleanliness in houses ; an elf ; a fay.
> Nan Page, my daughter, and my little son,
> And three or four more of their growth, we'll dress
> Like urchins, ouphes, and *fairies,* green and white. *Shakspeare.*

> Then let them all encircle him about,
> And *fairy* like too pinch the unclean knight ;
> And ask him, why, that hour of *fairy* revel,
> In their so sacred paths he dares to tread
> In shape prophane. *Shaks. Merry Wives of Windsor.*
> By the idea any one has of *fairies,* or centaurs, he cannot know that things, answering those ideas, exist. *Locke.*

> Fays, fairies, genii, elves, and demons; hear. *Pope.*

2. Enchantress. *Warburton.*
> To this great *fairy* I'll commend thy acts,
> Make her thanks bless thee. *Shaks. Ant. and Cleop.*

FA´IRY. *adj.*

1. Given by fairies.
> Be secret and discrete: these *fairy* favours Are lost when not conceal'd. *Dryd. Spanish Friar.*
> Such borrowed wealth, like *fairy* money, though it were gold in the hand from which he received it, will be but leaves and dust when it comes to use. *Locke.*

2. Belonging to fairies.
> This is the *fairy* land : oh, spight of spights,
> We talk with goblins, owls, and elvish sprights. *Shakspeare.*

FA´IRYSTONE. *n. s.* [*fairy* and *stone.*] A stone found in gravel pits.

FAITH. *n. s.* [*foi,* Fr. *fede,* Ital. *fides,* Lat.]

1. Belief of the revealed truths of religion.
> The name of *faith* being properly and strictly taken, it must needs have reference unto some uttered word, as the object of belief. *Hooker.*
> Faith, if it have not works, is dead. *James ii. 17.*
> Vision in the next life is the perfecting of that *faith* in this life, or that *faith* here is turned into vision there, as hope into enjoying. *Hammond.*
> Then *faith* shall fail, and holy hope shall die ;
> One lost in certainty, and one in joy. *Prior.*

2. The system of revealed truths held by the Christian church ; the *credenda.*
> Felix heard Paul concerning the *faith. Acts* xxiv. 24.
> This is the catholick *faith. Common Prayer.*

3. Trust in God.
> Faith is an entire dependence upon the truth, the power, the justice, and the mercy of God ; which dependence will certainly incline us to obey him in all things. *Swift.*

4. Tenet held.
> Which to believe of her,
> Must be a *faith,* that reason, without miracle,
> Should never plant in me. *Shakspeare's King Lear.*

5. Trust in the honesty or veracity of another.
> Her failing, while her *faith* to me remains,
> I should conceal. *Milton's Paradise Lost.*

6. Fidelity ; unshaken adherence.

7. Honour ; social confidence.
> For you alone
> I broke my *faith* with injured Palamon. *Dryden.*

8. Sincerity ; honesty ; veracity.
> Sir, in good *faith,* in meer verity. *Shaks. King Lear.*
> They are a very froward generation, children in whom is no *faith. Deuteronomy* xxxii. 20.

9. Promise given.
> I have been forsworn,
> In breaking *faith* with Julia whom I lov'd. *Shaks.*

FA´ITHBREACH. *n. s.* [*faith* and *breach.*] Breach of fidelity ; disloyalty ; perfidy.
> Now minutely revolts upbraid his *faithbreach* ;
> Those he commands, move only in command,
> Nothing in love. *Shakspeare's Macbeth.*

FA´ITHED. *adj.* [from *faith.*] Honest ; sincere. A word not in use.
> Thou bastard ! would the reposal
> Of any trust, virtue, or worth in thee,
> Make thy words *faith'd*? *Shakspeare's King Lear.*

FA´ITHFUL. *adj.* [*faith* and *full.*]

1. Firm in adherence to the truth of religion.
> To the saints which are at Ephesus, and the *faithful* in Christ Jesus. *Ephesians* i. 1.

Be thou *faithful* unto death, and I will give thee a crown of life. *Revelations* ii. 10.

2. Of true fidelity; loyal; true to the allegiance or duty professed.

I have this day receiv'd a traitor's judgment,
And by that name must die; yet, heav'n bear witness,
And, if I have a conscience, let it sink me,
Ev'n as the axe falls, if I be not *faithful*. *Shakspeare*.
So spake the seraph Abdiel, *faithful* found;
Among the faithless, *faithful* only he. *Milton*.

3. Honest; upright; without fraud.

My servant Moses is *faithful* in all mine house. *Numbers*.

4. Observant of compact or promise; true to his contract; sincere; veracious.

Well I know him;
Of easy temper, naturally good,
And *faithful* to his word. *Dryden's Don Sebastian*.

FA'ITHFULLY. *adv* [from *faithful*.]

1. With firm belief in religion.

2. With full confidence in God.

3. With strict adherence to duty and allegiance.

His noble grace would have some pity
Upon my wretched women, that so long
Have follow'd both my fortunes *faithfully*. *Shak*.

4. Without failure of performance; honestly; exactly.

If on my wounded breast thou drop a tear,
Think for whose sake my breast that wound did bear;
And *faithfully* my last desires fulfil,
As I perform my cruel father's will. *Dryden's Ovid*.

5. With earnest professions; with strong promises.

For his own part he did *faithfully* promise to be still in the king's power. *Bacon's Henry VII*.

6. Honestly; without fraud, trick, or ambiguity.

They suppose the nature of things to be truly and *faithfully* signified by their names, and thereupon believe as they hear, and practise as they believe. *South's Sermons*.

7. In *Shakspeare*, according to Mr. *Warburton*, fervently; perhaps rather, confidently; steadily.

If his occasions were not virtuous,
I should not urge it half so *faithfully*. *Shaks. Timon*.

FA'ITHFULNESS. *n. s.* [from *faithful*.]

1. Honesty; veracity.

For there is no *faithfulness* in your mouth; your inward part is very wickedness. *Psalm* lix.
The band that knits together and supports all compacts, is truth and *faithfulness*. *South*.

2. Adherence to duty; loyalty.

The same zeal and *faithfulness* continues in your blood, which animated one of your noble ancestors to sacrifice his life in the quarrel of his sovereign. *Dryd*.

FA'ITHLESS. *adj.* [from *faith*.]

1. Without belief in the revealed truths of religion; unconverted.

Whatsoever our hearts be to God and to his truth, believe we, or be we as yet *faithless*, for our conversion or confirmation, the force of natural reason is great. *Hooker*.

Never dare misfortune cross her foot,
Unless she doth it under this excuse,
That she is issue to a *faithless* Jew. *Shakspeare*.

2. Perfidious; disloyal; not true to duty, profession, promise, or allegiance.

Fell by our servants, by those men we lov'd most;
A most unnatural and *faithless* service. *Shakspeare*.
Abdiel, faithful found,
Among the faithless. *Milton's Paradise Lost*.

FA'ITHLESSNESS. *n. s.* [from *faithless*.]

1. Treachery; perfidy.

2. Unbelief as to revealed religion.

FA'ITOUR. *n. s.* [*faitard*, Fr.] A scoundrel; a rascal; a mean fellow; a poltroon. An old word now obsolete.

To Philemon, false *faitour*, Philemon,
I cast to pay, that I so dearly bought. *Fairy Queen*.
Into new woes unweeting I was cast,
By this false *faitour*. *Fairy Queen*.

FAKE. *n. s.* [Among seamen.] A coil of rope. *Harris*.

FALCA'DE. *n. s.* [from *falx, falcis*, Lat.]

A horse is said to make *falcades* when he throws himself upon his haunches two or three times, as in very quick curvets; therefore a *falcade* is that action of the haunches and of the legs, which bend very low, when you make a stop and half a stop. *Far. Dict.*

FA'LCATED. *adj.* [*falcatus*, Lat.] Hooked; bent like a reaping hook or scythe.

The enlightened part of the moon appears in the form of a sickle, or reaping hook, which is while she is moving from the conjunction to the opposition, or from the new moon to the full; but from full to a new again, the enlightened part appears gibbous, and the dark *falcated*. *Harris*.

FALCA'TION. *n. s.* [*falcis*, Lat.] Crookedness; form like that of a reaper's hook.

The locusts have antennæ, or long horns before, with a long *falcation* or forcipated tail behind. *Brown*.

FA'LCHION. *n. s.* [*ensis falcatus*; in Fr. *fauchon*.] A short crooked sword; a cimeter.

I've seen the day, with my good biting *falchion*,
I would have made them skip: I am old now. *Shaks*.
Old *falchions* are new temper'd in the fires;
The sounding trumpet every soul inspires. *Dry. Æn.*
What sighs and tears
Hath Eugene caused! how many widows curse
His cleaving *falchion*! *Philips*.

FA'LCON. *n. s.* [*faulcon*, Fr. *falconne*, Ital. *falco*, Lat. *Credo, a rostro falcato* sive *adunco*, from the falcated or crooked bill.]

1. A hawk trained for sport.

As Venus' bird, the white, swift, lovely dove,
O' happy dove that art compar'd to her,
Doth on her wings her utmost swiftness prove,
Finding the gripe of *falcon* fierce not far. *Sidney*.
Air stops not the high soaring of my noble *falcon*. *Walton*.

Apulian farms, for the rich soil admired,
And thy large fields where *falcons* may be tir'd. *Dry*.
Say, will the *falcon*, stooping from above,
Smit with her varying plumage, spare the dove? *Pope*.

2. A sort of cannon, whose diameter at the bore is five inches and a quarter, weight seven hundred and fifty pounds, length seven foot, load two pounds and a quarter, shot two inches and a half diameter, and two pounds and a half weight. *Harris*.

FA'LCONER. *n. s.* [*faulconier*, Fr.] One who breeds and trains hawks; one who follows the sport of fowling with hawks.

Hist! Romeo, hist! O for a *falc'ner's* voice,
To lure this tarsel gentle back again. *Shakspeare*.
The universal remedy was swallowing of pebblestones, in imitation of *falconers* curing hawks. *Temp*.
I have learned of a *falconer* never to feed up a hawk when I would have him fly. *Dryden's Don Sebast.*
A *falconer* Henry is, when Emma hawks;
With her of tarsels and of lures he talks. *Prior*.

FA'LCONET. *n. s.* [*falconette*, Fr.] A sort of ordnance, whose diameter at the bore is four inches and a quarter, weight four hundred pounds, length six foot, load one pound and quarter, shot something more than two inches diameter, and one pound and a quarter weight. *Harris*.

Mahomet sent janizaries and nimble footmen, with certain *falconets* and other small pieces, to take the streights. *Knolles*.

FA'LDAGE. *n. s.* [*faldagium*, barbarous Lat.] A privilege which anciently several lords reserved to themselves of setting up folds for sheep, in any fields within their manors, the better to manure them; and this not only with their own, but their tenants' sheep. This *faldage* in some places they call a foldcourse or freefold. *Harris*.

FA'LDFEE. *n. s.* [*fald* and *fee*.] A composition paid anciently by tenants for the privilege of faldage. *Dict*.

FA'LDING. *n. s.* A kind of coarse cloth. *Dict*.

FA'LDSTOOL. *n. s.* [*fald* or *fold* and *stool*.] A kind of stool placed at the south side of the altar, at which the kings of England kneel at their coronation.

To FALL. *v. n.* pret. *I fell ;* compound pret. *I have fallen,* or *faln.* [ᚠeallan, Sax. *fallen,* Germ.]

1. To drop from a higher place.

> Thou shalt make a battlement for thy roof, that thou bring not blood upon thine house, if any man *fall* from thence. *Deuteronomy.*

> I shall *fall*
> Like a bright exhalation in the evening,
> And no man see me more. *Shakspeare's Henry VIII.*

2. To drop from an erect to a prone posture.

> Saul *fell* all along on the earth. 1 *Sam.* xxviii. 20.

> That is a step,
> On which I must *fall* down, or else o'erleap ;
> For in my way it lies. *Shakspeare's Macbeth.*

3. To drop ; to be held or adhere no longer.

> His chains *fell* off from his hands. *Acts* xii. 7.

4. To move down any descent.

> All liquid bodies are diffusive ; for their parts being in motion, have no connexion one with another, but glide and *fall* off any way, as gravity and the air presseth them *Burnet.*

5. To drop ripe from the tree.

> As the leaf *falleth* off from the vine, and as a *falling* fig from the fig-tree. *Isaiah* xxxiv. 4.

6. To pass at the outlet : as a river.

> Cæsar therefore gave orders to build his gallies on the Loir, and the rivers that *fall* into it. *Arbuthnot.*

7. To be determined to some particular direction.

> Birds and fowls that rest one foot to ease the other, naturally lay their heads under their wings, that the centre of gravity may *fall* upon the foot they stand on. *Cheyne.*

8. To apostatise ; to depart from faith or goodness.

> Labour to enter into that rest, lest any man *fall* after the same example of unbelief. *Hebrews* iv. 11.

> They brought scandal
> To Israel, diffidence of God, and doubt
> In feeble hearts, propense enough before
> To waver or *fall* off, and join with idols. *Milton.*

> Whether some spirit on holy purpose bent,
> Or some *fall'n* angel from below broke loose,
> Who comes with envious eyes, and curst intent,
> To view this world and its created Lord. *Dryden.*

9. To die by violence.

> God and good angels fight on Richmond's side,
> And Richard *fall* in height of all his pride. *Shaks.*

> If one should be a prey, how much the better
> To *fall* before the lion than the wolf ! *Shakspeare.*

> What other oath,
> Than honesty, to honesty engag'd ?
> That this shall be, or we will *fall* for it. *Shakspeare.*

> A thousand shall *fall* at thy side, and ten thousand at thy right hand : but it shall not come nigh thee. *Psalm* xci. 7.

> Ye shall chase your enemies, and they shall *fall* before you by the sword. *Leviticus* xxvi. 7.

> They not obeying,
> Incurr'd, what could they less ? the penalty ;
> And manifold in sin, deserv'd to *fall*. *Milton.*

> Almon *falls,* old Tyrrheus' eldest care,
> Pierc'd with an arrow from the distant war ? *Dryden.*

10. To come to a sudden end.

> The greatness of these Irish lords suddenly *fell* and vanished, when their oppressions and extortions were taken away. *Davies.*

> He first the fate of Cæsar did foretell,
> And pity'd Rome when Rome in Cæsar *fell* ;
> In iron clouds conceal'd the publick light,
> And impious mortals fear'd eternal night. *Dryden.*

11. To be degraded from an high station ; to sink into meanness or disgrace ; to be plunged into sudden misery.

> What can be their business
> With a poor weak woman *fall'n* from favour ! *Shaks.*

12. To decline from power or empire ; to be overthrown.

> What men could do,
> Is done already : heaven and earth will witness,
> If Rome must *fall,* that we are innocent. *Addison.*

13. To enter into any state worse than the former.

> He *fell* at difference with Ludovico Sfortia, who carried the keys which brought him in, and shut him out. *Bacon's Henry VII.*

> Some painters taking precepts too literal a sense, have *fallen* thereby into great inconveniences. *Dryd.*

14. To come into any state of weakness, terrour, òr misery.

> These, by obtruding the beginning of a change for the entire work of new life, will *fall* under the former guilt. *Hammond.*

> One would wonder how so many learned men could *fall* into so great an absurdity, as to believe this river could preserve itself unmixed with the lake. *Addison on Italy.*

> The best men *fall* under the severest pressures. *Wake.*

15. To decrease ; to be diminished, as in weight.

> From the pound weight, as Pliny tells us, the As *fell* to two ounces in the first Punick war : when Hannibal invaded Italy, to one ounce ; then, by the Papirian law, to half an ounce. *Arbuthnot.*

16. To ebb ; to grow shallow : as, *the river* falls.

17. To decrease in value ; to bear less price.

> When the price of corn *falleth,* men generally break no more ground than will supply their own turn. *Carew.*

> But now her price is *fall'n*. *Shaks. King Lear.*

> Rents will *fall,* and incomes every day lessen, 'till industry and frugality, joined to a well ordered trade, shall restore to the kingdom the riches it had formerly. *Locke.*

18. To sink , not to amount to the full.

> The greatness of an estate, in bulk and territory, doth *fall* under measure ; and the greatness of finances and revenue doth *fall* under computation. *Bacon.*

19. To be rejected ; to become null.

> This book must stand or *fall* with thee ; not by any opinion I have of it, but thy own. *Locke.*

20. To decline from violence to calmness ; from intenseness to remission.

> He was stirr'd,
> And something spoke in choler, ill and hasty ;
> But he *fell* to himself again, and sweetly
> In all the rest shew'd a most noble patience. *Shaks.*

> At length her fury *fell,* her foaming censʼd ;
> And ebbing in her soul, the god decreasʼd. *Dryden.*

21. To enter into any new state of the body or mind.

> In sweet musick is such art,
> Killing care and grief of heart,
> *Fall* asleep, or hearing die. *Shakspeare.*

> Solyman, chafed with the loss of his gallies and best soldiers, and with the double injury done unto him by the Venetians, *fell* into such a rage that he cursed Barbarossa. *Knolles.*

> When about twenty, upon the falseness of a lover, she *fell* distracted. *Temple.*

> A spark like thee of the man-killing trade,
> *Fell* sick, and thus to his physician said ;
> Methinks I am not right in ev'ry part,
> I feel a kind of trembling at my heart ;
> My pulse unequal, and my breath is strong :
> Besides a filthy furr upon my tongue. *Dryden's Pref.*

> And you have known none in health who have pitied you ? and behold, they are gone before you, even since you fell into this distemper. *Wake.*

> He died calmly, and with all the easiness of a man *falling* asleep. *Atterbury.*

> Portius himself oft *falls* in tears before me,
> As if he mourn'd his rival's ill success. *Addison.*

> For as his own bright image he survey'd,
> He *fell* in love with the fantastick shade. *Addison.*

> I *fell* in love with the character of Pomponius Atticus ; I longed to imitate him. *Blount to Pope.*

22. To sink into an air of discontent or dejection of the look.

> If thou persuade thyself that they shall not be taken, let not thy countenance *fall*. *Judith* vi. 9.

> If you have any other request to make, hide it not ; for ye shall find we will not make your countenance to *fall* by the answer ye shall receive. *Bacon.*

> I have observ'd of late thy looks are *fallen,*
> O'ercast with gloomy cares and discontent. *Addison.*

23. To sink below something in comparison.

> Fame of thy beauty and thy youth,
> Among the rest me hither brought,
> Finding this fame *fall* short of truth,
> Made me stay longer than I thought. *Waller.*

24. To happen ; to befall.

> For such things as do *fall* scarce once in many ages, it did suffice to take such order as was requisite when they *fell*. *Hooker.*

> Oft it *falls* out, that while one thinks too much of his doing, he leaves to do the effect of this thinking. *Sidney.*

A long advertent and deliberate connexing of consequents, which *falls* not in the common road of ordinary men. *Hale.*

Since this fortune *falls* to you,
Be content and seek no new. *Shakspeare.*

If the worst *fall* that ever *fell*, I hope I shall make shift to go without him. *Shakspeare.*

O, how feeble is man's power,
That, if good fortune *fall*,
Cannot add another hour,
Nor a lost hour recall! *Donne.*

Since both cannot possess what both pursue,
I'm griev'd, my friend, the chance should *fall* on you. *Dryden.*

I had more leisure, and disposition, than have since *fallen* to my share. *Swift.*

25. To come by chance; to light on.

I have two boys
Seek Percy and thyself about the field;
But seeing thou *fall'st* on me so luckily,
I will assay thee. *Shakspeare's Henry IV.*

The Romans *fell* upon this model by chance, but the Spartans by thought and design. *Swift.*

26 To come in a stated method.

The odd hours at the end of the solar year, are not indeed fully six, but are deficient 10' 44''; which deficiency, in 134 years, collected, amounts to a whole day: and hence may be seen the reason why the vernal equinox, which at the time of the Nicene council *fell* upon the 21st of March, *falls* now about ten days sooner. *Holder on Time.*

It does not *fall* within my subject to lay down the rules of odes. *Felton on the Classicks.*

27. To come unexpectedly.

I am *fallen* upon the mention of mercuries. *Boyle.*

It happened this evening that we *fell* into a very pleasing walk, at a distance from his house. *Addison.*

28. To begin any thing with ardour and vehemence.

The king, understanding of their adventure, suddenly *falls* to take pride in making much of them. *Sidney.*

Each of us *fell* in praise of our country mistresses. *Shakspeare.*

And the mixt multitude *fell* a lusting. *Numb. ii. 4.*

It is better to sound a person afar off, than to *fall* upon the point at first; except you mean to surprise him by some short question. *Bacon.*

When a horse is hungry, and comes to a good pasture, he *falls* to his food immediately. *Hale.*

They *fell* to blows, insomuch that the Argonauts slew the most part of the Deliones. *L'Estrange.*

29. To handle or treat directly.

We must immediately *fall* into our subject, and treat every part of it in a lively manner. *Addison.*

30. To come vindictively: as a punishment.

There *fell* wrath for it against Israel. *2 Chronicles.*

31. To come by any mischance to any new possessor.

The stout bishop could not well brook that his province should *fall* into their hands. *Knolles.*

32. To drop or pass by carelessness or imprudence.

Ulysses let no partial favours *fall*,
The people's parent, he protected all. *Pope's Odyssey.*

Some expressions *fell* from him, not very favourable to the people of Ireland. *Swift.*

33. To come forcibly and irresistibly.

Fear *fell* on them all. *Acts xix. 17.*

A kind refreshing sleep is *fallen* upon him:
I saw him stretch'd at ease, his fancy lost
In pleasing dreams. *Addison's Cato.*

34. To become the property of any one by lot, chance, inheritance, or otherwise.

All the lands, which will *fall* to her majesty thereabouts, are large enough to contain them. *Spenser.*

If you do chance to hear of that blind traitor,
Preferment *falls* on him that cuts him off. *Shakspeare.*

Then 'tis most like
The sovereignty will *fall* upon Macbeth. *Shakspeare.*

After the flood, arts to Chaldea *fell*;
The father of the faithful there did dwell,
Who both their parent and instructor was. *Denham.*

You shall see a great estate *fall* to you, which you would have lost the relish of, had you known yourself born to it. *Addison.*

If to her share some female errours *fall*,
Look on her face, and you'll forget them all. *Pope.*

In their spiritual and temporal courts the labour *falls* to their vicars-general, proctors, apparitors, and seneschals. *Swift.*

35. To languish; to grow faint.

Their hopes or fears for the common cause rose or *fell* with your lordship's interest. *Addison on Italy.*

36. To be born; to be yeaned.

Lambs must have taken of them at their first *falling*, else, while they are weak, the crows and magpies will be apt to pick out their eyes. *Mortimer.*

37. To fall away. To grow lean.

Watery vegetables are proper, and fish rather than flesh; in a Lent diet people commonly *fall away*. *Arbuthnot on Diet.*

38. To fall away. To revolt; to change allegiance.

The fugitives *fell away* to the king of Babylon. *2 Kings.*

39. To fall away. To apostatise; to sink into wickedness.

These for a while believe, and in time of temptation *fall away*. *Luke viii. 13.*

Say not thou, it is through the Lord that I *fell away*; for thou oughtest not to do the things that he hateth. *Ecclus. xv.*

40. To fall away. To perish; to be lost.

Still propagate; for still they *fall away*:
'Tis prudence to prevent th' entire decay. *Dry. Virg.*

How can it enter into the thoughts of man, that the soul, which is capable of such immense perfections, and of receiving new improvement to all eternity, shall *fall away* into nothing, almost as soon as it is created? *Addison. Spectator.*

41. To fall away. To decline gradually; to fade; to languish.

In a curious brede of needlework one colour *falls away* by such just degrees, and another rises so insensibly, that we see the variety, without being able to distinguish the total vanishing of the one from the first appearance of the other. *Addison.*

42. To fall back. To fail of a promise or purpose.

We have often *fallen back* from our resolutions. *Taylor.*

43. To fall back. To recede; to give way.

44. To fall down. [*down* is sometimes added to *fall*, though it adds little to the signification.] To prostrate himself in adoration.

All kings shall *fall down* before him; all nations shall serve him. *Psalm lxxii. 11.*

Shall I *fall down* to the stock of a tree? *Is. xliv. 11.*

45. To fall down. To sink; not to stand.

As she was speaking she *fell down* for faintness. *Esther xv.*

Down fell the beauteous youth; the yawning wound
Gush'd out a purple stream, and stain'd the ground. *Dryden.*

46. To fall down. To bend as a suppliant.

They shall *fall down* unto thee; they shall make supplication unto thee. *Isaiah xlv. 14.*

47. To fall from. To revolt; to depart from adherence.

Clarence
Is very likely now to *fall from* him. *Shaks. Henry VI.*

The emperor, being much solicited by the Scots not to be a help to ruin their kingdom, *fell* by degrees from the king of England. *Hayward.*

48. To fall in. To concur; to coincide.

Objections *fall in* here, and are the clearest and most convincing arguments of the truth. *Woodward.*

His reasonings in this chapter seem to *fall in* with each other; yet, upon a closer investigation, we shall find them proposed with great variety and distinction. *Atterbury.*

Any single paper that *falls in* with the popular taste, and pleases more than ordinary, brings one in a great return of letters. *Addison.*

When the war was begun, there soon *fell in* other incidents at home, which made the continuance of it necessary. *Swift.*

49. To fall in. To comply; to yield to.

Our fine young ladies readily *fall in* with the direction of the graver sort. *Spectator.*

It is a double misfortune to a nation, which is thus given to change, when they have a sovereign that is prone to *fall in* with all the turns and veerings of the people. *Addison.*

You will find it difficult to persuade learned men to *fall in* with your projects. *Addison on Medals.*

That prince applied himself first to the church of England; and, upon their refusal to *fall in* with his measures, made the like advances to the dissenters. *Swift.*

50. *To fall off.* To separate; to be broken.

Love cools, friendship *falls off*, brothers divide; in cities, mutinies; in countries, discord. *Shakspeare.*

51. *To fall off.* To perish; to die away.

Languages need recruits to supply the place of those words that are continually *falling off* through disuse. *Felton.*

52. *To fall off.* To apostatise; to revolt; to forsake.

Oh, Hamlet, what a *falling off* was there! *Shaks.*
Revolted Mortimer!
—He never did *fall off*, my sovereign liege,
But by the chance of war. *Shakspeare's Henry IV.*
They, accustomed to afford at other times either silence or short assent to what he did purpose, did then *fall off* and forsake him. *Hayward.*
What cause
Mov'd our grand parents, in that happy state,
Favour'd of Heav'n so highly, to *fall off*
From their Creator, and transgress his will? *Milton.*
Those captive tribes *fell off*
From God to worship calves. *Milton's Par. Lost.*
Were I always grave, one half of my readers would *fall off* from me. *Addison. Spectator.*

53. *To fall on.* To begin eagerly to do any thing.

Some coarse cold salad is before thee set;
Bread with the bran, perhaps, and broken meat;
Fall on, and try thy appetite to eat. *Dryd. Persius.*

54. *To fall on.* To make an assault; to begin the attack.

They *fell on*, I made good my place; at length they came to the broomstaff with me; I defied 'em still. *Shakspeare's Henry VIII.*
Fall on, fall on, and hear him not;
But spare his person for his father's sake. *Dryden.*
Draw all; and when I give the word, *fall on*. *Oedipus.*
He pretends, amongst the rest, to quarrel with me, to have *fallen* foul on priesthood. *Dryden.*

55. *To fall over.* To revolt; to desert from one side to the other.

And do'st thou now *fall over* to my foes?
Thou wear a lion's hide! doff it, for shame,
And hang a calve's skin on those recreant limbs. *Shakspeare's King John.*

56. *To fall out.* To quarrel; to jar; to grow contentious.

Little needed those proofs to one who would have *fallen out* with herself, rather than make any conjectures to Zelmane's speeches. *Sidney.*
How *fell* you out, say that?
—No contraries hold more antipathy,
Than I and such a knave. *Shakspeare's King Lear.*
Meeting her of late behind the wood,
Seeking sweet favours for this hateful fool,
I did upbraid her, and *fall out* with her. *Shakspeare.*
The cedar, by the instigation of the loyalists, *fell out* with the homebians, who had elected him to be their king. *Howel.*
A soul exasperated in ills, *falls out*
With every thing, its friend, itself. *Addison's Cato.*
It has been my misfortune to live among quarrelsome neighbours; there is but one thing can make us *fall out*, and that is the inheritance of lord Strut's estate. *Arbuthnot's John Bull.*

57. *To fall out.* To happen; to befall.

Who think you is my Dorus *fallen out* to be? *Sidn.*
Now, for the most part, it so *falleth out*, touching things which generally are received, that although in themselves they be most certain, yet, because men presume them granted of all, we are hardliest able to bring proof of their certainty. *Hooker.*
It so *fell out*, that certain players
We o'er-rode on the way; of those we told him. *Shak.*
Yet so it may *fall out*, because their end
Is hate, not help to me. *Milton's Agonistes.*
There *fell out* a bloody quarrel betwixt the frogs and the mice. *L'Estrange.*
If it so *fall out* that thou art miserable for ever, thou hast no reason to be surprised, as if some unexpected thing had happened. *Tillotson.*

58. *To fall to.* To begin eagerly to eat.

The men were fashion'd in a larger mould,
The women fit for labour, big and bold;
Gigantick hinds, as soon as work was done,
To their huge pots of boiling pulse would run;
Fall to, with eager joy, on homely food. *Dryden.*

59. *To fall to.* To apply himself to.

They would need *fall to* the practice of those virtues which they before learned. *Sidney.*

I know thee not, old man; *fall to* thy prayers:
How ill white hairs become a fool and jester. *Shaks.*
Having been brought up an idle horseboy, he will never after *fall to* labour: but is only made fit for the halter. *Spenser.*
They *fell* to raising money under pretence of the relief of Ireland. *Clarendon.*
My lady *falls* to play: so bad her chance,
He must repair it. *Pope.*

60. *To fall under.* To be subject to; to become the subject of.

We know the effects of heat will be such as will scarce *fall under* the conceit of men, if the force of it be altogether kept in. *Bacon's Natural History.*
Those things which are wholly in the choice of another, *fall under* our deliberation. *Taylor.*
The idea of the painter and the sculptor is undoubtedly that perfect and excellent example of the mind, by imitation of which imagined form, all things are represented which *fall under* human sight. *Dry. Duf.*

61. *To fall under.* To be ranged with; to be reckoned with.

No rules that relate to pastoral can affect the Georgicks, which *fall under* that class of poetry which consists in giving plain instructions to the reader. *Addison on the Georgicks.*

62. *To fall on.* To attack; to invade; to assault.

Auria, *falling upon* these gallies, had with them a cruel and deadly fight. *Knolles.*
An infection in a town first *falls upon* children, weak constitutions, or those that are subject to other diseases; but, spreading farther, seizes upon the most healthy. *Temple.*
Man *falls upon* every thing that comes in his way; not a berry or mushroom can escape him. *Add. Spec.*
To get rid of fools and scoundrels was one part of my design in *falling upon* these authors. *Pope.*

63. *To fall upon.* To attempt.

I do not intend to *fall upon* nice philosophical disquisitions about the nature of time. *Holder.*

64. *To fall upon.* To rush against.

At the same time that the storm bears upon the whole species, we are *falling* foul *upon* one another. *Addison.*

65. *Fall* is one of those general words of which it is very difficult to ascertain or detail the full signification. It retains in most of its senses some part of its primitive meaning, and implies either literally or figuratively descent, violence, or suddenness. In many of its senses it is opposed to *rise*; but in others has no counterpart or correlative.

To FALL. *v. a.*

1. To drop; to let fall.

To-morrow in the battle think on me,
And *fall* thy edgeless sword, despair and die. *Shaks.*
If that the earth could teem with woman's tears,
Each drop she *falls* would prove a crocodile. *Shaks.*
Draw together;
And when I rear my hand, do you the like,
To *fall* it on Gonzalo. *Shakspeare's Tempest.*
I am willing to *fall* this argument: 'tis free for every man to write or not to write in verse, as he thinks it is or is not his talent, or as he imagines the audience will receive it. *Dryden.*

2. To sink; to depress; the contrary to *raise.*

If a man would endeavour to raise or *fall* his voice still by half notes, like the stops of a lute, or by whole notes alone without halfs, as far as an eight, he will not be able to frame his voice unto it. *Bacon's Natural History.*

3. To diminish; to let sink: opposed to *raise.*

Upon lessening interest to four *per cent.* you *fall* the price of your native commodities, or lessen your trade, or else prevent not the high use. *Locke.*

4. To yean; to bring forth.

They then conceiving, did, in yeaning time,
Fall party-colour'd lambs, and those were Jacob's. *Shakspeare.*

FALL. *n. s.* [from the verb.]

1. The act of dropping from on high.

High o'er their heads a mould'ring rock is plac'd,
That promises a *fall*, and shakes at every blast. *Dry.*

2. The act of tumbling from an erect posture.

I saw him run after a gilded butterfly ; and when he caught it, he let it go again, and after it again ; and over and over he comes, and up again, and caught it again ; or whether his *fall* enraged him, or how it was, he did so set his teeth, and did tear it. *Shaks.*

3. The violence suffered in dropping from on high.

My son, coming into his marriage-chamber happened to have a *fall*, and died. *2 Esdras x. 48.*

Spirit of wine, mingled with common water, if the first *fall* be broken by means of a sop or otherwise, stayeth above ; and once if mingled, it severeth not again as old doth. *Bacon's Physical Remains*

A fever or *fall* may take away my reason. *Locke.*

Some were hurt by the *falls* they got by leaping upon the ground. *Gulliver's Travels.*

4. Death ; overthrow ; destruction incurred.

Wail his *fall*,
Whom I myself struck down. *Shakspeare's Macbeth.*

Our fathers were given to the sword, and for a spoil, and had a great *fall* before our enemies. *Judith viii. 9.*

I will begin to pray before thee for myself and for them ; for I see the *falls* of us that dwell in the land. *2 Esdras viii. 17.*

5. Ruin ; dissolution.

Paul's, the late theme of such a muse, whose flight
Has bravely reach'd and soar'd above thy height :
Now shalt thou stand, though sword, or time, or fire,
Or zeal more fierce than they, thy *fall* conspire.
Denham.

6. Downfall ; loss of greatness ; declension from eminence ; degradation ; state of being deposed from a high station ; plunge from happiness or greatness into misery or meanness, or from virtue to corruption. In a sense like this we say the *fall* of man, and the *fall* of angels.

Her memory served as an accuser of her change,
and her own handwriting was there to bear testimony
against her *fall*. *Sidney.*

Perhaps thou talk'st of me, and dost enquire
Of my restraint : why here I live alone ;
And pitiest this my miserable *fall*. *Daniel's Civ. War.*

He, careless now of int'rest, fame, or fate,
Perhaps forgets that Oxford e'er was great ;
Or deeming meanest what we greatest call,
Beholds thee glorious only in thy *fall*. *Pope to Parn.*

7. Declension of greatness, power, or dominion.

Till the empire came to be settled in Charles the Great, the *fall* of the Romans' huge dominion concurring with other universal evils, caused those times to be days of much affliction and trouble throughout the world. *Hooker.*

8. Diminution ; decrease of value.

That the improvement of Ireland is the principal cause why our lands in purchase rise not, as naturally they should, with the *fall* of our interest, appears evidently from the effect the *fall* of interest hath had upon houses in London. *Child.*

9. Declination or diminution of sound, cadence ; close of musick.

That strain again ; it had a dying *fall* :
O, it came o'er my ear, like the sweet south
That breathes upon a bank of violets,
Stealing and giving odours. *Shaks. Twelfth Night.*

How sweetly did they float upon the wings
Of silence, through the empty-vaulted night,
At ev'ry *fall* smoothing the raven down
Of darkness 'till it smil'd ! *Milton.*

10. Declivity ; steep descent.

Waters when beat upon the shore, or straitened, as the *falls* of bridges, or dashed against themselves by winds, give a roaring noise. *Bacon's Nat. History.*

11. Cataract ; cascade ; rush of water down a steep place.

There will we sit upon the rocks,
And see the shepherds feed their flocks
By shallow rivers, to whose *falls*
Melodious birds sing madrigals. *Shakspeare.*

A whistling wind, or a melodious noise of birds, among the spreading branches, or a pleasing *fall* of water running violently, these things made them to swoon for fear. *Wisdom*

Down through the crannies of the living walls,
The crystal streams descend in murm'ring *falls*. *Dry.*

The swain, in barren deserts, with surprise
Sees lilies spring, and sudden verdure rise ;
And starts, amidst the thirsty wilds, to hear
New *falls* of water murm'ring in his ear. *Pope.*

Now under hanging mountains,
Beside the *falls* of fountains,
He makes his moan ;
And calls her ghost,
For ever, ever, ever lost ! *Pope's St. Cecilia.*

12. The outlet of a current into any other water.

Before the *fall* of the Po into the gulph, it receives into its channel considerable rivers. *Addis. on Italy.*

13. Autumn ; the fall of the leaf ; the time when the leaves drop from the trees.

What crouds of patients the town doctor kills,
Or how last *fall* he rais'd the weekly bills. *Dryden.*

14. Any thing that comes down in great quantities.

Upon a great *fall* of rain the current carried away a huge heap of apples. *L'Estrange.*

15. The act of felling or cutting down : as, the *fall* of timber.

FALLA'CIOUS. *adj.* [*fallax*, Lat. *fallacieux*, Fr.]

1. Producing mistake ; sophistical. It is never used of men, but of writings, pro positions, or things.

The Jews believed and assented to things neither evident nor certain, nor yet so much as probable, but actually false and *fallacious* ; such as the absurd doctrines and stories of their rabbies. *South's Sermons.*

2. Deceitful ; mocking expectation.

The force of that *fallacious* fruit,
That with exhilarating vapour bland
About their spirits had play'd, and inmost pow'rs
Made err, was now exhal'd. *Milton's Paradise Lost.*

False philosophy inspires
Fallacious hope. *Milton.*

FALLA'CIOUSLY. *adv.* [from *fallacious*.] Sophistically ; with purpose to deceive ; with unsound reasoning.

We shall so far encourage contradiction, as to promise not to oppose any pen that shall *fallaciously* refute us. *Brown.*

We have seen how *fallaciously* the author has stated the cause, by supposing that nothing but unlimited mercy, or unlimited punishment, are the methods that can be made use of. *Addison.*

FALLA'CIOUSNESS. *n. s.* [from *fallacious*.] Tendency to deceive ; inconclusiveness.

FA'LLACY. *n. s.* [*fallacia*, Lat. *fallace*, Fr.] Sophism ; logical artifice ; deceit ; deceitful argument ; delusory mode of ratiocination.

Most princes make themselves another thing from the people by a *fallacy* of argument, thinking themselves most kings when the subject is most basely subjected. *Sidney.*

Until I know this sure uncertainty,
I'll entertain the favour'd *fallacy*. *Shakspeare.*

It were a mere *fallacy* and mistaking, to ascribe that to the force of imagination upon another body, which is but the force of imagination upon the proper body. *Bacon.*

All men, who can see an inch before them, may easily detect gross *fallacies*. *Dryden.*

FALLIBI'LITY. *n. s.* [from *fallible*.] Liableness to be deceived ; uncertainty ; possibility of errour.

There is a great deal of *fallibility* in the testimony of men ; yet some things we may be almost as certain of, as that the sun shines, or that five twenties make an hundred. *Watts.*

FA'LLIBLE. *adj.* [*fallo*, Lat.] Liable to errour ; such as may be deceived.

Do not falsify your resolution with hopes that are *fallible* : to-morrow you must die. *Shakspeare.*

He that creates to himself thousands of little hopes, uncertain in the promise, *fallible* in the event, and depending upon a thousand circumstances, often fail his expectations. *Taylor.*

Our intellectual or rational powers need some assistance, because they are so frail and *fallible* in the present state. *Watts.*

FA'LLING. } *n. s.* [from *fall*.] Indentings
FA'LLING in. } opposed to prominence.

It shows the nose and eyebrows, with the several prominences and *fallings* in of the features, much more distinctly than any other kind of figure. *Addis.*

The History of Rasselas, Prince of Abyssinia

I. *Description of a Palace in a Valley*

Ye who listen with credulity to the whispers of fancy, and pursue with eagerness the phantoms of hope; who expect that age will perform the promises of youth, and that the deficiencies of the present day will be supplied by the morrow; attend to the history of Rasselas prince of Abyssinia.

Rasselas was the fourth son of the mighty emperor in whose dominions the Father of waters° begins his course; whose bounty pours down the streams of plenty, and scatters over half the world the harvests of Egypt.

According to the custom which has descended from age to age among the monarchs of the torrid zone, Rasselas was confined in a private palace, with the other sons and daughters of Abyssinian royalty, till the order of succession should call him to the throne.

The place which the wisdom or policy of antiquity had destined for the residence of the Abyssinian princes was a spacious valley in the kingdom of Amhara,° surrounded on every side by mountains, of which the summits overhang the middle part. The only passage by which it could be entered was a cavern that passed under a rock, of which it has long been disputed whether it was the work of nature or of human industry. The outlet of the cavern was concealed by a thick wood, and the mouth which opened into the valley was closed with gates of iron, forged by the artificers of ancient days, so massy that no man could, without the help of engines, open or shut them.

From the mountains on every side, rivulets descended that filled all the valley with verdure and fertility, and formed a lake in the middle inhabited by fish of every species, and frequented by every fowl whom nature has taught to dip the wing in water. This lake discharged its superfluities by a stream which entered a dark cleft of the mountain on the northern side, and fell with dreadful noise from precipice to precipice till it was heard no more.

The sides of the mountains were covered with trees, the banks of the brooks were diversified with flowers; every blast shook spices from the rocks, and every month dropped fruits upon the ground. All animals that bite the grass, or browse the shrub, whether wild or tame, wandered in this extensive circuit, secured from beasts of prey by the mountains which confined them. On one part were flocks and herds feeding in the pastures, on another all the beasts of chase frisking in the lawns; the sprightly kid was bounding on the rocks, the subtle monkey frolicking in the trees, and the solemn elephant reposing in the shade. All the diversities of the world were brought together, the blessings of nature were collected, and its evils extracted and excluded.

The valley, wide and fruitful, supplied its inhabitants with the necessaries of life, and all delights and superfluities were added at the annual visit which the emperor paid his children, when the iron gate was opened to the sound of music; and during eight days every one that resided in the valley was required to propose whatever might contribute to make seclusion pleasant, to fill up the vacancies of attention, and lessen the tediousness of time. Every desire was immediately granted. All the artificers of pleasure were called to gladden the festivity; the musicians exerted the power of harmony, and the dancers showed their activity before the princes, in hope that they should pass their lives in this blissful captivity, to which these only were admitted whose performance was thought able to add novelty to luxury. Such was the appearance of security and delight which this retirement afforded that they to whom it was new always desired that it might be perpetual; and as those on whom the iron gate had once closed were never suffered to return, the effect of longer experience could not be known. Thus every year produced new schemes of delight, and new competitors for imprisonment.

The palace stood on an eminence raised about thirty paces above the surface of the lake. It was divided into many squares or courts, built with greater or less magnificence according to the rank of those for whom they were designed. The roofs were turned into arches of massy stone joined with a cement that grew harder by time, and the building stood from century to century, deriding the solstitial rains and equinoctial hurricanes, without need of reparation.

This house, which was so large as to be fully known to none but some ancient officers who successively inherited the secrets of the place, was built as if suspicion herself had dictated the plan. To every room there was an open and secret passage, every square had a communication with the rest, either from the upper stories by private galleries, or by subterranean passages° from the lower apartments. Many of the columns had unsuspected cavities, in which a long race of monarchs had reposited their treasures. They then closed up the opening with marble, which was never to be removed but in the utmost exigencies of the kingdom; and recorded their accumulations in a book which was itself concealed in a tower not entered but by the emperor attended by the prince who stood next in succession.

II. *The Discontent of Rasselas in the Happy Valley*

Here the sons and daughters of Abyssinia lived only to know the soft vicissitudes of pleasure and repose, attended by all that were skilful to delight, and gratified with whatever the senses can enjoy. They wandered in gardens of fragrance, and slept in the fortresses of security. Every art was practised to make them pleased with their own condition. The sages who instructed them told them of nothing but the miseries of public life, and described all beyond the mountains as regions of calamity, where discord was always raging, and where man preyed upon man.

To heighten their opinion of their own felicity, they were daily entertained with songs, the subject of which was the *happy valley*. Their appetites were excited by frequent enumerations of different enjoyments, and revelry and merriment was the business of every hour from the dawn of morning to the close of even.

These methods were generally successful; few of the princes had ever wished to enlarge their bounds, but passed their lives in full conviction that they had all within their reach that art or nature could bestow, and pitied those whom fate had excluded from this seat of tranquility, as the sport of chance, and the slaves of misery.

Thus they rose in the morning, and lay down at night, pleased with each other and with themselves, all but Rasselas,° who, in the twenty-sixth year of his age, began to withdraw himself from their pastimes and assemblies, and to delight in solitary walks and silent meditation. He often sat before tables covered with luxury, and forgot to taste the dainties that were placed before him: he rose abruptly in the midst of the song, and hastily retired beyond the sound of music. His attendants observed the change and endeavoured to renew his love of pleasure: he neglected their officiousness, repulsed their invitations, and spent day after day on the banks of rivulets sheltered with trees, where he sometimes listened to the birds in the branches, sometimes observed the fish playing in the stream, and anon cast his eyes upon the pastures and mountains filled with animals, of which some were biting the herbage, and some sleeping among the bushes.

This singularity of his humour made him much observed. One of the sages in whose conversation he had formerly delighted followed him secretly, in hope of discovering the cause of his disquiet. Rasselas, who knew not that any one was near him, having for some time fixed his eyes upon the goats that were browsing among the rocks, began to compare their condition with his own.

'What,' said he, 'makes the difference between man and all the rest of the animal creation? Every beast that strays beside me has the same corporal necessities with myself; he is hungry and crops the grass, he is thirsty and drinks the stream, his thirst and hunger are appeased, he is satisfied and sleeps; he rises again and is hungry, he is again fed and is at rest. I am hungry and thirsty like him, but when thirst and hunger cease I am not at rest; I am, like him, pained with want, but am not, like him, satisfied with fullness. The intermediate hours are tedious and gloomy; I long again to be hungry that I may again quicken my attention. The birds peck the berries or the corn, and fly away to the groves where they sit in seeming happiness on the branches, and waste their lives in tuning one unvaried series of sounds. I likewise can call the lutanist and the singer, but the sounds that pleased me yesterday weary me today, and will grow yet more wearisome tomorrow. I can discover within me no power of perception which is not glutted with its proper pleasure, yet I do not feel myself delighted. Man has surely some latent sense for which this place affords no gratification, or he has some desires distinct from sense which must be satisfied before he can be happy.'

After this he lifted up his head, and seeing the moon rising, walked towards the palace. As he passed through the fields, and saw the animals around him, 'Ye,' said he, 'are happy, and need not envy me that walk thus among you, burdened with myself; nor do I, ye gentle beings, envy your felicity; for it is not the felicity of man. I have many distresses from which ye are free; I fear pain when I do not feel it; I sometimes shrink at evils recollected, and sometimes start at evils anticipated: surely the equity of providence has balanced peculiar sufferings with peculiar enjoyments.'

With observations like these the prince amused himself as he returned, uttering them with a plaintive voice, yet with a look that discovered him to feel some complacence in his own perspicacity, and to receive some solace of the miseries of life, from consciousness of the delicacy with which he felt, and the eloquence with which he bewailed them. He mingled cheerfully in the diversions of the evening, and all rejoiced to find that his heart was lightened.

III. *The Wants of Him That Wants Nothing*

On the next day his old instructor, imagining that he had now made himself acquainted with his disease of mind, was in hope of curing it by counsel, and officiously sought an opportunity of conference, which the prince, having long considered him as one whose intellects were exhausted, was not very willing to afford: 'Why,' said he, 'does this man thus intrude upon me; shall I be never suffered to forget those lectures which pleased only while they were new, and to become new again must be forgotten?' He then walked into the wood, and composed himself to his usual meditations; when, before his thoughts had taken any settled form, he perceived his pursuer at his side, and was at first prompted by his impatience to go hastily away; but, being unwilling to offend a man whom he had once reverenced and still loved, he invited him to sit down with him on the bank.

The old man, thus encouraged, began to lament the change which had been lately observed in the prince, and to enquire why he so often retired from the pleasures of the palace, to loneliness and silence. 'I fly from pleasure,' said the prince, 'because pleasure has ceased to please; I am lonely because I am miserable, and am unwilling to cloud with my presence the happiness of others.' 'You, sir,' said the sage, 'are the first who has complained of misery in the *happy valley*. I hope to convince you that your complaints have no real cause. You are here in full possession of all that the emperor of Abyssinia can bestow; here is neither labour to be endured nor danger to be dreaded, yet here is all that labour or danger can procure or purchase. Look round and tell me which of your wants is without supply: if you want nothing, how are you unhappy?'

'That I want nothing,' said the prince, 'or that I know not what I want, is the cause of my complaint; if I had any known want, I should have a certain wish; that wish would excite endeavour, and I should not then repine to see the sun move so slowly towards the western mountain, or lament when the day breaks and sleep will no longer hide me from myself. When I see the kids and the lambs chasing one another, I fancy that I should be happy if I had something to pursue. But, possessing all that I can want, I find one day and one hour exactly like another, except that the latter is still more tedious than the former. Let your experience inform me how the day may now seem as short as in my childhood, while nature was yet fresh, and every moment showed me what I never had observed before. I have already enjoyed too much; give me something to desire.'

The old man was surprised at this new species of affliction, and knew not what to reply, yet was unwilling to be silent. 'Sir,' said he, 'if you had seen the miseries of the world, you would know how to value your present state.' 'Now,' said the prince, 'you have given me something to desire; I shall long to see the miseries of the world, since the sight of them is necessary to happiness.'

IV. *The Prince Continues to Grieve and Muse*

At this time the sound of music proclaimed the hour of repast, and the conversation was concluded. The old man went away sufficiently discontented to find that his reasonings had produced the only conclusion which they were intended to prevent. But in the decline of life shame and grief are of short duration; whether it be that we bear easily what we have borne long, or that, finding ourselves in age less regarded, we less regard others; or that we look with slight regard upon afflictions to which we know that the hand of death is about to put an end.

The prince, whose views were extended to a wider space, could not speedily quiet his emotions. He had been before terrified at the length of life which nature promised him, because he considered that in a long time much must be endured; he now rejoiced in his youth, because in many years much might be done.

This first beam of hope that had been ever darted into his mind rekindled youth in his cheeks, and doubled the lustre of his eyes. He was fired with the desire of doing something, though he knew not yet with distinctness either end or means.

He was now no longer gloomy and unsocial; but considering himself as master of a secret stock of happiness, which he could enjoy only by concealing it, he affected to be busy in all schemes of diversion, and endeavoured to make others pleased with the state of which he himself was weary. But pleasures never can be so multiplied or continued as not to leave much of life unemployed; there were many hours, both of the night and day, which he could spend without suspicion in solitary thought. The load of life was much lightened: he went eagerly into the assemblies, because he supposed the frequency of his presence necessary to the success of his purposes; he retired gladly to privacy, because he had now a subject of thought.

His chief amusement was to picture to himself that world which he had never seen; to place himself in various conditions; to be entangled in imaginary difficulties, and to be engaged in wild adventures: but his benevolence always terminated his projects in the relief of distress, the detection of fraud, the defeat of oppression, and the diffusion of happiness.

Thus passed twenty months of the life of Rasselas. He busied himself so intensely in visionary bustle that he forgot his real solitude; and, amidst hourly preparations for the various incidents of human affairs, neglected to consider by what means he should mingle with mankind.

One day, as he was sitting on a bank, he feigned to himself an orphan virgin robbed of her little portion by a treacherous lover, and crying after him for restitution and redress. So strongly was the image impressed upon his mind that he started up in the maid's defence, and ran forward to seize the plunderer with all the eagerness of real pursuit. Fear naturally quickens the flight of guilt. Rasselas could not catch the fugitive with his utmost efforts; but, resolving to weary, by perseverance, him whom he could not surpass in speed, he pressed on till the foot of the mountain stopped his course.

Here he recollected himself, and smiled at his own useless impetuosity. Then raising his eyes to the mountain, 'This,' said he, 'is the fatal obstacle that hinders at once the enjoyment of pleasure, and the exercise of virtue. How long is it that my hopes and wishes have flown beyond this boundary of my life, which yet I never have attempted to surmount!'

Struck with this reflection, he sat down to muse, and remembered that since he first resolved to escape from his confinement, the sun had passed twice over him in his annual course. He now felt a degree of regret with which he had never been before acquainted. He considered how much might have been done in the time which had passed, and left nothing real behind it. He compared twenty months with the life of man. 'In life,' said he, 'is not to be counted the ignorance of infancy, or imbecility of age. We are long before we are able to think, and we soon cease from the power of acting. The true period of human existence may be reasonably estimated as forty years, of which I have mused away the four and twentieth part. What I have lost was certain, for I have certainly possessed it; but of twenty months to come who can assure me?'

The consciousness of his own folly pierced him deeply, and he was long before he could be reconciled to himself. 'The rest of my time,' said he, 'has been lost by the crime or folly of my ancestors, and the absurd institutions of my country; I remember it with disgust, yet without remorse: but the months that have passed since new light darted into my soul, since I formed a scheme of reasonable felicity, have been squandered by my own fault. I have lost that which can never be restored: I have seen the sun rise and set for twenty months, an idle gazer on the light of heaven. In this time the birds have left the nest of their mother, and committed themselves to the woods and to the skies: the kid has forsaken the teat, and learned by degrees to climb the rocks in quest of independent sustenance. I only have made no advances, but am still helpless and ignorant. The moon by more than twenty changes admonished me of the flux of life; the stream that rolled before my feet upbraided my inactivity. I sat feasting on intellectual luxury, regardless alike of the examples of the earth, and the instructions of the planets. Twenty months are past, who shall restore them!'

These sorrowful meditations fastened upon his mind; he passed four months in resolving to lose no more time in idle resolves, and was awakened to more vigorous exertion by hearing a maid who had broken a porcelain cup remark that what cannot be repaired is not to be regretted.

This was obvious; and Rasselas reproached himself that he had not discovered it, having not known, or not considered, how many useful hints are obtained by chance, and how often the mind, hurried by her own ardour to distant views, neglects the truths that lie open before her. He, for a few hours, regretted his regret, and from that time bent his whole mind upon the means of escaping from the valley of happiness.

v. *The Prince Meditates His Escape*

He now found that it would be very difficult to effect that which it was very easy to suppose effected. When he looked round about him, he saw himself confined by the bars of nature which had never yet been broken, and by the gate, through which none that once had passed it were ever able to return. He was now impatient as an eagle in a grate. He passed week after week in clambering the mountains, to see if there was any aperture which the bushes might conceal, but found all the summits inaccessible by their prominence. The iron gate he despaired to open; for it was not only secured with all the power of art, but was always watched by successive sentinels, and was by its position exposed to the perpetual observation of all the inhabitants.

He then examined the cavern through which the waters of the lake were discharged; and, looking down at a time when the sun shone strongly upon its mouth, he discovered it to be full of broken rocks, which, though they permitted the stream to flow through many narrow passages, would stop any body of solid bulk. He returned discouraged and dejected; but, having now known the blessing of hope, resolved never to despair.

In these fruitless searches he spent ten months. The time, however, passed cheerfully away: in the morning he rose with new hope, in the evening applauded his own diligence, and in the night slept sound after his fatigue. He met a thousand amusements which beguiled his labour, and diversified his thoughts. He discerned the various instincts of animals, and properties of plants, and found the place replete with wonders, of which he purposed to solace himself with the contemplation, if he should never be able to accomplish his flight; rejoicing that his endeavours, though yet unsuccessful, had supplied him with a source of inexhaustible inquiry.

But his original curiosity was not yet abated; he resolved to obtain some knowledge of the ways of men. His wish still continued, but his hope grew less. He ceased to survey any longer the walls of his prison, and spared to search by new toils for interstices which he knew could not be found, yet determined to keep his design always in view, and lay hold on any expedient that time should offer.

VI. *A Dissertation on the Art of Flying*

Among the artists that had been allured into the happy valley, to labour for the accommodation and pleasure of its inhabitants, was a man eminent for his knowledge of the mechanic powers, who had contrived many engines both of use and recreation. By a wheel, which the stream turned, he forced the water into a tower, whence it was distributed to all the apartments of the palace. He erected a pavilion in the garden, around which he kept the air always cool by artificial showers. One of the groves, appropriated to the ladies, was ventilated by fans, to which the rivulet that run through it gave a constant motion; and instruments of soft music were placed at proper distances, of which some played by the impulse of the wind, and some by the power of the stream.

This artist was sometimes visited by Rasselas, who was pleased with every kind of knowledge, imagining that the time would come when all his acquisitions should be of use to him in the open world. He came one day to amuse himself in his usual manner, and found the master busy in building a sailing chariot: he saw that the design was practicable upon a level surface, and with expressions of great esteem solicited its completion. The workman was pleased to find himself so much regarded by the prince, and resolved to gain yet higher honours. 'Sir,' said he, 'you have seen but a small part of what the mechanic sciences can perform. I have been long of opinion that, instead of the tardy conveyance of ships and chariots, man might use the swifter migration of wings; that the fields of air are open to knowledge, and that only ignorance and idleness need crawl upon the ground.'

This hint rekindled the prince's desire of passing the mountains; having seen what the mechanist had already performed, he was willing to fancy that he could do more; yet resolved to inquire further before he suffered hope to afflict him by disappointment. 'I am afraid,' said he to the artist, 'that your imagination prevails over your skill, and that you now tell me rather what you wish than what you know. Every animal has his element assigned him; the birds have the air, and man and beasts the earth.' 'So,' replied the mechanist, 'fishes have the water, in which yet beasts can swim by nature, and men by art. He that can swim needs not despair to fly: to swim is to fly in a grosser fluid, and to fly is to swim in a subtler. We are only to proportion our power of resistance to the different density of the matter through which we are to pass. You will be necessarily upborne by the air, if you can renew any impulse upon it faster than the air can recede from the pressure.'

'But the exercise of swimming,' said the prince, 'is very laborious; the strongest limbs are soon wearied; I am afraid the act of flying will be yet more violent, and wings will be of no great use, unless we can fly further than we can swim.'

'The labour of rising from the ground,'° said the artist, 'will be great, as we see it in the heavier domestic fowls; but, as we mount higher, the earth's attraction, and the body's gravity, will be gradually diminished, till we shall arrive at a region where the man will float in the air without any tendency to fall: no care will then be necessary but to move forwards, which the gentlest impulse will effect. You, sir, whose curiosity is so extensive, will easily conceive with what pleasure a philosopher, furnished with wings, and hovering in the sky, would see the earth, and all its inhabitants, rolling beneath him, and presenting to him successively, by its diurnal motion, all the countries within the same parallel. How must it amuse the pendent spectator to see the moving scene of land and ocean, cities and deserts! To survey with equal security the marts of trade, and the fields of battle; mountains infested by barbarians, and fruitful regions gladdened by plenty, and lulled by peace! How easily shall we then trace the Nile through all his passage; pass over to distant regions, and examine the face of nature from one extremity of the earth to the other!'

'All this,' said the prince, 'is much to be desired, but I am afraid that no man will be able to breathe in these regions of speculation and tranquility. I have been told that respiration is difficult upon lofty mountains, yet from these precipices, though so high as to produce great tenuity of the air, it is very easy to fall: therefore I suspect that from any height where life can be supported there may be danger of too quick descent.'

'Nothing,' replied the artist, 'will ever be attempted, if all possible objections must be first overcome. If you will favour my project I will try the first flight at my own hazard. I have considered the structure of all volant animals, and find the folding continuity of the bat's wings most easily accommodated to the human form. Upon this model I shall begin my task tomorrow, and in a year expect to tower into the air beyond the malice or pursuit of man. But I will work only on this condition, that the art shall not be divulged, and that you shall not require me to make wings for any but ourselves.'

'Why,' said Rasselas, 'should you envy others so great an advantage? All skill ought to be exerted for universal good; every man has owed much to others, and ought to repay the kindness that he has received.'

'If men were all virtuous,' returned the artist, 'I should with great alacrity teach them all to fly. But what would be the security of the good, if the bad could at pleasure invade them from the sky? Against an army sailing through the clouds neither walls, nor mountains, nor seas, could afford any security. A flight of northern savages might hover in the wind, and light at once with irresistible violence upon the capital of a fruitful region that was rolling under them. Even this valley, the retreat of princes, the abode of happiness, might be violated by the sudden descent of some of the naked nations that swarm on the coast of the southern sea.'

The prince promised secrecy, and waited for the performance, not wholly hopeless of success. He visited the work from time to time, observed its progress, and remarked many ingenious contrivances to facilitate motion, and unite levity with strength. The artist was every day more certain that he should leave vultures and eagles behind him, and the contagion of his confidence seized upon the prince.

In a year the wings were finished, and, on a morning appointed, the maker appeared furnished for flight on a little promontory: he waved his pinions a while to gather air, then leaped from his stand, and in an instant dropped into the lake. His wings, which were of no use in the air, sustained him in the water, and the prince drew him to land, half dead with terror and vexation.

VII. *The Prince Finds a Man of Learning*

The prince was not much afflicted by this disaster, having suffered himself to hope for a happier event only because he had no other means of escape in view. He still persisted in his design to leave the happy valley by the first opportunity.

His imagination was now at a stand; he had no prospect of entering into the world; and, notwithstanding all his endeavours to support himself, discontent by degrees preyed upon him, and he began again to lose his thoughts in sadness, when the rainy season, which in these countries is periodical, made it inconvenient to wander in the woods.

The rain continued longer and with more violence than had been ever known: the clouds broke on the surrounding mountains, and the torrents streamed into the plain on every side, till the cavern was too narrow to discharge the water. The lake overflowed its banks, and all the level of the valley was covered with the inundation. The eminence on which the palace was built and some other spots of rising ground were all that the eye could now discover. The herds and flocks left the pastures, and both the wild beasts and the tame retreated to the mountains.

This inundation confined all the princes to domestic amusements, and the attention of Rasselas was particularly seized by a poem which Imlac° rehearsed upon the various conditions of humanity. He commanded the poet to attend him in his apartment, and recite his verses a second time; then entering into familiar talk, he thought himself happy in having found a man who knew the world so well, and could so skilfully paint the scenes of life. He asked a thousand questions about things to which, though common to all other mortals, his confinement from childhood had kept him a stranger. The poet pitied his ignorance, and loved his curiosity, and entertained him from day to day with novelty and instruction, so that the prince regretted the necessity of sleep, and longed till the morning should renew his pleasure.

As they were sitting together, the prince commanded Imlac to relate his history, and to tell by what accident he was forced, or by what motive induced, to close his life in the happy valley. As he was going to begin his narrative, Rasselas was called to a concert, and obliged to restrain his curiosity till the evening.

VIII. *The History of Imlac*

The close of the day is, in the regions of the torrid zone, the only season of diversion and entertainment, and it was therefore midnight before the music ceased, and the princesses retired. Rasselas then called for his companion and required him to begin the story of his life.

'Sir,' said Imlac, 'my history will not be long: the life that is devoted to knowledge passes silently away, and is very little diversified by events. To talk in public, to think in solitude, to read and to hear, to inquire, and answer inquiries, is the business of a scholar. He wanders about the world without pomp or terror, and is neither known nor valued but by men like himself.

'I was born in the kingdom of Goiama, at no great distance from the fountain of the Nile. My father was a wealthy merchant, who traded between the inland countries of Africk and the ports of the Red Sea. He was honest, frugal and diligent, but of mean sentiments, and narrow comprehension: he desired only to be rich, and to conceal his riches, lest he should be spoiled by the governors of the province.'

'Surely,' said the prince, 'my father must be negligent of his charge, if any man in his dominions dares take that which belongs to another. Does he not know that kings are accountable for injustice permitted as well as done? If I were emperor, not the meanest of my subjects should be oppressed with impunity. My blood boils when I am told that a merchant durst not enjoy his honest gains for fear of losing them by the rapacity of power. Name the governor who robbed the people, that I may declare his crimes to the emperor.'

'Sir,' said Imlac, 'your ardour is the natural effect of virtue animated by youth: the time will come when you will acquit your father, and perhaps hear with less impatience of the governor. Oppression is, in the Abyssinian dominions, neither frequent nor tolerated; but no form of government has been yet discovered by which cruelty can be wholly prevented. Subordination supposes power on one part and subjection on the other; and if power be in the hands of men, it will sometimes be abused. The vigilance of the supreme magistrate may do much, but much will still remain undone. He can never know all the crimes that are committed, and can seldom punish all that he knows.'

'This,' said the prince, 'I do not understand, but I had rather hear thee than dispute. Continue thy narration.'

'My father,' proceeded Imlac, 'originally intended that I should have no other education than such as might qualify me for commerce; and discovering in me great strength of memory, and quickness of apprehension, often declared his hope that I should be some time the richest man in Abyssinia.'

'Why,' said the prince, 'did thy father desire the increase of his wealth, when it was already greater than he durst discover or enjoy? I am unwilling to doubt thy veracity, yet inconsistencies cannot both be true.'

'Inconsistencies,' answered Imlac, 'cannot both be right, but, imputed to man, they may both be true. Yet diversity is not inconsistency. My father might expect a time of greater security. However, some desire is necessary to keep life in motion, and he whose real wants are supplied must admit those of fancy.'

'This,' said the prince, 'I can in some measure conceive. I repent that I interrupted thee.'

'With this hope,' proceeded Imlac, 'he sent me to school; but when I had once found the delight of knowledge, and felt the pleasure of intelligence and the pride of invention, I began silently to despise riches, and determined to disappoint the purpose of my father, whose grossness of conception raised my pity. I was twenty years old before his tenderness would expose me to the fatigue of travel, in which time I had been instructed, by successive masters, in all the literature of my native country. As every hour taught me something new, I lived in a continual course of gratifications; but, as I advanced towards manhood, I lost much of the reverence with which I had been used to look on my instructors; because, when the lesson was ended, I did not find them wiser or better than common men.

'At length my father resolved to initiate me in commerce, and, opening one of his subterranean treasuries, counted out ten thousand pieces of gold. "This, young man," said he, "is the stock with which you must negotiate. I began with less than the fifth part, and you see how diligence and parsimony have increased it. This is your own to waste or to improve. If you squander it by negligence or caprice, you must wait for my death before you will be rich: if, in four years, you double your stock, we will thenceforward let subordination cease, and live together as friends and partners; for he shall always be equal with me who is equally skilled in the art of growing rich."

'We laid our money upon camels, concealed in bales of cheap goods, and travelled to the shore of the Red Sea. When I cast my eye on the expanse of waters my heart bounded like that of a prisoner escaped. I felt an unextinguishable curiosity kindle in my mind, and resolved to snatch this opportunity of seeing the manners of other nations, and of learning sciences unknown in Abyssinia.

'I remembered that my father had obliged me to the improvement of my stock, not by a promise which I ought not to violate, but by a penalty which I was at liberty to incur; and therefore determined to gratify my predominant desire, and by drinking at the fountains of knowledge, to quench the thirst of curiosity.

'As I was supposed to trade without connexion with my father, it was easy for me to become acquainted with the master of a ship, and procure a passage to some other country. I had no motives of choice to regulate my voyage; it was sufficient for me that, wherever I wandered, I should see a country which I had not seen before. I therefore entered a ship bound for Surat, having left a letter for my father declaring my intention.

IX. *The History of Imlac Continued*

'When I first entered upon the world of waters, and lost sight of land, I looked round about me with pleasing terror, and thinking my soul enlarged by the boundless prospect, imagined that I could gaze round for ever without satiety; but, in a short time, I grew weary of looking on barren uniformity, where I could only see again what I had already seen. I then descended into the ship, and doubted for a while whether all my future pleasures would not end like this in disgust and disappointment. "Yet, surely," said I, "the ocean and the land are very different; the only variety of water is rest and motion, but the earth has mountains and valleys, deserts and cities: it is inhabited by men of different customs and contrary opinions; and I may hope to find variety in life, though I should miss it in nature."

'With this thought I quieted my mind; and amused myself during the voyage, sometimes by learning from the sailors the art of navigation, which I have never practised, and sometimes by forming schemes for my conduct in different situations, in not one of which I have been ever placed.

'I was almost weary of my naval amusements when we landed safely at Surat. I secured my money, and purchasing some commodities for show, joined myself to a caravan that was passing into the inland country. My companions, for some reason or other, conjecturing that

I was rich, and, by my inquiries and admiration, finding that I was ignorant, considered me as a novice whom they had a right to cheat, and who was to learn at the usual expense the art of fraud. They exposed me to the theft of servants, and the exaction of officers, and saw me plundered upon false pretences, without any advantage to themselves, but that of rejoicing in the superiority of their own knowledge.'

'Stop a moment,' said the prince. 'Is there such depravity in man, as that he should injure another without benefit to himself? I can easily conceive that all are pleased with superiority; but your ignorance was merely accidental, which, being neither your crime nor your folly, could afford them no reason to applaud themselves; and the knowledge which they had, and which you wanted, they might as effectually have shown by warning, as betraying you.'

'Pride,' said Imlac, 'is seldom delicate, it will please itself with very mean advantages; and envy feels not its own happiness, but when it may be compared with the misery of others. They were my enemies because they grieved to think me rich, and my oppressors because they delighted to find me weak.'

'Proceed,' said the prince: 'I doubt not of the facts which you relate, but imagine that you impute them to mistaken motives.'

'In this company,' said Imlac, 'I arrived at Agra, the capital of Indostan, the city in which the great Mogul commonly resides. I applied myself to the language of the country, and in a few months was able to converse with the learned men; some of whom I found morose and reserved, and others easy and communicative; some were unwilling to teach another what they had with difficulty learned themselves; and some showed that the end of their studies was to gain the dignity of instructing.

'To the tutor of the young princes I recommended myself so much that I was presented to the emperor as a man of uncommon knowledge. The emperor asked me many questions concerning my country and my travels; and though I cannot now recollect any thing that he uttered above the power of a common man, he dismissed me astonished at his wisdom, and enamoured of his goodness.

'My credit was now so high that the merchants with whom I had travelled applied to me for recommendations to the ladies of the court. I was surprised at their confidence of solicitation, and gently reproached them with their practices on the road. They heard me with cold indifference, and showed no tokens of shame or sorrow.

'They then urged their request with the offer of a bribe; but what I would not do for kindness I would not do for money; and refused them, not because they had injured me, but because I would not enable them to injure others; for I knew they would have made use of my credit to cheat those who should buy their wares.

'Having resided at Agra till there was no more to be learned, I travelled into Persia, where I saw many remains of ancient magnificence, and observed many new accommodations of life. The Persians are a nation eminently social, and their assemblies afforded me daily opportunities of remarking characters and manners, and of tracing human nature through all its variations.

'From Persia I passed into Arabia, where I saw a nation at once pastoral and warlike; who live without any settled habitation; whose only wealth is their flocks and herds; and who have yet carried on, through all ages, an hereditary war with all mankind, though they neither covet nor envy their possessions.

x. *Imlac's History Continued. A Dissertation upon Poetry*

'Wherever I went, I found that poetry was considered as the highest learning, and regarded with a veneration somewhat approaching to that which man would pay to the angelic nature. And it yet fills me with wonder that, in almost all countries, the most ancient poets are considered as the best: whether it be that every other kind of knowledge is an acquisition gradually attained, and poetry is a gift conferred at once; or that the first poetry of every nation surprised them as a novelty, and retained the credit by consent which it received by accident at first: or whether, as the province of poetry is to describe nature and passion, which are always the same, the first writers took possession of the most striking objects for description, and the most probable occurrences for fiction, and left nothing to those that followed them but transcription of the same events, and new combinations of the same images. Whatever be the reason, it is commonly observed that the early writers are in possession of nature, and their followers of art: that the first excel in strength and invention, and the latter in elegance and refinement.

'I was desirous to add my name to this illustrious fraternity. I read all the poets of Persia and Arabia, and was able to repeat by memory the volumes that are suspended in the mosque of Mecca. But I soon found that no man was ever great by imitation. My desire of excellence impelled me to transfer my attention to nature and to life. Nature was to be my subject, and men to be my auditors: I could never describe what I had not seen: I could not hope to move those with delight or terror whose interests and opinions I did not understand.

'Being now resolved to be a poet, I saw every thing with a new purpose; my sphere of attention was suddenly magnified: no kind of knowledge was to be overlooked. I ranged mountains and deserts for images and resemblances, and pictured upon my mind every tree of the forest and flower of the valley. I observed with equal care the crags of the rock and the pinnacles of the palace. Sometimes I wandered along the mazes of the rivulet, and sometimes watched the changes of the summer clouds. To a poet nothing can be useless. Whatever is beautiful, and whatever is dreadful, must be familiar to his imagination: he must be conversant with all that is awfully vast or elegantly little. The plants of the garden, the animals of the wood, the minerals of the earth, and meteors of the sky, must all concur to store his mind with inexhaustible variety: for every idea is useful for the enforcement or decoration of moral or religious truth; and he who knows most will have most power of diversifying his scenes, and of gratifying his reader with remote allusions and unexpected instruction.

'All the appearances of nature I was therefore careful to study, and every country which I have surveyed has contributed something to my poetical powers.'

'In so wide a survey,' said the prince, 'you must surely have left much unobserved. I have lived, till now, within the circuit of these mountains, and yet cannot walk abroad without the sight of something which I had never beheld before, or never heeded.'

'The business of a poet,' said Imlac, 'is to examine, not the individual, but the species; to remark general properties and large appearances: he does not number the streaks of the tulip,° or describe the different shades in the verdure of the forest. He is to exhibit in his portraits of nature such prominent and striking features as recall the original to every mind; and must neglect the minuter discriminations, which one may have remarked, and another have neglected, for those characteristics which are alike obvious to vigilance and carelessness.

'But the knowledge of nature is only half the task of a poet; he must be acquainted likewise with all the modes of life. His character requires that he estimate the happiness and misery of every condition; observe the power of all the passions in all their combinations, and trace the changes of the human mind as they are modified by various institutions and accidental influences of climate or custom, from the spriteliness of infancy to the despondence of decrepitude. He must divest himself of the prejudices of his age or country; he must consider right and wrong in their abstracted and invariable state; he must disregard present laws and opinions, and rise to general and transcendental truths, which will always be the same: he must therefore content himself with the slow progress of his name; contemn the applause of his own time, and commit his claims to the justice of posterity. He must write as the interpreter of nature, and the legislator of mankind,° and consider himself as presiding over the thoughts and manners of future generations; as a being superior to time and place.

'His labour is not yet at an end: he must know many languages and many sciences; and, that his style may be worthy of his thoughts, must, by incessant practice, familiarize to himself every delicacy of speech and grace of harmony.'

XI. *Imlac's Narrative Continued. A Hint on Pilgrimage*

Imlac now felt the enthusiastic fit, and was proceeding to aggrandize his own profession, when the prince cried out, 'Enough! Thou hast convinced me that no human being can ever be a poet. Proceed with thy narration.'

'To be a poet,' said Imlac, 'is indeed very difficult.' 'So difficult,' returned the prince, 'that I will at present hear no more of his labours. Tell me whither you went when you had seen Persia.'

'From Persia,' said the poet, 'I travelled through Syria, and for three years resided in Palestine, where I conversed with great numbers of the northern and western nations of Europe; the nations which are now in possession of all power and all knowledge; whose armies are irresistible, and whose fleets command the remotest parts of the globe. When I compared these men with the natives of our own kingdom, and those that surround us, they appeared almost another order of beings. In their countries it is difficult to wish for any thing that may not be obtained: a thousand arts of which we never heard are continually labouring for their convenience and pleasure; and whatever their own climate has denied them is supplied by their commerce.'

'By what means,' said the prince, 'are the Europeans thus powerful? Or why, since they can so easily visit Asia and Africa for trade or conquest, cannot the Asiatics and Africans invade their coasts, plant colonies in their ports, and give laws to their natural princes? The same wind that carries them back would bring us thither.'

'They are more powerful, sir, than we,' answered Imlac, 'because they are wiser; knowledge will always predominate over ignorance, as man governs the other animals. But why their knowledge is more than ours, I know not what reason can be given but the unsearchable will of the Supreme Being.'

'When,' said the prince with a sigh, 'shall I be able to visit Palestine, and mingle with this mighty confluence of nations? Till that happy moment shall arrive, let me fill up the time with such representations as thou canst give me. I am not ignorant of the motive that assembles such numbers in that place, and cannot but consider it as the centre of wisdom and piety, to which the best and wisest men of every land must be continually resorting.'

'There are some nations,' said Imlac, 'that send few visitants to Palestine; for many numerous and learned sects in Europe concur to censure pilgrimage as superstitious, or deride it as ridiculous.'

'You know,' said the prince, 'how little my life has made me acquainted with diversity of opinions: it will be too long to hear the arguments on both sides; you, that have considered them, tell me the result.'

'Pilgrimage,' said Imlac, 'like many other acts of piety, may be reasonable or superstitious, according to the principles upon which it is performed. Long journeys in search of truth are not commanded. Truth such as is necessary to the regulation of life is always found where it is honestly sought. Change of place is no natural cause of the increase of piety, for it inevitably produces dissipation of mind. Yet, since men go every day to view the fields where great actions have been performed, and return with stronger impressions of the event, curiosity of the same kind may naturally dispose us to view that country whence our religion had its beginning; and I believe no man surveys those awful scenes without some confirmation of holy resolutions. That the Supreme Being may be more easily propitiated in one place than in another is the dream of idle superstition; but that some places may operate upon our own minds in an uncommon manner is an opinion which hourly experience will justify. He who supposes that his vices may be more successfully combated in Palestine will, perhaps, find himself mistaken, yet he may go thither without folly: he who thinks they will be more freely pardoned dishonours at once his reason and religion.'

'These,' said the prince, 'are European distinctions. I will consider them another time. What have you found to be the effect of knowledge? Are those nations happier than we?'

'There is so much infelicity,' said the poet, 'in the world, that scarce any man has leisure from his own distresses to estimate the comparative happiness of others. Knowledge is certainly one of the means of pleasure, as is confessed by the natural desire which every mind feels of increasing its ideas. Ignorance is mere privation, by which nothing can be produced: it is a vacuity in which the soul sits motionless and torpid for want of attraction; and, without knowing why, we always rejoice when we learn, and grieve when we forget. I am therefore inclined to conclude that, if nothing counteracts the natural consequence of learning, we grow more happy as our minds take a wider range.

'In enumerating the particular comforts of life we shall find many advantages on the side of the Europeans. They cure wounds and diseases with which we languish and perish. We suffer inclemencies of weather which they can obviate. They have engines for the despatch of many laborious works which we must perform by manual industry. There is such communication between distant places that one friend can hardly be said to be absent from another. Their policy removes all public inconveniencies: they have roads cut through their mountains, and bridges laid upon their rivers. And, if we descend to the privacies of life, their habitations are more commodious, and their possessions are more secure.'

'They are surely happy,' said the prince, 'who have all these conveniencies, of which I envy none so much as the facility with which separated friends interchange their thoughts.'

'The Europeans,' answered Imlac, 'are less unhappy than we, but they are not happy. Human life is everywhere a state in which much is to be endured, and little to be enjoyed.'

XII. *The Story of Imlac Continued*

'I am not yet willing,' said the prince, 'to suppose that happiness is so parsimoniously distributed to mortals; nor can believe but that, if I had the choice of life, I should be able to fill every day with pleasure. I would injure no man, and should provoke no resentment: I would relieve every distress, and should enjoy the benedictions of gratitude. I would choose my friends among the wise, and my wife among the virtuous; and therefore should be in no danger from treachery, or unkindness. My children should, by my care, be learned and pious, and would repay to my age what their childhood had received. What would dare to molest him who might call on every side to thousands enriched by his bounty, or assisted by his power? And why should not life glide quietly away in the soft reciprocation of protection and reverence? All this may be done without the help of European refinements, which appear by their effects to be rather specious than useful. Let us leave them and pursue our journey.'

'From Palestine,' said Imlac, 'I passed through many regions of Asia; in the more civilized kingdoms as a trader, and among the barbarians of the mountains as a pilgrim. At last I began to long for my native country, that I might repose after my travels, and fatigues, in the places where I had spent my earliest years, and gladden my old companions with the recital of my adventures. Often did I figure to myself those with whom I had sported away the gay hours of dawning life sitting round me in its evening, wondering at my tales, and listening to my counsels.

'When this thought had taken possession of my mind, I considered every moment as wasted which did not bring me nearer to Abyssinia. I hastened into Egypt, and, notwithstanding my impatience, was detained ten months in the contemplation of its ancient magnificence, and in inquiries after the remains of its ancient learning. I found in Cairo a mixture of all nations; some brought thither by the love of knowledge, some by the hope of gain, and many by the desire of living after their own manner without observation, and of lying hid in the obscurity of multitudes: for, in a city populous as Cairo it is possible to obtain at the same time the gratifications of society, and the secrecy of solitude.

'From Cairo I travelled to Suez, and embarked on the Red Sea, passing along the coast till I arrived at the port from which I had departed twenty years before. Here I joined myself to a caravan and re-entered my native country.

'I now expected the caresses of my kinsmen, and the congratulations of my friends, and was not without hope that my father, whatever value he had set upon riches, would own with gladness and pride a son who was able to add to the felicity and honour of the nation. But I was soon convinced that my thoughts were vain. My father had been dead fourteen years, having divided his wealth among my brothers, who were removed to some other provinces. Of my companions the greater part was in the grave, of the rest some could with difficulty remember me, and some considered me as one corrupted by foreign manners.

'A man used to vicissitudes is not easily dejected. I forgot, after a time, my disappointment, and endeavoured to recommend myself to the nobles of the kingdom: they admitted me to their tables, heard my story, and dismissed me. I opened a school, and was prohibited to teach. I then resolved to sit down in the quiet of domestic life, and addressed a lady that was fond of my conversation, but rejected my suit, because my father was a merchant.

'Wearied at last with solicitation and repulses, I resolved to hide myself for ever from the world, and depend no longer on the opinion or caprice of others. I waited for the time when the gate of the *happy valley* should open, that I might bid farewell to hope and fear: the day came; my performance was distinguished with favour, and I resigned myself with joy to perpetual confinement.'

'Hast thou here found happiness at last?' said Rasselas. 'Tell me without reserve; art thou content with thy condition? or dost thou wish to be again wandering and inquiring? All the inhabitants of this valley celebrate their lot, and, at the annual visit of the emperor, invite others to partake of their felicity.'

'Great prince,' said Imlac, 'I shall speak the truth: I know not one of all your attendants who does not lament the hour when he entered this retreat. I am less unhappy than the rest, because I have a mind replete with images, which I can vary and combine at pleasure. I can amuse my solitude by the renovation of the knowledge which begins to fade from my memory, and by recollection of the accidents of my past life. Yet all this ends in the sorrowful consideration that my acquirements are now useless, and that none of my pleasures can be again enjoyed. The rest, whose minds have no impression but of the present moment, are either corroded by malignant passions, or sit stupid in the gloom of perpetual vacancy.'

'What passions can infest those,' said the prince, 'who have no rivals? We are in a place where impotence precludes malice, and where all envy is repressed by community of enjoyments.'

'There may be community,' said Imlac, 'of material possessions, but there can never be community of love or of esteem. It must happen that one will please more than another; he that knows himself despised will always be envious; and still more envious and malevolent, if he is condemned to live in the presence of those who despise him. The invitations by which they allure others to a state which they feel to be wretched proceed from the natural malignity of hopeless misery. They are weary of themselves, and of each other, and expect to find relief in new companions. They envy the liberty which their folly has forfeited, and would gladly see all mankind imprisoned like themselves.

'From this crime, however, I am wholly free. No man can say that he is wretched by my persuasion. I look with pity on the crowds who are annually soliciting admission to captivity, and wish that it were lawful for me to warn them of their danger.'

'My dear Imlac,' said the prince, 'I will open to thee my whole heart. I have long meditated an escape from the happy valley. I have examined the mountains on every side, but find myself insuperably barred: teach me the way to break my prison; thou shalt be the companion of my flight, the guide of my rambles, the partner of my fortune, and my sole director in the *choice of life*.'

'Sir,' answered the poet, 'your escape will be difficult, and, perhaps, you may soon repent your curiosity. The world, which you figure to yourself smooth and quiet as the lake in the valley, you will find a sea foaming with tempests, and boiling with whirlpools: you will be sometimes overwhelmed by the waves of violence, and sometimes dashed against the rocks of treachery. Amidst wrongs and frauds, competitions and anxieties, you will wish a thousand times for these seats of quiet, and willingly quit hope to be free from fear.'

'Do not seek to deter me from my purpose,' said the prince: 'I am impatient to see what thou hast seen; and, since thou art thyself weary of the valley, it is evident that thy former state was better than this. Whatever be the consequence of my experiment, I am resolved to judge with my own eyes of the various conditions of men, and then to make deliberately my *choice of life*.'

'I am afraid,' said Imlac, 'you are hindered by stronger restraints than my persuasions; yet, if your determination is fixed, I do not counsel you to despair. Few things are impossible to diligence and skill.'

XIII. *Rasselas Discovers the Means of Escape*

The prince now dismissed his favourite to rest, but the narrative of wonders and novelties filled his mind with perturbation. He revolved all that he had heard, and prepared innumerable questions for the morning.

Much of his uneasiness was now removed. He had a friend to whom he could impart his thoughts, and whose experience could assist him in his designs. His heart was no longer condemned to swell with silent vexation. He thought that even the *happy valley* might be endured with such a companion, and that, if they could range the world together, he should have nothing further to desire.

In a few days the water was discharged, and the ground dried. The prince and Imlac then walked out together to converse without the notice of the rest. The prince, whose thoughts were always on the wing, as he passed by the gate, said, with a countenance of sorrow, 'Why art thou so strong, and why is man so weak?'

'Man is not weak,' answered his companion; 'knowledge is more than equivalent to force. The master of mechanics laughs at strength. I can burst the gate, but cannot do it secretly. Some other expedient must be tried.'

As they were walking on the side of the mountain, they observed that the conies, which the rain had driven from their burrows, had taken shelter among the bushes, and formed holes behind them, tending upwards in an oblique line. 'It has been the opinion of antiquity,' said Imlac, 'that human reason borrowed many arts from the instinct of animals; let us, therefore, not think ourselves degraded by learning from the cony. We may escape by piercing the mountain in the same direction. We will begin where the summit hangs over the middle part, and labour upward till we shall issue out beyond the prominence.'

The eyes of the prince, when he heard this proposal, sparkled with joy. The execution was easy, and the success certain.

No time was now lost. They hastened early in the morning to choose a place proper for their mine. They clambered with great fatigue among crags and brambles, and returned without having discovered any part that favoured their design. The second and the third day were spent in the same manner, and with the same frustration. But, on the fourth, they found a small cavern, concealed by a thicket, where they resolved to make their experiment.

Imlac procured instruments proper to hew stone and remove earth, and they fell to their work on the next day with more eagerness than vigour. They were presently exhausted by their efforts, and sat down to pant upon the grass. The prince, for a moment, appeared to be discouraged. 'Sir,' said his companion, 'practice will enable us to continue our labour for a longer time; mark, however, how far we have advanced, and you will find that our toil will some time have an end. Great works are performed, not by strength, but perseverance: yonder palace was raised by single stones, yet you see its height and spaciousness. He that shall walk with vigour three hours a day will pass in seven years a space equal to the circumference of the globe.'

They returned to their work day after day, and, in a short time, found a fissure in the rock, which enabled them to pass far with very little obstruction. This Rasselas considered as a good omen. 'Do not disturb your mind,' said Imlac, 'with other hopes or fears than reason may suggest: if you are pleased with prognostics of good, you will be terrified likewise with tokens of evil, and your whole life will be a prey to superstition. Whatever facilitates our work is more than an omen, it is a cause of success. This is one of those pleasing surprises which often happen to active resolution. Many things difficult to design prove easy to performance.'

XIV. *Rasselas and Imlac Receive an Unexpected Visit*

They had now wrought their way to the middle, and solaced their toil with the approach of liberty, when the prince, coming down to refresh himself with air, found his sister Nekayah standing before the mouth of the cavity. He started and stood confused, afraid to tell his design, and yet hopeless to conceal it. A few moments determined him to repose on her fidelity, and secure her secrecy by a declaration without reserve.

'Do not imagine,' said the princess, 'that I came hither as a spy: I had long observed from my window that you and Imlac directed your walk every day towards the same point, but I did not suppose you had any better reason for the preference than a cooler shade, or more fragrant bank; nor followed you with any other design than to partake of your conversation. Since then not suspicion but fondness has detected you, let me not lose the advantage of my discovery. I am equally weary of confinement with yourself, and not less desirous of knowing what is done or suffered in the world. Permit me to fly with you from this tasteless tranquility, which will yet grow more loathsome when you have left me. You may deny me to accompany you, but cannot hinder me from following.'

The prince, who loved Nekayah above his other sisters, had no inclination to refuse her request, and grieved that he had lost an opportunity of showing his confidence by a voluntary communication. It was therefore agreed that she should leave the valley with them; and that, in the mean time, she should watch, lest any other straggler should, by chance or curiosity, follow them to the mountain.

At length their labour was at an end; they saw the light beyond the prominence, and, issuing to the top of the mountain, beheld the Nile, yet a narrow current, wandering beneath them.

The prince looked round with rapture, anticipated all the pleasures of travel, and in thought was already transported beyond his father's dominions. Imlac, though very joyful at his escape, had less expectation of pleasure in the world, which he had before tried, and of which he had been weary.

Rasselas was so much delighted with a wider horizon that he could not soon be persuaded to return into the valley. He informed his sister that the way was open, and that nothing now remained but to prepare for their departure.

xv. *The Prince and Princess Leave the Valley and See Many Wonders*

The prince and princess had jewels sufficient to make them rich whenever they came into a place of commerce, which, by Imlac's direction, they hid in their clothes and, on the night of the next full moon, all left the valley. The princess was followed only by a single favourite, who did not know whither she was going.

They clambered through the cavity, and began to go down on the other side. The princess and her maid turned their eyes towards every part, and, seeing nothing to bound their prospect, considered themselves as in danger of being lost in a dreary vacuity. They stopped and trembled. 'I am almost afraid,' said the princess, 'to begin a journey of which I cannot perceive an end, and to venture into this immense plain where I may be approached on every side by men whom I never saw.' The prince felt nearly the same emotions, though he thought it more manly to conceal them.

Imlac smiled at their terror, and encouraged them to proceed; but the princess continued irresolute till she had been imperceptibly drawn forward too far to return.

In the morning they found some shepherds in the field, who set milk and fruits before them. The princess wondered that she did not see a palace ready for her reception, and a table spread with delicacies; but, being faint and hungry, she drank the milk and eat the fruits, and thought them of a higher flavour than the products of the valley.

They travelled forward by easy journeys, being all unaccustomed to toil or difficulty, and knowing, that though they might be missed, they could not be pursued. In a few days they came into a more populous region, where Imlac was diverted with the admiration which his companions expressed at the diversity of manners, stations, and employments.

Their dress was such as might not bring upon them the suspicion of having any thing to conceal, yet the prince, wherever he came, expected to be obeyed, and the princess was frighted, because those that came into her presence did not prostrate themselves before her. Imlac was forced to observe them with great vigilance, lest they should betray their rank by their unusual behaviour, and detained them several weeks in the first village to accustom them to the sight of common mortals.

By degrees the royal wanderers were taught to understand that they had for a time laid aside their dignity, and were to expect only such regard as liberality and courtesy could procure. And Imlac, having, by many admonitions, prepared them to endure the tumults of a port, and the ruggedness of the commercial race, brought them down to the sea-coast.

The prince and his sister, to whom every thing was new, were gratified equally at all places, and therefore remained for some months at the port without any inclination to pass further. Imlac was content with their stay, because he did not think it safe to expose them, unpractised in the world, to the hazards of a foreign country.

At last he began to fear lest they should be discovered, and proposed to fix a day for their departure. They had no pretensions to judge for themselves, and referred the whole scheme to his direction. He therefore took passage in a ship to Suez; and, when the time came, with great difficulty prevailed on the princess to enter the vessel. They had a quick and prosperous voyage, and from Suez travelled by land to Cairo.

XVI. *They Enter Cairo, and Find Every Man Happy*

As they approached the city, which filled the strangers with astonishment, 'This,' said Imlac to the prince, 'is the place where travellers and merchants assemble from all the corners of the earth. You will here find men of every character, and every occupation. Commerce is here honourable: I will act as a merchant, and you shall live as strangers who have no other end of travel than curiosity; it will soon be observed that we are rich; our reputation will procure us access to all whom we shall desire to know; you will see all the conditions of humanity, and enable yourself at leisure to make your *choice of life*.'

They now entered the town, stunned by the noise, and offended by the crowds. Instruction had not yet so prevailed over habit but that they wondered to see themselves pass undistinguished along the street, and met by the lowest of the people without reverence or notice. The princess could not at first bear the thought of being levelled with the vulgar, and, for some days, continued in her chamber, where she was served by her favourite Pekuah as in the palace of the valley.

Imlac, who understood traffic, sold part of the jewels the next day, and hired a house, which he adorned with such magnificence that he was immediately considered as a merchant of great wealth. His politeness attracted many acquaintance, and his generosity made him courted by many dependants. His table was crowded by men of every nation, who all admired his knowledge, and solicited his favour. His companions, not being able to mix in the conversation, could make no discovery of their ignorance or surprise, and were gradually initiated in the world as they gained knowledge of the language.

The prince had, by frequent lectures, been taught the use and nature of money; but the ladies could not, for a long time, comprehend what the merchants did with small pieces of gold and silver, or why things of so little use should be received as equivalent to the necessaries of life.

They studied the language two years, while Imlac was preparing to set before them the various ranks and conditions of mankind. He grew acquainted with all who had any thing uncommon in their fortune or conduct. He frequented the voluptuous and the frugal, the idle and the busy, the merchants and the men of learning.

The prince, being now able to converse with fluency, and having learned the caution necessary to be observed in his intercourse with strangers, began to accompany Imlac to places of resort, and to enter into all assemblies, that he might make his *choice of life*.

For some time he thought choice needless, because all appeared to him equally happy. Wherever he went he met gaiety and kindness, and heard the song of joy, or the laugh of carelessness. He began to believe that the world overflowed with universal plenty, and that nothing was withheld either from want or merit; that every hand showered liberality, and every heart melted with benevolence: 'And who then,' says he, 'will be suffered to be wretched?'

Imlac permitted the pleasing delusion, and was unwilling to crush the hope of inexperience; till one day, having sat a while silent, 'I know not,' said the prince, 'what can be the reason that I am more unhappy than any of our friends. I see them perpetually and unalterably cheerful, but feel my own mind restless and uneasy. I am unsatisfied with those pleasures which I seem most to court; I live in the crowds of jollity, not so much to enjoy company as to shun myself, and am only loud and merry to conceal my sadness.'

'Every man,' said Imlac, 'may, by examining his own mind, guess what passes in the minds of others: when you feel that your own gaiety is counterfeit, it may justly lead you to suspect that of your companions not to be sincere. Envy is commonly reciprocal. We are long before we are convinced that happiness is never to be found, and each believes it possessed by others, to keep alive the hope of obtaining it for himself. In the assembly where you passed the last night there appeared such spriteliness of air, and volatility of fancy, as might have suited beings of an higher order, formed to inhabit serener regions inaccessible to care or sorrow: yet, believe me, prince, there was not one who did not dread the moment when solitude should deliver him to the tyranny of reflection.'

'This,' said the prince, 'may be true of others, since it is true of me; yet, whatever be the general infelicity of man, one condition is more happy than another, and wisdom surely directs us to take the least evil in the *choice of life*.'

'The causes of good and evil,' answered Imlac, 'are so various and uncertain, so often entangled with each other, so diversified by various relations, and so much subject to accidents which cannot be foreseen that he who would fix his condition upon incontestable reasons of preference, must live and die inquiring and deliberating.'

'But surely,' said Rasselas, 'the wise men to whom we listen with reverence and wonder chose that mode of life for themselves which they thought most likely to make them happy.'

'Very few,' said the poet, 'live by choice. Every man is placed in his present condition by causes which acted without his foresight, and with which he did not always willingly co-operate; and therefore you will rarely meet one who does not think the lot of his neighbour better than his own.'

'I am pleased to think,' said the prince, 'that my birth has given me at least one advantage over others, by enabling me to determine for myself. I have here the world before me; I will review it at leisure: surely happiness is somewhere to be found.'

XVII. *The Prince Associates with Young Men of Spirit and Gaiety*

Rasselas rose next day, and resolved to begin his experiments upon life. 'Youth,' cried he, 'is the time of gladness: I will join myself to the young men whose only business is to gratify their desires, and whose time is all spent in a succession of enjoyments.'

To such societies he was readily admitted, but a few days brought him back weary and disgusted. Their mirth was without images, their laughter without motive; their pleasures were gross and sensual, in which the mind had no part; their conduct was at once wild and mean; they laughed at order and at law, but the frown of power dejected, and the eye of wisdom abashed them.

The prince soon concluded that he should never be happy in a course of life of which he was ashamed. He thought it unsuitable to a reasonable being to act without a plan, and to be sad or cheerful only by chance. 'Happiness,' said he, 'must be something solid and permanent, without fear and without uncertainty.'

But his young companions had gained so much of his regard by their frankness and courtesy that he could not leave them without warning and remonstrance. 'My friends,' said he, 'I have seriously considered our manners and our prospects, and find that we have mistaken our own interest. The first years of man must make provision for the last. He that never thinks never can be wise. Perpetual levity must end in ignorance; and intemperance, though it may fire the spirits for an hour, will make life short or miserable. Let us consider that youth is of no long duration, and that in maturer age, when the enchantments of fancy shall cease, and phantoms of delight dance no more about us, we shall have no comforts but the esteem of wise men, and the means of doing good. Let us, therefore, stop, while to stop is in our power: let us live as men who are sometime to grow old, and to whom it will be the most dreadful of all evils not to count their past years but by follies, and to be reminded of their former luxuriance of health only by the maladies which riot has produced.'

They stared a while in silence one upon another, and, at last, drove him away by a general chorus of continued laughter.

The consciousness that his sentiments were just, and his intentions kind, was scarcely sufficient to support him against the horror of derision. But he recovered his tranquility, and pursued his search.

XVIII. *The Prince Finds a Wise and Happy Man*

As he was one day walking in the street, he saw a spacious building which all were, by the open doors, invited to enter: he followed the stream of people, and found it a hall or school of declamation, in which professors read lectures to their auditory. He fixed his eye upon a sage raised above the rest, who discoursed with great energy on the government of the passions. His look was venerable, his action graceful, his pronunciation clear, and his diction elegant. He showed, with great strength of sentiment, and variety of illustration, that human nature is degraded and debased when the lower faculties predominate over the higher; that when fancy, the parent of passion, usurps the dominion of the mind, nothing ensues but the natural effect of unlawful government, perturbation and confusion; that she betrays the fortresses of the intellect to rebels, and excites her children to sedition against reason their lawful sovereign. He compared reason to the sun, of which the light is constant, uniform, and lasting; and fancy to a meteor, of bright but transitory lustre, irregular in its motion, and delusive in its direction.

He then communicated the various precepts given from time to time for the conquest of passion, and displayed the happiness of those who had obtained the important victory, after which man is no longer the slave of fear, nor the fool of hope; is no more emaciated by envy, inflamed by anger, emasculated by tenderness, or depressed by grief; but walks on calmly through the tumults or the privacies of life, as the sun pursues alike his course through the calm or the stormy sky.

He enumerated many examples of heroes immovable by pain or pleasure, who looked with indifference on those modes or accidents to which the vulgar give the names of good and evil. He exhorted his hearers to lay aside their prejudices, and arm themselves against the shafts of malice or misfortune by invulnerable patience; concluding that this state only was happiness, and that this happiness was in every one's power.

Rasselas listened to him with the veneration due to the instructions of a superior being, and, waiting for him at the door, humbly implored the liberty of visiting so great a master of true wisdom. The lecturer hesitated a moment, when Rasselas put a purse of gold into his hand, which he received with a mixture of joy and wonder.

'I have found,' said the prince, at his return to Imlac, 'a man who can teach all that is necessary to be known, who, from the unshaken throne of rational fortitude, looks down on the scenes of life changing beneath him. He speaks, and attention watches his lips. He reasons, and conviction closes his periods. This man shall be my future guide: I will learn his doctrines, and imitate his life.'

'Be not too hasty,' said Imlac, 'to trust, or to admire, the teachers of morality: they discourse like angels, but they live like men.'

Rasselas, who could not conceive how any man could reason so forcibly without feeling the cogency of his own arguments, paid his visit in a few days, and was denied admission. He had now learned the power of money, and made his way by a piece of gold to the inner apartment, where he found the philosopher in a room half darkened, with his eyes misty, and his face pale. 'Sir,' said he, 'you are come at a time when all human friendship is useless; what I suffer cannot be remedied, what I have lost cannot be supplied. My daughter, my only daughter, from whose tenderness I expected all the comforts of my age, died last night of a fever. My views, my purposes, my hopes are at an end: I am now a lonely being disunited from society.'

'Sir,' said the prince, 'mortality is an event by which a wise man can never be surprised: we know that death is always near, and it should therefore always be expected.' 'Young man,' answered the philosopher, 'you speak like one that has never felt the pangs of separation.' 'Have you then forgot the precepts,' said Rasselas, 'which you so powerfully enforced? Has wisdom no strength to arm the heart against calamity? Consider that external things are naturally variable, but truth and reason are always the same.' 'What comfort,' said the mourner, 'can truth and reason afford me? Of what effect are they now, but to tell me that my daughter will not be restored?'°

The prince, whose humanity would not suffer him to insult misery with reproof, went away convinced of the emptiness of rhetorical sound, and the inefficacy of polished periods and studied sentences.

XIX. *A Glimpse of Pastoral Life*

He was still eager upon the same inquiry; and, having heard of a hermit that lived near the lowest cataract of the Nile, and filled the whole country with the fame of his sanctity, resolved to visit his retreat, and inquire whether that felicity which public life could not afford was to be found in solitude; and whether a man whose age and virtue made him venerable could teach any peculiar art of shunning evils, or enduring them.

Imlac and the princess agreed to accompany him, and, after the necessary preparations, they began their journey. Their way lay through fields where shepherds tended their flocks, and the lambs were playing upon the pasture. 'This,' said the poet, 'is the life which has been often celebrated for its innocence and quiet: let us pass the heat of the day among the shepherds' tents, and know whether all our searches are not to terminate in pastoral simplicity.'

The proposal pleased them, and they induced the shepherds, by small presents and familiar questions, to tell their opinion of their own state: they were so rude and ignorant, so little able to compare the good with the evil of the occupation, and so indistinct in their narratives and descriptions, that very little could be learned from them. But it was evident that their hearts were cankered with discontent; that they considered themselves as condemned to labour for the luxury of the rich, and looked up with stupid malevolence toward those that were placed above them.

The princess pronounced with vehemence that she would never suffer these envious savages to be her companions, and that she should not soon be desirous of seeing any more specimens of rustic happiness; but could not believe that all the accounts of primeval pleasures were fabulous, and was yet in doubt whether life had any thing that could be justly preferred to the placid gratifications of fields and woods. She hoped that the time would come when with a few virtuous and elegant companions she should gather flowers planted by her own hand, fondle the lambs of her own ewe, and listen, without care, among brooks and breezes, to one of her maidens reading in the shade.

xx. *The Danger of Prosperity*

On the next day they continued their journey, till the heat compelled them to look round for shelter. At a small distance they saw a thick wood, which they no sooner entered than they perceived that they were approaching the habitations of men. The shrubs were diligently cut away to open walks where the shades were darkest; the boughs of opposite trees were artificially interwoven; seats of flowery turf were raised in vacant spaces, and a rivulet that wantoned along the side of a winding path had its banks sometimes opened into small basins, and its stream sometimes obstructed by little mounds of stone heaped together to increase its murmurs.

They passed slowly through the wood, delighted with such unexpected accommodations, and entertained each other with conjecturing what, or who, he could be that, in those rude and unfrequented regions, had leisure and art for such harmless luxury.

As they advanced, they heard the sound of music, and saw youths and virgins dancing in the grove; and, going still further, beheld a stately palace built upon a hill surrounded with woods. The laws of eastern hospitality allowed them to enter, and the master welcomed them like a man liberal and wealthy.

He was skilful enough in appearances soon to discern that they were no common guests, and spread his table with magnificence. The eloquence of Imlac caught his attention, and the lofty courtesy of the princess excited his respect. When they offered to depart he entreated their stay, and was the next day still more unwilling to dismiss them than before. They were easily persuaded to stop, and civility grew up in time to freedom and confidence.

The prince now saw all the domestics cheerful, and all the face of nature smiling round the place, and could not forbear to hope that he should find here what he was seeking; but when he was congratulating the master upon his possessions, he answered with a sigh, 'My condition has indeed the appearance of happiness, but appearances are delusive. My prosperity puts my life in danger; the Bassa of Egypt is my enemy, incensed only by my wealth and popularity. I have been hitherto protected against him by the princes of the country; but, as the favour of the great is uncertain, I know not how soon my defenders may be persuaded to share the plunder with the Bassa. I have sent my treasures into a distant country, and, upon the first alarm, am prepared to follow them. Then will my enemies riot in my mansion, and enjoy the gardens which I have planted.'

They all joined in lamenting his danger, and deprecating his exile; and the princess was so much disturbed with the tumult of grief and indignation that she retired to her apartment. They continued with their kind inviter a few days longer, and then went forward to find the hermit.

XXI. *The Happiness of Solitude. The Hermit's History*

They came on the third day, by the direction of the peasants, to the hermit's cell: it was a cavern in the side of a mountain, over-shadowed with palm-trees; at such a distance from the cataract that nothing more was heard than a gentle uniform murmur, such as composed the mind to pensive meditation, especially when it was assisted by the wind whistling among the branches. The first rude essay of nature had been so much improved by human labour that the cave contained several apartments, appropriated to different uses, and often afforded lodging to travellers whom darkness or tempests happened to overtake.

The hermit sat on a bench at the door, to enjoy the coolness of the evening. On one side lay a book with pens and papers, on the other mechanical instruments of various kinds. As they approached him unregarded, the princess observed that he had not the countenance of a man that had found, or could teach, the way to happiness.

They saluted him with great respect, which he repaid like a man not unaccustomed to the forms of courts. 'My children,' said he, 'if you have lost your way, you shall be willingly supplied with such conveniencies for the night as this cavern will afford. I have all that nature requires, and you will not expect delicacies in a hermit's cell.'

They thanked him, and, entering, were pleased with the neatness and regularity of the place. The hermit set flesh and wine before them, though he fed only upon fruits and water. His discourse was cheerful without levity, and pious without enthusiasm. He soon gained the esteem of his guests, and the princess repented of her hasty censure.

At last Imlac began thus: 'I do not now wonder that your reputation is so far extended; we have heard at Cairo of your wisdom, and came hither to implore your direction for this young man and maiden in the *choice of life*.'

'To him that lives well,' answered the hermit, 'every form of life is good; nor can I give any other rule for choice than to remove from all apparent evil.'

'He will remove most certainly from evil,' said the prince, 'who shall devote himself to that solitude which you have recommended by your example.'

'I have indeed lived fifteen years in solitude,' said the hermit, 'but have no desire that my example should gain any imitators. In my youth I professed arms, and was raised by degrees to the highest military rank. I have traversed wide countries at the head of my troops, and seen many battles and sieges. At last, being disgusted by the preferment of a younger officer, and feeling that my vigour was beginning to decay, I resolved to close my life in peace, having found the world full of snares, discord, and misery. I had once escaped from the pursuit of the enemy by the shelter of this cavern, and therefore choose it for my final residence. I employed artificers to form it into chambers, and stored it with all that I was likely to want.

'For some time after my retreat, I rejoiced like a tempest-beaten sailor at his entrance into the harbour, being delighted with the sudden change of the noise and hurry of war to stillness and repose. When the pleasure of novelty went away, I employed my hours in examining the plants which grow in the valley, and the minerals which I collected from the rocks. But that inquiry is now grown tasteless and irksome. I have been for some time unsettled and distracted: my mind is disturbed with a thousand perplexities of doubt, and vanities of imagination, which hourly prevail upon me, because I have no opportunities of relaxation or diversion. I am sometimes ashamed to think that I could not secure myself from vice but by retiring from the exercise of virtue, and begin to suspect that I was rather impelled by resentment, than led by devotion, into solitude. My fancy riots in scenes of folly, and I lament that I have lost so much, and have gained so little. In solitude, if I escape the example of bad men, I want likewise the counsel and conversation of the good. I have been long comparing the evils with the advantages of society, and resolve to return into the world tomorrow. The life of a solitary man will be certainly miserable, but not certainly devout.'

They heard his resolution with surprise, but, after a short pause, offered to conduct him to Cairo. He dug up a considerable treasure which he had hid among the rocks, and accompanied them to the city, on which, as he approached it, he gazed with rapture.

XXII. *The Happiness of a Life Led According to Nature*

Rasselas went often to an assembly of learned men, who met at stated times to unbend their minds, and compare their opinions. Their manners were somewhat coarse, but their conversation was instructive, and their disputations acute, though sometimes too violent, and often continued till neither controvertist remembered upon what question they began. Some faults were almost general among them: every one was desirous to dictate to the rest, and every one was pleased to hear the genius or knowledge of another depreciated.

In this assembly Rasselas was relating his interview with the hermit, and the wonder with which he heard him censure a course of life which he had so deliberately chosen, and so laudably followed. The sentiments of the hearers were various. Some were of opinion that the folly of his choice had been justly punished by condemnation to perpetual perseverance. One of the youngest among them, with great vehemence, pronounced him an hypocrite. Some talked of the right of society to the labour of individuals, and considered retirement as a desertion of duty. Others readily allowed that there was a time when the claims of the public were satisfied, and when a man might properly sequester himself, to review his life, and purify his heart.

One, who appeared more affected with the narrative than the rest, thought it likely that the hermit would, in a few years, go back to his retreat, and, perhaps, if shame did not restrain, or death intercept him, return once more from his retreat into the world: 'For the hope of happiness,' said he, 'is so strongly impressed that the longest experience is not able to efface it. Of the present state, whatever it be, we feel, and are forced to confess, the misery, yet, when the same state is again at a distance, imagination paints it as desirable. But the time will surely come when desire will be no longer our torment, and no man shall be wretched but by his own fault.'

'This,' said a philosopher, who had heard him with tokens of great impatience, 'is the present condition of a wise man. The time is already come when none are wretched but by their own fault. Nothing is more idle than to inquire after happiness, which nature has kindly placed within our reach. The way to be happy is to live according to nature,° in obedience to that universal and unalterable law with which every heart is originally impressed; which is not written on it by precept, but engraven by destiny, not instilled by education, but infused at our nativity. He that lives according to nature will suffer nothing from the delusions of hope, or importunities of desire: he will receive and reject with equability of temper,° and act or suffer as the reason of things shall alternately prescribe. Other men may amuse themselves with subtle definitions, or intricate ratiocination. Let them learn to be wise by easier means: let them observe the hind of the forest, and the linnet of the grove: let them consider the life of animals, whose motions are regulated by instinct; they obey their guide and are happy. Let us therefore, at length, cease to dispute, and learn to live; throw away the encumbrance of precepts which they who utter them with so much pride and pomp do not understand, and carry with us this simple and intelligible maxim, that deviation from nature is deviation from happiness.'

When he had spoken, he looked round him with a placid air, and enjoyed the consciousness of his own beneficence. 'Sir,' said the prince, with great modesty, 'as I, like all the rest of mankind, am desirous of felicity, my closest attention has been fixed upon your discourse: I doubt not the truth of a position which a man so learned has so confidently advanced. Let me only know what it is to live according to nature.'

'When I find young men so humble and so docile,' said the philosopher, 'I can deny them no information which my studies have enabled me to afford. To live according to nature is to act always with due regard to the fitness arising from the relations and qualities of causes and effects; to concur with the great and unchangeable scheme of universal felicity; to co-operate with the general disposition and tendency of the present system of things.'

The prince soon found that this was one of the sages whom he should understand less as he heard him longer. He therefore bowed and was silent, and the philosopher, supposing him satisfied, and the rest vanquished, rose up and departed with the air of a man that had co-operated with the present system.

XXIII. *The Prince and His Sister Divide Between Them the Work of Observation*

Rasselas returned home full of reflections, doubtful how to direct his future steps, Of the way to happiness he found the learned and simple equally ignorant; but, as he was yet young, he flattered himself that he had time remaining for more experiments, and further inquiries. He communicated to Imlac his observations and his doubts, but was answered by him with new doubts, and remarks that gave him no comfort. He therefore discoursed more frequently and freely with his sister, who had yet the same hope with himself, and always assisted him to give some reason why, though he had been hitherto frustrated, he might succeed at last.

'We have hitherto,' said she, 'known but little of the world: we have never yet been either great or mean. In our own country, though we had royalty, we had no power, and in this we have not yet seen the private recesses of domestic peace. Imlac favours not our search, lest we should in time find him mistaken. We will divide the task between us: you shall try what is to be found in the splendour of courts, and I will range the shades of humbler life. Perhaps command and authority may be the supreme blessings, as they afford most opportunities of doing good: or, perhaps, what this world can give may be found in the modest habitations of middle fortune; too low for great designs, and too high for penury and distress.'

XXIV. *The Prince Examines the Happiness of High Stations*

Rasselas applauded the design, and appeared next day with a splendid retinue at the court of the Bassa. He was soon distinguished for his magnificence, and admitted, as a prince whose curiosity had brought him from distant countries, to an intimacy with the great officers, and frequent conversation with the Bassa himself.

He was at first inclined to believe that the man must be pleased with his own condition whom all approached with reverence, and heard with obedience, and who had the power to extend his edicts to a whole kingdom. 'There can be no pleasure,' said he, 'equal to that of feeling at once the joy of thousands all made happy by wise administration. Yet, since, by the law of subordination, this sublime delight can be in one nation but the lot of one, it is surely reasonable to think that there is some satisfaction more popular and accessible, and that millions can hardly be subjected to the will of a single man only to fill his particular breast with incommunicable content.'

These thoughts were often in his mind, and he found no solution of the difficulty. But as presents and civilities gained him more familiarity, he found that almost every man who stood high in employment hated all the rest, and was hated by them, and that their lives were a continual succession of plots and detections, stratagems and escapes, faction and treachery. Many of those who surrounded the Bassa were sent only to watch and report his conduct; every tongue was muttering censure and every eye was searching for a fault.

At last the letters of revocation arrived, the Bassa was carried in chains to Constantinople, and his name was mentioned no more.

'What are we now to think of the prerogatives of power,' said Rasselas to his sister; 'is it without any efficacy to good? Or is the subordinate degree only dangerous, and the supreme safe and glorious? Is the Sultan the only happy man in his dominions? Or is the Sultan himself subject to the torments of suspicion, and the dread of enemies?'

In a short time the second Bassa was deposed. The Sultan that had advanced him was murdered by the Janissaries, and his successor had other views and different favourites.

XXV. *The Princess Pursues Her Inquiry with More Diligence than Success*

The princess, in the mean time, insinuated herself into many families; for there are few doors through which liberality, joined with good humour, cannot find its way. The daughters of many houses were airy and cheerful, but Nekayah had been too long accustomed to the conversation of Imlac and her brother to be much pleased with childish levity and prattle which had no meaning. She found their thoughts narrow, their wishes low, and their merriment often artificial. Their pleasures, poor as they were, could not be preserved pure, but were embittered by petty competitions and worthless emulation. They were always jealous of the beauty of each other; of a quality to which solicitude can add nothing, and from which detraction can take nothing away. Many were in love with triflers like themselves, and many fancied that they were in love when in truth they were only idle. Their affection was seldom fixed on sense or virtue, and therefore seldom ended but in vexation. Their grief, however, like their joy, was transient; every thing floated in their mind unconnected with the past or future, so that one desire easily gave way to another, as a second stone cast into the water effaces and confounds the circles of the first.

With these girls she played as with inoffensive animals, and found them proud of her countenance, and weary of her company.

But her purpose was to examine more deeply, and her affability easily persuaded the hearts that were swelling with sorrow to discharge their secrets in her ear: and those whom hope flattered, or prosperity delighted, often courted her to partake their pleasures.

The princess and her brother commonly met in the evening in a private summer-house on the bank of the Nile, and related to each other the occurrences of the day. As they were sitting together, the princess cast her eyes upon the river that flowed before her. 'Answer,' said she, 'great father of waters, thou that rollest thy floods through eighty nations, to the invocations of the daughter of thy native king. Tell me if thou waterest, through all thy course, a single habitation from which thou dost not hear the murmurs of complaint?'

'You are then,' said Rasselas, 'not more successful in private houses than I have been in courts.' 'I have, since the last partition of our provinces,' said the princess, 'enabled myself to enter familiarly into many families where there was the fairest show of prosperity and peace, and know not one house that is not haunted by some fury that destroys its quiet.

'I did not seek ease among the poor, because I concluded that there it could not be found. But I saw many poor whom I had supposed to live in affluence. Poverty has, in large cities, very different appearances: it is often concealed in splendour, and often in extravagance. It is the care of a very great part of mankind to conceal their indigence from the rest: they support themselves by temporary expedients, and every day is lost in contriving for the morrow.

'This, however, was an evil, which, though frequent, I saw with less pain, because I could relieve it. Yet some have refused my bounties; more offended with my quickness to detect their wants than pleased with my readiness to succour them: and others, whose exigencies compelled them to admit my kindness, have never been able to forgive their benefactress. Many, however, have been sincerely grateful without the ostentation of gratitude, or the hope of other favours.'

XXVI. *The Princess Continues Her Remarks upon Private Life*

Nekayah, perceiving her brother's attention fixed, proceeded in her narrative.

'In families, where there is or is not poverty, there is commonly discord:° if a kingdom be, as Imlac tells us, a great family, a family likewise is a little kingdom, torn with factions and exposed to revolutions. An unpractised observer expects the love of parents and children to be constant and equal; but this kindness seldom continues beyond the years of infancy: in a short time the children become rivals to their parents. Benefits are allayed by reproaches, and gratitude debased by envy.

'Parents and children seldom act in concert: each child endeavours to appropriate the esteem or fondness of the parents, and the parents, with yet less temptation, betray each other to their children; thus some place their confidence in the father, and some in the mother, and, by degrees, the house is filled with artifices and feuds.

'The opinions of children and parents, of the young and the old, are naturally opposite, by the contrary effects of hope and despondence, of expectation and experience, without crime or folly on either side. The colours of life in youth and age appear different as the face of nature in spring and winter. And how can children credit the assertions of parents which their own eyes show them to be false?

'Few parents act in such a manner as much to enforce their maxims by the credit of their lives. The old man trusts wholly to slow contrivance and gradual progression: the youth expects to force his way by genius, vigour, and precipitance. The old man pays regard to riches, and the youth reverences virtue. The old man deifies prudence: the youth commits himself to magnanimity and chance. The young man, who intends no ill, believes that none is intended, and therefore acts with openness and candour: but his father, having suffered the injuries of fraud, is impelled to suspect, and too often allured to practise it. Age looks with anger on the temerity of youth, and youth with contempt on the scrupulosity of age. Thus parents and children, for the greatest part, live on to love less and less: and, if those whom nature has thus closely united are the torments of each other, where shall we look for tenderness and consolation?'

'Surely,' said the prince, 'you must have been unfortunate in your choice of acquaintance: I am unwilling to believe that the most tender of all relations is thus impeded in its effects by natural necessity.'

'Domestic discord,' answered she, 'is not inevitably and fatally necessary; but yet is not easily avoided. We seldom see that a whole family is virtuous: the good and evil cannot well agree; and the evil can yet less agree with one another: even the virtuous fall sometimes to variance, when their virtues are of different kinds, and tending to extremes. In general, those parents have most reverence who most deserve it: for he that lives well cannot be despised.

'Many other evils infest private life. Some are the slaves of servants whom they have trusted with their affairs. Some are kept in continual anxiety to the caprice of rich relations, whom they cannot please, and dare not offend. Some husbands are imperious, and some wives perverse: and, as it is always more easy to do evil than good, though the wisdom or virtue of one can very rarely make many happy, the folly or vice of one may often make many miserable.'

'If such be the general effect of marriage,' said the prince, 'I shall, for the future, think it dangerous to connect my interest with that of another, lest I should be unhappy by my partner's fault.'

'I have met,' said the princess, 'with many who live single for that reason; but I never found that their prudence ought to raise envy. They dream away their time without friendship, without fondness, and are driven to rid themselves of the day for which they have no use by childish amusements, or vicious delights. They act as beings under the constant sense of some known inferiority, that fills their minds with rancour, and their tongues with censure. They are peevish at home, and malevolent abroad; and, as the outlaws of human nature, make it their business and their pleasure to disturb that society which debars them from its privileges. To live without feeling or exciting sympathy, to be fortunate without adding to the felicity of others, or afflicted without tasting the balm of pity, is a state more gloomy than solitude: it is not retreat but exclusion from mankind. Marriage has many pains, but celibacy has no pleasures.'

'What then is to be done?' said Rasselas. 'The more we inquire, the less we can resolve. Surely he is most likely to please himself that has no other inclination to regard.'

XXVII. *Disquisition upon Greatness*

The conversation had a short pause. The prince, having considered his sister's observations, told her that she had surveyed life with prejudice, and supposed misery where she did not find it. 'Your narrative,' says he, 'throws yet a darker gloom upon the prospects of futurity: the predictions of Imlac were but faint sketches of the evils painted by Nekayah. I have been lately convinced that quiet is not the daughter of grandeur, or of power: that her presence is not to be bought by wealth, nor enforced by conquest. It is evident that as any man acts in a wider compass, he must be more exposed to opposition from enmity or miscarriage from chance; whoever has many to please or to govern must use the ministry of many agents, some of whom will be wicked, and some ignorant; by some he will be misled, and by others betrayed. If he gratifies one he will offend another: those that are not favoured will think themselves injured; and, since favours can be conferred but upon few, the greater number will be always discontented.'

'The discontent,' said the princess, 'which is thus unreasonable, I hope that I shall always have spirit to despise, and you power to repress.'

'Discontent,' answered Rasselas, 'will not always be without reason under the most just or vigilant administration of public affairs. None, however attentive, can always discover that merit which indigence or faction may happen to obscure; and none, however powerful, can always reward it. Yet he that sees inferior desert advanced above him will naturally impute that preference to partiality or caprice; and, indeed, it can scarcely be hoped that any man, however magnanimous by nature, or exalted by condition, will be able to persist for ever in fixed and inexorable justice of distribution: he will sometimes indulge his own affections, and sometimes those of his favourites; he will permit some to please him who can never serve him; he will discover in those whom he loves qualities which in reality they do not possess; and to those from whom he receives pleasure he will in his turn endeavour to give it. Thus will recommendations sometimes prevail which were purchased by money, or by the more destructive bribery of flattery and servility.

'He that has much to do will do something wrong, and of that wrong must suffer the consequences; and, if it were possible that he should always act rightly, yet when such numbers are to judge of his conduct, the bad will censure and obstruct him by malevolence, and the good sometimes by mistake.

'The highest stations cannot therefore hope to be the abodes of happiness, which I would willingly believe to have fled from thrones and palaces to seats of humble privacy and placid obscurity. For what can hinder the satisfaction, or intercept the expectations, of him whose abilities are adequate to his employments, who sees with his own eyes the whole circuit of his influence, who chooses by his own knowledge all whom he trusts, and whom none are tempted to deceive by hope or fear? Surely he has nothing to do but to love and to be loved, to be virtuous and to be happy.'

'Whether perfect happiness would be procured by perfect goodness,' said Nekayah, 'this world will never afford an opportunity of deciding. But this, at least, may be maintained, that we do not always find visible happiness in proportion to visible virtue. All natural and almost all political evils are incident alike to the bad and good: they are confounded in the misery of a famine, and not much distinguished in the fury of a faction; they sink together in a tempest, and are driven together from their country by invaders. All that virtue can afford is quietness of conscience, a steady prospect of a happier state; this may enable us to endure calamity with patience; but remember that patience must suppose pain.'

XXVIII. *Rasselas and Nekayah Continue Their Conversation*

'Dear princess,' said Rasselas, 'you fall into the common error of exaggeratory declamation by producing, in a familiar disquisition, examples of national calamities, and scenes of extensive misery, which are found in books rather than in the world, and which, as they are horrid, are ordained to be rare. Let us not imagine evils which we do not feel, nor injure life by misrepresentations. I cannot bear that querulous eloquence which threatens every city with a siege like that of Jerusalem, that makes famine attend on every flight of locusts, and suspends pestilence on the wing of every blast that issues from the south.

'On necessary and inevitable evils, which overwhelm kingdoms at once, all disputation is vain: when they happen they must be endured. But it is evident that these bursts of universal distress are more dreaded than felt: thousands and ten thousands flourish in youth, and wither in age, without the knowledge of any other than domestic evils, and share the same pleasures and vexations whether their kings are mild or cruel, whether the armies of their country pursue their enemies, or retreat before them. While courts are disturbed with intestine competitions, and ambassadors are negotiating in foreign countries, the smith still plies his anvil, and the husbandman drives his plow forward; the necessaries of life are required and obtained, and the successive business of the seasons continues to make its wonted revolutions.

'Let us cease to consider what, perhaps, may never happen, and what, when it shall happen, will laugh at human speculation. We will not endeavour to modify the motions of the elements, or to fix the destiny of kingdoms. It is our business to consider what beings like us may perform; each labouring for his own happiness, by promoting within his circle, however narrow, the happiness of others.

'Marriage is evidently the dictate of nature; men and women were made to be companions of each other, and therefore I cannot be persuaded but that marriage is one of the means of happiness.'

'I know not,' said the princess, 'whether marriage be more than one of the innumerable modes of human misery. When I see and reckon the various forms of connubial infelicity, the unexpected causes of lasting discord, the diversities of temper, the oppositions of opinion, the rude collisions of contrary desire where both are urged by violent impulses, the obstinate contests of disagreeing virtues, where both are supported by consciousness of good intention, I am sometimes disposed to think with the severer casuists of most nations that marriage is rather permitted than approved, and that none, but by the instigation of a passion too much indulged, entangle themselves with indissoluble compacts.'

'You seem to forget,' replied Rasselas, 'that you have, even now, represented celibacy as less happy than marriage. Both conditions may be bad, but they cannot both be worst. Thus it happens when wrong opinions are entertained, that they mutually destroy each other, and leave the mind open to truth.'

'I did not expect,' answered the princess, 'to hear that imputed to falsehood which is the consequence only of frailty. To the mind, as to the eye, it is difficult to compare with exactness objects vast in their extent, and various in their parts. Where we see or conceive the whole at once we readily note the discriminations and decide the preference: but of two systems of which neither can be surveyed by any human being in its full compass of magnitude and multiplicity of complication, where is the wonder that judging of the whole by parts, I am alternately affected by one and the other as either presses on my memory or fancy? We differ from ourselves just as we differ from each other, when we see only part of the question, as in the multifarious relations of politics and morality: but when we perceive the whole at once, as in numerical computations, all agree in one judgment, and none ever varies his opinion.'

'Let us not add,' said the prince, 'to the other evils of life, the bitterness of controversy, nor endeavour to vie with each other in subtleties of argument. We are employed in a search of which both are equally to enjoy the success, or suffer by the miscarriage. It is therefore fit that we assist each other. You surely conclude too hastily from the infelicity of marriage against its institution; will not the misery of life prove equally that life cannot be the gift of heaven? The world must be peopled by marriage, or peopled without it.'

'How the world is to be peopled,' returned Nekayah, 'is not my care, and needs not be yours. I see no danger that the present generation should omit to leave successors behind them: we are not now inquiring for the world, but for ourselves.'

XXIX. *The Debate on Marriage Continued*

'The good of the whole,' says Rasselas, 'is the same with the good of all its parts. If marriage be best for mankind it must be evidently best for individuals, or a permanent and necessary duty must be the cause of evil, and some must be inevitably sacrificed to the convenience of others. In the estimate which you have made of the two states, it appears that the incommodities of a single life are, in a great measure, necessary and certain, but those of the conjugal state accidental and avoidable.

'I cannot forbear to flatter myself that prudence and benevolence will make marriage happy. The general folly of mankind is the cause of general complaint. What can be expected but disappointment and repentance from a choice made in the immaturity of youth, in the ardour of desire, without judgment, without foresight, without inquiry after conformity of opinions, similarity of manners, rectitude of judgment, or purity of sentiment.

'Such is the common process of marriage. A youth and maiden meeting by chance, or brought together by artifice, exchange glances, reciprocate civilities, go home, and dream of one another. Having little to divert attention, or diversify thought, they find themselves uneasy when they are apart, and therefore conclude that they shall be happy together. They marry, and discover what nothing but voluntary blindness had before concealed; they wear out life in altercations, and charge nature with cruelty.

'From those early marriages proceeds likewise the rivalry of parents and children: the son is eager to enjoy the world before the father is willing to forsake it, and there is hardly room at once for two generations. The daughter begins to bloom before the mother can be content to fade, and neither can forbear to wish for the absence of the other.

'Surely all these evils may be avoided by that deliberation and delay which prudence prescribes to irrevocable choice. In the variety and jollity of youthful pleasures life may be well enough supported without the help of a partner. Longer time will increase experience, and wider views will allow better opportunities of enquiry and selection: one advantage, at least, will be certain; the parents will be visibly older than their children.'

'What reason cannot collect,' said Nekayah, 'and what experiment has not yet taught, can be known only from the report of others. I have been told that late marriages are not eminently happy. This is a question too important to be neglected, and I have often proposed it to those whose accuracy of remark, and comprehensiveness of knowledge, made their suffrages worthy of regard. They have generally determined that it is dangerous for a man and woman to suspend their fate upon each other at a time when opinions are fixed, and habits are established; when friendships have been contracted on both sides, when life has been planned into method, and the mind has long enjoyed the contemplation of its own prospects.

'It is scarcely possible that two travelling through the world under the conduct of chance should have been both directed to the same path, and it will not often happen that either will quit the track which custom has made pleasing. When the desultory levity of youth has settled into regularity, it is soon succeeded by pride ashamed to yield, or obstinacy delighting to contend. And even though mutual esteem produces mutual desire to please, time itself, as it modifies unchangeably the external mien, determines likewise the direction of the passions, and gives an inflexible rigidity to the manners. Long customs are not easily broken: he that attempts to change the course of his own life very often labours in vain; and how shall we do that for others which we are seldom able to do for ourselves?'

'But surely,' interposed the prince, 'you suppose the chief motive of choice forgotten or neglected. Whenever I shall seek a wife, it shall be my first question whether she be willing to be led by reason.'

'Thus it is,' said Nekayah, 'that philosophers are deceived. There are a thousand familiar disputes which reason never can decide; questions that elude investigation, and make logic ridiculous; cases where something must be done, and where little can be said. Consider the state of mankind, and inquire how few can be supposed to act upon any occasions, whether small or great, with all the reasons of action present to their minds. Wretched would be the pair above all names of wretchedness who should be doomed to adjust by reason every morning all the minute detail of a domestic day.

'Those who marry at an advanced age will probably escape the encroachments of their children; but, in diminution of this advantage, they will be likely to leave them, ignorant and helpless, to a guardian's mercy: or, if that should not happen, they must at least go out of the world before they see those whom they love best either wise or great.

'From their children, if they have less to fear, they have less also to hope, and they lose, without equivalent, the joys of early love, and the convenience of uniting with manners pliant, and minds susceptible of new impressions, which might wear away their dissimilitudes by long cohabitation, as soft bodies, by continual attrition, conform their surfaces to each other.

'I believe it will be found that those who marry late are best pleased with their children, and those who marry early with their partners.'

'The union of these two affections,' said Rasselas, 'would produce all that could be wished. Perhaps there is a time when marriage might unite them, a time neither too early for the father, nor too late for the husband.'

'Every hour,' answered the princess, 'confirms my prejudice in favour of the position so often uttered by the mouth of Imlac, "That nature sets her gifts on the right hand and on the left." Those conditions which flatter hope and attract desire are so constituted that, as we approach one, we recede from another. There are goods so opposed that we cannot seize both, but, by too much prudence, may pass between them at too great a distance to reach either. This is often the fate of long consideration; he does nothing who endeavours to do more than is allowed to humanity. Flatter not yourself with contrarieties of pleasure. Of the blessings set before you make your choice, and be content. No man can taste the fruits of autumn while he is delighting his scent with the flowers of the spring: no man can, at the same time, fill his cup from the source and from the mouth of the Nile.'

xxx. *Imlac Enters, and Changes the Conversation*

Here Imlac entered, and interrupted them. 'Imlac,' said Rasselas, 'I have been taking from the princess the dismal history of private life, and am almost discouraged from further search.'

'It seems to me,' said Imlac, 'that while you are making the choice of life, you neglect to live. You wander about a single city, which, however large and diversified, can now afford few novelties, and forget that you are in a country famous among the earliest monarchies for the power and wisdom of its inhabitants; a country where the sciences first dawned that illuminate the world, and beyond which the arts cannot be traced of civil society or domestic life.

'The old Egyptians have left behind them monuments of industry and power before which all European magnificence is confessed to fade away. The ruins of their architecture are the schools of modern builders, and from the wonders which time has spared we may conjecture, though uncertainly, what it has destroyed.'

'My curiosity,' said Rasselas, 'does not very strongly lead me to survey piles of stone, or mounds of earth; my business is with man. I came hither not to measure fragments of temples, or trace choked aqueducts, but to look upon the various scenes of the present world.'

'The things that are now before us,' said the princess, 'require attention, and deserve it. What have I to do with the heroes or the monuments of ancient times? With times which never can return, and heroes whose form of life was different from all that the present condition of mankind requires or allows.'

'To know any thing,' returned the poet, 'we must know its effects; to see men we must see their works, that we may learn what reason has dictated, or passion has incited, and find what are the most powerful motives of action. To judge rightly of the present we must oppose it to the past; for all judgment is comparative, and of the future nothing can be known. The truth is that no mind is much employed upon the present: recollection and anticipation fill up almost all our moments. Our passions are joy and grief, love and hatred, hope and fear. Of joy and grief the past is the object, and the future of hope and fear; even love and hatred respect the past, for the cause must have been before the effect.

'The present state of things is the consequence of the former, and it is natural to inquire what were the sources of the good that we enjoy, or of the evil that we suffer. If we act only for ourselves, to neglect the study of history is not prudent: if we are entrusted with the care of others, it is not just. Ignorance, when it is voluntary, is criminal; and he may properly be charged with evil who refused to learn how he might prevent it.

'There is no part of history so generally useful as that which relates the progress of the human mind, the gradual improvement of reason, the successive advances of science, the vicissitudes of learning and ignorance, which are the light and darkness of thinking beings, the extinction and resuscitation of arts, and all the revolutions of the intellectual world. If accounts of battles and invasions are peculiarly the business of princes, the useful or elegant arts are not to be neglected; those who have kingdoms to govern have understandings to cultivate.

'Example is always more efficacious than precept. A soldier is formed in war, and a painter must copy pictures. In this, contemplative life has the advantage: great actions are seldom seen, but the labours of art are always at hand for those who desire to know what art has been able to perform.

'When the eye or the imagination is struck with any uncommon work the next transition of an active mind is to the means by which it was performed. Here begins the true use of such contemplation; we enlarge our comprehension by new ideas, and perhaps recover some art lost to mankind, or learn what is less perfectly known in our own country. At least we compare our own with former times, and either rejoice at our improvements, or, what is the first motion towards good, discover our defects.'

'I am willing,' said the prince, 'to see all that can deserve my search.' 'And I,' said the princess, 'shall rejoice to learn something of the manners of antiquity.'

'The most pompous monument of Egyptian greatness, and one of the most bulky works of manual industry,' said Imlac, 'are the pyramids; fabrics raised before the time of history, and of which the earliest narratives afford us only uncertain traditions. Of these the greatest is still standing, very little injured by time.'

'Let us visit them tomorrow,' said Nekayah. 'I have often heard of the Pyramids, and shall not rest till I have seen them within and without with my own eyes.'

XXXI. *They Visit the Pyramids*

The resolution being thus taken, they set out the next day. They laid tents upon their camels, being resolved to stay among the pyramids till their curiosity was fully satisfied. They travelled gently, turned aside to every thing remarkable, stopped from time to time and conversed with the inhabitants, and observed the various appearances of towns ruined and inhabited, of wild and cultivated nature.

When they came to the great pyramid they were astonished at the extent of the base, and the height of the top. Imlac explained to them the principles upon which the pyramidal form was chosen for a fabric intended to co-extend its duration with that of the world: he showed that its gradual diminution gave it such stability as defeated all the common attacks of the elements, and could scarcely be overthrown by earthquakes themselves, the least resistible of natural violence. A concussion that should shatter the pyramid would threaten the dissolution of the continent.

They measured all its dimensions, and pitched their tents at its foot. Next day they prepared to enter its interior apartments, and having hired the common guides climbed up to the first passage, when the favourite of the princess, looking into the cavity, stepped back and trembled. 'Pekuah,' said the princess, 'of what art thou afraid?' 'Of the narrow entrance,' answered the lady, 'and of the dreadful gloom. I dare not enter a place which must surely be inhabited by unquiet souls. The original possessors of these dreadful vaults will start up before us, and, perhaps, shut us in for ever.' She spoke, and threw her arms round the neck of her mistress.

'If all your fear be of apparitions,' said the prince, 'I will promise you safety: there is no danger from the dead; he that is once buried will be seen no more.'

'That the dead are seen no more,' said Imlac, 'I will not undertake to maintain against the concurrent and unvaried testimony of all ages, and of all nations. There is no people, rude or learned, among whom apparitions of the dead are not related and believed. This opinion, which, perhaps, prevails as far as human nature is diffused, could become universal only by its truth: those that never heard of one another would not have agreed in a tale which nothing but experience can make credible. That it is doubted by single cavillers can very little weaken the general evidence, and some who deny it with their tongues confess it by their fears.

'Yet I do not mean to add new terrors to those which have already seized upon Pekuah. There can be no reason why spectres should haunt the pyramid more than other places, or why they should have power or will to hurt innocence and purity. Our entrance is no violation of their privileges; we can take nothing from them, how then can we offend them?'

'My dear Pekuah,' said the princess, 'I will always go before you, and Imlac shall follow you. Remember that you are the companion of the princess of Abyssinia.'

'If the princess is pleased that her servant should die,' returned the lady, 'let her command some death less dreadful than enclosure in this horrid cavern. You know I dare not disobey you: I must go if you command me; but, if I once enter, I never shall come back.'

The princess saw that her fear was too strong for expostulation or reproof, and embracing her, told her that she should stay in the tent till their return. Pekuah was yet not satisfied, but entreated the princess not to pursue so dreadful a purpose as that of entering the recesses of the pyramid. 'Though I cannot teach courage,' said Nekayah, 'I must not learn cowardice; nor leave at last undone what I came hither only to do.'

XXXII. *They Enter the Pyramid*

Pekuah descended to the tents, and the rest entered the pyramid: they passed through the galleries, surveyed the vaults of marble, and examined the chest in which the body of the founder is supposed to have been reposited. They then sat down in one of the most spacious chambers to rest a while before they attempted to return.

'We have now,' said Imlac, 'gratified our minds with an exact view of the greatest work of man, except the wall of China.

'Of the wall it is very easy to assign the motives. It secured a wealthy and timorous nation from the incursions of barbarians, whose unskilfulness in arts made it easier for them to supply their wants by rapine than by industry, and who from time to time poured in upon the habitations of peaceful commerce, as vultures descend upon domestic fowl. Their celerity and fierceness made the wall necessary, and their ignorance made it efficacious.

'But for the pyramids no reason has ever been given adequate to the cost and labour of the work. The narrowness of the chambers proves that it could afford no retreat from enemies, and treasures might have been reposited at far less expense with equal security. It seems to have been erected only in compliance with that hunger of imagination which preys incessantly upon life, and must be always appeased by some employment. Those who have already all that they can enjoy must enlarge their desires. He that has built for use, till use is supplied, must begin to build for vanity, and extend his plan to the utmost power of human performance, that he may not be soon reduced to form another wish.

'I consider this mighty structure as a monument of the insufficiency of human enjoyments. A king whose power is unlimited, and whose treasures surmount all real and imaginary wants, is compelled to solace, by the erection of a pyramid, the satiety of dominion and tastelessness of pleasures, and to amuse the tediousness of declining life, by seeing thousands labouring without end, and one stone, for no purpose, laid upon another. Whoever thou art that, not content with a moderate condition, imaginest happiness in royal magnificence, and dreamest that command or riches can feed the appetite of novelty with perpetual gratifications, survey the pyramids, and confess thy folly!'

XXXIII. *The Princess Meets with an Unexpected Misfortune*

They rose up, and returned through the cavity at which they had entered, and the princess prepared for her favourite a long narrative of dark labyrinths, and costly rooms, and of the different impressions which the varieties of the way had made upon her. But, when they came to their train, they found every one silent and dejected: the men discovered shame and fear in their countenances, and the women were weeping in the tents.

What had happened they did not try to conjecture, but immediately inquired. 'You had scarcely entered into the pyramid,' said one of the attendants, 'when a troop of Arabs rushed upon us: we were too few to resist them, and too slow to escape. They were about to search the tents, set us on our camels, and drive us along before them, when the approach of some Turkish horsemen put them to flight; but they seized the lady Pekuah with her two maids, and carried them away: the Turks are now pursuing them by our instigation, but I fear they will not be able to overtake them.'

The princess was overpowered with surprise and grief. Rasselas, in the first heat of his resentment, ordered his servants to follow him, and prepared to pursue the robbers with his sabre in his hand. 'Sir,' said Imlac, 'what can you hope from violence or valour? The Arabs are mounted on horses trained to battle and retreat; we have only beasts of burden. By leaving our present station we may lose the princess, but cannot hope to regain Pekuah.'

In a short time the Turks returned, having not been able to reach the enemy. The princess burst out into new lamentations, and Rasselas could scarcely forbear to reproach them with cowardice; but Imlac was of opinion that the escape of the Arabs was no addition to their misfortune, for, perhaps, they would have killed their captives rather than have resigned them.

XXXIV. *They Return to Cairo Without Pekuah*

There was nothing to be hoped from longer stay. They returned to Cairo repenting of their curiosity, censuring the negligence of the government, lamenting their own rashness which had neglected to procure a guard, imagining many expedients by which the loss of Pekuah might have been prevented, and resolving to do something for her recovery, though none could find any thing proper to be done.

Nekayah retired to her chamber, where her women attempted to comfort her by telling her that all had their troubles, and that lady Pekuah had enjoyed much happiness in the world for a long time, and might reasonably expect a change of fortune. They hoped that some good would befall her wheresoever she was, and that their mistress would find another friend who might supply her place.

The princess made them no answer, and they continued the form of condolence, not much grieved in their hearts that the favourite was lost.

Next day the prince presented to the Bassa a memorial of the wrong which he had suffered, and a petition for redress. The Bassa threatened to punish the robbers, but did not attempt to catch them, nor, indeed, could any account or description be given by which he might direct the pursuit.

It soon appeared that nothing would be done by authority. Governors, being accustomed to hear of more crimes than they can punish, and more wrongs than they can redress, set themselves at ease by indiscriminate negligence, and presently forget the request when they lose sight of the petitioner.

Imlac then endeavoured to gain some intelligence by private agents. He found many who pretended to an exact knowledge of all the haunts of the Arabs, and to regular correspondence with their chiefs, and who readily undertook the recovery of Pekuah. Of these, some were furnished with money for their journey, and came back no more; some were liberally paid for accounts which a few days discovered to be false. But the princess would not suffer any means, however improbable, to be left untried. While she was doing something she kept her hope alive. As one expedient failed, another was suggested; when one messenger returned unsuccessful, another was despatched to a different quarter.

Two months had now passed, and of Pekuah nothing had been heard; the hopes which they had endeavoured to raise in each other grew more languid, and the princess, when she saw nothing more to be tried, sunk down inconsolable in hopeless dejection. A thousand times she reproached herself with the easy compliance by which she permitted her favourite to stay behind her. 'Had not my fondness,' said she, 'lessened my authority, Pekuah had not dared to talk of her terrors. She ought to have feared me more than spectres. A severe look would have overpowered her; a peremptory command would have compelled obedience. Why did foolish indulgence prevail upon me? Why did I not speak and refuse to hear?'

'Great princess,' said Imlac, 'do not reproach yourself for your virtue, or consider that as blameable by which evil has accidentally been caused. Your tenderness for the timidity of Pekuah was generous and kind. When we act according to our duty, we commit the event to him by whose laws our actions are governed, and who will suffer none to be finally punished for obedience. When, in prospect of some good, whether natural or moral, we break the rules prescribed us, we withdraw from the direction of superior wisdom, and take all consequences upon ourselves. Man cannot so far know the connexion of causes and events as that he may venture to do wrong in order to do right. When we pursue our end by lawful means, we may always console our miscarriage by the hope of future recompense. When we consult only our own policy, and attempt to find a nearer way to good, by overleaping the settled boundaries of right and wrong, we cannot be happy even by success, because we cannot escape the consciousness of our fault; but, if we miscarry, the disappointment is irremediably embittered. How comfortless is the sorrow of him who feels at once the pangs of guilt, and the vexation of calamity which guilt has brought upon him!

'Consider, princess, what would have been your condition, if the lady Pekuah had entreated to accompany you, and, being compelled to stay in the tents, had been carried away; or how would you have borne the thought, if you had forced her into the pyramid, and she had died before you in agonies of terror.'

'Had either happened,' said Nekayah, 'I could not have endured life till now: I should have been tortured to madness by the remembrance of such cruelty, or must have pined away in abhorrence of myself.'

'This at least,' said Imlac, 'is the present reward of virtuous conduct, that no unlucky consequence can oblige us to repent it.'

xxxv. *The Princess Languishes for Want of Pekuah*

Nekayah, being thus reconciled to herself, found that no evil is insupportable but that which is accompanied with consciousness of wrong. She was, from that time, delivered from the violence of tempestuous sorrow, and sunk into silent pensiveness and gloomy tranquillity. She sat from morning to evening recollecting all that had been done or said by her Pekuah, treasured up with care every trifle on which Pekuah had set an accidental value, and which might recall to mind any little incident or careless conversation. The sentiments of her whom she now expected to see no more were treasured in her memory as rules of life, and she deliberated to no other end than to conjecture on any occasion what would have been the opinion and counsel of Pekuah.

The women by whom she was attended knew nothing of her real condition, and therefore she could not talk to them but with caution and reserve. She began to remit her curiosity, having no great care to collect notions which she had no convenience of uttering. Rasselas endeavoured first to comfort and afterwards to divert her; he hired musicians, to whom she seemed to listen, but did not hear them, and procured masters to instruct her in various arts, whose lectures, when they visited her again, were again to be repeated. She had lost her taste of pleasure and her ambition of excellence. And her mind, though forced into short excursions, always recurred to the image of her friend.

Imlac was every morning earnestly enjoined to renew his inquiries, and was asked every night whether he had yet heard of Pekuah, till not being able to return the princess the answer that she desired, he was less and less willing to come into her presence. She observed his backwardness, and commanded him to attend her. 'You are not,' said she, 'to confound impatience with resentment, or to suppose that I charge you with negligence because I repine at your unsuccessfulness. I do not much wonder at your absence; I know that the unhappy are never pleasing, and that all naturally avoid the contagion of misery. To hear complaints is wearisome alike to the wretched and the happy; for who would cloud by adventitious grief the short gleams of gaiety which life allows us? Or who, that is struggling under his own evils, will add to them the miseries of another?

'The time is at hand when none shall be disturbed any longer by the sighs of Nekayah: my search after happiness is now at an end. I am resolved to retire from the world with all its flatteries and deceits, and will hide myself in solitude, without any other care than to compose my thoughts, and regulate my hours by a constant succession of innocent occupations, till, with a mind purified from all earthly desires, I shall enter into that state to which all are hastening, and in which I hope again to enjoy the friendship of Pekuah.'

'Do not entangle your mind,' said Imlac, 'by irrevocable determinations, nor increase the burden of life by a voluntary accumulation of misery: the weariness of retirement will continue or increase when the loss of Pekuah is forgotten. That you have been deprived of one pleasure is no very good reason for rejection of the rest.'

'Since Pekuah was taken from me,' said the princess, 'I have no pleasure to reject or to retain. She that has no one to love or trust has little to hope. She wants the radical principle of happiness. We may, perhaps, allow that what satisfaction this world can afford must arise from the conjunction of wealth, knowledge, and goodness: wealth is nothing but as it is bestowed, and knowledge nothing but as it is communicated: they must therefore be imparted to others, and to whom could I now delight to impart them? Goodness affords the only comfort which can be enjoyed without a partner, and goodness may be practised in retirement.'

'How far solitude may admit goodness, or advance it, I shall not,' replied Imlac, 'dispute at present. Remember the confession of the pious hermit. You will wish to return into the world when the image of your companion has left your thoughts.' 'That time,' said Nekayah, 'will never come. The generous frankness, the modest obsequiousness, and the faithful secrecy of my dear Pekuah will always be more missed as I shall live longer to see vice and folly.'

'The state of a mind oppressed with a sudden calamity,' said Imlac, 'is like that of the fabulous inhabitants of the new created earth, who, when the first night came upon them, supposed that day never would return. When the clouds of sorrow gather over us, we see nothing beyond them, nor can imagine how they will be dispelled: yet a new day succeeded to the night, and sorrow is never long without a dawn of ease. But they who restrain themselves from receiving comfort do as the savages would have done had they put out their eyes when it was dark. Our minds, like our bodies, are in continual flux; something is hourly lost, and something acquired. To lose much at once is inconvenient to either, but while the vital powers remain uninjured, nature will find the means of reparation. Distance has the same effect on the mind as on the eye, and while we glide along the stream of time, whatever we leave behind us is always lessening, and that which we approach increasing in magnitude. Do not suffer life to stagnate; it will grow muddy for want of motion: commit yourself again to the current of the world; Pekuah will vanish by degrees; you will meet in your way some other favourite, or learn to diffuse yourself in general conversation.'

'At least,' said the prince, 'do not despair before all remedies have been tried: the inquiry after the unfortunate lady is still continued, and shall be carried on with yet greater diligence, on condition that you will promise to wait a year for the event, without any unalterable resolution.'

Nekayah thought this a reasonable demand, and made the promise to her brother, who had been advised by Imlac to require it. Imlac had, indeed, no great hope of regaining Pekuah, but he supposed that if he could secure the interval of a year, the princess would be then in no danger of a cloister.

XXXVI. *Pekuah Is Still Remembered. The Progress of Sorrow*

Nekayah, seeing that nothing was omitted for the recovery of her favourite, and having, by her promise, set her intention of retirement at a distance, began imperceptibly to return to common cares and common pleasures. She rejoiced without her own consent at the suspension of her sorrows, and sometimes caught herself with indignation in the act of turning away her mind from the remembrance of her whom yet she resolved never to forget.

She then appointed a certain hour of the day for meditation on the merits and fondness of Pekuah, and for some weeks retired constantly at the time fixed, and returned with her eyes swollen and her countenance clouded. By degrees she grew less scrupulous, and suffered any important and pressing avocation to delay the tribute of daily tears. She then yielded to less occasions; sometimes forgot what she was indeed afraid to remember, and, at last, wholly released herself from the duty of periodical affliction.

Her real love of Pekuah was yet not diminished. A thousand occurrences brought her back to memory, and a thousand wants which nothing but the confidence of friendship can supply made her frequently regretted. She, therefore, solicited Imlac never to desist from inquiry, and to leave no art of intelligence untried, that, at least, she might have the comfort of knowing that she did not suffer by negligence or sluggishness. 'Yet what,' said she, 'is to be expected from our pursuit of happiness, when we find the state of life to be such that happiness itself is the cause of misery? Why should we endeavour to attain that of which the possession cannot be secured? I shall henceforward fear to yield my heart to excellence, however bright, or to fondness, however tender, lest I should lose again what I have lost in Pekuah.'

XXXVII. *The Princess Hears News of Pekuah*

In seven months, one of the messengers who had been sent away upon the day when the promise was drawn from the princess returned, after many unsuccessful rambles, from the borders of Nubia, with an account that Pekuah was in the hands of an Arab chief who possessed a castle or fortress on the extremity of Egypt. The Arab, whose revenue was plunder, was willing to restore her, with her two attendants, for two hundred ounces of gold.

The price was no subject of debate. The princess was in ecstasies when she heard that her favourite was alive, and might so cheaply be ransomed. She could not think of delaying for a moment Pekuah's happiness or her own, but entreated her brother to send back the messenger with the sum required. Imlac, being consulted, was not very confident of the veracity of the relator, and was still more doubtful of the Arab's faith, who might, if he were too liberally trusted, detain at once the money and the captives. He thought it dangerous to put themselves in the power of the Arab by going into his district, and could not expect that the rover would so much expose himself as to come into the lower country, where he might be seized by the forces of the Bassa.

It is difficult to negotiate where neither will trust. But Imlac, after some deliberation, directed the messenger to propose that Pekuah should be conducted by ten horsemen to the monastery of St Anthony,° which is situated in the deserts of Upper-Egypt, where she should be met by the same number, and her ransom should be paid.

That no time might be lost, as they expected that the proposal would not be refused, they immediately began their journey to the monastery and, when they arrived, Imlac went forward with the former messenger to the Arab's fortress. Rasselas was desirous to go with them, but neither his sister nor Imlac would consent. The Arab, according to the custom of his nation, observed the laws of hospitality with great exactness to those who put themselves into his power, and, in a few days, brought Pekuah with her maids, by easy journeys, to their place appointed, where receiving the stipulated price, he restored her with great respect to liberty and her friends, and undertook to conduct them back towards Cairo beyond all danger of robbery or violence.

The princess and her favourite embraced each other with transport too violent to be expressed, and went out together to pour the tears of tenderness in secret, and exchange professions of kindness and gratitude. After a few hours they returned into the refectory of the convent, where, in the presence of the prior and his brethren, the prince required of Pekuah the history of her adventures.

XXXVIII. *The Adventures of the Lady Pekuah*

'At what time, and in what manner, I was forced away,' said Pekuah, 'your servants have told you. The suddenness of the event struck me with surprise, and I was at first rather stupified than agitated with any passion of either fear or sorrow. My confusion was increased by the speed and tumult of our flight while we were followed by the Turks, who, as it seemed, soon despaired to overtake us, or were afraid of those whom they made a show of menacing.

'When the Arabs saw themselves out of danger they slackened their course, and, as I was less harassed by external violence, I began to feel more uneasiness in my mind. After some time we stopped near a spring shaded with trees in a pleasant meadow, where we were set upon the ground, and offered such refreshments as our masters were partaking. I was suffered to sit with my maids apart from the rest, and none attempted to comfort or insult us. Here I first began to feel the full weight of my misery. The girls sat weeping in silence, and from time to time looked on me for succour. I knew not to what condition we were doomed, nor could conjecture where would be the place of our captivity, or whence to draw any hope of deliverance. I was in the hands of robbers and savages, and had no reason to suppose that their pity was more than their justice, or that they would forbear the gratification of any ardour of desire, or caprice of cruelty. I, however, kissed my maids, and endeavoured to pacify them by remarking that we were yet treated with decency, and that, since we were now carried beyond pursuit, there was no danger of violence to our lives.

'When we were to be set again on horseback, my maids clung round me, and refused to be parted, but I commanded them not to irritate those who had us in their power. We travelled the remaining part of the day through an unfrequented and pathless country, and came by moonlight to the side of a hill, where the rest of the troop was stationed. Their tents were pitched, and their fires kindled, and our chief was welcomed as a man much beloved by his dependants.

'We were received into a large tent, where we found women who had attended their husbands in the expedition. They set before us the supper which they had provided, and I eat it rather to encourage my maids than to comply with any appetite of my own. When the meat was taken away they spread the carpets for repose. I was weary, and hoped to find in sleep that remission of distress which nature seldom denies. Ordering myself therefore to be undressed, I observed that the women looked very earnestly upon me, not expecting, I supposed, to see me so submissively attended. When my upper vest was taken off, they were apparently struck with the splendour of my clothes and one of them timorously laid her hand upon the embroidery. She then went out, and, in a short time, came back with another woman, who seemed to be of higher rank, and greater authority. She did, at her entrance, the usual act of reverence, and, taking me by the hand, placed me in a smaller tent, spread with finer carpets, where I spent the night quietly with my maids.

'In the morning, as I was sitting on the grass, the chief of the troop came towards me. I rose up to receive him, and he bowed with great respect. "Illustrious lady," said he, "my fortune is better than I had presumed to hope; I am told by my women that I have a princess in my camp." "Sir," answered I, "your women have deceived themselves and you; I am not a princess, but an unhappy stranger who intended soon to have left this country, in which I am now to be imprisoned for ever." "Whoever, or whencesoever, you are," returned the Arab, "your dress, and that of your servants, show your rank to be high, and your wealth to be great. Why should you, who can so easily procure your ransom, think yourself in danger of perpetual captivity? The purpose of my incursions is to increase my riches, or more properly to gather tribute. The sons of Ishmael are the natural and hereditary lords of this part of the continent, which is usurped by late invaders, and low-born tyrants, from whom we are compelled to take by the sword what is denied to justice. The violence of war admits no distinction; the lance that is lifted at guilt and power will sometimes fall on innocence and gentleness."

'"How little," said I, "did I expect that yesterday it should have fallen upon me."

'"Misfortunes," answered the Arab, "should always be expected. If the eye of hostility could learn reverence or pity, excellence like yours had been exempt from injury. But the angels of affliction spread their toils alike for the virtuous and the wicked, for the mighty and the mean. Do not be disconsolate; I am not one of the lawless and cruel rovers of the desert; I know the rules of civil life: I will fix your ransom, give a passport to your messenger, and perform my stipulation with nice punctuality."

'You will easily believe that I was pleased with his courtesy; and finding that his predominant passion was desire of money, I began now to think my danger less, for I knew that no sum would be thought too great for the release of Pekuah. I told him that he should have no reason to charge me with ingratitude, if I was used with kindness, and that any ransom which could be expected for a maid of common rank would be paid, but that he must not persist to rate me as a princess. He said he would consider what he should demand, and then, smiling, bowed and retired.

'Soon after the women came about me, each contending to be more officious than the other, and my maids themselves were served with reverence. We travelled onward by short journeys. On the fourth day the chief told me that my ransom must be two hundred ounces of gold, which I not only promised him, but told him that I would add fifty more if I and my maids were honourably treated.

'I never knew the power of gold before. From that time I was the leader of the troop. The march of every day was longer or shorter as I commanded, and the tents were pitched where I chose to rest. We now had camels and other conveniencies for travel, my own women were always at my side, and I amused myself with observing the manners of the vagrant nations, and with viewing remains of ancient edifices with which these deserted countries appear to have been, in some distant age, lavishly embellished.

'The chief of the band was a man far from illiterate: he was able to travel by the stars or the compass, and had marked in his erratic expeditions such places as are most worthy the notice of a passenger. He observed to me that buildings are always best preserved in places little frequented, and difficult of access: for, when once a country declines from its primitive splendour, the more inhabitants are left the quicker ruin will be made. Walls supply stones more easily than quarries, and palaces and temples will be demolished to make stables of granite, and cottages of porphyry.

XXXIX. *The Adventures of Pekuah Continued*

'We wandered about in this manner for some weeks, whether, as our chief pretended, for my gratification, or, as I rather suspected, for some convenience of his own. I endeavoured to appear contented where sullenness and resentment would have been of no use, and that endeavour conduced much to the calmness of my mind; but my heart was always with Nekayah, and the troubles of the night much overbalanced the amusements of the day. My women, who threw all their cares upon their mistress, set their minds at ease from the time when they saw me treated with respect, and gave themselves up to the incidental alleviations of our fatigue without solicitude or sorrow. I was pleased with their pleasure, and animated with their confidence. My condition had lost much of its terror, since I found that the Arab ranged the country merely to get riches. Avarice is an uniform and tractable vice: other intellectual distempers are different in different constitutions of mind; that which soothes the pride of one will offend the pride of another; but to the favour of the covetous there is a ready way, bring money and nothing is denied.

'At last we came to the dwelling of our chief, a strong and spacious house built with stone in an island of the Nile which lies, as I was told, under the tropic. "Lady," said the Arab, "you shall rest after your journey a few weeks in this place, where you are to consider yourself as sovereign. My occupation is war: I have therefore chosen this obscure residence, from which I can issue unexpected, and to which I can retire unpursued. You may now repose in security: here are few pleasures, but here is no danger." He then led me into the inner apartments, and seating me on the richest couch, bowed to the ground. His women, who considered me as a rival, looked on me with malignity; but being soon informed that I was a great lady detained only for my ransom, they began to vie with each other in obsequiousness and reverence.

'Being again comforted with new assurances of speedy liberty, I was for some days diverted from impatience by the novelty of the place. The turrets overlooked the country to a great distance, and afforded a view of many windings of the stream. In the day I wandered from one place to another as the course of the sun varied the splendor of the prospect, and saw many things which I had never seen before. The crocodiles and river-horses are common in this unpeopled region, and I often looked upon them with terror, though I knew that they could not hurt me. For some time I expected to see mermaids and tritons, which, as Imlac has told me, the European travellers have stationed in the Nile, but no such beings ever appeared, and the Arab, when I inquired after them, laughed at my credulity.

'At night the Arab always attended me to a tower set apart for celestial observations, where he endeavoured to teach me the names and courses of the stars. I had no great inclination to this study, but an appearance of attention was necessary to please my instructor, who valued himself for his skill, and, in a little while, I found some employment requisite to beguile the tediousness of time, which was to be passed always amidst the same objects. I was weary of looking in the morning on things from which I had turned away weary in the evening: I therefore was at last willing to observe the stars rather than do nothing, but could not always compose my thoughts, and was very often thinking on Nekayah when others imagined me contemplating the sky. Soon after the Arab went upon another expedition, and then my only pleasure was to talk with my maids about the accident by which we were carried away, and the happiness that we should all enjoy at the end of our captivity.'

'There were women in your Arab's fortress,' said the princess, 'why did you not make them your companions, enjoy their conversation, and partake their diversions? In a place where they found business or amusement, why should you alone sit corroded with idle melancholy? Or why could not you bear for a few months that condition to which they were condemned for life?'

'The diversions of the women,' answered Pekuah, 'were only childish play,° by which the mind accustomed to stronger operations could not be kept busy. I could do all which they delighted in doing by powers merely sensitive, while my intellectual faculties were flown to Cairo. They ran from room to room as a bird hops from wire to wire in his cage. They danced for the sake of motion, as lambs frisk in a meadow. One sometimes pretended to be hurt that the rest might be alarmed, or hid herself that another might seek her. Part of their time passed in watching the progress of light bodies that floated on the river, and part in marking the various forms into which clouds broke in the sky.

'Their business was only needlework, in which I and my maids sometimes helped them; but you know that the mind will easily straggle from the fingers, nor will you suspect that captivity and absence from Nekayah could receive solace from silken flowers.

'Nor was much satisfaction to be hoped from their conversation: for of what could they be expected to talk? They had seen nothing; for they had lived from early youth in that narrow spot: of what they had not seen they could have no knowledge, for they could not read. They had no ideas but of the few things that were within their view, and had hardly names for any thing but their clothes and their food. As I bore a superior character, I was often called to terminate their quarrels, which I decided as equitably as I could. If it could have amused me to hear the complaints of each against the rest, I might have been often detained by long stories, but the motives of their animosity were so small that I could not listen without intercepting the tale.'

'How,' said Rasselas, 'can the Arab, whom you represented as a man of more than common accomplishments, take any pleasure in his seraglio, when it is filled only with women like these? Are they exquisitely beautiful?'

'They do not,' said Pekuah, 'want that unaffecting and ignoble beauty which may subsist without spriteliness or sublimity, without energy of thought or dignity of virtue. But to a man like the Arab such beauty was only a flower casually plucked and carelessly thrown away. Whatever pleasures he might find among them, they were not those of friendship or society. When they were playing about him he looked on them with inattentive superiority: when they vied for his regard he sometimes turned away disgusted. As they had no knowledge, their talk could take nothing from the tediousness of life: as they had no choice, their fondness, or appearance of fondness, excited in him neither pride nor gratitude; he was not exalted in his own esteem by the smiles of a woman who saw no other man, nor was much obliged by that regard of which he could never know the sincerity, and which he might often perceive to be exerted not so much to delight him as to pain a rival. That which he gave, and they received, as love, was only a careless distribution of superfluous time, such love as man can bestow upon that which he despises, such as has neither hope nor fear, neither joy nor sorrow.'

'You have reason, lady, to think yourself happy,' said Imlac, 'that you have been thus easily dismissed. How could a mind, hungry for knowledge, be willing, in an intellectual famine, to lose such a banquet as Pekuah's conversation?'

'I am inclined to believe,' answered Pekuah, 'that he was for some time in suspense; for, notwithstanding his promise, whenever I proposed to dispatch a messenger to Cairo, he found some excuse for delay. While I was detained in his house he made many incursions into the neighbouring countries, and, perhaps, he would have refused to discharge me, had his plunder been equal to his wishes. He returned always courteous, related his adventures, delighted to hear my observations and endeavoured to advance my acquaintance with the stars. When I importuned him to send away my letters, he soothed me with professions of honour and sincerity; and, when I could be no longer decently denied, put his troop again in motion, and left me to govern in his absence. I was much afflicted by this studied procrastination, and was sometimes afraid that I should be forgotten;

that you would leave Cairo, and I must end my days in an island of the Nile.

'I grew at last hopeless and dejected, and cared so little to entertain him that he for a while more frequently talked with my maids. That he should fall in love with them, or with me, might have been equally fatal, and I was not much pleased with the growing friendship. My anxiety was not long; for, as I recovered some degree of cheerfulness, he returned to me, and I could not forbear to despise my former uneasiness.

'He still delayed to send for my ransom, and would, perhaps, never have determined, had not your agent found his way to him. The gold which he would not fetch he could not reject when it was offered. He hastened to prepare for our journey hither, like a man delivered from the pain of an intestine conflict. I took leave of my companions in the house, who dismissed me with cold indifference.'

Nekayah, having heard her favourite's relation, rose and embraced her, and Rasselas gave her an hundred ounces of gold, which she presented to the Arab for the fifty that were promised.

XL. *The History of a Man of Learning*°

They returned to Cairo, and were so well pleased at finding themselves together that none of them went much abroad. The prince began to love learning, and one day declared to Imlac that he intended to devote himself to science, and pass the rest of his days in literary solitude.

'Before you make your final choice,' answered Imlac, 'you ought to examine its hazards, and converse with some of those who are grown old in the company of themselves. I have just left the observatory of one of the most learned astronomers in the world, who has spent forty years in unwearied attention to the motions and appearances of the celestial bodies, and has drawn out his soul in endless calculations. He admits a few friends once a month to hear his deductions and enjoy his discoveries. I was introduced as a man of knowledge worthy of his notice. Men of various ideas and fluent conversation are commonly welcome to those whose thoughts have been long fixed upon a single point, and who find the images of other things stealing away. I delighted him with my remarks, he smiled at the narrative of my travels, and was glad to forget the constellations, and descend for a moment into the lower world.

'On the next day of vacation I renewed my visit, and was so

fortunate as to please him again. He relaxed from that time the severity of his rule, and permitted me to enter at my own choice. I found him always busy, and always glad to be relieved. As each knew much which the other was desirous of learning, we exchanged our notions with great delight. I perceived that I had every day more of his confidence, and always found new cause of admiration in the profundity of his mind. His comprehension is vast, his memory capacious and retentive, his discourse is methodical, and his expression clear.

'His integrity and benevolence are equal to his learning. His deepest researches and most favourite studies are willingly interrupted for any opportunity of doing good by his counsel or his riches. To his closest retreat, at his most busy moments, all are admitted that want his assistance: "For though I exclude idleness and pleasure, I will never," says he, "bar my doors against charity. To man is permitted the contemplation of the skies, but the practice of virtue is commanded."'

'Surely,' said the princess, 'this man is happy.'

'I visited him,' said Imlac, 'with more and more frequency, and was every time more enamoured of his conversation: he was sublime without haughtiness, courteous without formality, and communicative without ostentation. I was at first, great princess, of your opinion, thought him the happiest of mankind, and often congratulated him on the blessing that he enjoyed. He seemed to hear nothing with indifference but the praises of his condition, to which he always returned a general answer, and diverted the conversation to some other topic.

'Amidst this willingness to be pleased, and labour to please, I had quickly reason to imagine that some painful sentiment pressed upon his mind. He often looked up earnestly towards the sun, and let his voice fall in the midst of his discourse. He would sometimes, when we were alone, gaze upon me in silence with the air of a man who longed to speak what he was yet resolved to suppress. He would often send for me with vehement injunctions of haste, though, when I came to him, he had nothing extraordinary to say. And sometimes, when I was leaving him, would call me back, pause a few moments and then dismiss me.

XLI. *The Astronomer Discovers the Cause of His Uneasiness*

'At last the time came when the secret burst his reserve. We were sitting together last night in the turret of his house, watching the emersion of a satellite of Jupiter. A sudden tempest clouded the sky, and disappointed our observation. We sat a while silent in the dark, and then he addressed himself to me in these words: "Imlac, I have long considered thy friendship as the greatest blessing of my life. Integrity without knowledge is weak and useless, and knowledge without integrity is dangerous and dreadful. I have found in thee all the qualities requisite for trust, benevolence, experience, and fortitude. I have long discharged an office which I must soon quit at the call of nature, and shall rejoice in the hour of imbecility and pain to devolve it upon thee."

'I thought myself honoured by this testimony, and protested that whatever could conduce to his happiness would add likewise to mine.

'"Hear, Imlac, what thou wilt not without difficulty credit. I have possessed for five years the regulation of weather, and the distribution of the seasons: the sun has listened to my dictates, and passed from tropic to tropic by my direction; the clouds, at my call, have poured their waters, and the Nile has overflowed at my command; I have restrained the rage of the dog-star, and mitigated the fervours of the crab. The winds alone, of all the elemental powers, have hitherto refused my authority, and multitudes have perished by equinoctial tempests which I found myself unable to prohibit or restrain. I have administered this great office with exact justice, and made to the different nations of the earth an impartial dividend of rain and sunshine. What must have been the misery of half the globe, if I had limited the clouds to particular regions, or confined the sun to either side of the equator?"

XLII. *The Opinion of the Astronomer is Explained and Justified*

'I suppose he discovered in me, through the obscurity of the room, some tokens of amazement and doubt, for, after a short pause, he proceeded thus:

'"Not to be easily credited will neither surprise nor offend me; for I am, probably, the first of human beings to whom this trust has been imparted. Nor do I know whether to deem this distinction a reward or punishment; since I have possessed it I have been far less happy than before, and nothing but the consciousness of good intention could have enabled me to support the weariness of unremitted vigilance."

'"How long, Sir," said I, "has this great office been in your hands?"

'"About ten years ago," said he, "my daily observations of the changes of the sky led me to consider whether, if I had the power of the seasons, I could confer greater plenty upon the inhabitants of the earth. This contemplation fastened on my mind, and I sat days and nights in imaginary dominion, pouring upon this country and that the showers of fertility, and seconding every fall of rain with a due proportion of sunshine. I had yet only the will to do good, and did not imagine that I should ever have the power.

'"One day as I was looking on the fields withering with heat, I felt in my mind a sudden wish that I could send rain on the southern mountains, and raise the Nile to an inundation. In the hurry of my imagination I commanded rain to fall, and, by comparing the time of my command with that of the inundation, I found that the clouds had listened to my lips."

'"Might not some other cause," said I, "produce this concurrence? The Nile does not always rise on the same day."

'"Do not believe," said he with impatience, "that such objections could escape me: I reasoned long against my own conviction, and laboured against truth with the utmost obstinacy. I sometimes suspected myself of madness, and should not have dared to impart this secret but to a man like you, capable of distinguishing the wonderful from the impossible, and the incredible from the false."

'"Why, Sir," said I, "do you call that incredible which you know, or think you know, to be true?"

'"Because," said he, "I cannot prove it by any external evidence; and I know too well the laws of demonstration to think that my conviction ought to influence another who cannot, like me, be conscious of its force. I, therefore, shall not attempt to gain credit by disputation. It is sufficient that I feel this power, that I have long possessed, and every day exerted it. But the life of man is short, the infirmities of age increase upon me, and the time will soon come when the regulator of the year must mingle with the dust. The care of appointing a successor has long disturbed me; the night and the day have been spent in comparisons of all the characters which have come to my knowledge, and I have yet found none so worthy as thyself.

XLIII. *The Astronomer Leaves Imlac His Directions*

'"Hear, therefore, what I shall impart, with attention, such as the welfare of a world requires. If the task of a king be considered as difficult, who has the care only of a few millions to whom he cannot do much good or harm, what must be the anxiety of him on whom

depend the action of the elements, and the great gifts of light and heat!
—Hear me therefore with attention.

'"I have diligently considered the position of the earth and sun, and
formed innumerable schemes in which I changed their situation. I
have sometimes turned aside the axis of the earth, and sometimes
varied the ecliptic of the sun: but I have found it impossible to make a
disposition by which the world may be advantaged; what one region
gains, another loses by any imaginable alteration, even without
considering the distant parts of the solar system with which we are
unacquainted. Do not, therefore, in thy administration of the year,
indulge thy pride by innovation; do not please thyself with thinking
that thou canst make thyself renowned to all future ages by
disordering the seasons. The memory of mischief is no desirable fame.
Much less will it become thee to let kindness or interest prevail. Never
rob other countries of rain to pour it on thine own. For us the Nile is
sufficient."

'I promised that when I possessed the power, I would use it with
inflexible integrity, and he dismissed me, pressing my hand. "My
heart," said he, "will be now at rest, and my benevolence will no more
destroy my quiet: I have found a man of wisdom and virtue, to whom
I can cheerfully bequeath the inheritance of the sun."'

The prince heard this narration with very serious regard, but the
princess smiled, and Pekuah convulsed herself with laughter. 'Ladies,'
said Imlac, 'to mock the heaviest of human afflictions is neither
charitable nor wise. Few can attain this man's knowledge, and few
practise his virtues; but all may suffer his calamity. Of the
uncertainties of our present state, the most dreadful and alarming is
the uncertain continuance of reason.'

The princess was recollected, and the favourite was abashed.
Rasselas, more deeply affected, enquired of Imlac whether he thought
such maladies of the mind frequent, and how they were contracted.

XLIV. *The Dangerous Prevalence of Imagination*°

'Disorders of intellect,' answered Imlac, 'happen much more often
than superficial observers will easily believe. Perhaps, if we speak with
rigorous exactness, no human mind is in its right state. There is no
man whose imagination does not sometimes predominate over his
reason, who can regulate his attention wholly by his will, and whose
ideas will come and go at his command. No man will be found in
whose mind airy notions do not sometimes tyrannize, and force him to

hope or fear beyond the limits of sober probability. All power of fancy over reason is a degree of insanity; but while this power is such as we can control and repress, it is not visible to others, nor considered as any depravation of the mental faculties: it is not pronounced madness but when it comes ungovernable, and apparently influences speech or action.

'To indulge the power of fiction, and send imagination out upon the wing, is often the sport of those who delight too much in silent speculation. When we are alone we are not always busy; the labour of excogitation is too violent to last long; the ardour of inquiry will sometimes give way to idleness or satiety. He who has nothing external that can divert him must find pleasure in his own thoughts, and must conceive himself what he is not; for who is pleased with what he is? He then expatiates in boundless futurity, and culls from all imaginable conditions that which for the present moment he should most desire, amuses his desires with impossible enjoyments, and confers upon his pride unattainable dominion. The mind dances from scene to scene, unites all pleasures in all combinations, and riots in delights which nature and fortune, with all their bounty, cannot bestow.

'In time some particular train of ideas fixes the attention, all other intellectual gratifications are rejected, the mind, in weariness or leisure, recurs constantly to the favourite conception, and feasts on the luscious falsehood whenever she is offended with the bitterness of truth. By degrees the reign of fancy is confirmed; she grows first imperious, and in time despotic. Then fictions begin to operate as realities, false opinions fasten upon the mind, and life passes in dreams of rapture or of anguish.

'This, sir, is one of the dangers of solitude, which the hermit has confessed not always to promote goodness, and the astronomer's misery has proved to be not always propitious to wisdom.'

'I will no more,' said the favourite, 'imagine myself the queen of Abyssinia. I have often spent the hours which the princess gave to my own disposal in adjusting ceremonies and regulating the court; I have repressed the pride of the powerful, and granted the petitions of the poor; I have built new palaces in more happy situations, planted groves upon the tops of mountains, and have exulted in the beneficence of royalty, till, when the princess entered, I had almost forgotten to bow down before her.'

'And I,' said the princess, 'will not allow myself any more to play the shepherdess in my waking dreams. I have often soothed my thoughts with the quiet and innocence of pastoral employments, till I have in my chamber heard the winds whistle, and the sheep bleat; sometimes freed the lamb entangled in the thicket, and sometimes with my crook encountered the wolf. I have a dress like that of the village maids, which I put on to help my imagination, and a pipe on which I play softly, and suppose myself followed by my flocks.'

'I will confess,' said the prince, 'an indulgence of fantastic delight more dangerous than yours. I have frequently endeavoured to image the possibility of a perfect government, by which all wrong should be restrained, all vice reformed, and all the subjects preserved in tranquility and innocence. This thought produced innumerable schemes of reformation, and dictated many useful regulations and salutary edicts. This has been the sport and sometimes the labour of my solitude; and I start when I think with how little anguish I once supposed the death of my father and my brothers.'

'Such,' says Imlac, 'are the effects of visionary schemes: when we first form them we know them to be absurd, but familiarize them by degrees, and in time lose sight of their folly.'

XLV. *They Discourse with an Old Man*

The evening was now far past, and they rose to return home. As they walked along the bank of the Nile, delighted with the beams of the moon quivering on the water, they saw at a small distance an old man, whom the prince had often heard in the assembly of the sages. 'Yonder,' said he, 'is one whose years have calmed his passions, but not clouded his reason: let us close the disquisitions of the night by inquiring what are his sentiments of his own state, that we may know whether youth alone is to struggle with vexation, and whether any better hope remains for the latter part of life.'

Here the sage approached and saluted them. They invited him to join their walk, and prattled a while as acquaintance that had unexpectedly met one another. The old man was cheerful and talkative, and the way seemed short in his company. He was pleased to find himself not disregarded, accompanied them to their house, and, at the prince's request, entered with them. They placed him in the seat of honour, and set wine and conserves before him.

'Sir,' said the princess, 'an evening walk must give to a man of learning, like you, pleasures which ignorance and youth can hardly conceive. You know the qualities and the causes of all that you behold, the laws by which the river flows, the periods in which the planets perform their revolutions. Every thing must supply you with contemplation, and renew the consciousness of your own dignity.'

'Lady,' answered he, 'let the gay and the vigorous expect pleasure in their excursions, it is enough that age can obtain ease. To me the world has lost its novelty: I look round, and see what I remember to have seen in happier days. I rest against a tree, and consider that in the same shade I once disputed upon the annual overflow of the Nile with a friend who is now silent in the grave. I cast my eyes upwards, fix them on the changing moon, and think with pain on the vicissitudes of life. I have ceased to take much delight in physical truth; for what have I to do with those things which I am soon to leave?'

'You may at least recreate yourself,' said Imlac, 'with the recollection of an honourable and useful life, and enjoy the praise which all agree to give you.'

'Praise,' said the sage, with a sigh, 'is to an old man an empty sound. I have neither mother to be delighted with the reputation of her son, nor wife to partake the honours of her husband. I have outlived my friends and my rivals. Nothing is now of much importance; for I cannot extend my interest beyond myself. Youth is delighted with applause, because it is considered as the earnest of some future good, and because the prospect of life is far extended: but to me, who am now declining to decrepitude, there is little to be feared from the malevolence of men, and yet less to be hoped from their affection or esteem. Something they may yet take away, but they can give me nothing. Riches would now be useless, and high employment would be pain. My retrospect of life recalls to my view many opportunities of good neglected, much time squandered upon trifles, and more lost in idleness and vacancy. I leave many great designs unattempted, and many great attempts unfinished. My mind is burdened with no heavy crime, and therefore I compose myself to tranquility; endeavour to abstract my thoughts from hopes and cares, which, though reason knows them to be vain, still try to keep their old possession of the heart; expect, with serene humility, that hour which nature cannot long delay; and hope to possess in a better state that happiness which here I could not find, and that virtue which here I have not attained.'

He rose and went away, leaving his audience not much elated with the hope of long life. The prince consoled himself with remarking that it was not reasonable to be disappointed by this account; for age had never been considered as the season of felicity, and, if it was possible to be easy in decline and weakness, it was likely that the days of vigour and alacrity might be happy: that the moon of life might be bright, if the evening could be calm.

The princess suspected that age was querulous and malignant, and delighted to repress the expectations of those who had newly entered the world. She had seen the possessors of estates look with envy on their heirs, and known many who enjoy pleasure no longer than they can confine it to themselves.

Pekuah conjectured that the man was older than he appeared, and was willing to impute his complaints to delirious dejection; or else supposed that he had been unfortunate, and was therefore discontented: 'For nothing,' said she, 'is more common than to call our own condition the condition of life.'

Imlac, who had no desire to see them depressed, smiled at the comforts which they could so readily procure to themselves, and remembered that at the same age, he was equally confident of unmingled prosperity, and equally fertile of consolatory expedients. He forbore to force upon them unwelcome knowledge, which time itself would too soon impress. The princess and her lady retired; the madness of the astronomer hung upon their minds, and they desired Imlac to enter upon his office, and delay next morning the rising of the sun.

XLVI. *The Princess and Pekuah Visit the Astronomer*

The princess and Pekuah, having talked in private of Imlac's astronomer, thought his character at once so amiable and so strange that they could not be satisfied without a nearer knowledge, and Imlac was requested to find the means of bringing them together.

This was somewhat difficult; the philosopher had never received any visits from women, though he lived in a city that had in it many Europeans who followed the manners of their own countries, and many from other parts of the world that lived there with European liberty. The ladies would not be refused, and several schemes were proposed for the accomplishment of their design. It was proposed to introduce them as strangers in distress, to whom the sage was always accessible; but, after some deliberation, it appeared that by this artifice no acquaintance could be formed, for their conversation would be short, and they could not decently importune him often. 'This,' said Rasselas, 'is true; but I have yet a stronger objection against the misrepresentation of your state. I have always considered it as treason against the great republic of human nature to make any man's virtues the means of deceiving him, whether on great or little occasions. All imposture weakens confidence and chills benevolence. When the sage finds that you are not what you seemed, he will feel the resentment natural to a man who, conscious of great abilities, discovers that he has been tricked by understandings meaner than his own, and, perhaps, the distrust, which he can never afterwards wholly lay aside, may stop the voice of counsel, and close the hand of charity; and where will you find the power of restoring his benefactions to mankind, or his peace to himself?'

To this no reply was attempted, and Imlac began to hope that their curiosity would subside; but, next day, Pekuah told him, she had now found an honest pretence for a visit to the astronomer, for she would solicit permission to continue under him the studies in which she had been initiated by the Arab, and the princess might go with her either as a fellow-student, or because a woman could not decently come alone. 'I am afraid,' said Imlac, 'that he will be soon weary of your company: men advanced far in knowledge do not love to repeat the elements of their art, and I am not certain that even of the elements, as he will deliver them connected with inferences, and mingled with reflections, you are a very capable auditress.' 'That,' said Pekuah, 'must be my care: I ask of you only to take me thither. My knowledge is, perhaps, more than you imagine it, and by concurring always with his opinions I shall make him think it greater than it is.'

The astronomer, in pursuance of this resolution, was told that a foreign lady, travelling in search of knowledge, had heard of his reputation, and was desirous to become his scholar. The uncommonness of the proposal raised at once his surprise and curiosity, and when, after a short deliberation, he consented to admit her, he could not stay without impatience till the next day.

The ladies dressed themselves magnificently, and were attended by Imlac to the astronomer, who was pleased to see himself approached with respect by persons of so splendid an appearance. In the exchange of the first civilities he was timorous and bashful; but when the talk became regular, he recollected his powers, and justified the character which Imlac had given. Inquiring of Pekuah what could have turned her inclination towards astronomy, he received from her a history of her adventure at the pyramid, and of the time passed in the Arab's island. She told her tale with ease and elegance, and her conversation took possession of his heart. The discourse was then turned to astronomy: Pekuah displayed what she knew: he looked upon her as a prodigy of genius, and entreated her not to desist from a study which she had so happily begun.

They came again and again, and were every time more welcome than before. The sage endeavoured to amuse them, that they might prolong their visits, for he found his thoughts grow brighter in their company; the clouds of solicitude vanished by degrees, as he forced himself to entertain them, and he grieved when he was left at their departure to his old employment of regulating the seasons.

The princess and her favourite had now watched his lips for several months, and could not catch a single word from which they could judge whether he continued, or not, in the opinion of his preternatural commission. They often contrived to bring him to an open declaration, but he easily eluded all their attacks, and on which side soever they pressed him escaped from them to some other topic.

As their familiarity increased they invited him often to the house of Imlac, where they distinguished him by extraordinary respect. He began gradually to delight in sublunary pleasures. He came early and departed late; laboured to recommend himself by assiduity and compliance; excited their curiosity after new arts, that they might still want his assistance; and when they made any excursion of pleasure or enquiry, entreated to attend them.

By long experience of his integrity and wisdom, the prince and his sister were convinced that he might be trusted without danger; and lest he should draw any false hopes from the civilities which he received, discovered to him their condition, with the motives of their journey, and required his opinion on the choice of life.

'Of the various conditions which the world spreads before you, which you shall prefer,' said the sage, 'I am not able to instruct you. I can only tell that I have chosen wrong. I have passed my time in study without experience; in the attainment of sciences which can, for the most part, be but remotely useful to mankind. I have purchased knowledge at the expense of all the common comforts of life: I have missed the endearing elegance of female friendship, and the happy commerce of domestic tenderness. If I have obtained any prerogatives above other students, they have been accompanied with fear, disquiet, and scrupulosity; but even of these prerogatives, whatever they were, I have, since my thoughts have been diversified by more intercourse with the world, begun to question the reality. When I have been for a few days lost in pleasing dissipation, I am always tempted to think that my inquiries have ended in error, and that I have suffered much, and suffered it in vain.'

Imlac was delighted to find that the sage's understanding was breaking through its mists, and resolved to detain him from the planets till he should forget his task of ruling them, and reason should recover its original influence.

From this time the astronomer was received into familiar friendship, and partook of all their projects and pleasures: his respect kept him attentive, and the activity of Rasselas did not leave much time unengaged. Something was always to be done; the day was spent in making observations which furnished talk for the evening, and the evening was closed with a scheme for the morrow.

The sage confessed to Imlac that since he had mingled in the gay tumults of life, and divided his hours by a succession of amusements, he found the conviction of his authority over the skies fade gradually from his mind, and began to trust less to an opinion which he never could prove to others, and which he now found subject to variation from causes in which reason had no part. 'If I am accidentally left alone for a few hours,' said he, 'my inveterate persuasion rushes upon my soul, and my thoughts are chained down by some irresistible violence, but they are soon disentangled by the prince's conversation, and instantaneously released at the entrance of Pekuah. I am like a man habitually afraid of spectres, who is set at ease by a lamp, and wonders at the dread which harassed him in the dark, yet, if his lamp be extinguished, feels again the terrors which he knows that when it is light he shall feel no more. But I am sometimes afraid lest I indulge my quiet by criminal negligence, and voluntarily forget the great charge with which I am intrusted. If I favour myself in a known error, or am determined by my own ease in a doubtful question of this importance, how dreadful is my crime!'

'No disease of the imagination,' answered Imlac, 'is so difficult of cure as that which is complicated with the dread of guilt: fancy and conscience then act interchangeably upon us, and so often shift their places that the illusions of one are not distinguished from the dictates of the other. If fancy presents images not moral or religious, the mind drives them away when they give it pain, but when melancholic notions take the form of duty, they lay hold on the faculties without opposition, because we are afraid to exclude or banish them. For this reason the superstitious are often melancholy, and the melancholy almost always superstitious.

'But do not let the suggestions of timidity overpower your better reason: the danger of neglect can be but as the probability of the obligation, which when you consider it with freedom, you find very little, and that little growing every day less. Open your heart to the influence of the light which, from time to time, breaks in upon you: when scruples importune you, which you in your lucid moments know to be vain, do not stand to parley, but fly to business or to Pekuah, and keep this thought always prevalent, that you are only one atom of the mass of humanity, and have neither such virtue nor vice, as that you should be singled out for supernatural favours or afflictions.'

XLVII. *The Prince Enters and Brings a New Topic*

'All this,' said the astronomer, 'I have often thought, but my reason has been so long subjugated by an uncontrollable and overwhelming idea that it durst not confide in its own decisions. I now see how fatally I betrayed my quiet, by suffering chimeras to prey upon me in secret; but melancholy shrinks from communication, and I never found a man before, to whom I could impart my troubles, though I had been certain of relief. I rejoice to find my own sentiments confirmed by yours, who are not easily deceived, and can have no motive or purpose to deceive. I hope that time and variety will dissipate the gloom that has so long surrounded me, and the latter part of my days will be spent in peace.'

'Your learning and virtue,' said Imlac, 'may justly give you hopes.'

Rasselas then entered with the princess and Pekuah, and inquired whether they had contrived any new diversion for the next day. 'Such,' said Nekayah, 'is the state of life, that none are happy but by the anticipation of change: the change itself is nothing; when we have made it, the next wish is to change again. The world is not yet exhausted; let me see something tomorrow which I never saw before.'

'Variety,' said Rasselas, 'is so necessary to content that even the happy valley disgusted me by the recurrence of its luxuries; yet I could not forbear to reproach myself with impatience when I saw the monks of St Anthony support without complaint a life, not of uniform delight, but uniform hardship.'

'Those men,' answered Imlac, 'are less wretched in their silent convent than the Abyssinian princes in their prison of pleasure. Whatever is done by the monks is incited by an adequate and reasonable motive. Their labour supplies them with necessaries; it therefore cannot be omitted, and is certainly rewarded. Their devotion prepares them for another state, and reminds them of its approach, while it fits them for it. Their time is regularly distributed;

one duty succeeds another, so that they are not left open to the distraction of unguided choice, nor lost in the shades of listless inactivity. There is a certain task to be performed at an appropriated hour; and their toils are cheerful, because they consider them as acts of piety by which they are always advancing towards endless felicity.'

'Do you think,' said Nekayah, 'that the monastic rule is a more holy and less imperfect state than any other? May not he equally hope for future happiness who converses openly with mankind, who succours the distressed by his charity, instructs the ignorant by his learning, and contributes by his industry to the general system of life; even though he should omit some of the mortifications which are practised in the cloister, and allow himself such harmless delights as his condition may place within his reach?'

'This,' said Imlac, 'is a question which has long divided the wise, and perplexed the good. I am afraid to decide on either part. He that lives well in the world is better than he that lives well in a monastery. But, perhaps, every one is not able to stem the temptations of public life; and, if he cannot conquer, he may properly retreat. Some have little power to do good, and have likewise little strength to resist evil. Many are weary of their conflicts with adversity, and are willing to eject those passions which have long busied them in vain. And many are dismissed by age and diseases from the more laborious duties of society. In monasteries the weak and timorous may be happily sheltered, the weary may repose, and the penitent may meditate. Those retreats of prayer and contemplation have something so congenial to the mind of man that, perhaps, there is scarcely one that does not purpose to close his life in pious abstraction with a few associates serious as himself.'

'Such,' said Pekuah, 'has often been my wish, and I have heard the princess declare that she should not willingly die in a crowd.'

'The liberty of using harmless pleasures,' proceeded Imlac, 'will not be disputed; but it is still to be examined what pleasures are harmless. The evil of any pleasure that Nekayah can image is not in the act itself, but in its consequences. Pleasure, in itself harmless, may become mischievous, by endearing to us a state which we know to be transient and probatory, and withdrawing our thoughts from that of which every hour brings us nearer to the beginning, and of which no length of time will bring us to the end. Mortification is not virtuous in itself, nor has any other use but that it disengages us from the allurements of sense. In the state of future perfection to which we all aspire, there will be pleasure without danger, and security without restraint.'

The princess was silent, and Rasselas, turning to the astronomer, asked him whether he could not delay her retreat by showing her something which she had not seen before.

'Your curiosity,' said the sage, 'has been so general, and your pursuit of knowledge so vigorous, that novelties are not now very easily to be found: but what you can no longer procure from the living may be given by the dead. Among the wonders of this country are the catacombs, or the ancient repositories in which the bodies of the earliest generations were lodged, and where, by the virtue of the gums which embalmed them, they yet remain without corruption.'

'I know not,' said Rasselas, 'what pleasure the sight of the catacombs can afford; but, since nothing else is offered, I am resolved to view them, and shall place this with many other things which I have done because I would do something.'

They hired a guard of horsemen, and the next day visited the catacombs. When they were about to descend into the sepulchral caves, 'Pekuah,' said the princess, 'we are now again invading the habitations of the dead; I know that you will stay behind; let me find you safe when I return.' 'No, I will not be left,' answered Pekuah; 'I will go down between you and the prince.'

They then all descended, and roved with wonder through the labyrinth of subterraneous passages, where the bodies were laid in rows on either side.

XLVIII. *Imlac Discourses on the Nature of the Soul°*

'What reason,' said the prince, 'can be given why the Egyptians should thus expensively preserve those carcasses which some nations consume with fire, others lay to mingle with the earth, and all agree to remove from their sight, as soon as decent rites can be performed?'

'The original of ancient customs,' said Imlac, 'is commonly unknown; for the practice often continues when the cause has ceased; and concerning superstitious ceremonies it is vain to conjecture; for what reason did not dictate reason cannot explain. I have long believed that the practice of embalming arose only from tenderness to the remains of relations or friends, and to this opinion I am more inclined because it seems impossible that this care should have been general: had all the dead been embalmed, their repositories must in time have been more spacious than the dwellings of the living. I suppose only the rich or honourable were secured from corruption, and the rest left to the course of nature.

'But it is commonly supposed that the Egyptians believed the soul to live as long as the body continued undissolved, and therefore tried this method of eluding death.'

'Could the wise Egyptians,' said Nekayah, 'think so grossly of the soul? If the soul could once survive its separation, what could it afterwards receive or suffer from the body?'

'The Egyptians would doubtless think erroneously,' said the astronomer, 'in the darkness of heathenism, and the first dawn of philosophy. The nature of the soul is still disputed amidst all our opportunities of clearer knowledge: some yet say that it may be material who, nevertheless, believe it to be immortal.'

'Some,' answered Imlac, 'have indeed said that the soul is material, but I can scarcely believe that any man has thought it who knew how to think; for all the conclusions of reason enforce the immateriality of mind, and all the notices of sense and investigations of science concur to prove the unconsciousness of matter.

'It was never supposed that cogitation is inherent in matter, or that every particle is a thinking being. Yet, if any part of matter be devoid of thought, what part can we suppose to think? Matter can differ from matter only in form, density, bulk, motion, and direction of motion: to which of these, however varied or combined, can consciousness be annexed? To be round or square, to be solid or fluid, to be great or little, to be moved slowly or swiftly one way or another, are modes of material existence, all equally alien from the nature of cogitation. If matter be once without thought it can only be made to think by some new modification, but all the modifications which it can admit are equally unconnected with cogitative powers.'

'But the materialists,' said the astronomer, 'urge that matter may have qualities with which we are unacquainted.'

'He who will determine,' returned Imlac, 'against that which he knows because there may be something which he knows not; he that can set hypothetical possibility against acknowledged certainty is not to be admitted among reasonable beings. All that we know of matter is that matter is inert, senseless and lifeless; and if this conviction cannot be opposed but by referring us to something that we know not, we have all the evidence that human intellect can admit. If that which is known may be overruled by that which is unknown, no being not omniscient can arrive at certainty.'

'Yet let us not,' said the astronomer, 'too arrogantly limit the Creator's power.'

'It is no limitation of omnipotence,' replied the poet, 'to suppose that one thing is not consistent with another, that the same proposition cannot be at once true and false, that the same number cannot be even and odd, that cogitation cannot be conferred on that which is created incapable of cogitation.'

'I know not,' said Nekayah, 'any great use of this question. Does that immateriality, which, in my opinion, you have sufficiently proved, necessarily include eternal duration?'

'Of immateriality,' said Imlac, 'our ideas are negative, and therefore obscure. Immateriality seems to imply a natural power of perpetual duration as a consequence of exemption from all causes of decay: whatever perishes is destroyed by the solution of its contexture, and separation of its parts; nor can we conceive how that which has no parts, and therefore admits no solution, can be naturally corrupted or impaired.'

'I know not,' said Rasselas, 'how to conceive any thing without extension: what is extended must have parts, and you allow that whatever has parts may be destroyed.'

'Consider your own conceptions,' replied Imlac, 'and the difficulty will be less. You will find substance without extension. An ideal form is no less real than material bulk: yet an ideal form has no extension. It is no less certain, when you think on a pyramid, that your mind possesses the idea of a pyramid, than that the pyramid itself is standing. What space does the idea of a pyramid occupy more than the idea of a grain of corn? Or how can either idea suffer laceration? As is the effect such is the cause; as thought is, such is the power that thinks; a power impassive and indiscerptible.'

'But the Being,' said Nekayah, 'whom I fear to name, the Being which made the soul, can destroy it.'

'He, surely, can destroy it,' answered Imlac, 'since, however unperishable, it receives from a superior nature its power of duration. That it will not perish by any inherent cause of decay, or principle of corruption, may be shown by philosophy; but philosophy can tell no more. That it will not be annihilated by him that made it we must humbly learn from higher authority.'

The whole assembly stood a while silent and collected. 'Let us return,' said Rasselas, 'from this scene of mortality. How gloomy would be these mansions of the dead to him who did not know that he shall never die; that what now acts shall continue its agency, and what now thinks shall think on for ever. Those that lie here stretched before us, the wise and the powerful of ancient times, warn us to remember the shortness of our present state; they were, perhaps, snatched away while they were busy, like us, in the choice of life.'

'To me,' said the princess, 'the choice of life is become less important; I hope hereafter to think only on the choice of eternity.'

They then hastened out of the caverns, and, under the protection of their guard, returned to Cairo.

XLIX. *The Conclusion, in Which Nothing Is Concluded*

It was now the time of the inundation of the Nile: a few days after their visit to the catacombs, the river began to rise.

They were confined to their house. The whole region being under water gave them no invitation to any excursions, and, being well supplied with materials for talk, they diverted themselves with comparisons of the different forms of life which they had observed, and with various schemes of happiness which each of them had formed.

Pekuah was never so much charmed with any place as the convent of St Anthony, where the Arab restored her to the princess, and wished only to fill it with pious maidens, and to be made prioress of the order: she was weary of expectation and disgust, and would gladly be fixed in some unvariable state.

The princess thought that of all sublunary° things, knowledge was the best. She desired first to learn all sciences, and then purposed to found a college of learned women, in which she would preside, that, by conversing with the old, and educating the young, she might divide her time between the acquisition and communication of wisdom, and raise up for the next age models of prudence, and patterns of piety.

The prince desired a little kingdom, in which he might administer justice in his own person, and see all the parts of government with his own eyes; but he could never fix the limits of his dominion, and was always adding to the number of his subjects.

Imlac and the astronomer were contented to be driven along the stream of life without directing their course to any particular port.

Of these wishes that they had formed they well knew that none could be obtained. They deliberated a while what was to be done, and resolved, when the inundation should cease, to return to Abyssinia.°

The Plays of William Shakespeare

PREFACE°

That praises are without reason lavished on the dead, and that the honours due only to excellence are paid to antiquity, is a complaint likely to be always continued by those who, being able to add nothing to truth, hope for eminence from the heresies of paradox; or those who, being forced by disappointment upon consolatory expedients, are willing to hope from posterity what the present age refuses, and flatter themselves that the regard which is yet denied by envy will be at last bestowed by time.

Antiquity, like every other quality that attracts the notice of mankind, has undoubtedly votaries that reverence it, not from reason, but from prejudice. Some seem to admire indiscriminately whatever has been long preserved, without considering that time has sometimes co-operated with chance; all perhaps are more willing to honour past than present excellence; and the mind contemplates genius through the shades of age, as the eye surveys the sun through artificial opacity. The great contention of criticism is to find the faults of the moderns, and the beauties of the ancients. While an author is yet living we estimate his powers by his worst performance, and when he is dead we rate them by his best.

To works, however, of which the excellence is not absolute and definite, but gradual and comparative; to works not raised upon principles demonstrative and scientific, but appealing wholly to observation and experience, no other test can be applied than length of duration and continuance of esteem. What mankind have long possessed they have often examined and compared, and if they persist to value the possession, it is because frequent comparisons have confirmed opinion in its favour. As among the works of nature no man can properly call a river deep or a mountain high without the knowledge of many mountains and many rivers; so in the productions of genius, nothing can be styled excellent till it has been compared with other works of the same kind. Demonstration immediately displays its power, and has nothing to hope or fear from the flux of years; but works tentative and experimental must be estimated by their proportion to the general and collective ability of man as it is discovered in a long succession of endeavours. Of the first building that was raised, it might be with certainty determined that it was round or square, but whether it was spacious or lofty must have been referred to time. The Pythagorean scale of numbers was at once discovered to be perfect; but the poems of Homer we yet know not to transcend the common limits of human intelligence but by remarking that nation after nation, and century after century, has been able to do little more than transpose his incidents, new name his characters, and paraphrase his sentiments.

The reverence due to writings that have long subsisted arises therefore not from any credulous confidence in the superior wisdom of past ages, or gloomy persuasion of the degeneracy of mankind, but is the consequence of acknowledged and indubitable positions, that what has been longest known has been most considered, and what is most considered is best understood.

The poet of whose works I have undertaken the revision may now begin to assume the dignity of an ancient, and claim the privilege of established fame and prescriptive veneration. He has long outlived his century, the term commonly fixed as the test of literary merit. Whatever advantages he might once derive from personal allusions, local customs, or temporary opinions, have for many years been lost; and every topic of merriment or motive of sorrow which the modes of artificial life afforded him now only obscure the scenes which they once illuminated. The effects of favour and competition are at an end; the tradition of his friendships and his enmities has perished; his works support no opinion with arguments, nor supply any faction with invectives; they can neither indulge vanity nor gratify malignity, but are read without any other reason than the desire of pleasure, and are therefore praised only as pleasure is obtained; yet, thus unassisted by interest or passion, they have passed through variations of taste and changes of manners, and, as they devolved from one generation to another, have received new honours at every transmission.

But because human judgment, though it be gradually gaining upon certainty, never becomes infallible; and approbation, though long continued, may yet be only the approbation of prejudice or fashion; it is proper to inquire by what peculiarities of excellence Shakespeare has gained and kept the favour of his countrymen.

Nothing can please many, and please long, but just representations of general nature. Particular manners can be known to few, and therefore few only can judge how nearly they are copied. The irregular combinations of fanciful invention may delight a while, by that novelty of which the common satiety of life sends us all in quest; but the pleasures of sudden wonder are soon exhausted, and the mind can only repose on the stability of truth.

Shakespeare is above all writers, at least above all modern writers, the poet of nature; the poet that holds up to his readers a faithful mirror° of manners and of life. His characters are not modified by the customs of particular places, unpractised by the rest of the world; by the peculiarities of studies or professions, which can operate but upon small numbers; or by the accidents of transient fashions or temporary opinions: they are the genuine progeny of common humanity, such as the world will always supply, and observation will always find. His persons act and speak by the influence of those general passions and principles by which all minds are agitated, and the whole system of life is continued in motion. In the writings of other poets a character is too often an individual; in those of Shakespeare it is commonly a species.

It is from this wide extension of design that so much instruction is derived. It is this which fills the plays of Shakespeare with practical axioms and domestic wisdom. It was said of Euripides that every verse was a precept; and it may be said of Shakespeare that from his works may be collected a system of civil and economical prudence. Yet his real power is not shown in the splendour of particular passages, but by the progress of his fable, and the tenor of his dialogue; and he that tries to recommend him by select quotations will succeed like the pedant in Hierocles, who, when he offered his house to sale, carried a brick in his pocket as a specimen.

It will not easily be imagined how much Shakespeare excels in accommodating his sentiments to real life but by comparing him with other authors. It was observed of the ancient schools of declamation that the more diligently they were frequented, the more was the student disqualified for the world, because he found nothing there which he should ever meet in any other place. The same remark may be applied to every stage but that of Shakespeare. The theatre, when it is under any other direction, is peopled by such characters as were never seen, conversing in a language which was never heard, upon topics which will never arise in the commerce of mankind. But the dialogue of this author is often so evidently determined by the incident which produces it, and is pursued with so much ease and simplicity, that it seems scarcely to claim the merit of fiction, but to have been gleaned by diligent selection out of common conversation, and common occurrences.

Upon every other stage the universal agent is love, by whose power all good and evil is distributed, and every action quickened or retarded. To bring a lover, a lady, and a rival into the fable; to entangle them in contradictory obligations, perplex them with oppositions of interest, and harass them with violence of desires inconsistent with each other; to make them meet in rapture and part in agony; to fill their mouths with hyperbolical joy and outrageous sorrow; to distress them as nothing human ever was distressed; to deliver them as nothing human ever was delivered is the business of a modern dramatist. For this, probability is violated, life is misrepresented, and language is depraved. But love is only one of many passions, and as it has no great influence upon the sum of life, it has little operation in the dramas of a poet who caught his ideas from the living world, and exhibited only what he saw before him. He knew that any other passion, as it was regular or exorbitant, was a cause of happiness or calamity.

Characters thus ample and general were not easily discriminated and preserved, yet perhaps no poet ever kept his personages more distinct from each other. I will not say with Pope that every speech may be assigned to the proper speaker, because many speeches there are which have nothing characteristical; but perhaps, though some may be equally adapted to every person, it will be difficult to find any that can be properly transferred from the present possessor to another claimant. The choice is right, when there is reason for choice.

Other dramatists can only gain attention by hyperbolical or aggravated characters, by fabulous and unexampled excellence or depravity, as the writers of barbarous romances invigorated the reader by a giant and a dwarf; and he that should form his expectations of human affairs from the play, or from the tale, would be equally deceived. Shakespeare has no heroes; his scenes are occupied only by men, who act and speak as the reader thinks that he should himself have spoken or acted on the same occasion. Even where the agency is supernatural the dialogue is level with life. Other writers disguise the most natural passions and most frequent incidents; so that he who contemplates them in the book will not know them in the world: Shakespeare approximates the remote,° and familiarizes the wonderful; the event which he represents will not happen, but if it were possible, its effects would probably be such as he has assigned; and it may be said that he has not only shown human nature as it acts in real exigences, but as it would be found in trials to which it cannot be exposed.

This therefore is the praise of Shakespeare, that his drama is the mirror of life; that he who has mazed his imagination, in following the phantoms which other writers raise up before him, may here be cured of his delirious ecstasies, by reading human sentiments in human language; by scenes from which a hermit may estimate the transactions of the world, and a confessor predict the progress of the passions.

His adherence to general nature has exposed him to the censure of critics, who form their judgments upon narrower principles. Dennis and Rhymer° think his Romans not sufficiently Roman; and Voltaire censures his kings as not completely royal. Dennis is offended that Menenius, a senator of Rome, should play the buffoon; and Voltaire perhaps thinks decency violated when the Danish usurper is represented as a drunkard. But Shakespeare always makes nature predominate over accident; and if he preserves the essential character, is not very careful of distinctions superinduced and adventitious. His story requires Romans or kings, but he thinks only on men. He knew that Rome, like every other city, had men of all dispositions; and wanting a buffoon, he went into the senate-house for that which the senate-house would certainly have afforded him. He was inclined to show an usurper and a murderer not only odious but despicable; he therefore added drunkenness to his other qualities, knowing that kings love wine like other men, and that wine exerts its natural power upon kings. These are the petty cavils of petty minds;° a poet overlooks the casual distinction of country and condition, as a painter, satisfied with the figure, neglects the drapery.

The censure which he has incurred by mixing comic and tragic scenes, as it extends to all his works, deserves more consideration. Let the fact be first stated, and then examined.

Shakespeare's plays are not in the rigorous and critical sense either tragedies or comedies, but compositions of a distinct kind; exhibiting the real state of sublunary nature, which partakes of good and evil, joy and sorrow, mingled with endless variety of proportion and innumerable modes of combination; and expressing the course of the world, in which the loss of one is the gain of another; in which, at the same time, the reveller is hasting to his wine, and the mourner burying his friend; in which the malignity of one is sometimes defeated by the frolic of another; and many mischiefs and many benefits are done and hindered without design.

Out of this chaos of mingled purposes and casualties the ancient poets, according to the laws which custom had prescribed, selected some the crimes of men, and some their absurdities; some the momentous vicissitudes of life, and some the lighter occurrences; some the terror of distress, and some the gaieties of prosperity. Thus rose the two modes of imitation known by the names of tragedy and comedy, compositions intended to promote different ends by contrary means, and considered as so little allied that I do not recollect among the Greeks or Romans a single writer who attempted both.

Shakespeare has united the powers of exciting laughter and sorrow not only in one mind but in one composition. Almost all his plays are divided between serious and ludicrous characters, and, in the successive evolutions of the design, sometimes produce seriousness and sorrow, and sometimes levity and laughter.

That this is a practice contrary to the rules of criticism° will be readily allowed; but there is always an appeal open from criticism to nature. The end of writing is to instruct; the end of poetry is to instruct by pleasing.° That the mingled drama may convey all the instruction of tragedy or comedy cannot be denied, because it includes both in its alternations of exhibition, and approaches nearer than either to the appearance of life, by showing how great machinations and slender designs may promote or obviate one another, and the high and the low co-operate in the general system by unavoidable concatenation.

It is objected that by this change of scenes the passions are interrupted in their progression, and that the principal event, being not advanced by a due graduation of preparatory incidents, wants at last the power to move, which constitutes the perfection of dramatic poetry. This reasoning is so specious that it is received as true even by those who in daily experience feel it to be false. The interchanges of mingled scenes seldom fail to produce the intended vicissitudes of passion. Fiction cannot move so much but that the attention may be easily transferred; and though it must be allowed that pleasing melancholy be sometimes interrupted by unwelcome levity, yet let it be considered likewise that melancholy is often not pleasing, and that the disturbance of one man may be the relief of another; that different auditors have different habitudes; and that, upon the whole, all pleasure consists in variety.

The players, who in their edition divided our author's works into comedies, histories, and tragedies, seem not to have distinguished the three kinds by any very exact or definite ideas.

An action which ended happily to the principal persons, however serious or distressful through its intermediate incidents, in their opinion constituted a comedy. This idea of a comedy continued long amongst us, and plays were written which, by changing the catastrophe, were tragedies today and comedies tomorrow.

Tragedy was not in those times a poem of more general dignity or elevation than comedy; it required only a calamitous conclusion, with which the common criticism of that age was satisfied, whatever lighter pleasure it afforded in its progress.

History was a series of actions, with no other than chronological succession, independent on each other, and without any tendency to introduce or regulate the conclusion. It is not always very nicely distinguished from tragedy. There is not much nearer approach to unity of action in the tragedy of *Antony and Cleopatra* than in the history of *Richard the Second*. But a history might be continued through many plays; as it had no plan, it had no limits.

Through all these denominations of the drama, Shakespeare's mode of composition is the same; an interchange of seriousness and merriment, by which the mind is softened at one time, and exhilarated at another. But whatever be his purpose, whether to gladden or depress, or to conduct the story, without vehemence or emotion, through tracts of easy and familiar dialogue, he never fails to attain his purpose; as he commands us, we laugh or mourn, or sit silent with quiet expectation, in tranquillity without indifference.

When Shakespeare's plan is understood, most of the criticisms of Rhymer and Voltaire vanish away. The play of *Hamlet* is opened, without impropriety, by two sentinels; Iago bellows at Brabantio's window, without injury to the scheme of the play, though in terms which a modern audience would not easily endure; the character of Polonius is seasonable and useful; and the grave–diggers themselves may be heard with applause.

Shakespeare engaged in dramatic poetry with the world open before him; the rules of the ancients were yet known to few; the public judgment was unformed; he had no example of such fame as might force him upon imitation, nor critics of such authority as might restrain his extravagance. He therefore indulged his natural disposition, and his disposition, as Rhymer has remarked, led him to comedy. In tragedy he often writes with great appearance of toil and study what is written at last with little felicity; but in his comic scenes, he seems to produce without labour what no labour can improve. In tragedy he is always struggling after some occasion to be comic, but in comedy he seems to repose, or to luxuriate, as in a mode of thinking congenial to his nature. In his tragic scenes there is always something wanting, but his comedy often surpasses expectation or desire. His comedy pleases by the thoughts and the language, and his tragedy for the greater part by incident and action. His tragedy seems to be skill, his comedy to be instinct.

The force of his comic scenes has suffered little diminution from the changes made by a century and a half in manners or in words. As his personages act upon principles arising from genuine passion, very little modified by particular forms, their pleasures and vexations are communicable to all times and to all places; they are natural, and therefore durable; the adventitious peculiarities of personal habits are only superficial dyes, bright and pleasing for a little while, yet soon fading to a dim tint, without any remains of former lustre; but the discriminations of true passion are the colours of nature; they pervade the whole mass, and can only perish with the body that exhibits them. The accidental compositions of heterogeneous modes are dissolved by the chance which combined them; but the uniform simplicity of primitive qualities neither admits increase, nor suffers decay. The sand heaped by one flood is scattered by another, but the rock always continues in its place. The stream of time, which is continually washing the dissoluble fabrics of other poets, passes without injury by the adamant of Shakespeare.

If there be, what I believe there is, in every nation, a style which never becomes obsolete, a certain mode of phraseology so consonant and congenial to the analogy and principles of its respective language as to remain settled and unaltered; this style is probably to be sought in the common intercourse of life, among those who speak only to be understood, without ambition of elegance. The polite are always catching modish innovations, and the learned depart from established forms of speech, in hope of finding or making better; those who wish for distinction forsake the vulgar when the vulgar is right; but there is a conversation above grossness and below refinement, where propriety resides, and where this poet seems to have gathered his comic dialogue. He is therefore more agreeable to the ears of the present age than any other author equally remote, and among his other excellencies deserves to be studied as one of the original masters of our language.

These observations are to be considered not as unexceptionably constant, but as containing general and predominant truth. Shakespeare's familiar dialogue is affirmed to be smooth and clear, yet not wholly without ruggedness or difficulty, as a country may be eminently fruitful, though it has spots unfit for cultivation. His characters are praised as natural, though their sentiments are sometimes forced, and their actions improbable, as the earth upon the whole is spherical, though its surface is varied with protuberances and cavities.

Shakespeare with his excellencies has likewise faults, and faults sufficient to obscure and overwhelm any other merit. I shall show them in the proportion in which they appear to me, without envious malignity or superstitious veneration. No question can be more innocently discussed than a dead poet's pretensions to renown; and little regard is due to that bigotry which sets candour higher than truth.

His first defect is that to which may be imputed most of the evil in books or in men. He sacrifices virtue to convenience, and is so much more careful to please than to instruct that he seems to write without any moral purpose. From his writings indeed a system of social duty may be selected, for he that thinks reasonably must think morally; but his precepts and axioms drop casually from him; he makes no just distribution of good or evil, nor is always careful to show in the virtuous a disapprobation of the wicked;° he carries his persons indifferently through right and wrong, and at the close dismisses them without further care, and leaves their examples to operate by chance. This fault the barbarity of his age cannot extenuate; for it is always a writer's duty to make the world better, and justice is a virtue independent on time or place.

The plots are often so loosely formed that a very slight consideration may improve them, and so carelessly pursued that he seems not always fully to comprehend his own design. He omits opportunities of instructing or delighting which the train of his story seems to force upon him, and apparently rejects those exhibitions which would be more affecting, for the sake of those which are more easy.

It may be observed that in many of his plays the latter part is evidently neglected. When he found himself near the end of his work, and in view of his reward, he shortened the labour, to snatch the profit. He therefore remits his efforts where he should most vigorously exert them, and his catastrophe is improbably produced or imperfectly represented.

He had no regard to distinction of time or place, but gives to one age or nation, without scruple, the customs, institutions, and opinions of another, at the expense not only of likelihood, but of possibility. These faults Pope has endeavoured, with more zeal than judgment, to transfer to his imagined interpolators. We need not wonder to find Hector quoting Aristotle, when we see the loves of Theseus and Hippolyta combined with the Gothic mythology of fairies. Shakespeare, indeed, was not the only violator of chronology, for in the same age Sidney, who wanted not the advantages of learning, has, in his *Arcadia*, confounded the pastoral with the feudal times, the days of innocence, quiet, and security, with those of turbulence, violence, and adventure.

In his comic scenes he is seldom very successful when he engages his characters in reciprocations of smartness and contests of sarcasm; their jests are commonly gross, and their pleasantry licentious; neither his gentlemen nor his ladies have much delicacy, nor are sufficiently distinguished from his clowns by any appearance of refined manners. Whether he represented the real conversation of his time is not easy to determine; the reign of Elizabeth is commonly supposed to have been a time of stateliness, formality, and reserve, yet perhaps the relaxations of that severity were not very elegant. There must, however, have been always some modes of gaiety preferable to others, and a writer ought to choose the best.

In tragedy his performance seems constantly to be worse as his labour is more. The effusions of passion which exigence forces out are for the most part striking and energetic; but whenever he solicits his invention, or strains his faculties, the offspring of his throes is tumour, meanness, tediousness, and obscurity.

In narration he affects a disproportionate pomp of diction and a wearisome train of circumlocution, and tells the incident imperfectly in many words which might have been more plainly delivered in few. Narration in dramatic poetry is naturally tedious as it is unanimated and inactive, and obstructs the progress of the action; it should therefore always be rapid, and enlivened by frequent interruption. Shakespeare found it an encumbrance, and instead of lightening it by brevity, endeavoured to recommend it by dignity and splendour.

His declamations or set speeches are commonly cold and weak, for his power was the power of nature; when he endeavoured, like other tragic writers, to catch opportunities of amplification, and instead of inquiring what the occasion demanded, to show how much his stores of knowledge could supply, he seldom escapes without the pity or resentment of his reader.

It is incident to him to be now and then entangled with an unwieldy sentiment which he cannot well express, and will not reject; he struggles with it a while, and if it continues stubborn, comprises it in words such as occur, and leaves it to be disentangled and evolved by those who have more leisure to bestow upon it.

Not that always where the language is intricate the thought is subtle, or the image always great where the line is bulky; the equality of words to things is very often neglected, and trivial sentiments and vulgar ideas disappoint the attention to which they are recommended by sonorous epithets and swelling figures.

But the admirers of this great poet have most reason to complain when he approaches nearest to his highest excellence, and seems fully resolved to sink them in dejection, and mollify them with tender emotions by the fall of greatness, the danger of innocence, or the crosses of love. What he does best, he soon ceases to do. He is not long soft and pathetic without some idle conceit, or contemptible equivocation. He no sooner begins to move than he counteracts himself; and terror and pity, as they are rising in the mind, are checked and blasted by sudden frigidity.

A quibble° is to Shakespeare what luminous vapours are to the traveller; he follows it at all adventures, it is sure to lead him out of his way, and sure to engulf him in the mire. It has some malignant power over his mind, and its fascinations are irresistible. Whatever be the dignity or profundity of his disquisition, whether he be enlarging knowledge or exalting affection, whether he be amusing attention with incidents, or enchaining it in suspense, let but a quibble spring up before him, and he leaves his work unfinished. A quibble is the golden apple for which he will always turn aside from his career, or stoop from his elevation. A quibble, poor and barren as it is, gave him such delight that he was content to purchase it by the sacrifice of reason, propriety and truth. A quibble was to him the fatal Cleopatra for which he lost the world, and was content to lose it.

It will be thought strange that, in enumerating the defects of this writer, I have not yet mentioned his neglect of the unities; his violation of those laws which have been instituted and established by the joint authority of poets and of critics.

For his other deviations from the art of writing, I resign him to critical justice, without making any other demand in his favour than that which must be indulged to all human excellence; that his virtues be rated with his failings. But from the censure which this irregularity may bring upon him, I shall, with due reverence to that learning which I must oppose, adventure to try how I can defend him.

His histories, being neither tragedies nor comedies, are not subject to any of their laws; nothing more is necessary to all the praise which they expect than that the changes of action be so prepared as to be understood, that the incidents be various and affecting, and the characters consistent, natural, and distinct. No other unity is intended, and therefore none is to be sought.

In his other works he has well enough preserved the unity of action. He has not, indeed, an intrigue regularly perplexed and regularly unravelled; he does not endeavour to hide his design only to discover it, for this is seldom the order of real events, and Shakespeare is the poet of nature. But his plan has commonly what Aristotle requires, a beginning, a middle, and an end; one event is concatenated with another, and the conclusion follows by easy consequence. There are perhaps some incidents that might be spared, as in other poets there is much talk that only fills up time upon the stage; but the general system makes gradual advances, and the end of the play is the end of expectation.

To the unities of time and place he has shown no regard, and perhaps a nearer view of the principles on which they stand will diminish their value, and withdraw from them the veneration which, from the time of Corneille,° they have very generally received, by discovering that they have given more trouble to the poet than pleasure to the auditor.

The necessity of observing the unities of time and place arises from the supposed necessity of making the drama credible. The critics hold it impossible that an action of months or years can be possibly believed to pass in three hours; or that the spectator can suppose himself to sit in the theatre, while ambassadors go and return between distant kings, while armies are levied and towns besieged, while an exile wanders and returns, or till he whom they saw courting his mistress shall lament the untimely fall of his son. The mind revolts from evident falsehood, and fiction loses its force when it departs from the resemblance of reality.

From the narrow limitation of time necessarily arises the contraction of place. The spectator who knows that he saw the first act at Alexandria cannot suppose that he sees the next at Rome, at a distance to which not the dragons of Medea could, in so short a time, have transported him; he knows with certainty that he has not changed his place; and he knows that place cannot change itself; that what was a house cannot become a plain; that what was Thebes can never be Persepolis.

Such is the triumphant language with which a critic exults over the misery of an irregular poet, and exults commonly without resistance or reply. It is time therefore to tell him, by the authority of Shakespeare, that he assumes as an unquestionable principle a position which, while his breath is forming it into words, his understanding pronounces to be false. It is false that any representation is mistaken for reality; that any dramatic fable in its materiality was ever credible, or, for a single moment, was ever credited.

The objection arising from the impossibility of passing the first hour at Alexandria, and the next at Rome, supposes that when the play opens the spectator really imagines himself at Alexandria, and believes that his walk to the theatre has been a voyage to Egypt, and that he lives in the days of Antony and Cleopatra. Surely he that imagines this may imagine more. He that can take the stage at one time for the palace of the Ptolemies may take it in half an hour for the promontory of Actium. Delusion, if delusion be admitted, has no certain limitation; if the spectator can be once persuaded that his old acquaintance are Alexander and Caesar, that a room illuminated with candles is the plain of Pharsalia, or the bank of Granicus, he is in a state of elevation above the reach of reason, or of truth, and from the heights of empyrean poetry, may despise the circumscriptions of terrestrial nature. There is no reason why a mind thus wandering in ecstasy should count the clock, or why an hour should not be a century in that calenture of the brains that can make the stage a field.

The truth is that the spectators are always in their senses, and know, from the first act to the last, that the stage is only a stage, and that the players are only players. They come to hear a certain number of lines recited with just gesture and elegant modulation. The lines relate to some action, and an action must be in some place; but the different actions that complete a story may be in places very remote from each other; and where is the absurdity of allowing that space to represent first Athens, and then Sicily, which was always known to be neither Sicily nor Athens, but a modern theatre?

By supposition, as place is introduced, time may be extended; the time required by the fable elapses for the most part between the acts; for, of so much of the action as is represented, the real and poetical duration is the same. If, in the first act, preparations for war against Mithridates are represented to be made in Rome, the event of the war may, without absurdity, be represented, in the catastrophe, as happening in Pontus; we know that there is neither war, nor preparation for war; we know that we are neither in Rome nor Pontus; that neither Mithridates nor Lucullus are before us. The drama exhibits successive imitations of successive actions, and why may not the second imitation represent an action that happened years after the first, if it be so connected with it that nothing but time can be supposed to intervene? Time is, of all modes of existence, most obsequious to the imagination; a lapse of years is as easily conceived as a passage of hours. In contemplation we easily contract the time of real actions, and therefore willingly permit it to be contracted when we only see their imitation.

It will be asked how the drama moves, if it is not credited. It is credited with all the credit due to a drama. It is credited, whenever it moves, as a just picture of a real original; as representing to the auditor what he would himself feel if he were to do or suffer what is there feigned to be suffered or to be done. The reflection that strikes the heart is not that the evils before us are real evils, but that they are evils to which we ourselves may be exposed. If there be any fallacy, it is not that we fancy the players but that we fancy ourselves unhappy for a moment; but we rather lament the possibility than suppose the presence of misery, as a mother weeps over her babe when she remembers that death may take it from her. The delight of tragedy proceeds from our consciousness of fiction; if we thought murders and treasons real, they would please no more.

Imitations produce pain or pleasure, not because they are mistaken for realities, but because they bring realities to mind. When the imagination is recreated by a painted landscape, the trees are not supposed capable to give us shade, or the fountains coolness; but we consider how we should be pleased with such fountains playing beside us, and such woods waving over us. We are agitated in reading the history of Henry the Fifth, yet no man takes his book for the field of Agincourt. A dramatic exhibition is a book recited with concomitants that increase or diminish its effect. Familiar comedy is often more powerful on the theatre than in the page; imperial tragedy is always less. The humour of Petruchio may be heightened by grimace; but what voice or what gesture can hope to add dignity or force to the soliloquy of Cato?

A play read affects the mind like a play acted. It is therefore evident that the action is not supposed to be real, and it follows that between the acts a longer or shorter time may be allowed to pass, and that no more account of space or duration is to be taken by the auditor of a drama than by the reader of a narrative, before whom may pass in an hour the life of a hero, or the revolutions of an empire.

Whether Shakespeare knew the unities, and rejected them by design, or deviated from them by happy ignorance, it is, I think, impossible to decide, and useless to inquire. We may reasonably suppose that, when he rose to notice, he did not want the counsels and admonitions of scholars and critics, and that he at last deliberately persisted in a practice which he might have begun by chance. As nothing is essential to the fable but unity of action, and as the unities of time and place arise evidently from false assumptions, and, by circumscribing the extent of the drama, lessen its variety, I cannot think it much to be lamented that they were not known by him, or not observed. Nor, if such another poet could arise, should I very vehemently reproach him that his first act passed at Venice, and his next in Cyprus. Such violations of rules merely positive become the comprehensive genius of Shakespeare, and such censures are suitable to the minute and slender criticism of Voltaire:

> Non usque adeo permiscuit imis
> Longus summa dies, ut non, si voce Metelli
> Serventur leges, malint a Caesare tolli.°

Yet when I speak thus slightly of dramatic rules, I cannot but recollect how much wit and learning may be produced against me; before such authorities I am afraid to stand, not that I think the present question one of those that are to be decided by mere authority, but because it is to be suspected that these precepts have not been so easily received but for better reasons than I have yet been able to find. The result of my inquiries, in which it would be ludicrous to boast of impartiality, is that the unities of time and place are not essential to a just drama, that though they may sometimes conduce to pleasure, they are always to be sacrificed to the nobler beauties of variety and instruction; and that a play written with nice observation of critical rules is to be contemplated as an elaborate curiosity, as the product of superfluous and ostentatious art, by which is shown rather what is possible than what is necessary.

He that, without diminution of any other excellence, shall preserve all the unities unbroken deserves the like applause with the architect who shall display all the orders of architecture in a citadel without any deduction from its strength, but the principal beauty of a citadel is to exclude the enemy; and the greatest graces of a play are to copy nature and instruct life.

Perhaps what I have here not dogmatically but deliberately written may recall the principles of the drama to a new examination. I am almost frighted at my own temerity; and when I estimate the fame and the strength of those that maintain the contrary opinion am ready to sink down in reverential silence,° as Æneas withdrew from the defence of Troy, when he saw Neptune shaking the wall, and Juno heading the besiegers.

Those whom my arguments cannot persuade to give their approbation to the judgment of Shakespeare will easily, if they consider the condition of his life, make some allowance for his ignorance.

Every man's performances, to be rightly estimated, must be compared with the state of the age in which he lived, and with his own particular opportunities; and though to the reader a book be not worse or better for the circumstances of the author, yet as there is always a silent reference of human works to human abilities, and as the inquiry how far man may extend his designs, or how high he may rate his native force is of far greater dignity than in what rank we shall place any particular performance, curiosity is always busy to discover the instruments, as well as to survey the workmanship, to know how much is to be ascribed to original powers, and how much to casual and adventitious help. The palaces of Peru or Mexico were certainly mean and incommodious habitations, if compared to the houses of European monarchs; yet who could forbear to view them with astonishment who remembered that they were built without the use of iron?

The English nation, in the time of Shakespeare, was yet struggling to emerge from barbarity. The philology of Italy had been transplanted hither in the reign of Henry the Eighth; and the learned languages had been successfully cultivated by Lilly, Linacre, and More; by Pole, Cheke, and Gardiner; and afterwards by Smith, Clerk, Haddon, and Ascham. Greek was now taught to boys in the principal schools; and those who united elegance with learning read, with great diligence, the Italian and Spanish poets. But literature was yet confined to professed scholars, or to men and women of high rank. The public was gross and dark; and to be able to read and write was an accomplishment still valued for its rarity.

Nations, like individuals, have their infancy. A people newly awakened to literary curiosity, being yet unacquainted with the true state of things, knows not how to judge of that which is proposed as its resemblance. Whatever is remote from common appearances is always welcome to vulgar, as to childish credulity; and of a country unenlightened by learning, the whole people is the vulgar. The study of those who then aspired to plebeian learning was laid out upon adventures, giants, dragons, and enchantments. *The Death of Arthur* was the favourite volume.

The mind which has feasted on the luxurious wonders of fiction has no taste of the insipidity of truth. A play which imitated only the common occurrences of the world would, upon the admirers of *Palmerin* and *Guy of Warwick*, have made little impression; he that wrote for such an audience was under the necessity of looking round for strange events and fabulous transactions, and that incredibility by which maturer knowledge is offended was the chief recommendation of writings to unskilful curiosity.

Our author's plots are generally borrowed from novels, and it is reasonable to suppose that he chose the most popular, such as were read by many, and related by more; for his audience could not have followed him through the intricacies of the drama, had they not held the thread of the story in their hands.

The stories which we now find only in remoter authors were in his time accessible and familiar. The fable of *As You Like It*, which is supposed to be copied from Chaucer's *Gamelyn*, was a little pamphlet of those times; and old Mr Cibber remembered the tale of Hamlet in plain English prose, which the critics have now to seek in Saxo Grammaticus.

His English histories he took from English chronicles and English ballads; and as the ancient writers were made known to his countrymen by versions, they supplied him with new subjects; he dilated some of Plutarch's lives into plays, when they had been translated by North.

His plots, whether historical or fabulous, are always crowded with incidents, by which the attention of a rude people was more easily caught than by sentiment or argumentation; and such is the power of the marvellous even over those who despise it that every man finds his mind more strongly seized by the tragedies of Shakespeare than of any other writer; others please us by particular speeches, but he always makes us anxious for the event, and has perhaps excelled all but Homer in securing the first purpose of a writer, by exciting restless and unquenchable curiosity, and compelling him that reads his work to read it through.

The shows and bustle with which his plays abound have the same original. As knowledge advances, pleasure passes from the eye to the ear, but returns, as it declines, from the ear to the eye. Those to whom our author's labours were exhibited had more skill in pomps or processions than in poetical language, and perhaps wanted some visible and discriminated events as comments on the dialogue. He knew how he should most please; and whether his practice is more agreeable to nature, or whether his example has prejudiced the nation, we still find that on our stage something must be done as well as said, and inactive declamation is very coldly heard, however musical or elegant, passionate or sublime.

Voltaire expresses his wonder that our author's extravagances are endured by a nation which has seen the tragedy of *Cato*. Let him be answered that Addison speaks the language of poets, and Shakespeare of men. We find in *Cato* innumerable beauties which enamour us of its author, but we see nothing that acquaints us with human sentiments or human actions; we place it with the fairest and the noblest progeny which judgment propagates by conjunction with learning, but *Othello* is the vigorous and vivacious offspring of observation impregnated by genius. *Cato* affords a splendid exhibition of artificial and fictitious manners, and delivers just and noble sentiments, in diction easy, elevated, and harmonious, but its hopes and fears communicate no vibration to the heart; the composition refers us only to the writer; we pronounce the name of *Cato*, but we think on Addison.

The work of a correct and regular writer is a garden accurately formed and diligently planted, varied with shades, and scented with flowers; the composition of Shakespeare is a forest, in which oaks extend their branches, and pines tower in the air, interspersed sometimes with weeds and brambles, and sometimes giving shelter to myrtles and to roses; filling the eye with awful pomp, and gratifying the mind with endless diversity. Other poets display cabinets of precious rarities, minutely finished, wrought into shape, and polished into brightness. Shakespeare opens a mine which contains gold and diamonds in unexhaustible plenty, though clouded by incrustations, debased by impurities, and mingled with a mass of meaner minerals.

It has been much disputed, whether Shakespeare owed his excellence to his own native force, or whether he had the common helps of scholastic education, the precepts of critical science, and the examples of ancient authors.

There has always prevailed a tradition that Shakespeare wanted learning, that he had no regular education, nor much skill in the dead languages. Jonson, his friend, affirms that *he had small Latin, and less Greek*; who, besides that he had no imaginable temptation to falsehood, wrote at a time when the character and acquisitions of Shakespeare were known to multitudes. His evidence ought therefore to decide the controversy, unless some testimony of equal force could be opposed.

Some have imagined that they have discovered deep learning in many imitations of old writers; but the examples which I have known urged were drawn from books translated in his time; or were such easy coincidencies of thought as will happen to all who consider the same subjects; or such remarks on life or axioms of morality as float in conversation, and are transmitted through the world in proverbial sentences.

I have found it remarked that, in this important sentence, 'Go before, I'll follow', we read a translation of *I prae, sequar*. I have been told that when Caliban, after a pleasing dream, says, 'I cried to sleep again', the author imitates Anacreon, who had, like every other man, the same wish on the same occasion.

There are a few passages which may pass for imitations, but so few that the exception only confirms the rule; he obtained them from accidental quotations, or by oral communication, and as he used what he had, would have used more if he had obtained it.

The *Comedy of Errors* is confessedly taken from the *Menaechmi* of Plautus; from the only play of Plautus which was then in English. What can be more probable than that he who copied that would have copied more; but that those which were not translated were inaccessible?

Whether he knew the modern languages is uncertain. That his plays have some French scenes proves but little; he might easily procure them to be written, and probably, even though he had known the language in the common degree, he could not have written it without assistance. In the story of Romeo and Juliet he is observed to have followed the English translation where it deviates from the Italian; but this on the other part proves nothing against his knowledge of the original. He was to copy, not what he knew himself, but what was known to his audience.

It is most likely that he had learned Latin sufficiently to make him acquainted with construction, but that he never advanced to an easy perusal of the Roman authors. Concerning his skill in modern languages, I can find no sufficient ground of determination; but as no imitations of French or Italian authors have been discovered, though the Italian poetry was then high in esteem, I am inclined to believe that he read little more than English, and chose for his fables only such tales as he found translated.

That much knowledge is scattered over his works is very justly observed by Pope, but it is often such knowledge as books did not supply. He that will understand Shakespeare must not be content to study him in the closet, he must look for his meaning sometimes among the sports of the field, and sometimes among the manufactures of the shop.

There is however proof enough that he was a very diligent reader, nor was our language then so indigent of books but that he might very liberally indulge his curiosity without excursion into foreign literature. Many of the Roman authors were translated, and some of the Greek; the Reformation had filled the kingdom with theological learning; most of the topics of human disquisition had found English writers; and poetry had been cultivated, not only with diligence, but success. This was a stock of knowledge sufficient for a mind so capable of appropriating and improving it.

But the greater part of his excellence was the product of his own genius. He found the English stage in a state of the utmost rudeness; no essays either in tragedy or comedy had appeared from which it could be discovered to what degree of delight either one or other might be carried. Neither character nor dialogue were yet understood. Shakespeare may be truly said to have introduced them both amongst us, and in some of his happier scenes to have carried them both to the utmost height.

By what gradations of improvement he proceeded is not easily known; for the chronology of his works is yet unsettled. Rowe is of opinion that 'perhaps we are not to look for his beginning, like those of other writers, in his least perfect works; art had so little, and nature so large a share in what he did, that for aught I know,' says he, 'the performances of his youth, as they were the most vigorous, were the best.' But the power of nature is only the power of using to any certain purpose the materials which diligence procures, or opportunity supplies. Nature gives no man knowledge, and when images are collected by study and experience, can only assist in combining or applying them. Shakespeare, however favoured by nature, could impart only what he had learned; and as he must increase his ideas, like other mortals, by gradual acquisition, he, like them, grew wiser as he grew older, could display life better, as he knew it more, and instruct with more efficacy, as he was himself more amply instructed.

There is a vigilance of observation and accuracy of distinction which books and precepts cannot confer; from this almost all original and native excellence proceeds. Shakespeare must have looked upon mankind with perspicacity, in the highest degree curious and attentive. Other writers borrow their characters from preceding writers, and diversify them only by the accidental appendages of present manners; the dress is a little varied, but the body is the same. Our author had both matter and form to provide; for except the characters of Chaucer, to whom I think he is not much indebted, there were no writers in English, and perhaps not many in other modern languages, which showed life in its native colours.

The contest about the original benevolence or malignity of man had not yet commenced. Speculation had not yet attempted to analyse the mind, to trace the passions to their sources, to unfold the seminal principles of vice and virtue, or sound the depths of the heart for the motives of action. All those inquiries which from that time that human nature became the fashionable study have been made sometimes with nice discernment, but often with idle subtlety, were yet unattempted. The tales with which the infancy of learning was satisfied exhibited only the superficial appearances of action, related the events but omitted the causes, and were formed for such as delighted in wonders rather than in truth. Mankind was not then to be studied in the closet; he that would know the world was under the necessity of gleaning his own remarks, by mingling as he could in its business and amusements.

Boyle congratulated himself upon his high birth, because it favoured his curiosity, by facilitating his access. Shakespeare had no such advantage; he came to London a needy adventurer, and lived for a time by very mean employments. Many works of genius and learning have been performed in states of life that appear very little favourable to thought or to inquiry; so many that he who considers them is inclined to think that he sees enterprise and perseverance predominating over all external agency, and bidding help and hindrance vanish before them. The genius of Shakespeare was not to be depressed by the weight of poverty, nor limited by the narrow conversation to which men in want are inevitably condemned; the encumbrances of his fortune were shaken from his mind, *as dewdrops from a lion's mane.*°

Though he had so many difficulties to encounter, and so little assistance to surmount them, he has been able to obtain an exact knowledge of many modes of life, and many casts of native dispositions; to vary them with great multiplicity; to mark them by nice distinctions; and to show them in full view by proper combinations. In this part of his performances he had none to imitate, but has himself been imitated by all succeeding writers; and it may be doubted whether from all his successors more maxims of theoretical knowledge, or more rules of practical prudence, can be collected than he alone has given to his country.

Nor was his attention confined to the actions of men; he was an exact surveyor of the inanimate world; his descriptions have always some peculiarities, gathered by contemplating things as they really exist. It may be observed that the oldest poets of many nations preserve their reputation, and that the following generations of wit, after a short celebrity, sink into oblivion. The first, whoever they be, must take their sentiments and descriptions immediately from knowledge; the resemblance is therefore just, their descriptions are verified by every eye, and their sentiments acknowledged by every breast. Those whom their fame invites to the same studies copy partly them, and partly nature, till the books of one age gain such authority as to stand in the place of nature to another, and imitation, always deviating a little, becomes at last capricious and casual. Shakespeare, whether life or nature be his subject, shows plainly that he has seen with his own eyes; he gives the image which he receives, not weakened or distorted by the intervention of any other mind; the ignorant feel his representations to be just, and the learned see that they are complete.

Perhaps it would not be easy to find any author except Homer who invented so much as Shakespeare, who so much advanced the studies which he cultivated, or effused so much novelty upon his age or country. The form, the characters, the language, and the shows of the English drama are his. 'He seems,' says Dennis, 'to have been the very original of our English tragical harmony, that is, the harmony of blank verse, diversified often by disyllable and trisyllable terminations. For the diversity distinguishes it from heroic harmony, and by bringing it nearer to common use makes it more proper to gain attention, and more fit for action and dialogue. Such verse we make when we are writing prose; we make such verse in common conversation.'

I know not whether this praise is rigorously just. The disyllable termination, which the critic rightly appropriates to the drama, is to be found, though, I think, not in *Gorboduc*, which is confessedly before our author, yet in *Hieronimo*, of which the date is not certain, but which there is reason to believe at least as old as his earliest plays. This however is certain, that he is the first who taught either tragedy or comedy to please, there being no theatrical piece of any older writer of which the name is known except to antiquaries and collectors of books, which are sought because they are scarce, and would not have been scarce, had they been much esteemed.

To him we must ascribe the praise, unless Spenser may divide it with him, of having first discovered to how much smoothness and harmony the English language could be softened. He has speeches, perhaps sometimes scenes, which have all the delicacy of Rowe, without his effeminacy. He endeavours indeed commonly to strike by the force and vigour of his dialogue, but he never executes his purpose better than when he tries to soothe by softness.

Yet it must be at last confessed that as we owe every thing to him, he owes something to us; that, if much of his praise is paid by perception and judgment, much is likewise given by custom and veneration. We fix our eyes upon his graces, and turn them from his deformities, and endure in him what we should in another loathe or despise. If we endured without praising, respect for the father of our drama might excuse us; but I have seen, in the book of some modern critic, a collection of anomalies, which show that he has corrupted language by every mode of depravation, but which his admirer has accumulated as a monument of honour.

He has scenes of undoubted and perpetual excellence, but perhaps not one play which, if it were now exhibited as the work of a contemporary writer, would be heard to the conclusion. I am indeed far from thinking that his works were wrought to his own ideas of perfection; when they were such as would satisfy the audience, they satisfied the writer. It is seldom that authors, though more studious of fame than Shakespeare, rise much above the standard of their own age; to add a little to what is best will always be sufficient for present praise, and those who find themselves exalted into fame are willing to credit their encomiasts, and to spare the labour of contending with themselves.

It does not appear that Shakespeare thought his works worthy of posterity, that he levied any ideal tribute upon future times, or had any further prospect than of present popularity and present profit. When his plays had been acted, his hope was at an end; he solicited no addition of honour from the reader. He therefore made no scruple to repeat the same jests in many dialogues, or to entangle different plots by the same knot of perplexity, which may be at least forgiven him by those who recollect that of Congreve's four comedies, two are concluded by a marriage in a mask, by a deception which perhaps never happened, and which, whether likely or not, he did not invent.

So careless was this great poet of future fame that, though he retired to ease and plenty, while he was yet little *declined into the vale of years*,° before he could be disgusted with fatigue, or disabled by infirmity, he made no collection of his works, nor desired to rescue those that had been already published from the depravations that obscured them, or secure to the rest a better destiny, by giving them to the world in their genuine state.

Of the plays which bear the name of Shakespeare in the late editions, the greater part were not published till about seven years after his death, and the few which appeared in his life are apparently thrust into the world without the care of the author, and therefore probably without his knowledge.

Of all the publishers, clandestine or professed, the negligence and unskilfulness has by the late revisers been sufficiently shown. The faults of all are indeed numerous and gross, and have not only corrupted many passages perhaps beyond recovery, but have brought others into suspicion which are only obscured by obsolete phrase-ology, or by the writer's unskilfulness and affectation. To alter is more easy than to explain, and temerity is a more common quality than diligence. Those who saw that they must employ conjecture to a certain degree were willing to indulge it a little further. Had the author published his own works, we should have sat quietly down to disentangle his intricacies, and clear his obscurities; but now we tear what we cannot loose, and eject what we happen not to understand.

The faults are more than could have happened without the concurrence of many causes. The style of Shakespeare was in itself ungrammatical, perplexed and obscure; his works were transcribed for the players by those who may be supposed to have seldom understood them; they were transmitted by copiers equally unskilful, who still multiplied errors; they were perhaps sometimes mutilated by the actors, for the sake of shortening the speeches; and were at last printed without correction of the press.

In this state they remained, not as Dr Warburton supposes, because they were unregarded, but because the editor's art was not yet applied to modern languages, and our ancestors were accustomed to so much negligence of English printers that they could very patiently endure it. At last an edition was undertaken by Rowe; not because a poet was to be published by a poet, for Rowe seems to have thought very little on correction or explanation, but that our author's works might appear like those of his fraternity, with the appendages of a life and recommendatory preface. Rowe has been clamorously blamed for not performing what he did not undertake, and it is time that justice be done him by confessing that though he seems to have had no thought of corruption beyond the printer's errors, yet he has made many emendations, if they were not made before, which his successors have received without acknowledgement, and which, if they had produced them, would have filled pages and pages with censures of the stupidity by which the faults were committed, with displays of the absurdities which they involved, with ostentatious expositions of the new reading, and self-congratulations on the happiness of discovering it.

As of the other editors I have preserved the prefaces, I have likewise borrowed the author's life from Rowe, though not written with much elegance or spirit; it relates however what is now to be known, and therefore deserves to pass through all succeeding publications.

The nation had been for many years content enough with Mr Rowe's performance, when Mr Pope made them acquainted with the true state of Shakespeare's text, showed that it was extremely corrupt, and gave reason to hope that there were means of reforming it. He collated the old copies, which none had thought to examine before, and restored many lines to their integrity; but, by a very compendious criticism, he rejected whatever he disliked, and thought more of amputation than of cure.

I know not why he is commended by Dr Warburton for distinguishing the genuine from the spurious plays. In this choice he exerted no judgment of his own; the plays which he received were given by Heming and Condell, the first editors; and those which he rejected, though, according to the licentiousness of the press in those times, they were printed during Shakespeare's life, with his name, had been omitted by his friends, and were never added to his works before the edition of 1664, from which they were copied by the later printers.

This was a work which Pope seems to have thought unworthy of his abilities, being not able to suppress his contempt of *the dull duty of an editor*. He understood but half his undertaking. The duty of a collator is indeed dull, yet, like other tedious tasks, is very necessary; but an emendatory critic would ill discharge his duty without qualities very different from dullness. In perusing a corrupted piece, he must have before him all possibilities of meaning, with all possibilities of expression. Such must be his comprehension of thought, and such his copiousness of language. Out of many readings possible, he must be able to select that which best suits with the state, opinions, and modes of language prevailing in every age, and with his author's particular cast of thought, and turn of expression. Such must be his knowledge, and such his taste. Conjectural criticism demands more than humanity possesses, and he that exercises it with most praise has very frequent need of indulgence. Let us now be told no more of the dull duty of an editor.

Confidence is the common consequence of success. They whose excellence of any kind has been loudly celebrated are ready to conclude that their powers are universal. Pope's edition fell below his own expectations, and he was so much offended, when he was found to have left any thing for others to do, that he passed the latter part of his life in a state of hostility with verbal criticism.

I have retained all his notes, that no fragment of so great a writer may be lost; his preface, valuable alike for elegance of composition and justness of remark, and containing a general criticism on his author so extensive that little can be added, and so exact that little can be disputed, every editor has an interest to suppress, but that every reader would demand its insertion.

Pope was succeeded by Theobald, a man of narrow comprehension and small acquisitions, with no native and intrinsic splendour of genius, with little of the artificial light of learning, but zealous for minute accuracy, and not negligent in pursuing it. He collated the ancient copies, and rectified many errors. A man so anxiously scrupulous might have been expected to do more, but what little he did was commonly right.

In his reports of copies and editions he is not to be trusted without examination. He speaks sometimes indefinitely of copies, when he has only one. In his enumeration of editions, he mentions the two first folios as of high, and the third folio as of middle authority; but the truth is that the first is equivalent to all others, and that the rest only deviate from it by the printer's negligence. Whoever has any of the folios has all, excepting those diversities which mere reiteration of editions will produce. I collated them all at the beginning, but afterwards used only the first.

Of his notes I have generally retained those which he retained himself in his second edition, except when they were confuted by subsequent annotators, or were too minute to merit preservation. I have sometimes adopted his restoration of a comma, without inserting the panegyric in which he celebrated himself for his achievement. The exuberant excrescence of his diction I have often lopped, his triumphant exultations over Pope and Rowe I have sometimes suppressed, and his contemptible ostentation I have frequently concealed; but I have in some places shown him, as he would have shown himself, for the reader's diversion, that the inflated emptiness of some notes may justify or excuse the contraction of the rest.

Theobald, thus weak and ignorant, thus mean and faithless, thus petulant and ostentatious, by the good luck of having Pope for his enemy, has escaped, and escaped alone, with reputation, from this undertaking. So willingly does the world support those who solicit favour against those who command reverence; and so easily is he praised whom no man can envy.

Our author fell then into the hands of Sir Thomas Hanmer, the Oxford editor, a man, in my opinion, eminently qualified by nature for such studies. He had, what is the first requisite to emendatory criticism, that intuition by which the poet's intention is immediately discovered, and that dexterity of intellect which despatches its work by the easiest means. He had undoubtedly read much; his acquaintance with customs, opinions, and traditions, seems to have been large; and he is often learned without show. He seldom passes what he does not understand without an attempt to find or to make a meaning, and sometimes hastily makes what a little more attention would have found. He is solicitous to reduce to grammar what he could not be sure that his author intended to be grammatical. Shakespeare regarded more the series of ideas than of words; and his language, not being designed for the reader's desk, was all that he desired it to be if it conveyed his meaning to the audience.

Hanmer's care of the metre has been too violently censured. He found the measure reformed in so many passages, by the silent labours of some editors, with the silent acquiescence of the rest, that he thought himself allowed to extend a little further the license which had already been carried so far without reprehension; and of his corrections in general, it must be confessed that they are often just, and made commonly with the least possible violation of the text.

But, by inserting his emendations, whether invented or borrowed, into the page, without any notice of varying copies, he has appropriated the labour of his predecessors, and made his own edition of little authority. His confidence indeed, both in himself and others, was too great; he supposes all to be right that was done by Pope and Theobald; he seems not to suspect a critic of fallibility, and it was but reasonable that he should claim what he so liberally granted.

As he never writes without careful inquiry and diligent consideration, I have received all his notes, and believe that every reader will wish for more.

Of the last editor° it is more difficult to speak. Respect is due to high place, tenderness to living reputation, and veneration to genius and learning; but he cannot be justly offended at that liberty of which he has himself so frequently given an example, nor very solicitous what is thought of notes which he ought never to have considered as part of his serious employments, and which, I suppose, since the ardour of composition is remitted, he no longer numbers among his happy effusions.

The original and predominant error of his commentary is acquiescence in his first thoughts; that precipitation which is produced by consciousness of quick discernment; and that confidence which presumes to do, by surveying the surface, what labour only can perform by penetrating the bottom. His notes exhibit sometimes perverse interpretations, and sometimes improbable conjectures; he at one time gives the author more profundity of meaning than the sentence admits, and at another discovers absurdities where the sense is plain to every other reader. But his emendations are likewise often happy and just; and his interpretation of obscure passages learned and sagacious.

Of his notes, I have commonly rejected those against which the general voice of the public has exclaimed, or which their own incongruity immediately condemns, and which, I suppose, the author himself would desire to be forgotten. Of the rest, to part I have given the highest approbation, by inserting the offered reading in the text; part I have left to the judgment of the reader, as doubtful, though specious; and part I have censured without reserve, but I am sure without bitterness of malice, and, I hope, without wantonness of insult.

It is no pleasure to me, in revising my volumes, to observe how much paper is wasted in confutation. Whoever considers the revolutions of learning, and the various questions of greater or less importance upon which wit and reason have exercised their powers must lament the unsuccessfulness of inquiry, and the slow advances of truth, when he reflects that great part of the labour of every writer is only the destruction of those that went before him. The first care of the builder of a new system is to demolish the fabrics which are standing. The chief desire of him that comments an author is to show how much other commentators have corrupted and obscured him. The opinions prevalent in one age, as truths above the reach of controversy, are confuted and rejected in another, and rise again to reception in remoter times. Thus the human mind is kept in motion without progress. Thus sometimes truth and error, and sometimes contrarieties of error, take each other's place by reciprocal invasion. The tide of seeming knowledge which is poured over one generation retires and leaves another naked and barren; the sudden meteors of intelligence, which for a while appear to shoot their beams into the regions of obscurity, on a sudden withdraw their lustre, and leave mortals again to grope their way.

These elevations and depressions of renown, and the contradictions to which all improvers of knowledge must for ever be exposed, since they are not escaped by the highest and brightest of mankind, may surely be endured with patience by critics and annotators, who can rank themselves but as the satellites of their author. 'How canst thou beg for life,' says Homer's hero to his captive, 'when thou knowest that thou art now to suffer only what must another day be suffered by Achilles?'

Dr Warburton had a name sufficient to confer celebrity on those who could exalt themselves into antagonists, and his notes have raised a clamour too loud to be distinct. His chief assailants are the authors° of *The Canons of Criticism* and of the *Revisal of Shakespeare's Text*; of whom one ridicules his errors with airy petulance, suitable enough to the levity of the controversy; the other attacks them with gloomy malignity, as if he were dragging to justice an assassin or incendiary. The one stings like a fly, sucks a little blood, takes a gay flutter, and returns for more; the other bites like a viper, and would be glad to leave inflammations and gangrene behind him. When I think on one, with his confederates, I remember the danger of Coriolanus, who was afraid that 'girls with spits, and boys with stones, should slay him in puny battle'; when the other crosses my imagination, I remember the prodigy in *Macbeth*,

> A falcon towering in his pride of place,
> Was by a mousing owl hawked at and killed.

Let me however do them justice. One is a wit, and one a scholar. They have both shown acuteness sufficient in the discovery of faults, and have both advanced some probable interpretations of obscure passages; but when they aspire to conjecture and emendation, it appears how falsely we all estimate our own abilities, and the little which they have been able to perform might have taught them more candour to the endeavours of others.

Before Dr Warburton's edition, *Critical Observations on Shakespeare* had been published by Mr Upton, a man skilled in languages, and acquainted with books, but who seems to have had no great vigour of genius or nicety of taste. Many of his explanations are curious and useful, but he likewise, though he professed to oppose the licentious confidence of editors, and adhere to the old copies, is unable to restrain the rage of emendation, though his ardour is ill seconded by his skill. Every cold empiric, when his heart is expanded by a successful experiment, swells into a theorist, and the laborious collator at some unlucky moment frolics in conjecture.

Critical, Historical, and Explanatory Notes have been likewise published upon Shakespeare by Dr Grey, whose diligent perusal of the old English writers has enabled him to make some useful observations. What he undertook he has well enough performed, but as he neither attempts judicial nor emendatory criticism, he employs rather his memory than his sagacity. It were to be wished that all would endeavour to imitate his modesty who have not been able to surpass his knowledge.

I can say with great sincerity of all my predecessors, what I hope will hereafter be said of me, that not one has left Shakespeare without improvement, nor is there one to whom I have not been indebted for assistance and information. Whatever I have taken from them it was my intention to refer to its original author, and it is certain that what I have not given to another I believed when I wrote it to be my own. In some perhaps I have been anticipated; but if I am ever found to encroach upon the remarks of any other commentator, I am willing that the honour, be it more or less, should be transferred to the first claimant, for his right, and his alone, stands above dispute; the second can prove his pretensions only to himself, nor can himself always distinguish invention with sufficient certainty from recollection.

They have all been treated by me with candour, which they have not been careful of observing to one another. It is not easy to discover from what cause the acrimony of a scholiast can naturally proceed. The subjects to be discussed by him are of very small importance; they involve neither property nor liberty; nor favour the interest of sect or party. The various readings of copies, and different interpretations of a passage, seem to be questions that might exercise the wit, without engaging the passions. But, whether it be that *small things make mean men proud*,° and vanity catches small occasions; or that all contrariety of opinion, even in those that can defend it no longer, makes proud men angry; there is often found in commentaries a spontaneous strain of invective and contempt, more eager and venomous than is vented by the most furious controvertist in politics against those whom he is hired to defame.

Perhaps the lightness of the matter may conduce to the vehemence of the agency; when the truth to be investigated is so near to inexistence as to escape attention, its bulk is to be enlarged by rage and exclamation: that to which all would be indifferent in its original state may attract notice when the fate of a name is appended to it. A commentator has indeed great temptations to supply by turbulence what he wants of dignity, to beat his little gold to a spacious surface, to work that to foam which no art or diligence can exalt to spirit.

The notes which I have borrowed or written are either illustrative, by which difficulties are explained; or judicial, by which faults and beauties are remarked; or emendatory, by which depravations are corrected.

The explanations transcribed from others, if I do not subjoin any other interpretation, I suppose commonly to be right, at least I intend by acquiescence to confess that I have nothing better to propose.

After the labours of all the editors, I found many passages which appeared to me likely to obstruct the greater number of readers, and thought it my duty to facilitate their passage. It is impossible for an expositor not to write too little for some, and too much for others. He can only judge what is necessary by his own experience; and how long soever he may deliberate will at last explain many lines which the learned will think impossible to be mistaken, and omit many for which the ignorant will want his help. These are censures merely relative, and must be quietly endured. I have endeavoured to be neither superfluously copious, nor scrupulously reserved, and hope that I have made my author's meaning accessible to many who before were frighted from perusing him, and contributed something to the public by diffusing innocent and rational pleasure.

The complete explanation of an author not systematic and consequential, but desultory and vagrant, abounding in casual allusions and light hints, is not to be expected from any single scholiast. All personal reflections, when names are suppressed, must be in a few years irrecoverably obliterated; and customs too minute to attract the notice of law such as modes of dress, formalities of conversation, rules of visits, disposition of furniture, and practices of ceremony, which naturally find places in familiar dialogue, are so fugitive and unsubstantial that they are not easily retained or recovered. What can be known will be collected by chance, from the recesses of obscure and obsolete papers perused commonly with some other view. Of this knowledge every man has some, and none has much; but when an author has engaged the public attention, those who can add any thing to his illustration communicate their discoveries, and time produces what had eluded diligence.

To time I have been obliged to resign many passages which, though I did not understand them, will perhaps hereafter be explained, having, I hope, illustrated some which others have neglected or mistaken, sometimes by short remarks, or marginal directions, such as every editor has added at his will, and often by comments more laborious than the matter will seem to deserve; but that which is most difficult is not always most important, and to an editor nothing is a trifle by which his author is obscured.

The poetical beauties or defects I have not been very diligent to observe. Some plays have more and some fewer judicial observations, not in proportion to their difference of merit, but because I gave this part of my design to chance and to caprice. The reader, I believe, is seldom pleased to find his opinion anticipated; it is natural to delight more in what we find or make than in what we receive. Judgment, like other faculties, is improved by practice, and its advancement is hindered by submission to dictatorial decisions, as the memory grows torpid by the use of a table book. Some initiation is however necessary; of all skill, part is infused by precept, and part is obtained by habit; I have therefore shown so much as may enable the candidate of criticism to discover the rest.

To the end of most plays, I have added short strictures, containing a general censure of faults, or praise of excellence; in which I know not how much I have concurred with the current opinion; but I have not, by any affectation of singularity, deviated from it. Nothing is minutely and particularly examined, and therefore it is to be supposed that in the plays which are condemned there is much to be praised, and in those which are praised much to be condemned.

The part of criticism in which the whole succession of editors has laboured with the greatest diligence, which has occasioned the most arrogant ostentation, and excited the keenest acrimony, is the emendation of corrupted passages, to which the public attention having been first drawn by the violence of the contention between Pope and Theobald has been continued by the persecution which, with a kind of conspiracy, has been since raised against all the publishers of Shakespeare.

That many passages have passed in a state of depravation through all the editions is indubitably certain; of these the restoration is only to be attempted by collation of copies or sagacity of conjecture. The collator's province is safe and easy, the conjecturer's perilous and difficult. Yet as the greater part of the plays are extant only in one copy, the peril must not be avoided, nor the difficulty refused.

Of the readings which this emulation of amendment has hitherto produced, some from the labours of every publisher I have advanced into the text; those are to be considered as in my opinion sufficiently supported; some I have rejected without mention, as evidently erroneous; some I have left in the notes without censure or approbation, as resting in equipoise between objection and defence;

and some, which seemed specious but not right, I have inserted with a subsequent animadversion.

Having classed the observations of others, I was at last to try what I could substitute for their mistakes, and how I could supply their omissions. I collated such copies as I could procure, and wished for more, but have not found the collectors of these rarities very communicative. Of the editions which chance or kindness put into my hands I have given an enumeration, that I may not be blamed for neglecting what I had not the power to do.

By examining the old copies, I soon found that the later publishers, with all their boasts of diligence, suffered many passages to stand unauthorised, and contented themselves with Rowe's regulation of the text, even where they knew it to be arbitrary, and with a little consideration might have found it to be wrong. Some of these alterations are only the ejection of a word for one that appeared to him more elegant or more intelligible. These corruptions I have often silently rectified; for the history of our language, and the true force of our words, can only be preserved by keeping the text of authors free from adulteration. Others, and those very frequent, smoothed the cadence, or regulated the measure; on these I have not exercised the same rigour; if only a word was transposed, or a particle inserted or omitted, I have sometimes suffered the line to stand; for the inconstancy of the copies is such as that some liberties may be easily permitted. But this practice I have not suffered to proceed far, having restored the primitive diction wherever it could for any reason be preferred.

The emendations which comparison of copies supplied I have inserted in the text; sometimes where the improvement was slight, without notice, and sometimes with an account of the reasons of the change.

Conjecture, though it be sometimes unavoidable, I have not wantonly nor licentiously indulged. It has been my settled principle that the reading of the ancient books is probably true, and therefore is not to be disturbed for the sake of elegance, perspicuity, or mere improvement of the sense. For though much credit is not due to the fidelity, nor any to the judgment of the first publishers, yet they who had the copy before their eyes were more likely to read it right than we who read it only by imagination. But it is evident that they have often made strange mistakes by ignorance or negligence, and that therefore something may be properly attempted by criticism, keeping the middle way between presumption and timidity.

Such criticism I have attempted to practise, and where any passage appeared inextricably perplexed, have endeavoured to discover how it may be recalled to sense with least violence. But my first labour is always to turn the old text on every side, and try if there be any interstice through which light can find its way; nor would Huetius himself condemn me as refusing the trouble of research for ambition of alteration. In this modest industry I have not been unsuccessful. I have rescued many lines from the violations of temerity, and secured many scenes from the inroads of correction. I have adopted the Roman sentiment, that it is more honourable to save a citizen than to kill an enemy, and have been more careful to protect than to attack.

I have preserved the common distribution of the plays into acts, though I believe it to be in almost all the plays void of authority. Some of those which are divided in the later editions have no division in the first folio, and some that are divided in the folio have no division in the preceding copies. The settled mode of the theatre requires four intervals in the play, but few, if any, of our author's compositions can be properly distributed in that manner. An act is so much of the drama as passes without intervention of time or change of place. A pause makes a new act. In every real, and therefore in every imitative action, the intervals may be more or fewer, the restriction of five acts being accidental and arbitrary. This Shakespeare knew, and this he practised; his plays were written, and at first printed, in one unbroken continuity, and ought now to be exhibited with short pauses, interposed as often as the scene is changed, or any considerable time is required to pass. This method would at once quell a thousand absurdities.

In restoring the author's works to their integrity, I have considered the punctuation as wholly in my power; for what could be their care of colons and commas who corrupted words and sentences? Whatever could be done by adjusting points is therefore silently performed, in some plays with much diligence, in others with less; it is hard to keep a busy eye steadily fixed upon evanescent atoms, or a discursive mind upon evanescent truth.

The same liberty has been taken with a few particles, or other words of slight effect. I have sometimes inserted or omitted them without notice. I have done that sometimes which the other editors have done always, and which indeed the state of the text may sufficiently justify.

The greater part of readers, instead of blaming us for passing trifles, will wonder that on mere trifles so much labour is expended, with such importance of debate, and such solemnity of diction. To these I answer with confidence that they are judging of an art which they do not understand; yet cannot much reproach them with their ignorance, nor promise that they would become in general, by learning criticism, more useful, happier, or wiser.

As I practised conjecture more, I learned to trust it less; and after I had printed a few plays, resolved to insert none of my own readings in the text. Upon this caution I now congratulate myself, for every day increases my doubt of my emendations.

Since I have confined my imagination to the margin, it must not be considered as very reprehensible if I have suffered it to play some freaks in its own dominion. There is no danger in conjecture, if it be proposed as conjecture; and while the text remains uninjured, those changes may be safely offered which are not considered even by him that offers them as necessary or safe.

If my readings are of little value, they have not been ostentatiously displayed or importunately obtruded. I could have written longer notes, for the art of writing notes is not of difficult attainment. The work is performed, first by railing at the stupidity, negligence, ignorance, and asinine tastelessness of the former editors, and showing, from all that goes before and all that follows, the inelegance and absurdity of the old reading; then by proposing something which to superficial readers would seem specious, but which the editor rejects with indignation; then by producing the true reading, with a long paraphrase, and concluding with loud acclamations on the discovery, and a sober wish for the advancement and prosperity of genuine criticism.

All this may be done, and perhaps done sometimes without impropriety. But I have always suspected that the reading is right which requires many words to prove it wrong; and the emendation wrong that cannot without so much labour appear to be right. The justness of a happy restoration strikes at once, and the moral precept may be well applied to criticism, *quod dubitas ne feceris*.

To dread the shore which he sees spread with wrecks is natural to the sailor. I had before my eye so many critical adventures ended in miscarriage that caution was forced upon me. I encountered in every page Wit struggling with its own sophistry, and Learning confused by the multiplicity of its views. I was forced to censure those whom I admired, and could not but reflect, while I was dispossessing their emendations, how soon the same fate might happen to my own, and how many of the readings which I have corrected may be by some other editor defended and established.

Critics I saw that others' names efface,
And fix their own, with labour, in the place;
Their own, like others, soon their place resigned,
Or disappeared, and left the first behind.

Pope.

That a conjectural critic should often be mistaken cannot be wonderful, either to others or himself, if it be considered that in his art there is no system, no principal and axiomatical truth that regulates subordinate positions. His chance of error is renewed at every attempt; an oblique view of the passage, a slight misapprehension of a phrase, a casual inattention to the parts connected, is sufficient to make him not only fail, but fail ridiculously; and when he succeeds best, he produces perhaps but one reading of many probable, and he that suggests another will always be able to dispute his claims.

It is an unhappy state in which danger is hid under pleasure. The allurements of emendation are scarcely resistible. Conjecture has all the joy and all the pride of invention, and he that has once started a happy change is too much delighted to consider what objections may rise against it.

Yet conjectural criticism has been of great use in the learned world; nor is it my intention to depreciate a study that has exercised so many mighty minds, from the revival of learning to our own age, from the Bishop of Aleria° to English Bentley. The critics on ancient authors have, in the exercise of their sagacity, many assistances which the editor of Shakespeare is condemned to want. They are employed upon grammatical and settled languages, whose construction contributes so much to perspicuity that Homer has fewer passages unintelligible than Chaucer. The words have not only a known regimen, but invariable quantities, which direct and confine the choice. There are commonly more manuscripts than one; and they do not often conspire in the same mistakes. Yet Scaliger could confess to Salmasius how little satisfaction his emendations gave him. *Illudunt nobis conjecturae nostrae, quarum nos pudet, posteaquam in meliores codices incidimus.*° And Lipsius could complain that critics were making faults by trying to remove them, *Ut olim vitiis, ita nunc remediis laboratur.*° And indeed, where mere conjecture is to be used, the emendations of Scaliger and Lipsius, notwithstanding their wonderful sagacity and erudition, are often vague and disputable, like mine or Theobald's.

Perhaps I may not be more censured for doing wrong than for doing little; for raising in the public expectations which at last I have not answered. The expectation of ignorance is indefinite, and that of knowledge is often tyrannical. It is hard to satisfy those who know not what to demand, or those who demand by design what they think impossible to be done. I have indeed disappointed no opinion more than my own; yet I have endeavoured to perform my task with no slight solicitude. Not a single passage in the whole work has appeared to me corrupt which I have not attempted to restore; or obscure, which I have not endeavoured to illustrate. In many I have failed like others; and from many, after all my efforts, I have retreated, and confessed the repulse. I have not passed over, with affected superiority, what is equally difficult to the reader and to myself, but where I could not instruct him, have owned my ignorance. I might easily have accumulated a mass of seeming learning upon easy scenes; but it ought not to be imputed to negligence that, where nothing was necessary, nothing has been done, or that, where others have said enough, I have said no more.

Notes are often necessary, but they are necessary evils. Let him that is yet unacquainted with the powers of Shakespeare, and who desires to feel the highest pleasure that the drama can give, read every play from the first scene to the last, with utter negligence of all his commentators. When his fancy is once on the wing, let it not stoop at correction or explanation. When his attention is strongly engaged, let it disdain alike to turn aside to the name of Theobald and of Pope. Let him read on through brightness and obscurity, through integrity and corruption; let him preserve his comprehension of the dialogue and his interest in the fable. And when the pleasures of novelty have ceased, let him attempt exactness, and read the commentators.

Particular passages are cleared by notes, but the general effect of the work is weakened. The mind is refrigerated by interruption; the thoughts are diverted from the principal subject; the reader is weary, he suspects not why; and at last throws away the book which he has too diligently studied.

Parts are not to be examined till the whole has been surveyed; there is a kind of intellectual remoteness necessary for the comprehension of any great work in its full design and its true proportions; a close approach shows the smaller niceties, but the beauty of the whole is discerned no longer.

It is not very grateful to consider how little the succession of editors has added to this author's power of pleasing. He was read, admired, studied, and imitated while he was yet deformed with all the improprieties which ignorance and neglect could accumulate upon him; while the reading was yet not rectified, nor his allusions understood; yet then did Dryden° pronounce that

Shakespeare was the man, who, of all modern and perhaps ancient poets, had the largest and most comprehensive soul. All the images of nature were still present to him, and he drew them not laboriously, but luckily. When he describes any thing, you more than see it, you feel it too. Those who accuse him to have wanted learning give him the greater commendation: he was naturally learned: he needed not the spectacles of books to read nature; he looked inwards, and found her there. I cannot say he is every where alike; were he so, I should do him injury to compare him with the greatest of mankind. He is many times flat and insipid; his comic wit degenerating into clenches, his serious swelling into bombast. But he is always great when some great occasion is presented to him. No man can say he ever had a fit subject for his wit, and did not then raise himself as high above the rest of poets,

Quantum lenta solent inter viburna cupressi.°

It is to be lamented that such a writer should want a commentary; that his language should become obsolete, or his sentiments obscure. But it is vain to carry wishes beyond the condition of human things; that which must happen to all has happened to Shakespeare, by accident and time; and more than has been suffered by any other writer since the use of types, has been suffered by him through his own negligence of fame, or perhaps by that superiority of mind which despised its own performances when it compared them with its powers, and judged those works unworthy to be preserved which the critics of following ages were to contend for the fame of restoring and explaining.

Among these candidates of inferior fame, I am now to stand the judgment of the public; and wish that I could confidently produce my commentary as equal to the encouragement which I have had the honour of receiving. Every work of this kind is by its nature deficient, and I should feel little solicitude about the sentence, were it to be pronounced only by the skilful and the learned.

ACT III. SCENE I.

The Prison.

Enter Duke, Claudio, and Provost.

DUKE.

SO, then you've hope of pardon from lord *Angelo?*
  Claud. The miserable have no other medicine,
But only Hope: I've hope to live, and am prepar'd to
    die.
  Duke. Be absolute for death: ⁹ or death, or life,
Shall thereby be the sweeter.   Reason thus with life;
If I do lose thee, I do lose a thing,
That none but fools would keep; ¹ a breath thou art,
Servile to all the skiey influences
That do this habitation, ² where thou keep'st,

---

⁹ *Be absolute for death.*] Be
determined to die, without any
hope of life.   *Horace,* ——
— *The hour which exceeds expecta-*
  tion will be welcome.
  ¹ *That none but fools would*
keep.] But this reading is not
only contrary to all Sense and
Reason; but to the Drift of this
moral Discourse. The *Duke,* in
his assum'd Character of a *Friar,*
is endeavouring to instil into the
condemn'd Prisoner a Resignation of Mind to his Sentence;
but the Sense of the Lines, in
this Reading, is a direct Persua-
sive to *Suicide* : I make no Doubt,
but the Poet wrote,
  That none but Fools would reck.
i. e. care for, be anxious about,
regret the loss of. So in the

Tragedy of *Tancred and Gis-*
munda, Act 4. Scene 3.
    —— *Not that she* RECKS *this*
      life ——
And *Shakespeare* in *The Two Gen-*
tlemen of Verona,
  Recking *as little what betideth*
  me ——
                    WARBURTON.
  The meaning seems plainly
this, that *none but fools would* wish
to keep life ; or, *none but fools*
would keep it, if choice were
allowed. A sense, which, whether true or not, is certainly innocent.
  ² *That do this habitation.*]
This reading is substituted by
Sir *Thomas* Hanmer, for *that*
dost.

Hourly

MEASURE FOR MEASURE.   313

Hourly afflict; meerly thou art death's fool; [3]
For him thou labour'st by thy flight to shun,
And yet runn'st tow'rd him still. Thou art not noble;
For all th' accommodations, that thou bear'st,
Are nurs'd by baseness: [4] thou'rt by no means va-
    liant;
For thou dost fear the soft and tender fork
Of a poor worm. [5]   Thy best of Rest is sleep, [6]
And that thou oft provok'st; yet grosly fear'st

                                                    Thy

[3] —— *meerly thou art* Death's
Fool;
For him thou labour'st by thy
  flight to shun,
And yet runn'st tow'rd him still.]
In those old Farces called MO-
RALITIES, the *Fool* of the piece,
in order to shew the inevitable
approaches of Death, is made
to employ all his stratagems to
avoid him: which, as the matter is ordered, bring the *Fool*, at
every turn, into his very jaws.
So that the representations of
these scenes would afford a great
deal of good *mirth* and *morals*
mixed together. And from such
circumstances, in the genius of
our ancestors publick diversions,
I suppose it was, that the old
proverb arose, of *being merry and*
wise.   WARBURTON.
[4] *Are nurs'd by baseness.*] Dr.
Warburton is undoubtedly mistaken in supposing that by *base-*
ness is meant *self-love* here assigned as the motive of all human actions. *Shakespear* meant
only to observe, that a minute
analysis of life at once destroys
that splendour which dazzles the
imagination. Whatever grandeur can display, or luxury enjoy, is procured by *baseness*, by

offices of which the mind shrinks
from the contemplation. All the
delicacies of the table may be
traced back to the shambles and
the dunghill, all magnificence of
building was hewn from the
quarry, and all the pomp of ornaments, dug from among the
damps and darkness of the mine.
[5] —— *the soft and tender fork*
  Of a poor worm.——] *Worm*
is put for any creeping thing or
serpent. Shakespear supposes
falsely, but according to the vulgar notion, that a serpent wounds
with his tongue, and that his
tongue is *forked.* He confounds
reality and fiction, a serpent's
tongue is *soft* but not *forked*
nor hurtful. If it could hurt, it
could not be soft. In *Midsummer-*
Night's Dream he has the same
notion.

———— *With* doubler *tongue*
Than thine, O serpent, never ad-
  der stung.
[6] — *thy best of rest is sleep,*
And that thou oft provok'st; yet
  grosly fear'st
Thy death which is no more.——]
Evidently from the following
passage of *Cicero: Habes somnum*
imaginem Mortis, eamque quotidie
induis, & dubitas quin sensus in
                            morte

314 MEASURE FOR MEASURE.

Thy death, which is no more. [7] Thou'rt not thyself;
For thou exist'st on many a thousand grains,
That issue out of dust. Happy thou art not;
For what thou hast not, still thou striv'st to get;
And what thou hast forget'st. Thou are not certain;
For thy complexion shifts to strange effects, [8]
After the moon. If thou art rich, thou'rt poor;
For, like an ass, whose back with ingots bows,
Thou bear'st thy heavy riches but a journey,
And death unloadeth thee. Friend hast thou none;
For thy own bowels, which do call thee Sire,
The meer effusion of thy proper loins,
Do curse the *Gout*, *Serpigo*, and the *Rheum*,
For ending thee no sooner. Thou hast nor youth,
  nor age; [9]
But as it were an after-dinner's sleep,
Dreaming on both; for all thy blessed youth [1]
         Becomes

morte nullus sit, cum in ejus simu-
lacro videas esse nullum sensum.
But the Epicurean insinuation is,
with great judgment, omitted in
the imitation. WARBURTON.

Here Dr. *Warburton* might
have found a sentiment worthy
of his animadversion. I cannot
without indignation find *Shake-*
spear saying, that *death is only*
sleep, lengthening out his exhortation by a sentence which in the
Friar is impious, in the reasoner
is foolish, and in the poet trite
and vulgar.

7 — *Thou'rt not thyself.*] Thou
art perpetually repaired and re-
novated by external assistance,
thou subsistest upon foreign matter, and hast no power of producing or continuing thy own
being.

8 — *strange effects.*] For *ef-*
fects read *affects*; that is, *affections*,

passions of mind, or disorders of
body variously *affected*. So in
Othello, The young affects.

9 — *Thou hast nor youth, nor*
 age;
But as it were an after-dinner's
 sleep,
Dreaming on both.] This is exquisitely imagined. When we
are young we busy ourselves in
forming schemes for succeeding
time, and miss the gratifications
that are before us; when we are
old we amuse the languour of
age with the recollection of
youthful pleasures or performances; so that our life, of which
no part is filled with the business
of the present time, resembles
our dreams after dinner, when
the events of the morning are
mingled with the designs of the
evening.

1 — *For all thy blessed youth*
    Becomes

MEASURE FOR MEASURE.   315

Becomes as aged, and doth beg the alms
Of palsied Eld; and when thou'rt old and rich,
Thou haft neither heat, affection, limb, nor beauty ª

To

*Becomes as aged, and doth beg
the alms
Of palsied Eld; and when thou'rt
old and rich,
Thou haft neither heat, &c.*—]
The drift of this period is to
prove, that neither youth nor age
can be faid to be really enjoyed,
which, in poetical language, is,
—*We have neither youth nor age.*
But how is this made out? That
Age is not enjoyed he proves, by
recapitulating the infirmities of
it, which deprive that period of
life of all fenfe of pleafure. To
prove that *Youth* is not enjoyed,
he ufes thefe words, *For all thy
bleſſed youth becomes as aged, and
doth beg the alms of palsied Eld.*
Out of which, he that can deduce the concluſion, has a better
knack at logic than I have. I
ſuppoſe the Poet wrote,

—*for pall'd, thy blazed youth
Becomes* aſſuaged; *and doth beg
the alms
Of palsied Eld;*———

i. e. when thy youthful appetite
becomes palled, as it will be in the
very enjoyment, the blaze of youth
is at once aſſuaged, and thou immediately contracteſt the infirmities of old age; as, particularly,
the palſie and other nervous dif-
orders, confequent on the inordinate uſe of fenfual pleafures.
This is to the purpoſe; and proves
Youth is not enjoyed by ſhewing
the ſhort duration of it.
WARBURTON.

Here again I think Dr. *Warburton* totally miſtaken. *Shake-
ſpeare* declares that Man has *neither youth nor age,* for in *youth,*
which is the *happieſt* time, or
which might be the happieſt, he
commonly wants means to obtain what he could enjoy; he is
dependant on *palsied eld; muſt beg
alms* from the coffers of hoary
avarice; and being very niggardly fupplied *becomes as aged,* looks,
like an old man, on happinefs,
which is beyond his reach. And
when *he is old and rich,* when he
has wealth enough for the pur-
chafe of all that formerly excited
his defires, he has no longer the
powers of enjoyment.

———*has neither heat, affection,
limb, nor beauty
To make* his *riches pleafant.*

I have explained this paſſage
according to the prefent reading,
which may ſtand without much
inconvenience; yet I am willing
to perfuade my reader, becauſe
I have almoſt perfuaded myfelf,
that our authour wrote,

———*for all thy* blaſted *youth
Becomes as aged*———

ª ———*heat, affection, limb, nor
beauty.*] But how does beauty
make *riches pleafant?* We ſhould
read BOUNTY, which compleats
the fenfe. and is this; Thou haft
neither the pleafure of enjoying
riches thy felf, for thou wanteſt
vigour: nor of feeing it enjoyed
by

316 MEASURE FOR MEASURE.

To make thy riches pleasant.   What's yet in this,
That bears the name of life? yet in this life
Lye hid more thousand deaths; [3] yet death we fear,
That makes these odds all even.

   Claud. I humbly thank you.
To sue to live, I find, I seek to die;
And, seeking death, find life: let it come on.

Enter Isabella.

   Isab. What, ho? peace here, grace and good com-
      pany!
   Prov. Who's there? come in: the wish deserves a
      welcome.
   Duke. Dear Sir, ere long I'll visit you again.
   Claud. Most holy Sir, I thank you.
   Isab. My business is a word, or two, with *Claudio.*
   Prov. And very welcome.   Look, Signior, here's
      your sister.
   Duke. Provost, a word with you.
   Prov. As many as you please.
   Duke. Bring them to speak where I may be con-
      ceal'd,
Yet hear them.   [*Exeunt* Duke *and* Provost.

by others, for thou wantest *bounty*. Where the making the want
of *bounty* as inseparable from old
age as the want of *health*, is extremely satyrical tho' not altogether just.   WARBURTON.

  I am inclined to believe that
neither man nor woman will have
much difficulty to tell how *beauty
makes riches pleasant*. Surely this
emendation, though it is elegant
and ingenious, is not such as that

an opportunity of inserting it
should be purchased by declaring
ignorance of what every one
knows, by confessing insensibility of what every one feels.

  [3] —— *more thousand deaths.*]
For this Sir *T. Hanmer* reads, *a
thousand deaths :* the meaning is
not only *a thousand deaths*, but
a thousand deaths besides what
have been mentioned.

Concluding Notes°

ALL'S WELL THAT ENDS WELL

This play has many delightful scenes, though not sufficiently probable, and some happy characters, though not new, nor produced by any deep knowledge of human nature. Parolles is a boaster and a coward, such as has always been the sport of the stage, but perhaps never raised more laughter or contempt than in the hands of Shakespeare.

I cannot reconcile my heart to Bertram; a man noble without generosity, and young without truth; who marries Helen as a coward, and leaves her as a profligate: when she is dead by his unkindness, sneaks home to a second marriage, is accused by a woman whom he has wronged, defends himself by falsehood, and is dismissed to happiness.

The story of Bertram and Diana had been told before of Mariana and Angelo, and, to confess the truth, scarcely merited to be heard a second time.

The story is copied from a novel of Boccace, which may be read in *Shakespear Illustrated*, with remarks not more favourable to Bertram than my own.

JULIUS CAESAR

Of this tragedy many particular passages deserve regard, and the contention and reconcilement of Brutus and Cassius is universally celebrated; but I have never been strongly agitated in perusing it, and think it somewhat cold and unaffecting, compared with some other of Shakespeare's plays; his adherence to the real story, and to Roman manners, seems to have impeded the natural vigour of his genius.

HENRY IV, PART II

None of Shakespeare's plays are more read than the *First and Second Parts of Henry the Fourth*. Perhaps no author has ever in two plays afforded so much delight. The great events are interesting, for the fate of kingdoms depends upon them; the slighter occurrences are diverting, and, except one or two, sufficiently probable; the incidents are multiplied with wonderful fertility of invention, and the characters diversified with the utmost nicety of discernment, and the profoundest skill in the nature of man.

The Prince, who is the hero both of the comic and tragic part, is a young man of great abilities and violent passions, whose sentiments are right, though his actions are wrong; whose virtues are obscured by negligence, and whose understanding is dissipated by levity. In his idle hours he is rather loose than wicked, and when the occasion forces out his latent qualities, he is great without effort, and brave without tumult. The trifler is roused into a hero, and the hero again reposes in the trifler. This character is great, original, and just.

Percy is a rugged soldier, choleric, and quarrelsome, and has only the soldier's virtues, generosity and courage.

But Falstaff, unimitated, unimitable Falstaff, how shall I describe thee? Thou compound of sense and vice; of sense which may be admired but not esteemed, of vice which may be despised, but hardly detested. Falstaff is a character loaded with faults, and with those faults which naturally produce contempt. He is a thief, and a glutton, a coward, and a boaster, always ready to cheat the weak, and prey upon the poor; to terrify the timorous and insult the defenceless. At once obsequious and malignant, he satirises in their absence those whom he lives by flattering. He is familiar with the Prince only as an agent of vice, but of this familiarity he is so proud as not only to be supercilious and haughty with common men, but to think his interest of importance to the Duke of Lancaster. Yet the man thus corrupt, thus despicable, makes himself necessary to the prince that despises him, by the most pleasing of all qualities, perpetual gaiety, by an unfailing power of exciting laughter, which is the more freely indulged, as his wit is not of the splendid or ambitious kind, but consists in easy escapes and sallies of levity, which make sport but raise no envy. It must be observed that he is stained with no enormous or sanguinary crimes, so that his licentiousness is not so offensive but that it may be borne for his mirth.

The moral to be drawn from this representation is that no man is more dangerous than he that with a will to corrupt hath the power to please; and that neither wit nor honesty ought to think themselves safe with such a companion when they see Henry seduced by Falstaff.

KING LEAR

The tragedy of Lear is deservedly celebrated among the dramas of Shakespeare. There is perhaps no play which keeps the attention so strongly fixed; which so much agitates our passions and interests our curiosity. The artful involutions of distinct interests, the striking opposition of contrary characters, the sudden changes of fortune, and the quick succession of events fill the mind with a perpetual tumult of indignation, pity, and hope. There is no scene which does not contribute to the aggravation of the distress or conduct of the action, and scarce a line which does not conduce to the progress of the scene. So powerful is the current of the poet's imagination that the mind which once ventures within it is hurried irresistibly along.

On the seeming improbability of Lear's conduct it may be observed that he is represented according to histories at that time vulgarly received as true. And perhaps if we turn our thoughts upon the barbarity and ignorance of the age to which this story is referred, it will appear not so unlikely as while we estimate Lear's manners by our own. Such preference of one daughter to another, or resignation of dominion on such conditions, would be yet credible if told of a petty prince of Guinea or Madagascar. Shakespeare, indeed, by the mention of his earls and dukes, has given us the idea of times more civilised, and of life regulated by softer manners; and the truth is that though he so nicely discriminates, and so minutely describes the characters of men, he commonly neglects and confounds the characters of ages, by mingling customs ancient and modern, English and foreign.

My learned friend Mr Warton, who has in the *Adventurer* very minutely criticised this play, remarks that the instances of cruelty are too savage and shocking, and that the intervention of Edmund destroys the simplicity of the story. These objections may, I think, be answered by repeating that the cruelty of the daughters is an historical fact, to which the poet has added little, having only drawn it into a series by dialogue and action. But I am not able to apologise with equal plausibility for the extrusion of Gloucester's eyes, which seems an act too horrid to be endured in dramatic exhibition, and such as must always compel the mind to relieve its distress by incredulity. Yet let it be remembered that our author well knew what would please the audience for which he wrote.

The injury done by Edmund to the simplicity of the action is abundantly recompensed by the addition of variety, by the art with which he is made to co-operate with the chief design, and the opportunity which he gives the poet of combining perfidy with perfidy, and connecting the wicked son with the wicked daughters, to impress this important moral, that villainy is never at a stop, that crimes lead to crimes, and at last terminate in ruin.

But though this moral be incidentally enforced, Shakespeare has suffered the virtue of Cordelia to perish in a just cause, contrary to the natural ideas of justice, to the hope of the reader, and, what is yet more strange, to the faith of chronicles. Yet this conduct is justified by the Spectator, who blames Tate for giving Cordelia success and happiness in his alteration, and declares that in his opinion *the tragedy has lost half its beauty*. Dennis has remarked, whether justly or not, that, to secure the favourable reception of *Cato*, *the town was poisoned with much false and abominable criticism*, and that endeavours had been used to discredit and decry poetical justice. A play in which the wicked prosper, and the virtuous miscarry, may doubtless be good, because it is a just representation of the common events of human life: but since all reasonable beings naturally love justice, I cannot easily be persuaded that the observation of justice makes a play worse; or, that if other excellencies are equal, the audience will not always rise better pleased from the final triumph of persecuted virtue.

In the present case the public has decided. Cordelia, from the time of Tate, has always retired with victory and felicity. And, if my sensations could add any thing to the general suffrage, I might relate that I was many years ago so shocked by Cordelia's death that I know not whether I ever endured to read again the last scenes of the play till I undertook to revise them as an editor.

There is another controversy among the critics concerning this play. It is disputed whether the predominant image in Lear's disordered mind be the loss of his kingdom or the cruelty of his daughters. Mr Murphy, a very judicious critic, has evinced by induction of particular passages that the cruelty of his daughters is the primary source of his distress, and that the loss of royalty affects him only as a secondary and subordinate evil; he observes with great justness that Lear would move our compassion but little, did we not rather consider the injured father than the degraded king . . . .

OTHELLO

The beauties of this play impress themselves so strongly upon the attention of the reader that they can draw no aid from critical illustration. The fiery openness of Othello, magnanimous, artless, and credulous, boundless in his confidence, ardent in his affection, inflexible in his resolution, and obdurate in his revenge; the cool malignity of Iago, silent in his resentment, subtle in his designs, and studious at once of his interest and his vengeance; the soft simplicity of Desdemona, confident of merit, and conscious of innocence, her artless perseverance in her suit, and her slowness to suspect that she can be suspected are such proofs of Shakespeare's skill in human nature as, I suppose, it is vain to seek in any modern writer. The gradual progress which Iago makes in the Moor's conviction, and the circumstances which he employs to inflame him, are so artfully natural that, though it will perhaps not be said of him as he says of himself, that he is *a man not easily jealous*, yet we cannot but pity him when at last we find him *perplexed in the extreme*.

There is always danger lest wickedness conjoined with abilities should steal upon esteem, though it misses of approbation; but the character of Iago is so conducted that he is from the first scene to the last hated and despised.

Even the inferior characters of this play would be very conspicuous in any other piece, not only for their justness but their strength. Cassio is brave, benevolent, and honest, ruined only by his want of stubbornness to resist an insidious invitation. Roderigo's suspicious credulity, and impatient submission to the cheats which he sees practised upon him, and which by persuasion he suffers to be repeated, exhibit a strong picture of a weak mind betrayed by unlawful desires to a false friend; and the virtue of Aemilia is such as we often find, worn loosely, but not cast off, easy to commit small crimes, but quickened and alarmed at atrocious villanies.

The scenes from the beginning to the end are busy, varied by happy interchanges, and regularly promoting the progression of the story; and the narrative in the end, though it tells but what is known already, yet is necessary to produce the death of Othello.

Had the scene opened in Cyprus, and the preceding incidents been occasionally related, there had been little wanting to a drama of the most exact and scrupulous regularity.

Sermon 5°

Howbeit thou art just in all that is brought upon us, for
thou hast done right, but we have done wickedly.

Nehemiah ix. 33

There is nothing upon which more writers, in all ages, have laid out
their abilities than the miseries of life; and it affords no pleasing
reflections to discover that a subject so little agreeable is not yet
exhausted.

Some have endeavoured to engage us in the contemplation of the
evils of life for a very wise and good end. They have proposed, by
laying before us the uncertainty of prosperity, the vanity of pleasure,
and the inquietudes of power, the difficult attainment of most earthly
blessings, and the short duration of them all, to divert our thoughts
from the glittering follies and tempting delusions that surround us, to
an enquiry after more certain and permanent felicity; felicity not
subject to be interrupted by sudden vicissitudes, or impaired by the
malice of the revengeful, the caprice of the inconstant, or the envy of
the ambitious. They have endeavoured to demonstrate and have in
reality demonstrated to all those who will steal a few moments from
noise and show, and luxury, to attend to reason and to truth, that
nothing is worthy of our ardent wishes, or intense solicitude, that
terminates in this state of existence, and that those only make the true
use of life that employ it in obtaining the favour of God, and securing
everlasting happiness.

Others have taken occasion from the dangers that surround and the
troubles that perplex us to dispute the wisdom or justice of the
Governor of the world, or to murmur at the laws of divine Providence,
as the present state of the world, the disorder and confusion of every
thing about us, the casual and certain evils to which we are exposed,
and the disquiet and disgust which either accompany, or follow, those
few pleasures that are within our reach, seem, in their opinion, to
carry no marks of infinite benignity. This has been the reasoning by
which the wicked and profligate, in all ages, have attempted to harden
their hearts against the reproaches of conscience, and delude others
into a participation of their crimes. By this argument weak minds have
been betrayed into doubts and distrust, and decoyed by degrees into a
dangerous state of suspense, though perhaps never betrayed to
absolute infidelity. For few men have been made infidels by argument

and reflection; their actions are not generally the result of their reasonings, but their reasonings of their actions. Yet these reasonings, though they are not strong enough to pervert a good mind, may yet, when they coincide with interest, and are assisted by prejudice, contribute to confirm a man already corrupted in his impieties, and at least retard his reformation, if not entirely obstruct it.

Besides, notions thus derogatory from the providence of God tend, even in the best men, if not timely eradicated, to weaken those impressions of reverence and gratitude which are necessary to add warmth to his devotions, and vigour to his virtue; for as the force of corporeal motion is weakened by every obstruction, though it may not be entirely overcome by it, so the operations of the mind are by every false notion impeded and embarrassed, and though they are not wholly diverted or suppressed, proceed at least with less regularity, and with less celerity.

But these doubts may easily be removed, and these arguments confuted, by a calm and impartial attention to religion and to reason; it will appear upon examination that though the world be full of misery and disorder, yet God is not to be charged with disregard of his creation; that if we suffer, we suffer by our own fault, and that *he has done right, but we have done wickedly*.

We are informed by the Scriptures that God is not the Author of our present state, that when he created man, he created him for happiness; happiness indeed dependent upon his own choice, and to be preserved by his own conduct; for such must necessarily be the happiness of every reasonable being: that this happiness was forfeited by a breach of the conditions to which it was annexed, and that the posterity of him that broke the covenant were involved in the consequences of his fault. Thus religion shows us that physical and moral evil entered the world together, and reason and experience assure us that they continue for the most part so closely united that, to avoid misery, we must avoid sin, and that while it is in our power to be virtuous, it is in our power to be happy, at least to be happy to such a degree as may have little room for murmur and complaints.

Complaints are doubtless irrational in themselves, and unjust with respect to God, if the remedies of the evils we lament are in our hands; for what more can be expected from the beneficence of our Creator than that he should place good and evil before us, and then direct us in our choice?

That God has not been sparing of his bounties to mankind, or left them, even since the original transgression of his command, in a state so calamitous as discontent and melancholy have represented it, will evidently appear if we reflect,

First, how few of the evils of life can justly be ascribed to God.

Secondly, how far a general piety might exempt any community from those evils.

Thirdly, how much in the present corrupt state of the world, particular men may, by the practice of the duties of religion, promote their own happiness.

First, how few of the evils of life can justly be ascribed to God.

In examining what part of our present misery is to be imputed to God, we must carefully distinguish that which is actually appointed by him from that which is only permitted, or that which is the consequence of something done by ourselves, and could not be prevented but by the interruption of those general and settled laws which we term the course of nature, or the established order of the universe. Thus it is decreed by God that all men should die; and therefore the death of each man may justly be ascribed to God, but the circumstances and time of his death are very much in his own power, or in the power of others. When a good man falls by the hand of an assassin, or is condemned by the testimony of false witnesses, or the sentence of a corrupt judge, his death may, in some measure, be called the work of God, but his murder is the action of men. That he was mortal is the effect of the divine decree, but that he was deprived of life unjustly is the crime of his enemies.

If we examine all the afflictions of mind, body, and estate by this rule, we shall find God not otherwise accessory to them than as he works no miracles to prevent them, as he suffers men to be masters of themselves, and restrains them only by coercions applied to their reason. If God should, by a particular exertion of his omnipotence, hinder murder or oppression, no man could then be a murderer or an oppressor, because he would be withheld from it by an irresistible power; but then that power, which prevented crimes, would destroy virtue; for virtue is the consequence of choice. Men would be no longer rational, or would be rational to no purpose, because their actions would not be the result of free-will, determined by moral motives; but the settled and predestined motions of a machine impelled by necessity.

Thus it appears that God would not act as the Governor of rational and moral agents if he should lay any other restraints upon them than the hope of rewards, or fear of punishments; and that to destroy or obviate the consequences of human actions would be to destroy the present constitution of the world.

When therefore any man suffers pain from an injury offered him, that pain is not the act of God, but the effect of a crime, to which his enemy was determined by his own choice. He was created susceptible of pain, but not necessarily subjected to that particular injury which he now feels, and he is therefore not to charge God with his afflictions. The materials for building are naturally combustible, but when a city is fired by incendiaries, God is not the author of its destruction.

God may indeed, by special acts of providence, sometimes hinder the designs of bad men from being successfully executed, or the execution of them from producing such consequences as it naturally tends to; but this, whenever it is done, is a real, though not always a visible miracle, and is not to be expected in the ordinary occurrences of life, or the common transactions of the world.

In making an estimate therefore of the miseries that arise from the disorders of the body, we must consider how many diseases proceed from our own laziness, intemperance, or negligence; how many the vices or follies of our ancestors have transmitted to us, and beware of imputing to God the consequences of luxury, riot, and debauchery.

There are indeed distempers which no caution can secure us from, and which appear to be more immediately the strokes of Heaven; but these are not of the most painful or lingering kind, they are for the most part acute and violent, and quickly terminate, either in recovery, or death; and it is always to be remembered that nothing but wickedness makes death an evil.

Nor are the disquietudes of the mind less frequently excited by ourselves. Pride is the general source of our infelicity. A man that has a high opinion of his own merits, of the extent of his capacity, of the depth of his penetration, and the force of his eloquence naturally forms schemes of employment, and promotion, adequate to those abilities he conceives himself possessed of; he exacts from others the same esteem which he pays to himself, and imagines his deserts disregarded if they are not rewarded to the extent of his wishes. He claims more than he has a right to hope for, finds his exorbitant demands rejected, retires to obscurity and melancholy, and charges Heaven with his disappointments.

Men are very seldom disappointed, except when their desires are immoderate, or when they suffer their passions to overpower their reason, and dwell upon delightful scenes of future honours, power, or riches, till they mistake probabilities for certainties, or wild wishes for rational expectations. If such men, when they awake from these voluntary dreams, find the pleasing phantom vanish away, what can they blame but their own folly?

With no greater reason can we impute to Providence the fears and anxieties that harass and distract us; for they arise from too close an adherence to those things from which we are commanded to disengage our affections. We fail of being happy, because we determine to obtain felicity by means different from those which God hath appointed. We are forbidden to be too solicitous about future events, and is the Author of that prohibition to be accused, because men make themselves miserable by disregarding it?

Poverty indeed is not always the effect of wickedness, it may often be the consequence of virtue; but it is not certain that poverty is an evil. If we exempt the poor man from all the miseries to which his condition exposes him from the wickedness of others, if we secure him from the cruelty of oppression, and the contumelies of pride; if we suppose him to rate no enjoyment of this life beyond its real and intrinsic value; and to indulge no desire more than reason and religion allow; the inferiority of his station will very little diminish his happiness; and therefore the poverty of the virtuous reflects no reproach upon Providence. But poverty, like many other miseries of life, is often little more than an imaginary calamity. Men often call themselves poor, not because they want necessaries, but because they have not more than they want. This indeed is not always the case, nor ought we ever to harden our hearts against the cries of those who implore our assistance by supposing that they feel less than they express; but let us all relieve the necessitous according to our abilities, and real poverty will soon be banished out of the world.

To these general heads may be reduced almost all the calamities that embitter the life of man. To enumerate particular evils would be of little use. It is evident that most of our miseries are either imaginary, or the consequences either of our own faults, or the faults of others; and that it is therefore worthy of enquiry,

Secondly, how far a general piety might exempt any community from those evils.

It is an observation very frequently made that there is more tranquillity and satisfaction diffused through the inhabitants of uncultivated and savage countries than is to be met with in nations filled with wealth and plenty, polished with civility, and governed by laws. It is found happy to be free from contention, though that exemption be obtained by having nothing to contend for; and an equality of condition, though that condition be far from eligible, conduces more to the peace of society than an established and legal subordination, in which every man is perpetually endeavouring to exalt himself to the rank above him, though by degrading others already in possession of it, and every man exerting his efforts to hinder his inferiors from rising to the level with himself. It appears that it is better to have no property than to be in perpetual apprehensions of fraudulent artifices, or open invasions; and that the security arising from a regular administration of government is not equal to that which is produced by the absence of ambition, envy, or discontent.

Thus pleasing is the prospect of savage countries, merely from the ignorance of vice, even without the knowledge of virtue; thus happy are they, amidst all the hardships and distresses that attend a state of nature, because they are in a great measure free from those which men bring upon one another.

But a community in which virtue should generally prevail, of which every member should fear God with his whole heart, and love his neighbour as himself, where every man should labour to make himself *perfect, even as his Father which is in heaven is perfect,*° and endeavour, with his utmost diligence, to imitate the divine justice, and benevolence would have no reason to envy those nations whose quiet is the effect of their ignorance.

If we consider it with regard to public happiness, it would be opulent without luxury, and powerful without faction; its counsels would be steady, because they would be just; and its efforts vigorous, because they would be united. The governors would have nothing to fear from the turbulence of the people, nor the people any thing to apprehend from the ambition of their governors. The encroachments of foreign enemies they could not always avoid, but would certainly repulse, for scarce any civilized nation has been ever enslaved till it was first corrupted.

With regard to private men, not only that happiness which necessarily descends to particulars from the public prosperity would be enjoyed; but even those blessings which constitute the felicity of domestic life, and are less closely connected with the general good. Every man would be industrious to improve his property, because he would be in no danger of seeing his improvements torn from him. Every man would assist his neighbour, because he would be certain of receiving assistance, if he should himself be attacked by necessity. Every man would endeavour after merit, because merit would always be rewarded. Every tie of friendship and relation would add to happiness, because it would not be subject to be broken by envy, rivalship, or suspicion. Children would honour their parents, because all parents would be virtuous; all parents would love their children, because all children would be obedient. The grief which we naturally feel at the death of those that are dear to us could not perhaps be wholly prevented, but would be much more moderate than in the present state of things, because no man could ever want a friend, and his loss would therefore be less, because his grief, like his other passions, would be regulated by his duty. Even the relations of subjection would produce no uneasiness, because insolence would be separated from power, and discontent from inferiority. Difference of opinions would never disturb this community, because every man would dispute for truth alone, look upon the ignorance of others with compassion, and reclaim them from their errors with tenderness and modesty. Persecution would not be heard of among them, because there would be no pride on one side, nor obstinacy on the other. Disputes about property would seldom happen, because no man would grow rich by injuring another, and when they did happen, they would be quickly terminated, because each party would be equally desirous of a just sentence. All care and solicitude would be almost banished from this happy region, because no man would either have false friends, or public enemies. The immoderate desire of riches would be extinguished where there was no vanity to be gratified. The fear of poverty would be dispelled, where there was no man suffered to want what was necessary to his support, or proportioned to his deserts. Such would be the state of a community generally virtuous, and this happiness would probably be derived to future generations; since the earliest impressions would be in favour of virtue, since those to whom the care of education should be committed would make themselves venerable by the observation of their own precepts, and the minds of the young and unexperienced would not be tainted with false notions, nor their conduct influenced by bad examples.

Such is the state at which any community may arrive by the general practice of the duties of religion. And can Providence be accused of cruelty or negligence, when such happiness as this is within our power? Can man be said to have received his existence as a punishment, or a curse, when he may attain such a state as this; when even this is only preparatory to greater happiness, and the same course of life will secure him from misery, both in this world and in a future state?

Let no man charge this prospect of things with being a train of airy phantoms; a visionary scene, with which a gay imagination may be amused in solitude and ease, but which the first survey of the world will show him to be nothing more than a pleasing delusion. Nothing has been mentioned which would not certainly be produced in any nation by a general piety. To effect all this, no miracle is required; men need only unite their endeavours, and exert those abilities which God has conferred upon them, in conformity to the laws of religion.

To general happiness indeed is required a general concurrence in virtue; but we are not to delay the amendment of our own lives in expectation of this favourable juncture. A universal reformation must be begun somewhere, and every man ought to be ambitious of being the first. He that does not promote it, retards it; for every man must, by his conversation, do either good or hurt. Let every man therefore endeavour to make the world happy, by a strict performance of his duty to God and man, and the mighty work will soon be accomplished.

Governors have yet a harder task; they have not only their own actions, but those of others, to regulate, and are not only chargeable with their own faults, but with all those which they neglect to prevent or punish. As they are entrusted with the government for the sake of the people, they are under the strongest obligations to advance their happiness, which they can only do by encouragement of virtue.

But since the care of governors may be frustrated, since public happiness, which must be the result of public virtue, seems to be at a great distance from us, let us consider,

Thirdly, how much in the present corrupt state of the world particular men may, by the practice of the duties of religion, promote their own happiness.

He is very ignorant of the nature of happiness who imagines it to consist wholly in the outward circumstances of life, which being in themselves transient and variable, and generally dependent upon the will of others, can never be the true basis of a solid satisfaction. To be wealthy, to be honoured, to be loved, or to be feared, is not always to be happy. The man who considers himself as a being accountable to God, as a being sent into the world only to secure immortal happiness by his obedience to those laws which he has received from his Creator, will not be very solicitous about his present condition, which will soon give way to a state permanent and unchangeable, in which nothing will avail him but his innocence, or disturb him but his crimes. While this reflection is predominant in the mind, all the good and evil of life sinks into nothing. While he presses forward towards eternal felicity, honours and reproaches are equally contemptible. If he be injured, he will soon cease to feel the wrong; if he be calumniated, the day is coming in which all the nations of the earth, and all the host of heaven, shall be witnesses of his justification. If his friends forsake, or betray him, he alleviates his concern, by considering that the divine promises are never broken, and that the favour of God can only be forfeited by his own fault. In all his calamities he remembers that it is in his own power to make them subservient to his own advantage, and that patience is one of those virtues which he is commanded to practise, and which God has determined to reward. That man can never be miserable to whom persecution is a blessing; nor can his tranquillity be interrupted who places all his happiness in his prospect of eternity.

Thus it appears that by the practice of our duty, even our present state may be made pleasing and desirable; and that if we languish under calamities, they are brought upon us, not by the immediate hand of Providence, but by our own folly and disobedience; that happiness will be diffused, as virtue prevails; and *that God has done right, but we have done wickedly*.

The Life of Dr Francis Cheynel°

There is always this advantage in contending with illustrious adversaries, that the combatant is equally immortalized by conquest or defeat. He that dies by the sword of a hero will always be mentioned when the acts of his enemy are mentioned. The man of whose life the following account is offered to the public was indeed eminent among his own party, and had qualities which, employed in a good cause, would have given him some claim to distinction; but no one is now so much blinded with bigotry as to imagine him equal either to Hammond or Chillingworth,° nor would his memory perhaps have been preserved, had he not, by being conjoined with such illustrious names, become the object of public curiosity.

Francis Cheynel was born in 1608, at Oxford, where his father, Dr John Cheynel, who had been fellow of Corpus Christi college, practised physic with great reputation. He was educated in one of the grammar schools of his native city, and, in the beginning of the year 1623, became a member of the university.

It is probable that he lost his father when he was very young; for it appears that before 1629, his mother had married Dr Abbot, bishop of Salisbury, whom she had likewise buried. From this marriage he received great advantage; for his mother, being now allied to Dr Brent, then Warden of Merton college, exerted her interest so vigorously that he was admitted there a probationer, and afterwards obtained a fellowship.

Having taken the degree of master of arts, he was admitted to orders according to the rites of the Church of England, and held a curacy near Oxford, together with his fellowship. He continued in his college till he was qualified by his years of residence for the degree of bachelor of divinity, which he attempted to take in 1641, but was denied his grace° for disputing concerning predestination, contrary to the king's injunctions.

This refusal of his degree he mentions in his dedication to his account of Mr Chillingworth: 'Do not conceive that I snatch up my pen in an angry mood, that I might vent my dangerous wit, and ease my overburdened spleen. No, no, I have almost forgot the *visitation* at Merton college, *and the denial of my grace, the plundering of my house, and little library*: I know when, and where, and of whom, to demand satisfaction for all these injuries and indignities. I have learnt *centum plagas Spartana nobilitate concoquere*.° I have not learnt how to plunder others of goods, or living, and make myself amends, by force of arms. I will not take a living which belonged to any civil, studious, learned delinquent: unless it be the much neglected *commendam* of some lordly prelate, condemned by the known laws of the land, and the highest court of the kingdom, for some offence of the first magnitude.'

It is observable that he declares himself to have almost forgot his injuries and indignities, though he recounts them with an appearance of acrimony, which is no proof that the impression is much weakened: and insinuates his design of demanding, at a proper time, satisfaction for them.

These vexations were the consequence rather of the abuse of learning, than the want of it; no one that reads his works can doubt that he was turbulent, obstinate, and petulant: and ready to instruct his superiors when he most needed instruction from them. Whatever he believed (and the warmth of his imagination naturally made him precipitate in forming his opinions) he thought himself obliged to profess; and what he professed he was ready to defend, without the modesty which is always prudent, and generally necessary; and which, though it was not agreeable to Mr Cheynel's temper, and therefore readily condemned by him, is a very useful associate to truth, and often introduces her, by degrees, where she never could have forced her way by argument or declamation.

A temper of this kind is generally inconvenient and offensive in any society; but in a place of education is least to be tolerated; for, as authority is necessary to instruction, whoever endeavours to destroy subordination, by weakening that reverence which is claimed by those to whom the guardianship of youth is committed by their country, defeats at once the institution; and may be justly driven from a society by which he thinks himself too wise to be governed, and in which he is too young to teach, and too opinionative to learn.

This may be readily supposed to have been the case of Cheynel; and I know not how those can be blamed for censuring his conduct, or punishing his disobedience, who had a right to govern him, and who might certainly act with equal sincerity, and with greater knowledge.

With regard to the visitation of Merton college, the account is equally obscure; visitors are well known to be generally called to regulate the affairs of colleges when the members disagree with their head, or with one another; and the temper that Dr Cheynel discovers will easily incline his readers to suspect that he could not long live in any place without finding some occasion for debate; nor debate any question without carrying opposition to such a length as might make a moderator necessary. Whether this was his conduct at Merton, or whether an appeal to the visitor's authority was made by him, or his adversaries, or any other member of the college is not to be known; it appears only that there was a visitation; that he suffered by it, and resented his punishment.

He was afterwards presented to a living of great value, near Banbury, where he had some dispute with Archbishop Laud. Of this dispute I have found no particular account. Calamy° only says, *he had a ruffle with Bishop Laud, while at his height.*

Had Cheynel been equal to his adversary in greatness° and learning, it had not been easy to have found either a more proper opposite; for they were both to the last degree zealous, active, and pertinacious, and would have afforded mankind a spectacle of resolution and boldness not often to be seen. But the amusement of beholding the struggle would hardly have been without danger, as they were too fiery not to have communicated their heat, though it should have produced a conflagration of their country.

About the year 1641, when the whole nation was engaged in the controversy about the rights of the church, and necessity of episcopacy, he declared himself a presbyterian, and an enemy to bishops, liturgies, ceremonies; and was considered as one of the most learned and acute of his party; for having spent much of his life in a college, it cannot be doubted that he had a considerable knowledge of books, which the vehemence of his temper enabled him often to display when a more timorous man would have been silent, though in learning not his inferior.

When the war broke out, Mr Cheynel in consequence of his principles declared himself for the parliament, and as he appears to have held it as a first principle that all great and noble spirits abhor neutrality, there is no doubt but that he exerted himself to gain proselytes, and to promote the interest of that party which he had thought it his duty to espouse. These endeavours were so much regarded by the parliament that, having taken the covenant, he was nominated one of the assembly of divines who were to meet at Westminster for the settlement of the new discipline.

This distinction drew necessarily upon him the hatred of the cavaliers; and his living being not far distant from the king's headquarters, he received a visit from some of the troops, who, as he affirms, plundered his house, and drove him from it. His living, which was, I suppose, considered as forfeited by his absence (though he was not suffered to continue upon it) was given to a clergyman, of whom he says that he would become a stage better than a pulpit; a censure which I can neither confute nor admit, because I have not discovered who was his successor. He then retired into Sussex, to exercise his ministry among his friends, *in a place where*, as he observes, *there had been little of the power of religion either known or practised*. As no reason can be given why the inhabitants of Sussex should have less knowledge or virtue than those of other places, it may be suspected that he means nothing more than a place where the presbyterian discipline or principles had never been received. We now observe that the methodists, where they scatter their opinions, represent themselves as preaching the gospel to unconverted nations. And enthusiasts of all kinds have been inclined to disguise their particular tenets with pompous appellations, and to imagine themselves the great instruments of salvation. Yet it must be confessed that all places are not equally enlightened; that in the most civilized nations there are many corners which may yet be called barbarous, where neither politeness, nor religion, not the common arts of life, have yet been cultivated; and it is likewise certain that the inhabitants of Sussex have been sometimes mentioned as remarkable for brutality.°

From Sussex he went often to London, where in 1643 he preached three times before the parliament, and, returning in November to Chichester,° to keep the monthly fast there, as was his custom, he obtained a convoy of sixteen soldiers, whose bravery or good fortune was such that they faced and put to flight more than two hundred of the king's forces.

In this journey he found Mr Chillingworth in the hands of the parliament's troops, of whose sickness and death he gave the account which has been sufficiently made known to the learned world by Mr Maizeaux, in his life of Chillingworth.

With regard to this relation, it may be observed that it is written with an air of fearless veracity, and with the spirit of a man who thinks his cause just, and his behaviour without reproach; nor does there appear any reason for doubting that Cheynel spoke and acted as he relates. For he does not publish an apology, but a challenge, and writes not so much to obviate calumnies as to gain from others that applause which he seems to have bestowed very liberally upon himself for his behaviour on that occasion.

Since, therefore, this relation is credible, a great part of it being supported by evidence which cannot be refuted, Dr Maizeaux seems very justly in his life of Mr Chillingworth to oppose the common report that his life was shortened by the inhumanity of those to whom he was a prisoner; for Cheynel appears to have preserved, amidst all his detestation of the opinions which he imputed to him, a great kindness to his person, and veneration for his capacity; nor does he appear to have been cruel to him, otherwise than by that incessant importunity of disputation to which he was doubtless incited by a sincere belief of the danger of his soul, if he should die without renouncing some of his opinions.

The same kindness which made him desirous to convert him before his death would incline him to preserve him from dying before he was converted; and accordingly we find that, when the castle was yielded, he took care to procure him a commodious lodging; when he was to have been unseasonably removed, he attempted to shorten a journey which he knew would be dangerous; when the physician was disgusted by Chillingworth's distrust, he prevailed upon him, as the symptoms grew more dangerous, to renew his visits; and when death left no other act of kindness to be practised, procured him the rites of burial which some would have denied him.

Having done thus far justice to the humanity of Cheynel, it is proper to enquire how far he deserves blame. He appears to have extended none of that kindness to the opinions of Chillingworth which he showed to his person; for he interprets every word in the worst sense, and seems industrious to discover in every line heresies which might have escaped for ever any other apprehension; he appears always suspicious of some latent malignity, and ready to persecute what he only suspects with the same violence as if it had been openly avowed: in all his procedure he shows himself sincere, but without candour.

About this time Cheynel, in pursuance of his natural ardour, attended the army under the command of the Earl of Essex, and added the praise of valour to that of learning; for he distinguished himself so much by his personal bravery, and obtained so much skill in the science of war, that his commands were obeyed by the colonels with as much respect as those of the general. He seems, indeed, to have been born a soldier; for he had an intrepidity which was never to be shaken by any danger, and a spirit of enterprise not to be discouraged by difficulty; which were supported by an unusual degree of bodily strength. His services of all kinds were thought of so much importance by the parliament that they bestowed upon him the living of Petworth in Sussex. This living was of the value of 700*l.* per annum, from which they had ejected a man remarkable for his loyalty; and, therefore, in their opinion, not worthy of such revenues. And it may be enquired whether, in accepting this preferment, Cheynel did not violate the protestation which he makes in the passage already recited, and whether he did not suffer his resolution to be overborne by the temptations of wealth.

In 1646, when Oxford was taken by the forces of the Parliament, and the reformation of the University was resolved, Mr Cheynel was sent with six others to prepare the way for a visitation; being authorised by the Parliament to preach in any of the churches, without regard to the right of the members of the University, that their doctrine might prepare their hearers for the changes which were intended.

When they arrived at Oxford, they began to execute their commission by possessing themselves of the pulpits; but, if the relation of Wood is to be regarded, were heard with very little veneration. Those who had been accustomed to the preachers of Oxford, and the liturgy of the church of England, were offended at the emptiness of their discourses, which were noisy and unmeaning; at the unusual gestures, the wild distortions, and the uncouth tone with which they were delivered; at the coldness of their prayers for the king, and the vehemence and exuberance of those which they did not fail to utter for *the blessed councils* and actions of the Parliament and army; and at, what was surely not to be remarked without indignation, their omission of the Lord's Prayer.

But power easily supplied the want of reverence, and they proceeded in their plan of reformation; and thinking sermons not so efficacious to conversion as private interrogatories and exhortations, they established a weekly meeting for *freeing tender consciences from scruple*, at a house that, from the business to which it was appropriated, was called the *Scruple-shop*.

With this project they were so well pleased that they sent to the Parliament an account of it, which was afterwards printed, and is ascribed by Wood to Mr Cheynel. They continued for some weeks to hold their meetings regularly, and to admit great numbers, whom curiosity, or a desire of conviction, or a compliance with the prevailing party brought thither. But their tranquillity was quickly disturbed by the turbulence of the independents, whose opinions then prevailed among the soldiers, and were very industriously propagated by the discourses of William Earbury, a preacher of great reputation among them, who one day gathering a considerable number of his most zealous followers went to the house appointed for the resolution of scruples, on a day which was set apart for the disquisition of the dignity and office of a minister, and began to dispute with great vehemence against the presbyterians, whom he denied to have any true ministers among them, and whose assemblies he affirmed not to be the true church. He was opposed with equal heat by the presbyterians, and at length they agreed to examine the point another day, in a regular disputation. Accordingly they appointed the 12th of November for an enquiry, *whether in the Christian church the office of minister is committed to any particular persons.*

On the day fixed, the antagonists appeared, each attended by great numbers; but, when the question was proposed, they began to wrangle, not about the doctrine which they had engaged to examine, but about the terms of the proposition, which the independent alleged to be changed since their agreement; and at length the soldiers insisted that the question should be *whether those who call themselves ministers have more right or power to preach the gospel than any other man that is a Christian.* This question was debated for some time with great vehemence and confusion; but without any prospect of a conclusion. At length one of the soldiers, who thought they had an equal right with the rest to engage in the controversy, demanded of the presbyterians whence they themselves received their orders, whether from bishops, or any other persons. This unexpected interrogatory put them to great difficulties; for it happened that they were all ordained by the bishops, which they durst not acknowledge, for fear of exposing themselves to a general censure; and being convicted from their own declarations, in which they had frequently condemned episcopacy as contrary to Christianity; nor durst they deny it, because they might have been confuted, and must at once have sunk into contempt. The soldiers, seeing their perplexity, insulted them; and went away, boasting of their victory; nor did the presbyterians, for some time, recover spirit enough to renew their meetings, or to proceed in the work of easing consciences.

Earbury, exulting at the victory which not his own abilities but the subtlety of the soldier had procured him, began to vent his notions of every kind without scruple and, at length, asserted, that *the saints had an equal measure of the divine nature with our Saviour, though not equally manifest.* At the same time he took upon him the dignity of a prophet, and began to utter predictions relating to the affairs of England and Ireland.

His prophecies were not much regarded, but his doctrine was censured by the presbyterians in their pulpits; and Mr Cheynel challenged him to a disputation, to which he agreed, and at his first appearance in St Mary's church addressed his audience in the following manner:

Christian friends, kind fellow-soldiers, and worthy students, I, the humble servant of all mankind, am this day drawn, against my will, out of my cell into this public assembly, by the double chain of accusation and a challenge from the pulpit; I have been charged with heresy, I have been challenged to come hither, in a letter written by Mr Francis Cheynel. Here then I stand in defence of myself and my doctrine, which I shall introduce with only this declaration, that I claim not the office of a minister on account of any outward call, though I formerly received ordination, nor do I boast of *illumination*, or the knowledge of our Saviour, though I have been held in esteem by others, and formerly by myself. For I now declare that I know and am nothing, nothing, nor would I be thought of otherwise than as an enquirer and seeker.

He then advanced his former position in stronger terms, and with additions equally destestable, which Cheynel attacked with the vehemence which, in so warm a temper, such horrid assertions might naturally excite. The dispute, frequently interrupted by the clamours of the audience, and tumults raised to disconcert Cheynel, who was very unpopular, continued about four hours, and then both the controvertists grew weary and retired. The presbyterians afterwards thought they should more speedily put an end to the heresies of Earbury by power than by argument; and, by soliciting General Fairfax, procured his removal.

Mr Cheynel published an account of this dispute, under the title of *Faith triumphing over Error and Heresy in a Revelation, &c.*, nor can it be doubted but he had the victory, where his cause gave him so great superiority.

Somewhat before this, his captious and petulant disposition engaged him in a controversy from which he could not expect to gain equal reputation. Dr Hammond had, not long before, published his *Practical Catechism*, in which Mr Cheynel, according to his custom, found many errors implied, if not asserted; and, therefore, as it was much read, thought it convenient to censure it in the pulpit. Of this Dr Hammond, being informed, desired him, in a letter, to communicate his objections; to which Mr Cheynel returned an answer written with his usual temper, and, therefore, somewhat perverse. The controversy was drawn out to a considerable length, and the papers on both sides were afterwards made public by Dr Hammond.

In 1647, it was determined by Parliament that the reformation of Oxford should be more vigorously carried on; and Mr Cheynel was nominated one of the visitors. The general process of the visitation, the firmness and fidelity of the students, the address by which the enquiry was delayed, and the steadiness with which it was opposed, which are very particularly related by Wood, and after him by Walker, it is not necessary to mention here, as they relate not more to Dr Cheynel's life than to those of his associates.

There is indeed some reason to believe that he was more active and virulent than the rest, because he appears to have been charged in a particular manner with some of their most unjustifiable measures. He was accused of proposing that the members of the university should be denied the assistance of counsel, and was lampooned by name as a madman in a satire written on the visitation.

One action, which shows the violence of his temper, and his disregard both of humanity and decency, when they came into competition with his passions, must not be forgotten. The visitors, being offended at the obstinacy of Dr Fell, Dean of Christ Church and Vice-chancellor of the University, having first deprived him of the Vice-chancellorship, determined afterwards to dispossess him of his deanery; and, in the course of their proceedings, thought it proper to seize upon his chambers in the college. This was an act which most men would willingly have referred to the officers to whom the law assigned it; but Cheynel's fury prompted him to a different conduct. He, and three more of the visitors, went and demanded admission; which being steadily refused them, they obtained by the assistance of a file of soldiers, who forced the doors with pickaxes. Then entering, they saw Mrs Fell in the lodgings, Dr Fell being in prison at London, and ordered her to quit them; but found her not more obsequious than her husband. They repeated their orders with menaces, but were not able to prevail upon her to remove. They then retired, and left her exposed to the brutality of the soldiers, whom they commanded to keep possession, which Mrs Fell, however, did not leave. About nine days afterwards she received another visit of the same kind from the new Chancellor, the Earl of Pembroke; who having, like the others, ordered her to depart without effect, treated her with reproachful language, and at last commanded the soldiers to take her up in her chair, and carry her out of doors. Her daughters and some other gentlewomen that were with her were afterwards treated in the same manner; one of whom predicted, without dejection, that she should enter the house again with less difficulty at some other time; nor was she mistaken in her conjecture, for Dr Fell lived to be restored to his deanery.

At the reception of the Chancellor, Cheynel, as the most accomplished of the visitors, had the province of presenting him with
the ensigns of his office, some of which were counterfeit, and
addressing him with a proper oration. Of this speech, which Wood has
preserved, I shall give some passages, by which a judgment may be
made of his oratory.

Of the staves of the beadles he observes that 'some are stained with
double guilt, that some are pale with fear, and that others have been
made use of as crutches, for the support of bad causes and desperate
fortunes'; and he remarks of the book of statutes which he delivers
that 'the ignorant may perhaps admire the splendour of the cover, but
the learned know that the real treasure is within'. Of these two
sentences it is easily discovered that the first is forced and unnatural,
and the second trivial and low.

Soon afterwards Mr Cheynel was admitted to the degree of
bachelor of divinity, for which his grace had been denied him in
1641, and as he then suffered for an ill-timed assertion of the
presbyterian doctrines, he obtained that his degree should be dated
from the time at which he was refused it; an honour which however
did not secure him from being soon after publicly reproached as a
madman.

But the vigour of Cheynel was thought by his companions to
deserve profit, as well as honour; and Dr Bailey, the President of St
John's college, being not more obedient to the authority of the
parliament than the rest, was deprived of his revenues and authority,
with which Mr Cheynel was immediately invested; who, with his
usual coolness and modesty, took possession of the lodgings soon
after by breaking open the doors.

This preferment being not thought adequate to the deserts or
abilities of Mr Cheynel, it was, therefore, desired, by the committee of
parliament, that the visitors would recommend him to the lectureship
of divinity founded by the Lady Margaret. To recommend him and to
choose was at that time the same; and he had now the pleasure of
propagating his darling doctrine of predestination without interruption and without danger.

Being thus flushed with power and success, there is little reason for
doubting that he gave way to his natural vehemence, and indulged
himself in the utmost excesses of raging zeal, by which he was indeed
so much distinguished that, in a satire mentioned by Wood, he is
dignified by the title of Arch-visitor; an appellation which he seems to
have been industrious to deserve by severity and inflexibility: for, not

contented with the commission which he and his colleagues had already received, he procured six or seven of the members of parliament to meet privately in Mr Rouse's lodgings, and assume the style and authority of a committee, and from them obtained a more extensive and tyrannical power, by which the visitors were enabled to force the *solemn League and Covenant*, and the *negative oath* upon all the members of the University, and to prosecute those for a contempt who did not appear to a citation, at whatever distance they might be, and whatever reasons they might assign for their absence.

By this method he easily drove great numbers from the University, whose places he supplied with men of his own opinion, whom he was very industrious to draw from other parts, with promises of making a liberal provision for them out of the spoils of heretics and malignants.

Having in time almost extirpated those opinions which he found so prevalent at his arrival, or, at least, obliged those who would not recant to an appearance of conformity, he was at leisure for employments which deserve to be recorded with greater commendation. About this time, many Socinian writers began to publish their notions with great boldness, which the presbyterians, considering as heretical and impious, thought it necessary to confute; and, therefore, Cheynel, who had now obtained his doctor's degree, was desired in 1649 to write a vindication of the doctrine of the Trinity, which he performed, and published the next year.

He drew up likewise a confutation of some Socinian tenets advanced by John Fry, a man who spent great part of his life in ranging from one religion to another, and who sat as one of the judges on the king; but was expelled afterwards from the House of Commons, and disabled from sitting in parliament. Dr Cheynel is said to have shown himself evidently superior to him in the controversy, and was answered by him only with an opprobrious book against the presbyterian clergy.

Of the remaining part of his life there is found only an obscure and confused account. He quitted the presidentship of St John's, and the professorship, in 1650, as Calamy relates, because he would not take the engagement; and gave a proof that he could suffer as well as act in a cause which he believed just. We have indeed no reason to question his resolution, whatever occasion might be given to exert it; nor is it probable that he feared affliction more than danger, or that he would not have borne persecution himself for those opinions which inclined him to persecute others.

He did not suffer much on this occasion: for he retained the living

of Petworth, to which he thenceforward confined his labours, and
where he was very assiduous, and, as Calamy affirms, very successful
in the exercise of his ministry, it being his peculiar character to be
warm and zealous in all his undertakings.

This heat of his disposition, increased by the uncommon turbulence of the time in which he lived, and by the opposition to which the
unpopular nature of some of his employments exposed him, was at last
heightened to distraction, so that he was for some time disordered in
his understanding, as both Wood and Calamy relate, but with such
difference as might be expected from their opposite principles. Wood
appears to think that a tendency to madness was discoverable in a
great part of his life; Calamy, that it was only transient and accidental,
though, in his additions to his first narrative, he pleads it as an
extenuation of that fury with which his kindest friends confess him to
have acted on some occasions. Wood declares that he died little better
than distracted; Calamy, that he was perfectly recovered to a sound
mind before the restoration, at which time he retired to Preston, a
small village in Sussex, being turned out of his living of Petworth.

It does not appear that he kept his living till the general ejection of
the Nonconformists; and it is not unlikely that the asperity of his
carriage, and the known virulence of his temper, might have raised
him enemies, who were willing to make him feel the effects of
persecution which he had so furiously incited against others; but of
this incident of his life there is no particular account.

After his deprivation, he lived (till his death, which happened in
1665) at a small village near Chichester, upon a paternal estate, not
augmented by the large preferments wasted upon him in the triumphs
of his party; having been remarkable, throughout his life, for
hospitality and contempt of money.

Review of Joseph Warton, *An Essay on the Writings and Genius of Pope*°

This is a very curious and entertaining miscellany of critical remarks and literary history. Though the book promises nothing but observations on the writings of Pope, yet no opportunity is neglected of introducing the character of any other writer, or the mention of any performance or event in which learning is interested. From Pope, however, he always takes his hint, and to Pope he returns again from his digressions. The facts which he mentions, though they are seldom *anecdotes*,° in a rigorous sense, are often such as are very little known, and such as will delight more readers than naked criticism.

As he examines the works of this great poet in an order nearly chronological he necessarily begins with his pastorals, which, considered as representations of any kind of life, he very justly censures; for there is in them a mixture of Grecian and English, of ancient and modern images. Windsor is coupled with Hybla, and Thames with Pactolus. He then compares some passages which Pope has imitated or translated with the imitation, or version, and gives the preference to the originals, perhaps not always upon convincing arguments.

Theocritus makes his lover wish to be a bee, that he might creep among the leaves that form the chaplet of his mistress. Pope's enamoured swain longs to be made the captive bird that sings in his fair one's bower, that she might listen to his songs, and reward him with her kisses. The critic prefers the image of Theocritus, as more wild, more delicate, and more uncommon.

It is natural for a lover to wish that he might be any thing that could come near to his lady. But we more naturally desire to be that which she fondles and caresses than that which she would avoid, at least would neglect. The superior delicacy of Theocritus I cannot discover, nor can, indeed, find that either in the one or the other image there is any want of delicacy. Which of the two images was less common in the time of the poet who used it, for on that consideration the merit of novelty depends, I think it is now out of any critic's power to decide.

He remarks, I am afraid with too much justice, that there is not a single new thought in the pastorals, and, with equal reason, declares that their chief beauty consists in their *correct and musical versification, which has so influenced the English ear as to render every moderate rhymer harmonious.*

In his examination of the *Messiah*, he justly observes some deviations from the inspired author, which weaken the imagery, and dispirit the expression.

On *Windsor-Forest*, he declares, I think without proof, that descriptive poetry was by no means the excellence of Pope; he draws this inference from the few images introduced in this poem which would not equally belong to any other place. He must inquire whether *Windsor-Forest* has, in reality, any thing peculiar.

The Stag-chase *is not*, he says, *so full*, *so animated*, *and so circumstantiated* as Somerville's.° Barely to say that one performance is not so good as another is to criticise with little exactness. But Pope has directed that we should in *every work regard the author's end*. The stag-chase is the main subject of Somerville, and might, therefore, be properly dilated into all its circumstances; in Pope, it is only incidental, and was to be dispatched in a few lines.

He makes a just observation, that

the description of the external beauties of nature is usually the first effort° of a young genius, before he hath studied nature and passions. Some of Milton's most early, as well as most exquisite pieces, are his *Lycidas*,° *l'Allegro*, and *il Penseroso*, if we may except his ode on the nativity of Christ, which is, indeed, prior in order of time, and in which a penetrating critic might have observed the seeds of that boundless imagination, which was, one day, to produce the *Paradise Lost*.

Mentioning Thomson, and other descriptive poets, he remarks that writers fail in their copies for want of acquaintance with originals, and justly ridicules those who think they can form just ideas of valleys, mountains, and rivers in a garret of the Strand. For this reason, I cannot regret, with this author, that Pope laid aside his design of writing American pastorals; for, as he must have painted scenes which he never saw, and manners he never knew, his performance, though it might have been a pleasing amusement of fancy, would have exhibited no representation of nature or of life.

After the pastorals, the critic considers the lyric poetry of Pope, and dwells longest on the ode on St Cecilia's day, which he, like the rest of mankind, places next to that of Dryden, and not much below it. He remarks, after Mr Spence, that the first stanza is a perfect concert, the second he thinks a little flat; he justly commends the fourth, but without notice of the best line in that stanza, or in the poem,

> Transported demigods stood round,
> And men grew heroes at the sound.

In the latter part of the ode, he objects to the stanza of triumph:

Thus song could prevail,   &c.

as written in a measure *ridiculous* and *burlesque*, and justifies his
answer by observing that Addison uses the same numbers in the scene
of *Rosamond*, between Grideline and Sir Trusty:

How unhappy is he,   &c.

That the measure is the same in both passages must be confessed, and
both poets, perhaps, chose their numbers properly; for they both
meant to express a kind of airy hilarity. The two passions of
merriment and exultation are undoubtedly different; they are as
different as a gambol and a triumph, but each is a species of joy; and
poetical measures have not in any language been so far refined as to
provide for the subdivisions of passion. They can only be adapted to
general purposes, but the particular and minuter propriety must be
sought only in the sentiment and language. Thus the numbers are the
same in *Colin's Complaint*° and in the ballad of *Darby and Joan*,
though, in one, sadness is represented, and, in the other, tranquillity;
so the measure is the same of Pope's *Unfortunate Lady*, and the *Praise
of Voiture*.

He observes very justly that the odes both of Dryden and Pope
conclude unsuitably and unnaturally with epigram.

He then spends a page upon Mr Handel's music to Dryden's ode,
and speaks of him with that regard which he has generally obtained
among the lovers of sound. He finds something amiss in the air *With
ravished ears*, but has overlooked, or forgotten, the grossest fault° in
that composition, which is that in this line,

Revenge, revenge, Timotheus cries,

he has laid much stress upon the two latter words, which are merely
words of connexion, and ought in music to be considered as
parenthetical.

From this ode is struck out a digression on the nature of odes, and
the comparative excellence of the ancients and moderns. He mentions
the chorus which Pope wrote for the duke of Buckingham, and thence
takes occasion to treat of the chorus of the ancients. He then comes to
another ode, of *the dying Christian to his Soul*; in which finding an
apparent imitation of Flatman,° he falls into a pleasing and learned
speculation on the resembling passages to be found in different poets.

He mentions, with great regard, Pope's ode on *solitude*, written when he was but twelve years old, but omits to mention the poem on *Silence*, composed, I think, as early, with much greater elegance of diction, music of numbers, extent of observation, and force of thought. If he had happened to think on Baillet's° chapter of *Enfans célèbres*, he might have made, on this occasion, a very entertaining dissertation on early excellence.

He comes next to the *Essay on Criticism*, the stupendous performance of a youth not yet twenty years old; and after having detailed the felicities of condition to which he imagines Pope to have owed his wonderful prematurity of mind, he tells us that he is well informed this essay was first written in prose. There is nothing improbable in the report, nothing, indeed, but what is more likely than the contrary; yet I cannot forbear to hint to this writer and all others the danger and weakness of trusting too readily to information. Nothing but experience could evince the frequency of false information, or enable any man to conceive that so many groundless reports should be propagated as every man of eminence may hear of himself. Some men relate what they think as what they know; some men, of confused memories and habitual inaccuracy, ascribe to one man what belongs to another; and some talk on, without thought or care. A few men are sufficient to broach falsehoods, which are afterwards innocently diffused by successive relaters.

He proceeds on, examining passage after passage of this essay; but we must pass over all these criticisms to which we have not something to add or to object, or where this author does not differ from the general voice of mankind. We cannot agree with him in his censure of the comparison of a student advancing in science with a traveller passing the Alps, which is perhaps, the best simile in our language; that in which the most exact resemblance is traced between things in appearance utterly unrelated to each other. That *the last line conveys no new idea*° is not true; it makes particular what was before general. Whether the description which he adds from another author be, as he says, more *full* and *striking* than that of Pope is not to be inquired. Pope's description is relative, and can admit of no greater length than is usually allowed to a simile, nor any other particulars than such as form the correspondence.

Unvaried rhymes, says this writer, *highly disgust readers of a good ear*. It is surely not the ear, but the mind that is offended; the fault arising from the use of common rhymes is that by reading the first° line, the second may be guessed, and half the composition loses the grace of novelty.

On occasion of the mention of an alexandrine, the critic observes that *the alexandrine may be thought a modern measure, but that Robert of Gloucester's verse° is an alexandrine, with the addition of two syllables; and that Sternhold and Hopkins translated the psalms in the same measure of fourteen syllables, though they are printed otherwise.*

This seems not to be accurately conceived or expressed: an alexandrine with the addition of two syllables is no more an alexandrine than with the detraction of two syllables. Sternhold and Hopkins did generally write in the alternate measure of eight and six syllables; but Hopkins commonly rhymed the first and third, Sternhold only the second and fourth: so that Sternhold may be considered as writing couplets of long lines; but Hopkins wrote regular stanzas. From the practice of printing the long lines of fourteen syllables in two short lines arose the licence of some of our poets, who, though professing to write in stanzas, neglect the rhymes of the first and third lines.

Pope has mentioned Petronius among the great names of criticism, as the remarker justly observes, without any critical merit. It is to be suspected that Pope had never read his book, and mentioned him on the credit of two or three sentences which he had often seen quoted, imagining that where there was so much there must necessarily be more. Young men in haste to be renowned too frequently talk of books which they have scarcely seen.

The revival of learning, mentioned in this poem, affords an opportunity of mentioning the chief periods of literary history, of which this writer reckons five, that of Alexander, of Ptolemy Philadelphus, of Augustus, of Leo the tenth, of queen Anne.

These observations are concluded with a remark which deserves great attention: 'In no polished nation, after criticism has been much studied, and the rules of writing established, has any very extraordinary book ever appeared.'

The *Rape of the Lock* was always regarded by Pope as the highest production of his genius. On occasion of this work the history of the comic heroic is given; and we are told that it descended from Tassoni to Boileau, from Boileau to Garth,° and from Garth to Pope. Garth is mentioned perhaps with too much honour; but all are confessed to be inferior to Pope. There is in his remarks on this work no discovery of any latent beauty, nor any thing subtle or striking; he is indeed commonly right, but has discussed no difficult question.

The next pieces to be considered are the *Verses to the Memory of an Unfortunate Lady*, the *Prologue to Cato*, and *Epilogue to Jane Shore*.

The first piece he commends; on occasion of the second he digresses, according to his custom, into a learned dissertation on tragedies, and compares the English and French with the Greek stage. He justly censures *Cato* for want of action and of characters, but scarcely does justice to the sublimity of some speeches and the philosophical exactness in the sentiments. *The simile of mount Atlas, and that of the Numidian traveller, smothered in the sands, are, indeed, in character,* says the critic, *but sufficiently obvious.* The simile of the mountain is indeed common, but that of the traveller I do not remember. That it is obvious is easy to say, and easy to deny.—Many things are obvious, when they are taught.

He proceeds to criticise the other works of Addison, till the epilogue calls his attention to Rowe, whose character he discusses in the same manner, with sufficient freedom and sufficient candour.

The translation of the epistle of *Sappho to Phaon* is next considered, but Sappho and Ovid are more the subjects of this disquisition than Pope. We shall therefore pass over it to a piece of more importance, the epistle of Eloisa to Abelard, which may justly be regarded as one of the works on which the reputation of Pope will stand in future times.

The critic pursues Eloisa through all the changes of passion, produces the passages of her letters to which any allusion is made, and intersperses many agreeable particulars and incidental relations. There is not much profundity of criticism, because the beauties are sentiments of nature, which the learned and the ignorant feel alike. It is justly remarked by him that the wish of Eloisa for the happy passage of Abelard into the other world is formed according to the ideas of mystic devotion.

These are the pieces examined in this volume; whether the remaining part of the work will be one volume or more, perhaps the writer himself cannot yet inform us.° This piece is however a complete work, so far as it goes, and the writer is of opinion that he has dispatched the chief part of his task; for he ventures to remark that the reputation of Pope, as a poet, among posterity, will be principally founded on his *Windsor Forest, Rape of the Lock,* and *Eloisa to Abelard*; while the facts and characters alluded to in his late writings will be forgotten and unknown and their poignancy and propriety little relished; for wit and satire are transitory and perishable, but nature and passion are eternal.

He has interspersed some passages of Pope's life, with which most readers will be pleased. When Pope was yet a child, his father, who had been a merchant in London, retired to Binfield. He was taught to read by an aunt; and learned to write, without a master, by copying printed books. His father used to order him to make English verses, and would oblige him to correct and retouch them over and over, and at last could say, 'These are good rhymes.'

At eight years of age he was committed to one Taverner, a priest, who taught him the rudiments of the Latin and Greek. At this time, he met with Ogleby's Homer, which seized his attention; he fell next upon Sandys's Ovid, and remembered these two translations with pleasure to the end of his life.

About ten, being at school near Hyde-park Corner, he was taken to the playhouse, and was so struck with the splendour of the drama that he formed a kind of play out of Ogleby's Homer, intermixed with verses of his own. He persuaded the head-boys to act this piece, and Ajax was performed by his master's gardener; they were habited according to the pictures in Ogleby. At twelve he retired, with his father to Windsor forest, and formed himself by the study in the best English poets.

In this extract it was thought convenient to dwell chiefly upon such observations as relate immediately to Pope, without deviating with the author into incidental inquiries. We intend to kindle, not to extinguish, curiosity, by this slight sketch of a work abounding with curious quotations and pleasing disquisitions. He must be much acquainted with literary history both of remote and late times who does not find in this essay many things which he did not know before; and if there be any too learned to be instructed in facts or opinions, he may yet properly read this book as a just specimen of literary moderation.

Review of Thomas Blackwell, *Memoirs of the Court of Augustus*°

The first effect which this book has upon the reader is that of disgusting him with the author's vanity. He endeavours to persuade the world that here are some new treasures of literature spread before his eyes; that something is discovered which, to this happy day, had been concealed in darkness; that, by his diligence, time has been robbed of some valuable monument which he was on the point of devouring; and that names and facts doomed to oblivion are now restored to fame.

How must the unlearned reader be surprised when he shall be told that Mr Blackwell has neither digged in the ruins of any demolished city; nor found out the way to the library of Fez; nor had a single book in his hands that has not been in the possession of every man that was inclined to read it for years and ages; and that his book relates to a people who above all others have furnished employment to the studious, and amusements to the idle, who have scarcely left behind them a coin or a stone which has not been examined and explained a thousand times, and whose dress, and food, and household stuff it has been the pride of learning to understand.

A man need not fear to incur the imputation of vicious diffidence or affected humility who should have forborne to promise many novelties when he perceived such multitudes of writers possessed of the same materials, and intent upon the same purpose. Mr Blackwell knows well the opinion of Horace concerning those that open their undertakings with magnificent promises, and he knows likewise the dictates of common sense and common honesty, names of greater authority than that of Horace, who direct that no man should promise what he cannot perform.

I do not mean to declare that this volume has nothing new, or that the labours of those who have gone before our author have made his performance an useless addition to the burden of literature. New works may be constructed with old materials, the disposition of the parts may show contrivance, the ornaments interspersed may discover elegance.

It is not always without good effect that men of proper qualifications write in succession on the same subject, even when the latter add nothing to the information given by the former; for the same ideas may be delivered more intelligibly or more delightfully by one than by another, or with attractions that may lure minds of a different form. No writer pleases all, and every writer may please some.

But after all, to inherit is not to acquire; to decorate is not to make, and the man who had nothing to do but to read the ancient authors who mention the Roman affairs, and reduce them to commonplaces, ought not to boast himself as a great benefactor to the studious world.

After a preface of boast, and a letter of flattery, in which he seems to imitate the address of Horace, in his *vile potabis modicis Sabinum*,° he opens his book with telling us, that the

Roman republic, after the horrible proscription, was no more a *bleeding Rome*. The regal power of her consuls, the authority of her senate, and the majesty of her people, were now trampled under foot; those divine laws and hallowed customs, that had been the essence of her constitution—were set at nought, and her best friends were lying exposed in their blood.

These were surely very dismal times to those who suffered; but I know not why any one but a schoolboy in his declamation should whine over the commonwealth of Rome, which grew great only by the misery of the rest of mankind. The Romans, like others, as soon as they grew rich grew corrupt, and, in their corruption, sold the lives and freedoms of themselves, and of one another.

About this time, Brutus had his patience put to the *highest* trial: he had been married to Clodia; but whether the family did not please him, or whether he was dissatisfied with the lady's behaviour during his absence, he soon entertained thoughts of a separation. *This raised a good deal of talk*, and the women of the Clodian family inveighed bitterly against Brutus—but he married Portia, who was worthy of such a father as M. Cato, and such a husband as M. Brutus. She had a soul capable of an *exalted passion*, and found a proper object to raise and give it a sanction; she did not only love, but adored her husband; his worth, his truth, his every shining and heroic quality, made her gaze on him like a god, while the endearing returns of esteem and tenderness she met with, brought her joy, her pride, her every wish to centre in her beloved Brutus.

When the reader has been awakened by this rapturous preparation, he hears the whole story of Portia in the same luxuriant style, till she breathed out her last, a little before the *bloody proscription*, and 'Brutus complained heavily of his friends at Rome, as not having paid due attention to his *lady* in the declining state of her health.'

He is a great lover of modern terms. His senators and their wives are *gentlemen* and *ladies*. In this review of Brutus's army, who *was under the command of gallant men, not braver officers than true patriots*, he tells us, 'that Sextus the questor was *paymaster, secretary at war, and commissary general,* and that the *sacred discipline* of the Romans required the closest connection, like that of father and son, to subsist between the general of an army and his questor. Cicero was *general of the cavalry,* and the next *general officer* was Flavius, *master of the artillery,* the elder Lentulus was *admiral,* and the younger *rode* in the *band of volunteers;* under these the tribunes, *with many others too tedious to name.*' Lentulus, however, was but a subordinate officer; for we are informed afterwards that the Romans had made Sextus Pompeius *lord high admiral in all the seas of their dominions.*

Among other affectations of this writer is a furious and unnecessary zeal for liberty, or rather, for one form of government as preferable to another. This indeed might be suffered, because political institution is a subject in which men have always differed, and if they continue to obey their lawful governors, and attempt not to make innovations for the sake of their favourite schemes, they may differ for ever without any just reproach from one another. But who can bear the hardy champion who ventures nothing? who in full security undertakes the defence of the assassination of Caesar, and declares his resolution *to speak plain?* Yet let not just sentiments be overlooked; he has justly observed that the greater part of mankind will be naturally prejudiced against Brutus, for all feel the benefits of private friendship; but few can discern the advantages of a well-constituted government.

We know not whether some apology may not be necessary for the distance between the first account of this book and its continuation.° The truth is that this work, not being forced upon our attention by much public applause or censure, was sometimes neglected, and sometimes forgotten, nor would it, perhaps, have been now resumed, but that we might avoid to disappoint our readers by an abrupt desertion of any subject.

It is not our design to criticise the facts of this history but the style; not the veracity, but the address of the writer; for an account of the ancient Romans, as it cannot nearly interest any present reader, and must be drawn from writings that have been long known, can owe its value only to the language in which it is delivered, and the reflections with which it is accompanied. Dr Blackwell, however, seems to have heated his imagination so as to be much affected with every event, and to believe that he can affect others. Enthusiasm is indeed sufficiently contagious, but I never found any of his readers much enamoured of the *glorious Pompey, the patriot approved,* or much incensed against the *lawless Caesar*, whom this author probably stabs every day and night in his sleeping or waking dreams.

He is come too late into the world with his fury for freedom, with his Brutus and Cassius. We have all on this side of the Tweed long since settled our opinions; his zeal for Roman liberty and declamations against the violators of the republican constitution only stand now in the reader's way who wishes to proceed in the narrative without the interruption of epithets and exclamations. It is not easy to forbear laughter at a man so bold in fighting shadows, so busy in a dispute two thousand years past, and so zealous for the honour of a people who while they were poor robbed mankind, and as soon as they became rich robbed one another. Of these robberies our author seems to have no very quick sense, except when they are committed by Caesar's party, for every act is sanctified by the name of a patriot.

If this author's skill in ancient literature were less generally acknowledged, one might sometimes suspect that he had too frequently consulted the French writers. He tells us that Archelaus the Rhodian made a speech to Cassius, and, *in so saying*, dropped some tears, and that Cassius after the reduction of Rhodes was *covered with glory*.—Deiotarus was a keen and happy spirit—the ingrate Castor kept his court.

His great delight is to show his universal acquaintance with terms of art, with words that every other polite writer has avoided and despised.

When Pompey conquered the pirates, he destroyed fifteen hundred ships of the line.—The Xanthian parapets were tore down.—Brutus, suspecting that his troops were plundering, commanded the trumpets to sound to their colours.—Most people understood the act of attainder passed by the senate.—The Numidian troopers were unlikely in their appearance.—The Numidians beat up one quarter after another.—Salvidienus resolved to pass his men over in boats of leather, and he gave orders for equipping a sufficient number of that sort of small craft.—Pompey had light agile frigates, and fought in a strait where the current and caverns occasion swirls and a roll.—A sharp out-look was kept by the admiral.—It is a run of about fifty Roman miles.—Brutus broke Lipella in the sight of the army.—Mark Antony garbled the senate. He was a brave man, well qualified for a commodore.

In his choice of phrases he frequently uses words with great solemnity which every other mouth and pen has appropriated to jocularity and levity!

The Rhodians gave up the contest and in poor plight fled back to Rhodes.—Boys and girls were easily kidnapped.—Deiotarus was a mighty believer of augury.—Deiotarus destroyed his ungracious progeny.—The regularity of the Romans was their mortal aversion.—They desired the consuls to curb such heinous doings.—He had such a shrewd invention that no side of a question came amiss to him.—Brutus found his mistress a coquettish creature.

He sometimes with most unlucky dexterity mixes the grand and the burlesque together: *the violation of faith, Sir,* says Cassius, *lies at the door of the Rhodians by reiterated acts of perfidy.*—The iron grate fell down, crushed those under it to death, and catched the rest as in a trap.—When the Xanthians heard the military shout and saw the flame mount they concluded there would be no mercy. It was now about sunset, and they had been at hot work since noon.

He has often words or phrases with which our language has hitherto had no knowledge.

One was a heart friend to the republic. A deed was expeded. The Numidians begun to reel and were in hazard of falling into confusion.—The tutor embraced his pupil close in his arms.—Four hundred women were taxed who have no doubt been the wives of the best Roman citizens.—Men not born to action are inconsequential in government.—Collectitious troops.—The foot by their violent attack began the fatal break in the Pharsaliac field. He and his brother with a politic common to other countries had taken opposite sides.

His epithets are of the gaudy or hyperbolical kind. The glorious news—eager hopes and dismal fears—bleeding Rome—divine laws and hallowed customs—merciless war—intense anxiety.

Sometimes the reader is suddenly ravished with a sonorous sentence, of which when the noise is past the meaning does not long remain.

When Brutus set his legions to fill a moat, instead of heavy dragging and slow toil, they set about it with huzzas and racing, as if they had been striving at the Olympic games. They hurled impetuous down the huge trees and stones and with shouts forced them into the water, so that the work expected to continue half the campaign was with rapid toil completed in a few days. Brutus's soldiers fell to the gate with resistless fury, it gave way at last with hideous crash.—This great and good man, doing his duty to his country, received a mortal wound, and glorious fell in the cause of Rome; may his memory be ever dear to all lovers of liberty, learning, and humanity!—This promise ought ever to embalm his memory.—The queen of nations was torn by no foreign invaders. Rome fell a sacrifice to her own sons, and was ravaged by her unnatural offspring, all the great men of the state, all the good, all the holy were openly murdered by the wickedest and worst.—Little islands cover the harbour of Brindisi, and form the narrow outlet from the numerous creeks that compose its capacious port.—At the appearance of Brutus and Cassius a shout of joy rent the heavens from the surrounding multitudes.

Such are the flowers which may be gathered by every hand in every part of this garden of eloquence. But having thus freely mentioned our author's faults, it remains that we acknowledge his merit, and confess that this book is the work of a man of letters, that it is full of events displayed with accuracy, and related with vivacity, and though it is sufficiently defective to crush the vanity of its author, it is sufficiently entertaining to invite readers.

Observations on the Present State of Affairs°

The time is now come in which every Englishman expects to be informed of the national affairs, and in which he has a right to have that expectation gratified. For whatever may be urged by ministers, or those whom vanity or interest make the followers of ministers, concerning the necessity of confidence in our governors, and the presumption of prying with profane eyes into the recesses of policy, it is evident that this reverence can be claimed only by counsels yet unexecuted, and projects suspended in deliberation. But when a design has ended in miscarriage or success, when every eye and every ear is witness to general discontent, or general satisfaction, it is then a proper time to disentangle confusion and illustrate obscurity, to show by what causes every event was produced, and in what effects it is likely to terminate: to lay down with distinct particularity what rumour always huddles in general exclamations, or perplexes by undigested narratives; to show whence happiness or calamity is derived, and whence it may be expected, and honestly to lay before the people what inquiry can gather of the past, and conjecture can estimate of the future.

The general subject of the present war is sufficiently known. It is allowed on both sides that hostilities began in America, and that the French and English quarrelled about the boundaries of their settlements, about grounds and rivers to which, I am afraid, neither can show any other right than that of power, and which neither can occupy but by usurpation, and the dispossession of the natural lords and original inhabitants. Such is the contest that no honest man can heartily wish success to either party.

It may indeed be alleged that the Indians have granted large tracts of land both to one and to the other; but these grants can add little to the validity of our titles till it be experienced how they were obtained: for if they were extorted by violence, or induced by fraud; by threats, which the miseries of other nations had shown not to be vain, or by promises of which no performance was ever intended, what are they but new modes of usurpation, but new instances of cruelty and treachery?

And indeed what but false hope or resistless terror can prevail upon a weaker nation to invite a stronger into their country, to give their lands to strangers whom no affinity of manners or similitude of opinion can be said to recommend, to permit them to build towns from which the natives are excluded, to raise fortresses by which they are intimidated, to settle themselves with such strength that they cannot afterwards be expelled, but are for ever to remain the masters of the original inhabitants, the dictators of their conduct, and the arbiters of their fate?

When we see men acting thus against the precepts of reason, and the instincts of nature, we cannot hesitate to determine that by some means or other they were debarred from choice; that they were lured or frighted into compliance; that they either granted only what they found impossible to keep, or expected advantages upon the faith of their new inmates, which there was no purpose to confer upon them. It cannot be said that the Indians originally invited us to their coasts; we went uncalled and unexpected to nations who had no imagination that the earth contained any inhabitants so distant and so different from themselves. We astonished them with our ships, with our arms, and with our general superiority. They yielded to us as to beings of another and higher race, sent among them from some unknown regions, with power which naked Indians could not resist, and which they were therefore, by every act of humility, to propitiate, that they who could so easily destroy might be induced to spare.

To this influence, and to this only, are to be attributed all the cessions and submissions of the Indian princes, if indeed any such cessions were ever made, of which we have no witness but those who claim from them, and there is no great malignity in suspecting that those who have robbed have also lied.

Some colonies indeed have been established more peaceably than others. The utmost extremity of wrong has not always been practised; but those that have settled in the new world on the fairest terms have no other merit than that of a scrivener who ruins in silence over a plunderer that seizes by force; all have taken what had other owners, and all have had recourse to arms, rather than quit the prey on which they had fastened.

The American dispute between the French and us is therefore only the quarrel of two robbers for the spoils of a passenger, but as robbers have terms of confederacy, which they are obliged to observe as members of the gang, so the English and French may have relative rights, and do injustice to each other, while both are injuring the Indians. And such, indeed, is the present contest: they have parted the northern continent of America between them, and are now disputing about their boundaries, and each is endeavouring the destruction of the other by the help of the Indians, whose interest it is that both should be destroyed.

Both nations clamour with great vehemence about infraction of limits, violation of treaties, open usurpation, insidious artifices, and breach of faith. The English rail at the perfidious French, and the French at the encroaching English; they quote treaties on each side, charge each other with aspiring to universal monarchy, and complain on either part of the insecurity of possession near such turbulent neighbours.

Through this mist of controversy it can raise no wonder that the truth is not easily discovered. When a quarrel has been long carried on between individuals, it is often very hard to tell by whom it was begun. Every fact is darkened by distance, by interest, and by multitudes. Information is not easily procured from far; those whom the truth will not favour will not step voluntarily forth to tell it, and where there are many agents, it is easy for every single action to be concealed.

All these causes concur to the obscurity of the question, by whom were hostilities in America commenced? Perhaps there never can be remembered a time in which hostilities had ceased. Two powerful colonies inflamed with immemorial rivalry, and placed out of the superintendence of the mother nations, were not likely to be long at rest. Some opposition was always going forward, some mischief was every day done or meditated, and the borderers were always better pleased with what they could snatch from their neighbours than what they had of their own.

In this disposition to reciprocal invasion a cause of dispute never could be wanting. The forests and deserts of America are without landmarks, and therefore cannot be particularly specified in stipulations; the appellations of those wide extended regions have in every mouth a different meaning, and are understood on either side as inclination happens to contract or extend them. Who has yet pretended to define how much of America is included in Brazil, Mexico, or Peru? It is almost as easy to divide the Atlantic Ocean by a line as clearly to ascertain the limits of those uncultivated, uninhabitable, unmeasured regions.

It is likewise to be considered that contracts concerning boundaries are often left vague and indefinite without necessity, by the desire of each party to interpret the ambiguity to its own advantage when a fit opportunity shall be found. In forming stipulations, the commissaries are often ignorant, and often negligent; they are sometimes weary with debate, and contract a tedious discussion into general terms, or refer it to a former treaty, which was never understood. The weaker part is always afraid of requiring explanations, and the stronger always has an interest in leaving the question undecided: thus it will happen without great caution on either side that after long treaties solemnly ratified, the rights that had been disputed are still equally open to controversy.

In America it may easily be supposed that there are tracts of land yet claimed by neither party, and therefore mentioned in no treaties, which yet one or the other may be afterwards inclined to occupy; but to these vacant and unsettled countries each nation may pretend, as each conceives itself entitled to all that is not expressly granted to the other.

Here then is a perpetual ground of contest, every enlargement of the possessions of either will be considered as something taken from the other, and each will endeavour to regain what had never been claimed, but that the other occupied it.

Thus obscure in its original is the American contest. It is difficult to find the first invader, or to tell where invasion properly begins; but I suppose it is not to be doubted that after the last war, when the French had made peace with such apparent superiority, they naturally began to treat us with less respect in distant parts of the world, and to consider us as a people from whom they had nothing to fear, and who could no longer presume to contravene their designs, or to check their progress.

The power of doing wrong with impunity seldom waits long for the will, and it is reasonable to believe that in America the French would avow their purpose of aggrandising themselves with at least as little reserve as in Europe. We may therefore readily believe that they were unquiet neighbours, and had no great regard to right which they believed us no longer able to enforce.

That in forming a line of forts behind our colonies, if in no other part of their attempt, they had acted against the general intention, if not against the literal terms of treaties, can scarcely be denied; for it never can be supposed that we intended to be enclosed between the sea and the French garrisons, or preclude ourselves from extending our plantations backwards to any length that our convenience should require.

With dominion is conferred every thing that can secure dominion. He that has the coast has likewise the sea to a certain distance; he that possesses a fortress has the right of prohibiting another fortress to be built within the command of its cannon. When therefore we planted the coast of North America we supposed the possession of the inland region granted to an indefinite extent, and every nation that settled in that part of the world seems, by the permission of every other nation, to have made the same supposition in its own favour.

Here then, perhaps, it will be safest to fix the justice of our cause; here we are apparently and indisputably injured, and this injury may, according to the practice of nations, be justly resented. Whether we have not in return made some encroachments upon them must be left doubtful till our practices on the Ohio shall be stated and vindicated. There are no two nations confining on each other between whom a war may not always be kindled with plausible pretences on either part, as there is always passing between them a reciprocation of injuries and fluctuation of encroachments.

From the conclusion of the last peace perpetual complaints of the supplantations and invasions of the French have been sent to Europe from our colonies, and transmitted to our ministers at Paris, where good words were sometimes given us, and the practices of the American commanders were sometimes disowned, but no redress was ever obtained, nor is it probable that any prohibition was sent to America. We were still amused with such doubtful promises as those who are afraid of war are ready to interpret in their own favour, and the French pushed forward their line of fortresses, and seemed to resolve that before our complaints were finally dismissed, all remedy should be hopeless.

We likewise endeavoured at the same time to form a barrier against the Canadians by sending a colony to New Scotland,° a cold uncomfortable tract of ground, of which we had long the nominal possession before we really began to occupy it. To this those were invited whom the cessation of war deprived of employment, and made burdensome to their country, and settlers were allured thither by many fallacious descriptions of fertile valleys and clear skies. What effect these pictures of American happiness had upon my countrymen I was never informed, but I suppose very few sought provision in those frozen regions whom guilt or poverty did not drive from their native country. About the boundaries of this new colony there were some disputes, but as there was nothing yet worth a contest, the power of the French was not much exerted on that side: some disturbance was however given and some skirmishes ensued. But perhaps being peopled chiefly with soldiers, who would rather live by plunder than by agriculture, and who consider war as their best trade, New

Scotland would be more obstinately defended than some settlements of far greater value, and the French are too well informed of their own interest to provoke hostility for no advantage, or to select that country for invasion where they must hazard much, and can win little. They therefore pressed on southward behind our ancient and wealthy settlements, and built fort after fort at such distances that they might conveniently relieve one another, invade our colonies with sudden incursions, and retire to places of safety before our people could unite to oppose them.

This design of the French has been long formed, and long known, both in America and Europe, and might at first have been easily repressed had force been used instead of expostulation. When the English attempted a settlement upon the Island of St Lucia, the French, whether justly or not, considering it as neutral and forbidden to be occupied by either nation, immediately landed upon it, and destroyed the houses, wasted the plantations, and drove or carried away the inhabitants. This was done in the time of peace, when mutual professions of friendship were daily exchanged by the two courts, and was not considered as any violation of treaties, nor was any more than a very soft remonstrance made on our part.

The French therefore taught us how to act, but an Hanoverian quarrel with the house of Austria for some time induced us to court, at any expense, the alliance of a nation whose very situation makes them our enemies. We suffered them to destroy our settlements, and to advance their own, which we had an equal right to attack. The time however came at last when we ventured to quarrel with Spain, and then France no longer suffered the appearance of peace to subsist between us, but armed in defence of her ally.

The events of the war are well known, we pleased ourselves with victory at Dettingen, where we left our wounded men to the care of our enemies, but our army was broken at Fontenoy and Val; and though after the disgrace which we suffered in the Mediterranean we had some naval success, and an accidental dearth made peace necessary for the French, yet they prescribed the conditions, obliged us to give hostages, and acted as conquerors, though as conquerors of moderation.

In this war the Americans distinguished themselves in a manner unknown and unexpected. The New English raised an army, and under the command of Pepperel took Cape Breton, with the assistance of the fleet. This is the most important fortress in America. We pleased ourselves so much with the acquisition that we could not think of restoring it, and among the arguments used to inflame the people against Charles Stuart, it was very clamorously urged that if he gained the kingdom, he would give Cape Breton back to the French.

The French however had a more easy expedient to regain Cape Breton than by exalting Charles Stuart to the English throne; they took in their turn Fort St George, and had our East India company wholly in their power, whom they restored at the peace to their former possessions, that they may continue to export our silver.

Cape Breton therefore was restored, and the French were re-established in America, with equal power and greater spirit, having lost nothing by the war which they had before gained.

To the general reputation of their arms, and that habitual superiority which they derive from it, they owe their power in America, rather than to any real strength, or circumstances of advantage. Their numbers are yet not great; their trade, though daily improved, is not very extensive; their country is barren, their fortresses, though numerous, are weak, and rather shelters from wild beasts, or savage nations, than places built for defence against bombs or cannons. Cape Breton has been found not to be impregnable; nor, if we consider the state of the places possessed by the two nations in America, is there any reason upon which the French should have presumed to molest us but that they thought our spirit so broken that we durst not resist them, and in this opinion our long forbearance easily confirmed them.

We forgot, or rather avoided to think, that what we delayed to do must be done at last, and done with more difficulty as it was delayed longer; that while we were complaining, and they were eluding, or answering our complaints, fort was rising upon fort, and one invasion made a precedent for another.

This confidence of the French is exalted by some real advantages. If they possess in those countries less than we, they have more to gain, and less to hazard; if they are less numerous, they are better united.

The French compose one body with one head. They have all the same interest, and agree to pursue it by the same means. They are subject to a governor commissioned by an absolute monarch, and participating the authority of his master. Designs are therefore formed without debate, and executed without impediment. They have yet more martial than mercantile ambition, and seldom suffer their military schemes to be entangled with collateral projects of gain: they have no wish but for conquest, of which they justly consider riches as the consequence.

Some advantages they will always have as invaders. They make war at the hazard of their enemies: the contest being carried on in our territories, we must lose more by a victory than they will suffer by a defeat. They will subsist, while they stay, upon our plantations, and perhaps destroy them when they can stay no longer. If we pursue them and carry the war into their dominions, our difficulties will increase every step as we advance, for we shall leave plenty behind us, and find nothing in Canada but lakes and forests barren and trackless, our enemies will shut themselves up in their forts, against which it is difficult to bring cannon through so rough a country, and which if they are provided with good magazines will soon starve those who besiege them.

All these are the natural effects of their government, and situation; they are accidentally more formidable as they are less happy. But the favour of the Indians which they enjoy, with very few exceptions, among all the nations of the northern continent, we ought to consider with other thoughts; this favour we might have enjoyed, if we had been careful to deserve it. The French by having these savage nations on their side are always supplied with spies, and guides, and with auxiliaries, like the Tartars to the Turks or the Hussars to the Germans, of no great use against troops ranged in order of battle, but very well qualified to maintain a war among woods and rivulets, where much mischief may be done by unexpected onsets, and safety be obtained by quick retreats. They can waste a colony by sudden inroads, surprise the straggling planters, frighten the inhabitants into towns, hinder the cultivation of lands, and starve those whom they are not able to conquer.

(To be continued.)°

Review of [Jonas Hanway], *A Journal of Eight Days' Journey from Portsmouth to Kingston upon Thames ... with miscellaneous thoughts, moral and religious ... to which is added An Essay on Tea, considered as pernicious to health, obstructing industry, and impoverishing the Nation: Also an account of its Growth, and great Consumption in these Kingdoms; with several political Reflections; and thoughts on Public Love. ... By Mr H——Y.*°

Our readers may perhaps remember that we gave them a short account of this book, with a letter extracted from it, in November 1756. The author then sent us an injunction to forbear his work till a second edition should appear: this prohibition was rather too magisterial; for an author is no longer the sole master of a book which he has given to the public; yet he has been punctually obeyed; we had no desire to offend him, and if his character may be estimated by his book, he is a man whose failings may well be pardoned for his virtues.

The second edition is now sent into the world, *corrected and enlarged*, and yielded up by the author to the attacks of criticism. But he shall find in us no malignity of censure. We wish, indeed, that among other corrections he had submitted his pages to the inspection of a grammarian, that the elegancies of one line might not have been disgraced by the improprieties of another; but with us, to mean well is a degree of merit, which over-balances much greater errors than impurity of style.

We have already given, in our collections, one of the letters in which Mr Hanway endeavours to show that the consumption of tea is injurious to the interest of our country. We shall now endeavour to follow him regularly through all his observations on this modern luxury; but it can scarcely be candid not to make a previous declaration that he is to expect little justice from the author of this extract, a hardened and shameless tea-drinker, who has, for twenty years, diluted his meals with only the infusion of this fascinating plant, whose kettle has scarcely time to cool, who with tea amuses the evening, with tea solaces the midnights, and, with tea, welcomes the morning.

He begins by refuting a popular notion, that bohea and green tea are leaves of the same shrub, gathered at different times of the year. He is of opinion that they are produced by different shrubs. The leaves of tea are gathered in dry weather; then dried and curled over the fire, in copper pans. The Chinese use little green tea, imagining that it hinders digestion and excites fevers. How it should have either effect is not easily discovered, and, if we consider the innumerable prejudices which prevail concerning our own plants, we shall very little regard these opinions of the Chinese vulgar which experience does not confirm.

When the Chinese drink tea, they infuse it slightly, and extract only the more volatile parts, but though this seems to require great quantities at a time, yet the author believes, perhaps only because he has an inclination to believe it, that the English and Dutch use more than all the inhabitants of that extensive empire. The Chinese drink it sometimes with acids, seldom with sugar; and this practice our author, who has no intention to find anything right at home, recommends to his countrymen.

The history of the rise and progress of tea-drinking is truly curious. Tea was first imported, from Holland, by the earls of Arlington and Ossory, in 1666: from their ladies the women of quality learned its use. Its price was then three pounds a pound, and continued the same to 1707. In 1715, we began to use green tea, and the practice of drinking it descended to the lower class of the people. In 1720, the French began to send it hither by a clandestine commerce. From 1717 to 1726, we imported annually seven hundred thousand pounds. From 1732 to 1742, a million and two hundred thousand pounds were every year brought to London; in some years afterwards three millions, and in 1755, near four millions of pounds, or two thousand tons, in which we are not to reckon that which is surreptitiously introduced, which, perhaps, is nearly as much. Such quantities are, indeed, sufficient to alarm us; it is at least worth enquiry to know what are the qualities of such a plant, and what the consequences of such a trade.°

He then proceeds to enumerate the mischiefs of tea, and seems willing to charge upon it every mischief that he can find. He begins, however, by questioning the virtues ascribed to it, and denies that the crews of the Chinese ships are preserved, in their voyage homewards, from the scurvy by tea. About this report I have made some enquiry, and though I cannot find that these crews are wholly exempt from scorbutic maladies, they seem to suffer them less than other mariners, in any course of equal length. This I ascribe to the tea, not as possessing any medicinal qualities, but as tempting them to drink more water, to dilute their salt food more copiously, and, perhaps, to forbear punch, or other strong liquors.

He then proceeds in the pathetic strain to tell the ladies how, by drinking tea, they injure their health, and, what is yet more dear, their beauty.

To what can we ascribe the numerous complaints which prevail? How many *sweet creatures* of your sex languish with a *weak digestion*, *low spirits*, *lassitudes*, *melancholy*, and twenty disorders, which, in spite of the *faculty*, have yet no names, except the general one of *nervous complaints*? Let them change their diet, and among other articles leave off drinking tea, it is more than probable the greatest part of them will be restored to health.

Hot water is also very hurtful to the teeth. The Chinese do not drink their tea so hot as we do, and yet they have bad teeth. This cannot be ascribed entirely to sugar, for they use very little, as already observed, but we all know that *hot* or *cold* things, which *pain* the teeth, destroy them also. If we drank less tea, and used gentle *acids* for the gums and teeth, particularly *sour oranges*, though we had a less number of French *dentists*, I fancy this *essential* part of beauty would be much *better* preserved.

The women in the United Provinces, who *sip tea* from morning till night, are also as remarkable for *bad teeth*. They also look pallid, and many are troubled with certain feminine disorders arising from a relaxed habit. The Portuguese ladies, on the other hand, entertain with *sweetmeats*, and yet they have very *good teeth*; but their food in general is more of the farinaceous and vegetable kind than ours. They also *drink cold water* instead of *sipping hot*, and never taste any fermented liquors; for these reasons, the use of sugar does not seem to be at all pernicious to them.

Men seem to have lost their stature and comeliness, and women their beauty. I am not *young*, but methinks there is not quite so much *beauty* in this land as there was. Your very *chambermaids* have lost their bloom, I suppose by *sipping tea*. Even the agitations of the passions at *cards* are not so great enemies to female charms. What Shakespeare ascribes to the concealment of love is *in this age* more frequently occasioned by the use of tea.

To raise the fright still higher, he quotes an account of a pig's tail scalded with tea, on which however he does not much insist.

Of these dreadful effects, some are perhaps imaginary, and some may have another cause. That there is less beauty in the present race of females than in those who entered the world with us, all of us are inclined to think on whom beauty has ceased to smile; but our fathers and grandfathers made the same complaint before us; and our posterity will still find beauties irresistibly powerful.

That the diseases commonly called nervous, tremors, fits, habitual depression, and all the maladies which proceed from laxity and debility, are more frequent than in any former time, is, I believe, true, however deplorable. But this new race of evils will not be expelled by the prohibition of tea. This general languor is the effect of general luxury, of general idleness. If it be most to be found among tea drinkers, the reason is that tea is one of the stated amusements of the idle and luxurious. The whole mode of life is changed; every kind of voluntary labour, every exercise that strengthened the nerves, and hardened the muscles, is fallen into disuse. The inhabitants are crowded together in populous cities, so that no occasion of life requires much motion; every one is near to all that he wants; and the rich and delicate seldom pass from one street to another, but in carriages of pleasure. Yet we eat and drink, or strive to eat and drink, like the hunters and huntresses, the farmers and the housewives, of the former generation, and they that pass ten hours in bed, and eight at cards, and the greater part of the other six at the table, are taught to impute to tea all the diseases which a life unnatural in all its parts may chance to bring upon them.

Tea, among the greater part of those who use it most, is drunk in no great quantity. As it neither exhilarates the heart, nor stimulates the palate, it is commonly an entertainment merely nominal, a pretence for assembling to prattle, for interrupting business or diversifying idleness. They who drink one cup, and who drink twenty, are equally punctual in preparing or partaking it; and, indeed, there are few but discover, by their indifference about it, that they are brought together not by the tea, but the tea table. Three cups make the common quantity, so slightly impregnated that, perhaps, they might be tinged with the Athenian cicuta,° and produce less effects than these letters charge upon tea.

Our author proceeds to show yet other bad qualities of this hated leaf.

Green tea, when made strong even by infusion, is an emetic; nay, I am told, it is used as such in China, a decoction of it certainly performs this operation, yet by long use is drank by many without such an effect. The infusion also, when it is made strong, and stands long to draw the grosser particles, will *convulse* the bowels: even in the manner *commonly* used it has this effect on some constitutions, as I have already remarked to you from my *own experience*.

You see I confess my *weakness* without reserve, but those who are very fond of tea, if their digestion is weak, and they find themselves disordered, they generally ascribe it to any *cause*, except the *true* one. I am aware that the effect just mentioned is imputed to the hot water; let it be so, and my argument is still good: but who pretends to say, it is not *partly* owing to particular kinds of tea; perhaps, such as partake of *copperas*, which, there is cause to apprehend, is sometimes the case: if we judge from the manner in which it is said to be cured, together with its ordinary effects, there is some foundation for this opinion. Put a drop of strong tea, either *green* or *bohea*, but chiefly the former, on the blade of a knife, though it is not corrosive, in the same manner as vitriol, yet there appears to be a corrosive quality in it, very different from that of fruit which stain the knife.

He afterwards quotes Paulli,° to prove that tea is a *desiccative, and ought not to be used after the fortieth year*. I have, then, long exceeded the limits of permission, but I comfort myself that all the enemies of tea cannot be in the right. If tea be a desiccative, according to Paulli, it cannot weaken the fibres, as our author imagines; if it be emetic, it must constringe the stomach, rather than relax it.

The formidable quality of tinging the knife, it has in common with acorns, the bark, and leaves of oak, and every astringent bark or leaf: the copperas, which is given to the tea, is really in the knife. Ink may be made of any ferruginous matter, and astringent vegetable, as it is generally made of galls and copperas.

From tea the writer digresses to spirituous liquors, about which he will have no controversy with the *Literary Magazine*; we shall, therefore, insert almost his whole letter, and add to it one testimony, that the mischiefs arising, on every side, from this compendious mode of drunkenness, are enormous and insupportable; equally to be found among the great and the mean; filling palaces with disquiet, and distraction, harder to be borne, as it cannot be mentioned; and overwhelming multitudes with incurable diseases, and unpitied poverty.

Though tea and gin have spread their baneful influence over this island, and his majesty's other dominions, yet you may be well assured that the governors of the Foundling Hospital will exert their utmost skill and vigilance, to prevent the children, under their care, from being poisoned, or enervated by one or the other. This, however, is not the case of *workhouses*: it is well known, to the shame of those who are charged with the care of them, that gin has been too often permitted to enter their gates; and the debauched appetites of the people, who inhabit these houses, has been urged as a reason for it.

Desperate diseases require *desperate* remedies: if laws are rigidly executed against murderers in the highway, those who provide a draught of gin, which we see is *murderous*, ought not to be *countenanced*. I am now informed, that in certain hospitals, where the number of the *sick* used to be about 5600 in 14 years,

From 1704 to 1718, they increased to 8189;

From 1718 to 1734, still augmented to 12 710;

And from 1734 to 1749, multiplied to 38 147.

What a dreadful spectre does this exhibit! nor must we wonder, when satisfactory evidence was given, before the great council of the nation, that near eight millions of gallons of distilled spirits, at the standard it is commonly reduced to for drinking, was actually consumed annually in drams! the shocking difference in the numbers of the *sick*, and, we may presume, of the *dead* also, was supposed to keep pace with *gin*: and the most ingenious and unprejudiced physicians ascribed it to this cause. What is to be done under these melancholy circumstances? shall we still countenance the *distillery*, for the sake of the *revenue*; out of tenderness to the *few*, who will suffer by its being abolished; for fear of the madness of the people; or that foreigners will run it in upon us? There can be no *evil* so great as that we now suffer, except the making the same consumption, and paying for it to foreigners in *money*, which I hope never will be the case.

As to the *revenue*, it certainly may be replaced by taxes upon the *necessaries* of life, even upon the *bread we eat*, or, in other words, upon the *land*, which is the great source of supply to the *public*, and to *individuals*. Nor can I persuade myself, but that the people may be *weaned* from the habit of poisoning themselves. The difficulty of *smuggling* a bulky *liquid*, joined to the severity which *ought* to be exercised towards smugglers, whose *illegal* commerce is of so *infernal* a nature, must, in time, produce the effect desired. Spirituous liquors being abolished, instead of having the most undisciplined and abandoned poor, we might soon boast a race of men, temperate, religious, and industrious, even to a *proverb*. We should soon see the *ponderous* burden of the poors-rate decrease, and the *beauty* and *strength* of the land rejuvenate. Schools, workhouses, and hospitals, might then be sufficient to clear our streets of distress and misery, which never will be the case, whilst the love of poison prevails, and the means of ruin is sold in above one thousand houses in the *city* of London, in two thousand two hundred in Westminster, and one thousand nine hundred and thirty in Holborn and St Giles's.

But if other uses still demand *liquid fire*, I would really suppose, that it should be sold only in quart bottles, sealed up, with the king's seal, with a very high duty, and none sold without being mixed with a *strong emetic*.

Many become objects of charity by their *intemperance*, and this excludes others, who are such by the unavoidable accidents of life, or who cannot, by any means, support themselves. Hence it appears, that the introducing *new habits* of life, is the most substantial charity: and that the *regulation* of charity-schools, hospitals, and workhouses, not the augmentation of their number, can make them answer the wise ends, for which they were instituted.

The children of beggars should be also taken from them, and bred up to labour, as children of the public. Thus the *distressed* might be relieved, at a sixth part of the present expense; the idle be compelled to *work*, or *starve*; and the *mad* be sent to Bedlam. We should not see human nature disgraced by the aged, the maimed, the sickly, and young children, begging their bread, nor would compassion be abused by those, who have reduced it to an *art* to catch the unwary. Nothing is wanting but common sense and *honesty* in the execution of *laws*.

To prevent such abuse in the *streets*, seems more practicable than to abolish *bad habits within doors*, where *greater* numbers perish. We see, in many familiar instances, the fatal effects of example. The careless spending of time among *servants*, who are charged with the care of infants, is often fatal: the nurse frequently destroys the child! the poor infant, being left neglected, expires whilst she is sipping her tea! This may appear to you as *rank prejudice*, or *jest*; but, I am assured, from the most *indubitable* evidence, that many very extraordinary cases of this kind have *really* happened, among those whose *duty* does not permit of such kind of habits.

It is partly from such causes, that nurses of the children of the *public* often *forget* themselves, and become *impatient* when infants cry; the next step to this is using extraordinary means to quiet them. I have already mentioned the term *killing nurse*, as known in some workhouses: *Venice treacle*, *poppy water*, and *Godfrey's cordial*, have been the kind instruments of lulling the child to his *everlasting* rest. If these *pious* women could send up an ejaculation, when the child expired, all was *well*, and no questions *asked* by the *superiors*. An ingenious friend of mine informs me, that this has been so often the case, in some workhouses, that *Venice treacle* has acquired the appellation of *the Lord have mercy upon me*, in allusion to the nurses' *hackneyed* expression of *pretended* grief, when infants expire! Farewell.

I know not upon what observation Mr Hanway founds his confidence in the governors of the Foundling Hospital, men of whom I have not any knowledge, but whom I entreat to consider a little the minds, as well as bodies, of the children. I am inclined to believe irreligion equally pernicious with gin and tea, and, therefore, think it not unseasonable to mention that, when, a few months ago, I wandered through the hospital, I found not a child that seemed to have heard of his creed, or the commandments. To breed up children in this manner is to rescue them from an early grave that they may find employment for the gibbet; from dying in innocence, that they may perish by their crimes.°

Having considered the effects of tea upon the health of the drinker, which, I think, he has aggravated in the vehemence of his zeal, and which, after soliciting them by this watery luxury, year after year, I have not yet felt, he proceeds to examine how it may be shown to affect our interest; and first calculates the national loss by the time spent in drinking tea. I have no desire to appear captious, and shall, therefore, readily admit that tea is a liquor not proper for the lower classes of the people, as it supplies no strength to labour, or relief to disease, but gratifies the taste, without nourishing the body. It is a barren superfluity, to which those who can hardly procure what nature requires cannot prudently habituate themselves. Its proper use is to amuse the idle, and relax the studious, and dilute the full meals of those who cannot use exercise, and will not use abstinence. That time is lost in this insipid entertainment cannot be denied; many trifle away at the tea table those moments which would be better spent; but that any national detriment can be inferred from this waste of time does not evidently appear, because I know not that any work remains undone for want of hands. Our manufactures seem to be limited, not by the possibility of work, but by the possibility of sale.

His next argument is more clear. He affirms that one hundred and fifty thousand pounds, in silver, are paid to the Chinese, annually, for three millions of pounds of tea, and, that for two millions more, brought clandestinely from the neighbouring coasts, we pay, at twenty-pence a pound, one hundred sixty-six thousand six hundred and sixty-six pounds. The author justly conceives that this computation will waken us; for, says he: 'The loss of health, the loss of time, the injury of morals, are not very sensibly felt by some who are alarmed when you talk of the loss of money.' But he excuses the East-India company, as men not obliged to be political arithmeticians, or to enquire so much what the nation loses as how themselves may grow rich. It is certain that they who drink tea have no right to complain of those that import it, but if Mr Hanway's computation be just, the importation, and the use of it, ought at once to be stopped by a penal law.

The author allows one slight argument in favour of tea, which, in my opinion, might be, with far greater justice, urged both against that and many other parts of our naval trade. 'The tea-trade employs,' he tells us, 'six ships, and five or six hundred seamen, sent annually to China. It, likewise, brings in a revenue of three hundred and sixty thousand pounds, which, as a tax on luxury, may be considered as of great utility to the state.' The utility of this tax I cannot find; a tax on luxury is no better than another tax, unless it hinders luxury, which cannot be said of the impost upon tea while it is thus used by the great and the mean, the rich and the poor. The truth is that, by the loss of one hundred and fifty thousand pounds, we procure the means of shifting three hundred and sixty thousand, at best, only from one hand to another; but, perhaps, sometimes into hands by which it is not very honestly employed. Of the five or six hundred seamen sent to China, I am told that sometimes half, commonly a third part, perish in the voyage; so that, instead of setting this navigation against the inconveniencies already alleged, we may add to them the yearly loss of two hundred men in the prime of life; and reckon that the trade of China has destroyed ten thousand men since the beginning of this century.

If tea be thus pernicious, if it impoverishes our country, if it raises temptation, and gives opportunity to illicit commerce, which I have always looked on as one of the strongest evidences of the inefficacy of our law, the weakness of our government, and the corruption of our people, let us, at once, resolve to prohibit it for ever.

If the *question* was, how to promote industry most *advantageously*, in lieu of our tea-trade, supposing every branch of our commerce to be already fully supplied with men and money? *If* a *quarter* the sum now spent in tea were laid out, annually, in plantations, in making public gardens, in paving and widening streets, in making *roads*, in rendering *rivers* navigable, erecting *palaces*, building *bridges*, or neat and convenient *houses*, where are now only *huts*; *draining* lands, or rendering those, which are now *barren*, of some *use*; should we not be gainers, and provide more for health, pleasure, and long life, compared with the consequences of the *tea-trade*?

Our riches would be much better employed to these purposes; but if this project does not please, let us first resolve to save our money, and we shall afterwards very easily find ways to spend it.

Reply to a Paper in the *Gazetteer* of May 26, 1757°

It is observed in Le Sage's° *Gil Blas* that an exasperated author is not easily pacified. I have, therefore, very little hope of making my peace with the writer of the Eight Days' Journey. Indeed so little that I have long deliberated whether I should not rather sit silently down under his displeasure than aggravate my misfortune by a defence of which my heart forebodes the ill success. Deliberation is often useless. I am afraid that I have, at last, made the wrong choice, and that I might better have resigned my cause without a struggle to time and fortune, since I shall run the hazard of a new offence, by the necessity of asking him *why he is angry*.

Distress and terror often discover to us those faults with which we should never have reproached ourselves in a happy state. Yet, dejected as I am when I review the transaction between me and this writer, I cannot find that I have been deficient in reverence. When his book was first printed, he hints that I procured a sight of it before it was published. How the sight of it was procured, I do not now very exactly remember; but, if my curiosity was greater than my prudence, if I laid rash hands on the fatal volume, I have surely suffered, like him who burst the box° from which evil rushed into the world.

I took it, however, and inspected it, as the work of an author not higher than myself, and was confirmed in my opinion, when I found that these letters were *not written to be printed*. I concluded, however, that, though not *written* to be *printed*, they were *printed* to be *read*, and inserted one of them in the collection of November last. Not many days after, I received a note informing me that I ought to have waited for a more correct edition. This injunction was obeyed. The edition appeared, and I supposed myself at liberty to tell my thoughts upon it, as upon any other book, upon a royal manifesto, or an act of parliament. But see the fate of ignorant temerity! I now find, but find too late, that, instead of a writer, whose only power is in his pen, I have irritated an important member of an important corporation; a man, who, as he tells us in his letters, puts horses to his chariot.

It was allowed to the disputant of old to yield up the controversy, with little resistance, to the master of forty legions. Those who know how weakly naked truth can defend her advocates would forgive me, if I should pay the same respect to a governor of the foundlings. Yet the consciousness of my own rectitude of intention incites me to ask once again, how I have offended?

There are only three subjects upon which my unlucky pen has happened to venture: tea; the author of the journal; and the foundling hospital.

Of tea, what have I said? That I have drank it twenty years, without hurt, and, therefore, believe it not to be poison. That, if it dries the fibres, it cannot soften them, that, if it constringes, it cannot relax. I have modestly doubted whether it has diminished the strength of our men, or the beauty of our women, and whether it much hinders the progress of our woollen or iron manufactures; but I allowed it to be a barren superfluity, neither medicinal nor nutritious, that neither supplied strength nor cheerfulness, neither relieved weariness, nor exhilarated sorrow: I inserted, without charge or suspicion of falsehood, the sums exported to purchase it; and proposed a law to prohibit it for ever.

Of the author I unfortunately said that his injunction was somewhat too magisterial. This I said before I knew that he was a governor of the foundlings; but he seems inclined to punish this failure of respect, as the Czar of Muscovy made war upon Sweden, because he was not treated with sufficient honours when he passed through the country in disguise. Yet was not this irreverence without extenuation. Something was said of the merit of *meaning well*, and the journalist was declared to be a man *whose failings might well be pardoned for his virtues*. This is the highest praise which human gratitude can confer upon human merit, praise that would have more than satisfied Titus or Augustus, but which I must own to be inadequate and penurious when offered to the member of an important corporation.

I am asked whether I meant to *satirize* the man, or *criticise* the writer, when I say that *he believes, only perhaps because he has inclination to believe it, that the English and Dutch consume more tea than the vast empire of China*. Between the writer and the man, I did not, at that time, consider the distinction. The writer I found not of more than mortal might, and I did not immediately recollect that the man put horses to his chariot. But I did not write wholly without consideration. I knew but two causes of belief, evidence and inclination. What evidence the journalist could have of the Chinese consumption of tea, I was not able to discover. The officers of the East India company° are excluded, they best know why, from the towns and the country of China; they are treated as we treat gypsies and vagrants, and obliged to retire, every night, to their own hovel. What intelligence such travellers may bring is of no great importance. And, though the missionaries boast of having once penetrated further, I think they have never calculated the tea drank by the Chinese. There being thus no evidence for his opinion, to what could I ascribe it but inclination?

I am yet charged, more heavily, for having said that *he has no intention to find any thing right at home*. I believe every reader restrained this imputation to the subject which produced it, and supposed me to insinuate only that he meant to spare no part of the tea-table, whether essence or circumstance. But this line he has selected as an instance of virulence and acrimony, and confutes it by a lofty and splendid panegyric on himself. He asserts that he finds many things right at home, and that he loves his country almost to enthusiasm.

I had not the least doubt that he found, in his country, many things to please him; nor did I suppose that he desired the same inversion of every part of life as of the use of tea. The proposal of drinking tea sour showed, indeed, such a disposition to practical paradoxes that there was reason to fear lest some succeeding letter should recommend the dress of the Picts, or the cookery of the Eskimaux. However, I met with no other innovations, and, therefore, was willing to hope that he found something right at home.

But his love of his country seemed not to rise quite to enthusiasm when, amidst his rage against tea, he made a smooth apology for the East India company, as men who might not think themselves obliged to be political arithmeticians. I hold, though no enthusiastic patriot, that every man who lives and trades under the protection of a community is obliged to consider whether he hurts or benefits those who protect him, and that the most which can be indulged to private interest is a neutral traffic, if any such can be, by which our country is not injured, though it may not be benefited.

But he now renews his declamation against tea, notwithstanding the greatness or power of those that have interest or inclination to support it. I know not of what power or greatness he may dream. The importers only have an interest in defending it. I am sure they are not great, and I hope they are not powerful. Those whose inclination leads them to continue this practice are too numerous, but I believe their power is such as the journalist may defy without enthusiasm. The love of our country, when it rises to enthusiasm, is an ambiguous and uncertain virtue: when a man is enthusiastic he ceases to be reasonable; and, when he once departs from reason, what will he do but drink sour tea? As the journalist, though enthusiastically zealous for his country, has, with regard to smaller things, the placid happiness of philosophical indifference, I can give him no disturbance by advising him to restrain even the love of his country within due limits, lest it should, sometimes, swell too high, fill the whole capacity of his soul, and leave less room for the love of truth.

Nothing now remains but that I review my positions concerning the Foundling Hospital. What I declared last month, I declare now, once more, that I found none of the children that appeared to have heard of the catechism. It is enquired how I wandered, and how I examined? There is, doubtless, subtlety in the question; I know not well how to answer it. Happily I did not wander alone, I attended some ladies, with another gentleman, who all heard and assisted the inquiry, with equal grief and indignation. I did not conceal my observations. Notice was given of this shameful defect soon after, at my request, to one of the highest names of the society. This, I am now told, is incredible; but, since it is true, and the past is out of human power, the most important corporation cannot make it false. But, why is it incredible? Because, in the rules of the hospital, the children are ordered to learn the rudiments of religion. Orders are easily made, but they do not execute themselves. They say their catechism, at stated times, under an able master. But this able master was, I think, not elected before last February; and my visit happened, if I mistake not, in November. The children were shy, when interrogated by a stranger. This may be true, but the same shyness I do not remember to have hindered them from answering other questions, and I wonder why children so much accustomed to new spectators should be eminently shy.

My opponent, in the first paragraph, calls the inference that I made from this negligence a hasty conclusion: to the decency of this expression I had nothing to object. But, as he grew hot in his career, his enthusiasm began to sparkle; and, in the vehemence of his postscript, he charges my assertions, and my reasons for advancing them, with folly and malice. His argumentation, being somewhat enthusiastical, I cannot fully comprehend, but it seems to stand thus. My insinuations are foolish or malicious, since I know not one of the governors of the hospital; for he that knows not the governors of the hospital must be very foolish or malicious.

He has, however, so much kindness for me that he advises me to consult my safety when I talk of corporations. I know not what the most important corporation can do, becoming manhood, by which my safety is endangered. My reputation is safe, for I can prove the fact; my quiet is safe, for I meant well; and for any other safety, I am not used to be very solicitous.

I am always sorry when I see any being labouring in vain; and, in return for the journalist's attention to my safety, I will confess some compassion for his tumultuous resentment; since all his invectives fume into the air with so little effect upon me that I still esteem him, as one that has the *merit of meaning well*, and still believe him to be a man *whose failings may be justly pardoned for his virtues*.

Review of [Soame Jenyns], *A Free Inquiry into the Nature and Origin of Evil*°

This is a treatise, consisting of six letters, upon a very difficult and important question, which, I am afraid, this author's endeavours will not free from the perplexity which has entangled the speculatists of all ages, and which must always continue while *we see* but *in part*. He calls it a *Free* enquiry and indeed his *freedom* is, I think, greater than his modesty. Though he is far from the contemptible arrogance, or the impious licentiousness of Bolingbroke, yet he decides too easily upon questions out of the reach of human determination, with too little consideration of mortal weakness, and with too much vivacity for the necessary caution.

In the first letter, *on evil in general*, he observes that 'it is the solution of this important question *whence came evil?* alone that can ascertain the moral characteristic of God, without which there is an end of all distinction between good and evil'. Yet he begins this enquiry by this declaration: 'That there is a supreme being, infinitely powerful, wise, and benevolent, the great creator and preserver of all things, is a truth so clearly demonstrated that it shall be here taken for granted.' What is this but to say that we have already reason to grant the existence of those attributes of God which the present enquiry is designed to prove? The present enquiry is then surely made to no purpose. The attributes to the demonstration of which the solution of this great question is necessary have been demonstrated without any solution, or by means of the solution of some former writer.

He rejects the Manichean system,° but imputes to it an absurdity from which, amidst all its absurdities, it seems to be free, and adopts the system of Mr Pope.

That pain is no evil, if asserted with regard to the individuals who suffer it, is downright nonsense; but if considered as it affects the universal system, is an undoubted truth, and means only that there is no more pain in it than what is necessary to the production of happiness. How many soever of these evils then force themselves into the creation, so long as the good preponderates, it is a work well worthy of infinite wisdom and benevolence; and, notwithstanding the imperfections of its parts, the whole is, most undoubtedly, perfect.

And, in the former part of the letter, he gives the principle of his system in these words:

Omnipotence cannot work contradictions; it can only effect all possible things. But so little are we acquainted with the whole system of nature that we know not what are possible, and what are not; but if we may judge from that constant mixture of pain with pleasure, and inconveniency with advantage which we must observe in every thing around us, we have reason to conclude that to endue created beings with perfection, that is, to produce good exclusive of evil, is one of those impossibilities which even infinite power cannot accomplish.

This is elegant and acute, but will by no means calm discontent or silence curiosity; for whether evil can be wholly separated from good or not, it is plain that they may be mixed in various degrees, and as far as human eyes can judge, the degree of evil might have been less without any impediment to good.

The second letter, *on the evils of imperfection*, is little more than a paraphrase of Pope's epistles, or yet less than a paraphrase, a mere translation of poetry into prose. This is surely to attack difficulty with very disproportionate abilities, to cut the Gordian knot with very blunt instruments. When we are told of the insufficiency of former solutions, why is one of the latest, which no man can have forgotten, given us again? I am told that this pamphlet is not the effect° of hunger; what can it be then but the product of vanity? And yet, how can vanity be gratified by plagiarism or transcription? When this speculatist finds himself prompted to another performance, let him consider whether he is about to disburden his mind or employ his fingers; and if I might venture to offer him a subject, I should wish that he would solve this question, Why he that has nothing to write should desire to be a writer?

Yet is not this letter without some sentiments which, though not new, are of great importance, and may be read with pleasure in the thousandth repetition.

Whatever we enjoy is purely a free gift from our Creator; but that we enjoy no more can never sure be deemed an injury, or a just reason to question his infinite benevolence. All our happiness is owing to his goodness; but that it is no greater is owing only to ourselves, that is, to our not having any inherent right to any happiness, or even to any existence at all. This is no more to be imputed to God than the wants of a beggar to the person who has relieved him: that he had something was owing to his benefactor: but that he had no more, only to his own original poverty.

Thus far he speaks what every man must approve, and what every wise man has said before him. He then gives us the system of subordination,° not invented, for it was known I think to the Arabian metaphysicians, but adopted by Pope; and from him borrowed by the diligent researches of this great investigator.

No system can possibly be formed, even in imagination, without a subordination of parts. Every animal body must have different members, subservient to each other; every picture must be composed of various colours, and of light and shade; all harmony must be formed of trebles, tenors, and basses; every beautiful and useful edifice must consist of higher and lower, more and less magnificent apartments. This is in the very essence of all created things, and therefore cannot be prevented by any means whatever, unless by not creating them at all.

These instances are used, instead of Pope's oak and weeds, or Jupiter and his satellites; but neither Pope nor this writer have much contributed to solve the difficulty. Perfection or imperfection of unconscious beings has no meaning as referred to themselves; the bass and the treble are equally perfect; the mean and magnificent apartments feel no pleasure or pain from the comparison. Pope might ask the weed why it was less than the oak, but the weed would never ask the question for itself. The bass and treble differ only to the hearer, meanness and magnificence only to the inhabitant. There is no evil but must inhere in a conscious being, or be referred to it; that is, evil must be felt before it is evil. Yet even on this subject many questions might be offered which human understanding has not yet answered, and which the present haste of this extract will not suffer me to dilate.

He proceeds to an humble detail of Pope's opinion:

The universe is a system whose very essence consists in subordination; a scale of beings descending, by insensible degrees, from infinite perfection to absolute nothing: in which, though we may justly expect to find perfection in the whole, could we possibly comprehend it; yet would it be the highest absurdity to hope for it in all its parts, because the beauty and happiness of the whole depend altogether on the just inferiority of its parts, that is, on the comparative imperfections of the several beings of which it is composed.

It would have been no more an instance of God's wisdom to have created no beings but of the highest and most perfect order than it would be of a painter's art to cover his whole piece with one single colour, the most beautiful he could compose. Had he confined himself to such, nothing could have existed but demigods, or archangels, and then all inferior orders must have been void and uninhabited: but as it is surely more agreeable to infinite benevolence that all these should be filled up with beings capable of enjoying happiness themselves, and contributing to that of others, they must necessarily be filled with inferior beings, that is, with such as are less perfect, but from whose existence, notwithstanding that less perfection, more felicity upon the whole accrues to the universe than if no such had been created. It is, moreover, highly probable that there is such a connection between all ranks and orders by subordinate degrees that they mutually support each other's existence, and every one in its place is absolutely necessary towards sustaining the whole vast and magnificent fabric.

Our pretences for complaint could be of this only, that we are not so high in the scale of existence as our ignorant ambition may desire; a pretence which must eternally subsist, because, were we ever so much higher, there would be still room for infinite power to exalt us; and since no link in the chain can be broke, the same reason for disquiet must remain to those who succeed to that chasm which must be occasioned by our preferment. A man can have no reason to repine that he is not an angel; nor a horse that he is not a man; much less that in their several stations they possess not the faculties of another; for this would be an insufferable misfortune.

This doctrine of the regular subordination of beings, the scale of existence, and the chain of nature I have often considered, but always left the inquiry in doubt and uncertainty.

That every being not infinite, compared with infinity, must be imperfect is evident to intuition; that whatever is imperfect must have a certain line which it cannot pass is equally certain. But the reason which determined this limit, and for which such being was suffered to advance thus far and no further, we shall never be able to discern. Our discoverers tell us the Creator has made beings of all orders, and that therefore one of them must be such as man. But this system seems to be established on a concession which if it be refused cannot be extorted.

Every reason which can be brought to prove that there are beings of every possible sort will prove that there is the greatest number possible of every sort of beings; but this, with respect to man, we know, if we know any thing, not to be true.

It does not appear even to the imagination that of three orders of being, the first and the third receive any advantage from the imperfection of the second, or that indeed they may not equally exist, though the second had never been, or should cease to be, and why should that be concluded necessary which cannot be proved even to be useful?

The scale of existence from infinity to nothing cannot possibly have being. The highest being not infinite must be, as has been often observed, at an infinite distance below infinity. Cheyne,° who, with the desire inherent in mathematicians to reduce every thing to mathematical images, considers all existence as a *cone*, allows that the basis is at an infinite distance from the body, and in this distance between finite and infinite, there will be room for ever for an infinite series of indefinable existence.

Between the lowest positive existence and nothing, wherever we suppose positive existence to cease, is another chasm infinitely deep; where there is room again for endless orders of subordinate nature, continued for ever and for ever, and yet infinitely superior to non-existence.

To these meditations humanity is unequal. But yet we may ask, not of our maker, but of each other, since on the one side creation, wherever it stops, must stop infinitely below infinity, and on the other infinitely above nothing, what necessity there is that it should proceed so far either way that beings so high or so low should ever have existed? We may ask; but I believe no created wisdom can give an adequate answer.

Nor is this all. In the scale, wherever it begins or ends, are infinite vacuities. At whatever distance we suppose the next order of beings to be above man, there is room for an intermediate order of beings between them; and if for one order then for infinite orders; since every thing that admits of more or less, and consequently all the parts of that which admits them, may be infinitely divided. So that, as far as we can judge, there may be room in the vacuity between any two steps of the scale or between any two points of the cone of being, for infinite exertion of infinite power.

Thus it appears how little reason those who repose their reason upon the scale of being have to triumph over them who recur to any other expedient of solution, and what difficulties arise on every side to repress the rebellions of presumptuous decision: *Qui pauca considerat, facile pronunciat.*° In our passage through the boundless ocean of disquisition we often take fogs for land, and after having long toiled to approach them find, instead of repose and harbours, new storms of objection and fluctuations of uncertainty.

We are next entertained with Pope's alleviations of those evils which we are doomed to suffer.

Poverty, or the want of riches, is generally compensated by having more hopes and fewer fears, by a greater share of health, and a more exquisite relish of the smallest enjoyments, than those who possess them are usually blessed with. The want of taste and genius, with all the pleasures that arise from them, are commonly recompensed by a more useful kind of common sense, together with a wonderful delight, as well as success, in the busy pursuits of a scrambling world. The sufferings of the sick are greatly relieved by many trifling gratifications, imperceptible to others, and sometimes almost repaid by the inconceivable transports occasioned by the return of health and vigour. Folly cannot be very grievous, because imperceptible; and I doubt not but there is some truth in that rant of a mad poet, that there is a pleasure in being mad which none but madmen know. Ignorance, or the want of knowledge and literature, the appointed lot of all born to poverty and the drudgeries of life, is the only opiate capable of infusing that insensibility which can enable them to endure the miseries of the one, and the fatigues of the other. It is a cordial administered by the gracious hand of providence, of which they ought never to be deprived by an ill-judged and improper education. It is the basis of all subordination, the support of society, and the privilege of individuals: and I have ever thought it a most remarkable instance of the divine wisdom that, whereas in all animals, whose individuals rise little above the rest of their species, knowledge is instinctive; in man, whose individuals are so widely different, it is acquired by education; by which means the prince and the labourer, the philosopher and the peasant, are, in some measure, fitted for their respective situations.

Much of these positions is perhaps true, and the whole paragraph might well pass without censure, were not objections necessary to the establishment of knowledge. *Poverty* is very gently paraphrased by *want of riches*. In that sense almost every man may in his own opinion be poor. But there is another poverty which is *want of competence*, of all that can soften the miseries of life, of all that can diversify attention, or delight imagination. There is yet another poverty which is *want of necessaries*, a species of poverty° which no care of the public, no charity of particulars, can preserve many from feeling openly, and many secretly.

That hope and fear are inseparably or very frequently connected with poverty and riches° my surveys of life have not informed me. The milder degrees of poverty are sometimes supported by hope, but the more severe often sink down in motionless despondence. Life must be seen before it can be known. This author and Pope perhaps never saw the miseries which they imagine thus easy to be borne. The poor, indeed, are insensible of many little vexations, which sometimes embitter the possessions and pollute the enjoyments of the rich. They are not pained by casual incivility, or mortified by the mutilation of a compliment; but this happiness is like that of a malefactor who ceases to feel the cords that bind him when the pincers are tearing his flesh.°

That want of taste for one enjoyment is supplied by the pleasures of some other may be fairly allowed; but the compensations of sickness I have never found near to equivalence, and the transports of recovery only prove the intenseness of the pain.

With folly no man is willing to confess himself very intimately acquainted, and therefore its pains and pleasures are kept secret. But what the author says of its happiness seems applicable only to fatuity, or gross dullness, for that inferiority of understanding which makes one man without any other reason the slave, or tool, or property of another, which makes him sometimes useless, and sometimes ridiculous, is often felt with very quick sensibility. On the happiness of madmen, as the case is not very frequent, it is not necessary to raise a disquisition, but I cannot forbear to observe that I never yet knew disorders of mind increase felicity: every madman is either arrogant and irascible, or gloomy and suspicious, or possessed by some passion or notion destructive to his quiet. He has always discontent in his look, and malignity in his bosom. And, if we had the power of choice, he would soon repent who should resign his reason to secure his peace.

Concerning the portion of ignorance necessary to make the condition of the lower classes of mankind safe to the public and tolerable to themselves, both morals and policy exact a nicer enquiry than will be very soon or very easily made. There is undoubtedly a degree of knowledge which will direct a man to refer all to providence, and to acquiesce in the condition with which omniscient goodness has determined to allot him; to consider this world as a phantom that must soon glide from before his eyes, and the distresses and vexations that encompass him as dust scattered in his path, as a blast that chills him for a moment, and passes off for ever.

Such wisdom, arising from the comparison of a part with the whole of our existence, those that want it most cannot possibly obtain from philosophy, nor, unless the method of education and the general tenor of life are changed, will very easily receive it from religion. The bulk of mankind is not likely to be very wise or very good, and I know not whether there are not many states of life in which all knowledge less than the highest wisdom will produce discontent and danger. I believe it may be sometimes found that a *little learning* is to a poor man a *dangerous thing*.° But such is the condition of humanity that we easily see, or quickly feel the wrong, but cannot always distinguish the right. Whatever knowledge is superfluous, in irremediable poverty, is hurtful, but the difficulty is to determine when poverty is irremediable, and at what point superfluity begins. Gross ignorance every man has found equally dangerous with perverted knowledge. Men left wholly to their appetites and their instincts, with little sense of moral or religious obligation, and with very faint distinctions of right and wrong, can never be safely employed or confidently trusted: they can be honest only by obstinacy, and diligent only by compulsion or caprice. Some instruction, therefore, is necessary, and much, perhaps, may be dangerous.

Though it should be granted that those who are *born to poverty and drudgery* should not be *deprived* by an *improper education* of the *opiate of ignorance*, even this concession will not be of much use to direct our practice, unless it be determined who are those that are *born to poverty*. To entail irreversible poverty upon generation after generation only because the ancestor happened to be poor is in itself cruel, if not unjust, and is wholly contrary to the maxims of a commercial nation, which always suppose and promote a rotation of property, and offer every individual a chance of mending his condition by his diligence. Those who communicate literature to the son of a poor man consider him as one not born to poverty, but to the necessity of deriving a better fortune from himself. In this attempt, as in others, many fail, and many succeed. Those that fail will feel their misery more acutely; but since poverty is now confessed to be such a calamity as cannot be borne without the opiate of insensibility, I hope the happiness of those whom education enables to escape from it may turn the balance against that exacerbation which the others suffer.

I am always afraid of determining on the side of envy or cruelty. The privileges of education may sometimes be improperly bestowed, but I shall always fear to withhold them, lest I should be yielding to the suggestions of pride, while I persuade myself that I am following the maxims of policy; and under the appearance of salutary restraints, should be indulging the lust of dominion, and that malevolence which delights in seeing others depressed.

Pope's doctrine is at last exhibited in a comparison which, like other proofs of the same kind, is better adapted to delight the fancy than convince the reason.

Thus the universe resembles a large and well regulated family, in which all the officers and servants, and even the domestic animals, are subservient to each other in a proper subordination: each enjoys the privileges and perquisites peculiar to his place, and at the same time contributes by that just subordination to the magnificence and happiness of the whole.

The magnificence of a house is of use or pleasure always to the master, and sometimes to the domestics. But the magnificence of the universe adds nothing to the supreme Being; for any part of its inhabitants with which human knowledge is acquainted, an universe much less spacious or splendid would have been sufficient; and of happiness it does not appear that any is communicated from the beings of a lower world to those of a higher.

The enquiry after the cause of *natural evil* is continued in the third letter, in which, as in the former, there is mixture of borrowed truth and native folly, of some notions just and trite, with others uncommon and ridiculous.

His opinion of the value and importance of happiness is certainly just, and I shall insert it; not that it will give any information to any reader, but it may serve to show how the most common notion may be swelled in sound, and diffused in bulk, till it shall perhaps astonish the author himself.

Happiness is the only thing of real value in existence; neither riches, nor power, nor wisdom, nor learning, nor strength, nor beauty, nor virtue, nor religion, nor even life itself being of any importance but as they contribute to its production. All these are in themselves neither good nor evil: happiness alone is their great end, and they are desirable only as they tend to promote it.

Success produces confidence. After this discovery of the value of happiness, he proceeds without any distrust of himself to tell us what has been hid from all former enquirers.

The true solution of this important question, so long and so vainly searched for by the philosophers of all ages and all countries, I take to be at last no more than this, that these real evils proceed from the same source as those imaginary ones of imperfection before treated of, namely, from that subordination without which no created system can subsist; all subordination implying imperfection, all imperfection evil, and all evil some kind of inconveniency or suffering: so that there must be particular inconveniencies and sufferings annexed to every particular rank of created beings by the circumstances of things, and their modes of existence.

God indeed might have made us quite other creatures, and placed us in a world quite differently constituted; but then we had been no longer men, and whatever beings had occupied our stations in the universal system, they must have been liable to the same inconveniencies.

In all this, there is nothing that can silence the enquiries of curiosity, or calm the perturbations of doubt. Whether subordination implies imperfection may be disputed. The means respecting themselves may be as perfect as the end. The weed as a weed is no less perfect than the oak as an oak. That *imperfection implies evil, and evil suffering* is by no means evident. Imperfection may imply privative evil, or the absence of some good, but this privation produces no suffering but by the help of knowledge. An infant at the breast is yet an imperfect man, but there is no reason for belief that he is unhappy by his immaturity, unless some positive pain be superadded.

When this author presumes to speak of the universe, I would advise him a little to distrust his own faculties, however large and comprehensive. Many words easily understood on common occasions become uncertain and figurative when applied to the works of Omnipotence. Subordination in human affairs is well understood, but when it is attributed to the universal system, its meaning grows less certain, like the petty distinctions of locality, which are of good use upon our own globe, but have no meaning with regard to infinite space, in which nothing is *high* or *low*.

That if man, by exaltation to a higher nature, were exempted from the evils which he now suffers, some other being must suffer them; that if man were not man, some other being must be man, is a position arising from his established notion of the scale of being. A notion to which Pope has given some importance by adopting it, and of which I have therefore endeavoured to show the uncertainty and inconsistency. This scale of being I have demonstrated to be raised by presumptuous imagination, to rest on nothing at the bottom, to lean on nothing at the top, and to have vacuities from step to step through which any order of being may sink into nihility without any inconvenience, so far as we can judge, to the next rank above or below it. We are therefore little enlightened by a writer who tells us that any being in the state of man must suffer what man suffers, when the only question that requires to be resolved is, Why any being is in this state?

Of poverty and labour he gives just and elegant representations, which yet do not remove the difficulty of the first and fundamental question, though supposing the present state of man necessary, they may supply some motives to content.

Poverty is what all could not possibly have been exempted from, not only by reason of the fluctuating nature of human possessions, but because the world could not subsist without it; for had all been rich, none could have submitted to the commands of another, or the necessary drudgeries of life; thence all governments must have been dissolved, arts neglected, and lands uncultivated, and so an universal penury have overwhelmed all, instead of now and then pinching a few. Hence, by the by, appears the great excellence of charity, by which men are enabled by a particular distribution of the blessings and enjoyments of life, on proper occasions, to prevent that poverty, which by a general one omnipotence itself could never have prevented; so that, by enforcing this duty, God as it were demands our assistance to promote universal happiness, and to shut out misery at every door where it strives to intrude itself.

Labour, indeed, God might easily have excused us from, since at his command, the earth would readily have poured forth all her treasures without our inconsiderable assistance: but if the severest labour cannot sufficiently subdue the malignity of human nature, what plots and machinations, what wars, rapine, and devastation, what profligacy and licentiousness, must have been the consequences of universal idleness! So that labour ought only to be looked upon as a task kindly imposed upon us by our indulgent creator, necessary to preserve our health, our safety, and our innocence.

I am afraid, that *the latter end of his commonwealth forgets the beginning.*° If God *could easily have excused us from labour*, I do not comprehend why *he could not possibly have exempted all from poverty*. For poverty, in its easier and more tolerable degree, is little more than necessity of labour; and, in its more severe and deplorable state, little more than inability for labour. To be poor is to work for others, or to want the succour of others without work. And the same exuberant fertility which would make work unnecessary might make poverty impossible.

Surely a man who seems not completely master of his own opinion should have spoken more cautiously of omnipotence, nor have presumed to say what it could perform, or what it could prevent. I am in doubt whether those who stand highest in *the scale of being* speak thus confidently of the dispensations of their maker.

For fools rush in, where angels fear to tread.°

Of our inquietudes of mind, his account is still less reasonable. 'Whilst men are injured, they must be inflamed with anger; and whilst they see cruelties, they must be melted with pity; whilst they perceive danger, they must be sensible of fear.' This is to give a reason for all evil, by showing that one evil produces another. If there is danger there ought to be fear; but if fear is an evil, why should there be danger? His vindication of pain is of the same kind: pain is useful to alarm us, that we may shun greater evils, but those greater evils must be presupposed that the fitness of pain may appear.

Treating on death, he has expressed the known and true doctrine with sprightliness of fancy, and neatness of diction. I shall therefore insert it. There are truths which, as they are always necessary, do not grow stale by repetition.

Death, the last and most dreadful of all evils, is so far from being one that it is the infallible cure for all others.

> To die is landing on some silent shore,
> Where billows never beat, nor tempests roar.
> Ere well we feel the friendly stroke, 'tis o'er.
>
> Garth

For, abstracted from the sickness and sufferings usually attending it, it is no more than the expiration of that term of life God was pleased to bestow on us, without any claim or merit on our part. But was it an evil ever so great, it could not be remedied but by one much greater, which is by living for ever; by which means our wickedness, unrestrained by the prospect of a future state, would grow so insupportable, our sufferings so intolerable by perseverance, and our pleasures so tiresome by repetition, that no being in the universe could be so completely miserable as a species of immortal men. We have no reason, therefore, to look upon death as an evil, or to fear it as a punishment, even without any supposition of a future life: but if we consider it as a passage to a more perfect state, or a remove only in an eternal succession of still improving states (for which we have the strongest reasons) it will then appear a new favour from the divine munificence; and a man must be as absurd to repine at dying as a traveller would be who proposed to himself a delightful tour through various unknown countries to lament that he cannot take up his residence at the first dirty inn, which he baits at on the road.

The instability of human life, or of the changes of its successive periods, of which we so frequently complain, are no more than the necessary progress of it to this necessary conclusion; and are so far from being evils deserving these complaints that they are the source of our greatest pleasures, as they are the source of all novelty, from which our greatest pleasures are ever derived. The continual succession of seasons in the human life, by daily presenting to us new scenes, render it agreeable, and like those of the year, afford us delights by their change, which the choicest of them could not give us by their continuance. In the spring of life, the gilding of the sunshine, the verdure of the fields, and the variegated paintings of the sky, are so exquisite in the eyes of infants at their first looking abroad into a new world as nothing perhaps afterwards can equal. The heat and vigour of the succeeding summer of youth ripens for us new pleasures, the blooming maid, the nightly revel, and the jovial chase: the serene autumn of complete manhood feasts us with the golden harvests of our worldly pursuits: nor is the hoary winter of old age destitute of its peculiar comforts and enjoyments, of which the recollection and relation of those past are perhaps none of the least: and at last death opens to us a new prospect, from whence we shall probably look back upon the diversions and occupations of this world with the same contempt we do now on our tops and hobby-horses, and with the same surprise that they could ever so much entertain or engage us.

I would not willingly detract from the beauty of this paragraph, and in gratitude to him who has so well inculcated such important truths, I will venture to admonish him, since the chief comfort of the old is the recollection of the past, so to employ his time and his thoughts that when the imbecility of age shall come upon him, he may be able to recreate its languors by the remembrance of hours spent, not in presumptuous decisions,° but modest inquiries; not in dogmatical limitations of omnipotence,° but in humble acquiescence and fervent adoration. Old age will show him that much of the book now before us has no other use than to perplex the scrupulous, and to shake the weak, to encourage impious presumption, or stimulate idle curiosity.

Having thus despatched the consideration of particular evils, he comes at last to a general reason for which *evil* may be said to be *our good*. He is of opinion that there is some inconceivable benefit in pain abstractedly considered; that pain however inflicted, or wherever felt, communicates some good to the general system of being, and that every animal is some way or other the better for the pain of every other animal. This opinion he carries so far as to suppose that there passes some principle of union through all animal life, as attraction is communicated to all corporeal nature, and that the evils suffered on this globe may by some inconceivable means contribute to the felicity of the inhabitants of the remotest planet.

How the origin of evil is brought nearer to human conception by any *inconceivable* means, I am not able to discover. We believed that the present system of creation was right, though we could not explain the adaptation of one part to the other, or for the whole succession of causes and consequences. Where has the enquirer added to the little knowledge that we had before? He has told us of the benefits of evil which no man feels, and relations between distant parts of the universe which he cannot himself conceive. There was enough in this question inconceivable before, and we have little advantage from a new inconceivable solution.

I do not mean to reproach this author for not knowing what is equally hidden from learning and from ignorance. The shame is to impose words for ideas upon ourselves or others. To imagine that we are going forward when we are only turning round. To think that there is any difference between him that gives no reason, and him that gives a reason which by his own confession cannot be conceived.

But that he may not be thought to conceive nothing but things inconceivable, he has at last thought on a way by which human sufferings may produce good effects. He imagines that as we have not only animals for food, but choose some for our diversion, the same privilege may be allowed to some beings above us, *who may deceive*,

torment, or destroy us for the ends only of their own pleasure or utility.
This he again finds impossible to be conceived, *but that impossibility lessens not the probability of the conjecture, which by analogy is so strongly confirmed.*

I cannot resist the temptation of contemplating this analogy, which I think he might have carried further very much to the advantage of his argument. He might have shown that these *hunters, whose game is man* have many sports analogous to our own. As we drown whelps and kittens, they amuse themselves now and then with sinking a ship, and stand round the fields of Blenheim, or the walls of Prague,° as we encircle a cockpit. As we shoot a bird flying, they take a man in the midst of his business or pleasure, and knock him down with an apoplexy. Some of them, perhaps, are virtuosi, and delight in the operations of an asthma, as a human philosopher in the effects of the air pump.° To swell a man with a tympany is as good sport as to blow a frog. Many a merry bout have these frolic beings at the vicissitudes of an ague, and good sport it is to see a man tumble with an epilepsy, and revive and tumble again, and all this he knows not why. As they are wiser and more powerful than we, they have more exquisite diversions; for we have no way of procuring any sport so brisk and so lasting as the paroxysms of the gout and stone, which undoubtedly must make high mirth, especially if the play be a little diversified with the blunders and puzzles of the blind and deaf. We know not how far their sphere of observation may extend. Perhaps now and then a merry being may place himself in such a situation as to enjoy at once all the varieties of an epidemical disease, or amuse his leisure with the tossings and contortions of every possible pain exhibited together.

One sport the merry malice of these beings has found means of enjoying to which we have nothing equal or similar. They now and then catch a mortal proud of his parts, and flattered either by the submission of those who court his kindness, or the notice of those who suffer him to court theirs. A head thus prepared for the reception of false opinions, and the projection of vain designs, they easily fill with idle notions, till in time they make their plaything an author; their first diversion commonly begins with an ode or an epistle, then rises perhaps to a political irony, and is at last brought to its height by a treatise of philosophy. Then begins the poor animal to entangle himself in sophisms, and flounder in absurdity, to talk confidently of the scale of being, and to give solutions which himself confesses impossible to be understood. Sometimes, however, it happens, that their pleasure is without much mischief. The author feels no pain, but while they are wondering at the extravagance of his opinion, and pointing him out to one another as a new example of human folly, he is enjoying his own applause and that of his companions, and perhaps is elevated with the hope of standing at the head of a new sect.

Many of the books which now crowd the world may be justly suspected to be written for the sake of some invisible order of beings, for surely they are of no use to any of the corporeal inhabitants of the world. Of the productions of the last bounteous year, how many can be said to serve any purpose of use or pleasure? The only end of writing is to enable the readers better to enjoy life, or better to endure it; and how will either of those be put more in our power by him who tells us that we are puppets, of which some creature not much wiser than ourselves manages the wires? That a set of beings unseen and unheard are hovering about us, trying experiments upon our sensibility, putting us in agonies to see our limbs quiver, torturing us to madness that they may laugh at our vagaries, sometimes obstructing the bile that they may see how a man looks when he is yellow; sometimes breaking a traveller's bones to try how he will get home; sometimes wasting a man to a skeleton, and sometimes killing him fat for the greater elegance of his hide?

This is an account of natural evil which though, like the rest, not quite new, is very entertaining, though I know not how much it may contribute to patience. The only reason why we should contemplate evil is that we may bear it better; and I am afraid nothing is much more placidly endured for the sake of making others sport.

The first pages of the fourth letter are such as incline me both to hope and wish that I shall find nothing to blame in the succeeding part. He offers a criterion of action, an account of virtue and vice, for which I have often contended, and which must be embraced by all who are willing to know why they act, or why they forbear to give any reason of their conduct to themselves or others.

In order to find out the true origin of moral evil, it will be necessary, in the first place, to enquire into its nature and essence; or what it is that constitutes one action evil, and another good. Various have been the opinions of various authors on this criterion of virtue; and this variety has rendered that doubtful which must otherwise have been clear and manifest to the meanest capacity. Some indeed have denied that there is any such thing, because different ages and nations have entertained different sentiments concerning it; but this is just as reasonable as to assert that there are neither sun, moon, nor stars, because astronomers have supported different systems of the motions and magnitudes of these celestial bodies. Some have placed it in conformity to truth, some to the fitness of things, and others to the will of God. But all this is merely superficial: they resolve us not why truth, or the fitness of things, are either eligible or obligatory, or why God should require us to act in one manner rather than another. The true reason of which can possibly be no other than this, because some actions produce happiness, and others misery: so that all moral good and evil are nothing more than the production of natural. This alone it is that makes truth preferable to falsehood, this that determines the fitness of things, and this that induces God to command some actions, and forbid others. They who extol the truth, beauty, and harmony of virtue, exclusive of its consequences, deal but in pompous nonsense; and they who would persuade us that good and evil are things indifferent, depending wholly on the will of God, do but confound the nature of things, as well as all our notions of God himself, by representing him capable of willing contradictions; that is, that we should be, and be happy, and at the same time that we should torment and destroy each other; for injuries cannot be made benefits, pain cannot be made pleasure, and, consequently vice cannot be made virtue by any power whatever. It is the consequences, therefore, of all human actions that must stamp their value. So far as the general practice of any action tends to produce good, and introduce happiness into the world, so far we may pronounce it virtuous; so much evil as it occasions, such is the degree of vice it contains. I say the general practice, because we must always remember, in judging by this rule, to apply it only to the general species of actions, and not to particular actions; for the infinite wisdom of God, desirous to set bounds to the destructive consequences which must otherwise have followed from the universal depravity of mankind, has so wonderfully contrived the nature of things that our most vicious actions may sometimes accidentally and collaterally produce good. Thus, for instance, robbery may disperse useless hoards to the benefit of the public; adultery may bring heirs, and good humour too, into many families where they would otherwise have been wanting; and murder free the world from tyrants and oppressors. Luxury maintains its thousands, and vanity its ten thousands. Superstition and arbitrary power contribute to the grandeur of many nations, and the liberties of others are preserved by the perpetual contentions of avarice, knavery, selfishness, and ambition; and thus the worst of vices, and the worst of men, are often compelled by providence to serve the most beneficial purposes, contrary to their own malevolent tendencies and inclinations; and thus private vices become public benefits by the force only of accidental circumstances. But this impeaches not the truth of the criterion of virtue before mentioned, the only solid foundation on which any true system of ethics can be built, the only plain, simple, and uniform rule by which we can pass any judgment on our actions; but by this we may be enabled, not only to determine which are good, and which are evil, but almost mathematically to demonstrate the proportion of virtue or vice which belongs to each, by comparing them with the degrees of happiness or misery which they occasion. But though the production of happiness is the essence of virtue, it is by no means the end: the great end is the probation of mankind, or the giving them an opportunity of exalting or degrading themselves in another state by their behaviour in the present. And thus indeed it answers two most important purposes; those are the conservation of our happiness, and the test of our obedience; for had not such a test seemed necessary to God's infinite wisdom, and productive of universal good, he would never have permitted the happiness of men, even in this life, to have depended on so precarious a tenure as their mutual good behaviour to each other. For it is observable that he who best knows our formation has trusted no one thing of importance to our reason or virtue: he trusts only to our appetites for the support of the individual, and the continuance of our species; to our vanity, or compassion, for our bounty to others; and to our fears, for the preservation of ourselves; often to our vices for the support of government, and sometimes to our follies for the preservation of our religion. But since some test of our obedience was necessary, nothing sure could have been commanded for that end so fit and proper, and at the same time so useful, as the practice of virtue; nothing could have been so justly rewarded with happiness as the production of happiness in conformity to the will of God. It is this conformity alone which adds merit to virtue, and constitutes the essential difference between morality and religion. Morality obliges men to live honestly and soberly, because such behaviour is most conducive to public happiness, and consequently to their own; religion, to pursue the same course, because conformable to the will of their creator. Morality induces them to embrace virtue from prudential considerations; religion from those of gratitude and obedience. Morality therefore, entirely abstracted from religion, can have nothing meritorious in it; it being but wisdom, prudence, or good economy, which, like health, beauty, or riches, are rather obligations conferred upon us by God than merits in us towards him; for though we may be justly punished for injuring ourselves, we can claim no reward for self-preservation; as suicide deserves punishment and infamy, but a man deserves no reward or honours for not being guilty of it. This I take to be the meaning of all those passages in our scriptures in which works are represented to have no merit without faith; that is, not without believing in historical facts, in creeds, and articles, but without being done in pursuance of our belief in God, and in obedience to his commands. And now, having mentioned scripture, I cannot omit observing that the Christian is the only religious or moral institution in the world that ever set in a right light these two material points, the essence and the end of virtue; that ever founded the one in the production of happiness, that is, in universal benevolence, or, in their language, charity to all men; the other, in the probation of man, and his obedience to his Creator. Sublime and magnificent as was the philosophy of the ancients, all their moral systems were deficient in these two important articles. They were all built on the sandy foundations of the innate beauty of virtue, or enthusiastic patriotism; and their great point in view was the contemptible reward of human glory; foundations which were by no means able to support the magnificent structures which they erected upon them; for the beauty of virtue independent of its effects is unmeaning nonsense; patriotism which injures mankind in general for the sake of a particular country is but a more extended selfishness, and really criminal; and all human glory but a mean and ridiculous delusion. The whole affair then of religion and morality, the subject of so many thousand volumes, is, in short, no more than this: the supreme being, infinitely good as well as powerful, desirous to diffuse happiness by all possible means, has created innumerable ranks and orders of beings, all subservient to each other by proper subordination. One of these is occupied by man, a creature endued with such a certain degree of knowledge, reason, and free-will as is suitable to his situation, and placed, for a time on this globe as in a school of probation and education. Here he has an opportunity given him of improving or debasing his nature, in such a manner as to render himself fit for a rank of higher perfection and happiness, or to degrade himself to a state of greater imperfection and misery; necessary indeed towards carrying on the business of the universe, but very grievous and burdensome to those individuals who, by their own misconduct, are obliged to submit to it. The test of this his behaviour is doing good, that is, co-operating with his Creator, as far as his narrow sphere of action will permit, in the production of happiness. And thus the happiness and misery of a future state will be the just reward or punishment of promoting or preventing happiness in this. So artificially° by this means is the nature of all human virtue and vice contrived that their rewards and punishments are woven as it were in their very essence; their immediate effects give us a foretaste of their future, and their fruits in the present life are the proper samples of what they must unavoidably produce in another. We have reason given us to distinguish these consequences, and regulate our conduct; and, lest that should neglect its post, conscience also is appointed as an instinctive kind of monitor, perpetually to remind us both of our interest and our duty.

Si sic omnia dixisset!° To this account of the essence of vice and virtue, it is only necessary to add that the consequences of human actions being sometimes uncertain, and sometimes remote, it is not possible in many cases for most men, nor in all cases for any man, to determine what actions will ultimately produce happiness, and therefore it was proper that *Revelation* should lay down a rule to be followed invariably in opposition to appearances, and in every change of circumstances, by which we may be certain to promote the general felicity, and be set free from the dangerous temptation of *doing evil that good may come*.

Because it may easily happen, and in effect will happen very frequently, that our own private happiness may be promoted by an act injurious to others, when yet no man can be obliged by nature to prefer ultimately the happiness of others to his own, therefore, to the instructions of infinite wisdom it was necessary that infinite power should add penal sanctions. That every man to whom those instructions shall be imparted may know that he can never ultimately injure himself by benefiting others, or ultimately by injuring others benefit himself; but that however the lot of the good and bad may be huddled together in the seeming confusion of our present state, the time shall undoubtedly come when the most virtuous will be most happy.

I am sorry that the remaining part of this letter is not equal to the first. The author has indeed engaged in a disquisition in which we need not wonder if he fails, in the solution of questions on which philosophers have employed their abilities from the earliest times,

And found no end, in wand'ring mazes lost.°

He denies that man was created *perfect*, because the system requires subordination, and because the power of losing his perfection, of *rendering himself wicked and miserable, is the highest imperfection imaginable*. Besides, the regular gradations of the scale of being required somewhere *such a creature as man, with all his infirmities about him, and the total removal of those would be altering his nature, and when he became perfect, he must cease to be man*.

I have already spent some considerations on the *scale of being*, of which yet I am obliged to renew the mention whenever a new argument is made to rest upon it, and I must therefore again remark that consequences cannot have greater certainty than the postulate from which they are drawn, and that no system can be more hypothetical than this, and perhaps no hypothesis more absurd.

He again deceives himself with respect to the perfection with which *man* is held to be originally vested. *That man came perfect, that is, endued with all possible perfection, out of the hands of his creator, is a false notion derived from the philosophers.—The universal system required subordination, and, consequently, comparative imperfection.* That *man was ever endued with all possible perfection*, that is, with all perfection of which the idea is not contradictory, or destructive of itself, is, undoubtedly, *false*. But it can hardly be called *a false notion*, because no man ever thought it, nor can it be derived from the *philosophers*; for, without pretending to guess what philosophers he may mean, it is very safe to affirm that no philosopher ever said it. Of those who now maintain that *man* was once perfect, who may very easily be found, let the author enquire whether *man* was ever omniscient, whether he was ever omnipotent; whether he ever had even the lower power of archangels or angels. Their answers will soon inform him that the supposed perfection of *man* was not absolute, but respective, that he was perfect in a sense consistent enough with subordination, perfect not as compared with different beings, but with himself in his present degeneracy, not perfect as an angel, but perfect as man.

From this perfection, whatever it was, he thinks it necessary that man should be debarred, because pain is necessary to the good of the universe; and the pain of one order of beings extending its salutary influence to innumerable orders above and below, it was necessary that man should suffer; but because it is not suitable to justice that pain should be inflicted on innocence, it was necessary that man should be criminal.

This is given as a satisfactory account of the original of moral evil, which amounts only to this, that God created beings whose guilt he foreknew, in order that he might have proper objects of pain, because the pain of part is, no man knows how or why, necessary to the felicity of the whole.

The perfection which man once had may be so easily conceived that, without any unusual strain of imagination, we can figure its revival. All the duties to God or man that are neglected we may fancy performed; all the crimes that are committed we may conceive forborne. Man will then be restored to his moral perfections, and into what head can it enter that by this change the universal system would be shaken, or the condition of any order of beings altered for the worse?

He comes in the fifth letter to political, and in the sixth to religious evils. Of political evil, if we suppose the origin of moral evil discovered, the account is by no means difficult: polity being only the conduct of immoral men in public affairs. The evils of each particular kind of government are very clearly and elegantly displayed, and from their secondary causes very rationally deduced, but the first cause lies still in its ancient obscurity. There is in this letter nothing new, nor anything eminently instructive; one of his practical deductions, that *from government, evils cannot be eradicated, and their excess only can be prevented*, has been always allowed; the question upon which all dissension arises is when that excess begins, at what point men shall cease to bear, and attempt to remedy.

Another of his precepts, though not new, well deserves to be transcribed, because it cannot be too frequently impressed.

What has here been said of their imperfections and abuses is by no means intended as a defence of them: every wise man ought to redress them to the utmost of his power; which can be effected by one method only, that is, by a reformation of manners: for, as all political evils derive their original from moral, these can never be removed until those are first amended. He, therefore, who strictly adheres to virtue and sobriety in his conduct, and enforces them by his example, does more real service to a state than he who displaces a minister, or dethrones a tyrant: this gives but a temporary relief, but that exterminates the cause of the disease. No immoral man then can possibly be a true patriot; and all those who profess outrageous zeal for the liberty and prosperity of their country, and at the same time infringe her laws, affront her religion, and debauch her people, are but despicable quacks, by fraud or ignorance increasing the disorders they pretend to remedy.

Of religion he has said nothing but what he has learned, or might have learned, from the divines, that it is not universal, because it must be received upon conviction, and successively received by those whom conviction reached; that its evidences and sanctions are not irresistible, because it was intended to induce, not to compel; and that it is obscure, because we want faculties to comprehend it. What he means by his assertion that it wants policy I do not well understand; he does not mean to deny that a good Christian will be a good governor, or a good subject, and he has before justly observed that the good man only is a patriot.

Religion has been, he says, corrupted by the wickedness of those to whom it was communicated, and has lost part of its efficacy by its connexion with temporal interest and human passion.

He justly observes that from all this no conclusion can be drawn against the divine original of Christianity, since the objections arise not from the nature of the revelation, but of him to whom it is communicated.

All this is known, and all this is true, but why, we have not yet discovered. Our author, if I understand him right, pursues the argument thus: the religion of man produces evils, because the morality of man is imperfect; his morality is imperfect, that he may be justly a subject of punishment; he is made subject to punishment, because the pain of part is necessary to the happiness of the whole; pain is necessary to happiness, no mortal can tell why or how.

Thus, after having clambered with great labour from one step of argumentation to another, instead of rising into the light of knowledge, we are devolved back into dark ignorance, and all our effort ends in belief that for the evils of life there is some good reason, and in confession that the reason cannot be found. This is all that has been produced by the revival of Chrysippus's untractableness of matter,°

and the Arabian scale of existence. A system has been raised which is so ready to fall to pieces of itself that no great praise can be derived from its destruction. To object is always easy, and it has been well observed by a late writer that *the hand which cannot build a hovel may demolish a temple.*°

Of the Duty of a Journalist°

It is an unpleasing consideration that virtue cannot be inferred from knowledge; that many can teach others those duties which they never practise themselves; yet, though there may be speculative knowledge without actual performance, there can be no performance without knowledge; and the present state of many of our papers is such that it may be doubted not only whether the compilers know their duty, but whether they have endeavoured or wished to know it.

A journalist is an historian, not indeed of the highest class, nor of the number of those whose works bestow immortality upon others or themselves; yet, like other historians, he distributes for a time reputation or infamy, regulates the opinion of the week, raises hopes and terrors, inflames or allays the violence of the people. He ought therefore to consider himself as subject at least to the first law of history, the obligation to tell truth. The journalist, indeed, however honest, will frequently deceive, because he will frequently be deceived himself. He is obliged to transmit the earliest intelligence before he knows how far it may be credited; he relates transactions yet fluctuating in uncertainty; he delivers reports of which he knows not the authors. It cannot be expected that he should know more than he is told, or that he should not sometimes be hurried down the current of a popular clamour. All that he can do is to consider attentively, and determine impartially, to admit no falsehoods by design, and to retract those which he shall have adopted by mistake.

This is not much to be required, and yet this is more than the writers of news seem to exact from themselves. It must surely sometimes raise indignation to observe with what serenity of confidence they relate on one day what they know not to be true, because they hope that it will please, and with what shameless tranquillity they contradict it on the next day, when they find that it will please no longer. How readily they receive any report that will disgrace our enemies, and how eagerly they accumulate praises upon a name which caprice or accident has made a favourite. They know, by experience, however destitute of reason, that what is desired will be credited without nice examination; they do not therefore always limit their narratives by possibility, but slaughter armies without battles, and conquer countries without invasions.

There are other violations of truth admitted only to gratify idle curiosity which yet are mischievous in their consequences, and hateful in their contrivance. Accounts are sometimes published of robberies and murders which never were committed, men's minds are terrified with fictitious dangers, the public indignation is raised, and the government of our country depreciated and contemned. These scribblers who give false alarms ought to be taught by some public animadversion that to relate crimes is to teach them, and that as most men are content to follow the herd, and to be like their neighbours, nothing contributes more to the frequency of wickedness than the representation of it as already frequent.

There is another practice of which the injuriousness is more apparent, and which, if the law could succour the poor, is now punishable by law. The advertisement of apprentices who have left their masters, and who are often driven away by cruelty or hunger; the minute descriptions of men whom the law has not considered as criminal, and the insinuations often published in such a manner that, though obscure to the public, they are well understood where they can do most mischief; and many other practices by which particular interests are injured are to be diligently avoided by an honest journalist, whose business is only to tell transactions of general importance, or uncontested notoriety, or by advertisements to promote private convenience without disturbance of private quiet.

Thus far the journalist is obliged to deviate from the common methods of his competitors by the laws of unvariable morality. Other improvements may be expected from him as conducive to delight or information. It is common to find passages in papers of intelligence which cannot be understood. Obscure places are sometimes mentioned without any information from geography or history. Sums of money are reckoned by coins or denominations of which the value is not known in this country. Terms of war and navigation are inserted which are utterly unintelligible to all who are not engaged in military or naval business. A journalist, above most other men, ought to be acquainted with the lower orders of mankind, that he may be able to judge what will be plain and what will be obscure; what will require a comment, and what will be apprehended without explanation. He is to consider himself not as writing to students or statesmen alone, but to women, shopkeepers, and artisans, who have little time to bestow upon mental attainments, but desire, upon easy terms, to know how the world goes; who rises, and who falls; who triumphs, and who is defeated.

If the writer of this journal shall be able to execute his own plan; if he shall carefully enquire after truth, and diligently impart it; if he shall resolutely refuse to admit into his paper whatever is injurious to private reputation; if he shall relate transactions with greater clearness than others, and sell more instruction at a cheaper rate, he hopes that his labours will not be overlooked. This he promises to endeavour; and, if his promise shall obtain the favour of an early attention, he desires that favour to be continued only as it is deserved.

Introduction to *Proceedings of the Committee Appointed to Manage the Contributions . . . for Clothing French Prisoners of War*°

The Committee entrusted with the money contributed to the relief of the subjects of France, now prisoners in the British Dominions, here lay before the public an exact account of all the sums received and expended; that the donors may judge how properly their benefactions have been applied.

Charity would lose its name, were it influenced by so mean a motive as human praise: it is, therefore, not intended to celebrate, by any particular memorial, the liberality of single persons, or distinct societies; it is sufficient that their works praise them.°

Yet he who is far from seeking honour may very justly obviate censure. If a good example has been set, it may lose its influence by misrepresentation; and to free charity from reproach is itself a charitable action.

Against the relief of the French, only one argument has been brought; but that one is so popular and specious that if it were to remain unexamined, it would by many be thought irrefragable. It has been urged that charity, like other virtues, may be improperly and unseasonably exerted; that while we are relieving Frenchmen, there remain many Englishmen unrelieved; that while we lavish pity on our enemies, we forget the misery of our friends.

Grant this argument all it can prove, and what is the conclusion?—that to relieve the French is a good action, but that a better may be conceived. This is all the result, and this all is very little. To do the best can seldom be the lot of man; it is sufficient if, when opportunities are presented, he is ready to do good. How little virtue could be practised, if beneficence were to wait always for the most proper objects, and the noblest occasions; occasions that may never happen, and objects that never may be found?

It is far from certain that a single Englishman will suffer by the charity to the French. New scenes of misery make new impressions; and much of the charity which produced these donations may be supposed to have been generated by a species of calamity never known among us before. Some imagine that the laws have provided all necessary relief in common cases, and remit the poor to the care of the public; some have been deceived by fictitious misery, and are afraid of encouraging imposture; many have observed want to be the effect of vice, and consider casual almsgivers as patrons of idleness. But all these difficulties vanish in the present case: we know that for the prisoners of war there is no legal provision; we see their distress, and are certain of its cause; we know that they are poor and naked, and poor and naked without a crime.

But it is not necessary to make any concessions. The opponents of this charity must allow it to be good, and will not easily prove it not to be the best. That charity is best of which the consequences are most extensive: the relief of enemies has a tendency to unite mankind in fraternal affection; to soften the acrimony of adverse nations, and dispose them to peace and amity: in the mean time, it alleviates captivity, and takes away something from the miseries of war. The rage of war, however mitigated, will always fill the world with calamity and horror:° let it not then be unnecessarily extended; let animosity and hostility cease together; and no man be longer deemed an enemy than while his sword is drawn against us.

The effects of these contributions may, perhaps, reach still further. Truth is best supported by virtue: we may hope from those who feel or who see our charity that they shall no longer detest as heresy that religion which makes its professors the followers of Him who has commanded us to *do good to them that hate us.*°

The Bravery of the English Common Soldiers°

By those who have compared the military genius of the English with that of the French nation, it is remarked, that 'the French officers will always lead, if the soldiers will follow'; and that 'the English soldiers will always follow, if their officers will lead'.

In all pointed sentences some degree of accuracy must be sacrificed to conciseness; and, in this comparison, our officers seem to lose what our soldiers gain. I know not any reason for supposing that the English officers are less willing than the French to lead; but it is, I think, universally allowed that the English soldiers are more willing to follow. Our nation may boast, beyond any other people in the world, of a kind of epidemic bravery, diffused equally through all its ranks. We can show a peasantry of heroes, and fill our armies with clowns whose courage may vie with that of their general.

There may be some pleasure in tracing the causes of this plebeian magnanimity. The qualities which commonly make an army for-midable are long habits of regularity, great exactness of discipline, and great confidence in the commander. Regularity may, in time, produce a kind of mechanical obedience to signals and commands, like that which the perverse Cartesians° impute to animals: discipline may impress such an awe upon the mind that any danger shall be less dreaded than the danger of punishment; and confidence in the wisdom or fortune of the general may induce the soldiers to follow him blindly to the most dangerous enterprise.

What may be done by discipline and regularity may be seen in the troops of the Russian Empress, and Prussian Monarch.° We find that they may be broken without confusion, and repulsed without flight.

But the English troops have none of these requisites in any eminent degree. Regularity is by no means part of their character: they are rarely exercised, and therefore show very little dexterity in their evolutions as bodies of men, or in the manual use of their weapons as individuals: they neither are thought by others, nor by themselves, more active or exact than their enemies, and therefore derive none of their courage from such imaginary superiority.

The manner in which they are dispersed in quarters over the country, during times of peace, naturally produces laxity of discipline: they are very little in sight of their officers; and, when they are not engaged in the slight duty of the guard, are suffered to live every man his own way.

The equality of English privileges, the impartiality of our laws, the freedom of our tenures,° and the prosperity of our trade dispose us very little to reverence of superiors. It is not to any great esteem of the officers that the English soldier is indebted for his spirit in the hour of battle; for perhaps it does not often happen that he thinks much better of his leader than of himself. The French Count° who has lately published the *Art of War* remarks how much soldiers are animated when they see all their dangers shared by those who were born to be their masters, and whom they consider as beings of a different rank. The Englishman despises such motives of courage: he was born without a master; and looks not on any man, however dignified by lace or titles, as deriving from Nature any claims to his respect, or inheriting any qualities superior to his own.

There are some, perhaps, who would imagine that every Englishman fights better than the subjects of absolute governments, because he has more to defend. But what has the English more than the French soldier? Property they are both commonly without. Liberty is, to the lowest rank of every nation, little more than the choice of working or starving; and this choice is, I suppose, equally allowed in every country. The English soldier seldom has his head very full of the constitution; nor has there been, for more than a century, any war that put the property or liberty of a single Englishman in danger.

Whence then is the courage of the English vulgar? It proceeds, in my opinion, from that dissolution of dependence which obliges every man to regard his own character. While every man is fed by his own hands, he has no need of any servile arts: he may always have wages for his labour; and is no less necessary to his employer than his employer is to him. While he looks for no protection from others, he is naturally roused to be his own protector; and having nothing to abate his esteem of himself, he consequently aspires to the esteem of others. Thus every man that crowds our streets is a man of honour, disdainful of obligation, impatient of reproach, and desirous of extending his reputation among those of his own rank; and as courage is in most frequent use, the fame of courage is most eagerly pursued. From this neglect of subordination I do not deny that some inconveniences may from time to time proceed: the power of the law does not always sufficiently supply the want of reverence, or maintain the proper distinction between different ranks: but good and evil will grow up in this world together; and they who complain, in peace, of the insolence of the populace, must remember that their insolence in peace is bravery in war.

Review of [William Tytler], *An Historical and Critical Enquiry into the Evidence Produced by the Earls of Moray and Morton against Mary, Queen of Scots with an Examination of the Rev. Dr Robertson's Dissertation and Mr Hume's History with Respect to That Evidence*°

We live in an age in which there is much talk of independence, of private judgment, of liberty of thought, and liberty of press. Our clamorous praises of liberty sufficiently prove that we enjoy it; and if by liberty nothing else be meant than security from the persecutions of power, it is so fully possessed by us that little more is to be desired, except that one should talk of it less, and use it better.

But a social being can scarcely rise to complete independence; he that has any wants which others can supply must study the gratification of them whose assistance he expects; this is equally true, whether his wants be wants of nature or of vanity. The writers of the present time are not always candidates for preferment, nor often the hirelings of a patron. They profess to serve no interest, and speak with loud contempt of sycophants and slaves.

There is, however, a power from whose influence neither they nor their predecessors have ever been free. Those who have set greatness at defiance have yet been the slaves of fashion. When an opinion has once become popular, very few are willing to oppose it. Idleness is more willing to credit than enquire; cowardice is afraid of controversy, and vanity of answer; and he that writes merely for sale is tempted to court purchasers by flattering the prejudices of the public.

It has now been fashionable for near half a century to defame and vilify the house of Stuart, and to exalt and magnify the reign of Elizabeth. The Stuarts have found few apologists, for the dead cannot pay for praise; and who will, without reward, oppose the tide of popularity? Yet there remains still among us, not wholly extinguished, a zeal for truth, a desire of establishing right, in opposition to fashion. The author whose work is now before us has attempted a vindication of Mary of Scotland, whose name has, for some years, been generally resigned to infamy, and who has been considered as the murderer of her husband, and condemned by her own letters.

Of these letters, the author of this vindication confesses the importance to be such that, *if they be genuine, the queen was guilty; and, if they be spurious, she was innocent.* He has therefore undertaken to prove them spurious, and divided his treatise into six parts.

In the first is contained the history of the letters from their discovery by the earl of Morton, their being produced against Queen Mary, and their several appearances in England, before Queen Elizabeth and her commissioners, until they were finally delivered back again to the earl of Morton.

The second contains a short abstract of Mr Goodall's arguments for proving the letters to be spurious and forged; and of Dr Robertson and Mr Hume's objections by way of answer to Mr Goodall,° with critical observations on these authors.

The third contains an examination of the arguments of Dr Robertson and Mr Hume in support of the authenticity of the letters.

The fourth contains an examination of the confession of Nicholas Hubert, commonly called *French Paris*, with observations showing the same to be a forgery.

The fifth contains a short recapitulation, or summary, of the arguments on both sides of the question. And,

The last is an historical collection of the direct or positive evidence still on record, tending to show what part the earls of Murray and Morton, and secretary Lethington, had in the murder of the lord Darnley.

The author apologizes for the length of this book, by observing that it necessarily comprises a great number of particulars, which could not easily be contracted: the same plea may be made for the imperfection of our extract, which will naturally fall below the force of the book, because we can only select parts of that evidence, which owes its strength to its concatenation, and which will be weakened whenever it is disjoined.

The account of the seizure of these controverted letters is thus given by the queen's enemies:

That in the castell of Edinburgh thair was left be the Erle of Bothwell, before his fleeing away, and was send for be ane George Dalgleish, his servand, who was taken be the Erle of Mortoun, ane small gylt coffer, not fully ane fute lang, garnisht in sindrie places with the roman letter F. under ane king's crowne; wharin were certane letteris and writings weel knawin, and be aithis to be affirmit to have been written with the Quene of Scottis awn hand to the Erle.

The papers in the box were said to be eight letters in French, some love sonnets in French also, and a promise of marriage by the Queen to Bothwell.

To the reality of these letters our author makes some considerable objections, from the nature of things, but as such arguments do not always convince we will pass to the evidence of facts.

On June 15, 1567, the queen delivered herself to Morton, and his party, who imprisoned her.

June 20, 1567, Dalgleish was seized, and, six days after, was examined by Morton; his examination is still extant, and there is no mention of this fatal box.

Dec. 4, 1567, Murray's secret council published an act, in which is the first mention of these letters, and in which they are said to be *written and subscrivit with her awin hand.* Ten days after, Murray's first parliament met, and passed an act, in which they mention *previe letters written halelie* [wholly] *with her awin hand.* The difference between *written and subscribed,* and *wholly written,* gives the author just reason to suspect, first, a forgery, and then a variation of the forgery. It is indeed very remarkable that the first account asserts more than the second, though the second contains all the truth, for the letters, whether *written* by the queen or not, were not *subscribed.* Had the second account differed from the first only by something added, the first might have contained truth, though not all the truth, but as the second corrects the first by diminution, the first cannot be cleared from falsehood.

In October, 1568, these letters were shown at York to Elizabeth's commissioners, by the agents of Murray, but not in their public character as commissioners, but by way of private information, and were not therefore exposed to Mary's commissioners. Mary, however, hearing that some letters were intended to be produced against her, directed her commissioners to require them for her inspection, and, in the mean time, to declare them *false and feigned, forged and invented,* observing that there were many that could counterfeit her hand.

To counterfeit a name is easy, to counterfeit a hand through eight letters very difficult. But it does not appear that the letters were ever shown to those who would desire to detect them, and to the English commissioners a rude and remote imitation might be sufficient, since they were not shown as judicial proofs; and why they were not shown as proofs no other reason can be given than they must have then been examined and that examination would have detected the forgery.

These letters, thus timorously and suspiciously communicated, were all the evidence against Mary; for the servants of Bothwell, executed for the murder of the king, acquitted the Queen, at the hour of death. These letters were so necessary to Murray that he alleges them as the reason of the queen's imprisonment, though he imprisoned her on the 16th, and pretended not to have intercepted the letters before the 20th of June.

Of these letters, on which the fate of princes and kingdoms was suspended, the authority should have been put out of doubt, yet that such letters were ever found, there is no witness but Morton, who accused the queen, and Crawfurd, a dependent on Lennox, another of her accusers. Dalgleish, the bearer, was hanged without any interrogatories concerning them; and Hulet, mentioned in them, though then in prison, was never called to authenticate them, nor was his confession produced against Mary till death had left him no power to disown it.

Elizabeth, indeed, was easily satisfied; she declared herself ready to receive the proofs against Mary, and absolutely refused Mary the liberty of confronting her accusers, and making her defence. Before such a judge, a very little proof would be sufficient. She gave the accusers of Mary leave to go to Scotland, and the box and letters were seen no more. They have been since lost, and the discovery, which comparison of writing might have made, is now no longer possible. Hume has, however, endeavoured to palliate the conduct of Elizabeth, but his *account*, says our author, *is contradicted almost in every sentence by the records which, it appears, he has himself perused.*

In the next part, the authenticity of the letters is examined, and it seems to be proved beyond contradiction that the French letters, supposed to have been written by Mary, are translated from the Scotch copy, and, if originals, which it was so much the interest of such numbers to preserve, are wanting, it is much more likely that they never existed than that they have been lost.

The arguments used by Dr Robertson to prove the genuineness of the letters are next examined. Robertson makes use principally of what he calls the *internal evidence*, which, amounting at most to conjecture, is opposed by conjecture equally probable.

In examining the confession of Nicholas Hubert, or French Paris, this new apologist of Mary seems to gain ground upon her accuser. Paris is mentioned in the letters as the bearer of them to Bothwell; when the rest of Bothwell's servants were executed, clearing the queen in the last moment, Paris, instead of suffering his trial with the rest at Edinburgh, was conveyed to St Andrew's, where Murray was absolute, put into a dungeon of Murray's citadel, and two years after condemned by Murray himself, nobody knew how. Several months after his death, a confession in his name, without the regular testifications, was sent to Cecil, at what exact time nobody can tell.

Of this confession, Lesly, bishop of Ross, openly denied the genuineness, in a book printed at London, and suppressed by Elizabeth; and another historian of that time declares that Paris died without any confession; and the confession itself was never shown to Mary, or to Mary's commissioners. The author makes this reflection:

From the violent presumptions that arise from their carrying this poor ignorant stranger from Edinburgh, the ordinary seat of justice; their keeping him hid from all the world, in a remote dungeon, and not producing him with their other evidences, so as he might have been publicly questioned; the positive and direct testimony of the author of Crawfurd's manuscript, then living, and on the spot at the time; with the public affirmation of the bishop of Ross at the time of Paris's death, that he had vindicated the queen with his dying breath; the behaviour of Murray, Morton, Buchanan, and even of Hay, the attester of this pretended confession, on that occasion; their close and reserved silence, at the time when they must have had this confession of Paris in their pocket; and their publishing every other circumstance that could tend to blacken the queen, and yet omitting this confession, the only direct evidence of her supposed guilt; all this duly and dispassionately considered, I think, one may safely conclude that it was judged not fit to expose so soon to light this piece of evidence against the queen; which a cloud of witnesses, living, and present at Paris's execution, would, surely, have given clear testimony against, as a notorious imposture.

Mr Hume, indeed, observes: 'It is in vain at present to seek for improbabilities in Nicholas Hubert's dying confession, and to magnify the smallest difficulties into a contradiction. It was certainly a *regular judicial* paper, given in regularly and judicially, and ought to have been canvassed at the time, if the persons whom it concerned had been assured of their innocence.' To which our author makes a reply, which cannot be shortened without weakening it:

Upon what does this author ground his sentence? Upon two very plain reasons, *first*, that the confession was a judicial one, that is, taken in presence, or by authority of a judge. And *secondly*, that it was regularly and judicially given in; that must be understood during the time of the conferences before queen Elizabeth and her council, in presence of Mary's commissioners; at which time she ought to have canvassed it [says our author] if she knew her innocence.

That it was not a judicial confession is evident: the paper itself does not bear any such mark; nor does it mention that it was taken in presence of any person, or by any authority whatsoever; and, by comparing it with the judicial examinations of Dalgleish, Hay, and Hepburn, in page 146, it is apparent, that it is destitute of every formality requisite in a judicial evidence. In what dark corner, then, this strange production was generated, our author may endeavour to find out, if he can.

As to his second assertion, that it was regularly and judicially given in, and, therefore, ought to have been canvassed by Mary during the conferences, we have already seen that this, likewise, is not fact. The conferences broke up in February, 1569: Nicholas Hubert was not hanged till August thereafter, and his dying confession, as Mr Hume calls it, is only dated the 10th of that month. How, then, can this gentleman gravely tell us that this confession was judicially given in, and ought to have been, at that very time, canvassed by queen Mary and her commissioners? Such positive assertions, apparently contrary to fact, are unworthy the character of an historian, and may, very justly, render his decision, with respect to evidences of a higher nature, very dubious. In answer, then, to Mr Hume: As the queen's accusers did not choose to produce this material witness, Paris, whom they had alive and in their hands, nor any declaration or confession from him, at the critical and proper time for having it canvassed by the queen, I apprehend our author's conclusion may fairly be used against himself; that it is in vain, at present, to support the improbabilities and absurdities in a confession taken in a clandestine way, nobody knows how; and produced, after Paris's death, by nobody knows whom; and, from every appearance, destitute of every formality, requisite and common to such sort of evidence: for these reasons, I am under no sort of hesitation to give sentence against Nicholas Hubert's confession, as a gross imposutre and forgery.

The state of the evidence relating to the letters is this:

Morton affirms that they were taken in the hands of Dalgleish. The examination of Dalgleish is still extant, and he appears never to have been once interrogated concerning the letters.

Morton and Murray affirm that they were written by the queen's hand; they were carefully concealed from Mary and her commissioners, and were never collated by one man who could desire to disprove them.

Several of the incidents mentioned in the letters are confirmed by the oath of Crawfurd, one of Lennox's dependants, and some of the incidents are so minute as that they could scarcely be thought on by a forger. Crawfurd's testimony is not without suspicion. Whoever practises forgery endeavours to make truth the vehicle of falsehood. Of a prince's life very minute incidents are known, and if any are too slight to be remarked, they may be safely feigned, for they are, likewise, too slight to be contradicted. But there are still more reasons for doubting the genuineness of these letters. They had no date of time or place, no seal, no direction, no superscription.

The only evidences that could prove their authenticity were Dalgleish and Paris, of which Dalgleish, at his trial, was never questioned about them, Paris was never publicly tried, though he was kept alive through the time of the conference.

The servants of Bothwell, who were put to death for the king's murder, cleared Mary with their last words.

The letters were first declared to be subscribed, and were then produced without subscription.

They were shown during the conferences at York privately to the English commissioners, but were concealed from the commissioners of Mary.

Mary always solicited the perusal of these letters, and was always denied it.

She demanded to be heard in person by Elizabeth, before the nobles of England and the ambassadors of other princes, and was refused.

When Mary persisted in demanding copies of the letters, her commissioners were dismissed with their box to Scotland, and the letters were seen no more.

The French letters, which for almost two centuries have been considered as originals by the enemies of Mary's memory, are now discovered to be forgeries, and acknowledged to be translations, and perhaps French translations of a Latin translation. And the modern accusers of Mary are forced to infer from these letters which now exist that other letters existed formerly, which have been lost, in spite of curiosity, malice, and interest.

The rest of this treatise is employed in an endeavour to prove that Mary's accusers were the murderers of Darnley: through this enquiry it is not necessary to follow him, only let it be observed that, if these letters were forged by them, they may easily be thought capable of other crimes. That the letters were forged is now made so probable that perhaps they will never more be cited as testimonies.

The Fountains: A Fairy Tale°

Felix qui potuit boni
Fontem visere lucidum.
Boethius°

As Floretta was wandering in a meadow at the foot of Plinlimmon, she heard a little bird cry in such a note as she had never observed before, and looking round her, saw a lovely goldfinch entangled by a lime-twig, and a hawk hovering over him, as at the point of seizing him in his talons.

Floretta longed to rescue the little bird, but was afraid to encounter the hawk, who looked fiercely upon her without any apparent dread of her approach, and as she advanced seemed to increase in bulk, and clapped his wings in token of defiance. Floretta stood deliberating a few moments, but seeing her mother at no great distance, took courage, and snatched the twig with the little bird upon it. When she had disengaged him she put him in her bosom, and the hawk flew away.

Floretta, showing her bird to her mother, told her from what danger she had rescued him; her mother, after admiring his beauty, said that he would be a very proper inhabitant of the little gilded cage which had hung empty since the starling died for want of water, and that he should be placed at the chamber window, for it would be wonderfully pleasant to hear him in the morning.

Floretta, with tears in her eyes, replied that he had better have been devoured by the hawk than die for want of water, and that she would not save him from a less evil to put him in danger of a greater. She therefore took him into her hand, cleaned his feathers from the bird-lime, looked upon him with great tenderness, and, having put his bill to her lips, dismissed him into the air.

He flew in circles round her as she went home, and perching on a tree before the door, delighted them awhile with such sweetness of song that her mother reproved her for not putting him in the cage. Floretta endeavoured to look grave, but silently approved her own act, and wished her mother more generosity. Her mother guessed her thoughts, and told her that when she was older she would be wiser.

Floretta however did not repent, but hoped to hear her little bird the next morning singing at liberty. She waked early and listened, but no goldfinch could she hear. She rose, and walking in the same meadow, went to view the bush where she had seen the lime-twig the day before.

When she entered the thicket, and was near the place for which she was looking, from behind a blossoming hawthorn advanced a female form of very low stature, but of elegant proportions and majestic air, arrayed in all the colours of the meadow, and sparkling as she moved like a dew-drop in the sun.

Floretta was too much disordered to speak or fly, and stood motionless between fear and pleasure, when the little lady took her by the hand.

'I am,' said she, 'one of that order of beings which some call fairies, and some piskies. We have always been known to inhabit the crags and caverns of Plinlimmon. The maids and shepherds when they wander by moonlight have often heard our music, and sometimes seen our dances.

'I am the chief of the fairies of this region, and am known among them by the name of Lady Lilinet of the Blue Rock. As I lived always in my own mountain, I had very little knowledge of human manners, and thought better of mankind than other fairies found them to deserve; I therefore often opposed the mischievous practices of my sisters without always enquiring whether they were just. I extinguished the light that was kindled to lead a traveller into a marsh, and found afterwards that he was hasting to corrupt a virgin: I dissipated a mist which assumed the form of a town, and was raised to decoy a monopolizer of corn from his way to the next market: I removed a thorn artfully planted to prick the foot of a churl that was going to hinder the poor from following his reapers; and defeated so many schemes of obstruction and punishment that I was cited before the Queen as one who favoured wickedness and opposed the execution of fairy justice.

'Having never been accustomed to suffer control, and thinking myself disgraced by the necessity of defence, I so much irritated the Queen by my sullenness and petulance that in her anger she transformed me into a goldfinch. "In this form," says she, "I doom thee to remain until some human being shall show thee kindness without any prospect of interest."

'I flew out of her presence not much dejected; for I did not doubt but every reasonable being must love that which having never offended could not be hated, and, having no power to hurt, could not be feared.

'I therefore fluttered about the villages, and endeavoured to force myself into notice.

'Having heard that nature was least corrupted among those who had no acquaintance with elegance and splendor, I employed myself for five years in hopping before the doors of cottages, and often sat singing on the thatched roof; my motions were seldom seen nor my notes heard, no kindness was ever excited, and all the reward of my officiousness was to be aimed at with a stone when I stood within a throw.

'The stones never hurt me, for I had still the power of a fairy.

'I then betook myself to spacious and magnificent habitations, and sung in bowers by the walks or on the banks of fountains.

'In these places where novelty was recommended by satiety, and curiosity excited by leisure, my form and my voice were soon distinguished, and I was known by the name of the pretty goldfinch; the inhabitants would walk out to listen to my music, and at last it was their practice to court my visits by scattering meat in my common haunts.

'This was repeated till I went about pecking in full security, and expected to regain my original form, when I observed two of my most liberal benefactors silently advancing with a net behind me. I flew off, and fluttering beside them pricked the leg of each, and left them halting and groaning with the cramp.

'I then went to another house, where for two springs and summers I entertained a splendid family with such melody as they had never heard in the woods before. The winter that followed the second summer was remarkably cold, and many little birds perished in the field. I laid myself in the way of one of the ladies as benumbed with cold and faint with hunger; she picked me up with great joy, telling her companions that she had found the goldfinch that sung so finely all summer in the myrtle hedge, that she would lay him where he should die, for she could not bear to kill him, and would then pick his fine feathers very carefully, and stick them in her muff.

'Finding that her fondness and her gratitude could give way to so slight an interest, I chilled her fingers that she could not hold me, then flew at her face, and with my beak gave her nose four pecks that left four black spots indelible behind them, and broke a match by which she would have obtained the finest equipage in the county.

'At length the Queen repented of her sentence, and being unable to revoke it, assisted me to try experiments upon man, to excite his tenderness, and attract his regard.

'We made many attempts in which we were always disappointed. At last she placed me in your way held by a lime-twig, and herself in the shape of a hawk made the show of devouring me. You, my dear, have rescued me from the seeming danger without desiring to detain me in captivity, or seeking any other recompense than the pleasure of benefiting a feeling creature.

'The Queen is so much pleased with your kindness that I am come, by her permission, to reward you with a greater favour than ever fairy bestowed before.

'The former gifts of fairies, though bounties in design, have proved commonly mischiefs in the event. We have granted mortals to wish according to their own discretion, and their discretion being small, and their wishes irreversible, they have rashly petitioned for their own destruction. But you, my dearest Floretta, shall have, what none have ever before obtained from us, the power of indulging your wish, and the liberty of retracting it. Be bold and follow me.'

Floretta was easily persuaded to accompany the fairy, who led her through a labyrinth of crags and shrubs, to a cavern covered by a thicket on the side of the mountain.

'This cavern,' said she, 'is the court of Lilinet your friend; in this place you shall find a certain remedy for all real evils.' Lilinet then went before her through a long subterraneous passage, where she saw many beautiful fairies, who came to gaze at the stranger, but who, from reverence to their mistress, gave her no disturbance. She heard from remote corners of the gloomy cavern the roar of winds and the fall of waters, and more than once entreated to return; but Lilinet assuring her that she was safe persuaded her to proceed till they came to an arch, into which the light found its way through a fissure of the rock.

There Lilinet seated herself and her guest upon a bench of agate, and pointing to two fountains that bubbled before them, said, 'Now attend, my dear Floretta, and enjoy the gratitude of a fairy. Observe the two fountains that spring up in the middle of the vault, one into a basin of alabaster, and the other into a basin of dark flint. The one is called the Spring of Joy, the other of Sorrow; they rise from distant veins in the rock, and burst out in two places, but after a short course unite their streams, and run ever after in one mingled current.

'By drinking of these fountains, which, though shut up from all other human beings, shall be always accessible to you, it will be in your power to regulate your future life.

'When you are drinking the water of joy from the alabaster fountain, you may form your wish, and it shall be granted. As you raise your wish higher, the water will be sweeter and sweeter to the taste; but beware that you are not tempted by its increasing sweetness to repeat your draughts, for the ill effects of your wish can only be removed by drinking the spring of sorrow from the basin of flint, which will be bitter in the same proportion as the water of joy was sweet. Now, my Floretta, make the experiment, and give me the first proof of moderate desires. Take the golden cup that stands on the margin of the spring of joy, form your wish and drink.'

Floretta wanted no time to deliberate on the subject of her wish; her first desire was the increase of her beauty. She had some disproportion of features. She took the cup and wished to be agreeable; the water was sweet, and she drank copiously; and in the fountain, which was clearer than crystal, she saw that her face was completely regular.

She then filled the cup again, and wished for a rosy bloom upon her cheeks: the water was sweeter than before, and the colour of her cheeks was heightened.

She next wished for a sparkling eye. The water grew yet more pleasant, and her glances were like the beams of the sun.

She could not yet stop; she drank again, desired to be made a perfect beauty, and a perfect beauty she became.

She had now whatever her heart could wish; and making an humble reverence to Lilinet, requested to be restored to her own habitation. They went back, and the fairies in the way wondered at the change of Floretta's form. She came home delighted to her mother, who, on seeing the improvement, was yet more delighted than herself.

Her mother from that time pushed her forward into public view. Floretta was at all the resorts of idleness and assemblies of pleasure; she was fatigued with balls, she was cloyed with treats, she was exhausted by the necessity of returning compliments. This life delighted her awhile, but custom soon destroyed its pleasure. She found that the men who courted her today resigned her on the morrow to other flatterers, and that the women attacked her reputation by whispers and calumnies, till without knowing how she had offended, she was shunned as infamous.

She knew that her reputation was destroyed by the envy of her beauty, and resolved to degrade herself from the dangerous pre-eminence. She went to the bush where she rescued the bird, and called for Lady Lilinet. Immediately Lilinet appeared, and discovered by

Floretta's dejected look that she had drank too much from the alabaster fountain.

'Follow me,' she cried, 'my Floretta, and be wiser for the future.'

They went to the fountains, and Floretta began to taste the waters of sorrow, which were so bitter that she withdrew more than once the cup from her mouth. At last she resolutely drank away the perfection of beauty, the sparkling eye and rosy bloom, and left herself only agreeable.

She lived for some time with great content; but content is seldom lasting. She had a desire in a short time again to taste the waters of joy: she called for the conduct of Lilinet, and was led to the alabaster fountain, where she drank, and wished for a faithful lover.

After her return she was soon addressed by a young man, whom she thought worthy of her affection. He courted, and flattered, and promised; till at last she yielded up her heart. He then applied to her parents; and, finding her fortune less than he expected, contrived a quarrel and deserted her.

Exasperated by her disappointment, she went in quest of Lilinet, and expostulated with her for the deceit which she had practised. Lilinet asked her with a smile for what she had been wishing; and being told, made her this reply. 'You are not, my dear, to wonder or complain. You may wish for yourself, but your wishes can have no effect upon another. You may become lovely by the efficacy of the fountain, but that you shall be loved is by no means a certain consequence; for you cannot confer upon another either discernment or fidelity. That happiness which you must derive from others it is not in my power to regulate or bestow.'

Floretta was for some time so dejected by this limitation of the fountain's power that she thought it unworthy of another visit; but being on some occasion thwarted by her mother's authority, she went to Lilinet, and drank at the alabaster fountain for a spirit to do her own way.

Lilinet saw that she drank immoderately, and admonished her of her danger; but *spirit* and *her own way* gave such sweetness to the water that she could not prevail upon herself to forbear, till Lilinet in pure compassion snatched the cup out of her hand.

When she came home every thought was contempt, and every action was rebellion. She had drunk into herself a spirit to resist, but could not give her mother a disposition to yield; the old lady asserted her right to govern; and, though she was often foiled by the impetuosity of her daughter, she supplied in pertinacity what she wanted in violence, so that the house was in continual tumult by the pranks of the daughter and opposition of the mother.

In time, Floretta was convinced that spirit had only made her a capricious termagant, and that her own ways ended in error, perplexity, and disgrace; she perceived that the vehemence of mind which to a man may sometimes procure awe and obedience produce to a woman nothing but detestation; she therefore went back, and by a large draught from the flinty fountain, though the water was very bitter, replaced herself under her mother's care, and quitted her spirit, and her own way.

Floretta's fortune was moderate, and her desires were not larger, till her mother took her to spend a summer at one of the places which wealth and idleness frequent, under pretence of drinking the waters. She was now no longer a perfect beauty, and therefore conversation in her presence took its course as in other company, opinions were freely told, and observations made without reserve. Here Floretta first learned the importance of money. When she saw a woman of mean air and empty talk draw the attention of the place, she always discovered upon enquiry that she had so many thousands to her fortune.

She soon perceived that where these golden goddesses appeared, neither birth, nor elegance, nor civility had any power of attraction, that every art of entertainment was devoted to them, and that the great and the wise courted their regard.

The desire after wealth was raised yet higher by her mother, who was always telling her how much neglect she suffered for want of fortune, and what distinctions if she had but a fortune her good qualities would obtain. Her narrative of the day was always that Floretta walked in the morning, but was not spoken to because she had a small fortune, and that Floretta danced at the ball better than any of them, but nobody minded her for want of a fortune.

This want, in which all other wants appeared to be included, Floretta was resolved to endure no longer, and came home flattering her imagination in secret with the riches which she was now about to obtain.

On the day after her return she walked out alone to meet Lady Lilinet, and went with her to the fountain. Riches did not taste so sweet as either beauty or spirit, and therefore she was not immoderate in her draught.

When they returned from the cavern, Lilinet gave her wand to a fairy that attended her, with an order to conduct Floretta to the Black Rock.

The way was not long, and they soon came to the mouth of a mine in which there was a hidden treasure, guarded by an earthy fairy deformed and shaggy, who opposed the entrance of Floretta till he recognized the wand of the Lady of the Mountain. Here Floretta saw vast heaps of gold and silver and gems, gathered and reposited in former ages, and entrusted to the guard of the fairies of the earth. The little fairy delivered the orders of her mistress, and the surly sentinel promised to obey them.

Floretta, wearied with her walk, and pleased with her success, went home to rest, and when she waked in the morning, first opened her eyes upon a cabinet of jewels, and looking into her drawers and boxes, found them filled with gold.

Floretta was now as fine as the finest. She was the first to adopt any expensive fashion, to subscribe to any pompous entertainment, to encourage any foreign artist, or engage in any frolic of which the cost was to make the pleasure.

She was on a sudden the favourite of every place. Report made her wealth thrice greater than it really was, and wherever she came, all was attention, reverence, and obedience. The ladies who had formerly slighted her, or by whom she had been formerly caressed, gratified her pride by open flattery and private murmurs. She sometimes overheard them railing at upstarts, and wondering whence some people came, or how their expenses were supplied. This inclined her to heighten the splendour of her dress, to increase the number of her retinue, and to make such propositions of costly schemes that her rivals were forced to desist from contest.

But she now began to find that the tricks which can be played with money will seldom bear to be repeated, that admiration is a short-lived passion, and that the pleasure of expense is gone when wonder and envy are no more excited. She found that respect was an empty form, and that all those who crowded round her were drawn to her by vanity or interest.

It was however pleasant to be able on any terms to elevate and to mortify, to raise hopes and fears; and she would still have continued to be rich, had not the ambition of her mother contrived to marry her to a lord, whom she despised as ignorant, and abhorred as profligate. Her mother persisted in her importunity, and Floretta having now lost the spirit of resistance, had no other refuge than to divest herself of her fairy fortune.

She implored the assistance of Lilinet, who praised her resolution. She drank cheerfully from the flinty fountain, and found the waters not extremely bitter. When she returned she went to bed, and in the morning perceived that all her riches had been conveyed away she knew not how, except a few ornamental jewels, which Lilinet had ordered to be carried back as a reward for her dignity of mind.

She was now almost weary of visiting the fountain, and solaced herself with such amusements as every day happened to produce. At last there arose in her imagination a strong desire to become a wit.

The pleasures with which this new character appeared to teem were so numerous and so great that she was impatient to enjoy them; and rising before the sun, hastened to the place where she knew that her fairy patroness was always to be found. Lilinet was willing to conduct her, but could now scarcely restrain her from leading the way but by telling her that if she went first the fairies of the cavern would refuse her passage.

They came in time to the fountain, and Floretta took the golden cup into her hand; she filled it and drank, and again she filled it, for wit was sweeter than riches, spirit, or beauty.

As she returned she felt new successions of imagery rise in her mind, and whatever her memory offered to her imagination assumed a new form, and connected itself with things to which it seemed before to have no relation. All the appearances about her were changed, but the novelties exhibited were commonly defects. She now saw that almost every thing was wrong, without often seeing how it could be better; and frequently imputed to the imperfection of art these failures which were caused by the limitation of nature.

Wherever she went, she breathed nothing but censure and reformation. If she visited her friends, she quarrelled with the situation of their houses, the disposition of their gardens, the direction of their walks, and the termination of their views. It was vain to show her fine furniture, for she was always ready to tell how it might be finer, or to conduct her through spacious apartments, for her thoughts were full of nobler fabrics, or airy palaces and hesperian gardens. She admired nothing and praised but little.

Her conversation was generally thought uncivil. If she received flatteries, she seldom repaid them; for she set no value upon vulgar praise. She could not hear a long story without hurrying the speaker on to the conclusion; and obstructed the mirth of her companions, for she rarely took notice of a good jest, and never laughed except when she was delighted.

This behaviour made her unwelcome wherever she went; nor did her speculation upon human manners much contribute to forward her reception. She now saw the disproportions between language and sentiment, between passion and exclamation; she discovered the defects of every action, and the uncertainty of every conclusion; she knew the malignity of friendship, the avarice of liberality, the anxiety of content, and the cowardice of temerity.

To see all this was pleasant, but the greatest of all pleasures was to show it. To laugh was something, but it was much more to make others laugh. As every deformity of character made a strong impression upon her, she could not always forbear to transmit it to others; as she hated false appearances, she thought it her duty to detect them, till, between wantonness and virtue, scarce any that she knew escaped without some wounds by the shafts of ridicule; not that her merriment was always the consequence of total contempt, for she often honoured virtue where she laughed at affectation.

For these practices, and who can wonder, the cry was raised against her from every quarter, and to hunt her down was generally determined. Every eye was watching for a fault, and every tongue was busy to supply its share of defamation. With the most unpolluted purity of mind, she was censured as too free of favours, because she was not afraid to talk with men. With generous sensibility of every human excellence, she was thought cold or envious, because she would not scatter praise with undistinguishing profusion. With tenderness that agonized at real misery, she was charged with delight in the pain of others, when she would not condole with those whom she knew to counterfeit affliction. She derided false appearances of kindness and of pity, and was therefore avoided as an enemy to society. As she seldom commended or censured but with some limitations and exceptions, the world condemned her as indifferent to the good and bad; and because she was often doubtful where others were confident, she was charged with laxity of principles, while her days were distracted and her rest broken by niceties of honour and scruples of morality.

Report had now made her so formidable that all flattered and all shunned her. If a lover gave a ball to his mistress and her friends, it was stipulated that Floretta should not be invited. If she entered a public room the ladies curtsied, and shrunk away, for there was no such thing as speaking but Floretta would find something to criticise. If a girl was more spritely than her aunt, she was threatened that in a little time she would be like Floretta. Visits were very diligently paid when Floretta was known not to be at home; and no mother trusted her daughter to herself without a caution, if she should meet Floretta to leave the company as soon as she could.

With all this Floretta made sport at first, but in time grew weary of general hostility. She would have been content with a few friends, but no friendship was durable; it was the fashion to desert her, and with the fashion what fidelity will contend? She could have easily amused herself in solitude, but that she thought it mean to quit the field to treachery and folly.

Persecution at length tired her constancy, and she implored Lilinet to rid her of her wit: Lilinet complied and walked up the mountain, but was often forced to stop and wait for her follower. When they came to the flinty fountain, Floretta filled a small cup and slowly brought it to her lips, but the water was insupportably bitter. She just tasted it, and dashed it to the ground, diluted the bitterness at the fountain of alabaster, and resolved to keep her wit with all its consequences.

Being now a wit for life, she surveyed the various conditions of mankind with such superiority of sentiment that she found few distinctions to be envied or desired, and therefore did not very soon make another visit to the fountain. At length being alarmed by sickness, she resolved to drink length of life from the golden cup. She returned elated and secure, for though the longevity acquired was indeterminate, she considered death as far distant, and therefore suffered it not to intrude upon her pleasures.

But length of life included not perpetual health. She felt herself continually decaying, and saw the world fading about her. The delights of her early days would delight no longer, and however widely she extended her view, no new pleasure could be found; her friends, her enemies, her admirers, her rivals dropped one by one into the grave, and with those who succeeded them she had neither community of joys nor strife of competition.

By this time she began to doubt whether old age were not dangerous to virtue; whether pain would not produce peevishness, and peevishness impair benevolence. She thought that the spectacle of life might be too long continued, and the vices which were often seen might raise less abhorrence; that resolution might be sapped by time, and let that virtue sink which in its firmest state it had not without difficulty supported; and that it was vain to delay the hour which must come at last, and might come at a time of less preparation and greater imbecility.

These thoughts led her to Lilinet, whom she accompanied to the flinty fountain; where, after a short combat with herself, she drank the bitter water. They walked back to the favourite bush pensive and silent. 'And now,' said she, 'accept my thanks for the last benefit that Floretta can receive.' Lady Lilinet dropped a tear, impressed upon her lips the final kiss, and resigned her, as she resigned herself, to the course of Nature.

Robert Chambers's Vinerian Lectures on the English Law°

PART II, LECTURE I. OF CRIMINAL LAW, AND FIRST OF THE GENERAL
NATURE OF PUNISHMENTS

Having in the lectures of the last part described the institution of the English government and traced it through its various modes of subordination, I now proceed to consider the ends proposed by this institution and the means by which they are prosecuted and attained and shall attempt in this and the following lecture to explain the principles and trace the progress of vindictive justice to show from the laws of nature why penalties were originally enacted and from the history of mankind how they have been varied.

The most striking effects of civil society are that power by which every community in vindication of its own laws inflicts punishment upon individuals and that acquiescence with which every man submits to the judgment of others in questions that regard not only his property but his life.

If society were now to begin we *might* conceive it credible that men would leave to the arbitration of others whether they should be rich or poor; but surely it must be difficult to persuade any man to trust the question whether he shall live or die to human wisdom or to human virtue. Such power, as it is evidently great, is evidently dangerous and would never have been committed by one man to another, but that experience proved it to be necessary.

The first purpose of every political society is *internal peace*, for as no man would submit to *any* polity if he were able by his own power to gratify his appetites and appease his fears, so he has submitted in vain to the diminution of his natural liberty unless he has obtained in return some additional stability of good and security from evil.

Society rightly adjusted and regularly administered imparts to every individual its collective strength and collective wisdom, by laws which direct the actions of those who are not able to judge for themselves and protect the persons and properties of those who are insufficient for their own defence.

When we consider in abstracted speculation the unequal distribution of the pleasures of life, when we observe that pride, the most general of all human passions, is gratified in one order of men only because it is ungratified in another and that the great pleasure of many possessions arises from the reflection that the possessor enjoys what multitudes desire; when it is apparent that many want the necessaries of nature, and many more the comforts and conveniences of life, that the idle live at ease by the fatigues of the diligent and the luxurious are pampered with delicacies untasted by those who supply them, when to him that glitters with jewels and slumbers in a palace multitudes may say what was said to Pompey,° *Nostrâ miseriâ tu es magnus*, when the greater number must always want what the smaller are enjoying and squandering, enjoying often without merit and squandering without use, it seems impossible to conceive that the peace of society can long subsist; it were natural to expect that no man would be left long in possession of superfluous enjoyments while such numbers are destitute of real necessaries, but that the wardrobe of Lucullus should be rifled by the naked and the dainties of Apicius° dispersed among the hungry, that almost every man should attempt to regulate that distribution which he thinks injurious to himself and supply his wants from the common stock.

An ingenious but whimsical French author gives us a very remarkable account of the opinions entertained on this subject by three savage American chieftains who came to Rouen at the time that Charles the 9th of France was there. 'The King (says he) discoursed a long time with them. They were shown our manner of living, our pomp and the several beauties of that great city. Some time after, a gentleman asked what it was that struck them most among the various objects they had seen. They answered three things, the last of which to my great regret I have forgot but the other two I remember. First they thought it very strange that so many tall men wearing beards, armed and standing round the King, should submit voluntarily to a child; and that they did not rather choose one of those tall men to govern them. Secondly that they had observed there were many among us, men who seemed rioting in superfluities of every kind, whilst their other half (a phrase used in their language) stood begging at their doors, quite pale and mortified through hunger and misery. Now they wondered extremely that this necessitous half should submit to such great injustice, and that they did not take the other half by the throat, or set fire to their houses' (Montaigne's *Essays*, pa: 169 of the 8ᵛᵒ edit: printed at Paris 1604). Such are naturally the first thoughts of an uninstructed mind concerning the unequal distribution of external goods; but the experience of many ages has taught every civilized nation that as in the physical disposition of the universe every planet is detained in its orbit by an exact equipoise of contrary tendencies, so in the economy of the moral world contrary passions debilitate each other. Every man desires to retain his own in proportion as he desires to seize what is another's, and no man can be allowed to rob, where none are willing to be robbed. We therefore mutually agree to protect and be protected, and every invader of property is opposed by the whole community, at least by all that part of it which has any thing to lose.

The same account may be given of the means by which the *irascible* passions are restrained. Every man would at some time be willing to hurt another but that he is afraid of being hurt himself. Of Achilles it was natural to expect that *Jura neget sibi nata*,° because the consequences of unlimited violence would be probably in his favour, but the rest of mankind would combine against him, and supply by their united power what was wanting to particular persons. Thus we permit anger and revenge to be restrained by law, because if they were once let loose upon mankind one mischief would for ever beget another, and he that had been oftenest conqueror would at last be conquered.

'I will tell you (says Thrasymachus in the first Book of Plato *De Republica* (v. I. pa: 86 of Massey's 8ᵛᵒ edition)) what is the nature of justice and what the original. It is the general opinion of men that to practise wrong is good, but to suffer it is evil, but that there is more evil in suffering wrong than good in doing it. So that after men have reciprocally done wrong and suffered it, and tasted the consequences of both, they discover that they cannot obtain the one and avoid the other, and find it convenient to contract with each other that wrong shall be no longer either done or suffered. From this time laws began to be made and compacts to be formed and henceforth what the law prescribed was termed legal and just.'

In explaining the formation of things matter is often considered as acting by its own properties, even among those philosophers who acknowledge creation to be the work of Omnipotence. So in the foregoing speculation society has been considered, not as modelled by any superior direction, but as forming itself by successive experiments and raising order by slow degrees out of confusion. This however was not the real opinion of Plato or of Socrates; and to us who have the advantage of Sacred History it must seem more probable that no society was thus formed. The laws of God revealed to Adam and to Noah were undoubtedly propagated through their descendants. Accordingly civil life may be traced backwards to the East, the laws of the Egyptians were borrowed by the Cretans, by them transmitted into Greece and from Greece adopted by the Romans. There are indeed some nations in the world lawless and barbarous. In every society one class of men will be more ignorant than another and the poor commonly more ignorant than the rich; nothing is more evident than that those who have least to lose will be most adventurous, and those most inclined to migrate who leave nothing behind them; it is therefore easy to conceive how a nation of regulated polity might send out a colony or drive out a troop very little qualified to retain or transmit civility. The knowledge of the first ages was not registered in books; the vulgar had little leisure to receive oral instruction and the little which they knew would easily be lost amidst the labours and distresses of a new settlement, in which every day was to struggle for itself without respect to the past or anticipation of the future. They that went out ignorant became quickly savage, and I know not that history furnishes an example of any savage race that was ever able to recover the maxims and practice of civil life, but as they were subdued by foreign power or enlightened by foreign information. Had mankind received no original instructions from a superior Being, they would probably have continued through all ages *mutum et turpe pecus*,° fattening in the summer and starving in the winter, worrying the kid and flying from the tiger. Such are the solitary savages sometimes caught on the borders of Poland and Russia, supposed to have been dropped there, when young, by flying Tartars; such was likewise Peter the wild youth caught in a forest in Hanover and sent over to England as a present to King George the First. See Salmon's *Modern Hist*: &c.

If it be enquired what is the use of supposing a state of life which is confessed never to have subsisted, it may be answered that in moral as in natural disquisitions objects must be magnified that they may be more clearly perceived. What would be true in its whole extent of savages becoming civil is true to a certain degree of the imperfect rudiments of every society. The desire of greater and greater security makes successive improvements in all political institutions. This first collected under chieftains the scattered tribes of our Gothic ancestors, ranged them by degrees in feudal subordination, by applying military authority to civil life, and has at last, partly by refinement of manners and partly by positive institutions, melted down the feudal system into equal laws and community of right.

While mankind continued in the state of gross barbarity in which all were eager to do wrong and all unwilling to suffer, it is apparent that every man's fear would be greater than his hope, for an individual, thinking himself at liberty to act merely for his own interest, would consider every other individual as his enemy who acted only by the same principle. When they came to deliberate how they should escape what many had felt and all dreaded, they would soon find that safety was only to be obtained by setting interest on the side of innocence, by such a scheme of regulation as should give every man a prospect of living more happily by forbearing than by usurping the property of another; and which should repress the passions of anger and revenge by making their gratification the cause of immediate misery.

This was the *first principle* of *penal laws*. Pleasure is forborne only for fear of pain, and to the imagination importuned by inordinate desires it is necessary to represent the terrific images of misery and death. While in a nation of *Nomades*, or wandering inhabitants, no other idea is present to the mind but that he who lessens his neighbour's flock shall increase his own, most men would be strongly instigated to secret theft or to open violence. But when law has determined that he who diminishes another's flock shall not only restore what he has stolen but add to it a double number of his own cattle, he then finds it safer to grow rich by natural increase than injurious invasion. This disposition to peace will be more and more increased as the forfeiture is doubled or trebled or made ten-fold, or as corporal punishment is superadded, or as the fact is to be followed by exile or by death.

The great strength of human laws arises from the constitution of things ordained by Providence, by which man is so formed and disposed that he can suffer more than he can enjoy. If the evil of penalty could not exceed the advantage of wickedness, the mind, so far as it is influenced merely by the laws of man, could never pass beyond an equipoise of passion, and the nearer good would generally outweigh the remoter evil. But such is the frame of man that the dread of evil may be always made more powerful than the appetite of good. He that possessing a hundred sheep shall steal a hundred more will by no means gain such a degree of happiness as he will lose if his own hundred be taken away. Even the *Lex Talionis*° has upon this principle a very powerful operation, for no man can have as much pleasure in pulling out the eyes of another as he will suffer pain from the pulling out of his own.

To this principle, which is easily discovered, society owes all its power over individuals. It was soon found that pain would be too powerful for pleasure, and the question then remaining was, on what occasions and in what proportions pain should be applied.

I have endeavoured in the first of my introductory lectures to give some account, partly from Sacred History and partly from conjecture, of the actual origin of civil society. To what I have there said it may be proper now to add that, as the most frequent cause of uniting men under one head was probably sudden fear of external force, it must be supposed that, in the formation of a new government, every thing would be left to the wisdom and discretion of the governor, and that in many instances his authority would cease of course when the occasion that gave rise to it was over.

In such a state of rudeness and barbarity, disputes about property could be but few, because possession was neither great nor multifarious, and those few must necessarily be decided by the governing power, when government was established, according to such notions of equity as might happen to prevail. Crimes would be considered as the objects rather of private vengeance than of public punishment.

The most atrocious offence that can be committed by one man against another is the act of taking away life, which seems to have been considered throughout the whole race of man as lawfully punishable with death, though death has not always been inflicted. The universality of this opinion may be referred to that natural justice which always dictates some proportion between the punishment and the crime, unless it may be more properly ascribed to the divine edict promulgated by Noah to the succeeding generation and amidst the dispersion of mankind preserved from oblivion by too frequent occasion of remembering and applying it.

When once the convenience of life began to be appropriated and men felt and understood the use of riches and the infelicity of poverty, there was immediately a passage opened for the influence of wealth and an easy method was discovered of making satisfaction for injuries; a satisfaction adequate and efficacious for violated property, and very often acceptable and pacificatory after the more atrocious guilt by which life has been destroyed. It became therefore usual to appease, by composition, the wrath of the person injured, or of his relations in case of murder.

The right of private vengeance, on which these compositions are founded and of which there is still some shadow remaining amongst us, is a principle so opposite to quiet, order, and security that every nation may be considered as more civilized and every government as nearer to perfection in proportion as it is more effectually repressed and extinguished. Yet by a late writer,° who has investigated with great ingenuity the original of criminal justice, it seems to be considered as one of the dictates of nature, as a legitimate passion which has a right to procure its own gratification. Revenge, he says, is one of the first movers of the human breast, every man naturally desires to do hurt to that from which hurt has been received, and revenge is therefore in his opinion the darling privilege of human nature.

No mind properly instructed will easily believe *that* to be in itself justifiable which the divine authority has interdicted, and against which, by this author's own confession, all the efforts of legislative wisdom have from age to age been constantly directed. It may reasonably be presumed, even though the fallacy by which he has deceived himself could not be immediately detected, that however some fallacy there is, and that nature never could approve what experience every where condemns.

The fallacy of his reasoning seems to consist in this, that he uses the *Law of nature* in different senses. When he speaks of the Law of nature as authorizing just punishment, he means, like other writers, a principle that nature suggests and that reason approves. When he considers the Law of nature as prompting revenge, he means by it a brute instinct which man shares in common with other animals, but which his reason is given him to moderate and govern. That this is his meaning may be learnt from his own instance, when he alleges that a man is inclined to break the stone against which he stumbles. It is true that, in savage and uncultivated minds, such storms of passion will sometimes rise as impel them not only to hurt others, but sometimes to hurt themselves, and at other times to vent their rage upon insensible subjects. But impulses thus violent and blind can be no principle of moral agency. It is impossible for a reasonable being, so far as he is reasonable, to fight the air because the wind is cold, or to beat a tree because it stands in his way; and it is equally impossible for reason to wish any evil but for the sake of good. That every man who feels himself injured desires the punishment of his enemy is true, but he can properly desire it only that his enemy may no more offend him, or that others may be deterred from doing him wrong. *Non quasi dulce sit vindicare*, says Seneca, *sed quasi utile*° (*De Ira*, II. 32). Between resentment and revenge there is no more necessary connection than between hunger and gluttony, between weariness and idleness. Hunger will incite a man to eat, and it is surely the law of nature that he shall eat not till he is sick but till he is refreshed. Resentment inclines men to give others pain, but reason will direct them to give no more pain than will benefit themselves. It is true that many are revengeful, and feast upon the misery of others. It is true likewise that many are gluttonous and lose the pleasure of refreshment in the disgust of satiety. The end of every law properly made, and such certainly are the laws of nature, is always either the promotion of good or the prevention of evil. That act therefore which produces more evil than good is done in opposition to the law of nature, and with the highest degree of opposition when its whole effect is unmingled evil; and such an act is the execution of revenge abstracted from all the purposes of punishment, of revenge that proposes neither reformation on one part nor security on the other. That revenge for its own sake is very generally desired may perhaps be true, but if desire could infer rectitude all positive law is pernicious and erroneous; for law is made for no other reason but that men may not do that which they desire.

Let it be observed that I am not here denying a fact but opposing a principle; it is possible that the first punishments might be the efforts of revenge and these punishments, whatever was their cause, might contribute to the restraint of violence and regularity of manners. But these effects, when they were not intended, must be considered as accidental, and, though they justified the permissions of Providence, supply no defence to the depravity of man.

Since revenge for its own sake cannot be justified, it will follow that the natural justice of punishment, as of every other act of man to man, must depend solely on its utility, and that its only lawful end is some good more than equivalent to the evil which it necessarily produces. Accordingly the ablest writers on the laws of nature have assigned to punishment a threefold end.

1. Benefit to the offender.
2. Benefit to the suffering party.
3. Benefit to the public in general.

Vel utilitas ejus qui peccavit, vel ejus cujus intererat non fuisse peccatum, vel indistincte quorumlibet (Grotius° *de J. B. & P*: L.2: C. 20: Sec. 6. Puff. *de Jure Nat*: *& Gent*: L. 8: C. 3: Sect. 9 & *de Off: Hom: & Civ*: L. 2: C. 13: S. 7).

1. *First* then the *good of the offender* himself is promoted by every punishment which has for its object his correction and amendment. For since the commission of every sinful act renders the mind somewhat flexible to sin and tends in some degree to create a habit of

offending, it is to be wished, even for the sake of the offender himself, that the approaches to vice may be strictly guarded and that every fault may be followed by chastisement, the pain of which may outweigh future temptation. This is the end and for the most part the only end of those punishments which parents are permitted to inflict on their children, teachers on their scholars, and masters on their hired servants and apprentices. For though it is probable that in the patriarchal ages every master of a family exercised a power of life and death over those who were his *subjects*, in a civil as well as an economical sense, a power which subsisted very long in the Roman Empire over children and slaves, yet now in almost every state which makes any near approach to political perfections, and particularly in this kingdom, domestic government implies no powers but such as are beneficial to the party governed. The good of the offender himself is likewise one end, though not the only end, proposed by those punishments which are inflicted by the civil magistrate but which do not entirely destroy life or liberty, but leave the criminal still a member of society entitled, as the case may be, either to all or to some of the privileges of a citizen.

2. The *second end* of punishment is the *good of him by whom injury has been sustained*. It is diligently to be noted that the present discourse is not of civil but of criminal justice, not of redressing wrongs, but of punishing the doer of wrong. By the good therefore of the person injured is not intended the satisfaction received when property unjustly withheld is resigned to the claimant or that which is taken away is returned to the owner, or when for an injury done to the body or the reputation a compensation is appointed by a judicial sentence; for no man can properly be said to be punished by losing that which he has no right to keep, or by repairing any mischief which he had no right to do. A reparation may indeed be accidentally punishment, as it may be more painful to pay a large sum than pleasant to defame a neighbour, and more burdensome to rebuild a house than it was agreeable to burn it. Reparation however can never be considered as passing beyond a mixed mode of justice partaking of civil judicature as it compensates the injury and of the criminal as it afflicts or intimidates the offender.

The advantage of the person injured such as justice purely criminal produces is for the most part not direct and peculiar, but consequential and communicated. When a thief is whipped for larceny no good direct and peculiar ensues to the person robbed from the operation of the law, but he is in less danger of being robbed again by the same or by any other thief, and as the number of robbers is made less he obtains his share in the increase of public security.

3. The *public security* is the principal end of public punishment, and therefore it is well said by the writers before quoted that the *third end of punishment* is *utilitas indistincte quorumlibet*. As by the unrestrained licentiousness of inordinate passions every man's possessions are endangered, by their punishment and coercion every man's property is protected and established, and all are preserved in continual possession of the most valuable of all goods, quiet and security.

We who have always lived under the shelter of legal protection and in the safe calm of a settled society are perhaps not sufficiently grateful to the care of legislators. Those who have never been sick have little sense of the comfort of health; and those feel not their obligation to the vigilance of the law who have never been under any necessity of watching for themselves. But he that should live for a very small portion of his life in a place where nothing was safe but as it was out of reach, where the day passed in suspicion and the night in anxiety, would soon discover that all have an interest in the penal laws, and that the punishment of every malefactor produces some good to every honest man.

The Patriot. Addressed to the Electors of Great Britain

> They bawl for freedom in their senseless mood,
> Yet still revolt when truth would set them free,
> License they mean, when they cry liberty,
> For who loves that must first be wise and good.
>
> Milton°

To improve the golden moment of opportunity, and catch the good that is within our reach, is the great art of life. Many wants are suffered which might once have been supplied; and much time is lost in regretting the time which had been lost before.

At the end of every seven years comes the Saturnalian season, when the freemen of Great Britain may please themselves with the choice of their representatives. This happy day has now arrived,° somewhat sooner than it could be claimed.

To select and depute those by whom laws are to be made, and taxes to be granted, is a high dignity and an important trust: and it is the business of every elector to consider how this dignity may be well sustained, and this trust faithfully discharged.

It ought to be deeply impressed on the minds of all who have voices in this national deliberation that no man can deserve a seat in Parliament who is not a Patriot. No other man will protect our rights, no other man can merit our confidence.

A *Patriot* is he whose public conduct is regulated by one single motive, the love of his country; who, as an agent in Parliament, has for himself neither hope nor fear, neither kindness nor resentment, but refers every thing to the common interest.

That of five hundred men, such as this degenerate age affords, a majority can be found thus virtuously abstracted, who will affirm? Yet there is no good in despondence: vigilance and activity often effect more than was expected. Let us take a Patriot where we can meet him; and that we may not flatter ourselves by false appearances, distinguish those marks which are certain from those which may deceive: for a man may have the external appearance of a Patriot, without the constituent qualities; as false coins have often lustre, though they want weight.

Some claim a place in the list of Patriots by an acrimonious and unremitting opposition to the Court.°

This mark is by no means infallible. Patriotism is not necessarily included in rebellion. A man may hate his king, yet not love his country. He that has been refused a reasonable or unreasonable request, who thinks his merit underrated, and sees his influence declining, begins soon to talk of natural equality, the absurdity of *many made for one*,° the original compact, the foundation of authority, and the majesty of the people. As his political melancholy increases, he tells, and perhaps dreams of the advances of the prerogative, and the dangers of arbitrary power; yet his design in all his declamation is not to benefit his country, but to gratify his malice.

These, however, are the most honest of the opponents of government; their patriotism is a species of disease; and they feel some part of what they express. But the greater, far the greater number of those who rave and rail, and enquire and accuse, neither suspect, nor fear, nor care for the public; but hope to force their way to riches by virulence and invective, and are vehement and clamorous only that they may be sooner hired to be silent.

A man sometimes starts up a Patriot only by disseminating discontent and propagating reports of secret influence, of dangerous counsels, of violated rights and encroaching usurpation.

This practice is no certain note of patriotism. To instigate the populace with rage beyond the provocation is to suspend public happiness, if not to destroy it. He is no lover of his country that unnecessarily disturbs its peace. Few errors and few faults of government can justify an appeal to the rabble; who ought not to judge of what they cannot understand, and whose opinions are not propagated by reason, but caught by contagion.

The fallaciousness of this note of patriotism is particularly apparent when the clamour continues after the evil is past. They who are still filling our ears with Mr Wilkes and the Freeholders of Middlesex lament a grievance that is now at an end. Mr Wilkes may be chosen, if any will choose him, and the precedent of his exclusion makes not any honest or any decent man think himself in danger.

It may be doubted whether the name of a Patriot can be fairly given as the reward of secret satire, or open outrage. To fill the newspapers with sly hints of corruption and intrigue, to circulate the *Middlesex Journal* and *London Pacquet*, may indeed be zeal; but it may likewise be interest and malice. To offer a petition not expected to be granted; to insult a king with a rude remonstrance,° only because there is no punishment for legal insolence, is not courage, for there is no danger; nor patriotism, for it tends to the subversion of order, and lets wickedness loose upon the land, by destroying the reverence due to sovereign authority.

It is the quality of patriotism to be jealous and watchful, to observe all secret machinations, and to see public dangers at a distance. The true *Lover of his country* is ready to communicate his fears and to sound the alarm whenever he perceives the approach of mischief. But he sounds no alarm when there is no enemy: he never terrifies his countrymen, till he is terrified himself. The patriotism therefore may be justly doubted of him who professes to be disturbed by incredibilities; who tells that the last peace° was obtained by bribing the Princess of Wales; that the King is grasping at arbitrary power; and that because the French in the new conquests enjoy their own laws, there is a design at court of abolishing in England the trial by juries.

Still less does the true Patriot circulate opinions which he knows to be false. No man who loves his country fills the nation with clamorous complaints that the Protestant religion is in danger, because *Popery is established in the extensive province of Quebec,*° a falsehood so open and shameless that it can need no confutation among those who know that of which it is almost impossible for the most unenlightened zealot to be ignorant,

That Quebec is on the other side of the Atlantic, at too great a distance to do much good or harm to the European world:

That the inhabitants, being French, were always Papists, who are certainly more dangerous as enemies than as subjects:

That though the province be wide, the people are few, probably not so many as may be found in one of the larger English counties:

That persecution is not more virtuous in a Protestant than a Papist; and that while we blame Lewis the Fourteenth, for his dragoons and his galleys,° we ought, when power comes into our hands, to use it with greater equity:

That when Canada with its inhabitants was yielded, the free enjoyment of their religion was stipulated; a condition, of which King William, who was no propagator of Popery, gave an example nearer home, at the surrender of Limerick:

That in an age where every mouth is open for *liberty of conscience*, it is equitable to show some regard to the conscience of a Papist, who may be supposed, like other men, to think himself safest in his own religion; and that those at least who enjoy a toleration° ought not to deny it to our new subjects.

If liberty of conscience be a natural right, we have no power to withhold it; if it be an indulgence, it may be allowed to Papists while it is not denied to other sects.

A Patriot is necessarily and invariably a lover of the people. But even this mark may sometimes deceive us.

The people is a very heterogeneous and confused mass of the wealthy and the poor, the wise and the foolish, the good and the bad. Before we confer on a man who caresses the people the title of Patriot, we must examine to what part of the people he directs his notice. It is proverbially said that he who dissembles his own character may be known by that of his companions.° If the candidate of patriotism endeavours to infuse right opinions into the higher ranks, and by their influence to regulate the lower; if he consorts chiefly with the wise, the temperate, the regular and the virtuous, his love of the people may be rational and honest. But if his first or principal application be to the indigent, who are always inflammable; to the weak, who are naturally suspicious; to the ignorant, who are easily misled; and to the profligate, who have no hope but from mischief and confusion; let his love of the people be no longer boasted. No man can reasonably be thought a lover of his country for roasting an ox, or burning a boot,° or attending the meeting at Mile-end, or registering his name in the Lumber-troop.° He may, among the drunkards, be a *hearty fellow*, and among sober handicraftsmen, a *free spoken gentleman*; but he must have some better distinction before he is a *Patriot*.

A Patriot is always ready to countenance the just claims, and animate the reasonable hopes of the people; he reminds them frequently of their rights, and stimulates them to resent encroachments, and to multiply securities.

But all this may be done in appearance, without real patriotism. He that raises false hopes to serve a present purpose only makes a way for disappointment and discontent. He who promises to endeavour what he knows his endeavours unable to effect means only to delude his followers by an empty clamour of ineffectual zeal.

A true Patriot is no lavish promiser: he undertakes not to shorten parliaments; to repeal laws; or to change the mode of representation transmitted by our ancestors: he knows that futurity is not in his power, and that all times are not alike favourable to change.

Much less does he make a vague and indefinite promise of obeying the mandates of his constituents. He knows the prejudices of faction, and the inconstancy of the multitude. He would first enquire how the opinion of his constituents shall be taken. Popular instructions are commonly the work, not of the wise and steady, but the violent and rash; meetings held for directing representatives are seldom attended but by the idle and the dissolute; and he is not without suspicion that of his constituents, as of other numbers of men, the smaller part may often be the wiser.

He considers himself as deputed to promote the public good, and to preserve his constituents, with the rest of his countrymen, not only from being hurt by others but from hurting themselves.

The common marks of patriotism having been examined, and shown to be such as artifice may counterfeit, or folly misapply, it cannot be improper to consider whether there are not some characteristical modes of speaking or acting which may prove a man to be *not a Patriot*.

In this enquiry, perhaps clearer evidence may be discovered, and firmer persuasion attained: for it is commonly easier to know what is wrong than what is right; to find what we should avoid, than what we should pursue.

As war is one of the heaviest of national evils, a calamity in which every species of misery is involved; as it sets the general safety to hazard, suspends commerce, and desolates the country; as it exposes great numbers to hardships, dangers, captivity and death; no man who desires the public prosperity will inflame general resentment by aggravating minute injuries, or enforcing disputable rights of little importance.

It may therefore be safely pronounced that those men are no Patriots who when the national honour was vindicated in the sight of Europe, and the Spaniards, having invaded what they call their own, had shrunk to a disavowal of their attempt and a relaxation of their claim, would still have instigated us to a war for a bleak and barren spot° in the Magellanic ocean, of which no use could be made, unless it were a place of exile for the hypocrites of patriotism.

Yet let it not be forgotten that by the howling violence of patriotic rage, the nation was for a time exasperated to such madness that for a barren rock under a stormy sky, we might have now been fighting and dying, had not our competitors been wiser than ourselves; and those who are now courting the favour of the people by noisy professions of public spirit would, while they were counting the profits of their artifice, have enjoyed the patriotic pleasure of hearing sometimes that thousands had been slaughtered in a battle, and sometimes that a navy had been dispeopled by poisoned air and corrupted food.

He that wishes to see his country robbed of its rights cannot be a Patriot.

That man therefore is no Patriot who justifies the ridiculous claims of American usurpation; who endeavours to deprive the nation of its natural and lawful authority over its own colonies: those colonies, which were settled under English protection; were constituted by an English charter; and have been defended by English arms.

To suppose that by sending out a colony, the nation established an independent power; that when, by indulgence and favour, emigrants are become rich, they shall not contribute to their own defence but at their own pleasure; and that they shall not be included, like millions of their fellow subjects, in the general system of representation involves such an accumulation of absurdity as nothing but the show of patriotism could palliate.

He that accepts protection stipulates obedience. We have always protected the Americans; we may therefore subject them to government.

The less is included in the greater. The power which can take away life may seize upon property. The Parliament may enact for America a law of capital punishment; it may therefore establish a mode and proportion of taxation.

But there are some who lament the state of the poor Bostonians,° because they cannot all be supposed to have committed acts of rebellion; yet all are involved in the penalty imposed. This, they say, is to violate the first rule of justice, by condemning the innocent to suffer with the guilty.

This deserves some notice, as it seems dictated by equity and humanity, however it may raise contempt by the ignorance which it betrays of the state of man, and the system of things. That the innocent should be confounded with the guilty is undoubtedly an evil; but it is an evil which no care or caution can prevent. National crimes require national punishments, of which many must necessarily have their part who have not incurred them by personal guilt. If rebels should fortify a town, the cannon of lawful authority will endanger equally the harmless burghers and the criminal garrison.

In some cases, those suffer most who are least intended to be hurt. If the French in the late war had taken an English city, and permitted the natives to keep their dwellings, how could it have been recovered, but by the slaughter of our friends? A bomb might as well destroy an Englishman as a Frenchman; and by famine we know that the inhabitants would be the first that should perish.

This infliction of promiscuous evil may therefore be lamented, but cannot be blamed. The power of lawful government must be maintained; and the miseries which rebellion produces can be charged only on the rebels.

That man likewise is *not a Patriot* who denies his governors their due praise, and who conceals from the people the benefits which they receive. Those therefore can lay no claim to this illustrious appellation who impute want of public spirit to the late Parliament; an assembly of men whom, notwithstanding some fluctuation of counsel, and some weakness of agency, the nation must always remember with gratitude, since it is indebted to them for a very ample concession in the resignation of protections,° and a wise and honest attempt to improve the constitution in the new judicature instituted for the trial of elections.°

The right of protection, which might be necessary when it was first claimed, and was very consistent with that liberality of immunities in which the feudal constitution delighted, was by its nature liable to abuse, and had in reality been sometimes misapplied, to the evasion of the law, and the defeat of justice. The evil was perhaps not adequate to the clamour; nor is it very certain that the possible good of this privilege was not more than equal to the possible evil. It is however plain that whether they gave any thing or not to the public, they at least lost something from themselves. They divested their dignity of a very splendid distinction, and showed that they were more willing than their predecessors to stand on a level with their fellow-subjects.

The new mode of trying elections, if it be found effectual, will diffuse its consequences further than seems yet to be foreseen. It is, I believe, generally considered as advantageous only to those who claim seats in Parliament; but, if to choose representatives be one of the most valuable rights of Englishmen, every voter must consider that law as adding to his happiness which makes his suffrage efficacious; since it was vain to choose, while the election could be controlled by any other power.

With what imperious contempt of ancient rights, and what audaciousness of arbitrary authority, former Parliaments have judged the disputes about elections, it is not necessary to relate. The claim of a candidate and the right of electors are said scarcely to have been, even in appearance, referred to conscience; but to have been decided by party, by passion, by prejudice, or by frolic. To have friends in the borough was of little use to him who wanted friends in the House; a pretence was easily found to evade a majority, and the seat was at last his that was chosen not by his electors, but his fellow-senators.

Thus the nation was insulted with a mock election, and the Parliament was filled with spurious representatives; one of the most important claims, that of a right to sit in the supreme council of the kingdom, was debated in jest, and no man could be confident of success from the justice of his cause.

A disputed election is now tried with the same scrupulousness and solemnity as any other title. The candidate that has deserved well of his neighbours may now be certain of enjoying the effect of their approbation; and the elector who has voted honestly for known merit may be certain that he has not voted in vain.

Such was the Parliament which some of those who are now aspiring to sit in another have taught the rabble to consider as an unlawful convention of men, worthless, venal, and prostitute, slaves of the court, and tyrants of the people.

That the next House of Commons may act upon the principles of the last, with more constancy and higher spirit, must be the wish of all who wish well to the public; and it is surely not too much to expect that the nation will recover from its delusion, and unite in a general abhorrence of those who, by deceiving the credulous with fictitious mischiefs, overbearing the weak by audacity of falsehood, by appealing to the judgment of ignorance, and flattering the vanity of meanness, by slandering honesty and insulting dignity, have gathered round them whatever the kingdom can supply of base, and gross, and profligate; and *raised by merit to this bad eminence,*° arrogate to themselves the name of *Patriots.*

Preface to Thomas Maurice, *Poems and Miscellaneous Pieces with a Free Translation of the Oedipus Tyrannus of Sophocles*°

The tragedy of which I have attempted to convey the beauties into the English language in a free translation stands amidst the foremost of the classical productions of antiquity. Of tragical writing it has ever been esteemed the model and the masterpiece. The grandeur of the subject is not less eminent than the dignity of the personages who are employed in it; and the design of the whole can only be rivalled by that art with which the particular parts are conducted. The subject is a nation labouring under calamities of the most dreadful and portentous kind; and the leading character is a wise and mighty prince, expiating by his punishment the involuntary crimes of which those calamities were the effect. The design is of the most interesting and important nature, to inculcate a due moderation in our passions, and an implicit obedience to that providence of which the decrees are equally unknown and irresistible.

So sublime a composition could not fail to secure the applause and fix the admiration of ages. The philosopher is exercised in the contemplation of its deep and awful morality; the critic is captivated by its dramatic beauties, and the man of feeling is interested by those strokes of genuine passion which prevail in almost every page—which every character excites, and every new event tends to diversify in kind or in degree.

The three grand unities of time, place, and action are observed with scrupulous exactness. However complicate its various parts may on the first view appear, on a nearer and more accurate examination we find every thing useful, every thing necessary; some secret spring of action laid open, some momentous truth inculcated, or some important end promoted: not one scene is superfluous, nor is there one episode that could be retrenched. The successive circumstances of the play arise gradually and naturally one out of the other, and are connected with such inimitable judgment that if the smallest part were taken away the whole would fall to the ground. The principal objection to this tragedy is that the punishment of Oedipus is much more than adequate to his crimes: that his crimes are only the effect of his ignorance, and that consequently the guilt of them is to be imputed not to Oedipus, but Apollo, who ordained and predicted them, and that he is only *Phoebi reus*,° as Seneca expresses himself. In vindication of Sophocles, it must be considered that the conduct of Oedipus is by no means so irreproachable as some have contended: for though his public character is delineated as that of a good king, anxious for the welfare of his subjects, and ardent in his endeavours to appease the gods by incense and supplication, yet we find him in private life choleric, haughty, inquisitive; impatient of control, and impetuous in resentment. His character, even as a king, is not free from the imputation of imprudence, and our opinion of his piety is greatly invalidated by his contemptuous treatment of the wise, the benevolent, the sacred Tiresias. The rules of tragic art scarcely permit that a perfectly virtuous man should be loaded with misfortunes. Had Sophocles presented to our view a character less debased by vice, or more exalted by virtue, the end of his performance would have been frustrated; instead of agonizing compassion, he would have raised in us indignation unmixed, and horror unabated. The intention of the poet would have been yet more frustrated on the return of our reason, and our indignation would have been transferred from Oedipus to the gods themselves—from Oedipus, who committed parricide, to the gods who first ordained, and then punished it. By making him criminal in a small degree, and miserable in a very great one, by investing him with some excellent qualities, and some imperfections, he at once inclines us to pity and to condemn. His obstinacy darkens the lustre of his other virtues; it aggravates his impiety, and almost justifies his sufferings. This is the doctrine of Aristotle and of nature, and shows Sophocles to have had an intimate knowledge of the human heart, and the springs by which it is actuated. That his crimes and punishment still seem disproportionate is not to be imputed as a fault to Sophocles, who proceeded only on the ancient and popular notion of Destiny; which we know to have been the basis of pagan theology.

It is not the intention of the translator to proceed farther in a critical discussion of the beauties and defects of a tragedy which hath already employed the pens of the most distinguished commentators; which hath wearied conjecture, and exhausted all the arts of unnecessary and unprofitable defence. The translator is no stranger to the merits of Dr Franklin,° whose character he reveres, and by whose excellent performance he has been animated and instructed. He thinks it necessary to disclaim every idea of rivalship with an author of such established and exalted reputation. The present translation, though it be executed with far less ability than that of Doctor Franklin, may deserve some notice, because professedly written on very different principles. The Doctor was induced by his plan, and enabled by his erudition, to encounter all the difficulties of *literal* translation. This work will be found by the reader, what it is called by the writer, a *free* translation. The author was not fettered by his text, but guided by it; he has however not forgotten the boundaries by which liberal translation is distinguished from that which is wild and licentious. He has always endeavoured to represent the sense of his original, he hopes sometimes to have caught its spirit, and he throws himself without reluctance, but not without diffidence, on the candour of those readers who understand and feel the difference that subsists between the Greek and English languages, between ancient and modern manners, between nature and refinement, between a Sophocles who appeals to posterity, and a writer who catches at the capricious taste of the day.

Dedication of Charles Burney, *An Account of the Musical Performances in Westminster-Abbey and the Pantheon . . . in Commemoration of Handel*°

TO THE KING

Greatness of mind is never more willingly acknowledged, nor more sincerely reverenced, than when it descends into the regions of general life, and by countenancing common pursuits, or partaking common amusements, shows that it borrows nothing from distance or formality.

By the notice which Your Majesty has been pleased to bestow upon the celebration of HANDEL's memory, You have condescended to add Your voice to public praise, and give Your sanction to musical emulation.

The delight which Music affords seems to be one of the first attainments of rational nature; wherever there is humanity, there is modulated sound. The mind set free from the resistless tyranny of painful want employs its first leisure upon some savage melody. Thus in those lands of unprovided wretchedness which Your Majesty's encouragement of naval investigation° has brought lately to the knowledge of the polished world, though all things else were wanted, every nation had its Music; an art of which the rudiments accompany the commencements, and the refinements adorn the completion of civility, in which the inhabitants of the earth seek their first refuge from evil, and, perhaps, may find at last the most elegant of their pleasures.

But that this pleasure may be truly elegant, science and nature must assist each other; a quick sensibility of Melody and Harmony is not always originally bestowed, and those who are born with this susceptibility of modulated sounds are often ignorant of its principles, and must therefore be in a great degree delighted by chance; but when Your Majesty is pleased to be present at Musical performances, the artists may congratulate themselves upon the attention of a judge in whom all requisites concur, who hears them not merely with instinctive emotion, but with rational approbation, and whose praise of HANDEL is not the effusion of credulity, but the emanation of Science.

How near, or how distant, the time may be when the art of combining sounds shall be brought to its highest perfection by the natives of Great Britain, this is not the place to enquire; but the efforts produced in other parts of knowledge° by Your Majesty's favour give hopes that Music may make quick advances now it is recommended by the attention, and dignified by the patronage of our Sovereign.

I am, With the most profound Humility, Your MAJESTY'S most dutiful and devoted Subject and Servant,

CHARLES BURNEY.

A Journey to the Western Islands of Scotland°

I had desired to visit the Hebrides, or Western Islands of Scotland, so long that I scarcely remember how the wish was originally excited; and was in the autumn of the year 1773 induced to undertake the journey by finding in Mr Boswell a companion whose acuteness would help my inquiry, and whose gaiety of conversation and civility of manners are sufficient to counteract the inconveniences of travel in countries less hospitable than we have passed.

On the eighteenth of August we left Edinburgh, a city too well known to admit description, and directed our course northward, along the eastern coast of Scotland, accompanied the first day by another gentleman, who could stay with us only long enough to show us how much we lost at separation.

As we crossed the Firth of Forth, our curiosity was attracted by Inch Keith, a small island, which neither of my companions had ever visited, though, lying within their view, it had all their lives solicited their notice. Here, by climbing with some difficulty over shattered crags, we made the first experiment of unfrequented coasts. Inch Keith is nothing more than a rock covered with a thin layer of earth, not wholly bare of grass, and very fertile of thistles. A small herd of cows grazes annually upon it in the summer. It seems never to have afforded to man or beast a permanent habitation.

We found only the ruins of a small fort, not so injured by time but that it might be easily restored to its former state. It seems never to have been intended as a place of strength, nor was built to endure a siege, but merely to afford cover to a few soldiers, who perhaps had the charge of a battery, or were stationed to give signals of approaching danger. There is therefore no provision of water within the walls, though the spring is so near that it might have been easily enclosed. One of the stones had this inscription: 'Maria Reg. 1564.' It has probably been neglected from the time that the whole island had the same king.

We left this little island with our thoughts employed awhile on the different appearance that it would have made if it had been placed at the same distance from London, with the same facility of approach; with what emulation of price a few rocky acres would have been purchased, and with what expensive industry they would have been cultivated and adorned.

When we landed, we found our chaise ready, and passed through

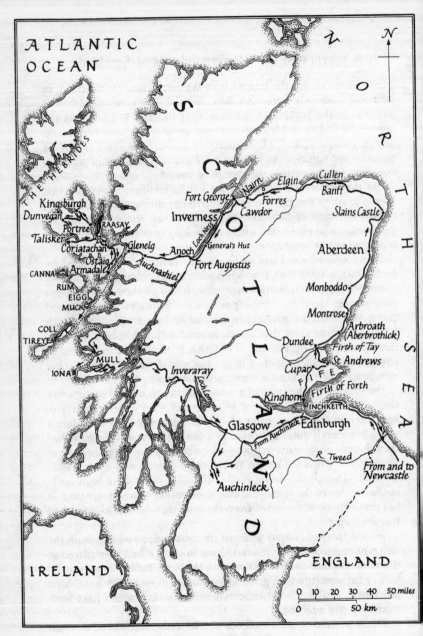

ATLANTIC
OCEAN

NORTH

SCOTLAND

THE HEBRIDES

Kingsburgh
Dunvegan
Portree RAASAY
Talisker
Coriatachan Glenelg
Ostaig Auchnashiel
Armadale
CANNA
RUM
EIGG
MUCK

COLL
TIREYE

MULL
IONA

Inveraray

Loch Ness

Fort George Nairn Elgin Cullen
Forres Banff
Inverness Cawdor
Slains Castle
Anoch General's Hut
Fort Augustus

Aberdeen

Monboddo

Montrose
Arbroath
(Aberbrothick)
Dundee Firth of Tay
Cupar St Andrews
FIFE
Kinghorn Firth of Forth
INCHKEITH
Glasgow Edinburgh
From Auchinleck

R. Tweed

Auchinleck

NORTH SEA

IRELAND

ENGLAND

From and to
Newcastle

Loch Lomond

0 10 20 30 40 50 miles
0   50 km

THE SCOTTISH TOUR

Kinghorn, Kirkaldy, and Cowpar, places not unlike the small or straggling market-towns in those parts of England where commerce and manufactures have not yet produced opulence.

Though we were yet in the most populous part of Scotland, and at so small a distance from the capital, we met few passengers.

The roads are neither rough nor dirty; and it affords a southern stranger a new kind of pleasure to travel so commodiously without the interruption of toll-gates. Where the bottom is rocky, as it seems commonly to be in Scotland, a smooth way is made indeed with great labour, but it never wants repairs; and in those parts where adventitious materials are necessary, the ground once consolidated is rarely broken; for the inland commerce is not great, nor are heavy commodities often transported otherwise than by water. The carriages in common use are small carts, drawn each by one little horse; and a man seems to derive some degree of dignity and importance from the reputation of possessing a two-horse cart.

ST ANDREWS

At an hour somewhat late we came to St Andrews, a city once archiepiscopal; where that university still subsists in which philosophy was formerly taught by Buchanan, whose name has as fair a claim to immortality as can be conferred by modern Latinity, and perhaps a fairer than the instability of vernacular languages admits.

We found that by the interposition of some invisible friend, lodgings had been provided for us at the house of one of the professors, whose easy civility quickly made us forget that we were strangers; and in the whole time of our stay we were gratified by every mode of kindness, and entertained with all the elegance of lettered hospitality.

In the morning we rose to perambulate a city which only history shows to have once flourished, and surveyed the ruins of ancient magnificence, of which even the ruins cannot long be visible, unless some care be taken to preserve them; and where is the pleasure of preserving such mournful memorials? They have been till very lately so much neglected that every man carried away the stones who fancied that he wanted them.

The cathedral, of which the foundations may be still traced, and a small part of the wall is standing, appears to have been a spacious and majestic building, not unsuitable to the primacy of the kingdom. Of the architecture, the poor remains can hardly exhibit, even to an artist, a sufficient specimen. It was demolished, as is well known, in the tumult and violence of Knox's reformation.

Not far from the cathedral, on the margin of the water, stands a fragment of the castle in which the archbishop anciently resided. It was never very large, and was built with more attention to security than pleasure. Cardinal Beatoun° is said to have had workmen employed in improving its fortifications at the time when he was murdered by the ruffians of reformation, in the manner of which Knox has given what he himself calls a merry narrative.

The change of religion in Scotland, eager and vehement as it was, raised an epidemical enthusiasm, compounded of sullen scrupulousness and warlike ferocity, which, in a people whom idleness resigned to their own thoughts, and who, conversing only with each other, suffered no dilution of their zeal from the gradual influx of new opinions, was long transmitted in its full strength from the old to the young, but by trade and intercourse with England is now visibly abating, and giving way too fast to that laxity of practice and indifference of opinion in which men not sufficiently instructed to find the middle point too easily shelter themselves from rigour and constraint.

The city of St Andrews, when it had lost its archiepiscopal preeminence, gradually decayed. One of its streets is now lost; and in those that remain, there is the silence and solitude of inactive indigence and gloomy depopulation.

The university, within a few years, consisted of three colleges, but is now reduced to two; the college of St Leonard being lately dissolved by the sale of its buildings and the appropriation of its revenues to the professors of the two others. The chapel of the alienated college is yet standing, a fabric not inelegant of external structure; but I was always, by some civil excuse, hindered from entering it. A decent attempt, as I was since told, has been made to convert it into a kind of greenhouse, by planting its area with shrubs. This new method of gardening is unsuccessful; the plants do not hitherto prosper. To what use it will next be put I have no pleasure in conjecturing. It is something that its present state is at least not ostentatiously displayed. Where there is yet shame, there may in time be virtue.

The dissolution of St Leonard's college was doubtless necessary; but of that necessity there is reason to complain. It is surely not without just reproach that a nation of which the commerce is hourly extending and the wealth increasing denies any participation of its prosperity to its literary societies; and while its merchants or its nobles are raising palaces, suffers its universities to moulder into dust.

Of the two colleges yet standing, one is by the institution of its founder appropriated to divinity. It is said to be capable of containing fifty students; but more than one must occupy a chamber. The library, which is of late erection, is not very spacious, but elegant and luminous.

The doctor by whom it was shown hoped to irritate or subdue my English vanity by telling me that we had no such repository of books in England.

Saint Andrews seems to be a place eminently adapted to study and education, being situated in a populous, yet a cheap country, and exposing the minds and manners of young men neither to the levity and dissoluteness of a capital city, not to the gross luxury of a town of commerce, places naturally unpropitious to learning; in one the desire of knowledge easily gives way to the love of pleasure, and in the other, is in danger of yielding to the love of money.

The students however are represented as at this time not exceeding a hundred. Perhaps it may be some obstruction to their increase that there is no episcopal chapel in the place. I saw no reason for imputing their paucity to the present professors; nor can the expense of an academical education be very reasonably objected. A student of the highest class may keep his annual session, or as the English call it, his term, which lasts seven months, for about fifteen pounds, and one of lower rank for less than ten; in which board, lodging, and instruction are all included. . . .

In walking among the ruins of religious buildings, we came to two vaults over which had formerly stood the house of the sub-prior. One of the vaults was inhabited by an old woman, who claimed the right of abode there, as the widow of a man whose ancestors had possessed the same gloomy mansion for no less than four generations. The right, however it began, was considered as established by legal prescription, and the old woman lives undisturbed. She thinks however that she has a claim to something more than sufferance; for as her husband's name was Bruce, she is allied to royalty, and told Mr Boswell that when there were persons of quality in the place, she was distinguished by some notice; that indeed she is now neglected, but she spins a thread, has the company of her cat, and is troublesome to nobody.

Having now seen whatever this ancient city offered to our curiosity, we left it with good wishes, having reason to be highly pleased with the attention that was paid us. But whoever surveys the world must see many things that give him pain. The kindness of the professors did not contribute to abate the uneasy remembrance of an university declining, a college alienated, and a church profaned and hastening to the ground.

St Andrews indeed has formerly suffered more atrocious ravages and more extensive destruction, but recent evils affect with greater force. We were reconciled to the sight of archiepiscopal ruins. The distance of a calamity from the present time seems to preclude the mind from contact or sympathy. Events long past are barely known; they are not considered. We read with as little emotion the violence of Knox and his followers, as the irruptions of Alaric and the Goths. Had the university been destroyed two centuries ago, we should not have regretted it; but to see it pining in decay and struggling for life fills the mind with mournful images and ineffectual wishes.

ABERBROTHICK

As we knew sorrow and wishes to be vain, it was now our business to mind our way. The roads of Scotland afford little diversion to the traveller, who seldom sees himself either encountered or overtaken, and who has nothing to contemplate but grounds that have no visible boundaries, or are separated by walls of loose stone. From the bank of the Tweed to St Andrews I had never seen a single tree which I did not believe to have grown up far within the present century. Now and then about a gentleman's house stands a small plantation, which in Scotch is called a *policy*, but of these there are few, and those few all very young. The variety of sun and shade is here utterly unknown. There is no tree for either shelter or timber. The oak and the thorn is equally a stranger, and the whole country is extended in uniform nakedness, except that in the road between Kirkaldy and Cowpar, I passed for a few yards between two hedges. A tree might be a show in Scotland as a horse in Venice. At St Andrews Mr Boswell found only one, and recommended it to my notice; I told him that it was rough and low, or looked as if I thought so. 'This,' said he, 'is nothing to another a few miles off.' I was still less delighted to hear that another tree was not to be seen nearer. 'Nay,' said a gentleman that stood by, 'I know but of this and that tree in the country.'

The Lowlands of Scotland had once undoubtedly an equal portion of woods with other countries. Forests are every where gradually diminished, as architecture and cultivation prevail by the increase of people and the introduction of arts. But I believe few regions have been denuded like this, where many centuries must have passed in waste without the least thought of future supply. Davies° observes in his account of Ireland that no Irishman had ever planted an orchard. For that negligence some excuse might be drawn from an unsettled state of life, and the instability of property; but in Scotland possession has long been secure, and inheritance regular, yet it may be doubted whether before the Union any man between Edinburgh and England had ever set a tree.

Of this improvidence no other account can be given than that it probably began in times of tumult, and continued because it had begun. Established custom is not easily broken till some great event shakes the whole system of things, and life seems to recommence upon new principles. That before the Union the Scots had little trade and little money is no valid apology; for plantation is the least expensive of all methods of improvement. To drop a seed into the ground can cost nothing, and the trouble is not great of protecting the young plant till it is out of danger; though it must be allowed to have some difficulty in places like these, where they have neither wood for palisades, nor thorns for hedges.

Our way was over the Firth of Tay, where, though the water was not wide, we paid four shillings for ferrying the chaise. In Scotland the necessaries of life are easily procured, but superfluities and elegancies are of the same price at least as in England, and therefore may be considered as much dearer.

We stopped a while at Dundee, where I remember nothing remarkable, and mounting our chaise again, came about the close of the day to Aberbrothick.

The monastery of Aberbrothick is of great renown in the history of Scotland. Its ruins afford ample testimony of its ancient magnificence. Its extent might, I suppose, easily be found by following the walls among the grass and weeds, and its height is known by some parts yet standing. The arch of one of the gates is entire, and of another only so far dilapidated as to diversify the appearance. A square apartment of great loftiness is yet standing; its use I could not conjecture, as its elevation was very disproportionate to its area. Two corner towers particularly attracted our attention. Mr Boswell, whose inquisitiveness is seconded by great activity, scrambled in at a high window, but found the stairs within broken, and could not reach the top. Of the other tower we were told that the inhabitants sometimes climbed it, but we did not immediately discern the entrance, and as the night was gathering upon us, thought proper to desist. Men skilled in architecture might do what we did not attempt: they might probably form an exact ground-plot of this venerable edifice. They may from some parts yet standing conjecture its general form, and perhaps by comparing it with other buildings of the same kind and the same age, attain an idea very near to truth. I should scarcely have regretted my journey, had it afforded nothing more than the sight of Aberbrothick.

[The travellers pass through Montrose, and visit Lord Monboddo at his house near by.]

The roads beyond Edinburgh, as they are less frequented, must be expected to grow gradually rougher; but they were hitherto by no means incommodious. We travelled on with the gentle pace of a Scotch driver, who having no rivals in expedition, neither gives himself nor his horses unnecessary trouble. We did not affect the impatience we did not feel, but were satisfied with the company of each other as well riding in the chaise as sitting at an inn. The night and the day are equally solitary and equally safe; for where there are so few travellers, why should there be robbers?

ABERDEEN

We came somewhat late to Aberdeen, and found the inn so full that we had some difficulty in obtaining admission till Mr Boswell made himself known. His name overpowered all objection, and we found a very good house and civil treatment.

I received the next day a very kind letter from Sir Alexander Gordon, whom I had formerly known in London, and after a cessation of all intercourse for near twenty years met here professor of physic in the King's College. Such unexpected renewals of acquaintance may be numbered among the most pleasing incidents of life.

The knowledge of one professor soon procured me the notice of the rest, and I did not want any token of regard, being conducted wherever there was any thing which I desired to see, and entertained at once with the novelty of the place, and the kindness of communication.

To write of the cities of our own island with the solemnity of geographical description, as if we had been cast upon a newly discovered coast, has the appearance of very frivolous ostentation; yet as Scotland is little known to the greater part of those who may read these observations, it is not superfluous to relate that under the name of Aberdeen are comprised two towns standing about a mile distant from each other, but governed, I think, by the same magistrates.

Old Aberdeen is the ancient episcopal city, in which are still to be seen the remains of the cathedral. It has the appearance of a town in decay, having been situated in times when commerce was yet unstudied, with very little attention to the commodities of the harbour.

New Aberdeen has all the bustle of prosperous trade, and all the show of increasing opulence. It is built by the waterside. The houses are large and lofty, and the streets spacious and clean. They build almost wholly with the granite used in the new pavement of the streets of London, which is well known not to want hardness, yet they shape it easily. It is beautiful and must be very lasting.

What particular parts of commerce are chiefly exercised by the merchants of Aberdeen, I have not inquired. The manufacture which forces itself upon a stranger's eye is that of knit-stockings, on which the women of the lower class are visibly employed.

In each of these towns there is a college, or in stricter language, a university; for in both there are professors of the same parts of learning, and the colleges hold their sessions and confer degrees separately, with total independence of one on the other.

In Old Aberdeen stands the King's College, of which the first president was Hector Boece, or Boethius, who may be justly reverenced one of the revivers of elegant learning. When he studied at Paris, he was acquainted with Erasmus, who afterwards gave him a public testimony of his esteem by inscribing to him a catalogue of his works. The style of Boethius, though, perhaps, not always rigorously pure, is formed with great diligence upon ancient models, and wholly uninfected with monastic barbarity. His history is written with elegance and vigour, but his fabulousness and credulity are justly blamed. His fabulousness, if he was the author of the fictions, is a fault for which no apology can be made; but his credulity may be excused in an age when all men were credulous. Learning was then rising on the world; but ages so long accustomed to darkness were too much dazzled with its light to see any thing distinctly. The first race of scholars, in the fifteenth century, and some time after, were, for the most part, learning to speak, rather than to think, and were therefore more studious of elegance than of truth. The contemporaries of Boethius thought it sufficient to know what the ancients had delivered. The examination of tenets and of facts was reserved for another generation. . . .

In both these colleges the methods of instruction are nearly the same; the lectures differing only by the accidental difference of diligence, or ability in the professors. The students wear scarlet gowns and the professors black, which is, I believe, the academical dress in all the Scottish universities, except that of Edinburgh, where the scholars are not distinguished by any particular habit. In the King's College there is kept a public table, but the scholars of the Marischal College are boarded in the town. The expense of living is here, according to the information that I could obtain, somewhat more than at St Andrews.

The course of education is extended to four years, at the end of which those who take a degree, who are not many, become masters of arts, and whoever is a master may, if he pleases, immediately commence doctor. The title of doctor, however, was for a considerable time bestowed only on physicians. The advocates are examined and approved by their own body; the ministers were not ambitious of titles, or were afraid of being censured for ambition; and the doctorate in every faculty was commonly given or sold into other countries. The ministers are now reconciled to distinction, and as it must always happen that some will excel others, have thought graduation a proper testimony of uncommon abilities or acquisitions.

The indiscriminate collation of degrees has justly taken away that respect which they originally claimed as stamps by which the literary value of men so distinguished was authoritatively denoted. That academical honours, or any others, should be conferred with exact proportion to merit is more than human judgment or human integrity have given reason to expect. Perhaps degrees in universities cannot be better adjusted by any general rule than by the length of time passed in the public profession of learning. An English or Irish doctorate cannot be obtained by a very young man, and it is reasonable to suppose, what is likewise by experience commonly found true, that he who is by age qualified to be a doctor has in so much time gained learning sufficient not to disgrace the title, or wit sufficient not to desire it.

[They go on to visit Slains Castle, 'built upon the margin of the sea', and are awed by the turbulent water of the Buller of Buchan.]

At night we came to Bamff, where I remember nothing that particularly claimed my attention. The ancient towns of Scotland have generally an appearance unusual to Englishmen. The houses, whether great or small, are for the most part built of stones. Their ends are now and then next the streets, and the entrance into them is very often by a flight of steps, which reaches up to the second story, the floor which is level with the ground being entered only by stairs descending within the house.

The art of joining squares of glass with lead is little used in Scotland, and in some places is totally forgotten. The frames of their windows are all of wood. They are more frugal of their glass than the English, and will often, in houses not otherwise mean, compose a square of two pieces, not joining like cracked glass, but with one edge laid perhaps half an inch over the other. Their windows do not move upon hinges, but are pushed up and drawn down in grooves, yet they are seldom accommodated with weights and pulleys. He that would have his window open must hold it with his hand, unless, what may be sometimes found among good contrivers, there be a nail which he may stick into a hole, to keep it from falling.

What cannot be done without some uncommon trouble or particular expedient will not often be done at all. The incommodiousness of the Scotch windows keeps them very closely shut. The necessity of ventilating human habitations has not yet been found by our northern neighbours; and even in houses well built and elegantly furnished, a stranger may be sometimes forgiven if he allows himself to wish for fresher air.

These diminutive observations seem to take away something from the dignity of writing, and therefore are never communicated but with hesitation, and a little fear of abasement and contempt. But it must be remembered that life consists not of a series of illustrious actions, or elegant enjoyments; the greater part of our time passes in compliance with necessities, in the performance of daily duties, in the removal of small inconveniencies, in the procurement of petty pleasures; and we are well or ill at ease as the main stream of life glides on smoothly, or is ruffled by small obstacles and frequent interruption. The true state of every nation is the state of common life. The manners of a people are not to be found in the schools of learning, or the palaces of greatness, where the national character is obscured or obliterated by travel or instruction, by philosophy or vanity; nor is public happiness to be estimated by the assemblies of the gay, or the banquets of the rich. The great mass of nations is neither rich nor gay: they whose aggregate constitutes the people are found in the streets, and the villages, in the shops and farms; and from them collectively considered must the measure of general prosperity be taken. As they approach to delicacy a nation is refined, as their conveniencies are multiplied, a nation, at least a commercial nation, must be denominated wealthy.

ELGIN

Finding nothing to detain us at Bamff, we set out in the morning, and having breakfasted at Cullen, about noon came to Elgin, where in the inn that we supposed the best a dinner was set before us which we could not eat. This was the first time, and except one, the last, that I found any reason to complain of a Scottish table; and such disappointments, I suppose, must be expected in every country where there is no great frequency of travellers.

The ruins of the cathedral of Elgin afforded us another proof of the waste of reformation. There is enough yet remaining to show that it was once magnificent. Its whole plot is easily traced. On the north side of the choir, the chapter-house, which is roofed with an arch of stone, remains entire; and on the south side, another mass of building, which we could not enter, is preserved by the care of the family of Gordon; but the body of the church is a mass of fragments.

A paper was here put into our hands which deduced from sufficient authorities the history of this venerable ruin. The church of Elgin had, in the intestine tumults of the barbarous ages, been laid waste by the irruption of a Highland chief whom the bishop had offended; but it was gradually restored to the state of which the traces may be now discerned, and was at last not destroyed by the tumultuous violence of Knox, but more shamefully suffered to dilapidate by deliberate robbery and frigid indifference. There is still extant, in the books of the council, an order, of which I cannot remember the date, but which was doubtless issued after the Reformation, directing that the lead which covers the two cathedrals of Elgin and Aberdeen shall be taken away, and converted into money for the support of the army. A Scotch army was in those times very cheaply kept; yet the lead of two churches must have borne so small a proportion to any military expense that it is hard not to believe the reason alleged to be merely popular, and the money intended for some private purse. The order however was obeyed; the two churches were stripped, and the lead was shipped to be sold in Holland. I hope every reader will rejoice that this cargo of sacrilege was lost at sea.

Let us not however make too much haste to despise our neighbours. Our own cathedrals are mouldering by unregarded dilapidation.° It seems to be part of the despicable philosophy of the time to despise monuments of sacred magnificence, and we are in danger of doing that deliberately which the Scots did not do but in the unsettled state of an imperfect constitution.

Those who had once uncovered the cathedrals never wished to cover them again; and being thus made useless, they were first neglected, and perhaps, as the stone was wanted, afterwards demolished.

[They spend the night at Forres ('the town to which Macbeth was travelling when he met the weird sisters in his way. This to an Englishman is classic ground'). Next day they pass through Nairn (where 'we may fix the verge of the Highlands; for here I first saw peat fires, and first heard the Erse language') and Calder (Cawdor) ('from which Macbeth drew his second title'), and visit the military post at Fort George.]

We did not regret the time spent at the fort, though in consequence of our delay we came somewhat late to Inverness, the town which may properly be called the capital of the Highlands. Hither the inhabitants of the inland parts come to be supplied with what they cannot make for themselves. Hither the young nymphs of the mountains and valleys are sent for education, and as far as my observation has reached, are not sent in vain.

INVERNESS

Inverness was the last place which had a regular communication by high roads with the southern counties. All the ways beyond it have, I believe, been made by the soldiers in this century. At Inverness therefore Cromwell, when he subdued Scotland, stationed a garrison, as at the boundary of the Highlands. The soldiers seem to have incorporated afterwards with the inhabitants, and to have peopled the place with an English race; for the language of this town has been long considered as peculiarly elegant.

Here is a castle, called the castle of Macbeth, the walls of which are yet standing. It was no very capacious edifice, but stands upon a rock so high and steep that I think it was once not accessible but by the help of ladders, or a bridge. Over against it, on another hill, was a fort built by Cromwell, now totally demolished; for no faction of Scotland loved the name of Cromwell, or had any desire to continue his memory.

Yet what the Romans did to other nations was in a great degree done by Cromwell to the Scots; he civilized them by conquests, and introduced by useful violence the arts of peace. I was told at Aberdeen that the people learned from Cromwell's soldiers to make shoes and to plant kail.°

How they lived without kail it is not easy to guess: they cultivate hardly any other plant for common tables, and when they had not kail they probably had nothing. The numbers that go barefoot are still sufficient to show that shoes may be spared: they are not yet considered as necessities of life; for tall boys, not otherwise meanly dressed, run without them in the streets; and in the islands the sons of gentlemen pass several of their first years with naked feet.

I know not whether it be not peculiar to the Scots to have attained the liberal, without the manual arts, to have excelled in ornamental knowledge, and to have wanted not only the elegancies, but the conveniencies of common life. Literature soon after its revival found its way to Scotland, and from the middle of the sixteenth century, almost to the middle of the seventeenth, the politer studies were very diligently pursued. The Latin poetry of *Deliciae Poëtarum Scotorum*° would have done honour to any nation, at least till the publication of May's *Supplement* the English had very little to oppose.

Yet men thus ingenious and inquisitive were content to live in total ignorance of the trades by which human wants are supplied, and to supply them by the grossest means. Till the Union made them acquainted with English manners, the culture of their lands was unskillful, and their domestic life unformed; their tables were coarse as the feasts of Eskimeaux, and their houses filthy as the cottages of Hottentots.

Since they have known that their condition was capable of improvement, their progress in useful knowledge has been rapid and uniform. What remains to be done they will quickly do, and then wonder, like me, why that which was so necessary and so easy was so long delayed. But they must be for ever content to owe to the English that elegance and culture, which, if they had been vigilant and active, perhaps the English might have owed to them.

Here the appearance of life began to alter. I had seen a few women with plaids at Aberdeen; but at Inverness the Highland manners are common. There is I think a kirk in which only the Erse language is used. There is likewise an English chapel, but meanly built, where on Sunday we saw a very decent congregation.

We were now to bid farewell to the luxury of travelling, and to enter a country upon which perhaps no wheel has ever rolled. We could indeed have used our post-chaise one day longer, along the military road to Fort Augustus, but we could have hired no horses beyond Inverness, and we were not so sparing of ourselves as to lead them, merely that we might have one day longer the indulgence of a carriage.

At Inverness therefore we procured three horses for ourselves and a servant, and one more for our baggage, which was no very heavy load. We found in the course of our journey the convenience of having disencumbered ourselves by laying aside whatever we could spare; for it is not to be imagined without experience how in climbing crags, and treading bogs, and winding through narrow and obstructed passages, a little bulk will hinder, and a little weight will burden; or how often a man that has pleased himself at home with his own resolution will, in the hour of darkness and fatigue, be content to leave behind him every thing but himself.

LOUGH NESS

We took two Highlanders to run beside us, partly to show us the way, and partly to take back from the sea-side the horses of which they were the owners. One of them was a man of great liveliness and activity, of whom his companion said that he would tire any horse in Inverness. Both of them were civil and ready-handed. Civility seems part of the national character of Highlanders. Every chieftain is a monarch, and politeness, the natural product of royal government, is diffused from the laird through the whole clan. But they are not commonly dexterous: their narrowness of life confines them to a few operations, and they are accustomed to endure little wants more than to remove them.

We mounted our steeds on the thirtieth of August, and directed our guides to conduct us to Fort Augustus. It is built at the head of Lough Ness, of which Inverness stands at the outlet. The way between them has been cut by the soldiers, and the greater part of it runs along a rock, levelled with great labour and exactness, near the water-side.

Most of this day's journey was very pleasant. The day, though bright, was not hot; and the appearance of the country, if I had not seen the Peak,° would have been wholly new. We went upon a surface so hard and level that we had little care to hold the bridle, and were therefore at full leisure for contemplation. On the left were high and steep rocks shaded with birch, the hardy native of the North, and covered with fern or heath. On the right the limpid waters of Lough Ness were beating their bank, and waving their surface by a gentle agitation. Beyond them were rocks sometimes covered with verdure, and sometimes towering in horrid nakedness. Now and then we espied a little corn-field, which served to impress more strongly the general barrenness. . . .

The road on which we travelled, and which was itself a source of entertainment, is made along the rock, in the direction of the lough, sometimes by breaking off protuberances, and sometimes by cutting the great mass of stone to a considerable depth. The fragments are piled in a loose wall on either side, with apertures left at very short spaces, to give a passage to the wintry currents. Part of it is bordered with low trees, from which our guides gathered nuts, and would have had the appearance of an English lane, except that an English lane is almost always dirty. It has been made with great labour, but has this advantage, that it cannot, without equal labour, be broken up.

Within our sight there were goats feeding or playing. The mountains have red deer, but they came not within view; and if what is said of their vigilance and subtlety be true, they have some claim to that palm of wisdom which the eastern philosopher whom Alexander interrogated gave to those beasts which live furthest from men.

Near the way, by the water-side, we espied a cottage. This was the first Highland hut that I had seen; and as our business was with life and manners, we were willing to visit it. To enter a habitation without leave seems to be not considered here as rudeness or intrusion. The old laws of hospitality still give this licence to a stranger.

A hut is constructed with loose stones, ranged for the most part with some tendency to circularity. It must be placed where the wind cannot act upon it with violence, because it has no cement; and where the water will run easily away, because it has no floor but the naked ground. The wall, which is commonly about six feet high, declines from the perpendicular a little inward. Such rafters as can be procured are then raised for a roof, and covered with heath, which makes a strong and warm thatch, kept from flying off by ropes of twisted heath, of which the ends, reaching from the centre of the thatch to the top of the wall, are held firm by the weight of a large stone. No light is admitted but at the entrance, and through a hole in the thatch, which gives vent to the smoke. This hole is not directly over the fire, lest the rain should extinguish it; and the smoke therefore naturally fills the place before it escapes. Such is the general structure of the houses in which one of the nations of this opulent and powerful island has been hitherto content to live. Huts however are not more uniform than palaces; and this which we were inspecting was very far from one of the meanest, for it was divided into several apartments; and its inhabitants possessed such property as a pastoral poet might exalt into riches.

When we entered, we found an old woman boiling goats-flesh in a kettle. She spoke little English, but we had interpreters at hand; and she was willing enough to display her whole system of economy. She has five children, of which none are yet gone from her. The eldest, a boy of thirteen, and her husband, who is eighty years old, were at work in the wood. Her two next sons were gone to Inverness to buy *meal*, by which oatmeal is always meant. Meal she considered as expensive food, and told us that in spring, when the goats gave milk, the children could live without it. She is mistress of sixty goats, and I saw many kids in an enclosure at the end of her house. She had also some poultry. By the lake we saw a potato-garden, and a small spot of ground on which stood four shucks, containing each twelve sheaves of barley. She has all this from the labour of their own hands, and for what is necessary to be bought, her kids and her chickens are sent to market.

With the true pastoral hospitality, she asked us to sit down and drink whisky. She is religious, and though the kirk is four miles off, probably eight English miles, she goes thither every Sunday. We gave her a shilling, and she begged snuff; for snuff is the luxury of a Highland cottage.

Soon afterwards we came to the General's Hut, so called because it was the temporary abode of Wade,° while he superintended the works upon the road. It is now a house of entertainment for passengers, and we found it not ill stocked with provisions.

[They spend the night at Fort Augustus, the guests of the army garrison, and next morning set out across the Highlands.]

ANOCH

Early in the afternoon we came to Anoch, a village in Glenmollison of three huts, one of which is distinguished by a chimney. Here we were to dine and lodge, and were conducted through the first room, that had the chimney, into another lighted by a small glass window. The landlord attended us with great civility, and told us what he could give us to eat and drink. I found some books on a shelf, among which were a volume or more of Prideaux's *Connection*.

This I mentioned as something unexpected, and perceived that I did not please him: I praised the propriety of his language, and was answered that I need not wonder, for he had learned it by grammar.

By subsequent opportunities of observation, I found that my host's diction had nothing peculiar. Those Highlanders that can speak English commonly speak it well, with few of the words, and little of the tone by which a Scotchman is distinguished. Their language seems to have been learned in the army or the navy, or by some communication with those who could give them good examples of accent and pronunciation. By their Lowland neighbours they would not willingly be taught; for they have long considered them as a mean and degenerate race. These prejudices are wearing fast away; but so much of them still remains that when I asked a very learned minister in the islands which they considered as their most savage clans: 'Those,' said he, 'that live next the Lowlands.'

As we came hither early in the day, we had time sufficient to survey the place. The house was built like other huts of loose stones, but the part in which we dined and slept was lined with turf and wattled with twigs, which kept the earth from falling. Near it was a garden of turnips and a field of potatoes. It stands in a glen, or valley, pleasantly watered by a winding river. But this country, however it may delight the gazer or amuse the naturalist, is of no great advantage to its owners. Our landlord told us of a gentleman who possesses lands, eighteen Scotch miles in length, and three in breadth; a space containing at least a hundred square English miles. He has raised his rents, to the danger of depopulating his farms, and he sells his timber, and by exerting every art of augmentation, has obtained an yearly revenue of four hundred pounds, which for a hundred square miles is three halfpence an acre.

Some time after dinner we were surprised by the entrance of a young woman, not inelegant either in mien or dress, who asked us whether we would have tea. We found that she was the daughter of our host, and desired her to make it. Her conversation, like her appearance, was gentle and pleasing. We knew that the girls of the Highlands are all gentlewomen, and treated her with great respect, which she received as customary and due, and was neither elated by it, nor confused, but repaid my civilities without embarrassment, and told me how much I honoured her country by coming to survey it.

She had been at Inverness to gain the common female qualifications, and had, like her father, the English pronunciation. I presented her with a book which I happened to have about me, and should not be pleased to think that she forgets me.

In the evening the soldiers whom we had passed on the road came to spend at our inn the little money that we had given them. They had the true military impatience of coin in their pockets, and had marched at least six miles to find the first place where liquor could be bought. Having never been before in a place so wild and unfrequented, I was glad of their arrival, because I knew that we had made them friends, and to gain still more of their good will, we went to them, where they were carousing in the barn, and added something to our former gift. All that we gave was not much, but it detained them in the barn, either merry or quarrelling, the whole night, and in the morning they went back to their work, with great indignation at the bad qualities of whisky.

We had gained so much the favour of our host that, when we left his house in the morning, he walked by us a great way, and entertained us with conversation both on his own condition, and that of the country. His life seemed to be merely pastoral, except that he differed from some of the ancient Nomads in having a settled dwelling. His wealth consists of one hundred sheep, as many goats, twelve milk-cows, and twenty-eight beeves ready for the drover.

From him we first heard of the general dissatisfaction which is now driving the Highlanders into the other hemisphere; and when I asked him whether they would stay at home, if they were well treated, he answered with indignation that no man willingly left his native country. Of the farm which he himself occupied, the rent had, in twenty-five years, been advanced from five to twenty pounds, which he found himself so little able to pay that he would be glad to try his fortune in some other place. Yet he owned the reasonableness of raising the Highland rents in a certain degree, and declared himself willing to pay ten pounds for the ground which he had formerly had for five.

Our host, having amused us for a time, resigned us to our guides. The journey of this day was long, not that the distance was great, but that the way was difficult. We were now in the bosom of the Highlands, with full leisure to contemplate the appearance and properties of mountainous regions, such as have been, in many countries, the last shelters of national distress, and are every where the scenes of adventures, stratagems, surprises and escapes. . . .

Of the hills many may be called with Homer's Ida *abundant in springs*, but few can deserve the epithet which he bestows upon Pelion by *waving their leaves*. They exhibit very little variety, being almost wholly covered with dark heath, and even that seems to be checked in its growth. What is not heath is nakedness, a little diversified by now and then a stream rushing down the steep. An eye accustomed to flowery pastures and waving harvests is astonished and repelled by this wide extent of hopeless sterility. The appearance is that of matter incapable of form or usefulness, dismissed by nature from her care and disinherited of her favours, left in its original elemental state, or quickened only with one sullen power of useless vegetation.

It will very readily occur that this uniformity of barrenness can afford very little amusement to the traveller; that it is easy to sit at home and conceive rocks and heath, and waterfalls; and that these journeys are useless labours, which neither impregnate the imagination, nor enlarge the understanding. It is true that of far the greater part of things, we must content ourselves with such knowledge as description may exhibit, or analogy supply; but it is true likewise that these ideas are always incomplete, and that at least, till we have compared them with realities, we do not know them to be just. As we see more, we become possessed of more certainties, and consequently gain more principles of reasoning, and found a wider basis of analogy.

Regions mountainous and wild, thinly inhabited, and little cultivated, make a great part of the earth, and he that has never seen them must live unacquainted with much of the face of nature, and with one of the great scenes of human existence.

As the day advanced towards noon, we entered a narrow valley not very flowery, but sufficiently verdant. Our guides told us that the horses could not travel all day without rest or meat, and entreated us to stop here, because no grass would be found in any other place. The request was reasonable and the argument cogent. We therefore willingly dismounted and diverted ourselves as the place gave us opportunity.

I sat down on a bank such as a writer of romance might have delighted to feign. I had indeed no trees to whisper over my head, but a clear rivulet streamed at my feet. The day was calm, the air soft, and all was rudeness, silence, and solitude. Before me, and on either side, were high hills, which by hindering the eye from ranging, forced the mind to find entertainment for itself. Whether I spent the hour well I know not; for here I first conceived the thought of this narration.

We were in this place at ease and by choice, and had no evils to suffer or to fear; yet the imaginations excited by the view of an unknown and untravelled wilderness are not such as arise in the artificial solitude of parks and gardens, a flattering notion of self-sufficiency, a placid indulgence of voluntary delusions, a secure expansion of the fancy, or a cool concentration of the mental powers. The phantoms which haunt a desert are want, and misery, and danger; the evils of dereliction rush upon the thoughts; man is made unwillingly acquainted with his own weakness, and meditation shows him only how little he can sustain, and how little he can perform. There were no traces of inhabitants, except a rude pile of clods called a summer hut, in which a herdsman had rested in the favourable seasons. Whoever had been in the place where I then sat, unprovided with provisions and ignorant of the country, might, at least before the roads were made, have wandered among the rocks till he had perished with hardship, before he could have found either food or shelter. Yet what are these hillocks to the ridges of Taurus, or these spots of wildness to the deserts of America? . . .

THE HIGHLANDS

As we continued our journey, we were at leisure to extend our speculations, and to investigate the reason of those peculiarities by which such rugged regions as these before us are generally distinguished.

Mountainous countries commonly contain the original, at least the oldest, race of inhabitants, for they are not easily conquered, because they must be entered by narrow ways, exposed to every power of mischief from those that occupy the heights; and every new ridge is a new fortress, where the defendants have again the same advantages. If the assailants either force the strait, or storm the summit, they gain only so much ground; their enemies are fled to take possession of the next rock, and the pursuers stand at gaze, knowing neither where the ways of escape wind among the steeps, nor where the bog has firmness to sustain them: besides that, mountaineers have an agility in climbing and descending distinct from strength or courage, and attainable only by use.

If the war be not soon concluded, the invaders are dislodged by hunger; for in those anxious and toilsome marches, provisions cannot easily be carried, and are never to be found. The wealth of mountains is cattle, which, while the men stand in the passes, the women drive away. Such lands at last cannot repay the expense of conquest, and therefore perhaps have not been so often invaded by the mere ambition of dominion, as by resentment of robberies and insults, or the desire of enjoying in security the more fruitful provinces.

As mountains are long before they are conquered, they are likewise

long before they are civilized. Men are softened by intercourse
mutually profitable, and instructed by comparing their own notions
with those of others. Thus Caesar found the maritime parts of Britain
made less barbarous by their commerce with the Gauls. Into a barren
and rough tract no stranger is brought either by the hope of gain or of
pleasure. The inhabitants having neither commodities for sale, nor
money for purchase, seldom visit more polished places, or if they do
visit them, seldom return.

It sometimes happens that by conquest, intermixture, or gradual
refinement, the cultivated parts of a country change their language.
The mountaineers then become a distinct nation, cut off by
dissimilitude of speech from conversation with their neighbours.
Thus in Biscay, the original Cantabrian, and in Dalecarlia, the old
Swedish still subsists. Thus Wales and the Highlands speak the
tongue of the first inhabitants of Britain, while the other parts have
received first the Saxon, and in some degree afterwards the French,
and then formed a third language between them.

That the primitive manners are continued where the primitive
language is spoken, no nation will desire me to suppose, for the
manners of mountaineers are commonly savage, but they are rather
produced by their situation than derived from their ancestors.

Such seems to be the disposition of man that whatever makes a
distinction produces rivalry. England, before other causes of enmity
were found, was disturbed for some centuries by the contests of the
northern and southern counties; so that at Oxford, the peace of study
could for a long time be preserved only by choosing annually one of
the Proctors° from each side of the Trent. A tract intersected by many
ridges of mountains naturally divides its inhabitants into petty
nations, which are made by a thousand causes enemies to each other.
Each will exalt its own chiefs, each will boast the valour of its men, or
the beauty of its women, and every claim of superiority irritates
competition; injuries will sometimes be done, and be more injuriously
defended; retaliation will sometimes be attempted, and the debt
exacted with too much interest.

In the Highlands it was a law that if a robber was sheltered from
justice, any man of the same clan might be taken in his place. This was
a kind of irregular justice, which, though necessary in savage times,
could hardly fail to end in a feud, and a feud once kindled among an
idle people with no variety of pursuits to divert their thoughts burnt
on for ages either sullenly glowing in secret mischief, or openly
blazing into public violence. Of the effects of this violent judicature,

there are not wanting memorials. The cave is now to be seen to which one of the Campbells, who had injured the Macdonalds, retired with a body of his own clan. The Macdonalds required the offender, and being refused, made a fire at the mouth of the cave, by which he and his adherents were suffocated together.

Mountaineers are warlike, because by their feuds and competitions they consider themselves as surrounded with enemies, and are always prepared to repel incursions, or to make them. Like the Greeks in their unpolished state, described by Thucydides, the Highlanders, till lately, went always armed, and carried their weapons to visits, and to church.

Mountaineers are thievish, because they are poor, and having neither manufactures nor commerce, can grow richer only by robbery. They regularly plunder their neighbours, for their neighbours are commonly their enemies; and having lost that reverence for property by which the order of civil life is preserved soon consider all as enemies whom they do not reckon as friends, and think themselves licensed to invade whatever they are not obliged to protect.

By a strict administration of the laws, since the laws have been introduced into the Highlands, this disposition to thievery is very much repressed. Thirty years ago no herd had ever been conducted through the mountains without paying tribute in the night to some of the clans; but cattle are now driven, and passengers travel without danger, fear, or molestation.

Among a warlike people, the quality of highest esteem is personal courage, and with the ostentatious display of courage are closely connected promptitude of offence and quickness of resentment. The Highlanders, before they were disarmed, were so addicted to quarrels that the boys used to follow any public procession or ceremony, however festive, or however solemn, in expectation of the battle which was sure to happen before the company dispersed.

Mountainous regions are sometimes so remote from the seat of government, and so difficult of access, that they are very little under the influence of the sovereign, or within the reach of national justice. Law is nothing without power; and the sentence of a distant court could not be easily executed, nor perhaps very safely promulgated, among men ignorantly proud and habitually violent, unconnected with the general system, and accustomed to reverence only their own lords. It has therefore been necessary to erect many particular jurisdictions, and commit the punishment of crimes, and the decision of right to the proprietors of the country who could enforce their own decrees. It immediately appears that such judges will be often ignorant, and often partial; but in the immaturity of political establishments no better expedient could be found. As government advances towards perfection, provincial judicature is perhaps in every empire gradually abolished.

Those who had thus the dispensation of law were by consequence themselves lawless. Their vassals had no shelter from outrages and oppressions; but were condemned to endure, without resistance, the caprices of wantonness, and the rage of cruelty.

In the Highlands, some great lords had an hereditary jurisdiction over counties; and some chieftains over their own lands; till the final conquest of the Highlands afforded an opportunity of crushing all the local courts, and of extending the general benefits of equal law to the low and the high, in the deepest recesses and obscurest corners.

While the chiefs had this resemblance of royalty, they had little inclination to appeal, on any question, to superior judicatures. A claim of lands between two powerful lairds was decided like a contest for dominion between sovereign powers. They drew their forces into the field, and right attended on the strongest. This was, in ruder times, the common practice, which the kings of Scotland could seldom control.

Even so lately as in the last years of King William, a battle was fought at Mull Roy, on a plain a few miles to the south of Inverness, between the clans of Mackintosh and Macdonald of Keppoch. Col. Macdonald, the head of a small clan, refused to pay the dues demanded from him by Mackintosh, as his superior lord. They disdained the interposition of judges and laws, and calling each his followers to maintain the dignity of the clan, fought a formal battle, in which several considerable men fell on the side of Mackintosh, without a complete victory to either. This is said to have been the last open war made between the clans by their own authority.

The Highland lords made treaties, and formed alliances, of which some traces may still be found, and some consequences still remain as lasting evidences of petty regality. The terms of one of these confederacies were that each should support the other in the right, or in the wrong, except against the king.

The inhabitants of mountains form distinct races, and are careful to preserve their genealogies. Men in a small district necessarily mingle blood by intermarriages, and combine at last into one family, with a common interest in the honour and disgrace of every individual. Then begins that union of affections, and co-operation of endeavours, that constitute a clan. They who consider themselves as ennobled by their family will think highly of their progenitors, and they who through successive generations live always together in the same place will preserve local stories and hereditary prejudices. Thus every Highlander can talk of his ancestors, and recount the outrages which they suffered from the wicked inhabitants of the next valley.

Such are the effects of habitation among mountains, and such were the qualities of the Highlanders, while their rocks secluded them from the rest of mankind, and kept them an unaltered and discriminated race. They are now losing their distinction, and hastening to mingle with the general community.

GLENELG

We left Auknasheals and the Macraes in the afternoon, and in the evening came to Ratiken, a high hill on which a road is cut, but so steep and narrow that it is very difficult. There is now a design of making another way round the bottom. Upon one of the precipices, my horse, weary with the steepness of the rise, staggered a little, and I called in haste to the Highlander to hold him. This was the only moment of my journey in which I thought myself endangered.

Having surmounted the hill at last, we were told that at Glenelg, on the sea-side, we should come to a house of lime and slate and glass. This image of magnificence raised our expectation. At last we came to our inn weary and peevish, and began to inquire for meat and beds.

Of the provisions the negative catalogue was very copious. Here was no meat, no milk, no bread, no eggs, no wine. We did not express much satisfaction. Here however we were to stay. Whisky we might have, and I believe at last they caught a fowl and killed it. We had some bread, and with that we prepared ourselves to be contented, when we had a very eminent proof of Highland hospitality. Along some miles of the way, in the evening, a gentleman's servant had kept us company on foot with very little notice on our part. He left us near Glenelg, and we thought on him no more till he came to us again, in about two hours, with a present from his master of rum and sugar. The man had mentioned his company, and the gentleman, whose name, I think, is Gordon, well knowing the penury of the place, had this attention to two men whose names perhaps he had not heard, by whom his kindness was not likely to be ever repaid, and who could be recommended to him only by their necessities.

We were now to examine our lodging. Out of one of the beds on which we were to repose started up, at our entrance, a man black as a Cyclops from the forge. Other circumstances of no elegant recital concurred to disgust us. We had been frighted by a lady at Edinburgh with discouraging representations of Highland lodgings. Sleep, however, was necessary. Our Highlanders had at last found some hay, with which the inn could not supply them. I directed them to bring a bundle into the room, and slept upon it in my riding coat. Mr Boswell, being more delicate, laid himself sheets with hay over and under him, and lay in linen like a gentleman.

SKY. ARMIDEL

In the morning, September the second, we found ourselves on the edge of the sea. Having procured a boat, we dismissed our Highlanders, whom I would recommend to the service of any future travellers, and were ferried over to the Isle of Sky. We landed at Armidel, where we were met on the sands by Sir Alexander Macdonald, who was at that time there with his lady, preparing to leave the island and reside at Edinburgh.

Armidel is a neat house, built where the Macdonalds had once a seat, which was burnt in the commotions that followed the Revolution. The walled orchard which belonged to the former house still remains. It is well shaded by tall ash trees, of a species, as Mr Janes the fossilist informed me, uncommonly valuable. This plantation is very properly mentioned by Dr Campbell, in his new account of the state of Britain, and deserves attention, because it proves that the present nakedness of the Hebrides is not wholly the fault of Nature.

As we sat at Sir Alexander's table, we were entertained, according to the ancient usage of the North, with the melody of the bagpipe. Every thing in those countries has its history. As the bagpiper was playing, an elderly gentleman informed us that in some remote time, the Macdonalds of Glengary having been injured, or offended by the inhabitants of Culloden, and resolving to have justice or vengeance, came to Culloden on a Sunday, where finding their enemies at worship, they shut them up in the church, which they set on fire; and 'this', said he, 'is the tune that the piper played while they were burning.'

Narrations like this, however uncertain, deserve the notice of a traveller, because they are the only records of a nation that has no historians, and afford the most genuine representation of the life and character of the ancient Highlanders.

Under the denomination of Highlander are comprehended in Scotland all that now speak the Erse language, or retain the primitive manners, whether they live among the mountains or in the islands; and in that sense I use the name, when there is not some apparent reason for making a distinction.

In Sky I first observed the use of brogues, a kind of artless shoes, stitched with thongs so loosely that though they defend the foot from stones, they do not exclude water. Brogues were formerly made of raw hides, with the hair inwards, and such are perhaps still used in rude and remote parts; but they are said not to last above two days. Where life is somewhat improved, they are now made of leather tanned with oak bark, as in other places, or with the bark of birch, or roots of tormentil, a substance recommended in defect of bark, about forty years ago, to the Irish tanners, by one to whom the parliament of that kingdom voted a reward. The leather of Sky is not completely penetrated by vegetable matter, and therefore cannot be very durable.

My inquiries about brogues gave me an early specimen of Highland information. One day I was told that to make brogues was a domestic art, which every man practised for himself, and that a pair of brogues was the work of an hour. I supposed that the husband made brogues as the wife made an apron, till next day it was told me that a brogue-maker was a trade, and that a pair would cost half a crown. It will easily occur that these representations may both be true, and that, in some places, men may buy them, and in others, make them for themselves; but I had both the accounts in the same house within two days.

Many of my subsequent inquiries upon more interesting topics ended in the like uncertainty. He that travels in the Highlands may easily saturate his soul with intelligence, if he will acquiesce in the first account. The Highlander gives to every question an answer so prompt and peremptory that skepticism itself is dared into silence, and the mind sinks before the bold reporter in unresisting credulity; but, if a second question be ventured, it breaks the enchantment; for it is immediately discovered that what was told so confidently was told at hazard, and that such fearlessness of assertion was either the sport of negligence, or the refuge of ignorance.

If individuals are thus at variance with themselves, it can be no wonder that the accounts of different men are contradictory. The traditions of an ignorant and savage people have been for ages negligently heard, and unskillfully related. Distant events must have been mingled together, and the actions of one man given to another. These, however, are deficiencies in story for which no man is now to be censured. It were enough if what there is yet opportunity of examining were accurately inspected, and justly represented; but such is the laxity of Highland conversation that the inquirer is kept in continual suspense, and by a kind of intellectual retrogradation, knows less as he hears more.

In the islands the plaid is rarely worn. The law° by which the Highlanders have been obliged to change the form of their dress, has, in all the places that we have visited, been universally obeyed. I have seen only one gentleman completely clothed in the ancient habit, and by him it was worn only occasionally and wantonly. The common people do not think themselves under any legal necessity of having coats; for they say that the law against plaids was made by Lord Hardwicke,° and was in force only for his life: but the same poverty that made it then difficult for them to change their clothing hinders them now from changing it again.

The fillibeg, or lower garment, is still very common, and the bonnet almost universal; but their attire is such as produces, in a sufficient degree, the effect intended by the law, of abolishing the dissimilitude of appearance between the Highlanders and the other inhabitants of Britain; and, if dress be supposed to have much influence, facilitates their coalition with their fellow-subjects.

What we have long used we naturally like, and therefore the Highlanders were unwilling to lay aside their plaid, which yet to an unprejudiced spectator must appear an incommodious and cumbersome dress; for hanging loose upon the body, it must flutter in a quick motion, or require one of the hands to keep it close. The Romans always laid aside the gown when they had any thing to do. It was a dress so unsuitable to war that the same word which signified a gown signified peace. The chief use of a plaid seems to be this, that they could commodiously wrap themselves in it, when they were obliged to sleep without a better cover.

In our passage from Scotland to Sky, we were wet for the first time with a shower. This was the beginning of the Highland winter, after which we were told that a succession of three dry days was not to be expected for many months. The winter of the Hebrides consists of little more than rain and wind. As they are surrounded by an ocean never frozen, the blasts that come to them over the water are too much softened to have the power of congelation. The salt loughs, or inlets of the sea, which shoot very far into the island, never have any ice upon them, and the pools of fresh water will never bear the walker. The snow that sometimes falls is soon dissolved by the air, or the rain.

This is not the description of a cruel climate, yet the dark months are here a time of great distress, because the summer can do little more than feed itself, and winter comes with its cold and its scarcity upon families very slenderly provided.

[Crossing Skye to the island of Raasay, which they have been invited by its chief, John Macleod, to visit, they spend the night at the house of Lachlan Mackinnon at Coriatachan (Coirechatachan).]

CORIATACHAN IN SKY

. . . .

The weather was next day too violent for the continuation of our journey; but we had no reason to complain of the interruption. We saw in every place, what we chiefly desired to know, the manners of the people. We had company, and, if we had chosen retirement, we might have had books.

I never was in any house of the Islands where I did not find books in more languages than one, if I stayed long enough to want them, except one from which the family was removed. Literature is not neglected by the higher rank of the Hebridians.

It need not, I suppose, be mentioned that in countries so little frequented as the Islands, there are no houses where travellers are entertained for money. He that wanders about these wilds either procures recommendations to those whose habitations lie near his way, or, when night and weariness come upon him, takes the chance of general hospitality. If he finds only a cottage, he can expect little more than shelter; for the cottagers have little more for themselves: but if his good fortune brings him to the residence of a gentleman, he will be glad of a storm to prolong his stay. There is, however, one inn by the sea-side at Sconsor in Sky, where the post-office is kept.

At the tables where a stranger is received, neither plenty nor delicacy is wanting. A tract of land so thinly inhabited must have much wild-fowl; and I scarcely remember to have seen a dinner without them. The moorgame is every where to be had. That the sea abounds with fish needs not be told, for it supplies a great part of Europe. The Isle of Sky has stags and roebucks, but no hares. They sell very numerous droves of oxen yearly to England, and therefore cannot be supposed to want beef at home. Sheep and goats are in great numbers, and they have the common domestic fowls.

But as here is nothing to be bought, every family must kill its own meat, and roast part of it somewhat sooner than Apicius° would prescribe. Every kind of flesh is undoubtedly excelled by the variety and emulation of English markets; but that which is not best may be yet very far from bad, and he that shall complain of his fare in the Hebrides has improved his delicacy more than his manhood.

Their fowls are not like those plumped for sale by the poulterers of London, but they are as good as other places commonly afford, except that the geese, by feeding in the sea, have universally a fishy rankness.

These geese seem to be of a middle race between the wild and domestic kinds. They are so tame as to own a home, and so wild as sometimes to fly quite away.

Their native bread is made of oats, or barley. Of oatmeal they spread very thin cakes, coarse and hard, to which unaccustomed palates are not easily reconciled. The barley cakes are thicker and softer; I began to eat them without unwillingness; the blackness of their colour raises some dislike, but the taste is not disagreeable. In most houses there is wheat flour, with which we were sure to be treated, if we stayed long enough to have it kneaded and baked. As neither yeast nor leaven are used among them, their bread of every kind is unfermented. They make only cakes, and never mould a loaf.

A man of the Hebrides, for of the women's diet I can give no account, as soon as he appears in the morning, swallows a glass of whisky; yet they are not a drunken race, at least I never was present at much intemperance; but no man is so abstemious as to refuse the morning dram, which they call a *skalk*.

The word *whisky* signifies water, and is applied by way of eminence to *strong water*, or distilled liquor. The spirit drunk in the North is drawn from barley. I never tasted it, except once for experiment at the inn in Inverary, when I thought it preferable to any English malt brandy. It was strong, but not pungent, and was free from the empyreumatic° taste or smell. What was the process I had no opportunity of inquiring, nor do I wish to improve the art of making poison pleasant.

Not long after the dram may be expected the breakfast, a meal in which the Scots, whether of the lowlands or mountains, must be confessed to excel us. The tea and coffee are accompanied not only with butter, but with honey, conserves, and marmalades. If an epicure could remove by a wish, in quest of sensual gratifications, wherever he had supped he would breakfast in Scotland.

In the Islands however, they do what I found it not very easy to endure. They pollute the tea-table by plates piled with large slices of Cheshire cheese, which mingles its less grateful odours with the fragrance of the tea.

Where many questions are to be asked, some will be omitted. I forgot to inquire how they were supplied with so much exotic luxury. Perhaps the French may bring them wine for wool, and the Dutch give them tea and coffee at the fishing season, in exchange for fresh provision. Their trade is unconstrained; they pay no customs, for there is no officer to demand them; whatever therefore is made dear only by impost is obtained here at an easy rate.

A dinner in the Western Islands differs very little from a dinner in England, except that in the place of tarts, there are always set different preparations of milk. This part of their diet will admit some improvement. Though they have milk, and eggs, and sugar, few of them know how to compound them in a custard. Their gardens afford them no great variety, but they have always some vegetables on the table. Potatoes at least are never wanting, which, though they have not known them long, are now one of the principal parts of their food. They are not of the mealy, but the viscous kind.

Their more elaborate cookery, or made dishes, an Englishman at the first taste is not likely to approve, but the culinary compositions of every country are often such as become grateful to other nations only by degrees; though I have read a French author who, in the elation of his heart, says that French cookery pleases all foreigners, but foreign cookery never satisfies a Frenchman.

Their suppers are, like their dinners, various and plentiful. The table is always covered with elegant linen. Their plates for common use are often of that kind of manufacture which is called cream coloured, or queen's ware. They use silver on all occasions where it is common in England, nor did I ever find the spoon of horn but in one house.

The knives are not often either very bright, or very sharp. They are indeed instruments of which the Highlanders have not been long acquainted with the general use. They were not regularly laid on the table before the prohibition of arms, and the change of dress. Thirty years ago the Highlander wore his knife as a companion to his dirk or dagger, and when the company sat down to meat, the men who had knives cut the flesh into small pieces for the women, who with their fingers conveyed it to their mouths.

There was perhaps never any change of national manners so quick, so great, and so general as that which has operated in the Highlands by the last conquest, and the subsequent laws. We came thither too late to see what we expected, a people of peculiar appearance, and a system of antiquated life. The clans retain little now of their original character, their ferocity of temper is softened, their military ardour is extinguished, their dignity of independence is depressed, their contempt of government subdued, and their reverence for their chiefs abated. Of what they had before the late conquest of their country, there remain only their language and their poverty. Their language is attacked on every side. Schools are erected in which English only is taught, and there were lately some who thought it reasonable to refuse them a version of the holy scriptures, that they might have no monument of their mother-tongue.

That their poverty is gradually abated cannot be mentioned among the unpleasing consequences of subjection. They are now acquainted with money, and the possibility of gain will by degrees make them industrious. Such is the effect of the late regulations that a longer journey than to the Highlands must be taken by him whose curiosity pants for savage virtues and barbarous grandeur.

RAASAY

Our reception exceeded our expectations. We found nothing but civility, elegance, and plenty. After the usual refreshments, and the usual conversation, the evening came upon us. The carpet was then rolled off the floor; the musician was called, and the whole company was invited to dance, nor did ever fairies trip with greater alacrity. The general air of festivity which predominated in this place, so far remote from all those regions which the mind has been used to contemplate as the mansions of pleasure, struck the imagination with a delightful surprise, analogous to that which is felt at an unexpected emersion from darkness into light.

When it was time to sup, the dance ceased, and six and thirty persons sat down to two tables in the same room. After supper the ladies sung Erse songs, to which I listened as an English audience to an Italian opera, delighted with the sound of words which I did not understand.

I inquired the subjects of the songs, and was told of one that it was a love song, and of another that it was a farewell composed by one of the

Islanders that was going, in this epidemical fury of emigration, to seek his fortune in America. What sentiments would rise, on such an occasion, in the heart of one who had not been taught to lament by precedent, I should gladly have known; but the lady by whom I sat thought herself not equal to the work of translating. . . .

The length of Raasay is, by computation, fifteen miles, and the breadth two. These countries have never been measured, and the computation by miles is negligent and arbitrary. We observed in travelling that the nominal and real distance of places had very little relation to each other. Raasay probably contains near a hundred square miles. It affords not much ground, notwithstanding its extent, either for tillage, or pasture; for it is rough, rocky, and barren. The cattle often perish by falling from the precipices. It is like the other islands, I think, generally naked of shade, but it is naked by neglect; for the laird has an orchard, and very large forest trees grow about his house. Like other hilly countries it has many rivulets. One of the brooks turns a corn-mill, and at least one produces trouts.

In the streams or fresh lakes of the Islands, I have never heard of any other fish than trouts and eels. The trouts which I have seen are not large; the colour of their flesh is tinged as in England. Of their eels I can give no account, having never tasted them; for I believe they are not considered as wholesome food.

It is not very easy to fix the principles upon which mankind have agreed to eat some animals, and reject others; and as the principle is not evident, it is not uniform. That which is selected as delicate in one country is by its neighbours abhorred as loathsome. The Neapolitans lately refused to eat potatoes in a famine. An Englishman is not easily persuaded to dine on snails with an Italian, on frogs with a Frenchman, or on horseflesh with a Tartar. The vulgar inhabitants of Sky, I know not whether of the other islands, have not only eels, but pork and bacon in abhorrence, and accordingly I never saw a hog in the Hebrides, except one at Dunvegan. . . .

The beasts of prey in the Islands are foxes, otters, and weasels. The foxes are bigger than those of England; but the otters exceed ours in a far greater proportion. I saw one at Armidel of a size much beyond that which I supposed them ever to attain; and Mr Maclean, the heir of Col, a man of middle stature, informed me that he once shot an otter of which the tail reached the ground when he held up the head to a level with his own. I expected the otter to have a foot particularly formed for the art of swimming; but upon examination, I did not find it differing much from that of a spaniel. As he preys in the sea, he does little visible mischief, and is killed only for his fur. White otters are sometimes seen.

In Raasay they might have hares and rabbits, for they have no foxes. Some depredations, such as were never made before, have caused a suspicion that a fox has been lately landed in the island by spite or wantonness. This imaginary stranger has never yet been seen, and therefore, perhaps, the mischief was done by some other animal. It is not likely that a creature so ungentle, whose head could have been sold in Sky for a guinea, should be kept alive only to gratify the malice of sending him to prey upon a neighbour: and the passage from Sky is wider than a fox would venture to swim, unless he were chased by dogs into the sea, and perhaps than his strength would enable him to cross. How beasts of prey came into any islands is not easy to guess. In cold countries they take advantage of hard winters, and travel over the ice: but this is a very scanty solution; for they are found where they have no discoverable means of coming.

The corn of this island is but little. I saw the harvest of a small field. The women reaped the corn, and the men bound up the sheaves. The strokes of the sickle were timed by the modulation of the harvest song, in which all their voices were united. They accompany in the Highlands every action which can be done in equal time with an appropriated strain, which has, they say, not much meaning; but its effects are regularity and cheerfulness. The ancient proceleusmatic° song by which the rowers of galleys were animated may be supposed to have been of this kind. There is now an oar-song used by the Hebridians. . . .

In nations where there is hardly the use of letters, what is once out of sight is lost for ever. They think but little, and of their few thoughts, none are wasted on the past, in which they are neither interested by fear nor hope. Their only registers are stated observances and practical representations. For this reason an age of ignorance is an age of ceremony. Pageants, and processions, and commemorations gradually shrink away, as better methods come into use of recording events, and preserving rights.

It is not only in Raasay that the chapel is unroofed and useless; through the few islands which we visited, we neither saw nor heard of any house of prayer, except in Sky, that was not in ruins. The malignant influence of Calvinism has blasted ceremony and decency together; and if the remembrance of papal superstition is obliterated, the monuments of papal piety are likewise effaced.

It has been, for many years, popular to talk of the lazy devotion of the Romish clergy; over the sleepy laziness of men that erected churches, we may indulge our superiority with a new triumph, by comparing it with the fervid activity of those who suffer them to fall.

Of the destruction of churches, the decay of religion must in time be the consequence; for while the public acts of the ministry are now performed in houses, a very small number can be present; and as the greater part of the Islanders make no use of books, all must necessarily live in total ignorance who want the opportunity of vocal instruction.

From these remains of ancient sanctity, which are every where to be found, it has been conjectured that, for the last two centuries, the inhabitants of the Islands have decreased in number. This argument, which supposes that the churches have been suffered to fall only because they were no longer necessary, would have some force if the houses of worship still remaining were sufficient for the people. But since they have now no churches at all, these venerable fragments do not prove the people of former times to have been more numerous, but to have been more devout. If the inhabitants were doubled with their present principles, it appears not that any provision for public worship would be made. Where the religion of a country enforces consecrated buildings, the number of those buildings may be supposed to afford some indication, however uncertain, of the populousness of the place; but where by a change of manners a nation is contented to live without them, their decay implies no diminution of inhabitants.

Some of these dilapidations are said to be found in islands now uninhabited; but I doubt whether we can thence infer that they were ever peopled. The religion of the middle age is well known to have placed too much hope in lonely austerities. Voluntary solitude was the great art of propitiation by which crimes were effaced, and conscience was appeased; it is therefore not unlikely that oratories were often built in places where retirement was sure to have no disturbance.

Raasay has little that can detain a traveller, except the Laird and his family; but their power wants no auxiliaries. Such a seat of hospitality, amidst the winds and waters, fills the imagination with a delightful contrariety of images. Without is the rough ocean and the rocky land, the beating billows and the howling storm: within is plenty and elegance, beauty and gaiety, the song and the dance. In Raasay, if I could have found a Ulysses, I had fancied a Phaeacia.°

[They cross to Portree on the main island and spend the night at Kingsburgh as guests of the famous Flora Macdonald and her husband. They visit

Dunvegan Castle, the seat of the chief of Clan Macleod, and the homes of other Macleods at Ulinish and Talisker, and pass several days at Ostaig and nearby Armadale waiting for fair weather in which to pursue their journey by boat. At this point in his narrative, Johnson sums up his observations in a remarkable essay in cultural anthropology that occupies one-fourth of his book. As well as the matters treated in the excerpts below, he discusses the flora and fauna of Skye, its schools, the effect of the disarming law and the abolition of the legal jurisdiction of chiefs of the clans, and 'second sight', the existence of which he thinks has not been disproven.]

OSTIG IN SKY

.   .   .   .

As this island lies in the fifty-seventh degree,° the air cannot be supposed to have much warmth. The long continuance of the sun above the horizon does indeed sometimes produce great heat in northern latitudes; but this can only happen in sheltered places, where the atmosphere is to a certain degree stagnant, and the same mass of air continues to receive for many hours the rays of the sun, and the vapours of the earth. Sky lies open on the west and north to a vast extent of ocean, and is cooled in the summer by perpetual ventilation, but by the same blasts is kept warm in winter. Their weather is not pleasing. Half the year is deluged with rain. From the autumnal to the vernal equinox, a dry day is hardly known, except when the showers are suspended by a tempest. Under such skies can be expected no great exuberance of vegetation. Their winter overtakes their summer, and their harvest lies upon the ground drenched with rain. The autumn struggles hard to produce some of our early fruits. I gathered gooseberries in September; but they were small, and the husk was thick. . . .

Their agriculture is laborious, and perhaps rather feeble than unskilful. Their chief manure is sea-weed, which, when they lay it to rot upon the field, gives them a better crop than those of the Highlands. They heap sea shells upon the dunghill, which in time moulder into a fertilising substance. When they find a vein of earth where they cannot use it, they dig it up, and add it to the mould of a more commodious place.

Their corn grounds often lie in such intricacies among the crags that there is no room for the action of a team and plow. The soil is then turned up by manual labour, with an instrument called a crooked spade, of a form and weight which to me appeared very incommodious, and would perhaps be soon improved in a country where workmen could be easily found and easily paid. It has a narrow blade of iron fixed to a long and heavy piece of wood, which must have, about a foot and a half above the iron, a knee or flexure with the angle downwards. When the farmer encounters a stone which is the great impediment of his operations, he drives the blade under it, and bringing the knee or angle to the ground, has in the long handle a very forcible lever.

They have lately found a manufacture considerably lucrative. Their rocks abound with kelp, a sea-plant, of which the ashes are melted into glass. They burn kelp in great quantities, and then send it away in ships, which come regularly to purchase them. This new source of riches has raised the rents of many maritime farms; but the tenants pay, like all other tenants, the additional rent with great unwillingness; because they consider the profits of the kelp as the mere product of personal labour, to which the landlord contributes nothing. However, as any man may be said to give what he gives the power of gaining, he has certainly as much right to profit from the price of kelp as any thing else found or raised upon his ground.

This new trade has excited a long and eager litigation between Macdonald and Macleod for a ledge of rocks which, till the value of kelp was known, neither of them desired the reputation of possessing.

The cattle of Sky are not so small as is commonly believed. Since they have sent their beeves in great numbers to southern marts, they have probably taken more care of their breed. At stated times the annual growth of cattle is driven to a fair by a general drover, and with the money, which he returns to the farmer, the rents are paid.

The price regularly expected is from two to three pounds a head; there was once one sold for five pounds. They go from the Islands very lean, and are not offered to the butcher till they have been long fatted in English pastures.

Of their black cattle, some are without horns, called by the Scots *humble* cows, as we call a bee an *humble* bee that wants a sting. Whether this difference be specific or accidental, though we inquired with great diligence, we could not be informed. We are not very sure that the bull is ever without horns, though we have been told that such bulls there are. What is produced by putting a horned and unhorned male and female together, no man has ever tried that thought the result worthy of observation.

Their horses are, like their cows, of a moderate size. I had no difficulty to mount myself commodiously by the favour of the gentlemen. I heard of very little cows in Barra, and very little horses in Rum, where perhaps no care is taken to prevent that diminution of size which must always happen where the greater and the less copulate promiscuously, and the young animal is restrained from growth by penury of sustenance.

The goat is the general inhabitant of the earth, complying with every difference of climate, and of soil. The goats of the Hebrides are like others: nor did I hear any thing of their sheep to be particularly remarked. . . .

The inhabitants of Sky, and of the other islands which I have seen, are commonly of the middle stature, with fewer among them very tall or very short than are seen in England, or perhaps, as their numbers are small, the chances of any deviation from the common measure are necessarily few. The tallest men that I saw are among those of higher rank. In regions of barrenness and scarcity, the human race is hindered in its growth by the same causes as other animals.

The ladies have as much beauty here as in other places, but bloom and softness are not to be expected among the lower classes, whose faces are exposed to the rudeness of the climate, and whose features are sometimes contracted by want, and sometimes hardened by the blasts. Supreme beauty is seldom found in cottages or work-shops, even where no real hardships are suffered. To expand the human face to its full perfection, it seems necessary that the mind should co-operate by placidness of content, or consciousness of superiority. . . .

In the Islands, as in most other places, the inhabitants are of different rank, and one does not encroach here upon another. Where there is no commerce nor manufacture, he that is born poor can scarcely become rich; and if none are able to buy estates, he that is born to land cannot annihilate his family by selling it. This was once the state of these countries. Perhaps there is no example till within a century and half of any family whose estate was alienated otherwise than by violence or forfeiture. Since money has been brought amongst them, they have found, like others, the art of spending more than they receive; and I saw with grief the chief of a very ancient clan, whose island was condemned by law to be sold for the satisfaction of his creditors.

The name of highest dignity is laird, of which there are in the extensive Isle of Sky only three, Macdonald, Macleod, and Mackinnon. The laird is the original owner of the land, whose natural power must be very great where no man lives but by agriculture; and where the produce of the land is not conveyed through the labyrinths of traffic but passes directly from the hand that gathers it to the mouth that eats it. The laird has all those in his power that live upon his farms. Kings can, for the most part, only exalt or degrade. The laird at pleasure can feed or starve, can give bread, or withhold it. This inherent power was yet strengthened by the kindness of consanguinity, and the reverence of patriarchal authority. The laird was the father of the clan, and his tenants commonly bore his name. And to these principles of original command was added, for many ages, an exclusive right of legal jurisdiction.

This multifarious and extensive obligation operated with force scarcely credible. Every duty, moral or political, was absorbed in affection and adherence to the chief. Not many years have passed since the clans knew no law but the laird's will. He told them to whom they should be friends or enemies, what king they should obey, and what religion they should profess.

When the Scots first rose in arms against the succession of the house of Hanover, Lovat, the chief of the Frasers, was in exile for a rape. The Frasers were very numerous, and very zealous against the government. A pardon was sent to Lovat. He came to the English camp, and the clan immediately deserted to him.

Next in dignity to the laird is the tacksman; a large taker or lease-holder of land, of which he keeps part, as a domain, in his own hand, and lets part to under tenants. The tacksman is necessarily a man capable of securing to the laird the whole rent, and is commonly a collateral relation. These 'tacks', or subordinate possessions, were long considered as hereditary, and the occupant was distinguished by the name of the place at which he resided. He held a middle station, by which the highest and the lowest orders were connected. He paid rent and reverence to the laird, and received them from the tenants. This tenure still subsists, with its original operation, but not with the primitive stability. Since the islanders, no longer content to live, have learned the desire of growing rich, an ancient dependant is in danger of giving way to a higher bidder, at the expense of domestic dignity and hereditary power. The stranger, whose money buys him preference, considers himself as paying for all that he has, and is indifferent about the laird's honour or safety. The commodiousness of money is indeed great; but there are some advantages which money cannot buy, and which therefore no wise man will by the love of money be tempted to forgo.

I have found in the hither parts of Scotland men not defective in judgment or general experience who consider the tacksman as a useless burden of the ground, as a drone who lives upon the product of an estate, without the right of property, or the merit of labour, and who impoverishes at once the landlord and the tenant. The land, say they, is let to the tacksman at six-pence an acre, and by him to the tenant at ten-pence. Let the owner be the immediate landlord to all the tenants; if he sets the ground at eight-pence, he will increase his revenue by a fourth part, and the tenant's burden will be diminished by a fifth.

Those who pursue this train of reasoning seem not sufficiently to inquire whither it will lead them, nor to know that it will equally show the propriety of suppressing all wholesale trade, of shutting up the shops of every man who sells what he does not make, and of extruding all whose agency and profit intervene between the manufacturer and the consumer. They may, by stretching their understandings a little wider, comprehend that all those who by undertaking large quantities of manufacture, and affording employment to many labourers, make themselves considered as benefactors to the public have only been robbing their workmen with one hand, and their customers with the other. If Crowley° had sold only what he could make, and all his smiths had wrought their own iron with their own hammers, he would have lived on less, and they would have sold their work for more. The salaries of superintendents and clerks would have been partly saved, and partly shared, and nails been sometimes cheaper by a farthing in a hundred. But then if the smith could not have found an immediate purchaser, he must have deserted his anvil; if there had by accident at any time been more sellers than buyers, the workmen must have reduced their profit to nothing, by underselling one another; and as no great stock could have been in any hand, no sudden demand of large quantities could have been answered, and the builder must have stood still till the nailer could supply him.

According to these schemes, universal plenty is to begin and end in universal misery. Hope and emulation will be utterly extinguished; and as all must obey the call of immediate necessity, nothing that requires extensive views, or provides for distant consequences, will ever be performed.

To the southern inhabitants of Scotland, the state of the mountains and the islands is equally unknown with that of Borneo or Sumatra. Of both they have only heard a little, and guess the rest. They are strangers to the language and the manners, to the advantages and wants of the people whose life they would model, and whose evils they would remedy.

Nothing is less difficult than to procure one convenience by the forfeiture of another. A soldier may expedite his march by throwing away his arms. To banish the tacksman is easy, to make a country plentiful by diminishing the people is an expeditious mode of husbandry; but that abundance which there is nobody to enjoy contributes little to human happiness. . . .

Such is the system of insular subordination, which, having little variety, cannot afford much delight in the view, nor long detain the mind in contemplation. The inhabitants were for a long time perhaps not unhappy; but their content was a muddy mixture of pride and ignorance, an indifference for pleasures which they did not know, a blind veneration for their chiefs, and a strong conviction of their own importance.

Their pride has been crushed by the heavy hand of a vindictive conqueror, whose severities have been followed by laws which, though they cannot be called cruel, have produced much discontent, because they operate upon the surface of life, and make every eye bear witness to subjection. To be compelled to a new dress has always been found painful.

Their chiefs, being now deprived of their jurisdiction, have already lost much of their influence; and as they gradually degenerate from patriarchal rulers to rapacious landlords, they will divest themselves of the little that remains.

That dignity which they derived from an opinion of their military importance, the law, which disarmed them, has abated. An old gentleman, delighting himself with the recollection of better days, related that forty years ago, a chieftain walked out attended by ten or twelve followers, with their arms rattling. That animating rabble has now ceased. The chief has lost his formidable retinue; and the Highlander walks his heath unarmed and defenceless, with the peaceable submission of a French peasant or English cottager.

Their ignorance grows every day less, but their knowledge is yet of little other use than to show them their wants. They are now in the period of education, and feel the uneasiness of discipline, without yet perceiving the benefit of instruction. . . .

There seems now, whatever be the cause, to be through a great part of the Highlands a general discontent. That adherence which was lately professed by every man to the chief of his name has now little prevalence; and he that cannot live as he desires at home, listens to the tale of fortunate islands, and happy regions, where every man may have land of his own, and eat the product of his labours without a superior.

Those who have obtained grants of American lands have, as is well known, invited settlers from all quarters of the globe; and among other places where oppression might produce a wish for new habitations, their emissaries would not fail to try their persuasions in the Isles of Scotland, where at the time when the clans were newly disunited from their chiefs, and exasperated by unprecedented exactions, it is no wonder that they prevailed.

Whether the mischiefs of emigration were immediately perceived may be justly questioned. They who went first were probably such as could best be spared; but the accounts sent by the earliest adventurers, whether true or false, inclined many to follow them; and whole neighbourhoods formed parties for removal; so that departure from their native country is no longer exile. He that goes thus accompanied carries with him all that makes life pleasant. He sits down in a better climate, surrounded by his kindred and his friends: they carry with them their language, their opinions, their popular songs, and hereditary merriment: they change nothing but the place of their abode; and of that change they perceive the benefit.

This is the real effect of emigration, if those that go away together settle on the same spot, and preserve their ancient union. But some relate that these adventurous visitants of unknown regions, after a voyage passed in dreams of plenty and felicity, are dispersed at last upon a sylvan wilderness, where their first years must be spent in toil, to clear the ground which is afterwards to be tilled, and that the whole effect of their undertaking is only more fatigue and equal scarcity.

Both accounts may be suspected. Those who are gone will endeavour by every art to draw others after them; for as their numbers are greater, they will provide better for themselves. When Nova Scotia was first peopled, I remember a letter published under the character of a New Planter, who related how much the climate put him in mind of Italy. Such intelligence the Hebridians probably receive from their transmarine correspondents. But with equal temptations of interest, and perhaps with no greater niceness of veracity, the owners of the islands spread stories of American hardships to keep their people content at home.

Some method to stop this epidemic desire of wandering, which spreads its contagion from valley to valley, deserves to be sought with great diligence. In more fruitful countries, the removal of one only makes room for the succession of another: but in the Hebrides, the loss of an inhabitant leaves a lasting vacuity; for nobody born in any other parts of the world will choose this country for his residence; and an island once depopulated will remain a desert as long as the present facility of travel gives every one who is discontented and unsettled the choice of his abode.

Let it be inquired whether the first intention of those who are fluttering on the wing, and collecting a flock that they may take their flight, be to attain good, or to avoid evil. If they are dissatisfied with that part of the globe which their birth has allotted them, and resolve not to live without the pleasures of happier climates; if they long for bright suns, and calm skies, and flowery fields, and fragrant gardens, I know not by what eloquence they can be persuaded, or what offers they can be hired to stay.

But if they are driven from their native country by positive evils, and disgusted by ill-treatment, real or imaginary, it were fit to remove their grievances, and quiet their resentment; since, if they have been hitherto undutiful subjects, they will not much mend their principles by American conversation. . . .

The religion of the Islands is that of the Kirk of Scotland. The gentlemen with whom I conversed are all inclined to the English liturgy; but they are obliged to maintain the established minister, and the country is too poor to afford payment to another, who must live wholly on the contribution of his audience.

They therefore all attend the worship of the Kirk, as often as a visit from their minister, or the practicability of travelling gives them opportunity; nor have they any reason to complain of insufficient pastors; for I saw not one in the Islands whom I had reason to think either deficient in learning, or irregular in life; but found several with whom I could not converse without wishing, as my respect increased, that they had not been Presbyterians.

The ancient rigour of puritanism is now very much relaxed, though all are not yet equally enlightened. I sometimes met with prejudices sufficiently malignant, but they were prejudices of ignorance. The ministers in the Islands had attained such knowledge as may justly be admired in men who have no motive to study but generous curiosity, or, what is still better, desire of usefulness; with such politeness as so narrow a circle of converse could not have supplied but to minds naturally disposed to elegance.

Reason and truth will prevail at last. The most learned of the Scottish doctors would now gladly admit a form of prayer, if the people would endure it. The zeal or rage of congregations has its different degrees. In some parishes the Lord's Prayer is suffered: in others it is still rejected as a form; and he that should make it part of his supplication would be suspected of heretical pravity.

The principle upon which extemporary prayer was originally introduced is no longer admitted. The minister formerly, in the effusion of his prayer, expected immediate, and perhaps perceptible inspiration, and therefore thought it his duty not to think before what he should say. It is now universally confessed that men pray as they speak on other occasions, according to the general measure of their abilities and attainments. Whatever each may think of a form prescribed by another, he cannot but believe that he can himself compose by study and meditation a better prayer than will rise in his mind at a sudden call; and if he has any hope of supernatural help, why may he not as well receive it when he writes as when he speaks?

In the variety of mental powers, some must perform extemporary prayer with much imperfection; and in the eagerness and rashness of contradictory opinions, if public liturgy be left to the private judgment of every minister, the congregation may often be offended or misled.

There is in Scotland, as among ourselves, a restless suspicion of popish machinations, and a clamour of numerous converts to the Romish religion. The report is, I believe, in both parts of the island equally false. The Romish religion is professed only in Egg and Canna, two small islands, into which the Reformation never made its way. If any missionaries are busy in the Highlands, their zeal entitles them to respect, even from those who cannot think favourably of their doctrine. . . .

In an unwritten speech, nothing that is not very short is transmitted from one generation to another. Few have opportunities of hearing a long composition often enough to learn it, or have inclination to repeat it so often as is necessary to retain it; and what is once forgotten is lost for ever. I believe there cannot be recovered, in the whole Erse language, five hundred lines of which there is any evidence to prove them a hundred years old. Yet I hear that the father of Ossian° boasts of two chests more of ancient poetry, which he suppresses, because they are too good for the English.

He that goes into the Highlands with a mind naturally acquiescent, and a credulity eager for wonders, may come back with an opinion very different from mine; for the inhabitants knowing the ignorance of all strangers in their language and antiquities perhaps are not very scrupulous adherents to truth; yet I do not say that they deliberately speak studied falsehood, or have a settled purpose to deceive. They have inquired and considered little, and do not always feel their own ignorance. They are not much accustomed to be interrogated by others; and seem never to have thought upon interrogating themselves; so that if they do not know what they tell to be true, they likewise do not distinctly perceive it to be false.

Mr Boswell was very diligent in his inquiries; and the result of his investigations was that the answer to the second question was commonly such as nullified the answer to the first.

We were a while told that they had an old translation of the scriptures; and told it till it would appear obstinacy to inquire again. Yet by continued accumulation of questions we found that the translation meant, if any meaning there were, was nothing else than the Irish Bible.

We heard of manuscripts that were, or that had been in the hands of somebody's father, or grandfather; but at last we had no reason to believe they were other than Irish. Martin°mentions Irish, but never any Erse manuscripts, to be found in the Islands in his time.

I suppose my opinion of the poems of Ossian is already discovered. I believe they never existed in any other form than that which we have seen. The editor, or author, never could show the original; nor can it be shown by any other; to revenge reasonable incredulity, by refusing evidence, is a degree of insolence with which the world is not yet acquainted; and stubborn audacity is the last refuge of guilt. It would be easy to show it if he had it; but whence could it be had? It is too long to be remembered, and the language formerly had nothing written. He has doubtless inserted names that circulate in popular stories, and may have translated some wandering ballads, if any can be found; and the names, and some of the images, being recollected, make an inaccurate auditor imagine, by the help of Caledonian bigotry, that he has formerly heard the whole.

I asked a very learned minister in Sky, who had used all arts to make me believe the genuineness of the book, whether at last he believed it himself? but he would not answer. He wished me to be deceived, for the honour of his country; but would not directly and formally deceive me. Yet has this man's testimony been publicly produced, as of one that held *Fingal* to be the work of Ossian.

It is said that some men of integrity profess to have heard parts of it, but they all heard them when they were boys; and it was never said that any of them could recite six lines. They remember names, and perhaps some proverbial sentiments; and, having no distinct ideas, coin a resemblance without an original. The persuasion of the Scots, however, is far from universal; and in a question so capable of proof, why should doubt be suffered to continue? The editor has been heard to say that part of the poem was received by him in the Saxon character. He has then found, by some peculiar fortune, an unwritten language, written in a character which the natives probably never beheld.

I have yet supposed no imposture but in the publisher, yet I am far from certainty that some translations have not been lately made that may now be obtruded as parts of the original work. Credulity on one part is a strong temptation to deceit on the other, especially to deceit of which no personal injury is the consequence, and which flatters the author with his own ingenuity. The Scots have something to plead for their easy reception of an improbable fiction: they are seduced by their fondness for their supposed ancestors. A Scotchman must be a very sturdy moralist who does not love Scotland better than truth: he will always love it better than inquiry; and if falsehood flatters his vanity, will not be very diligent to detect it. Neither ought the English to be much influenced by Scotch authority; for of the past and present state of the whole Erse nation, the Lowlanders are at least as ignorant as ourselves. To be ignorant is painful; but it is dangerous to quiet our uneasiness by the delusive opiate of hasty persuasion.

But this is the age in which those who could not read have been supposed to write; in which the giants of antiquated romance have been exhibited as realities. If we know little of the ancient Highlanders, let us not fill the vacuity with Ossian. If we have not searched the Magellanic regions, let us however forbear to people them with Patagons.°

[Escorted by Donald Maclean, its 'young Laird', whose enterprise in learning modern methods of agriculture Johnson highly praises, they visit the island of Col, after a stormy voyage from Skye, and then go on to view the remains of the early Christian mission on Inch Kenneth and Iona (Icolmkill), celebrated by one of Johnson's most famous passages.]

The evening was now approaching, and we were yet at a considerable distance from the end of our expedition. We could therefore stop no more to make remarks in the way, but set forward with some degree of eagerness. The day soon failed us, and the moon presented a very solemn and pleasing scene. The sky was clear, so that the eye commanded a wide circle: the sea was neither still nor turbulent: the wind neither silent nor loud. We were never far from one coast or another on which, if the weather had become violent, we could have found shelter, and therefore contemplated at ease the region through which we glided in the tranquillity of the night, and saw now a rock and now an island grow gradually conspicuous and gradually obscure. I committed the fault which I have just been censuring, in neglecting, as we passed, to note the series of this placid navigation.

We were very near an island, called Nun's Island, perhaps from an ancient convent. Here is said to have been dug the stone that was used in the buildings of Icolmkill. Whether it is now inhabited we could not stay to inquire.

At last we came to Icolmkill, but found no convenience for landing. Our boat could not be forced very near the dry ground, and our Highlanders carried us over the water.

We were now treading that illustrious island which was once the luminary of the Caledonian regions, whence savage clans and roving barbarians derived the benefits of knowledge, and the blessings of religion. To abstract the mind from all local emotion would be impossible, if it were endeavoured, and would be foolish, if it were possible. Whatever withdraws us from the power of our senses; whatever makes the past, the distant, or the future predominate over the present advances us in the dignity of thinking beings. Far from me and from my friends be such frigid philosophy as may conduct us indifferent and unmoved over any ground which has been dignified by wisdom, bravery, or virtue. That man is little to be envied whose patriotism would not gain force upon the plain of Marathon, or whose piety would not grow warmer among the ruins of Iona!

[Returning to the mainland, they are entertained by the Duke of Argyll at Inveraray, and by a cousin of Tobias Smollett at his family's home on Loch Lomond. They pass through Glasgow on their way to Boswell's family seat at Auchinleck, and finally make their way back to Edinburgh.]

We now returned to Edinburgh, where I passed some days with men of learning, whose names want no advancement from my commemoration, or with women of elegance, which perhaps disclaims a pedant's praise.

The conversation of the Scots grows every day less unpleasing to the English; their peculiarities wear fast away; their dialect is likely to become in half a century provincial and rustic, even to themselves. The great, the learned, the ambitious, and the vain all cultivate the English phrase, and the English pronunciation, and in splendid companies Scotch is not much heard, except now and then from an old lady.

There is one subject of philosophical curiosity to be found in

Edinburgh, which no other city has to show: a college of the deaf and dumb, who are taught to speak, to read, to write, and to practise arithmetic by a gentleman whose name is Braidwood. The number which attends him is, I think, about twelve, which he brings together into a little school, and instructs according to their several degrees of proficiency.

I do not mean to mention the instruction of the deaf as new. Having been first practised upon the son of a Constable of Spain, it was afterwards cultivated with much emulation in England by Wallis and Holder, and was lately professed by Mr Baker,° who once flattered me with hopes of seeing his method published. How far any former teachers have succeeded it is not easy to know; the improvement of Mr Braidwood's pupils is wonderful. They not only speak, write, and understand what is written, but if he that speaks looks towards them, and modifies his organs by distinct and full utterance, they know so well what is spoken that it is an expression scarcely figurative to say they hear with the eye. That any have attained to the power mentioned by Burnet of feeling sounds by laying a hand on the speaker's mouth, I know not; but I have seen so much that I can believe more; a single word, or a short sentence, I think, may possibly be so distinguished.

It will readily be supposed by those that consider this subject that Mr Braidwood's scholars spell accurately. Orthography is vitiated among such as learn first to speak, and then to write, by imperfect notions of the relation between letters and vocal utterance; but to those students every character is of equal importance; for letters are to them not symbols of names, but of things; when they write they do not represent a sound, but delineate a form.

This school I visited, and found some of the scholars waiting for their master, whom they are said to receive at his entrance with smiling countenances and sparkling eyes, delighted with the hope of new ideas. One of the young ladies had her slate before her, on which I wrote a question consisting of three figures, to be multiplied by two figures. She looked upon it, and quivering her fingers in a manner which I thought very pretty, but of which I know not whether it was art or play, multiplied the sum regularly in two lines, observing the decimal place; but did not add the two lines together, probably disdaining so easy an operation. I pointed at the place where the sum total should stand, and she noted it with such expedition as seemed to show that she had it only to write.

It was pleasing to see one of the most desperate of human calamities capable of so much help: whatever enlarges hope, will exalt courage; after having seen the deaf taught arithmetic, who would be afraid to cultivate the Hebrides?

Such are the things which this journey has given me an opportunity of seeing, and such are the reflections which that sight has raised. Having passed my time almost wholly in cities, I may have been surprised by modes of life and appearances of nature that are familiar to men of wider survey and more varied conversation. Novelty and ignorance must always be reciprocal, and I cannot but be conscious that my thoughts on national manners are the thoughts of one who has seen but little.

FINIS

Prefaces, Biographical and Critical, to the Works of the English Poets

Addison

Joseph Addison was born on the first of May, 1672, at Milston, of which his father, Lancelot Addison, was then rector, near Ambrosbury in Wiltshire, and appearing weak and unlikely to live he was christened the same day. After the usual domestic education, which from the character of his father may be reasonably supposed to have given him strong impressions of piety, he was committed to the care of Mr Naish at Ambrosbury, and afterwards of Mr Taylor at Salisbury.

Not to name the school or the masters of men illustrious for literature is a kind of historical fraud, by which honest fame is injuriously diminished. I would therefore trace him through the whole process of his education. In 1683, in the beginning of his twelfth year, his father, being made dean of Lichfield, naturally carried his family to his new residence, and, I believe, placed him for some time, probably not long, under Mr Shaw, then master of the school at Lichfield, father of the late Dr Peter Shaw. Of this interval his biographers have given no account, and I know it only from a story of a *barring-out*, told me when I was a boy by Andrew Corbet° of Shropshire, who had heard it from Mr Pigot his uncle.

The practice of *barring-out* was a savage license, practised in many schools to the end of the last century, by which the boys, when the periodical vacation drew near, growing petulant at the approach of liberty, some days before the time of regular recess, took possession of the school, of which they barred the doors, and bade their master defiance from the windows. It is not easy to suppose that on such occasions the master would do more than laugh, yet, if tradition may be credited, he often struggled hard to force or surprise the garrison. The master, when Pigot was a school-boy, was *barred-out* at Lichfield, and the whole operation, as he said, was planned and conducted by Addison.

To judge better of the probability of this story, I have enquired when he was sent to the Chartreux;° but, as he was not one of those who enjoyed the Founder's benefaction, there is no account preserved of his admission. At the school of the Chartreux, to which he was removed either from that of Salisbury or Lichfield, he pursued his juvenile studies under the care of Dr Ellis, and contracted that intimacy with Sir Richard Steele which their joint labours have so effectually recorded.

Of this memorable friendship the greater praise must be given to Steele. It is not hard to love those from whom nothing can be feared, and Addison never considered Steele as a rival; but Steele lived, as he confesses, under an habitual subjection to the predominating genius of Addison, whom he always mentioned with reverence and treated with obsequiousness.

Addison, who knew his own dignity, could not always forbear to show it by playing a little upon his admirer; but he was in no danger of retort: his jests were endured without resistance or resentment.

But the sneer of jocularity was not the worst. Steele, whose imprudence of generosity or vanity of profusion kept him always incurably necessitous, upon some pressing exigence in an evil hour borrowed a hundred pounds of his friend, probably without much purpose of repayment; but Addison, who seems to have had other notions of a hundred pounds, grew impatient of delay, and reclaimed his loan by an execution.° Steele felt with great sensibility the obduracy of his creditor; but with emotions of sorrow rather than of anger.

In 1687 he was entered into Queen's College in Oxford, where, in 1689, the accidental perusal of some Latin verses gained him the patronage of Dr Lancaster, afterwards provost of Queen's College; by whose recommendation he was elected into Magdalen College as a Demy, a term by which that society denominates those which are elsewhere called Scholars; young men who partake of the founder's benefaction and succeed in their order to vacant fellowships.

Here he continued to cultivate poetry and criticism, and grew first eminent by his Latin compositions, which are indeed entitled to particular praise. He has not confined himself to the imitation of any ancient author, but has formed his style from the general language, such as a diligent perusal of the productions of different ages happened to supply.

His Latin compositions seem to have had much of his fondness; for he collected a second volume of the *Musae Anglicanae*,° perhaps for a convenient receptacle, in which all his Latin pieces are inserted, and where his Poem on the Peace has the first place. He afterwards presented the collection to Boileau, who from that time 'conceived', says Tickell,° 'an opinion of the English genius for poetry'. Nothing is better known of Boileau than that he had an injudicious and peevish contempt of modern Latin, and therefore his profession of regard was probably the effect of his civility rather than approbation.

Three of his Latin poems are upon subjects on which perhaps he would not have ventured to have written in his own language: *The Battle of the Pygmies and Cranes,*° *The Barometer*, and *A Bowling-green*. When the matter is low or scanty a dead language, in which nothing is mean because nothing is familiar, affords great conveniences; and by the sonorous magnificence of Roman syllables the writer conceals penury of thought and want of novelty, often from the reader, and often from himself.

In his twenty-second year he first showed his power of English poetry by some verses addressed to Dryden; and soon afterwards published a translation of the greater part of the *Fourth Georgic upon Bees*; after which, says Dryden, 'my latter swarm is hardly worth the hiving'.

About the same time he composed the arguments prefixed to the several books of Dryden's *Virgil*; and produced an *Essay on the Georgics*, juvenile, superficial, and uninstructive, without much either of the scholar's learning or the critic's penetration.

His next paper of verses contained a character of the principal English poets, inscribed to Henry Sacheverell, who was then, if not a poet, a writer of verses, as is shown by his version of a small part of Virgil's *Georgics* published in the *Miscellanies*, and a Latin encomium on queen Mary in the *Musae Anglicanae*. These verses exhibit all the fondness of friendship; but on one side or the other friendship was afterwards too weak for the malignity of faction.

In this poem is a very confident and discriminative character of Spenser, whose work he had then never read. So little sometimes is criticism the effect of judgement. It is necessary to inform the reader that about this time he was introduced by Congreve to Montague,° then Chancellor of the Exchequer: Addison was then learning the trade of a courtier, and subjoined Montague as a poetical name to those of Cowley and of Dryden.

By the influence of Mr Montague, concurring, according to Tickell, with his natural modesty, he was diverted from his original design of entering into holy orders. Montague alleged the corruption of men who engaged in civil employments without liberal education; and declared that, though he was represented as an enemy to the Church, he would never do it any injury but by withholding Addison from it.

Soon after (in 1695) he wrote a poem to King William, with a rhyming introduction addressed to Lord Somers.° King William had no regard to elegance or literature: his study was only war; yet by a choice of ministers whose disposition was very different from his own he procured without intention a very liberal patronage to poetry. Addison was caressed both by Somers and Montague.

In 1697 appeared his Latin verses on the peace of Ryswick, which he dedicated to Montague, and which was afterwards called by Smith° 'the best Latin poem since the *Æneid*'. Praise must not be too rigorously examined; but the performance cannot be denied to be vigorous and elegant.

Having yet no public employment he obtained (in 1699) a pension of three hundred pounds a year, that he might be enabled to travel. He stayed a year at Blois, probably to learn the French language; and then proceeded in his journey to Italy, which he surveyed with the eyes of a poet.

While he was travelling at leisure he was far from being idle; for he not only collected his observations on the country, but found time to write his *Dialogues on Medals* and four Acts of *Cato*. Such at least is the relation of Tickell. Perhaps he only collected his materials, and formed his plan.

Whatever were his other employments in Italy he there wrote the letter to Lord Halifax, which is justly considered as the most elegant, if not the most sublime, of his poetical productions. But in about two years he found it necessary to hasten home; being, as Swift informs us, distressed by indigence, and compelled to become the tutor of a travelling Squire, because his pension was not remitted.

At his return he published his Travels, with a dedication to Lord Somers. As his stay in foreign countries was short his observations are such as might be supplied by a hasty view, and consist chiefly in comparisons of the present face of the country with the descriptions left us by the Roman poets, from whom he made preparatory collections, though he might have spared the trouble had he known that such collections had been made twice before by Italian authors.

The most amusing passage of his book is his account of the minute republic of San Marino; of many parts it is not a very severe censure to say that they might have been written at home. His elegance of language and variegation of prose and verse, however, gain upon the reader; and the book, though a while neglected, became in time so much the favourite of the public that before it was reprinted it rose to five times its price.

When he returned to England (in 1702), with a meanness of appearance which gave testimony of the difficulties to which he had been reduced, he found his old patrons out of power, and was therefore for a time at full leisure for the cultivation of his mind, and a mind so cultivated gives reason to believe that little time was lost.

But he remained not long neglected or useless. The victory at Blenheim (1704) spread triumph and confidence over the nation; and Lord Godolphin° lamenting to Lord Halifax that it had not been celebrated in a manner equal to the subject, desired him to propose it to some better poet. Halifax told him that there was no encouragement for genius; that worthless men were unprofitably enriched with public money, without any care to find or employ those whose appearance might do honour to their country. To this Godolphin replied that such abuses should in time be rectified, and that if a man could be found capable of the task then proposed he should not want an ample recompense. Halifax then named Addison, but required that the Treasurer should apply to him in his own person. Godolphin sent the message by Mr Boyle, afterwards Lord Carleton; and Addison, having undertaken the work, communicated it to the Treasurer while it was yet advanced no further than the simile of the Angel,° and was immediately rewarded by succeeding Mr Locke in the place of Commissioner of Appeals.

In the following year he was at Hanover with Lord Halifax; and the year after was made under-secretary of state, first to Sir Charles Hedges, and in a few months more to the Earl of Sunderland.

About this time the prevalent taste for Italian operas inclined him to try what would be the effect of a musical drama in our own language. He therefore wrote the opera of *Rosamond*, which, when exhibited on the stage, was either hissed or neglected; but trusting that the readers would do him more justice he published it, with an inscription to the Duchess of Marlborough,° a woman without skill or pretensions to skill in poetry or literature. His dedication was therefore an instance of servile absurdity, to be exceeded only by Joshua Barnes's dedication of a Greek *Anacreon* to the Duke.

His reputation had been somewhat advanced by *The Tender Husband*, a comedy which Steele dedicated to him, with a confession that he owed to him several of the most successful scenes. To this play Addison supplied a prologue.

When the Marquis of Wharton was appointed lord lieutenant of Ireland, Addison attended him as his secretary, and was made keeper of the records in Birmingham's Tower, with a salary of three hundred pounds a year. The office was little more than nominal, and the salary was augmented for his accommodation.

Interest and faction allow little to the operation of particular dispositions or private opinions. Two men of personal characters more opposite than those of Wharton and Addison could not easily be brought together. Wharton was impious, profligate, and shameless, without regard or appearance of regard to right and wrong: whatever is contrary to this may be said of Addison; but as agents of a party they were connected, and how they adjusted their other sentiments we cannot know.

Addison must, however, not be too hastily condemned. It is not necessary to refuse benefits from a bad man when the acceptance implies no approbation of his crimes; nor has the subordinate officer any obligation to examine the opinions or conduct of those under whom he acts, except that he may not be made the instrument of wickedness. It is reasonable to suppose that Addison counteracted, as far as he was able, the malignant and blasting influence of the Lieutenant, and that at least by his intervention some good was done, and some mischief prevented.

When he was in office he made a law to himself, as Swift has recorded, never to remit his regular fees in civility to his friends: 'For,' said he, 'I may have a hundred friends, and if my fee be two guineas I shall, by relinquishing my right, lose two hundred guineas, and no friend gain more than two; there is therefore no proportion between the good imparted and the evil suffered.'

He was in Ireland when Steele, without any communication of his design, began the publication of *The Tatler*; but he was not long concealed: by inserting a remark on Virgil, which Addison had given him, he discovered himself. It is indeed not easy for any man to write upon literature or common life so as not to make himself known to those with whom he familiarly converses, and who are acquainted with his track of study, his favourite topics, his peculiar notions, and his habitual phrases.

If Steele desired to write in secret he was not lucky; a single month detected him. His first *Tatler* was published April 22 (1709), and Addison's contribution appeared May 26. Tickell observes that *The Tatler* began and was concluded without his concurrence. This is doubtless literally true; but the work did not suffer much by his unconsciousness of its commencement or his absence at its cessation, for he continued his assistance to December 23, and the paper stopped on January 2. He did not distinguish his pieces by any signature; and I know not whether his name was not kept secret till the papers were collected into volumes.

To *The Tatler* in about two months succeeded *The Spectator*, a series of essays of the same kind, but written with less levity, upon a more regular plan, and published daily. Such an undertaking showed the writers not to distrust their own copiousness of materials or facility of composition, and their performance justified their confidence. They found, however, in their progress many auxiliaries. To attempt a single paper was no terrifying labour: many pieces were offered, and many were received.

Addison had enough of the zeal of party, but Steele had at that time almost nothing else. *The Spectator* in one of the first papers showed the political tenets of its authors; but a resolution was soon taken of courting general approbation by general topics, and subjects on which faction had produced no diversity of sentiments, such as literature, morality, and familiar life. To this practice they adhered with very few deviations. The ardour of Steele once broke out in praise of Marlborough; and when Dr Fleetwood prefixed to some sermons a preface overflowing with whiggish opinions, that it might be read by the Queen,° it was reprinted in *The Spectator*.

To teach the minuter decencies and inferior duties, to regulate the practice of daily conversation, to correct those depravities which are rather ridiculous than criminal, and remove those grievances which, if they produce no lasting calamities, impress hourly vexation, was first attempted by Casa° in his book of *Manners*, and Castiglione in his *Courtier*, two books yet celebrated in Italy for purity and elegance, and which, if they are now less read, are neglected only because they have effected that reformation which their authors intended, and their precepts now are no longer wanted. Their usefulness to the age in which they were written is sufficiently attested by the translations which almost all the nations of Europe were in haste to obtain.

This species of instruction was continued and perhaps advanced by the French; among whom La Bruyère's *Manners of the Age*, though, as Boileau remarked, it is written without connection, certainly deserves great praise for liveliness of description and justness of observation.

Before *The Tatler* and *Spectator*, if the writers for the theatre are excepted, England had no masters of common life. No writers had yet undertaken to reform either the savageness of neglect or the impertinence of civility; to show when to speak, or to be silent; how to refuse, or how to comply. We had many books to teach us our more important duties, and to settle opinions in philosophy or politics; but an *Arbiter elegantiarum*, a judge of propriety, was yet wanting, who should survey the track of daily conversation and free it from thorns and prickles, which tease the passer, though they do not wound him.

For this purpose nothing is so proper as the frequent publication of short papers, which we read not as study but amusement. If the subject be slight, the treatise likewise is short. The busy may find time, and the idle may find patience.

This mode of conveying cheap and easy knowledge began among us in the Civil War, when it was much the interest of either party to raise and fix the prejudices of the people. At that time appeared *Mercurius Aulicus*, *Mercurius Rusticus*, and *Mercurius Civicus*. It is said that when any title grew popular it was stolen by the antagonist, who by this stratagem conveyed his notions to those who would not have received him had he not worn the appearance of a friend. The tumult of those unhappy days left scarcely any man leisure to treasure up occasional compositions; and so much were they neglected that a complete collection is nowhere to be found.

These *Mercuries* were succeeded by L'Estrange's *Observator*, and that by Lesley's *Rehearsal*, and perhaps by others; but hitherto nothing had been conveyed to the people in this commodious manner but controversy relating to the Church or State: of which they taught many to talk whom they could not teach to judge.

It has been suggested that the Royal Society was instituted soon after the Restoration to divert the attention of the people from public discontent. *The Tatler* and *Spectator* had the same tendency; they were published at a time when two parties, loud, restless, and violent, each with plausible declarations, and each perhaps without any distinct termination of its views, were agitating the nation: to minds heated with political contest they supplied cooler and more inoffensive reflections; and it is said by Addison, in a subsequent work, that they had a perceptible influence upon the conversation of that time, and taught the frolic and the gay to unite merriment with decency—an effect which they can never wholly lose, while they continue to be among the first books by which both sexes are initiated in the elegances of knowledge.

The Tatler and *Spectator* adjusted, like Casa, the unsettled practice of daily intercourse by propriety and politeness; and, like La Bruyère, exhibited the 'Characters and Manners of the Age'. The personages introduced in these papers were not merely ideal; they were then known, and conspicuous in various stations. Of *The Tatler* this is told by Steele in his last paper, and of *The Spectator* by Budgell° in the Preface to *Theophrastus*; a book which Addison has recommended, and which he was suspected to have revised, if he did not write it. Of those portraits, which may be supposed to be sometimes embellished and sometimes aggravated, the originals are now partly known, and partly forgotten.

But to say that they united the plans of two or three eminent writers is to give them but a small part of their due praise: they superadded literature and criticism, and sometimes towered far above their predecessors; and taught, with great justness of argument and dignity of language, the most important duties and sublime truths.

All these topics were happily varied with elegant fictions and refined allegories, and illuminated with different changes of style and felicities of invention.

It is recorded by Budgell that of the characters feigned or exhibited in *The Spectator* the favourite of Addison was Sir Roger de Coverley, of whom he had formed a very delicate and discriminated idea, which he would not suffer to be violated; and therefore when Steele had shown him innocently picking up a girl in the Temple, and taking her to a tavern, he drew upon himself so much of his friend's indignation that he was forced to appease him by a promise of forbearing Sir Roger for the time to come.

The reason which induced Cervantes to bring his hero to the grave, 'para mi solo nacio Don Quixote, y yo para el',° made Addison declare, with an undue vehemence of expression, that he would kill Sir Roger; being of opinion that they were born for one another, and that any other hand would do him wrong.

It may be doubted whether Addison ever filled up his original delineation. He describes his Knight as having his imagination somewhat warped; but of this perversion he has made very little use. The irregularities in Sir Roger's conduct seem not so much the effects of a mind deviating from the beaten track of life by the perpetual pressure of some overwhelming idea as of habitual rusticity, and that negligence which solitary grandeur naturally generates.

The variable weather of the mind, the flying vapours of incipient madness, which from time to time cloud reason without eclipsing it, it requires so much nicety to exhibit that Addison seems to have been deterred from prosecuting his own design.

To Sir Roger, who, as a country gentleman, appears to be a Tory, or, as it is gently expressed, an adherent to the landed interest, is opposed Sir Andrew Freeport, a new man, a wealthy merchant, zealous for the moneyed interest, and a Whig. Of this contrariety of opinions it is probable more consequences were at first intended than could be produced when the resolution was taken to exclude party from the paper. Sir Andrew does but little, and that little seems not to have pleased Addison, who, when he dismissed him from the club, changed his opinions. Steele had made him, in the true spirit of unfeeling commerce, declare that he 'would not build an hospital for idle people'; but at last he buys land, settles in the country, and builds not a manufactory, but an hospital for twelve old husbandmen, for men with whom a merchant has little acquaintance, and whom he commonly considers with little kindness.

Of essays thus elegant, thus instructive, and thus commodiously distributed, it is natural to suppose the approbation general and the sale numerous. I once heard it observed that the sale may be calculated by the product of the tax,° related in the last number to produce more than twenty pounds a week, and therefore stated at one and twenty pounds, or three pounds ten shillings a day: this, at a half-penny a paper, will give sixteen hundred and eighty for the daily number.

This sale is not great; yet this, if Swift be credited, was likely to grow less; for he declares that 'the Spectator,' whom he ridicules for his endless mention of the 'fair sex,' had before his recess wearied his readers.

The next year (1713), in which *Cato* came upon the stage, was the grand climacteric of Addison's reputation. Upon the death of Cato he had, as is said, planned a tragedy in the time of his travels, and had for several years the four first acts finished, which were shown to such as were likely to spread their admiration. They were seen by Pope, and by Cibber, who relates that Steele when he took back the copy told him, in the despicable cant of literary modesty, that, whatever spirit his friend had shown in the composition, he doubted whether he would have courage sufficient to expose it to the censure of a British audience.

The time, however, was now come when those who affected to think liberty in danger affected likewise to think that a stage-play might preserve it; and Addison was importuned, in the name of the tutelary deities of Britain, to show his courage and his zeal by finishing his design.

To resume his work he seemed perversely and unaccountably unwilling; and by a request which perhaps he wished to be denied desired Mr Hughes° to add a fifth act. Hughes supposed him serious; and, undertaking the supplement, brought in a few days some scenes for his examination: but he had in the mean time gone to work himself, and produced half an act, which he afterwards completed, but with brevity irregularly disproportionate to the foregoing parts; like a task performed with reluctance, and hurried to its conclusion.

It may yet be doubted whether *Cato* was made public by any change of the author's purpose; for Dennis° charged him with raising prejudices in his own favour by false positions of preparatory criticism, and with 'poisoning the town' by contradicting in *The Spectator* the established rule of poetical justice, because his own hero, with all his virtues, was to fall before a tyrant. The fact is certain; the motives we must guess.

Addison was, I believe, sufficiently disposed to bar all avenues against all danger. When Pope brought him the prologue, which is properly accommodated to the play, there were these words, 'Britons, arise, be worth like this approved'; meaning nothing more than, Britons, erect and exalt yourselves to the approbation of public virtue. Addison was frighted lest he should be thought a promoter of insurrection, and the line was liquidated to 'Britons, attend'.

Now, 'heavily in clouds came on the day, the great, the important day',° when Addison was to stand the hazard of the theatre. That there might, however, be left as little to hazard as was possible on the first night, Steele, as himself relates, undertook to pack an audience. This, says Pope, had been tried for the first time in favour of *The Distrest Mother*;° and was now, with more efficacy, practised for *Cato*.

The danger was soon over. The whole nation was at that time on fire with faction. The Whigs applauded every line in which Liberty was mentioned, as a satire on the Tories; and the Tories echoed every clap, to show that the satire was unfelt. The story of Bolingbroke is well known. He called Booth to his box, and gave him fifty guineas for defending the cause of Liberty so well against a perpetual dictator.° The Whigs, says Pope, design a second present, when they can accompany it with as good a sentence.

The play, supported thus by the emulation of factious praise, was acted night after night for a longer time than, I believe, the public had allowed to any drama before; and the author, as Mrs Porter° long afterwards related, wandered through the whole exhibition behind the scenes with restless and unappeasable solicitude.

When it was printed notice was given that the Queen would be pleased if it was dedicated to her; 'but as he had designed that compliment elsewhere, he found himself obliged,' says Tickell, 'by his own duty on the one hand, and his honour on the other, to send it into the world without any dedication.'

Human happiness has always its abatements; the brightest sunshine of success is not without a cloud. No sooner was *Cato* offered to the reader than it was attacked by the acute malignity of Dennis, with all the violence of angry criticism. Dennis, though equally zealous, and probably by his temper more furious than Addison, for what they called liberty, and though a flatterer of the Whig ministry, could not sit quiet at a successful play; but was eager to tell friends and enemies that they had misplaced their admirations. The world was too stubborn for instruction: with the fate of the censurer of Corneille's *Cid* his animadversions showed his anger without effect, and *Cato* continued to be praised.

Pope had now an opportunity of courting the friendship of Addison by vilifying his old enemy, and could give resentment its full play without appearing to revenge himself. He therefore published *A Narrative of the Madness of John Dennis*; a performance which left the objections to the play in their full force, and therefore discovered more desire of vexing the critic than of defending the poet.

Addison, who was no stranger to the world, probably saw the selfishness of Pope's friendship, and, resolving that he should have the consequences of his officiousness to himself, informed Dennis by Steele that he was sorry for the insult; and that whenever he should think fit to answer his remarks, he would do it in a manner to which nothing could be objected.

The greatest weakness of the play is in the scenes of love, which are said by Pope to have been added to the original plan upon a subsequent review, in compliance with the popular practice of the stage. Such an authority it is hard to reject, yet the love is so intimately mingled with the whole action that it cannot easily be thought extrinsic and adventitious; for if it were taken away what would be left? Or how were the four acts filled in the first draught?

At the publication the Wits seemed proud to pay their attendance with encomiastic verses. The best are from an unknown hand, which will perhaps lose somewhat of their praise when the author is known to be Jeffreys.°

Cato had yet other honours. It was censured as a party-play by 'A Scholar of Oxford', and defended in a favourable examination by Dr Sewel.° It was translated by Salvini into Italian, and acted at Florence; and by the Jesuits of St Omer's into Latin, and played by their pupils. Of this version a copy was sent to Mr Addison: it is to be wished that it could be found, for the sake of comparing their version of the soliloquy with that of Bland.

A tragedy was written on the same subject by Des Champs, a French poet, which was translated, with a criticism on the English play. But the translator and the critic are now forgotten.

Dennis lived on unanswered, and, therefore, little read: Addison knew the policy° of literature too well to make his enemy important by drawing the attention of the public upon a criticism which, though sometimes intemperate, was often irrefragable.

While *Cato* was upon the stage another daily paper, called *The Guardian*, was published by Steele. To this Addison gave great assistance, whether occasionally or by previous engagement is not known.

The character of 'Guardian' was too narrow and too serious: it might properly enough admit both the duties and the decencies of life, but seemed not to include literary speculations, and was in some degree violated by merriment and burlesque. What had the Guardian of the Lizards° to do with clubs of tall or of little men, with nests of ants, or with Strada's prolusions?

Of this paper nothing is necessary to be said but that it found many contributors, and that it was a continuation of *The Spectator*, with the same elegance and the same variety, till some unlucky sparkle from a Tory paper set Steele's politics on fire, and wit at once blazed into faction. He was soon too hot for neutral topics, and quitted *The Guardian* to write *The Englishman*.

The papers of Addison are marked in *The Spectator* by one of the letters in the name of *Clio*, and in *The Guardian* by *a hand*; whether it was, as Tickell pretends to think, that he was unwilling to usurp the praise of others, or as Steele, with far greater likelihood, insinuates, that he could not without discontent impart to others any of his own. I have heard that his avidity did not satisfy itself with the air of renown, but that with great eagerness he laid hold on his proportion of the profits.

Many of these papers were written with powers truly comic, with nice discrimination of characters, and accurate observation of natural or accidental deviations from propriety, but it was not supposed that he had tried a comedy on the stage till Steele, after his death, declared him the author of *The Drummer*; this, however, Steele did not know to be true by any direct testimony, for when Addison put the play into his hands he only told him it was the work of 'a Gentleman in the Company'; and when it was received, as is confessed, with cold disapprobation, he was probably less willing to claim it. Tickell omitted it in his collection; but the testimony of Steele and the total silence of any other claimant has determined the public to assign it to

Addison, and it is now printed with his other poetry. Steele carried *The Drummer* to the playhouse, and afterwards to the press, and sold the copy for fifty guineas.

To the opinion of Steele may be added the proof supplied by the play itself, of which the characters are such as Addison would have delineated and the tendency such as Addison would have promoted. That it should have been ill received would raise wonder did we not daily see the capricious distribution of theatrical praise.

He was not all this time an indifferent spectator of public affairs. He wrote as different exigences required (in 1707) *The Present State of the War, and the Necessity of an Augmentation*; which, however judicious, being written on temporary topics and exhibiting no peculiar powers, laid hold on no attention, and has naturally sunk by its own weight into neglect. This cannot be said of the few papers entitled *The Whig Examiner*, in which is employed all the force of gay malevolence and humorous satire. Of this paper, which just appeared and expired, Swift remarks with exultation that 'it is now down among the dead men'. He might well rejoice at the death of that which he could not have killed. Every reader of every party, since personal malice is past and the papers which once inflamed the nation are read only as effusions of wit, must wish for more of the *Whig Examiners*; for on no occasion was the genius of Addison more vigorously exerted, and on none did the superiority of his powers more evidently appear. His *Trial of Count Tariff*, written to expose the treaty of commerce with France, lived no longer than the question that produced it.

Not long afterwards an attempt was made to revive *The Spectator*, at a time indeed by no means favourable to literature, when the succession of a new family to the throne filled the nation with anxiety, discord, and confusion; and either the turbulence of the times or the satiety of the readers put a stop to the publication after an experiment of eighty numbers, which were afterwards collected into an eighth volume, perhaps more valuable than any one of those that went before it. Addison produced more than a fourth part, and the other contributors are by no means unworthy of appearing as his associates. The time that had passed during the suspension of *The Spectator*, though it had not lessened his power of humour, seems to have increased his disposition to seriousness: the proportion of his religious to his comic papers is greater than in the former series.

The Spectator from its recommencement was published only three times a week; and no discriminative marks were added to the papers. To Addison Tickell has ascribed twenty-three.

The Spectator had many contributors; and Steele, whose negligence kept him always in a hurry, when it was his turn to furnish a paper, called loudly for the letters, of which Addison, whose materials were more, made little use; having recourse to sketches and hints, the product of his former studies, which he now reviewed and completed: among these are named by Tickell the *Essays on Wit*, those on the *Pleasures of the Imagination* and the *Criticism on Milton*.

When the House of Hanover took possession of the throne it was reasonable to expect that the zeal of Addison would be suitably rewarded. Before the arrival of King George he was made secretary to the regency, and was required by his office to send notice to Hanover that the Queen was dead, and that the throne was vacant. To do this would not have been difficult to any man but Addison, who was so overwhelmed with the greatness of the event and so distracted by choice of expression that the lords, who could not wait for the niceties of criticism, called Mr Southwell, a clerk in the house, and ordered him to dispatch the message.° Southwell readily told what was necessary in the common style of business, and valued himself upon having done what was too hard for Addison.

He was better qualified for *The Freeholder*, a paper which he published twice a week, from Dec. 23, 1715, to the middle of the next year. This was undertaken in defence of the established government, sometimes with argument, sometimes with mirth. In argument he had many equals; but his humour was singular and matchless. Bigotry itself must be delighted with the Tory Fox-hunter.

There are, however, some strokes less elegant and less decent; such as the Pretender's Journal, in which one topic of ridicule is his poverty. This mode of abuse had been employed by Milton against King Charles II.

> . . . *Jacobaei*
> Centum exulantis viscera marsupii regis.°

And Oldmixon delights to tell of some alderman of London that he had more money than the exiled princes; but that which might be expected from Milton's savageness or Oldmixon's meanness was not suitable to the delicacy of Addison.

Steele thought the humour of *The Freeholder* too nice and gentle for such noisy times; and is reported to have said that the ministry made use of a lute when they should have called for a trumpet.

This year (1716) he married the Countess dowager of Warwick, whom he had solicited by a very long and anxious courtship, perhaps with behaviour not very unlike that of Sir Roger to his disdainful widow; and who, I am afraid, diverted herself often by playing with his passion. He is said to have first known her by becoming tutor to her son. 'He formed,' said Tonson,° 'the design of getting that lady from the time when he was first recommended into the family.' In what part of his life he obtained the recommendation, or how long, and in what manner he lived in the family, I know not. His advances at first were certainly timorous, but grew bolder as his reputation and influence increased; till at last the lady was persuaded to marry him on terms much like those on which a Turkish princess is espoused, to whom the Sultan is reported to pronounce, 'Daughter, I give thee this man for thy slave.' The marriage, if uncontradicted report can be credited, made no addition to his happiness: it neither found them nor made them equal. She always remembered her own rank, and thought herself entitled to treat with very little ceremony the tutor of her son. Rowe's ballad of *The Despairing Shepherd* is said to have been written, either before or after marriage, upon this memorable pair; and it is certain that Addison has left behind him no encouragement for ambitious love.

The year after (1717) he rose to his highest elevation, being made Secretary of State. For this employment he might be justly supposed qualified by long practice of business and by his regular ascent through other offices: but expectation is often disappointed: it is universally confessed that he was unequal to the duties of his place. In the House of Commons he could not speak, and therefore was useless to the defence of the government. In the office, says Pope, he could not issue an order without losing his time in quest of fine expressions. What he gained in rank, he lost in credit; and, finding by experience his own inability, was forced to solicit his dismission, with a pension of fifteen hundred pounds a year. His friends palliated this relinquishment, of which both friends and enemies knew the true reason, with an account of declining health, and the necessity of recess and quiet.

He now returned to his vocation, and began to plan literary occupations for his future life. He purposed a tragedy on the death of Socrates; a story of which, as Tickell remarks, the basis is narrow, and to which I know not how love could have been appended. There would, however, have been no want either of virtue in the sentiments, or elegance in the language.

He engaged in a nobler work, a defence of the *Christian Religion*, of which part was published after his death; and he designed to have made a new poetical version of the Psalms.

These pious compositions Pope imputed to a selfish motive, upon the credit, as he owns, of Tonson, who, having quarrelled with Addison and not loving him, said that, when he laid down the secretary's office, he intended to take orders, and obtain a bishopric, 'for,' said he, 'I always thought him a priest in his heart.'

That Pope should have thought this conjecture of Tonson worth remembrance is a proof, but indeed so far as I have found, the only proof, that he retained some malignity from their ancient rivalry. Tonson pretended but to guess it; no other mortal ever suspected it; and Pope might have reflected that a man who had been Secretary of State in the ministry of Sunderland knew a nearer way° to a bishopric than by defending religion, or translating the Psalms.

It is related that he had once a design to make an English Dictionary, and that he considered Dr Tillotson° as the writer of highest authority. There was formerly sent to me by Mr Locker, clerk of the Leathersellers' Company, who was eminent for curiosity and literature, a collection of examples selected from Tillotson's works, as Locker said, by Addison. It came too late to be of use,° so I inspected it but slightly, and remember it indistinctly. I thought the passages too short.

Addison, however, did not conclude his life in peaceful studies, but relapsed when he was near his end to a political dispute.

It so happened that (1718–19) a controversy was agitated with great vehemence between those friends of long continuance, Addison and Steele. It may be asked, in the language of Homer, what power or what cause could set them at variance.° The subject of their dispute was of great importance. The Earl of Sunderland proposed an act called the *Peerage Bill*, by which the number of peers should be fixed, and the king restrained from any new creation of nobility, unless when an old family should be extinct. To this the Lords would naturally agree; and the king, who was yet little acquainted with his own prerogative and, as is now well known, almost indifferent to the possessions of the Crown, had been persuaded to consent. The only difficulty was found among the Commons, who were not likely to approve the perpetual exclusion of themselves and their posterity. The bill therefore was eagerly opposed, and among others by Sir Robert Walpole, whose speech was published.

The Lords might think their dignity diminished by improper advancements, and particularly by the introduction of twelve new peers at once, to produce a majority of Tories in the last reign; an act of authority violent enough, yet certainly legal, and by no means to be compared with that contempt of national right, with which some time afterwards, by the instigation of Whiggism, the Commons, chosen by the people for three years, chose themselves for seven.° But whatever might be the disposition of the Lords, the people had no wish to increase their power. The tendency of the bill, as Steele observed in a letter to the Earl of Oxford, was to introduce an aristocracy; for a majority in the House of Lords so limited would have been despotic and irresistible.

To prevent this subversion of the ancient establishment, Steele, whose pen readily seconded his political passions, endeavoured to alarm the nation by a pamphlet called *The Plebeian*; to this an answer was published by Addison, under the title of *The Old Whig*, in which it is not discovered that Steele was then known to be the advocate for the Commons. Steele replied by a second *Plebeian*, and, whether by ignorance or by courtesy, confined himself to his question without any personal notice of his opponent. Nothing hitherto was committed against the laws of friendship or proprieties of decency; but controvertists cannot long retain their kindness for each other. *The Old Whig* answered *The Plebeian*, and could not forbear some contempt of 'little *Dicky*,° whose trade it was to write pamphlets.' Dicky, however, did not lose his settled veneration for his friend, but contented himself with quoting some lines of *Cato*, which were at once detection and reproof. The bill was laid aside during that session, and Addison died before the next, in which its commitment was rejected by two hundred sixty-five to one hundred seventy-seven.

Every reader surely must regret that these two illustrious friends, after so many years passed in confidence and endearment, in unity of interest, conformity of opinion, and fellowship of study, should finally part in acrimonious opposition. Such a controversy was 'Bellum plusquam civile',° as Lucan expresses it. Why could not faction find other advocates? But, among the uncertainties of the human state, we are doomed to number the instability of friendship.

Of this dispute I have little knowledge but from the *Biographia Britannica*.° *The Old Whig* is not inserted in Addison's works, nor is it mentioned by Tickell in his *Life*; why it was omitted the biographers doubtless give the true reason: the fact was too recent, and those who had been heated in the contention were not yet cool.

The necessity of complying with times and of sparing persons is the great impediment of biography. History may be formed from permanent monuments and records; but Lives can only be written from personal knowledge, which is growing every day less, and in a short time is lost for ever. What is known can seldom be immediately told, and when it might be told it is no longer known. The delicate features of the mind, the nice discriminations of character, and the minute peculiarities of conduct are soon obliterated; and it is surely better that caprice, obstinacy, frolic, and folly, however they might delight in the description, should be silently forgotten than that by wanton merriment and unseasonable detection a pang should be given to a widow, a daughter, a brother, or a friend. As the process of these narratives is now bringing me among my contemporaries I begin to feel myself *walking upon ashes under which the fire is not extinguished*,° and coming to the time of which it will be proper rather to say *nothing that is false, than all that is true*.

The end of this useful life was now approaching.—Addison had for some time been oppressed by shortness of breath, which was now aggravated by a dropsy; and, finding his danger pressing, he prepared to die conformably to his own precepts and professions.

During this lingering decay he sent, as Pope relates, a message by the Earl of Warwick° to Mr Gay, desiring to see him: Gay, who had not visited him for some time before, obeyed the summons, and found himself received with great kindness. The purpose for which the interview had been solicited was then discovered: Addison told him that he had injured him, but that if he recovered he would recompense him. What the injury was he did not explain, nor did Gay ever know; but supposed that some preferment designed for him had, by Addison's intervention, been withheld.

Lord Warwick was a young man of very irregular life, and perhaps of loose opinions. Addison, for whom he did not want respect, had very diligently endeavoured to reclaim him; but his arguments and expostulations had no effect. One experiment, however, remained to be tried: when he found his life near its end he directed the young lord to be called, and when he desired with great tenderness to hear his last injunctions, told him, 'I have sent for you that you may see how a Christian can die.' What effect this awful scene had on the earl I know not; he likewise died himself in a short time.

In Tickell's excellent Elegy on his friend are these lines:

> He taught us how to live; and, oh! too high
> The price of knowledge, taught us how to die.

In which he alludes, as he told Dr Young, to this moving interview.

Having given directions to Mr Tickell for the publication of his works, and dedicated them on his death-bed to his friend Mr Craggs, he died June 17, 1719, at Holland-house, leaving no child but a daughter.

Of his virtue it is a sufficient testimony that the resentment of party has transmitted no charge of any crime. He was not one of those who are praised only after death; for his merit was so generally acknowledged that Swift, having observed that his election passed without a contest, adds that if he had proposed himself for king, he would hardly have been refused.

His zeal for his party did not extinguish his kindness for the merit of his opponents: when he was secretary in Ireland he refused to intermit his acquaintance with Swift.

Of his habits, or external manners, nothing is so often mentioned as that timorous or sullen taciturnity, which his friends called modesty by too mild a name. Steele mentions with great tenderness 'that remarkable bashfulness, which is a cloak that hides and muffles merit'; and tells us that 'his abilities were covered only by modesty, which doubles the beauties which are seen, and gives credit and esteem to all that are concealed'. Chesterfield affirms that 'Addison was the most timorous and awkward man that he ever saw'. And Addison, speaking of his own deficience in conversation, used to say of himself that, with respect to intellectual wealth, 'he could draw bills for a thousand pounds, though he had not a guinea in his pocket'.

That he wanted current coin for ready payment, and by that want was often obstructed and distressed; that he was oppressed by an improper and ungraceful timidity, every testimony concurs to prove: but Chesterfield's representation is doubtless hyperbolical. That man cannot be supposed very unexpert in the arts of conversation and practice of life who, without fortune or alliance, by his usefulness and dexterity became secretary of state, and who died at forty-seven, after having not only stood long in the highest rank of wit and literature, but filled one of the most important offices of state.

The time in which he lived had reason to lament his obstinacy of silence, 'for he was', said Steele, 'above all men in that talent called humour, and enjoyed it in such perfection that I have often reflected, after a night spent with him apart from all the world, that I had had the pleasure of conversing with an intimate acquaintance of Terence and Catullus, who had all their wit and nature, heightened with humour more exquisite and delightful than any other man ever possessed.' This is the fondness of a friend; let us hear what is told us by a rival. 'Addison's conversation,' says Pope, 'had something in it more charming than I have found in any other man. But this was only when familiar: before strangers, or perhaps a single stranger, he preserved his dignity by a stiff silence.'

This modesty was by no means inconsistent with a very high opinion of his own merit. He demanded to be the first name in modern wit; and, with Steele to echo him, used to depreciate Dryden, whom Pope and Congreve defended against them. There is no reason to doubt that he suffered too much pain from the prevalence of Pope's poetical reputation; nor is it without strong reason suspected that by some disingenuous acts he endeavoured to obstruct it: Pope was not the only man whom he insidiously injured, though the only man of whom he could be afraid.

His own powers were such as might have satisfied him with conscious excellence. Of very extensive learning he has indeed given no proofs. He seems to have had small acquaintance with the sciences, and to have read little except Latin and French; but of the Latin poets his *Dialogues on Medals* show that he had perused the works with great diligence and skill. The abundance of his own mind left him little need of adventitious sentiments: his wit always could suggest what the occasion demanded. He had read with critical eyes the important volume of human life, and knew the heart of man from the depths of stratagem to the surface of affectation.

What he knew he could easily communicate. 'This,' says Steele, 'was particular in this writer, that when he had taken his resolution or made his plan for what he designed to write, he would walk about a room and dictate it into language with as much freedom and ease as any one could write it down, and attend to the coherence and grammar of what he dictated.'

Pope, who can be less suspected of favouring his memory, declares that he wrote very fluently, but was slow and scrupulous in correcting; that many of his *Spectators* were written very fast, and sent immediately to the press; and that it seemed to be for his advantage not to have time for much revisal.

'He would alter,' says Pope, 'any thing to please his friends, before publication, but would not retouch his pieces afterwards: and I believe not one word in *Cato* to which I made an objection was suffered to stand.'

The last line of *Cato* is Pope's, having been originally written

> And, oh! 'twas this that ended Cato's life.

Pope might have made more objections to the six concluding lines. In the first couplet the words 'from hence' are improper, and the second line is taken from Dryden's *Virgil*. Of the next couplet the first verse, being included in the second, is therefore useless, and in the third *Discord* is made to produce *Strife*.

Of the course of Addison's familiar day before his marriage Pope has given a detail. He had in the house with him Budgell, and perhaps Philips. His chief companions were Steele, Budgell, Philips, Carey, Davenant, and Colonel Brett.° With one or other of these he always breakfasted. He studied all morning, then dined at a tavern, and went afterwards to Button's.

Button had been a servant in the Countess of Warwick's family, who, under the patronage of Addison, kept a coffee-house on the south side of Russell Street, about two doors from Covent Garden. Here it was that the wits of that time used to assemble. It is said that when Addison had suffered any vexation from the Countess he withdrew the company from Button's house.

From the coffee-house he went again to a tavern, where he often sat late and drank too much wine. In the bottle discontent seeks for comfort, cowardice for courage, and bashfulness for confidence. It is not unlikely that Addison was first seduced to excess by the manumission which he obtained from the servile timidity of his sober hours. He that feels oppression from the presence of those to whom he knows himself superior will desire to set loose his powers of conversation; and who that ever asked succour from Bacchus was able to preserve himself from being enslaved by his auxiliary?

Among those friends it was that Addison displayed the elegance of his colloquial accomplishments, which may easily be supposed such as Pope represents them. The remark of Mandeville, who, when he had passed an evening in his company, declared that he was a parson in tie-wig,° can detract little from his character: he was always reserved to strangers, and was not incited to uncommon freedom by a character like that of Mandeville.

From any minute knowledge of his familiar manners the intervention of sixty years has now debarred us. Steele once promised Congreve and the public a complete description of his character; but the promises of authors are like the vows of lovers. Steele thought no more on his design, or thought on it with anxiety that at last disgusted him, and left his friend in the hands of Tickell.

One slight lineament of his character Swift has preserved. It was hi practice when he found any man invincibly wrong to flatter his opinions by acquiescence, and sink him yet deeper in absurdity. This artifice of mischief was admired by Stella; and Swift seems to approve her admiration.

His works will supply some information. It appears from his various pictures of the world that, with all his bashfulness, he had conversed with many distinct classes of men, had surveyed their ways with very diligent observation, and marked with great acuteness the effects of different modes of life. He was a man in whose presence nothing reprehensible was out of danger: quick in discerning whatever was wrong or ridiculous, and not unwilling to expose it. 'There are,' says Steele, 'in his writings many oblique strokes upon some of the wittiest men of the age.' His delight was more to excite merriment than detestation, and he detects follies rather than crimes.

If any judgement be made from his books of his moral character nothing will be found but purity and excellence. Knowledge of mankind indeed, less extensive than that of Addison, will show that to write and to live are very different. Many who praise virtue do no more than praise it. Yet it is reasonable to believe that Addison's professions and practice were at no great variance, since, amidst that storm of faction in which most of his life was passed, though his station made him conspicuous and his activity made him formidable, the character given him by his friends was never contradicted by his enemies: of those with whom interest or opinion united him he had not only the esteem, but the kindness; and of others, whom the violence of opposition drove against him, though he might lose the love, he retained the reverence.

It is justly observed by Tickell that he employed wit on the side of virtue and religion. He not only made the proper use of wit himself, but taught it to others; and from his time it has been generally subservient to the cause of reason and of truth. He has dissipated the prejudice that had long connected gaiety with vice, and easiness of manners with laxity of principles. He has restored virtue to its dignity, and taught innocence not to be ashamed. This is an elevation of literary character, *above all Greek, above all Roman fame*.° No greater felicity can genius attain than that of having purified intellectual pleasure, separated mirth from indecency, and wit from licentiousness; of having taught a succession of writers to bring elegance and gaiety to the aid of goodness; and, if I may use expressions yet more awful, of having *turned many to righteousness*.°

Addison, in his life and for some time afterwards, was considered by the greater part of readers as supremely excelling both in poetry and criticism. Part of his reputation may be probably ascribed to the advancement of his fortune: when, as Swift observes, he became a statesman, and saw poets waiting at his levee, it is no wonder that praise was accumulated upon him. Much likewise may be more honourably ascribed to his personal character: he who, if he had claimed it, might have obtained the diadem, was not likely to be denied the laurel.

But time quickly puts an end to artificial and accidental fame; and Addison is to pass through futurity protected only by his genius. Every name which kindness or interest once raised too high is in danger lest the next age should by the vengeance of criticism sink it in the same proportion. A great writer° has lately styled him 'an indifferent poet, and a worse critic'.

His poetry is first to be considered; of which it must be confessed that it has not often those felicities of diction which give lustre to sentiments, or that vigour of sentiment that animates diction: there is little of ardour, vehemence, or transport; there is very rarely the awfulness of grandeur, and not very often the splendour of elegance. He thinks justly; but he thinks faintly. This is his general character; to which, doubtless, many single passages will furnish exceptions.

Yet, if he seldom reaches supreme excellence, he rarely sinks into dullness, and is still more rarely entangled in absurdity. He did not trust his powers enough to be negligent. There is in most of his compositions a calmness and equability, deliberate and cautious, sometimes with little that delights, but seldom with any thing that offends.

Of this kind seem to be his poems to Dryden, to Somers, and to the King. His *Ode on St Cecilia* has been imitated by Pope, and has something in it of Dryden's vigour. Of his *Account of the English Poets* he used to speak as 'a poor thing'; but it is not worse than his usual strain. He has said, not very judiciously, in his character of Waller:

> Thy verse could show ev'n Cromwell's innocence,
> And compliment the storms that bore him hence.
> O! had thy Muse not come an age too soon,
> But seen great Nassau on the British throne,
> How had his triumph glitter'd in thy page!—

What is this but to say that he who could compliment Cromwell had been the proper poet for King William? Addison, however, never printed the piece.

The *Letter from Italy* has been always praised, but has never been praised beyond its merit. It is more correct, with less appearance of labour, and more elegant, with less ambition of ornament, than any other of his poems. There is, however, one broken metaphor, of which notice may properly be taken:

> Fir'd with that name—
> I bridle in my struggling Muse with pain,
> That longs to launch into a nobler strain.

To *bridle* a *goddess* is no very delicate idea; but why must she be *bridled*? Because she *longs to launch*; an act which was never hindered by a *bridle*: and whither will she *launch*? Into a *nobler strain*. She is in the first line a *horse*, in the second a *boat*; and the care of the poet is to keep his *horse* or his *boat* from *singing*.

The next composition is the far-famed *Campaign*, which Dr Warton has termed a 'Gazette° in Rhyme', with harshness not often used by the good nature of his criticism. Before a censure so severe is admitted, let us consider that war is a frequent subject of poetry, and then enquire who has described it with more justness and force. Many of our own writers tried their powers upon this year of victory, yet Addison's is confessedly the best performance; his poem is the work of a man not blinded by the dust of learning: his images are not borrowed merely from books. The superiority which he confers upon his hero is not personal prowess, and 'mighty bone', but deliberate intrepidity, a calm command of his passions, and the power of consulting his own mind in the midst of danger. The rejection and contempt of fiction° is rational and manly.

It may be observed that the last line is imitated by Pope;

> Marlb'rough's exploits appear divinely bright,
> .   .   .   .   .   .
> Rais'd of themselves, their genuine charms they boast,
> And those that paint them truest, praise them most.

This Pope had in his thoughts; but, not knowing how to use what was not his own, he spoiled the thought when he had borrowed it:

> The well-sung woes shall soothe my ghost;
> He best can paint them who shall feel them most.°

Martial exploits may be *painted*; perhaps *woes* may be *painted*; but they are surely not *painted* by being *well-sung*: it is not easy to paint in song or to sing in colours.

No passage in *The Campaign* has been more often mentioned than the simile of the Angel,° which is said in *The Tatler* to be 'one of the noblest thoughts that ever entered into the heart of man', and is therefore worthy of attentive consideration. Let it be first enquired whether it be a simile. A poetical simile is the discovery of likeness between two actions in their general nature dissimilar, or of causes terminating by different operations in some resemblance of effect. But the mention of another like consequence from a like cause, or of a like performance by a like agency, is not a simile, but an exemplification. It is not a simile to say that the Thames waters fields as the Po waters fields; or that as Hecla vomits flames in Iceland, so Ætna vomits flames in Sicily. When Horace says of Pindar that he pours his violence and rapidity of verse as a river swollen with rain rushes from the mountain; or of himself that his genius wanders in quest of poetical decorations, as the bee wanders to collect honey; he, in either case, produces a simile: the mind is impressed with the resemblance of things generally unlike, as unlike as intellect and body. But if Pindar had been described as writing with the copiousness and grandeur of Homer, or Horace had told that he reviewed and finished his own poetry with the same care as Isocrates polished his orations, instead of similitude he would have exhibited almost identity: he would have given the same portraits with different names. In the poem now examined, when the English are represented as gaining a fortified pass by repetition of attack and perseverance of resolution, their obstinacy of courage and vigour of onset is well illustrated by the sea that breaks with incessant battery the dikes of Holland. This is a simile: but when Addison, having celebrated the beauty of Marlborough's person, tells us that 'Achilles thus was formed with every grace', here is no simile, but a mere exemplification. A simile may be compared to lines converging at a point and is more excellent as the lines approach from greater distance: an exemplification may be considered as two parallel lines which run together without approximation, never far separated, and never joined.

Marlborough is so like the angel in the poem that the action of both is almost the same, and performed by both in the same manner. Marlborough 'teaches the battle to rage'; the angel 'directs the storm': Marlborough is 'unmoved in peaceful thought'; the angel is 'calm and serene': Marlborough stands 'unmoved amidst the shock of hosts'; the angel rides 'calm in the whirlwind'. The lines on Marlborough are just and noble; but the simile gives almost the same images a second time.

But perhaps this thought, though hardly a simile, was remote from vulgar conceptions, and required great labour of research or dexterity of application. Of this Dr Madden,° a name which Ireland ought to honour, once gave me his opinion. 'If I had set,' said he, 'ten school-boys to write on the battle of Blenheim, and eight had brought me the Angel, I should not have been surprised.'

The opera of *Rosamond*, though it is seldom mentioned, is one of the first of Addison's compositions. The subject is well-chosen, the fiction is pleasing, and the praise of Marlborough, for which the scene gives an opportunity, is, what perhaps every human excellence must be, the product of good-luck improved by genius. The thoughts are sometimes great, and sometimes tender; the versification is easy and gay. There is doubtless some advantage in the shortness of the lines, which there is little temptation to load with expletive epithets. The dialogue seems commonly better than the songs. The two comic characters of Sir Trusty and Grideline, though of no great value, are yet such as the poet intended. Sir Trusty's account of the death of Rosamond is, I think, too grossly absurd. The whole drama is airy and elegant; engaging in its process, and pleasing in its conclusion. If Addison had cultivated the lighter parts of poetry he would probably have excelled.

The tragedy of *Cato*, which, contrary to the rule observed in selecting the works of other poets, has by the weight of its character forced its way into the late collection,° is unquestionably the noblest production of Addison's genius. Of a work so much read, it is difficult to say any thing new. About things on which the public thinks long it commonly attains to think right; and of *Cato* it has been not unjustly determined that it is rather a poem in dialogue than a drama, rather a succession of just sentiments in elegant language than a representation of natural affections, or of any state probable or possible in human life. Nothing here 'excites or assuages emotion'; here is 'no magical power of raising phantastic terror or wild anxiety'. The events are expected without solicitude, and are remembered without joy or sorrow. Of the agents we have no care: we consider not what they are doing, or what they are suffering; we wish only to know what they have to say. Cato is a being above our solicitude; a man of whom the gods take care, and whom we leave to their care with heedless confidence. To the rest, neither gods nor men can have much attention; for there is not one amongst them that strongly attracts either affection or esteem. But they are made the vehicles of such sentiments and such expression that there is scarcely a scene in the play which the reader does not wish to impress upon his memory.

When *Cato* was shown to Pope he advised the author to print it without any theatrical exhibition; supposing that it would be read more favourably than heard. Addison declared himself of the same opinion, but urged the importunity of his friends for its appearance on the stage. The emulation of parties made it successful beyond expectation, and its success has introduced or confirmed among us the use of dialogue too declamatory, of unaffecting elegance, and chill philosophy.

The universality of applause, however it might quell the censure of common mortals, had no other effect than to harden Dennis in fixed dislike; but his dislike was not merely capricious. He found and showed many faults: he showed them indeed with anger, but he found them with acuteness, such as ought to rescue his criticism from oblivion; though, at last, it will have no other life than it derives from the work which it endeavours to oppress.

Why he pays no regard to the opinion of the audience he gives his reason by remarking that

A deference is to be paid to a general applause when it appears that that applause is natural and spontaneous, but that little regard is to be had to it when it is affected and artificial; that of all the tragedies which in his memory have had vast and violent runs not one has been excellent, few have been tolerable, most have been scandalous . . . ; that when a poet writes a tragedy, who knows he has judgement and who feels he has genius, that poet presumes upon his own merit, and scorns to make a cabal; that people come coolly to the representation of such a tragedy, without any violent expectation, or delusive imagination, or invincible prepossession; that such an audience is liable to receive the impressions which the poem shall naturally make in them, and to judge by their own reason and their own judgements, and that reason and judgement are calm and serene, not formed by nature to make proselytes, and to control and lord it over the imaginations of others; but that when an author writes a tragedy who knows he has neither genius nor judgement he has recourse to the making a party, and he endeavours to make up in industry what is wanting in talent, and to supply by poetical craft the absence of poetical art: that such an author is humbly contented to raise men's passions by a plot without doors, since he despairs of doing it by that which he brings upon the stage; that party and passion and prepossession are clamorous and tumultuous things, and so much the more clamorous and tumultuous by how much the more erroneous; that they domineer and tyrannize over the imaginations of persons who want judgement, and sometimes too of those who have it, and, like a fierce and outrageous torrent, bear down all opposition before them.

He then condemns the neglect of poetical justice, which is always one of his favourite principles.

'Tis certainly the duty of every tragic poet, by the exact distribution of poetical justice, to imitate the Divine Dispensation, and to inculcate a particular Providence. 'Tis true, indeed, upon the stage of the world the wicked sometimes prosper, and the guiltless suffer. But that is permitted by the Governor of the world to show, from the attribute of his infinite justice, that there is compensation in futurity, to prove the immortality of the human soul, and the certainty of future rewards and punishments. But the poetical persons in tragedy exist no longer than the reading or the representation; the whole extent of their entity is circumscribed by those; and therefore, during that reading or representation, according to their merits or demerits, they must be punished or rewarded. If this is not done there is no impartial distribution of poetical justice, no instructive lecture of a particular Providence, and no imitation of the Divine Dispensation. And yet the author of this tragedy does not only run counter to this in the fate of his principal character, but every where throughout it makes virtue suffer and vice triumph; for not only Cato is vanquished by Caesar, but the treachery and perfidiousness of Syphax prevails over the honest simplicity and the credulity of Juba, and the sly subtlety and dissimulation of Portius over the generous frankness and open-heartedness of Marcus.

Whatever pleasure there may be in seeing crimes punished and virtue rewarded, yet, since wickedness often prospers in real life, the poet is certainly at liberty to give it prosperity on the stage. For if poetry has an imitation of reality,° how are its laws broken by exhibiting the world in its true form? The stage may sometimes gratify our wishes; but, if it be truly the *mirror of life*,° it ought to show us sometimes what we are to expect.

Dennis objects to the characters that they are not natural or reasonable; but as heroes and heroines are not beings that are seen every day, it is hard to find upon what principles their conduct shall be tried. It is, however, not useless to consider what he says of the manner in which Cato receives the account of his son's death:

Nor is the grief of Cato in the fourth act one jot more in nature than that of his son and Lucia in the third. Cato receives the news of his son's death not only with dry eyes, but with a sort of satisfaction; and in the same page sheds tears for the calamity of his country, and does the same thing in the next page upon the bare apprehension of the danger of his friends. Now, since the love of one's country is the love of one's countrymen, as I have shown upon another occasion, I desire to ask these questions: Of all our countrymen which do we love most, those whom we know, or those whom we know not? And of those whom we know which do we cherish most, our friends or our enemies? And of our friends, which are the dearest to us, those who are related to us, or those who are not? And of all our relations, for which have we most tenderness, for those who are near to us, or for those who are remote? And of our near relations which are the nearest, and consequently the dearest to us, our offspring or others? Our offspring, most certainly; as nature, or in other words Providence, has wisely contrived for the preservation of mankind. Now, does it not follow, from what has been said, that for a man to receive the news of his son's death with dry eyes, and to weep at the same time for the calamities of his country, is a wretched affectation, and a miserable inconsistency? Is not that, in plain English, to receive with dry eyes the news of the deaths of those for whose sake our country is a name so dear to us, and at the same time to shed tears for those for whose sakes our country is not a name so dear to us?

But this formidable assailant is least resistible when he attacks the probability of the action and the reasonableness of the plan. Every critical reader must remark that Addison has, with a scrupulosity almost unexampled on the English stage, confined himself in time to a single day, and in place to rigorous unity. The scene never changes, and the whole action of the play passes in the great hall of Cato's house at Utica. Much therefore is done in the hall for which any other place had been more fit; and this impropriety affords Dennis many hints of merriment and opportunities of triumph. The passage is long; but as such disquisitions are not common, and the objections are skilfully formed and vigorously urged, those who delight in critical controversy° will not think it tedious.

Upon the departure of Portius, Sempronius makes but one soliloquy, and immediately in comes Syphax, and then the two politicians are at it immediately. They lay their heads together with their snuff-boxes in their hands, as Mr Bayes° has it, and league it away. But, in the midst of that wise scene, Syphax seems to give a seasonable caution to Sempronius:

> *Syph.* But is it true, Sempronius, that your senate
> Is call'd together? Gods! thou must be cautious,
> Cato has piercing eyes.

There is a great deal of caution shown indeed, in meeting in a governor's own hall to carry on their plot against him. Whatever opinion they have of his eyes I suppose they had none of his ears, or they would never have talked at this foolish rate so near:

> Gods! thou must be cautious.

Oh! yes, very cautious: for if Cato should overhear you, and turn you off for politicians, Caesar would never take you; no, Caesar would never take you.

.   .   .   .

But let us come to the scenery of the Fifth Act. Cato appears first upon the scene, sitting in a thoughtful posture; in his hand Plato's treatise on the Immortality of the Soul, a drawn sword on the table by him. Now let us consider the place in which this sight is presented to us. The place, forsooth, is a long hall. Let us suppose that any one should place himself in this posture in the midst of one of our halls in London; that he should appear *solus*, in a sullen posture, a drawn sword on the table by him; in his hand Plato's treatise on the Immortality of the Soul, translated lately by Bernard Lintot: I desire the reader to consider whether such a person as this would pass with them who beheld him for a great patriot, a great philosopher, or a general, or for some whimsical person who fancied himself all these; and whether the people who belonged to the family would think that such a person had a design upon their midriffs or his own.

In short, that Cato should sit long enough in the aforesaid posture, in the midst of this large hall, to read over Plato's treatise on the Immortality of the Soul, which is a lecture of two long hours; that he should propose to himself to be private there upon that occasion; that he should be angry with his son for intruding there; then, that he should leave this hall upon the pretence of sleep, give himself the mortal wound in his bedchamber, and then be brought back into that hall to expire, purely to show his good-breeding, and save his friends the trouble of coming up to his bedchamber: all this appears to me to be improbable, incredible, impossible.

Such is the censure of Dennis. There is, as Dryden expresses it, perhaps 'too much horse-play in his raillery'; but if his jests are coarse, his arguments are strong. Yet as we love better to be pleased than to be taught, *Cato* is read, and the critic is neglected.

Flushed with consciousness of these detections of absurdity in the conduct, he afterwards attacked the sentiments of *Cato*; but he then amused himself with petty cavils, and minute objections.

Of Addison's smaller poems no particular mention is necessary: they have little that can employ or require a critic. The parallel of the Princes and Gods, in his verses to Kneller, is often happy, but is too well known to be quoted.

His translations, so far as I have compared them, want the exactness of a scholar. That he understood his authors cannot be doubted; but his versions will not teach others to understand them, being too licentiously paraphrastical. They are, however, for the most part smooth and easy, and, what is the first excellence of a translator, such as may be read with pleasure by those who do not know the originals.

His poetry is polished and pure: the product of a mind too judicious to commit faults, but not sufficiently vigorous to attain excellence. He has sometimes a striking line, or a shining paragraph; but in the whole he is warm rather than fervid, and shows more dexterity than strength. He was, however, one of our earliest examples of correctness.

The versification which he had learned from Dryden he debased rather than refined. His rhymes are often dissonant: in his *Georgics* he admits broken lines. He uses both triplets and alexandrines, but triplets more frequently in his translations than his other works. The mere structure of verses seems never to have engaged much of his care. But his lines are very smooth in *Rosamond*, and too smooth in *Cato*.

Addison is now to be considered as a critic; a name which the present generation is scarcely willing to allow him. His criticism is condemned as tentative or experimental rather than scientific, and he is considered as deciding by taste rather than by principles.°

It is not uncommon for those who have grown wise by the labour of others to add a little of their own, and overlook their masters. Addison is now despised by some who perhaps would never have seen his defects, but by the lights which he afforded them. That he always wrote as he would think it necessary to write now cannot be affirmed; his instructions were such as the character of his readers made proper. That general knowledge which now circulates in common talk was in his time rarely to be found. Men not professing learning were not ashamed of ignorance; and in the female world any acquaintance with books was distinguished only to be censured. His purpose was to infuse literary curiosity by gentle and unsuspected conveyance into the gay, the idle, and the wealthy; he therefore presented knowledge in the most alluring form, not lofty and austere, but accessible and familiar. When he showed them their defects, he showed them likewise that they might be easily supplied. His attempt succeeded; enquiry was awakened and comprehension expanded. An emulation of intellectual elegance was excited, and from his time to our own life has been gradually exalted, and conversation purified and enlarged.

Dryden had not many years before scattered criticism over his *Prefaces* with very little parsimony; but, though he sometimes condescended to be somewhat familiar, his manner was in general too scholastic for those who had yet their rudiments to learn, and found it not easy to understand their master. His observations were framed rather for those that were learning to write than for those that read only to talk.

An instructor like Addison was now wanting, whose remarks, being superficial, might be easily understood, and being just might prepare the mind for more attainments. Had he presented *Paradise Lost* to the public with all the pomp of system and severity of science, the criticism would perhaps have been admired, and the poem still have been neglected; but by the blandishments of gentleness and facility he has made Milton an universal favourite, with whom readers of every class think it necessary to be pleased.

He descended now and then to lower disquisitions; and by a serious display of the beauties of *Chevy Chase* exposed himself to the ridicule of 'Wagstaff', who bestowed a like pompous character on *Tom Thumb*;° and to the contempt of Dennis, who, considering the fundamental position of his criticism, that *Chevy Chase* pleases, and ought to please, because it is natural, observes 'that there is a way of deviating from nature, by bombast or tumour, which soars above nature, and enlarges images beyond their real bulk; by affectation, which forsakes nature in quest of something unsuitable; and by imbecility, which degrades nature by faintness and diminution, by obscuring its appearances and weakening its effects'. In *Chevy Chase* there is not much of either bombast or affectation; but there is chill and lifeless imbecility. The story cannot possibly be told in a manner that shall make less impression on the mind.

Before the profound observers of the present race repose too securely on the consciousness of their superiority to Addison, let them consider his *Remarks on Ovid*, in which may be found specimens of criticism sufficiently subtle and refined; let them peruse likewise his *Essays on Wit* and on *The Pleasures of Imagination*, in which he founds art on the base of nature, and draws the principles of invention from dispositions inherent in the mind of man with skill and elegance, such as his contemners will not easily attain.

As a describer of life and manners he must be allowed to stand perhaps the first of the first rank. His humour, which, as Steele observes, is peculiar to himself, is so happily diffused as to give the grace of novelty to domestic scenes and daily occurrences. He never 'outsteps the modesty of nature',° nor raises merriment or wonder by the violation of truth. His figures neither divert by distortion, nor amaze by aggravation. He copies life with so much fidelity that he can be hardly said to invent; yet his exhibitions have an air so much original that it is difficult to suppose them not merely the product of imagination.

As a teacher of wisdom he may be confidently followed. His religion has nothing in it enthusiastic or superstitious:° he appears neither weakly credulous nor wantonly sceptical; his morality is neither dangerously lax, nor impracticably rigid. All the enchantment of fancy and all the cogency of argument are employed to recommend to the reader his real interest, the care of pleasing the Author of his being.

Truth is shown sometimes as the phantom of a vision, sometimes appears half-veiled in an allegory, sometimes attracts regard in the robes of fancy, and sometimes steps forth in the confidence of reason. She wears a thousand dresses, and in all is pleasing.

Mille habet ornatus, mille decenter habet.°

His prose is the model of the middle style; on grave subjects not formal, on light occasions not groveling; pure without scrupulosity, and exact without apparent elaboration; always equable, and always easy, without glowing words or pointed sentences. Addison never deviates from his track to snatch a grace; he seeks no ambitious ornaments, and tries no hazardous innovations. His page is always luminous, but never blazes in unexpected splendour.

It was apparently his principal endeavour to avoid all harshness and severity of diction; he is therefore sometimes verbose in his transitions and connections, and sometimes descends too much to the language of conversation: yet if his language had been less idiomatical it might have lost somewhat of its genuine Anglicism. What he attempted, he performed; he is never feeble, and he did not wish to be energetic; he is never rapid, and he never stagnates. His sentences have neither studied amplitude, nor affected brevity; his periods, though not diligently rounded, are voluble and easy. Whoever wishes to attain an English style familiar but not coarse, and elegant but not ostentatious, must give his days and nights to the volumes of Addison.

Cowley

. . . .

Cowley, like other poets who have written with narrow views and, instead of tracing intellectual pleasure to its natural sources in the mind of man, paid their court to temporary prejudices, has been at one time too much praised and too much neglected at another.

Wit, like all other things subject by their nature to the choice of man, has its changes and fashions, and at different times takes different forms. About the beginning of the seventeenth century appeared a race of writers that may be termed the metaphysical° poets, of whom in a criticism on the works of Cowley it is not improper to give some account.

The metaphysical poets were men of learning, and to show their learning was their whole endeavour; but, unluckily resolving to show it in rhyme, instead of writing poetry they only wrote verses, and very often such verses as stood the trial of the finger better than of the ear; for the modulation was so imperfect that they were only found to be verses by counting the syllables.

If the father of criticism° has rightly denominated poetry τέχνη μιμητική, *an imitative art*, these writers will without great wrong lose their right to the name of poets, for they cannot be said to have imitated any thing: they neither copied nature nor life; neither painted the forms of matter nor represented the operations of intellect.

Those however who deny them to be poets allow them to be wits. Dryden confesses of himself and his contemporaries that they fall below Donne in wit, but maintains that they surpass him in poetry.

If wit be well described by Pope as being 'that which has been often thought, but was never before so well expressed',° they certainly never attained nor ever sought it, for they endeavoured to be singular in their thoughts, and were careless of their diction. But Pope's account of wit is undoubtedly erroneous; he depresses it below its natural dignity, and reduces it from strength of thought to happiness of language.

If by a more noble and more adequate conception that be considered as wit which is at once natural and new, that which though not obvious is, upon its first production, acknowledged to be just; if it be that which he that never found it wonders how he missed; to wit of this kind the metaphysical poets have seldom risen. Their thoughts are often new, but seldom natural; they are not obvious, but neither are they just; and the reader, far from wondering that he missed them, wonders more frequently by what perverseness of industry they were ever found.

But wit, abstracted from its effects upon the hearer, may be more rigorously and philosophically considered as a kind of *discordia concors*;° a combination of dissimilar images, or discovery of occult resemblances in things apparently unlike. Of wit, thus defined, they have more than enough. The most heterogeneous ideas are yoked by violence together;° nature and art are ransacked for illustrations, comparisons, and allusions; their learning instructs, and their subtlety surprises; but the reader commonly thinks his improvement dearly bought, and, though he sometimes admires, is seldom pleased.

From this account of their compositions it will be readily inferred that they were not successful in representing or moving the affections. As they were wholly employed on something unexpected and surprising they had no regard to that uniformity of sentiment which enables us to conceive and to excite the pains and the pleasure of other minds: they never enquired what on any occasion they should have said or done, but wrote rather as beholders than partakers of human nature; as beings looking upon good and evil, impassive and at leisure; as Epicurean deities making remarks on the actions of men and the vicissitudes of life, without interest and without emotion. Their courtship was void of fondness and their lamentation of sorrow. Their wish was only to say what they hoped had been never said before.

Nor was the sublime more within their reach than the pathetic; for they never attempted that comprehension and expanse of thought which at once fills the whole mind, and of which the first effect is sudden astonishment, and the second rational admiration. Sublimity is produced by aggregation, and littleness by dispersion. Great thoughts are always general,° and consist in positions not limited by exceptions, and in descriptions not descending to minuteness. It is with great propriety that subtlety, which in its original import means exility of particles, is taken in its metaphorical meaning for nicety of distinction. Those writers who lay on the watch for novelty could have little hope of greatness; for great things cannot have escaped former observation. Their attempts were always analytic: they broke every image into fragments, and could no more represent by their slender conceits and laboured particularities the prospects of nature or the scenes of life than he who dissects a sunbeam with a prism can exhibit the wide effulgence of a summer noon.

What they wanted however of the sublime they endeavoured to

supply by hyperbole; their amplification had no limits: they left not only reason but fancy behind them, and produced combinations of confused magnificence that not only could not be credited, but could not be imagined.

Yet great labour directed by great abilities is never wholly lost: if they frequently threw away their wit upon false conceits, they likewise sometimes struck out unexpected truth: if their conceits were far-fetched, they were often worth the carriage. To write on their plan it was at least necessary to read and think. No man could be born a metaphysical poet, nor assume the dignity of a writer by descriptions copied from descriptions, by imitations borrowed from imitations, by traditional imagery and hereditary similes, by readiness of rhyme and volubility of syllables.

In perusing the works of this race of authors the mind is exercised either by recollection or inquiry; either something already learned is to be retrieved, or something new is to be examined. If their greatness seldom elevates, their acuteness often surprises; if the imagination is not always gratified, at least the powers of reflection and comparison are employed; and in the mass of materials, which ingenious absurdity has thrown together, genuine wit and useful knowledge may be sometimes found, buried perhaps in grossness of expression, but useful to those who know their value, and such as, when they are expanded to perspicuity and polished to elegance, may give lustre to works which have more propriety though less copiousness of sentiment.

This kind of writing, which was, I believe, borrowed from Marino and his followers, had been recommended by the example of Donne, a man of very extensive and various knowledge, and by Jonson, whose manner resembled that of Donne more in the ruggedness of his lines than in the cast of his sentiments.

When their reputation was high they had undoubtedly more imitators than time has left behind. Their immediate successors, of whom any remembrance can be said to remain, were Suckling, Waller, Denham, Cowley, Cleveland, and Milton. Denham and Waller sought another way to fame, by improving the harmony of our numbers. Milton tried the metaphysic style only in his lines upon Hobson the Carrier. Cowley adopted it, and excelled his predecessors; having as much sentiment and more music. Suckling neither improved versification nor abounded in conceits. The fashionable style remained chiefly with Cowley: Suckling could not reach it, and Milton disdained it.

Critical remarks are not easily understood without examples, and I have therefore collected instances of the modes of writing by which this species of poets, for poets they were called by themselves and their admirers, was eminently distinguished.

As the authors of this race were perhaps more desirous of being admired than understood they sometimes drew their conceits from recesses of learning not very much frequented by common readers of poetry. Thus Cowley on *Knowledge*:

> The sacred tree midst the fair orchard grew;
>   The phoenix Truth did on it rest,
>   And built his perfum'd nest,
> That right Porphyrian tree which did true logick shew.
>   Each leaf did learned notions give,
>   And th' apples were demonstrative:
>   So clear their colour and divine,
> The very shade they cast did other lights outshine.

On Anacreon continuing a lover in his old age:

> Love was with thy life entwin'd,
> Close as heat with fire is join'd;
> A powerful brand prescrib'd the date
> Of thine, like Meleager's fate.
> Th' antiperistasis of age
> More enflam'd thy amorous rage.

. . . .

Thus Donne shows his medicinal knowledge in some encomiastic verses:

> In every thing there naturally grows
> A balsamum to keep it fresh and new,
> If 'twere not injur'd by extrinsique blows;
> Your youth and beauty are this balm in you.
>   But you, of learning and religion,
> And virtue and such ingredients, have made
>   A mithridate, whose operation
> Keeps off or cures what can be done or said.

. . . .

Of thoughts so far-fetched as to be not only unexpected but unnatural, all their books are full.

To a lady, who wrote poesies for rings:

> They, who above do various circles find,
> Say, like a ring th' equator heaven does bind.
> When heaven shall be adorn'd by thee
> (Which then more heaven than 'tis, will be),
> 'Tis thou must write the poesy there,
> For it wanteth one as yet,
> Though the sun pass through't twice a year,
> The sun, which is esteem'd the god of wit.
>
> Cowley.

The tears of lovers are always of great poetical account, but Donne has extended them into worlds. If the lines are not easily understood they may be read again.

> On a round ball
> A workman, that hath copies by, can lay
> An Europe, Afric, and an Asia,
> And quickly make that, which was nothing, all.
> So doth each tear,
> Which thee doth wear,
> A globe, yea world, by that impression grow,
> Till thy tears mixt with mine do overflow
> This world, by waters sent from thee my heaven dissolved so.

On reading the following lines the reader may perhaps cry out, 'Confusion worse confounded'.

> Here lies a she sun, and a he moon here,
> She gives the best light to his sphere,
> Or each is both, and all, and so
> They unto one another nothing owe.
>
> Donne.

Who but Donne would have thought that a good man is a telescope?

> Though God be our true glass, through which we see
> All, since the being of all things is he,
> Yet are the trunks, which do to us derive
> Things in proportion fit by perspective,
> Deeds of good men; for by their living here,
> Virtues, indeed remote, seem to be near.

Of enormous and disgusting hyperboles these may be examples:

> By every wind, that comes this way,
> Send me at least a sigh or two,
> Such and so many I'll repay
> As shall themselves make winds to get to you.
>
> Cowley.

> In tears I'll waste these eyes,
> By Love so vainly fed;
> So lust of old the Deluge punished.
>
> Cowley.

> All arm'd in brass the richest dress of war
> (A dismal glorious sight) he shone afar.
> The sun himself started with sudden fright,
> To see his beams return so dismal bright.
>
> Cowley.

Their fictions were often violent and unnatural.

> Of his Mistress bathing:
>
> The fish around her crowded, as they do
> To the false light that treacherous fishers shew,
> And all with as much ease might taken be,
> As she at first took me:
> For ne'er did light so clear
> Among the waves appear,
> Though every night the sun himself set there.
>
> Cowley.

Their conceits were sometimes slight and trifling.

> On an inconstant woman:
>
> He enjoys thy calmy sunshine now,
> And no breath stirring hears;
> In the clear heaven of thy brow,
> No smallest cloud appears.
> He sees thee gentle, fair and gay,
> And trusts the faithless April of thy May.
>
> Cowley.

Upon a paper written with the juice of lemon, and read by the fire:

> Nothing yet in thee is seen;
> But when a genial heat warms thee within,
> A new-born wood of various lines there grows;
> Here buds an L, and there a B,
> Here sprouts a V, and there a T,
> And all the flourishing letters stand in rows.

Cowley.

As they sought only for novelty they did not much enquire whether their allusions were to things high or low, elegant or gross; whether they compared the little to the great, or the great to the little.

> Physic and Chirurgery for a Lover:
>
> Gently, ah gently, madam, touch
>   The wound, which you yourself have made;
> That pain must needs be very much,
>   Which makes me of your hand afraid.
> Cordials of pity give me now,
> For I too weak for purgings grow.

Cowley.

> The World and a Clock:
>
> Mahol th' inferior world's fantastic face
> Through all the turns of matter's maze did trace;
> Great Nature's well-set clock in pieces took;
> On all the springs and smallest wheels did look
> Of life and motion; and with equal art
> Made up again the whole of every part.

Cowley.

A coal-pit has not often found its poet; but, that it may not want its due honour, Cleveland has paralleled it with the sun:

> The moderate value of our guiltless ore
> Makes no man atheist, and no woman whore;
> Yet why should hallow'd vestal's sacred shrine
> Deserve more honour than a flaming mine?
> These pregnant wombs of heat would fitter be
> Than a few embers, for a deity.
>   Had he our pits, the Persian would admire
> No sun, but warm's devotion at our fire:
> He'd leave the trotting whipster, and prefer
> Our profound Vulcan 'bove that waggoner.

> For wants he heat, or light? or would have store
> Of both? 'tis here: and what can suns give more?
> Nay, what's the sun but, in a different name,
> A coal-pit rampant, or a mine on flame!
> Then let this truth reciprocally run,
> The sun's heaven's coalery, and coals our sun.

Their thoughts and expressions were sometimes grossly absurd, and such as no figures or license can reconcile to the understanding. . . .

> A Lover's heart, a hand grenado:
>
> Woe to her stubborn heart, if once mine come
>   Into the self-same room,
>   'Twill tear and blow up all within,
> Like a grenado shot into a magazin.
> Then shall Love keep the ashes and torn parts
>   Of both our broken hearts:
>   Shall out of both one new one make;
> From her's th' allay, from mine the metal, take.
>
> Cowley.

They were in very little care to clothe their notions with elegance of dress, and therefore miss the notice and the praise which are often gained by those who think less, but are more diligent to adorn their thoughts. . . .

All that man has to do is to live and die; the sum of humanity is comprehended by Donne in the following lines:

> Think in how poor a prison thou didst lie
> After, enabled but to suck and cry.
> Think, when 'twas grown to most, 'twas a poor inn,
> A province pack'd up in two yards of skin,
> And that usurp'd, or threaten'd with a rage
> Of sicknesses, or their true mother, age.
> But think that death hath now enfranchis'd thee;
> Thou hast thy expansion now, and liberty;
> Think, that a rusty piece discharg'd is flown
> In pieces, and the bullet is his own,
> And freely flies: this to thy soul allow,
> Think thy shell broke, think thy soul hatch'd but now.

They were sometimes indelicate and disgusting. Cowley thus apostrophizes beauty:

—Thou tyrant, which leav'st no man free!
Thou subtle thief, from whom nought safe can be!
Thou murtherer, which hast kill'd, and devil, which would'st damn me!

. . . .

Thus he represents the meditations of a lover:

Though in thy thoughts scarce any tracts have been
So much as of original sin,
Such charms thy beauty wears as might
Desires in dying confest saints excite.
Thou with strange adultery
Dost in each breast a brothel keep;
Awake, all men do lust for thee,
And some enjoy thee when they sleep.

The true taste of Tears:
Hither with crystal vials, lovers, come,
And take my tears, which are Love's wine,
And try your mistress' tears at home;
For all are false that taste not just like mine.

Donne.

This is yet more indelicate:

As the sweet sweat of roses in a still,
As that which from chafed musk-cat's pores doth trill,
As the almighty balm of th' early East,
Such are the sweet drops of my mistress' breast.
And on her neck her skin such lustre sets,
They seem no sweat-drops, but pearl coronets
Rank sweaty froth thy mistress' brow defiles.

Donne.

Their expressions sometimes raise horror, when they intend perhaps to be pathetic:

As men in hell are from diseases free,
So from all other ills am I,
Free from their known formality:
But all pains eminently lie in thee.

Cowley.

They were not always strictly curious whether the opinions from which they drew their illustrations were true; it was enough that they were popular. Bacon remarks that some falsehoods are continued by tradition, because they supply commodious allusions.

> It gave a piteous groan, and so it broke;
> In vain it something would have spoke:
> The love within too strong for 't was,
> Like poison put into a Venice-glass.
>
> Cowley.

In forming descriptions they looked out not for images, but for conceits. Night has been a common subject, which poets have contended to adorn. Dryden's *Night*° is well known, Donne's is as follows:

> Thou seest me here at midnight; now all rest,
> Time's dead low-water; when all minds divest
> To-morrow's business; when the labourers have
> Such rest in bed, that their last church-yard grave,
> Subject to change, will scarce be a type of this.
> Now when the client, whose last hearing is
> To-morrow, sleeps; when the condemned man—
> Who when he opes his eyes must shut them then
> Again by death—although sad watch he keep,
> Doth practise dying by a little sleep;
> Thou at this midnight seest me.

It must be however confessed of these writers that if they are upon common subjects often unnecessarily and unpoetically subtle, yet where scholastic speculation can be properly admitted, their copiousness and acuteness may justly be admired. What Cowley has written upon hope shows an unequalled fertility of invention:

> Hope, whose weak being ruin'd is,
> Alike if it succeed, and if it miss;
> Whom good or ill does equally confound,
> And both the horns of Fate's dilemma wound;
> Vain shadow, which dost vanish quite,
> Both at full noon and perfect night!
> The stars have not a possibility
> Of blessing thee;
> If things then from their end we happy call,
> 'Tis Hope is the most hopeless thing of all.

Hope, thou bold taster of delight,
Who, whilst thou should'st but taste, devour'st it quite!
Thou bring'st us an estate, yet leav'st us poor,
By clogging it with legacies before!
  The joys which we entire should wed,
  Come deflower'd virgins to our bed,
Good fortunes without gain imported be,
  Such mighty custom's paid to thee:
For joy, like wine, kept close does better taste:
If it take air before, its spirits waste.

To the following comparison of a man that travels and his wife that stays at home with a pair of compasses, it may be doubted whether absurdity or ingenuity has the better claim:

Our two souls therefore, which are one,
  Though I must go, endure not yet
A breach, but an expansion,
  Like gold to airy thinness beat.

If they be two, they are two so
  As stiff twin-compasses are two:
Thy soul, the fixt foot, makes no show
  To move, but doth, if th' other do.

And though it in the centre sit,
  Yet when the other far doth roam,
It leans, and hearkens after it,
  And grows erect, as that comes home.

Such wilt thou be to me, who must,
  Like th' other foot, obliquely run;
Thy firmness makes my circle just,
  And makes me end where I begun.

                                        Donne.

In all these examples it is apparent that whatever is improper or vicious is produced by a voluntary deviation from nature in pursuit of something new and strange, and that the writers fail to give delight by their desire of exciting admiration.

Having thus endeavoured to exhibit a general representation of the style and sentiments of the metaphysical poets, it is now proper to examine particularly the works of Cowley, who was almost the last of that race and undoubtedly the best. . . .

In his poem on the death of Hervey there is much praise, but little passion, a very just and ample delineation of such virtues as a studious privacy admits, and such intellectual excellence as a mind not yet called forth to action can display. He knew how to distinguish and how to commend the qualities of his companions, but when he wishes to make us weep he forgets to weep himself, and diverts his sorrow by imagining how his crown of bays, if he had it, would *crackle* in the *fire*. It is the odd fate of this thought to be worse for being true. The bay-leaf crackles remarkably as it burns; as therefore this property was not assigned it by chance, the mind must be thought sufficiently at ease that could attend to such minuteness of physiology. But the power of Cowley is not so much to move the affections, as to exercise the understanding.

The Chronicle is a composition unrivalled and alone: such gaiety of fancy, such facility of expression, such varied similitude, such a succession of images, and such a dance of words, it is vain to expect from Cowley. His strength always appears in his agility; his volatility is not the flutter of a light, but the bound of an elastic mind. His levity never leaves his learning behind it; the moralist, the politician, and the critic mingle their influence even in this airy frolic of genius. To such a performance Suckling could have brought the gaiety, but not the knowledge; Dryden could have supplied the knowledge, but not the gaiety. . . .

These little pieces will be found more finished in their kind than any other of Cowley's works. The diction shows nothing of the mould of time, and the sentiments are at no great distance from our present habitudes of thought. Real mirth must be always natural, and nature is uniform. Men have been wise in very different modes; but they have always laughed the same way.

Levity of thought naturally produced familiarity of language, and the familiar part of language continues long the same: the dialogue of comedy, when it is transcribed from popular manners and real life, is read from age to age with equal pleasure. The artifice of inversion, by which the established order of words is changed, or of innovation, by which new words or new meanings of words are introduced, is practised, not by those who talk to be understood, but by those who write to be admired.

The *Anacreontiques* therefore of Cowley give now all the pleasure which they ever gave. If he was formed by nature for one kind of writing more than for another, his power seems to have been greatest in the familiar and the festive.

The next class of his poems is called *The Mistress*, of which it is not necessary to select any particular pieces for praise or censure. They have all the same beauties and faults, and nearly in the same proportion. They are written with exuberance of wit, and with copiousness of learning; and it is truly asserted by Sprat that the plenitude of the writer's knowledge flows in upon his page, so that the reader is commonly surprised into some improvement. But, considered as the verses of a lover, no man that has ever loved will much commend them. They are neither courtly nor pathetic, have neither gallantry nor fondness. His praises are too far-sought and too hyperbolical either to express love or to excite it: every stanza is crowded with darts and flames, with wounds and death, with mingled souls, and with broken hearts.

The principal artifice by which *The Mistress* is filled with conceits is very copiously displayed by Addison. Love is by Cowley as by other poets expressed metaphorically by flame and fire; and that which is true of real fire is said of love, or figurative fire, the same word in the same sentence retaining both significations. Thus, 'observing the cold regard of his mistress's eyes, and at the same time their power of producing love in him, he considers them as burning-glasses made of ice. Finding himself able to live in the greatest extremities of love he concludes the torrid zone to be habitable. Upon the dying of a tree, on which he had cut his loves, he observes that his flames had burnt up and withered the tree.'

These conceits Addison calls mixed wit, that is, wit which consists of thoughts true in one sense of the expression, and false in the other. Addison's representation is sufficiently indulgent: that confusion of images may entertain for a moment, but being unnatural it soon grows wearisome. Cowley delighted in it, as much as if he had invented it; but, not to mention the ancients, he might have found it full-blown in modern Italy.

> Aspice quam variis distringar, Vesbia, curis,
>   Uror, et heu! nostro manat ab igne liquor;
> Sum Nilus, sumque Ætna simul; restringite flammas
>   O lacrimae, aut lacrimas ebibe flamma meas.°

One of the severe theologians of that time censured him as having published 'a book of profane and lascivious Verses'. From the charge of profaneness the constant tenor of his life, which seems to have been eminently virtuous, and the general tendency of his opinions, which discover no irreverence of religion, must defend him; but that the accusation of lasciviousness is unjust, the perusal of his works will sufficiently evince.

Cowley's *Mistress* has no power of seduction; she 'plays round the head, but comes not at the heart'. Her beauty and absence, her kindness and cruelty, her disdain and inconstancy produce no correspondence of emotion. His poetical account of the virtues of plants and colours of flowers is not perused with more sluggish frigidity. The compositions are such as might have been written for penance by a hermit, or for hire by a philosophical rhymer who had only heard of another sex; for they turn the mind only on the writer, whom, without thinking on a woman but as the subject for his talk, we sometimes esteem as learned and sometimes despise as trifling, always admire as ingenious, and always condemn as unnatural. . . .

The fault of Cowley, and perhaps of all the writers of the metaphysical race, is that of pursuing his thoughts to their last ramifications, by which he loses the grandeur of generality, for of the greatest things the parts are little; what is little can be but pretty, and by claiming dignity becomes ridiculous. Thus all the power of description is destroyed by a scrupulous enumeration; and the force of metaphors is lost when the mind by the mention of particulars is turned more upon the original than the secondary sense, more upon that from which the illustration is drawn than that to which it is applied.

Of this we have a very eminent example in the ode intituled *The Muse*, who goes to 'take the air' in an intellectual chariot, to which he harnesses Fancy and Judgement, Wit and Eloquence, Memory and Invention: how he distinguished Wit from Fancy, or how Memory could properly contribute to Motion, he has not explained; we are however content to suppose that he could have justified his own fiction, and wish to see the Muse begin her career; but there is yet more to be done.

> Let the *postilion* Nature mount, and let
> The *coachman* Art be set;
> And let the airy *footmen*, running all beside,
> Make a long row of goodly pride,
> Figures, conceits, raptures, and sentences,
> In a well-worded dress,
> And innocent loves, and pleasant truths, and useful lies,
> In all their gaudy *liveries*.

Every mind is now disgusted with this cumber of magnificence; yet I cannot refuse myself the four next lines:

> Mount, glorious queen, thy travelling throne,
>> And bid it to put on;
>> For long though cheerful is the way,
>> And life alas! allows but one ill winter's day.

In the same ode, celebrating the power of the Muse, he gives her prescience or, in poetical language, the foresight of events hatching in futurity; but having once an egg in his mind he cannot forbear to show us that he knows what an egg contains:

> Thou into the close nests of Time dost peep,
>> And there with piercing eye
> Through the firm shell and the thick white dost spy
>> Years to come a-forming lie,
> Close in their sacred fecundine asleep.

. . . .

If the Pindaric style be what Cowley thinks it, 'the highest and noblest kind of writing in verse', it can be adapted only to high and noble subjects; and it will not be easy to reconcile the poet with the critic or to conceive how that can be the highest kind of writing in verse which, according to Sprat, 'is chiefly to be preferred for its near affinity to prose'.

This lax and lawless versification so much concealed the deficiencies of the barren and flattered the laziness of the idle that it immediately overspread our books of poetry; all the boys and girls caught the pleasing fashion, and they that could do nothing else could write like Pindar. The rights of antiquity were invaded, and disorder tried to break into the Latin: a poem on the Sheldonian Theatre, in which all kinds of verse are shaken together, is unhappily inserted in the *Musae Anglicanae*.° Pindarism prevailed above half a century, but at last died gradually away, and other imitations supply its place.

The *Pindarique Odes* have so long enjoyed the highest degree of poetical reputation that I am not willing to dismiss them with unabated censure; and surely, though the mode of their composition be erroneous, yet many parts deserve at least that admiration which is due to great comprehension of knowledge and great fertility of fancy. The thoughts are often new and often striking, but the greatness of one part is disgraced by the littleness of another; and total negligence of language gives the noblest conceptions the appearance of a fabric, august in the plan, but mean in the materials. Yet surely those verses are not without a just claim to praise of which it may be said with truth that no one but Cowley could have written them.

The *Davideis* now remains to be considered; a poem which the author designed to have extended to twelve books, merely, as he makes no scruple of declaring, because the *Æneid* had that number; but he had leisure or perseverance only to write the third part. Epic poems have been left unfinished by Virgil, Statius, Spenser, and Cowley. That we have not the whole *Davideis* is, however, not much to be regretted, for in this undertaking Cowley is, tacitly at least, confessed to have miscarried. There are not many examples of so great a work produced by an author generally read and generally praised that has crept through a century with so little regard. Whatever is said of Cowley is meant of his other works. Of the *Davideis* no mention is made: it never appears in books, nor emerges in conversation. By the *Spectator* it has once been quoted, by Rymer it has once been praised, and by Dryden, in *Mac Flecknoe*, it has once been imitated; nor do I recollect much other notice from its publication till now in the whole succession of English literature.

Of this silence and neglect if the reason be inquired, it will be found partly in the choice of the subject, and partly in the performance of the work.

Sacred history has been always read with submissive reverence, and an imagination over-awed and controlled. We have been accustomed to acquiesce in the nakedness and simplicity of the authentic narrative, and to repose on its veracity with such humble confidence as suppresses curiosity. We go with the historian as he goes, and stop with him when he stops. All amplification is frivolous and vain: all addition to that which is already sufficient for the purposes of religion seems not only useless, but in some degree profane.

Such events as were produced by the visible interposition of Divine Power are above the power of human genius to dignify. The miracle of Creation, however it may teem with images, is best described with little diffusion of language: 'He spake the word, and they were made.'

.   .   .   .

It is not only when the events are confessedly miraculous that fancy and fiction lose their effect: the whole system of life, while the Theocracy was yet visible, has an appearance so different from all other scenes of human action that the reader of the Sacred Volume habitually considers it as the peculiar mode of existence of a distinct species of mankind, that lived and acted with manners uncommunicable; so that it is difficult even for imagination to place us in the state of them whose story is related, and by consequence their joys and griefs are not easily adopted, nor can the attention be often interested in any thing that befalls them.

To the subject, thus originally indisposed to the reception of poetical embellishments, the writer brought little that could reconcile impatience or attract curiosity. Nothing can be more disgusting than a narrative spangled with conceits, and conceits are all that the *Davideis* supplies.

One of the great sources of poetical delight is description, or the power of presenting pictures to the mind. Cowley gives inferences instead of images, and shows not what may be supposed to have been seen, but what thoughts the sight might have suggested. When Virgil describes the stone which Turnus lifted against Æneas, he fixes the attention on its bulk and weight:

> Saxum circumspicit ingens,
> Saxum antiquum, ingens, campo quod forte jacebat,
> Limes agro positus, litem ut discerneret arvis.°

Cowley says of the stone with which Cain slew his brother,

> I saw him fling the stone, as if he meant
> At once his murther and his monument.

Of the sword taken from Goliah he says,

> A sword so great, that it was only fit
> To cut off his great head that came with it.

The dress of Gabriel deserves attention:

> He took for skin a cloud most soft and bright,
> That e'er the midday sun pierc'd through with light;
> Upon his cheeks a lively blush he spread,
> Wash'd from the morning beauties' deepest red;
> An harmless flattering meteor shone for hair,
> And fell adown his shoulders with loose care;
> He cuts out a silk mantle from the skies,
> Where the most sprightly azure pleas'd the eyes;
> This he with starry vapours sprinkles all,
> Took in their prime ere they grow ripe and tall;
> Of a new rainbow, ere it fret or fade,
> The choicest piece cut out, a scarf is made.

This is a just specimen of Cowley's imagery: what might in general expressions be great and forcible he weakens and makes ridiculous by branching it into small parts. That Gabriel was invested with the softest or brightest colours of the sky we might have been told, and been dismissed to improve the idea in our different proportions of conception; but Cowley could not let us go till he had related where Gabriel got first his skin, and then his mantle, then his lace, and then his scarf, and related it in the terms of the mercer and tailor.

. . . .

Rymer has declared the *Davideis* superior to the *Jerusalem* of Tasso, 'which,' says he, 'the poet, with all his care, has not totally purged from pedantry.' If by pedantry is meant that minute knowledge which is derived from particular sciences and studies, in opposition to the general notions supplied by a wide survey of life and nature, Cowley certainly errs by introducing pedantry far more frequently than Tasso. I know not, indeed, why they should be compared; for the resemblance of Cowley's work to Tasso's is only that they both exhibit the agency of celestial and infernal spirits, in which however they differ widely: for Cowley supposes them commonly to operate upon the mind by suggestion; Tasso represents them as promoting or obstructing events by external agency.

Of particular passages that can be properly compared I remember only the description of Heaven, in which the different manner of the two writers is sufficiently discernible. Cowley's is scarcely description, unless it be possible to describe by negatives; for he tells us only what there is not in heaven. Tasso endeavours to represent the splendours and pleasures of the regions of happiness. Tasso affords images, and Cowley sentiments.°. . .

In the perusal of the *Davideis*, as of all Cowley's works, we find wit and learning unprofitably squandered. Attention has no relief; the affections are never moved; we are sometimes surprised, but never delighted, and find much to admire, but little to approve. Still, however, it is the work of Cowley, of a mind capacious by nature, and replenished by study.

In the general review of Cowley's poetry it will be found that he wrote with abundant fertility, but negligent or unskilful selection; with much thought, but with little imagery; that he is never pathetic and rarely sublime, but always either ingenious or learned, either acute or profound.

It is said by Denham in his elegy:

> To him no author was unknown;
> Yet what he writ was all his own.

This wide position requires less limitation when it is affirmed of Cowley than perhaps of any other poet: he read much, and yet borrowed little.

His character of writing was indeed not his own: he unhappily adopted that which was predominant. He saw a certain way to present praise; and not sufficiently enquiring by what means the ancients have continued to delight through all the changes of human manners, he contented himself with a deciduous laurel, of which the verdure in its spring was bright and gay, but which time has been continually stealing from his brows.

He was in his own time considered as of unrivalled excellence. Clarendon represents him as having taken a flight beyond all that went before him; and Milton is said to have declared that the three greatest English poets were Spenser, Shakespeare, and Cowley.

His manner he had in common with others; but his sentiments were his own. Upon every subject he thought for himself, and such was his copiousness of knowledge that something at once remote and applicable rushed into his mind; yet it is not likely that he always rejected a commodious idea merely because another had used it; his known wealth was so great that he might have borrowed without loss of credit.

. . . .

His diction was in his own time censured as negligent. He seems not to have known, or not to have considered, that words being arbitrary must owe their power to association, and have the influence, and that only, which custom has given them. Language is the dress of thought; and as the noblest mien or most graceful action would be degraded and obscured by a garb appropriated to the gross employments of rustics or mechanics, so the most heroic sentiments will lose their efficacy, and the most splendid ideas drop their magnificence, if they are conveyed by words used commonly upon low and trivial occasions, debased by vulgar mouths, and contaminated by inelegant applications.

Truth indeed is always truth, and reason is always reason; they have an intrinsic and unalterable value, and constitute that intellectual gold which defies destruction: but gold may be so concealed in baser matter that only a chemist can recover it; sense may be so hidden in unrefined and plebeian words that none but philosophers can distinguish it; and both may be so buried in impurities as not to pay the cost of their extraction.

The diction, being the vehicle of the thoughts, first presents itself to the intellectual eye; and if the first appearance offends, a further knowledge is not often sought. Whatever professes to benefit by pleasing must please at once. The pleasures of the mind imply something sudden and unexpected; that which elevates must always surprise. What is perceived by slow degrees may gratify us with the consciousness of improvement, but will never strike with the sense of pleasure.

Of all this Cowley appears to have been without knowledge or without care. He makes no selection of words, nor seeks any neatness of phrase; he has no elegances either lucky or elaborate: as his endeavours were rather to impress sentences upon the understanding than images on the fancy he has few epithets, and those scattered without peculiar propriety or nice adaptation. It seems to follow from the necessity of the subject, rather than the care of the writer, that the diction of his heroic poem is less familiar than that of his slightest writings. He has given not the same numbers, but the same diction, to the gentle Anacreon and the tempestuous Pindar.

His versification seems to have had very little of his care; and if what he thinks be true, that his numbers are unmusical only when they are ill read, the art of reading them is at present lost; for they are commonly harsh to modern ears. He has indeed many noble lines, such as the feeble care of Waller never could produce. The bulk of his thoughts sometimes swelled his verse to unexpected and inevitable grandeur, but his excellence of this kind is merely fortuitous; he sinks willingly down to his general carelessness, and avoids with very little care either meanness or asperity.

. . . .

After so much criticism on his poems, the essays which accompany them must not be forgotten. What is said by Sprat of his conversation, that no man could draw from it any suspicion of his excellence in poetry, may be applied to these compositions. No author ever kept his verse and his prose at a greater distance from each other. His thoughts are natural, and his style has a smooth and placid equability, which has never yet obtained its due commendation. Nothing is far-sought, or hard-laboured; but all is easy without feebleness, and familiar without grossness.

It has been observed by Felton, in his *Essay on the Classics*, that Cowley was beloved by every Muse that he courted, and that he has rivalled the Ancients in every kind of poetry but tragedy.

It may be affirmed without any encomiastic fervour that he brought to his poetic labours a mind replete with learning, and that his pages are embellished with all the ornaments which books could supply; that he was the first who imparted to English numbers the enthusiasm of the greater ode, and the gaiety of the less; that he was equally qualified for spritely sallies and for lofty flights; that he was among those who freed translation from servility, and, instead of following his author at a distance, walked by his side; and that if he left versification yet improvable, he left likewise from time to time such specimens of excellence as enabled succeeding poets to improve it.

Milton

In the examination of Milton's poetical works I shall pay so much regard to time as to begin with his juvenile productions. For his earlier pieces he seems to have had a degree of fondness not very laudable: what he has once written he resolves to preserve, and gives to the public an unfinished poem, which he broke off because he was 'nothing satisfied with what he had done', supposing his readers less nice than himself. These preludes to his future labours are in Italian, Latin, and English. Of the Italian I cannot pretend to speak as a critic, but I have heard them commended by a man well qualified to decide their merit. The Latin pieces are lusciously elegant; but the delight which they afford is rather by the exquisite imitation of the ancient writers, by the purity of the diction, and the harmony of the numbers, than by any power of invention or vigour of sentiment. They are not all of equal value; the elegies excel the odes, and some of the exercises on Gunpowder Treason might have been spared.

The English poems, though they make no promises of *Paradise Lost*, have this evidence of genius, that they have a cast original and unborrowed. But their peculiarity is not excellence: if they differ from verses of others, they differ for the worse; for they are too often distinguished by repulsive harshness; the combinations of words are new, but they are not pleasing; the rhymes and epithets seem to be laboriously sought and violently applied.

That in the early parts of his life he wrote with much care appears from his manuscripts, happily preserved at Cambridge, in which many of his smaller works are found as they were first written, with the subsequent corrections. Such reliques show how excellence is acquired: what we hope ever to do with ease we may learn first to do with diligence.

Those who admire the beauties of this great poet sometimes force their own judgement into false approbation of his little pieces, and prevail upon themselves to think that admirable which is only singular. All that short compositions can commonly attain is neatness and elegance. Milton never learned the art of doing little things with grace; he overlooked the milder excellence of suavity and softness: he was a 'Lion' that had no skill 'in dandling the Kid'.

One of the poems on which much praise has been bestowed is *Lycidas*; of which the diction is harsh, the rhymes uncertain, and the numbers unpleasing. What beauty there is we must therefore seek in the sentiments and images. It is not to be considered as the effusion of real passion; for passion runs not after remote allusions and obscure opinions. Passion plucks no berries from the myrtle and ivy, nor calls upon Arethuse and Mincius, nor tells of 'rough satyrs and fauns with cloven heel'. Where there is leisure for fiction° there is little grief.

In this poem there is no nature, for there is no truth; there is no art, for there is nothing new. Its form is that of a pastoral, easy, vulgar,° and therefore disgusting: whatever images it can supply are long ago exhausted; and its inherent improbability always forces dissatisfaction on the mind. When Cowley tells of Hervey that they studied together, it is easy to suppose how much he must miss the companion of his labours and the partner of his discoveries; but what image of tenderness can be excited by these lines!

> We drove afield, and both together heard
> What time the grey fly winds her sultry horn,
> Battening our flocks with the fresh dews of night.

We know that they never drove afield, and that they had no flocks to batten; and though it be allowed that the representation may be allegorical, the true meaning is so uncertain and remote that it is never sought because it cannot be known when it is found.

Among the flocks and copses and flowers appear the heathen deities, Jove and Phoebus, Neptune and Æolus, with a long train of mythological imagery, such as a College easily supplies. Nothing can less display knowledge or less exercise invention than to tell how a shepherd has lost his companion and must now feed his flocks alone, without any judge of his skill in piping; and how one god asks another god what is become of Lycidas, and how neither god can tell. He who thus grieves will excite no sympathy; he who thus praises will confer no honour.

This poem has yet a grosser fault. With these trifling fictions are mingled the most awful and sacred truths, such as ought never to be polluted with such irreverent combinations. The shepherd likewise is now a feeder of sheep, and afterwards an ecclesiastical pastor, a superintendent of a Christian flock. Such equivocations are always unskilful; but here they are indecent, and at least approach to impiety, of which, however, I believe the writer not to have been conscious.

Such is the power of reputation justly acquired that its blaze drives away the eye from nice examination. Surely no man could have fancied that he read *Lycidas*° with pleasure had he not known its author.

Of the two pieces *L'Allegro* and *Il Penseroso*, I believe opinion is uniform; every man that reads them reads them with pleasure. The author's design is not, what Theobald has remarked, merely to show how objects derived their colours from the mind, by representing the operation of the same things upon the gay and the melancholy temper, or upon the same man as he is differently disposed; but rather how, among the successive variety of appearances, every disposition of mind takes hold on those by which it may be gratified.

The *cheerful* man hears the lark in the morning; the *pensive* man hears the nightingale in the evening. The *cheerful* man sees the cock strut, and hears the horn and hounds echo in the wood; then walks 'not unseen' to observe the glory of the rising sun or listen to the singing milk-maid, and view the labours of the plowman and the mower; then casts his eyes about him over scenes of smiling plenty, and looks up to the distant tower, the residence of some fair inhabitant: thus he pursues rural gaiety through a day of labour or of play, and delights himself at night with the fanciful narratives of superstitious ignorance.

The *pensive* man at one time walks 'unseen' to muse at midnight, and at another hears the sullen curfew. If the weather drives him home he sits in a room lighted only by 'glowing embers'; or by a lonely lamp outwatches the North Star to discover the habitation of separate souls, and varies the shades of meditation by contemplating the magnificent or pathetic scenes of tragic and epic poetry. When the morning comes, a morning gloomy with rain and wind, he walks into the dark trackless woods, falls asleep by some murmuring water, and with melancholy enthusiasm expects some dream of prognostication or some music played by aerial performers.

Both Mirth and Melancholy are solitary, silent inhabitants of the breast that neither receive nor transmit communication; no mention is therefore made of a philosophical friend or a pleasant companion. The seriousness does not arise from any participation of calamity, nor the gaiety from the pleasures of the bottle.

The man of *cheerfulness* having exhausted the country tries what 'towered cities' will afford, and mingles with scenes of splendor, gay assemblies, and nuptial festivities; but he mingles a mere spectator as, when the learned comedies of Jonson or the wild dramas of Shakespeare are exhibited, he attends the theatre.

The *pensive* man never loses himself in crowds, but walks the cloister or frequents the cathedral. Milton probably had not yet forsaken the Church.

Both his characters delight in music, but he seems to think that cheerful notes would have obtained from Pluto a complete dismission of Eurydice, of whom solemn sounds only procured a conditional release.

For the old age of Cheerfulness he makes no provision; but Melancholy he conducts with great dignity to the close of life. His Cheerfulness is without levity, and his Pensiveness without asperity.

Through these two poems the images are properly selected and nicely distinguished, but the colours of the diction seem not sufficiently discriminated. I know not whether the characters are kept sufficiently apart. No mirth can, indeed, be found in his melancholy; but I am afraid that I always meet some melancholy in his mirth. They are two noble efforts of imagination.

The greatest of his juvenile performances is the *Mask of Comus*, in which may very plainly be discovered the dawn or twilight of *Paradise Lost*. Milton appears to have formed very early that system of diction and mode of verse which his maturer judgement approved, and from which he never endeavoured nor desired to deviate.

Nor does *Comus* afford only a specimen of his language; it exhibits likewise his power of description and his vigour of sentiment, employed in the praise and defence of virtue. A work more truly poetical is rarely found; allusions, images, and descriptive epithets embellish almost every period with lavish decoration. As a series of lines, therefore, it may be considered as worthy of all the admiration with which the votaries have received it.

As a drama it is deficient. The action is not probable. A Masque, in those parts where supernatural intervention is admitted, must indeed be given up to all the freaks of imagination; but so far as the action is merely human it ought to be reasonable, which can hardly be said of the conduct of the two brothers, who, when their sister sinks with fatigue in a pathless wilderness, wander both away in search of berries too far to find their way back, and leave a helpless Lady to all the sadness and danger of solitude. This however is a defect over-balanced by its convenience.

What deserves more reprehension is that the prologue spoken in the wild wood by the attendant Spirit is addressed to the audience; a mode of communication so contrary to the nature of dramatic representation that no precedents can support it.

The discourse of the Spirit is too long, an objection that may be made to almost all the following speeches; they have not the spriteliness of a dialogue animated by reciprocal contention, but seem rather declamations deliberately composed and formally repeated on a moral question. The auditor therefore listens as to a lecture, without passion, without anxiety.

The song of Comus has airiness and jollity; but, what may recommend Milton's morals as well as his poetry, the invitations to pleasure are so general that they excite no distinct images of corrupt enjoyment, and take no dangerous hold on the fancy.

The following soliloquies of Comus and the Lady are elegant, but tedious. The song must owe much to the voice, if it ever can delight. At last the Brothers enter, with too much tranquillity; and when they have feared lest their sister should be in danger, and hoped that she is not in danger, the Elder makes a speech in praise of chastity, and the Younger finds how fine it is to be a philosopher.

Then descends the Spirit in form of a shepherd; and the Brother, instead of being in haste to ask his help, praises his singing, and enquires his business in that place. It is remarkable that at this interview the Brother is taken with a short fit of rhyming. The Spirit relates that the Lady is in the power of Comus, the Brother moralises again, and the Spirit makes a long narration, of no use because it is false, and therefore unsuitable to a good Being.

In all these parts the language is poetical and the sentiments are generous, but there is something wanting to allure attention.

The dispute between the Lady and Comus is the most animated and affecting scene of the drama, and wants nothing but a brisker reciprocation of objections and replies to invite attention and detain it.

The songs are vigorous and full of imagery; but they are harsh in their diction, and not very musical in their numbers.

Throughout the whole the figures are too bold and the language too luxuriant for dialogue: it is a drama in the epic style, inelegantly splendid, and tediously instructive.

The *Sonnets* were written in different parts of Milton's life upon different occasions. They deserve not any particular criticism; for of the best it can only be said that they are not bad, and perhaps only the eighth and the twenty-first are truly entitled to this slender commendation. The fabric of a sonnet, however adapted to the Italian language, has never succeeded in ours, which, having greater variety of termination, requires the rhymes to be often changed.

Those little pieces may be dispatched without much anxiety; a greater work calls for greater care. I am now to examine *Paradise Lost*, a poem which, considered with respect to design, may claim the first place, and with respect to performance the second, among the productions of the human mind.

By the general consent of critics, the first praise of genius is due to the writer of an epic poem, as it requires an assemblage of all the powers which are singly sufficient for other compositions. Poetry is the art of uniting pleasure with truth, by calling imagination to the help of reason. Epic poetry undertakes to teach the most important truths by the most pleasing precepts, and therefore relates some great event in the most affecting manner. History must supply the writer with the rudiments of narration, which he must improve and exalt by a nobler art, must animate by dramatic energy, and diversify by retrospection and anticipation; morality must teach him the exact bounds and different shades of vice and virtue; from policy and the practice of life he has to learn the discriminations of character and the tendency of the passions, either single or combined; and physiology must supply him with illustrations and images. To put these materials to poetical use is required an imagination capable of painting nature and realizing fiction. Nor is he yet a poet till he has attained the whole extension of his language, distinguished all the delicacies of phrase, and all the colours of words, and learned to adjust their different sounds to all the varieties of metrical modulation.

Bossu is of opinion that the poet's first work is to find a *moral*, which his fable is afterwards to illustrate and establish. This seems to have been the process only of Milton: the moral of other poems is incidental and consequent; in Milton's only it is essential and intrinsic. His purpose was the most useful and the most arduous: 'to vindicate° the ways of God to man'; to show the reasonableness of religion, and the necessity of obedience to the Divine Law.

To convey this moral there must be a *fable*, a narration artfully constructed so as to excite curiosity and surprise expectation. In this part of his work Milton must be confessed to have equalled every other poet. He has involved in his account of the Fall of Man the events which preceded, and those that were to follow it: he has interwoven the whole system of theology with such propriety that every part appears to be necessary, and scarcely any recital is wished shorter for the sake of quickening the progress of the main action.

The subject of an epic poem is naturally an event of great importance. That of Milton is not the destruction of a city, the conduct of a colony, or the foundation of an empire. His subject is the fate of worlds, the revolutions of heaven and of earth; rebellion against the Supreme King raised by the highest order of created beings; the overthrow of their host and the punishment of their crime; the creation of a new race of reasonable creatures; their original happiness and innocence, their forfeiture of immortality, and their restoration to hope and peace.

Great events can be hastened or retarded only by persons of elevated dignity. Before the greatness displayed in Milton's poem all other greatness shrinks away. The weakest of his agents are the highest and noblest of human beings, the original parents of mankind; with whose actions the elements consented; on whose rectitude or deviation of will depended the state of terrestrial nature and the condition of all the future inhabitants of the globe.

Of the other agents in the poem the chief are such as it is irreverence to name on slight occasions. The rest were lower powers;

> of which the least could wield
> Those elements, and arm him with the force
> Of all their regions;

powers which only the control of Omnipotence restrains from laying creation waste, and filling the vast expanse of space with ruin and confusion. To display the motives and actions of beings thus superior, so far as human reason can examine them or human imagination represent them, is the task which this mighty poet has undertaken and performed.

In the examination of epic poems much speculation is commonly employed upon the *characters*. The characters in the *Paradise Lost* which admit of examination are those of angels and of man; of angels good and evil, of man in his innocent and sinful state.

Among the angels the virtue of Raphael is mild and placid, of easy condescension and free communication; that of Michael is regal and lofty, and, as may seem, attentive to the dignity of his own nature. Abdiel and Gabriel appear occasionally, and act as every incident requires; the solitary fidelity of Abdiel is very amiably painted.

Of the evil angels the characters are more diversified. To Satan, as Addison observes, such sentiments are given as suit 'the most exalted and most depraved being'. Milton has been censured by Clarke for the impiety which sometimes breaks from Satan's mouth. For there are thoughts, as he justly remarks, which no observation of character can justify, because no good man would willingly permit them to pass, however transiently, through his own mind. To make Satan speak as a rebel, without any such expressions as might taint the reader's imagination, was indeed one of the great difficulties in Milton's undertaking, and I cannot but think that he has extricated himself with great happiness. There is in Satan's speeches little that can give pain to a pious ear. The language of rebellion cannot be the same with that of obedience. The malignity of Satan foams in haughtiness and obstinacy; but his expressions are commonly general, and no otherwise offensive than as they are wicked.

The other chiefs of the celestial rebellion are very judiciously discriminated in the first and second books; and the ferocious character of Moloch appears, both in the battle and the council, with exact consistency.

To Adam and to Eve are given during their innocence such sentiments as innocence can generate and utter. Their love is pure benevolence and mutual veneration; their repasts are without luxury and their diligence without toil. Their addresses to their Maker have little more than the voice of admiration and gratitude. Fruition left them nothing to ask, and Innocence left them nothing to fear.

But with guilt enter distrust and discord, mutual accusation, and stubborn self-defence; they regard each other with alienated minds, and dread their Creator as the avenger of their transgression. At last they seek shelter in his mercy, soften to repentance, and melt in supplication. Both before and after the Fall the superiority of Adam is diligently sustained.

Of the *probable* and the *marvellous*, two parts of a vulgar epic poem which immerge the critic in deep consideration, the *Paradise Lost* requires little to be said. It contains the history of a miracle, of Creation and Redemption; it displays the power and the mercy of the Supreme Being: the probable therefore is marvellous, and the marvellous is probable. The substance of the narrative is truth; and as truth allows no choice, it is, like necessity, superior to rule. To the accidental or adventitious parts, as to every thing human, some slight exceptions may be made. But the main fabric is immovably supported.

It is justly remarked by Addison that this poem has, by the nature of its subject, the advantage above all others, that it is universally and perpetually interesting. All mankind will, through all ages, bear the same relation to Adam and to Eve, and must partake of that good and evil which extend to themselves.

Of the *machinery*, so called from Θεὸς ἀπὸ μηχανῆς,° by which is meant the occasional interposition of supernatural power, another fertile topic of critical remarks, here is no room to speak, because every thing is done under the immediate and visible direction of

Heaven; but the rule is so far observed that no part of the action could have been accomplished by any other means.

Of *episodes* I think there are only two, contained in Raphael's relation of the war in heaven and Michael's prophetic account of the changes to happen in this world. Both are closely connected with the great action; one was necessary to Adam as a warning, the other as a consolation.

To the completeness or *integrity* of the design nothing can be objected; it has distinctly and clearly what Aristotle requires, a beginning, a middle, and an end. There is perhaps no poem of the same length from which so little can be taken without apparent mutilation. Here are no funeral games, nor is there any long description of a shield. The short digressions at the beginning of the third, seventh, and ninth books might doubtless be spared; but superfluities so beautiful who would take away? Or who does not wish that the author of the *Iliad* had gratified succeeding ages with a little knowledge of himself? Perhaps no passages are more frequently or more attentively read than those extrinsic paragraphs; and, since the end of poetry is pleasure, that cannot be unpoetical with which all are pleased.

The questions whether the action of the poem be strictly *one*, whether the poem can be properly termed *heroic*, and who is the hero, are raised by such readers as draw their principles of judgement rather from books than from reason. Milton, though he entitled *Paradise Lost* only a 'poem', yet calls it himself 'heroic song'. Dryden, petulantly and indecently, denies the heroism of Adam because he was overcome; but there is no reason why the hero should not be unfortunate except established practice, since success and virtue do not go necessarily together.° Cato is the hero of Lucan, but Lucan's authority will not be suffered by Quintilian to decide. However, if success be necessary, Adam's deceiver was at last crushed; Adam was restored to his Maker's favour, and therefore may securely resume his human rank.

After the scheme and fabric of the poem must be considered its component parts, the sentiments, and the diction.

The *sentiments*,° as expressive of manners or appropriated to characters, are for the greater part unexceptionably just.

Splendid passages containing lessons of morality or precepts of prudence occur seldom. Such is the original formation of this poem that as it admits no human manners till the Fall, it can give little assistance to human conduct. Its end is to raise the thoughts above sublunary° cares or pleasures. Yet the praise of that fortitude with which Abdiel maintained his singularity of virtue against the scorn of multitudes may be accommodated to all times; and Raphael's reproof of Adam's curiosity after the planetary motions, with the answer returned by Adam, may be confidently opposed to any rule of life which any poet has delivered.

The thoughts which are occasionally called forth in the progress are such as could only be produced by an imagination in the highest degree fervid and active, to which materials were supplied by incessant study and unlimited curiosity. The heat of Milton's mind might be said to sublimate his learning, to throw off into his work the spirit of science, unmingled with its grosser parts.

He had considered creation in its whole extent, and his descriptions are therefore learned. He had accustomed his imagination to unrestrained indulgence, and his conceptions therefore were extensive. The characteristic quality of his poem is sublimity. He sometimes descends to the elegant, but his element is the great. He can occasionally invest himself with grace; but his natural port is gigantic loftiness.° He can please when pleasure is required; but it is his peculiar power to astonish.

He seems to have been well acquainted with his own genius, and to know what it was that Nature had bestowed upon him more bountifully than upon others; the power of displaying the vast, illuminating the splendid, enforcing the awful, darkening the gloomy, and aggravating the dreadful: he therefore chose a subject on which too much could not be said, on which he might tire his fancy without the censure of extravagance.

The appearances of nature and the occurrences of life did not satiate his appetite of greatness. To paint things as they are requires a minute attention, and employs the memory rather than the fancy. Milton's delight was to sport in the wide regions of possibility; reality was a scene too narrow for his mind. He sent his faculties out upon discovery, into worlds where only imagination can travel, and delighted to form new modes of existence, and furnish sentiment and action to superior beings, to trace the counsels of hell, or accompany the choirs of heaven.

But he could not be always in other worlds: he must sometimes revisit earth, and tell of things visible and known. When he cannot raise wonder by the sublimity of his mind he gives delight by its fertility.

Whatever be his subject he never fails to fill the imagination. But his images and descriptions of the scenes or operations of Nature do not seem to be always copied from original form, nor to have the freshness, raciness, and energy of immediate observation. He saw Nature, as Dryden expresses it, 'through the spectacles of books'; and on most occasions calls learning to his assistance. The garden of Eden brings to his mind the vale of Enna, where Proserpine was gathering flowers. Satan makes his way through fighting elements, like Argo between the Cyanean rocks, or Ulysses between the two *Sicilian* whirlpools, when he shunned Charybdis 'on the larboard'. The mythological allusions have been justly censured, as not being always used with notice of their vanity; but they contribute variety to the narration, and produce an alternate exercise of the memory and the fancy.

His similes are less numerous and more various than those of his predecessors. But he does not confine himself within the limits of rigorous comparison: his great excellence is amplitude, and he expands the adventitious image beyond the dimensions which the occasion required. Thus, comparing the shield of Satan to the orb of the moon, he crowds the imagination with the discovery of the telescope and all the wonders which the telescope discovers.

Of his moral sentiments it is hardly praise to affirm that they excel those of all other poets; for this superiority he was indebted to his acquaintance with the sacred writings. The ancient epic poets, wanting the light of Revelation, were very unskilful teachers of virtue: their principal characters may be great, but they are not amiable. The reader may rise from their works with a greater degree of active or passive fortitude, and sometimes of prudence; but he will be able to carry away few precepts of justice, and none of mercy.

From the Italian writers it appears that the advantages of even Christian knowledge may be possessed in vain. Ariosto's pravity is generally known; and, though the *Deliverance of Jerusalem* may be considered as a sacred subject, the poet has been very sparing of moral instruction.

In Milton every line breathes sanctity of thought and purity of manners, except when the train of the narration requires the introduction of the rebellious spirits; and even they are compelled to acknowledge their subjection to God in such a manner as excites reverence and confirms piety.

Of human beings there are but two; but those two are the parents of mankind, venerable before their fall for dignity and innocence, and amiable after it for repentance and submission. In their first state their affection is tender without weakness, and their piety sublime without presumption. When they have sinned they show how discord begins in mutual frailty, and how it ought to cease in mutual forbearance; how confidence of the divine favour is forfeited by sin, and how hope of pardon may be obtained by penitence and prayer. A state of innocence we can only conceive, if indeed in our present misery it be possible to conceive it; but the sentiments and worship proper to a fallen and offending being we have all to learn, as we have all to practise.

The poet, whatever be done, is always great. Our progenitors in their first state conversed with angels; even when folly and sin had degraded them they had not in their humiliation 'the port of mean suitors'; and they rise again to reverential regard when we find that their prayers were heard.

As human passions did not enter the world before the Fall, there is in the *Paradise Lost* little opportunity for the pathetic; but what little there is has not been lost. That passion which is peculiar to rational nature, the anguish arising from the consciousness of transgression and the horrors attending the sense of the Divine Displeasure, are very justly described and forcibly impressed. But the passions are moved only on one occasion; sublimity is the general and prevailing quality in this poem—sublimity variously modified, sometimes descriptive, sometimes argumentative.

The defects and faults of *Paradise Lost*, for faults and defects every work of man must have, it is the business of impartial criticism to discover. As in displaying the excellence of Milton I have not made long quotations, because of selecting beauties there had been no end, I shall in the same general manner mention that which seems to deserve censure; for what Englishman can take delight in transcribing passages which, if they lessen the reputation of Milton, diminish in some degree the honour of our country?

The generality of my scheme does not admit the frequent notice of verbal inaccuracies which Bentley, perhaps better skilled in grammar than in poetry, has often found, though he sometimes made them, and which he imputed to the obtrusions of a reviser whom the author's blindness obliged him to employ. A supposition rash and groundless, if he thought it true; and vile and pernicious, if, as is said, he in private allowed it to be false.

The plan of *Paradise Lost* has this inconvenience, that it comprises neither human actions nor human manners. The man and woman who act and suffer are in a state which no other man or woman can ever know. The reader finds no transaction in which he can be engaged, beholds no condition in which he can by any effort of imagination place himself; he has, therefore, little natural curiosity or sympathy.

We all, indeed, feel the effects of Adam's disobedience; we all sin like Adam, and like him must all bewail our offences; we have restless and insidious enemies in the fallen angels, and in the blessed spirits we have guardians and friends; in the Redemption of mankind we hope to be included: in the description of heaven and hell we are surely interested, as we are all to reside hereafter either in the regions of horror or of bliss.

But these truths are too important to be new: they have been taught to our infancy; they have mingled with our solitary thoughts and familiar conversation, and are habitually interwoven with the whole texture of life. Being therefore not new they raise no unaccustomed emotion in the mind: what we knew before we cannot learn; what is not unexpected cannot surprise.

Of the ideas suggested by these awful scenes, from some we recede with reverence, except when stated hours require their association; and from others we shrink with horror or admit them only as salutary inflictions, as counterpoises to our interests and passions. Such images rather obstruct the career of fancy than incite it.

Pleasure and terror are indeed the genuine sources of poetry; but poetical pleasure must be such as human imagination can at least conceive, and poetical terror such as human strength and fortitude may combat. The good and evil of Eternity are too ponderous for the wings of wit; the mind sinks under them in passive helplessness, content with calm belief and humble adoration.

Known truths however may take a different appearance, and be conveyed to the mind by a new train of intermediate images. This Milton has undertaken, and performed with pregnancy and vigour of mind peculiar to himself. Whoever considers the few radical positions which the Scriptures afforded him will wonder by what energetic operations he expanded them to such extent and ramified them to so much variety, restrained as he was by religious reverence from licentiousness of fiction.

Here is a full display of the united force of study and genius; of a great accumulation of materials, with judgement to digest and fancy to combine them: Milton was able to select from nature or from story, from ancient fable or from modern science, whatever could illustrate or adorn his thoughts. An accumulation of knowledge impregnated his mind, fermented by study and exalted by imagination.

It has been therefore said without an indecent hyperbole by one of his encomiasts, that in reading *Paradise Lost* we read a book of universal knowledge.

But original deficience cannot be supplied. The want of human interest is always felt. *Paradise Lost* is one of the books which the reader admires and lays down, and forgets to take up again. None ever wished it longer than it is. Its perusal is a duty rather than a pleasure. We read Milton for instruction, retire harassed and overburdened, and look elsewhere for recreation; we desert our master, and seek for companions.

Another inconvenience of Milton's design is that it requires the description of what cannot be described, the agency of spirits. He saw that immateriality supplied no images, and that he could not show angels acting but by instruments of action; he therefore invested them with form and matter. This being necessary was therefore defensible; and he should have secured the consistency of his system by keeping immateriality out of sight, and enticing his reader to drop it from his thoughts. But he has unhappily perplexed his poetry with his philosophy. His infernal and celestial powers are sometimes pure spirit and sometimes animated body. When Satan walks with his lance upon the 'burning marle' he has a body; when in his passage between hell and the new world he is in danger of sinking in the vacuity and is supported by a gust of rising vapours he has a body; when he animates the toad he seems to be mere spirit that can penetrate matter at pleasure; when he 'starts up in his own shape', he has at least a determined form; and when he is brought before Gabriel he has 'a spear and a shield', which he had the power of hiding in the toad, though the arms of the contending angels are evidently material.

The vulgar inhabitants of Pandaemonium, being 'incorporeal spirits', are 'at large though without number' in a limited space, yet in the battle when they were overwhelmed by mountains their armour hurt them, 'crushed in upon their substance, now grown gross by sinning'. This likewise happened to the uncorrupted angels, who were overthrown 'the sooner for their arms, for unarmed they might easily as spirits have evaded by contraction or remove'. Even as spirits they are hardly spiritual, for 'contraction' and 'remove' are images of matter; but if they could have escaped without their armour, they might have escaped from it and left only the empty cover to be battered. Uriel, when he rides on a sun-beam, is material; Satan is material when he is afraid of the prowess of Adam.

The confusion of spirit and matter which pervades the whole

narration of the war of heaven fills it with incongruity; and the book in which it is related is, I believe, the favourite of children, and gradually neglected as knowledge is increased.

After the operation of immaterial agents which cannot be explained may be considered that of allegorical persons, which have no real existence. To exalt causes into agents, to invest abstract ideas with form, and animate them with activity has always been the right of poetry. But such airy beings are for the most part suffered only to do their natural office, and retire. Thus Fame tells a tale and Victory hovers over a general or perches on a standard; but Fame and Victory can do no more. To give them any real employment or ascribe to them any material agency is to make them allegorical no longer, but to shock the mind by ascribing effects to non-entity. In the *Prometheus* of Æschylus we see Violence and Strength, and in the *Alcestis* of Euripides we see Death, brought upon the stage, all as active persons of the drama; but no precedents can justify absurdity.

Milton's allegory of Sin and Death is undoubtedly faulty. Sin is indeed the mother of Death, and may be allowed to be the portress of hell; but when they stop the journey of Satan, a journey described as real, and when Death offers him battle, the allegory is broken. That Sin and Death should have shown the way to hell might have been allowed; but they cannot facilitate the passage by building a bridge, because the difficulty of Satan's passage is described as real and sensible, and the bridge ought to be only figurative. The hell assigned to the rebellious spirits is described as not less local than the residence of man. It is placed in some distant part of space, separated from the regions of harmony and order by a chaotic waste and an unoccupied vacuity; but Sin and Death worked up a 'mole of aggregated soil', cemented with asphaltus; a work too bulky for ideal architects.

This unskilful allegory appears to me one of the greatest faults of the poem; and to this there was no temptation but the author's opinion of its beauty.

To the conduct of the narrative some objections may be made. Satan is with great expectation brought before Gabriel in Paradise, and is suffered to go away unmolested. The creation of man is represented as the consequence of the vacuity left in heaven by the expulsion of the rebels; yet Satan mentions it as a report 'rife in heaven' before his departure.

To find sentiments for the state of innocence was very difficult; and something of anticipation perhaps is now and then discovered.

Adam's discourse of dreams seems not to be the speculation of a new-created being. I know not whether his answer to the angel's reproof for curiosity does not want something of propriety: it is the speech of a man acquainted with many other men. Some philosophical notions, especially when the philosophy is false, might have been better omitted. The angel in a comparison speaks of 'timorous deer', before deer were yet timorous, and before Adam could understand the comparison.

Dryden remarks that Milton has some flats among his elevations. This is only to say that all the parts are not equal. In every work one part must be for the sake of others; a palace must have passages, a poem must have transitions. It is no more to be required that wit should always be blazing than that the sun should always stand at noon. In a great work there is a vicissitude of luminous and opaque parts, as there is in the world a succession of day and night. Milton, when he has expatiated in the sky, may be allowed sometimes to revisit earth; for what other author ever soared so high or sustained his flight so long?

Milton, being well versed in the Italian poets, appears to have borrowed often from them; and, as every man catches something from his companions, his desire of imitating Ariosto's levity has disgraced his work with the 'Paradise of Fools'; a fiction not in itself ill-imagined, but too ludicrous for its place.

His play on words, in which he delights too often; his equivocations, which Bentley endeavours to defend by the example of the ancients; his unnecessary and ungraceful use of terms of art, it is not necessary to mention, because they are easily remarked and generally censured, and at last bear so little proportion to the whole that they scarcely deserve the attention of a critic.

Such are the faults of that wonderful performance *Paradise Lost*, which he who can put in balance with its beauties must be considered not as nice but as dull, as less to be censured for want of candour than pitied for want of sensibility.

Of *Paradise Regained* the general judgement seems now to be right, that it is in many parts elegant, and everywhere instructive. It was not to be supposed that the writer of *Paradise Lost* could ever write without great effusions of fancy and exalted precepts of wisdom. The basis of *Paradise Regained* is narrow; a dialogue without action can never please like an union of the narrative and dramatic powers. Had this poem been written, not by Milton but by some imitator, it would have claimed and received universal praise.

If *Paradise Regained* has been too much depreciated, *Samson Agonistes* has in requital been too much admired. It could only be by long prejudice and the bigotry of learning that Milton could prefer the ancient tragedies with their encumbrance of a chorus to the exhibitions of the French and English stages; and it is only by a blind confidence in the reputation of Milton that a drama can be praised in which the intermediate parts have neither cause nor consequence, neither hasten nor retard the catastrophe.

In this tragedy are however many particular beauties, many just sentiments and striking lines; but it wants that power of attracting attention which a well-connected plan produces.

Milton would not have excelled in dramatic writing; he knew human nature only in the gross, and had never studied the shades of character, nor the combinations of concurring or the perplexity of contending passions. He had read much and knew what books could teach; but had mingled little in the world, and was deficient in the knowledge which experience must confer.

Through all his greater works there prevails an uniform peculiarity of *diction*, a mode and cast of expression which bears little resemblance to that of any former writer, and which is so far removed from common use that an unlearned reader when he first opens his book finds himself surprised by a new language.

This novelty has been, by those who can find nothing wrong in Milton, imputed to his laborious endeavours after words suitable to the grandeur of his ideas. 'Our language,' says Addison, 'sunk under him.' But the truth is, that both in prose and verse, he had formed his style by a perverse and pedantic principle. He was desirous to use English words with a foreign idiom. This in all his prose is discovered and condemned, for there judgement operates freely, neither softened by the beauty nor awed by the dignity of his thoughts; but such is the power of his poetry that his call is obeyed without resistance, the reader feels himself in captivity to a higher and a nobler mind, and criticism sinks in admiration.

Milton's style was not modified by his subject: what is shown with greater extent in *Paradise Lost* may be found in *Comus*. One source of his peculiarity was his familiarity with the Tuscan poets: the disposition of his words is, I think, frequently Italian; perhaps sometimes combined with other tongues. Of him, at last, may be said what Jonson says of Spenser, that 'he wrote no language', but has formed what Butler calls 'a Babylonish Dialect', in itself harsh and barbarous, but made by exalted genius and extensive learning the vehicle of so much instruction and so much pleasure that, like other lovers, we find grace in its deformity.

Whatever be the faults of his diction he cannot want the praise of copiousness and variety; he was master of his language in its full extent, and has selected the melodious words with such diligence that from his book alone the Art of English Poetry might be learned.

After his diction something must be said of his versification. 'The measure,' he says, 'is the English heroic verse without rhyme.' Of this mode he had many examples among the Italians, and some in his own country. The Earl of Surrey is said to have translated one of Virgil's books without rhyme, and besides our tragedies a few short poems had appeared in blank verse; particularly one tending to reconcile the nation to Raleigh's wild attempt upon Guiana, and probably written by Raleigh himself. These petty performances cannot be supposed to have much influenced Milton, who more probably took his hint from Trissino's *Italia Liberata*; and, finding blank verse easier than rhyme, was desirous of persuading himself that it is better.

'Rhyme,' he says, and says truly, 'is no necessary adjunct of true poetry.' But perhaps of poetry as a mental operation metre or music is no necessary adjunct; it is however by the music of metre that poetry has been discriminated in all languages, and in languages melodiously constructed with a due proportion of long and short syllables metre is sufficient. But one language cannot communicate its rules to another; where metre is scanty and imperfect some help is necessary. The music of the English heroic line strikes the ear so faintly that it is easily lost, unless all the syllables of every line co-operate together; this co-operation can be only obtained by the preservation of every verse unmingled with another as a distinct system of sounds, and this distinctness is obtained and preserved by the artifice of rhyme. The variety of pauses so much boasted by the lovers of blank verse changes the measures of an English poet to the periods of a declaimer; and there are only a few skilful and happy readers of Milton who enable their audience to perceive where the lines end or begin. 'Blank verse,' said an ingenious critic,° 'seems to be verse only to the eye.'

Poetry may subsist without rhyme, but English poetry will not often please; nor can rhyme ever be safely spared but where the subject is able to support itself. Blank verse makes some approach to that which is called the 'lapidary style'; has neither the easiness of prose nor the melody of numbers, and therefore tires by long continuance. Of the Italian writers without rhyme whom Milton alleges as precedents not one is popular; what reason could urge in its defence has been confuted by the ear.

But whatever be the advantage of rhyme I cannot prevail on myself to wish that Milton had been a rhymer, for I cannot wish his work to be other than it is; yet like other heroes he is to be admired rather than imitated. He that thinks himself capable of astonishing may write blank verse, but those that hope only to please must condescend to rhyme.

The highest praise of genius is original invention. Milton cannot be said to have contrived the structure of an epic poem, and therefore owes reverence to that vigour and amplitude of mind to which all generations must be indebted for the art of poetical narration, for the texture of the fable, the variation of incidents, the interposition of dialogue, and all the stratagems that surprise and enchain attention. But of all the borrowers from Homer Milton is perhaps the least indebted. He was naturally a thinker for himself, confident of his own abilities and disdainful of help or hindrance; he did not refuse admission to the thoughts or images of his predecessors, but he did not seek them. From his contemporaries he neither courted nor received support; there is in his writings nothing by which the pride of other authors might be gratified or favour gained, no exchange of praise nor solicitation of support. His great works were performed under discountenance and in blindness, but difficulties vanished at his touch; he was born for whatever is arduous; and his work is not the greatest of heroic poems, only because it is not the first.

Dryden

. . . .

Dryden may be properly considered as the father of English criticism, as the writer who first taught us to determine upon principles the merit of composition. Of our former poets the greatest dramatist wrote without rules, conducted through life and nature by a genius that rarely misled, and rarely deserted him. Of the rest, those who knew the laws of propriety had neglected to teach them.

Two *Arts of English Poetry* were written in the days of Elizabeth by Webb and Puttenham, from which something might be learned, and a few hints had been given by Jonson and Cowley; but Dryden's *Essay on Dramatic Poetry* was the first regular and valuable treatise on the art of writing.

He who, having formed his opinions in the present age of English literature, turns back to peruse this dialogue will not perhaps find much increase of knowledge or much novelty of instruction; but he is to remember that critical principles were then in the hands of a few, who had gathered them partly from the Ancients, and partly from the Italians and French. The structure of dramatic poems was not then generally understood. Audiences applauded by instinct, and poets perhaps often pleased by chance.

A writer who obtains his full purpose loses himself in his own lustre. Of an opinion which is no longer doubted, the evidence ceases to be examined. Of an art universally practised, the first teacher is forgotten. Learning once made popular is no longer learning: it has the appearance of something which we have bestowed upon ourselves, as the dew appears to rise from the field which it refreshes.

To judge rightly of an author we must transport ourselves to his time, and examine what were the wants of his contemporaries, and what were his means of supplying them. That which is easy at one time was difficult at another. Dryden at least imported his science, and gave his country what it wanted before; or rather, he imported only the materials, and manufactured them by his own skill.

The dialogue on the Drama was one of his first essays of criticism, written when he was yet a timorous candidate for reputation, and therefore laboured with that diligence which he might allow himself somewhat to remit when his name gave sanction to his positions, and his awe of the public was abated, partly by custom, and partly by success. It will not be easy to find in all the opulence of our language a treatise so artfully variegated with successive representations of opposite probabilities, so enlivened with imagery, so brightened with illustrations. His portraits of the English dramatists are wrought with great spirit and diligence. The account of Shakespeare may stand as a perpetual model of encomiastic criticism; exact without minuteness, and lofty without exaggeration. The praise lavished by Longinus on the attestation of the heroes of Marathon by Demosthenes fades away before it. In a few lines is exhibited a character so extensive in its comprehension and so curious in its limitations that nothing can be added, diminished, or reformed; nor can the editors and admirers of Shakespeare, in all their emulation of reverence, boast of much more than of having diffused and paraphrased this epitome of excellence, of having changed Dryden's gold for baser metal, of lower value though of greater bulk.

In this, and in all his other essays on the same subject, the criticism of Dryden is the criticism of a poet; not a dull collection of theorems, nor a rude detection of faults, which perhaps the censor was not able to have committed; but a gay and vigorous dissertation, where delight is mingled with instruction, and where the author proves his right of judgement by his power of performance.

The different manner and effect with which critical knowledge may be conveyed was perhaps never more clearly exemplified than in the performances of Rymer° and Dryden. It was said of a dispute between two mathematicians, 'malim cum Scaligero errare, quam cum Clavio recte sapere'; that 'it was more eligible to go wrong with one than right with the other'. A tendency of the same kind every mind must feel at the perusal of Dryden's prefaces and Rymer's discourses. With Dryden we are wandering in quest of Truth, whom we find, if we find her at all, dressed in the graces of elegance; and if we miss her, the labour of the pursuit rewards itself: we are led only through fragrance and flowers. Rymer, without taking a nearer, takes a rougher way; every step is to be made through thorns and brambles, and Truth, if we meet her, appears repulsive by her mien and ungraceful by her habit. Dryden's criticism has the majesty of a queen; Rymer's has the ferocity of a tyrant.

As he had studied with great diligence the art of poetry, and enlarged or rectified his notions by experience perpetually increasing, he had his mind stored with principles and observations: he poured out his knowledge with little labour; for of labour, notwithstanding the multiplicity of his productions, there is sufficient reason to suspect that he was not a lover. To write *con amore*, with fondness for the

employment, with perpetual touches and retouches, with unwillingness to take leave of his own idea, and an unwearied pursuit of
unattainable perfection, was, I think, no part of his character.

His criticism may be considered as general or occasional. In his
general precepts, which depend upon the nature of things and the
structure of the human mind, he may doubtless be safely recommended to the confidence of the reader; but his occasional and
particular positions were sometimes interested, sometimes negligent,
and sometimes capricious. It is not without reason that Trapp,°
speaking of the praises which he bestows on *Palamon and Arcite*, says

Novimus judicium Drydeni de poemate quodam Chauceri, pulchro sane
illo, et admodum laudando, nimirum quod non modo vere epicum sit, sed
Iliada etiam atque *Æneida* aequet, imo superet. Sed novimus eodem tempore
viri illius maximi non semper accuratissimas esse censuras, nec ad sever-
issimam critices normam exactas: Illo judice id plerumque optimum est, quod
nunc prae manibus habet, et in quo nunc occupatur.

He is therefore by no means constant to himself. His defence and
desertion of dramatic rhyme is generally known. Spence, in his
remarks on Pope's *Odyssey*, produces what he thinks an unconquerable quotation from Dryden's preface to the *Æneid*, in favour
of translating an epic poem into blank verse; but he forgets that when
his author attempted the *Iliad*, some years afterwards, he departed
from his own decision, and translated into rhyme.

When he has any objection to obviate, or any license to defend, he is
not very scrupulous about what he asserts, nor very cautious, if the
present purpose be served, not to entangle himself in his own
sophistries. But when all arts are exhausted, like other hunted animals,
he sometimes stands at bay; when he cannot disown the grossness of
one of his plays, he declares that he knows not any law that prescribes
morality to a comic poet.

His remarks on ancient or modern writers are not always to be
trusted. His parallel of the versification of Ovid with that of Claudian
has been very justly censured by Sewel.° His comparison of the first
line of Virgil with the first of Statius is not happier. Virgil, he says, is
soft and gentle, and would have thought Statius mad if he had heard
him thundering out

Quae superimposito moles geminata colosso.°

Statius perhaps heats himself as he proceeds to exaggerations
somewhat hyperbolical; but undoubtedly Virgil would have been too

hasty if he had condemned him to straw° for one sounding line. Dryden wanted an instance, and the first that occurred was impressed into the service.

What he wishes to say, he says at hazard; he cited *Gorbuduc*, which he had never seen; gives a false account of Chapman's versification; and discovers in the preface to his *Fables* that he translated the first book of the *Iliad* without knowing what was in the second.

It will be difficult to prove that Dryden ever made any great advances in literature. As having distinguished himself at Westminster under the tuition of Busby, who advanced his scholars to a height of knowledge very rarely attained in grammar-schools, he resided afterwards at Cambridge, it is not to be supposed that his skill in the ancient languages was deficient compared with that of common students; but his scholastic acquisitions seem not proportionate to his opportunities and abilities. He could not, like Milton or Cowley, have made his name illustrious merely by his learning. He mentions but few books, and those such as lie in the beaten track of regular study; from which, if ever he departs, he is in danger of losing himself in unknown regions.

In his *Dialogue on the Drama* he pronounces with great confidence that the Latin tragedy of *Medea* is not Ovid's, because it is not sufficiently interesting and pathetic. He might have determined the question upon surer evidence, for it is quoted by Quintilian as the work of Seneca; and the only line which remains of Ovid's play, for one line is left us, is not there to be found. There was therefore no need of the gravity of conjecture, or the discussion of plot or sentiment, to find what was already known upon higher authority than such discussions can ever reach.

His literature, though not always free from ostentation, will be commonly found either obvious, and made his own by the art of dressing it; or superficial, which by what he gives shows what he wanted; or erroneous, hastily collected, and negligently scattered.

Yet it cannot be said that his genius is ever unprovided of matter, or that his fancy languishes in penury of ideas. His works abound with knowledge, and sparkle with illustrations. There is scarcely any science or faculty that does not supply him with occasional images and lucky similitudes; every page discovers a mind very widely acquainted both with art and nature, and in full possession of great stores of intellectual wealth. Of him that knows much it is natural to suppose that he has read with diligence; yet I rather believe that the knowledge of Dryden was gleaned from accidental intelligence and various conversation; by a quick apprehension, a judicious selection, and a happy memory, a keen appetite of knowledge, and a powerful digestion; by vigilance that permitted nothing to pass without notice, and a habit of reflection that suffered nothing useful to be lost. A mind like Dryden's, always curious, always active, to which every under-standing was proud to be associated, and of which every one solicited the regard by an ambitious display of himself, had a more pleasant, perhaps a nearer, way to knowledge than by the silent progress of solitary reading. I do not suppose that he despised books or intentionally neglected them; but that he was carried out by the impetuosity of his genius to more vivid and speedy instructors, and that his studies were rather desultory and fortuitous than constant and systematical.

It must be confessed that he scarcely ever appears to want book-learning but when he mentions books; and to him may be transferred the praise which he gives his master Charles:°

> His conversation, wit, and parts,
> His knowledge in the noblest useful arts,
> Were such, dead authors could not give,
> But habitudes of those that live;
> Who, lighting him, did greater lights receive:
> He drain'd from all, and all they knew,
> His apprehension quick, his judgement true:
> That the most learn'd with shame confess
> His knowledge more, his reading only less.

Of all this however if the proof be demanded I will not undertake to give it; the atoms of probability of which my opinion has been formed lie scattered over all his works: and by him who thinks the question worth his notice his works must be perused with very close attention.

Criticism, either didactic or defensive, occupies almost all his prose, except those pages which he has devoted to his patrons; but none of his prefaces were ever thought tedious. They have not the formality of a settled style, in which the first half of the sentence betrays the other. The clauses are never balanced, nor the periods modelled; every word seems to drop by chance, thought it falls into its proper place. Nothing is cold or languid; the whole is airy, animated, and vigorous: what is little is gay; what is great is splendid. He may be thought to mention himself too frequently; but while he forces himself upon our esteem, we cannot refuse him to stand high in his own. Everything is excused by the play of images and the spriteliness of expression. Though all is easy, nothing is feeble; though all seems careless, there is nothing harsh; and though since his earlier works more than a century has passed they have nothing yet uncouth or obsolete.

He who writes much will not easily escape a manner, such a recurrence of particular modes as may be easily noted. Dryden is always 'another and the same'; he does not exhibit a second time the same elegances in the same form, nor appears to have any art other than that of expressing with clearness what he thinks with vigour. His style could not easily be imitated, either seriously or ludicrously; for, being always equable and always varied, it has no prominent or discriminative characters. The beauty who is totally free from disproportion of parts and features cannot be ridiculed by an overcharged resemblance.

From his prose however Dryden derives only his accidental and secondary praise; the veneration with which his name is pronounced by every cultivator of English literature is paid to him as he refined the language, improved the sentiments, and tuned the numbers of English poetry.

After about half a century of forced thoughts and rugged metre some advances towards nature and harmony had been already made by Waller and Denham; they had shown that long discourses in rhyme grew more pleasing when they were broken into couplets, and that verse consisted not only in the number but the arrangement of syllables.

But though they did much, who can deny that they left much to do? Their works were not many, nor were their minds of very ample comprehension. More examples of more modes of composition were necessary for the establishment of regularity, and the introduction of propriety in word and thought.

Every language of a learned nation necessarily divides itself into diction scholastic and popular, grave and familiar, elegant and gross; and from a nice distinction of these different parts arises a great part of the beauty of style. But if we except a few minds, the favourites of nature, to whom their own original rectitude was in the place of rules, this delicacy of selection was little known to our authors: our speech lay before them in a heap of confusion, and every man took for every purpose what chance might offer him.

There was therefore before the time of Dryden no poetical diction: no system of words at once refined from the grossness of domestic use and free from the harshness of terms appropriated to particular arts. Words too familiar or too remote defeat the purpose of a poet. From those sounds which we hear on small or on coarse occasions, we do not easily receive strong impressions or delightful images; and words to which we are nearly strangers, whenever they occur, draw that attention on themselves which they should transmit to things.

Those happy combinations of words which distinguish poetry from prose had been rarely attempted; we had few elegances or flowers of speech: the roses had not yet been plucked from the bramble or different colours had not been joined to enliven one another.

It may be doubted whether Waller and Denham could have overborne the prejudices which had long prevailed, and which even then were sheltered by the protection of Cowley. The new versification, as it was called, may be considered as owing its establishment to Dryden, from whose time it is apparent that English poetry has had no tendency to relapse to its former savageness.

The affluence and comprehension of our language is very illustriously displayed in our poetical translations of ancient writers: a work which the French seem to relinquish in despair, and which we were long unable to perform with dexterity. Ben Jonson thought it necessary to copy Horace almost word by word; Feltham, his contemporary and adversary, considers it as indispensably requisite in a translation to give line for line. It is said that Sandys, whom Dryden calls the best versifier of the last age, has struggled hard to comprise every book of his English *Metamorphoses* in the same number of verses with the original. Holyday had nothing in view but to show that he understood his author, with so little regard to the grandeur of his diction, or the volubility of his numbers, that his metres can hardly be called verses; they cannot be read without reluctance, nor will the labour always be rewarded by understanding them. Cowley saw that such 'copiers' were a 'servile race'; he asserted his liberty, and spread his wings so boldly that he left his authors. It was reserved for Dryden to fix the limits of poetical liberty, and give us just rules and examples of translation.

When languages are formed upon different principles, it is impossible that the same modes of expression should always be elegant in both. While they run on together the closest translation may be considered as the best; but when they divaricate each must take its natural course. Where correspondence cannot be obtained it is necessary to be content with something equivalent. 'Translation therefore,' says Dryden, 'is not so loose as paraphrase, nor so close as metaphrase.'

All polished languages have different styles: the concise, the diffuse, the lofty, and the humble. In the proper choice of style consists the resemblance which Dryden principally exacts from the translator. He is to exhibit his author's thoughts in such a dress of diction as the author would have given them, had his language been English: rugged magnificence is not to be softened; hyperbolical ostentation is not to be repressed, nor sententious affectation to have its points blunted. A translator is to be like his author: it is not his business to excel him.

The reasonableness of these rules seems sufficient for their vindication; and the effects produced by observing them were so happy that I know not whether they were ever opposed but by Sir Edward Sherburne, a man whose learning was greater than his powers of poetry, and who, being better qualified to give the meaning than the spirit of Seneca, has introduced his version of three tragedies by a defence of close translation. The authority of Horace, which the new translators cited in defence of their practice, he has, by a judicious explanation, taken fairly from them; but reason wants not Horace to support it.

. . . .

Of Dryden's works it was said by Pope that 'he could select from them better specimens of every mode of poetry than any other English writer could supply'. Perhaps no nation ever produced a writer that enriched his language with such variety of models. To him we owe the improvement, perhaps the completion of our metre, the refinement of our language, and much of the correctness of our sentiments. By him we were taught *sapere et fari*, to think naturally and express forcibly. Though Davies has reasoned in rhyme before him, it may be perhaps maintained that he was the first who joined argument with poetry. He showed us the true bounds of a translator's liberty. What was said of Rome, adorned by Augustus, may be applied by an easy metaphor to English poetry embellished by Dryden, *lateritiam invenit, marmoream reliquit*,° he found it brick, and he left it marble.

Pope°

The person of Pope is well known not to have been formed by the nicest model. He has, in his account of the 'Little Club', compared himself to a spider, and by another is described as protuberant behind and before. He is said to have been beautiful in his infancy; but he was of a constitution originally feeble and weak, and as bodies of a tender frame are easily distorted his deformity was probably in part the effect of his application. His stature was so low that, to bring him to a level with common tables, it was necessary to raise his seat. But his face was not displeasing, and his eyes were animated and vivid.

By natural deformity or accidental distortion his vital functions were so much disordered that his life was a 'long disease'. His most frequent assailant was the headache, which he used to relieve by inhaling the steam of coffee, which he very frequently required.

Most of what can be told concerning his petty peculiarities was communicated by a female domestic of the Earl of Oxford, who knew him perhaps after the middle of life. He was then so weak as to stand in perpetual need of female attendance; extremely sensible of cold, so that he wore a kind of fur doublet under a shirt of very coarse warm linen with fine sleeves. When he rose he was invested in bodice made of stiff canvas, being scarce able to hold himself erect till they were laced, and he then put on a flannel waistcoat. One side was contracted. His legs were so slender that he enlarged their bulk with three pair of stockings, which were drawn on and off by the maid; for he was not able to dress or undress himself, and neither went to bed nor rose without help. His weakness made it very difficult for him to be clean.

His hair had fallen almost all away, and he used to dine sometimes with Lord Oxford, privately, in a velvet cap. His dress of ceremony was black, with a tie-wig and a little sword.

The indulgence and accommodation which his sickness required had taught him all the unpleasing and unsocial qualities of a valetudinary man. He expected that every thing should give way to his ease or humour, as a child whose parents will not hear her cry has an unresisted dominion in the nursery.

> C'est que l'enfant toujours est homme,
> C'est que l'homme est toujours enfant.

When he wanted to sleep he 'nodded in company'; and once

slumbered at his own table while the Prince of Wales was talking of poetry.

The reputation which his friendship gave procured him many invitations; but he was a very troublesome inmate. He brought no servant, and had so many wants that a numerous attendance was scarcely able to supply them. Wherever he was he left no room for another, because he exacted the attention and employed the activity of the whole family. His errands were so frequent and frivolous that the footmen in time avoided and neglected him, and the Earl of Oxford discharged some of the servants for their resolute refusal of his messages. The maids, when they had neglected their business, alleged that they had been employed by Mr Pope. One of his constant demands was of coffee in the night, and to the woman that waited on him in his chamber he was very burdensome; but he was careful to recompense her want of sleep, and Lord Oxford's servant declared that in a house where her business was to answer his call she would not ask for wages.

He had another fault, easily incident to those who suffering much pain think themselves entitled to whatever pleasures they can snatch. He was too indulgent to his appetite: he loved meat highly seasoned and of strong taste, and, at the intervals of the table, amused himself with biscuits and dry conserves. If he sat down to a variety of dishes he would oppress his stomach with repletion, and though he seemed angry when a dram was offered him, did not forbear to drink it. His friends, who knew the avenues to his heart, pampered him with presents of luxury, which he did not suffer to stand neglected. The death of great men is not always proportioned to the lustre of their lives. Hannibal, says Juvenal, did not perish by a javelin or a sword; the slaughters of Cannae were revenged by a ring.° The death of Pope was imputed by some of his friends to a silver saucepan, in which it was his delight to heat potted lampreys.

That he loved too well to eat is certain; but that his sensuality shortened his life will not be hastily concluded when it is remembered that a conformation so irregular lasted six and fifty years, notwithstanding such pertinacious diligence of study and meditation.

In all his intercourse with mankind he had great delight in artifice, and endeavoured to attain all his purposes by indirect and unsuspected methods. 'He hardly drank tea without a stratagem.' If at the house of his friends he wanted any accommodation he was not willing to ask for it in plain terms, but would mention it remotely as something convenient; though, when it was procured, he soon made it appear for whose sake it had been recommended. Thus he teased Lord Orrery till he obtained a screen. He practised his arts on such small occasions that Lady Bolingbroke used to say, in a French phrase, that 'he played the politician about cabbages and turnips'. His unjustifiable impression° of *The Patriot King*, as it can be imputed to no particular motive, must have proceeded from his general habit of secrecy and cunning: he caught an opportunity of a sly trick, and pleased himself with the thought of outwitting Bolingbroke.

In familiar or convivial conversation it does not appear that he excelled. He may be said to have resembled Dryden as being not one that was distinguished by vivacity in company. It is remarkable that, so near his time, so much should be known of what he has written, and so little of what he has said: traditional memory retains no sallies of raillery nor sentences of observation; nothing either pointed or solid, either wise or merry. One apophthegm only stands upon record. When an objection raised against his inscription for Shakespeare was defended by the authority of Patrick, he replied,—*horresco referens°*— that 'he would allow the publisher of a Dictionary to know the meaning of a single word, but not of two words put together'.

He was fretful and easily displeased, and allowed himself to be capriciously resentful. He would sometimes leave Lord Oxford silently, no one could tell why, and was to be courted back by more letters and messages than the footmen were willing to carry. The table was indeed infested by Lady Mary Wortley, who was the friend of Lady Oxford, and who, knowing his peevishness, could by no entreaties be restrained from contradicting him, till their disputes were sharpened to such asperity that one or the other quitted the house.

He sometimes condescended to be jocular with servants or inferiors; but by no merriment, either of others or his own, was he ever seen excited to laughter.

Of his domestic character frugality was a part eminently remarkable. Having determined not to be dependent he determined not to be in want, and therefore wisely and magnanimously rejected all temptations to expense unsuitable to his fortune. This general care must be universally approved; but it sometimes appeared in petty artifices of parsimony, such as the practice of writing his compositions on the back of letters, as may be seen in the remaining copy of the *Iliad*, by which perhaps in five years five shillings were saved; or in a niggardly reception of his friends and scantiness of entertainment, as when he had two guests in his house he would set at supper a single pint upon the table, and having himself taken two small glasses would retire and say, 'Gentlemen, I leave you to your wine.' Yet he tells his friends that 'he has a heart for all, a house for all, and, whatever they may think, a fortune for all'.

He sometimes, however, made a splendid dinner, and is said to have wanted no part of the skill or elegance which such performances require. That this magnificence should be often displayed, that obstinate prudence with which he conducted his affairs would not permit; for his revenue, certain and casual, amounted only to about eight hundred pounds a year, of which, however, he declares himself able to assign one hundred to charity.

Of this fortune, which as it arose from public approbation was very honourably obtained, his imagination seems to have been too full: it would be hard to find a man so well entitled to notice by his wit that ever delighted so much in talking of his money. In his letters and in his poems, his garden and his grotto, his quincunx and his vines, or some hints of his opulence, are always to be found. The great topic of his ridicule is poverty: the crimes with which he reproaches his antagonists are their debts, their habitation in the Mint, and their want of a dinner. He seems to be of an opinion, not very uncommon in the world, that to want money is to want every thing.

Next to the pleasure of contemplating his possessions seems to be that of enumerating the men of high rank with whom he was acquainted, and whose notice he loudly proclaims not to have been obtained by any practices of meanness or servility; a boast which was never denied to be true, and to which very few poets have ever aspired. Pope never set genius to sale: he never flattered those whom he did not love, or praised those whom he did not esteem. Savage, however, remarked that he began a little to relax his dignity when he wrote a distich for 'his Highness's dog'.

His admiration of the great seems to have increased in the advance of life. He passed over peers and statesmen to inscribe his *Iliad* to Congreve, with a magnanimity of which the praise had been complete had his friend's virtue been equal to his wit. Why he was chosen for so great an honour it is not now possible to know; there is no trace in literary history of any particular intimacy between them. The name of Congreve appears in the letters among those of his other friends, but without any observable distinction or consequence.

To his latter works, however, he took care to annex names dignified with titles, but was not very happy in his choice; for, except Lord Bathurst, none of his noble friends were such as that a good man would wish to have his intimacy with them known to posterity: he can derive little honour from the notice of Cobham, Burlington, or Bolingbroke.

Of his social qualities, if an estimate be made from his letters, an opinion too favourable cannot easily be formed; they exhibit a perpetual and unclouded effulgence of general benevolence and particular fondness. There is nothing but liberality, gratitude, constancy, and tenderness. It has been so long said as to be commonly believed that the true characters of men may be found in their letters, and that he who writes to his friend lays his heart open before him. But the truth is that such were simple friendships of the *Golden Age*, and are now the friendships only of children. Very few can boast of hearts which they dare lay open to themselves, and of which, by whatever accident exposed, they do not shun a distinct and continued view; and certainly what we hide from ourselves we do not show to our friends. There is, indeed, no transaction which offers stronger temptations to fallacy and sophistication than epistolary intercourse. In the eagerness of conversation the first emotions of the mind often burst out before they are considered; in the tumult of business interest and passion have their genuine effect; but a friendly letter is a calm and deliberate performance in the cool of leisure, in the stillness of solitude, and surely no man sits down to depreciate by design his own character.

Friendship has no tendency to secure veracity, for by whom can a man so much wish to be thought better than he is as by him whose kindness he desires to gain or keep? Even in writing to the world there is less constraint: the author is not confronted with his reader, and takes his chance of approbation among the different dispositions of mankind; but a letter is addressed to a single mind of which the prejudices and partialities are known, and must therefore please, if not by favouring them, by forbearing to oppose them.

To charge those favourable representations which men give of their own minds with the guilt of hypocritical falsehood would show more severity than knowledge. The writer commonly believes himself. Almost every man's thoughts, while they are general, are right; and most hearts are pure while temptation is away. It is easy to awaken generous sentiments in privacy; to despise death when there is no danger; to glow with benevolence when there is nothing to be given. While such ideas are formed they are felt, and self-love does not suspect the gleam of virtue to be the meteor of fancy.

If the letters of Pope are considered merely as compositions they seem to be premeditated and artificial. It is one thing to write because there is something which the mind wishes to discharge, and another to solicit the imagination because ceremony or vanity requires something to be written. Pope confesses his early letters to be vitiated with 'affectation and ambition': to know whether he disentangled himself from these perverters of epistolary integrity his book and his life must be set in comparison.

One of his favourite topics is contempt of his own poetry. For this, if it had been real, he would deserve no commendation, and in this he certainly was not sincere; for his high value of himself was sufficiently observed, and of what could he be proud but of his poetry? He writes, he says, when 'he has just nothing else to do': yet Swift complains that he was never at leisure for conversation because he 'had always some poetical scheme in his head'. It was punctually required that his writing-box should be set upon his bed before he rose; and Lord Oxford's domestic related that in the dreadful winter of Forty, she was called from her bed by him four times in one night to supply him with paper, lest he should lose a thought.

He pretends insensibility to censure and criticism, though it was observed by all who knew him that every pamphlet disturbed his quiet and that his extreme irritability laid him open to perpetual vexation; but he wished to despise his critics, and therefore hoped that he did despise them.

As he happened to live in two reigns when the Court paid little attention to poetry he nursed in his mind a foolish disesteem of kings, and proclaims that 'he never sees Courts'. Yet a little regard shown him by the Prince of Wales melted his obduracy, and he had not much to say when he was asked by his Royal Highness 'how he could love a Prince while he disliked Kings'.

He very frequently professes contempt of the world, and represents himself as looking on mankind, sometimes with gay indifference, as on emmets of a hillock below his serious attention, and sometimes with gloomy indignation, as on monsters more worthy of hatred than of pity. These were dispositions apparently counterfeited. How could he despise those whom he lived by pleasing, and on whose approbation his esteem of himself was superstructed? Why should he hate those to whose favour he owed his honour and his ease? Of things that terminate in human life the world is the proper judge: to despise its sentence, if it were possible, is not just; and if it were just is not possible. Pope was far enough from this unreasonable temper; he was sufficiently 'a fool to Fame', and his fault was that he pretended to neglect it. His levity and his sullenness were only in his letters; he passed through common life, sometimes vexed and sometimes pleased, with the natural emotions of common men.

His scorn of the great is repeated too often to be real: no man thinks much of that which he despises; and as falsehood is always in danger of inconsistency he makes it his boast at another time that he lives among them.

It is evident that his own importance swells often in his mind. He is afraid of writing lest the clerks of the Post-office should know his secrets; he has many enemies; he considers himself as surrounded by universal jealousy; 'after many deaths, and many dispersions, two or three of us,' says he, 'may still be brought together, not to plot, but to divert ourselves, and the world too, if it pleases'; and they can live together, and 'show what friends wits may be, in spite of all the fools in the world'. All this while it was likely that the clerks did not know his hand: he certainly had no more enemies than a public character like his inevitably excites, and with what degree of friendship the wits might live very few were so much fools as ever to enquire.

Some part of this pretended discontent he learned from Swift, and expresses it, I think, most frequently in his correspondence with him. Swift's resentment was unreasonable, but it was sincere; Pope's was the mere mimicry of his friend, a fictitious part which he began to play before it became him. When he was only twenty-five years old he related that 'a glut of study and retirement had thrown him on the world' and that there was danger lest 'a glut of the world should throw him back upon study and retirement'. To this Swift answered with great propriety that Pope had not yet either acted or suffered enough in the world to have become weary of it. And, indeed, it must be some very powerful reason that can drive back to solitude him who has once enjoyed the pleasures of society.

In the letters both of Swift and Pope there appears such narrowness of mind as makes them insensible of any excellence that has not some affinity with their own, and confines their esteem and approbation to so small a number that whoever should form his opinion of the age from their representation would suppose them to have lived amidst ignorance and barbarity, unable to find among their contemporaries either virtue or intelligence, and persecuted by those that could not understand them.

When Pope murmurs at the world, when he professes contempt of fame, when he speaks of riches and poverty, of success and disappointment, with negligent indifference, he certainly does not express his habitual and settled sentiments, but either wilfully disguises his own character, or, what is more likely, invests himself with temporary qualities, and sallies out in the colours of the present moment. His hopes and fears, his joys and sorrows, acted strongly upon his mind, and if he differed from others it was not by carelessness. He was irritable and resentful: his malignity to Philips, whom he had first made ridiculous, and then hated for being angry, continued too long. Of his vain desire to make Bentley contemptible, I never heard any adequate reason. He was sometimes wanton in his attacks, and before Chandos, Lady Wortley, and Hill was mean in his retreat.

The virtues which seem to have had most of his affection were liberality and fidelity of friendship, in which it does not appear that he was other than he describes himself. His fortune did not suffer his charity to be splendid and conspicuous, but he assisted Dodsley with a hundred pounds that he might open a shop; and of the subscription of forty pounds a year that he raised for Savage twenty were paid by himself. He was accused of loving money, but his love was eagerness to gain, not solicitude to keep it.

In the duties of friendship he was zealous and constant: his early maturity of mind commonly united him with men older than himself, and therefore, without attaining any considerable length of life, he saw many companions of his youth sink into the grave; but it does not appear that he lost a single friend by coldness or by injury: those who loved him once continued their kindness. His ungrateful mention of Allen in his will was the effect of his adherence to one whom he had known much longer, and whom he naturally loved with greater fondness. His violation of the trust reposed in him by Bolingbroke could have no motive inconsistent with the warmest affection; he either thought the action so near to indifferent that he forgot it, or so laudable that he expected his friend to approve it.

It was reported, with such confidence as almost to enforce belief, that in the papers entrusted to his executors was found a defamatory *Life of Swift*, which he had prepared as an instrument of vengeance to be used, if any provocation should be ever given. About this I enquired of the Earl of Marchmont, who assured me that no such piece was among his remains.

The religion in which he lived and died was that of the Church of Rome, to which in his correspondence with Racine he professes himself a sincere adherent. That he was not scrupulously pious in some part of his life is known by many idle and indecent applications of sentences taken from the Scriptures; a mode of merriment which a good man dreads for its profaneness, and a witty man disdains for its easiness and vulgarity. But to whatever levities he has been betrayed, it does not appear that his principles were ever corrupted, or that he ever lost his belief of Revelation. The positions which he transmitted from Bolingbroke he seems not to have understood, and was pleased with an interpretation that made them orthodox.

A man of such exalted superiority and so little moderation would naturally have all his delinquences observed and aggravated: those who could not deny that he was excellent would rejoice to find that he was not perfect.

Perhaps it may be imputed to the unwillingness with which the same man is allowed to possess many advantages that his learning has been depreciated. He certainly was in his early life a man of great literary curiosity, and when he wrote his *Essay on Criticism* had for his age a very wide acquaintance with books. When he entered into the living world it seems to have happened to him as to many others that he was less attentive to dead masters: he studied in the academy of Paracelsus, and made the universe his favourite volume. He gathered his notions fresh from reality, not from the copies of authors, but the originals of Nature. Yet there is no reason to believe that literature ever lost his esteem; he always professed to love reading, and Dobson, who spent some time at his house translating his *Essay on Man*, when I asked him what learning he found him to possess, answered, 'More than I expected.' His frequent references to history, his allusions to various kinds of knowledge, and his images selected from art and nature, with his observations on the operations of the mind and the modes of life, show an intelligence perpetually on the wing, excursive, vigorous, and diligent, eager to pursue knowledge, and attentive to retain it.

From this curiosity arose the desire of travelling, to which he alludes in his verses to Jervas, and which, though he never found an opportunity to gratify it, did not leave him till his life declined.

Of his intellectual character the constituent and fundamental principle was good sense, a prompt and intuitive perception of consonance and propriety. He saw immediately, of his own conceptions, what was to be chosen, and what to be rejected; and, in the works of others, what was to be shunned, and what to be copied.

But good sense alone is a sedate and quiescent quality, which manages its possessions well, but does not increase them; it collects few materials for its own operations, and preserves safety, but never gains supremacy. Pope had likewise genius; a mind active, ambitious, and adventurous, always investigating, always aspiring; in its widest searches still longing to go forward, in its highest flights still wishing to be higher; always imagining something greater than it knows, always endeavouring more than it can do.

To assist these powers he is said to have had great strength and exactness of memory. That which he had heard or read was not easily lost; and he had before him not only what his own meditation suggested, but what he had found in other writers that might be accommodated to his present purpose.

These benefits of nature he improved by incessant and unwearied diligence; he had recourse to every source of intelligence, and lost no opportunity of information; he consulted the living as well as the dead; he read his compositions to his friends, and was never content with mediocrity when excellence could be attained. He considered poetry as the business of his life, and, however he might seem to lament his occupation, he followed it with constancy: to make verses was his first labour, and to mend them was his last.

From his attention to poetry he was never diverted. If conversation offered anything that could be improved he committed it to paper; if a thought, or perhaps an expression more happy than was common, rose to his mind, he was careful to write it; an independent distich was preserved for an opportunity of insertion, and some little fragments have been found containing lines, or parts of lines, to be wrought upon at some other time.

He was one of those few whose labour is their pleasure, he was never elevated to negligence, nor wearied to impatience; he never passed a fault unamended by indifference, nor quitted it by despair. He laboured his works first to gain reputation, and afterwards to keep it.

Of composition there are different methods. Some employ at once memory and invention, and, with little intermediate use of the pen, form and polish large masses by continued meditation, and write their productions only when, in their own opinion, they have completed them. It is related of Virgil that his custom was to pour out a great number of verses in the morning, and pass the day in retrenching exuberances and correcting inaccuracies. The method of Pope, as may be collected from his translation, was to write his first thoughts in his first words, and gradually to amplify, decorate, rectify, and refine them.

With such faculties and such dispositions he excelled every other writer in *poetical prudence*; he wrote in such a manner as might expose him to few hazards. He used almost always the same fabric of verse; and, indeed, by those few essays which he made of any other, he did not enlarge his reputation. Of this uniformity the certain consequence was readiness and dexterity. By perpetual practice language had in his mind a systematical arrangement; having always the same use for words, he had words so selected and combined as to be ready at his call. This increase of facility he confessed himself to have perceived in the progress of his translation.

But what was yet of more importance, his effusions were always voluntary, and his subjects chosen by himself. His independence secured him from drudging at a task, and labouring upon a barren topic: he never exchanged praise for money, nor opened a shop of condolence or congratulation. His poems, therefore, were scarce ever temporary. He suffered coronations and royal marriages to pass without a song, and derived no opportunities from recent events, nor any popularity from the accidental disposition of his readers. He was never reduced to the necessity of soliciting the sun to shine upon a birth-day, of calling the Graces and Virtues to a wedding, or of saying what multitudes have said before him. When he could produce nothing new, he was at liberty to be silent.

His publications were for the same reason never hasty. He is said to have sent nothing to the press till it had lain two years under his inspection: it is at least certain that he ventured nothing without nice examination. He suffered the tumult of imagination to subside, and the novelties of invention to grow familiar. He knew that the mind is always enamoured of its own productions, and did not trust his first fondness. He consulted his friends, and listened with great willingness to criticism; and, what was of more importance, he consulted himself, and let nothing pass against his own judgement.

He professed to have learned his poetry from Dryden, whom, whenever an opportunity was presented, he praised through his whole life with unvaried liberality; and perhaps his character may receive some illustration if he be compared with his master.

Integrity of understanding and nicety of discernment were not allotted in a less proportion to Dryden than to Pope. The rectitude of Dryden's mind was sufficiently shown by the dismission of his poetical prejudices, and the rejection of unnatural thoughts and rugged numbers. But Dryden never desired to apply all the judgement that he had. He wrote, and professed to write, merely for the people; and when he pleased others, he contented himself. He spent no time in struggles to rouse latent powers; he never attempted to make that better which was already good, nor often to mend what he must have known to be faulty. He wrote, as he tells us, with very little consideration; when occasion or necessity called upon him, he poured out what the present moment happened to supply, and, when once it had passed the press, ejected it from his mind; for when he had no pecuniary interest, he had no further solicitude.

Pope was not content to satisfy; he desired to excel, and therefore always endeavoured to do his best: he did not court the candour, but dared the judgement of his reader, and, expecting no indulgence from others, he showed none to himself. He examined lines and words with minute and punctilious observation, and retouched every part with indefatigable diligence, till he had left nothing to be forgiven.

For this reason he kept his pieces very long in his hands, while he considered and reconsidered them. The only poems which can be supposed to have been written with such regard to the times as might hasten their publication were the two satires of *Thirty-eight*; of which Dodsley told me that they were brought to him by the author that they might be fairly copied. 'Almost every line,' he said, 'was then written twice over; I gave him a clean transcript, which he sent some time afterwards to me for the press, with almost every line written twice over a second time.'

His declaration that his care for his works ceased at their publication was not strictly true. His parental attention never abandoned them; what he found amiss in the first edition, he silently corrected in those that followed. He appears to have revised the *Iliad*, and freed it from some of its imperfections; and the *Essay on Criticism* received many improvements after its first appearance. It will seldom be found that he altered without adding clearness, elegance, or vigour. Pope had perhaps the judgement of Dryden; but Dryden certainly wanted the diligence of Pope.

In acquired knowledge the superiority must be allowed to Dryden, whose education was more scholastic, and who before he became an author had been allowed more time for study, with better means of information. His mind has a larger range, and he collects his images and illustrations from a more extensive circumference of science. Dryden knew more of man in his general nature, and Pope in his local manners. The notions of Dryden were formed by comprehensive speculation, and those of Pope by minute attention. There is more dignity in the knowledge of Dryden, and more certainty in that of Pope.

Poetry was not the sole praise of either, for both excelled likewise in prose; but Pope did not borrow his prose from his predecessor. The style of Dryden is capricious and varied, that of Pope is cautious and uniform; Dryden obeys the motions of his own mind, Pope constrains his mind to his own rules of composition. Dryden is sometimes vehement and rapid; Pope is always smooth, uniform, and gentle. Dryden's page is a natural field, rising into inequalities, and diversified by the varied exuberance of abundant vegetation; Pope's is a velvet lawn, shaven by the scythe, and levelled by the roller.

Of genius, that power which constitutes a poet; that quality without which judgement is cold and knowledge is inert; that energy which collects, combines, amplifies, and animates—the superiority must, with some hesitation, be allowed to Dryden. It is not to be inferred that of this poetical vigour Pope had only a little, because Dryden had more, for every other writer since Milton must give place to Pope; and even of Dryden it must be said that if he has brighter paragraphs, he has not better poems. Dryden's performances were always hasty, either excited by some external occasion, or extorted by domestic necessity; he composed without consideration, and published without correction. What his mind could supply at call, or gather in one excursion, was all that he sought, and all that he gave. The dilatory caution of Pope enabled him to condense his sentiments, to multiply his images, and to accumulate all that study might produce, or chance might supply. If the flights of Dryden therefore are higher, Pope continues longer on the wing. If of Dryden's fire the blaze is brighter, of Pope's the heat is more regular and constant. Dryden often surpasses expectation, and Pope never falls below it. Dryden is read with frequent astonishment, and Pope with perpetual delight.

This parallel will, I hope, when it is well considered, be found just; and if the reader should suspect me, as I suspect myself, of some partial fondness for the memory of Dryden, let him not too hastily condemn me; for meditation and enquiry may, perhaps, show him the reasonableness of my determination.

The works of Pope are now to be distinctly examined, not so much with attention to slight faults or petty beauties, as to the general character and effect of each performance.

It seems natural for a young poet to initiate himself by pastorals, which, not professing to imitate real life, require no experience, and, exhibiting only the simple operation of unmingled passions, admit no subtle reasoning or deep enquiry. Pope's *Pastorals* are not however composed but with close thought; they have reference to the times of the day, the seasons of the year, and the periods of human life. The last, that which turns the attention upon age and death, was the author's favourite. To tell of disappointment and misery, to thicken the darkness of futurity, and perplex the labyrinth of uncertainty, has been always a delicious employment of the poets. His preference was probably just. I wish, however, that his fondness had not overlooked a line in which the 'Zephyrs' are made 'to lament in silence'.

To charge these *Pastorals* with want of invention is to require what never was intended. The imitations are so ambitiously frequent that the writer evidently means rather to show his literature than his wit. It is surely sufficient for an author of sixteen not only to be able to copy the poems of antiquity with judicious selection, but to have obtained sufficient power of language and skill in metre to exhibit a series of versification which had in English poetry no precedent, nor has since had an imitation.

The design of *Windsor Forest* is evidently derived from *Cooper's Hill*, with some attention to Waller's poem on *The Park*; but Pope cannot be denied to excel his masters in variety and elegance, and the art of interchanging description, narrative, and morality. The objection made by Dennis is the want of plan, of a regular subordination of parts terminating in the principal and original design. There is this want in most descriptive poems, because as the scenes, which they must exhibit successively, are all subsisting at the same time, the order in which they are shown must by necessity be arbitrary, and more is not to be expected from the last part than from the first. The attention, therefore, which cannot be detained by suspense, must be excited by diversity, such as his poem offers to its reader.

But the desire of diversity may be too much indulged: the parts of *Windsor Forest* which deserve least praise are those which were added to enliven the stillness of the scene, the appearance of Father Thames and the transformation of Lodona. Addison had in his *Campaign* derided the 'Rivers' that 'rise from their oozy beds' to tell stories of heroes, and it is therefore strange that Pope should adopt a fiction not only unnatural but lately censured. The story of Lodona is told with sweetness; but a new metamorphosis is a ready and puerile expedient: nothing is easier than to tell how a flower was once a blooming virgin, or a rock an obdurate tyrant.

The Temple of Fame has, as Steele warmly declared, 'a thousand beauties'. Every part is splendid; there is great luxuriance of ornaments; the original vision of Chaucer was never denied to be much improved; the allegory is very skilfully continued, the imagery is properly selected and learnedly displayed: yet, with all this comprehension of excellence, as its scene is laid in remote ages, and its sentiments, if the concluding paragraph be excepted, have little relation to general manners or common life, it never obtained much notice, but is turned silently over, and seldom quoted or mentioned with either praise or blame.

That *The Messiah* excels the *Pollio* is no great praise, if it be considered from what original the improvements are derived.

The *Verses on the Unfortunate Lady* have drawn much attention by the illaudable singularity of treating suicide with respect, and they must be allowed to be written in some parts with vigorous animation, and in others with gentle tenderness; nor has Pope produced any poem in which the sense predominates more over the diction. But the tale is not skilfully told: it is not easy to discover the character of either the lady or her guardian. History relates that she was about to disparage herself by a marriage with an inferior; Pope praises her for the dignity of ambition, and yet condemns the uncle to detestation for his pride: the ambitious love of a niece may be opposed by the interest, malice, or envy of an uncle, but never by his pride. On such an occasion a poet may be allowed to be obscure, but inconsistency never can be right.

The *Ode for St Cecilia's Day* was undertaken at the desire of Steele: in this the author is generally confessed to have miscarried, yet he has miscarried only as compared with Dryden; for he has far outgone other competitors. Dryden's plan is better chosen; history will always take stronger hold of the attention than fable: the passions excited by Dryden are the pleasures and pains of real life, the scene of Pope is laid in imaginary existence. Pope is read with calm acquiescence, Dryden with turbulent delight; Pope hangs upon the ear, and Dryden finds the passes of the mind.

Both the odes want the essential constituent of metrical compositions, the stated recurrence of settled numbers. It may be alleged that Pindar is said by Horace to have written *numeris lege solutis*,° but as no such lax performances have been transmitted to us, the meaning of that expression cannot be fixed; and perhaps the like return might properly be made to a modern Pindarist, as Mr Cobb° received from Bentley, who, when he found his criticisms upon a Greek exercise, which Cobb had presented, refuted one after another by Pindar's authority, cried out at last, 'Pindar was a bold fellow, but thou art an impudent one.'

If Pope's Ode be particularly inspected it will be found that the first stanza consists of sounds well chosen indeed, but only sounds.

The second consists of hyperbolical commonplaces, easily to be found, and perhaps without much difficulty to be as well expressed.

In the third, however, there are numbers, images, harmony, and vigour, not unworthy the antagonist of Dryden. Had all been like this—but every part cannot be the best.

The next stanzas place and detain us in the dark and dismal regions of mythology, where neither hope nor fear, neither joy nor sorrow can be found: the poet however faithfully attends us; we have all that can be performed by elegance of diction or sweetness of versification; but what can form avail without better matter?

The last stanza recurs again to commonplaces. The conclusion is too evidently modelled by that of Dryden; and it may be remarked that both end with the same fault, the comparison of each is literal on one side, and metaphorical on the other.

Poets do not always express their own thoughts; Pope, with all this labour in the praise of music, was ignorant of its principles, and insensible of its effects.

One of his greatest though of his earliest works is the *Essay on Criticism*, which if he had written nothing else would have placed him among the first critics and the first poets, as it exhibits every mode of excellence that can embellish or dignify didactic composition, selection of matter, novelty of arrangement, justness of precept, splendour of illustration, and propriety of digression. I know not whether it be pleasing to consider that he produced this piece at twenty, and never afterwards excelled it: he that delights himself with observing that such powers may be so soon attained cannot but grieve to think that life was ever after at a stand.

To mention the particular beauties of the *Essay* would be unprofitably tedious; but I cannot forbear to observe that the comparison of a student's progress in the sciences with the journey of a traveller in the Alps is perhaps the best that English poetry can show.° A simile, to be perfect, must both illustrate and ennoble the subject; must show it to the understanding in a clearer view, and display it to the fancy with greater dignity: but either of these qualities may be sufficient to recommend it. In didactic poetry, of which the great purpose is instruction, a simile may be praised which illustrates, though it does not ennoble; in heroics, that may be admitted which ennobles, though it does not illustrate. That it may be complete it is required to exhibit, independently of its references, a pleasing image;

for a simile is said to be a short episode. To this antiquity was so attentive that circumstances were sometimes added which, having no parallels, served only to fill the imagination, and produced what Perrault ludicrously called 'comparisons with a long tail'. In their similes the greatest writers have sometimes failed: the ship-race, compared with the chariot-race, is neither illustrated nor aggrandised; land and water make all the difference: when Apollo running after Daphne is likened to a greyhound chasing a hare, there is nothing gained; the ideas of pursuit and flight are too plain to be made plainer, and a god and the daughter of a god are not represented much to their advantage by a hare and dog. The simile of the Alps has no useless parts, yet affords a striking picture by itself: it makes the foregoing position better understood, and enables it to take faster hold on the attention; it assists the apprehension, and elevates the fancy.

Let me likewise dwell a little on the celebrated paragraph, in which it is directed that 'the sound should seem an echo to the sense'; a precept which Pope is allowed to have observed beyond any other English poet.

This notion of representative metre, and the desire of discovering frequent adaptations of the sound to the sense, have produced, in my opinion, many wild conceits and imaginary beauties. All that can furnish this representation are the sounds of the words considered singly, and the time in which they are pronounced. Every language has some words framed to exhibit the noises which they express, as *thump*, *rattle*, *growl*, *hiss*. These, however, are but few, and the poet cannot make them more, nor can they be of any use but when sound is to be mentioned. The time of pronunciation was in the dactylic measures of the learned languages capable of considerable variety; but that variety could be accommodated only to motion or duration, and different degrees of motion were perhaps expressed by verses rapid or slow, without much attention of the writer, when the image had full possession of his fancy: but our language having little flexibility our verses can differ very little in the cadence. The fancied resemblances, I fear, arise sometimes merely from the ambiguity of words; there is supposed to be some relation between a *soft* line and a *soft* couch, or between *hard* syllables and *hard* fortune.

Motion, however, may be in some sort exemplified; and yet it may be suspected that even in such resemblances the mind often governs the ear, and the sounds are estimated by their meaning. One of the most successful attempts has been to describe the labour of Sisyphus:

> With many a weary step, and many a groan,
> Up a high hill he heaves a huge round stone;
> The huge round stone, resulting with a bound,
> Thunders impetuous down, and smokes along the ground.

Who does not perceive the stone to move slowly upward, and roll violently back? But set the same numbers to another sense;

> While many a merry tale, and many a song,
> Cheered the rough road, we wished the rough road long.
> The rough road then, returning in a round,
> Mock'd our impatient steps, for all was fairy ground.

We have now surely lost much of the delay, and much of the rapidity.

But to show how little the greatest master of numbers can fix the principles of representative harmony, it will be sufficient to remark that the poet, who tells us that

> When Ajax strives some rock's vast weight to throw,
> The line too labours and the words move slow:
> Not so when swift Camilla scours the plain,
> Flies o'er th' unbending corn, and skims along the main,

when he had enjoyed for about thirty years the praise of Camilla's lightness of foot, tried another experiment upon *sound* and *time*, and produced this memorable triplet:

> Waller was smooth; but Dryden taught to join ⎫
> The varying verse, the full resounding line, ⎬
> The long majestic march, and energy divine. ⎭

Here are the swiftness of the rapid race and the march of slow-paced majesty exhibited by the same poet in the same sequence of syllables, except that the exact prosodist will find the line of *swiftness* by one time longer than that of *tardiness*.

Beauties of this kind are commonly fancied; and when real are technical and nugatory, not to be rejected and not to be solicited.

To the praises which have been accumulated on *The Rape of the Lock* by readers of every class, from the critic to the waiting-maid, it is difficult to make any addition. Of that which is universally allowed to be the most attractive of all ludicrous compositions, let it rather be now enquired from what sources the power of pleasing is derived.

Dr Warburton, who excelled in critical perspicacity, has remarked that the preternatural agents are very happily adapted to the purposes of the poem. The heathen deities can no longer gain attention: we should have turned away from a contest between Venus and Diana.

The employment of allegorical persons always excites conviction of its own absurdity: they may produce effects, but cannot conduct actions; when the phantom is put in motion, it dissolves; thus Discord may raise a mutiny, but Discord cannot conduct a march, nor besiege a town. Pope brought into view a new race of Beings, with powers and passions proportionate to their operation. The sylphs and gnomes act at the toilet and the tea-table what more terrific and more powerful phantoms perform on the stormy ocean or the field of battle; they give their proper help, and do their proper mischief.

Pope is said by an objector not to have been the inventer of this petty nation; a charge which might with more justice have been brought against the author of the *Iliad*, who doubtless adopted the religious system of his country; for what is there but the names of his agents which Pope has not invented? Has he not assigned them characters and operations never heard of before? Has he not, at least, given them their first poetical existence? If this is not sufficient to denominate his work original, nothing original ever can be written.

In this work are exhibited in a very high degree the two most engaging powers of an author: new things are made familiar, and familiar things are made new. A race of aerial people never heard of before is presented to us in a manner so clear and easy that the reader seeks for no further information, but immediately mingles with his new acquaintance, adopts their interests and attends their pursuits, loves a sylph and detests a gnome.

That familiar things are made new every paragraph will prove. The subject of the poem is an event below the common incidents of common life; nothing real is introduced that is not seen so often as to be no longer regarded, yet the whole detail of a female day is here brought before us invested with so much art of decoration that, though nothing is disguised, every thing is striking, and we feel all the appetite of curiosity for that from which we have a thousand times turned fastidiously away.

The purpose of the Poet is, as he tells us, to laugh at 'the little unguarded follies of the female sex'. It is therefore without justice that Dennis charges *The Rape of the Lock* with the want of a moral, and for that reason sets it below *The Lutrin*, which exposes the pride and discord of the clergy. Perhaps neither Pope nor Boileau has made the world much better than he found it; but if they had both succeeded, it were easy to tell who would have deserved most from public gratitude. The freaks, and humours, and spleen, and vanity of women, as they embroil families in discord and fill houses with disquiet, do more to obstruct the happiness of life in a year than the ambition of the clergy in many centuries. It has been well observed that the misery of man proceeds not from any single crush of overwhelming evil, but from small vexations continually repeated.

It is remarked by Dennis likewise that the machinery is superfluous; that by all the bustle of preternatural operation the main event is neither hastened nor retarded. To this charge an efficacious answer is not easily made. The sylphs cannot be said to help or to oppose, and it must be allowed to imply some want of art that their power has not been sufficiently intermingled with the action. Other parts may likewise be charged with want of connection; the game at *ombre* might be spared, but if the lady had lost her hair while she was intent upon her cards, it might have been inferred that those who are too fond of play will be in danger of neglecting more important interests. Those perhaps are faults; but what are such faults to so much excellence!

The *Epistle of Eloise to Abelard* is one of the most happy productions of human wit: the subject is so judiciously chosen that it would be difficult, in turning over the annals of the world, to find another which so many circumstances concur to recommend. We regularly interest ourselves most in the fortune of those who most deserve our notice. Abelard and Eloise were conspicuous in their days for eminence of merit. The heart naturally loves truth. The adventures and misfortunes of this illustrious pair are known from undisputed history. Their fate does not leave the mind in hopeless dejection; for they both found quiet and consolation in retirement and piety. So new and so affecting is their story that it supersedes invention, and imagination ranges at full liberty without straggling into scenes of fable.

The story thus skilfully adopted has been diligently improved. Pope has left nothing behind him which seems more the effect of studious perseverance and laborious revisal. Here is particularly observable the *curiosa felicitas*,° a fruitful soil, and careful cultivation. Here is no crudeness of sense, nor asperity of language.

The sources from which sentiments which have so much vigour and efficacy have been drawn are shown to be the mystic writers by the learned author of the *Essay on the Life and Writings of Pope*;° a book which teaches how the brow of criticism may be smoothed, and how she may be enabled, with all her severity, to attract and to delight.

The train of my disquisition has now conducted me to that poetical wonder, the translation of the *Iliad*; a performance which no age or nation can pretend to equal. To the Greeks translation was almost unknown; it was totally unknown to the inhabitants of Greece. They had no recourse to the Barbarians for poetical beauties, but sought for every thing in Homer, where, indeed, there is but little which they might not find.

The Italians have been very diligent translators; but I can hear of no version, unless perhaps Anguillara's *Ovid* may be excepted, which is read with eagerness. The *Iliad* of Salvini every reader may discover to be punctiliously exact; but it seems to be the work of a linguist skilfully pedantic, and his countrymen, the proper judges of its power to please, reject it with disgust.

Their predecessors the Romans have left some specimens of translation behind them, and that employment must have had some credit in which Tully and Germanicus engaged; but unless we suppose, what is perhaps true, that the plays of Terence were versions of Menander, nothing translated seems ever to have risen to high reputation. The French, in the meridian hour of their learning, were very laudably industrious to enrich their own language with the wisdom of the ancients; but found themselves reduced, by whatever necessity, to turn the Greek and Roman poetry into prose. Whoever could read an author could translate him. From such rivals little can be feared.

The chief help of Pope in this arduous undertaking was drawn from the versions of Dryden. Virgil had borrowed much of his imagery from Homer, and part of the debt was now paid by his translator. Pope searched the pages of Dryden for happy combinations of heroic diction, but it will not be denied that he added much to what he found. He cultivated our language with so much diligence and art that he has left in his *Homer* a treasure of poetical elegances to posterity. His version may be said to have tuned the English tongue, for since its appearance no writer, however deficient in other powers, has wanted melody. Such a series of lines so elaborately corrected and so sweetly modulated took possession of the public ear; the vulgar was enamoured of the poem, and the learned wondered at the translation.

But in the most general applause discordant voices will always be heard. It has been objected by some who wish to be numbered among the sons of learning that Pope's version of Homer is not Homerical; that it exhibits no resemblance of the original and characteristic manner of the Father of Poetry, as it wants his awful simplicity, his artless grandeur, his unaffected majesty. This cannot be totally denied, but it must be remembered that *necessitas quod cogit defendit*, that may be lawfully done which cannot be forborne. Time and place will always enforce regard. In estimating this translation consideration must be had of the nature of our language, the form of our metre, and, above all, of the change which two thousand years have made in the modes of life and the habits of thought. Virgil wrote in a language of the same general fabric with that of Homer, in verses of the same measure, and in an age nearer to Homer's time by eighteen hundred years; yet he found even then the state of the world so much altered, and the demand for elegance so much increased, that mere nature would be endured no longer; and perhaps, in the multitude of borrowed passages, very few can be shown which he has not embellished.

There is a time when nations emerging from barbarity, and falling into regular subordination, gain leisure to grow wise, and feel the shame of ignorance and the craving pain of unsatisfied curiosity. To this hunger of the mind plain sense is grateful; that which fills the void removes uneasiness, and to be free from pain for a while is pleasure; but repletion generates fastidiousness, a saturated intellect soon becomes luxurious, and knowledge finds no willing reception till it is recommended by artificial diction. Thus it will be found in the progress of learning that in all nations the first writers are simple, and that every age improves in elegance. One refinement always makes way for another, and what was expedient to Virgil was necessary to Pope.

I suppose many readers of the English *Iliad*, when they have been touched with some unexpected beauty of the lighter kind, have tried to enjoy it in the original, where, alas! it was not to be found. Homer doubtless owes to his translator many Ovidian graces not exactly suitable to his character; but to have added can be no great crime if nothing be taken away. Elegance is surely to be desired if it be not gained at the expense of dignity. A hero would wish to be loved as well as to be reverenced.

To a thousand cavils one answer is sufficient: the purpose of a writer is to be read, and the criticism which would destroy the power of pleasing must be blown aside. Pope wrote for his own age and his own nation: he knew that it was necessary to colour the images and point the sentiments of his author; he therefore made him graceful, but lost him some of his sublimity.

The copious notes with which the version is accompanied and by which it is recommended to many readers, though they were undoubtedly written to swell the volumes, ought not to pass without praise: commentaries which attract the reader by the pleasure of perusal have not often appeared; the notes of others are read to clear difficulties, those of Pope to vary entertainment.

It has, however, been objected with sufficient reason that there is in the commentary too much of unseasonable levity and affected gaiety; that too many appeals are made to the ladies, and the ease which is so carefully preserved is sometimes the ease of a trifler. Every art has its terms and every kind of instruction its proper style; the gravity of common critics may be tedious, but is less despicable than childish merriment.

Of the *Odyssey* nothing remains to be observed; the same general praise may be given to both translations, and a particular examination of either would require a large volume. The notes were written by Broome, who endeavoured not unsuccessfully to imitate his master.

Of *The Dunciad* the hint is confessedly taken from Dryden's *Mac Flecknoe*, but the plan is so enlarged and diversified as justly to claim the praise of an original, and affords perhaps the best specimen that has yet appeared of personal satire ludicrously pompous.

That the design was moral, whatever the author might tell either his readers or himself, I am not convinced. The first motive was the desire of revenging the contempt with which Theobald had treated his *Shakespeare*, and regaining the honour which he had lost, by crushing his opponent. Theobald was not of bulk enough to fill a poem, and therefore it was necessary to find other enemies with other names, at whose expense he might divert the public.

In this design there was petulance and malignity enough; but I cannot think it very criminal. An author places himself uncalled before the tribunal of criticism, and solicits fame at the hazard of disgrace. Dullness or deformity are not culpable in themselves, but may be very justly reproached when they pretend to the honour of wit or the influence of beauty. If bad writers were to pass without reprehension what should restrain them? *Impune diem consumpserit ingens Telephus,*° and upon bad writers only will censure have much effect. The satire which brought Theobald and Moore into contempt, dropped impotent from Bentley, like the javelin of Priam.°

All truth is valuable, and satirical criticism may be considered as useful when it rectifies error and improves judgement: he that refines the public taste is a public benefactor.

The beauties of this poem are well known; its chief fault is the grossness of its images. Pope and Swift had an unnatural delight in ideas physically impure, such as every other tongue utters with unwillingness, and of which every ear shrinks from the mention.

But even this fault, offensive as it is, may be forgiven for the excellence of other passages; such as the formation and dissolution of Moore, the account of the Traveller, the misfortune of the Florist, and the crowded thoughts and stately numbers which dignify the concluding paragraph.

The alterations which have been made in *The Dunciad*, not always for the better, require that it should be published, as in the last collection, with all its variations.

The *Essay on Man*° was a work of great labour and long consideration, but certainly not the happiest of Pope's performances. The subject is perhaps not very proper for poetry, and the poet was not sufficiently master of his subject; metaphysical morality was to him a new study, he was proud of his acquisitions, and, supposing himself master of great secrets, was in haste to teach what he had not learned. Thus he tells us, in the first Epistle, that from the nature of the Supreme Being may be deduced an order of beings such as mankind, because Infinite Excellence can do only what is best. He finds out that these beings must be 'somewhere', and that 'all the question is whether man be in a wrong place'. Surely if, according to the poet's Leibnitian reasoning, we may infer that man ought to be only because he is, we may allow that his place is the right place, because he has it. Supreme Wisdom is not less infallible in disposing than in creating. But what is meant by 'somewhere' and 'place' and 'wrong place' it has been vain to ask Pope, who probably had never asked himself.

Having exalted himself into the chair of wisdom he tells us much that every man knows, and much that he does not know himself; that we see but little, and that the order of the universe is beyond our comprehension, an opinion not very uncommon; and that there is a chain of subordinate beings 'from infinite to nothing', of which himself and his readers are equally ignorant. But he gives us one comfort which, without his help, he supposes unattainable, in the position 'that though we are fools, yet God is wise'.

This *Essay* affords an egregious instance of the predominance of genius, the dazzling splendour of imagery, and the seductive powers of eloquence. Never were penury of knowledge and vulgarity of sentiment so happily disguised. The reader feels his mind full, though he learns nothing; and when he meets it in its new array no longer knows the talk of his mother and his nurse. When these wonder-working sounds sink into sense and the doctrine of the *Essay*, disrobed of its ornaments, is left to the powers of its naked excellence, what shall we discover? That we are, in comparison with our Creator, very weak and ignorant; that we do not uphold the chain of existence; and that we could not make one another with more skill than we are made. We may learn yet more: that the arts of human life were copied from the instinctive operations of other animals; that if the world be made for man, it may be said that man was made for geese. To these profound principles of natural knowledge are added some moral instructions equally new: that self-interest well under-stood will produce social concord; that men are mutual gainers by mutual benefits; that evil is sometimes balanced by good; that human advantages are unstable and fallacious, of uncertain duration and doubtful effect; that our true honour is not to have a great part, but to act it well; that virtue only is our own; and that happiness is always in our power.

Surely a man of no very comprehensive search may venture to say that he has heard all this before, but it was never till now recommended by such a blaze of embellishment or such sweetness of melody. The vigorous contraction of some thoughts, the luxuriant amplification of others, the incidental illustrations, and sometimes the dignity, sometimes the softness of the verses, enchain philosophy, suspend criticism, and oppress judgement by overpowering pleasure.

This is true of many paragraphs; yet if I had undertaken to exemplify Pope's felicity of composition before a rigid critic I should not select the *Essay on Man*, for it contains more lines unsuccessfully laboured, more harshness of diction, more thoughts imperfectly expressed, more levity without elegance, and more heaviness without strength than will easily be found in all his other works.

The *Characters of Men and Women* are the product of diligent speculation upon human life; much labour has been bestowed upon them, and Pope very seldom laboured in vain. That his excellence may be properly estimated I recommend a comparison of his *Characters of Women* with Boileau's *Satire*, it will then be seen with how much more perspicacity female nature is investigated and female excellence selected; and he surely is no mean writer to whom Boileau shall be found inferior. The *Characters of Men*, however, are written with more, if not with deeper, thought, and exhibit many passages exquisitely beautiful. 'The Gem and the Flower' will not easily be equalled. In the women's part are some defects: the character of Atossa is not so neatly finished as that of Clodio, and some of the female characters may be found perhaps more frequently among men; what is said of Philomede was true of Prior.

In the *Epistles to Lord Bathurst* and *Lord Burlington* Dr Warburton has endeavoured to find a train of thought which was never in the writer's head, and, to support his hypothesis, has printed that first which was published last. In one, the most valuable passage is perhaps the elogy on Good Sense, and in the other the End of the Duke of Buckingham.

The *Epistle to Arbuthnot*, now arbitrarily called the *Prologue to the Satires*, is a performance consisting, as it seems, of many fragments wrought into one design, which by this union of scattered beauties contains more striking paragraphs than could probably have been brought together into an occasional work. As there is no stronger motive to exertion than self-defence, no part has more elegance, spirit, or dignity than the poet's vindication of his own character. The meanest passage is the satire upon Sporus.

Of the two poems which derived their names from the year, and which are called the *Epilogue to the Satires*, it was very justly remarked by Savage that the second was in the whole more strongly conceived and more equally supported, but that it had no single passages equal to the contention in the first for the dignity of Vice and the celebration of the triumph of Corruption.

The *Imitations of Horace* seem to have been written as relaxations of his genius. This employment became his favourite by its facility; the plan was ready to his hand, and nothing was required but to accommodate as he could the sentiments of an old author to recent facts or familiar images; but what is easy is seldom excellent: such imitations cannot give pleasure to common readers. The man of learning may be sometimes surprised and delighted by an unexpected parallel; but the comparison requires knowledge of the original, which will likewise often detect strained applications. Between Roman images and English manners there will be an irreconcileable dissimilitude, and the work will be generally uncouth and parti-coloured; neither original nor translated, neither ancient nor modern.

Pope had, in proportions very nicely adjusted to each other, all the qualities that constitute genius. He had Invention, by which new trains of events are formed and new scenes of imagery displayed, as in *The Rape of the Lock*, and by which extrinsic and adventitious embellishments and illustrations are connected with a known subject, as in the *Essay on Criticism*; he had Imagination, which strongly impresses on the writer's mind and enables him to convey to the reader the various forms of nature, incidents of life, and energies of passion, as in his *Eloisa*, *Windsor Forest*, and the *Ethic Epistles*; he had

Judgement, which selects from life or nature what the present purpose requires, and, by separating the essence of things from its concomitants, often makes the representation more powerful than the reality; and he had colours of language always before him ready to decorate his matter with every grace of elegant expression, as when he accommodates his diction to the wonderful multiplicity of Homer's sentiments and descriptions.

Poetical expression includes sound as well as meaning. 'Music,' says Dryden, 'is inarticulate poetry'; among the excellences of Pope, therefore, must be mentioned the melody of his metre. By perusing the works of Dryden he discovered the most perfect fabric of English verse, and habituated himself to that only which he found the best; in consequence of which restraint his poetry has been censured as too uniformly musical, and as glutting the ear with unvaried sweetness. I suspect this objection to be the cant of those who judge by principles rather than perception; and who would even themselves have less pleasure in his works if he had tried to relieve attention by studied discords, or affected to break his lines and vary his pauses.

But though he was thus careful of his versification he did not oppress his powers with superfluous rigour. He seems to have thought with Boileau that the practice of writing might be refined till the difficulty should overbalance the advantage. The construction of his language is not always strictly grammatical; with those rhymes which prescription had conjoined he contented himself, without regard to Swift's remonstrances, though there was no striking consonance; nor was he very careful to vary his terminations or to refuse admission at a small distance to the same rhymes.

To Swift's edict for the exclusion of alexandrines and triplets he paid little regard; he admitted them, but, in the opinion of Fenton, too rarely: he uses them more liberally in his translation than his poems.

He has a few double rhymes, and always, I think, unsuccessfully, except once in *The Rape of the Lock*.

Expletives he very early ejected from his verses; but he now and then admits an epithet rather commodious than important. Each of the six first lines of the *Iliad* might lose two syllables with very little diminution of the meaning; and sometimes, after all his art and labour, one verse seems to be made for the sake of another. In his latter productions the diction is sometimes vitiated by French idioms, with which Bolingbroke had perhaps infected him.

I have been told that the couplet by which he declared his own ear to be most gratified was this:

> Lo, where Maeotis sleeps, and hardly flows
> The freezing Tanais thro' a waste of snows.°

But the reason of this preference I cannot discover.

It is remarked by Watts that there is scarcely a happy combination of words or a phrase poetically elegant in the English language which Pope has not inserted into his version of Homer. How he obtained possession of so many beauties of speech it were desirable to know. That he gleaned from authors, obscure as well as eminent, what he thought brilliant or useful, and preserved it all in a regular collection, is not unlikely. When, in his last years, Hall's *Satires* were shown him he wished that he had seen them sooner.

New sentiments and new images others may produce, but to attempt any further improvement of versification will be dangerous. Art and diligence have now done their best, and what shall be added will be the effort of tedious toil and needless curiosity.

After all this it is surely superfluous to answer the question that has once been asked, 'Whether Pope was a poet?'° otherwise than by asking in return, 'If Pope be not a poet, where is poetry to be found?' To circumscribe poetry by a definition will only show the narrowness of the definer, though a definition which shall exclude Pope will not easily be made. Let us look round upon the present time, and back upon the past; let us enquire to whom the voice of mankind has decreed the wreath of poetry; let their productions be examined and their claims stated, and the pretensions of Pope will be no more disputed. Had he given the world only his version the name of poet must have been allowed him; if the writer of the *Iliad* were to class his successors he would assign a very high place to his translator, without requiring any other evidence of genius.

Thomson

As a writer he is entitled to one praise of the highest kind: his mode of thinking and of expressing his thoughts is original. His blank verse is no more the blank verse of Milton or of any other poet than the rhymes of Prior are the rhymes of Cowley. His numbers, his pauses, his diction, are of his own growth, without transcription, without imitation. He thinks in a peculiar train, and he thinks always as a man of genius; he looks round on Nature and on Life with the eye which Nature bestows only on a poet, the eye that distinguishes in every thing presented to its view whatever there is on which imagination can delight to be detained, and with a mind that at once comprehends the vast, and attends to the minute. The reader of *The Seasons* wonders that he never saw before what Thomson shows him, and that he never yet has felt what Thomson impresses.

His is one of the works in which blank verse seems properly used; Thomson's wide expansion of general views, and his enumeration of circumstantial varieties, would have been obstructed and embarrassed by the frequent intersection of the sense, which are the necessary effects of rhyme.

His descriptions of extended scenes and general effects bring before us the whole magnificence of Nature, whether pleasing or dreadful. The gaiety of *Spring*, the splendour of *Summer*, the tranquillity of *Autumn*, and the horror of *Winter* take in their turns possession of the mind. The poet leads us through the appearances of things as they are successively varied by the vicissitudes of the year, and imparts to us so much of his own enthusiasm that our thoughts expand with his imagery and kindle with his sentiments. Nor is the naturalist without his part in the entertainment; for he is assisted to recollect and to combine, to arrange his discoveries, and to amplify the sphere of his contemplation.

The great defect of *The Seasons* is want of method; but for this I know not that there was any remedy. Of many appearances subsisting all at once, no rule can be given why one should be mentioned before another; yet the memory wants the help of order, and the curiosity is not excited by suspense or expectation.

His diction is in the highest degree florid and luxuriant, such as may be said to be to his images and thoughts 'both their lustre and their shade'; such as invests them with splendour, through which perhaps they are not always easily discerned. It is too exuberant, and sometimes may be charged with filling the ear more than the mind.

These poems with which I was acquainted at their first appearance I have since found altered and enlarged by subsequent revisals, as the author supposed his judgement to grow more exact, and as books or conversation extended his knowledge and opened his prospects. They are, I think, improved in general; yet I know not whether they have not lost part of what Temple calls their *race*, a word which, applied to wines, in its primitive sense, means the flavour of the soil.

Liberty, when it first appeared, I tried to read, and soon desisted. I have never tried again, and therefore will not hazard either praise or censure.

The highest praise which he has received ought not to be suppressed; it is said by Lord Lyttelton in the Prologue to his posthumous play that his works contained

No line which, dying, he could wish to blot.

The poems of Dr Watts were by my recommendation inserted in the late Collection; the readers of which are to impute to me whatever pleasure or weariness they may find in the perusal of Blackmore, Watts, Pomfret, and Yalden. . . .

The series of his works I am not able to deduce; their number and their variety show the intenseness of his industry, and the extent of his capacity.

He was one of the first authors that taught the Dissenters to court attention by the graces of language. Whatever they had among them before, whether of learning or acuteness, was commonly obscured and blunted by coarseness and inelegance of style. He showed them that zeal and purity might be expressed and enforced by polished diction.

He continued to the end of his life the teacher of a congregation, and no reader of his works can doubt his fidelity or diligence. In the pulpit, though his low stature, which very little exceeded five feet, graced him with no advantages of appearance, yet the gravity and propriety of his utterance made his discourses very efficacious. I once mentioned the reputation which Mr Foster° had gained by his proper delivery to my friend Dr Hawkesworth, who told me that in the art of pronunciation he was far inferior to Dr Watts.

Such was his flow of thoughts, and such his promptitude of language, that in the latter part of his life he did not precompose his cursory sermons; but having adjusted the heads, and sketched out some particulars, trusted for success to his extemporary powers.

He did not endeavour to assist his eloquence by any gesticulations; for, as no corporeal actions have any correspondence with theological truth, he did not see how they could enforce it.

At the conclusion of weighty sentences he gave time, by a short pause, for the proper impression.

To stated and public instruction he added familiar visits and personal application, and was careful to improve the opportunities which conversation offered of diffusing and increasing the influence of religion.

By his natural temper he was quick of resentment, but by his established and habitual practice he was gentle, modest, and inoffensive. His tenderness appeared in his attention to children and to the poor. To the poor, while he lived in the family of his friend, he allowed the third part of his annual revenue, though the whole was not a hundred a year; and for children he condescended to lay aside the scholar, the philosopher, and the wit, to write little poems of devotion and systems of instruction, adapted to their wants and capacities, from the dawn of reason through its gradations of advance in the morning of life. Every man acquainted with the common principles of human action will look with veneration on the writer who is at one time combating Locke, and at another making a catechism for children in their fourth year. A voluntary descent from the dignity of science is perhaps the hardest lesson that humility can teach.

As his mind was capacious, his curiosity excursive, and his industry continual, his writings are very numerous and his subjects various. With his theological works I am only enough acquainted to admire his meekness of opposition and his mildness of censure. It was not only in his book but in his mind that orthodoxy was united with charity.

Of his philosophical pieces his *Logic* has been received into the universities, and therefore wants no private recommendation: if he owes part of it to Le Clerc° it must be considered that no man who undertakes merely to methodise or illustrate a system pretends to be its author.

In his metaphysical disquisitions it was observed by the late learned Mr Dyer that he confounded the idea of *space* with that of *empty space* and did not consider that though space might be without matter, yet matter, being extended, could not be without space.

Few books have been perused by me with greater pleasure than his *Improvement of the Mind*, of which the radical principles may indeed be found in Locke's *Conduct of the Understanding*, but they are so expanded and ramified by Watts as to confer upon him the merit of a work in the highest degree useful and pleasing. Whoever has the care of instructing others may be charged with deficience in his duty if this book is not recommended.

I have mentioned his treatises of Theology as distinct from his other productions, but the truth is that whatever he took in hand was, by his incessant solicitude for souls, converted to Theology. As piety predominated in his mind, it is diffused over his works; under his direction it may be truly said, *Theologiae Philosophia ancillatur*, philosophy is subservient to evangelical instruction: it is difficult to read a page without learning, or at least wishing, to be better. The attention is caught by indirect instruction, and he that sat down only to reason is on a sudden compelled to pray.

It was therefore with great propriety that, in 1728, he received from

Edinburgh and Aberdeen an unsolicited diploma, by which he became a Doctor of Divinity. Academical honours would have more value if they were always bestowed with equal judgement.

He continued many years to study and to preach, and to do good by his instruction and example, till at last the infirmities of age disabled him from the more laborious part of his ministerial functions, and, being no longer capable of public duty, he offered to remit the salary appendant to it; but his congregation would not accept the resignation.

By degrees his weakness increased, and at last confined him to his chamber and his bed, where he was worn gradually away without pain, till he expired Nov. 25, 1748, in the seventy-fifth year of his age.

Few men have left behind such purity of character or such monuments of laborious piety. He has provided instruction for all ages, from those who are lisping their first lessons, to the enlightened readers of Malebranche and Locke; he has left neither corporeal nor spiritual nature unexamined; he has taught the art of reasoning, and the science of the stars.

His character, therefore, must be formed from the multiplicity and diversity of his attainments, rather than from any single performance; for it would not be safe to claim for him the highest rank in any single denomination of literary dignity: yet perhaps there was nothing in which he would not have excelled, if he had not divided his powers to different pursuits.

As a poet, had he been only a poet, he would probably have stood high among the authors with whom he is now associated. For his judgement was exact, and he noted beauties and faults with very nice discernment; his imagination, as the *Dacian Battle* proves, was vigorous and active, and the stores of knowledge were large by which his fancy was to be supplied. His ear was well-tuned, and his diction was elegant and copious. But his devotional poetry is, like that of others, unsatisfactory. The paucity of its topics enforces perpetual repetition, and the sanctity of the matter rejects the ornaments of figurative diction. It is sufficient for Watts to have done better than others what no man has done well.

His poems on other subjects seldom rise higher than might be expected from the amusements of a Man of Letters, and have different degrees of value as they are more or less laboured, or as the occasion was more or less favourable to invention.

He writes too often without regular measures, and too often in blank verse; the rhymes are not always sufficiently correspondent. He is particularly unhappy in coining names expressive of characters. His lines are commonly smooth and easy, and his thoughts always religiously pure; but who is there that, to so much piety and innocence, does not wish for a greater measure of spriteliness and vigour? He is at least one of the few poets with whom youth and ignorance may be safely pleased; and happy will be that reader whose mind is disposed by his verses or his prose to imitate him in all but his nonconformity, to copy his benevolence to man, and his reverence to God.

Collins

William Collins was born at Chichester on the twenty-fifth of December, about 1720. His father was a hatter of good reputation. He was in 1733, as Dr Warton has kindly informed me, admitted scholar of Winchester College, where he was educated by Dr Burton. His English exercises were better than his Latin.

He first courted the notice of the public by some verses *To a Lady Weeping*, published in *The Gentleman's Magazine*.

In 1740 he stood first in the list of the scholars to be received in succession at New College; but unhappily there was no vacancy. This was the original misfortune of his life. He became a Commoner of Queen's College, probably with a scanty maintenance; but was in about half a year elected a *Demy* of Magdalen College, where he continued till he had taken a Bachelor's degree, and then suddenly left the University, for what reason I know not that he told.

He now (about 1744) came to London a literary adventurer, with many projects in his head, and very little money in his pocket. He designed many works, but his great fault was irresolution, or the frequent calls of immediate necessity broke his schemes, and suffered him to pursue no settled purpose. A man doubtful of his dinner, or trembling at a creditor, is not much disposed to abstracted meditation or remote enquiries. He published proposals for a *History of the Revival of Learning*, and I have heard him speak with great kindness of Leo the Tenth, and with keen resentment of his tasteless successor. But probably not a page of the *History* was ever written. He planned several tragedies, but he only planned them. He wrote now and then odes and other poems, and did something, however little.

About this time I fell into his company. His appearance was decent and manly; his knowledge considerable, his views extensive, his conversation elegant, and his disposition cheerful. By degrees I gained his confidence; and one day was admitted to him when he was immured by a bailiff that was prowling in the street. On this occasion recourse was had to the booksellers, who, on the credit of a translation of Aristotle's *Poetics*, which he engaged to write with a large commentary, advanced as much money as enabled him to escape into the country. He showed me the guineas safe in his hand. Soon afterwards his uncle, Mr Martin, a lieutenant-colonel, left him about two thousand pounds; a sum which Collins could scarcely think exhaustible, and which he did not live to exhaust. The guineas were then repaid, and the translation neglected.

But man is not born for happiness. Collins, who, while he 'studied to live', felt no evil but poverty, no sooner 'lived to study' than his life was assailed by more dreadful calamities, disease and insanity.

Having formerly written his character,° while perhaps it was yet more distinctly impressed upon my memory, I shall insert it here.

Mr Collins was a man of extensive literature, and of vigorous faculties. He was acquainted not only with the learned tongues, but with the Italian, French, and Spanish languages. He had employed his mind chiefly upon works of fiction and subjects of fancy, and by indulging some peculiar habits of thought was eminently delighted with those flights of imagination which pass the bounds of nature, and to which the mind is reconciled only by a passive acquiescence in popular traditions. He loved fairies, genii, giants, and monsters; he delighted to rove through the meanders of enchantment, to gaze on the magnificence of golden palaces, to repose by the waterfalls of Elysian gardens.

This was, however, the character rather of his inclination than his genius; the grandeur of wildness and the novelty of extravagance were always desired by him, but were not always attained. Yet as diligence is never wholly lost, if his efforts sometimes caused harshness and obscurity, they likewise produced in happier moments sublimity and splendour. This idea which he had formed of excellence led him to oriental fictions and allegorical imagery, and perhaps, while he was intent upon description, he did not sufficiently cultivate sentiment. His poems are the productions of a mind not deficient in fire, nor unfurnished with knowledge either of books or life, but somewhat obstructed in its progress by deviation in quest of mistaken beauties.

His morals were pure, and his opinions pious; in a long continuance of poverty and long habits of dissipation it cannot be expected that any character should be exactly uniform. There is a degree of want by which the freedom of agency is almost destroyed; and long association with fortuitous companions will at last relax the strictness of truth, and abate the fervour of sincerity. That this man, wise and virtuous as he was, passed always unentangled through the snares of life, it would be prejudice and temerity to affirm; but it may be said that at least he preserved the source of action unpolluted, that his principles were never shaken, that his distinctions of right and wrong were never confounded, and that his faults had nothing of malignity or design, but proceeded from some unexpected pressure, or casual temptation.

The latter part of his life cannot be remembered but with pity and sadness. He languished some years under that depression of mind which enchains the faculties without destroying them, and leaves reason the knowledge of right without the power of pursuing it. These clouds which he perceived gathering on his intellects he endeavoured to disperse by travel, and passed into France;

but found himself constrained to yield to his malady, and returned. He was for some time confined in a house of lunatics, and afterwards retired to the care of his sister in Chichester, where death in 1756 came to his relief.

After his return from France the writer of this character paid him a visit at Islington, where he was waiting for his sister, whom he had directed to meet him: there was then nothing of disorder discernible in his mind by any but himself, but he had withdrawn from study, and travelled with no other book than an English Testament, such as children carry to the school; when his friend took it into his hand, out of curiosity to see what companion a Man of Letters had chosen, 'I have but one book,' said Collins, 'but that is the best.'

Such was the fate of Collins, with whom I once delighted to converse, and whom I yet remember with tenderness.

He was visited at Chichester in his last illness by his learned friends Dr Warton and his brother, to whom he spoke with disapprobation of his *Oriental Eclogues*, as not sufficiently expressive of Asiatic manners, and called them his 'Irish Eclogues'. He showed them at the same time an ode inscribed to Mr John Hume° on the superstitions of the Highlands, which they thought superior to his other works, but which no search has yet found.

His disorder was not alienation of mind, but general laxity and feebleness, a deficiency rather of his vital than intellectual powers. What he spoke wanted neither judgement nor spirit; but a few minutes exhausted him, so that he was forced to rest upon the couch, till a short cessation restored his powers, and he was again able to talk with his former vigour.

The approaches of this dreadful malady he began to feel soon after his uncle's death, and, with the usual weakness of men so diseased, eagerly snatched that temporary relief with which the table and the bottle flatter and seduce. But his health continually declined, and he grew more and more burdensome to himself.

To what I have formerly said of his writings may be added that his diction was often harsh, unskilfully laboured, and injudiciously selected. He affected the obsolete when it was not worthy of revival; and he puts his words out of the common order, seeming to think, with some later candidates for fame, that not to write prose is certainly to write poetry. His lines commonly are of slow motion, clogged and impeded with clusters of consonants. As men are often esteemed who cannot be loved, so the poetry of Collins may sometimes extort praise when it gives little pleasure.

Young

Of Young's poems it is difficult to give any general character, for he has no uniformity of manner: one of his pieces has no great resemblance to another. He began to write early and continued long, and at different times had different modes of poetical excellence in view. His numbers are sometimes smooth and sometimes rugged; his style is sometimes concatenated and sometimes abrupt, sometimes diffusive and sometimes concise. His plan seems to have started in his mind at the present moment, and his thoughts appear the effects of chance, sometimes adverse and sometimes lucky, with very little operation of judgement.

He was not one of the writers whom experience improves, and who observing their own faults become gradually correct. His poem on *The Last Day*, his first great performance, has an equability and propriety which he afterwards either never endeavoured or never attained. Many paragraphs are noble and few are mean, yet the whole is languid; the plan is too much extended, and a succession of images divides and weakens the general conception: but the great reason why the reader is disappointed is that the thought of the LAST DAY makes every man more than poetical by spreading over his mind a general obscurity of sacred horror, that oppresses distinction and disdains expression.

His story of *Jane Grey* was never popular. It is written with elegance enough, but Jane is too heroic to be pitied.

The Universal Passion is indeed a very great performance. It is said to be a series of epigrams; but if it be it is what the author intended; his endeavour was at the production of striking distichs and pointed sentences; and his distichs have the weight of solid sentiment, and his points the sharpness of resistless truth. His characters are often selected with discernment and drawn with nicety; his illustrations are often happy and his reflections often just. His species of satire is between those of Horace and of Juvenal: he has the gaiety of Horace without his laxity of numbers, and the morality of Juvenal with greater variation of images. He plays, indeed, only on the surface of life; he never penetrates the recesses of the mind, and therefore the whole power of his poetry is exhausted by a single perusal: his conceits please only when they surprise.

To translate he never condescended, unless his *Paraphrase on Job* may be considered as a version, in which he has not, I think, been unsuccessful; he indeed favoured himself by choosing those parts which most easily admit the ornaments of English poetry.

He had least success in his lyric attempts, in which he seems to have been under some malignant influence: he is always labouring to be great, and at last is only turgid.

In his *Night Thoughts* he has exhibited a very wide display of original poetry, variegated with deep reflections and striking allusions, a wilderness of thought in which the fertility of fancy scatters flowers of every hue and of every odour. This is one of the few poems in which blank verse could not be changed for rhyme but with disadvantage. The wild diffusion of the sentiments and the digressive sallies of imagination would have been compressed and restrained by confinement to rhyme. The excellence of this work is not exactness, but copiousness; particular lines are not to be regarded: the power is in the whole, and in the whole there is a magnificence of vast extent and endless diversity.

His last poem was the *Resignation*, in which he made, as he was accustomed, an experiment of a new mode of writing, and succeeded better than in his *Ocean* or his *Merchant*. It was very falsely represented as a proof of decaying faculties. There is Young in every stanza, such as he often was in his highest vigour.

His tragedies, not making part of the collection, I had forgotten, till Mr Steevens recalled them to my thoughts by remarking that he seemed to have one favourite catastrophe, as his three plays all concluded with lavish suicide, a method by which, as Dryden remarked, a poet easily rids his scene of persons whom he wants not to keep alive. In *Busiris* there are the greatest ebullitions of imagination; but the pride of Busiris is such as no other man can have, and the whole is too remote from known life to raise either grief, terror, or indignation. The *Revenge* approaches much nearer to human practices and manners, and therefore keeps possession of the stage; the first design seems suggested by *Othello*, but the reflections, the incidents, and the diction are original. The moral observations are so introduced and so expressed as to have all the novelty that can be required. Of *The Brothers* I may be allowed to say nothing, since nothing was ever said of it by the public.

It must be allowed of Young's poetry that it abounds in thought, but without much accuracy or selection. When he lays hold of an illustration he pursues it beyond expectation, sometimes happily, as in his parallel of quicksilver with pleasure, which I have heard repeated with approbation by a lady of whose praise he would have been justly proud, and which is very ingenious, very subtle, and almost exact; but sometimes he is less lucky, as when, in his *Night Thoughts*, having it dropped into his mind that the orbs, floating in space, might be called the 'cluster' of Creation, he thinks on a cluster of grapes, and says that they all hang on the great Vine, drinking the 'nectareous juice of immortal Life'.

His conceits are sometimes yet less valuable; in *The Last Day* he hopes to illustrate the re-assembly of the atoms that compose the human body at the 'Trump of Doom' by the collection of bees into a swarm at the tinkling of a pan.

The Prophet says of Tyre that her 'merchants are princes'; Young says of Tyre in his *Merchant*,

> Her merchants princes, and each *deck a throne*.

Let burlesque try to go beyond him.

He has the trick of joining the turgid and familiar: to buy the alliance of Britain, 'Climes were paid down'. Antithesis is his favourite: 'They for kindness hate', and 'because she's right, she's ever in the wrong'.

His versification is his own: neither his blank nor his rhyming lines have any resemblance to those of former writers; he picks up no hemistichs, he copies no favourite expressions; he seems to have laid up no stores of thought or diction, but to owe all to the fortuitous suggestions of the present moment. Yet I have reason to believe that, when once he had formed a new design, he then laboured it with very patient industry, and that he composed with great labour and frequent revisions.

His verses are formed by no certain model, for he is no more like himself in his different productions than he is like others. He seems never to have studied prosody, nor to have had any direction but from his own ear. But, with all his defects, he was a man of genius and a poet.

Gray

Gray's poetry is now to be considered, and I hope not to be looked on as an enemy to his name if I confess that I contemplate it with less pleasure than his life.

His *Ode on Spring* has something poetical, both in the language and the thought; but the language is too luxuriant, and the thoughts have nothing new. There has of late arisen a practice of giving to adjectives derived from substantives the termination of participles, such as the *cultured* plain, the *daisied* bank; but I was sorry to see, in the lines of a scholar like Gray, 'the *honied* Spring'. The morality is natural, but too stale; the conclusion is pretty.

The poem on the Cat was doubtless by its author considered as a trifle, but it is not a happy trifle. In the first stanza 'the azure flowers that blow' show resolutely a rhyme is sometimes made when it cannot easily be found. Selima, the Cat, is called a nymph, with some violence both to language and sense; but there is good use made of it when it is done; for of the two lines,

> What female heart can gold despise?
> What cat's averse to fish?

the first relates merely to the nymph, and the second only to the cat. The sixth stanza contains a melancholy truth, that 'a favourite has no friend', but the last ends in a pointed sentence of no relation to the purpose; if what glistered had been 'gold', the cat would not have gone into the water; and, if she had, would not less have been drowned.

The *Prospect of Eton College* suggests nothing to Gray which every beholder does not equally think and feel. His supplication to Father Thames to tell him who drives the hoop or tosses the ball is useless and puerile. Father Thames has no better means of knowing than himself. His epithet 'buxom° health' is not elegant; he seems not to understand the word. Gray thought his language more poetical as it was more remote from common use: finding in Dryden 'honey redolent° of Spring', an expression that reaches the utmost limits of our language, Gray drove it a little more beyond common apprehension, by making 'gales' to be 'redolent of joy and youth'.

Of the *Ode on Adversity* the hint was at first taken from 'O Diva, gratum quae regis Antium';° but Gray has excelled his original by the variety of his sentiments and by their moral application. Of this piece, at once poetical and rational, I will not by slight objections violate the dignity.

My process has now brought me to the 'Wonderful Wonder of Wonders', the two Sister Odes; by which, though either vulgar ignorance or common sense at first universally rejected them, many have been since persuaded to think themselves delighted. I am one of those that are willing to be pleased, and therefore would gladly find the meaning of the first stanza of *The Progress of Poetry*.

Gray seems in his rapture to confound the images of 'spreading sound' and 'running water'. A 'stream of music' may be allowed; but where does Music, however 'smooth and strong', after having visited the 'verdant vales', 'roll down the steep amain' so as that 'rocks and nodding groves rebellow to the roar'? If this be said of Music, it is nonsense; if it be said of Water, it is nothing to the purpose.

The second stanza, exhibiting Mars's car and Jove's eagle, is unworthy of further notice. Criticism disdains to chase a schoolboy to his commonplaces.

To the third it may likewise be objected that it is drawn from mythology, though such as may be more easily assimilated to real life. 'Idalia's velvet-green' has something of cant. An epithet or metaphor drawn from Nature ennobles Art; an epithet or metaphor drawn from Art degrades Nature. Gray is too fond of words arbitrarily compounded. 'Many-twinkling' was formerly censured as not analogical; we may say *many-spotted*, but scarcely *many-spotting*. This stanza, however, has something pleasing.

Of the second ternary of stanzas the first endeavours to tell something, and would have told it had it not been crossed by Hyperion; the second describes well enough the universal prevalence of poetry, but I am afraid that the conclusion will not rise from the premises. The caverns of the North and the plains of Chili are not the residences of 'Glory' and 'generous Shame'. But that Poetry and Virtue go always together is an opinion so pleasing that I can forgive him who resolves to think it true.

The third stanza sounds big with Delphi, and Egean, and Ilissus, and Meander, and 'hallowed fountain' and 'solemn sound'; but in all Gray's odes there is a kind of cumbrous splendour which we wish away. His position is at last false: in the time of Dante and Petrarch, from whom he derives our first school of poetry, Italy was overrun by 'tyrant power' and 'coward vice'; nor was our state much better when we first borrowed the Italian arts.

Of the third ternary the first gives a mythological birth of Shakespeare. What is said of that mighty genius is true; but it is not said happily: the real effects of this poetical power are put out of sight by the pomp of machinery. Where truth is sufficient to fill the mind, fiction is worse than useless; the counterfeit debases the genuine.

His account of Milton's blindness, if we suppose it caused by study in the formation of his poem, a supposition surely allowable, is poetically true, and happily imagined. But the 'car' of Dryden, with his 'two coursers' has nothing in it peculiar; it is a car in which any other rider may be placed.

The Bard appears at the first view to be, as Algarotti and others have remarked, an imitation of the prophecy of Nereus. Algarotti thinks it superior to its original, and, if preference depends only on the imagery and animation of the two poems, his judgement is right. There is in *The Bard* more force, more thought, and more variety. But to copy is less than to invent, and the copy has been unhappily produced at a wrong time. The fiction of Horace was to the Romans credible; but its revival disgusts us with apparent and unconquerable falsehood. 'Incredulus odi.'°

To select a singular event, and swell it to a giant's bulk by fabulous appendages of spectres and predictions, has little difficulty, for he that forsakes the probable may always find the marvellous. And it has little use: we are affected only as we believe; we are improved only as we find something to be imitated or declined. I do not see that *The Bard* promotes any truth, moral or political.

His stanzas are too long, especially his epodes; the ode is finished before the ear has learned its measures, and consequently before it can receive pleasure from their consonance and recurrence.

Of the first stanza the abrupt beginning has been celebrated; but technical beauties can give praise only to the inventor. It is in the power of any man to rush abruptly upon his subject that has read the ballad of *Johnny Armstrong*,

Is there ever a man in all Scotland—.

The initial resemblances, or alliterations, 'ruin', 'ruthless', 'helm nor hauberk', are below the grandeur of a poem that endeavours at sublimity.

In the second stanza the Bard is well described; but in the third we have the puerilities of obsolete mythology. When we are told that Cadwallo 'hush'd the stormy main', and that Modred 'made huge

Plinlimmon bow his cloud-top'd head', attention recoils from the repetition of a tale that, even when it was first heard, was heard with scorn.

The 'weaving' of the 'winding sheet' he borrowed, as he owns, from the northern Bards; but their texture, however, was very properly the work of female powers, as the art of spinning the thread of life in another mythology. Theft is always dangerous; Gray has made weavers of his slaughtered bards by a fiction outrageous and incongruous. They are then called upon to 'Weave the warp, and weave the woof' perhaps with no great propriety; for it is by crossing the woof with the warp that men weave the web or piece; and the first line was dearly bought by the admission of its wretched correspondent, 'Give ample room and verge enough'. He has, however, no other line as bad.

The third stanza of the second ternary is commended, I think, beyond its merit. The personification is indistinct. Thirst and Hunger are not alike, and their features, to make the imagery perfect, should have been discriminated. We are told, in the same stanza, how 'towers' are 'fed'. But I will no longer look for particular faults; yet let it be observed that the ode might have been concluded with an action of better example: but suicide° is always to be had without expense of thought.

These odes are marked by glittering accumulations of ungraceful ornaments: they strike, rather than please; the images are magnified by affectation; the language is laboured into harshness. The mind of the writer seems to work with unnatural violence. 'Double, double, toil and trouble.'° He has a kind of strutting dignity, and is tall by walking on tiptoe. His art and his struggle are too visible, and there is too little appearance of ease and nature.

To say that he has no beauties would be unjust: a man like him, of great learning and great industry, could not but produce something valuable. When he pleases least, it can only be said that a good design was ill directed.

His translations of Northern and Welsh Poetry deserve praise: the imagery is preserved, perhaps often improved; but the language is unlike the language of other poets.

In the character of his *Elegy* I rejoice to concur with the common reader; for by the common sense of readers uncorrupted with literary prejudices, after all the refinements of subtlety and the dogmatism of learning, must be finally decided all claim to poetical honours. The *Churchyard* abounds with images which find a mirror in every mind, and with sentiments to which every bosom returns an echo. The four stanzas beginning 'Yet even these bones' are to me original: I have never seen the notions in any other place; yet he that reads them here persuades himself that he has always felt them. Had Gray written often thus it had been vain to blame, and useless to praise him.

From *Diaries, Prayers, and Meditations*

SEPT. 7, 1709, I was born at Lichfield. My mother had a very difficult and dangerous labour, and was assisted by George Hector,° a man-midwife of great reputation. I was born almost dead, and could not cry for some time. When he had me in his arms, he said, 'Here is a brave boy.'

In a few weeks an inflammation was discovered on my buttock, which was at first, I think, taken for a burn; but soon appeared to be a natural disorder. It swelled, broke, and healed.

My Father being that year Sheriff of Lichfield, and to ride the circuit of the County next day, which was a ceremony then performed with great pomp; he was asked by my mother, 'Whom he would invite to the Riding?' and answered, 'All the town now.' He feasted the citizens with uncommon magnificence, and was the last but one that maintained the splendour of the Riding.

I was, by my father's persuasion, put to one Marclew, commonly called Bellison, the servant, or wife of a servant of my father, to be nursed in George Lane, where I used to call when I was a bigger boy, and eat fruit in the garden, which was full of trees. Here it was discovered that my eyes were bad; and an issue was cut in my left arm, of which I took no great notice, as I think my mother has told me, having my little hand in a custard. How long this issue was continued I do not remember. I believe it was suffered to dry when I was about six years old.

It is observable that, having been told of this operation, I always imagined that I remembered it, but I laid the scene in the wrong house. Such confusions of memory I suspect to be common.

My mother visited me every day, and used to go different ways, that her assiduity might not expose her to ridicule; and often left her fan or glove behind her, that she might have a pretence to come back unexpected; but she never discovered any token of neglect. Dr Swinfen° told me that the scrofulous sores which afflicted me proceeded from the bad humours of the nurse, whose son had the same distemper, and was likewise short-sighted, but both in a less degree. My mother thought my diseases derived from her family.

In ten weeks I was taken home, a poor, diseased infant, almost blind.

I remember my aunt Nath. Ford told me, when I was about . . . years old, that she would not have picked such a poor creature up in the street.

In . . . 67, when I was at Lichfield, I went to look for my nurse's house; and, inquiring somewhat obscurely, was told 'this is the house in which you were nursed'. I saw my nurse's son, to whose milk I succeeded, reading a large Bible, which my nurse had bought, as I was then told, some time before her death.

Dr Swinfen used to say, that he never knew any child reared with so much difficulty.

In the second year I know not what happened to me. I believe it was then that my mother carried me to Trysul, to consult Dr Atwood, an oculist of Worcester. My father and Mrs Harriots, I think, never had much kindness for each other. She was my mother's relation; and he had none so high to whom he could send any of his family. He saw her seldom himself, and willingly disgusted her by sending his horses from home on Sunday; which she considered, and with reason, as a breach of duty.° My father had much vanity, which his adversity hindered from being fully exerted. I remember, that, mentioning her legacy in the humility of distress, he called her *our good Cousin Harriots*. My mother had no value for his relations; those indeed whom we knew of were much lower than hers. This contempt began, I know not on which side, very early: but, as my father was little at home, it had not much effect.

My father and mother had not much happiness from each other. They seldom conversed; for my father could not bear to talk of his affairs; and my mother, being unacquainted with books, cared not to talk of any thing else. Had my mother been more literate, they had been better companions. She might have sometimes introduced her unwelcome topic with more success if she could have diversified her conversation. Of business she had no distinct conception; and therefore her discourse was composed only of complaint, fear, and suspicion. Neither of them ever tried to calculate the profits of trade, or the expenses of living. My mother concluded that we were poor, because we lost by some of our trades; but the truth was that my father, having in the early part of his life contracted debts, never had trade sufficient to enable him to pay them, and maintain his family; he got something, but not enough.

It was not till about 1768 that I thought to calculate the returns of my father's trade, and by that estimate his probable profits. This, I believe, my parents never did.

This year, in Lent—12, I was taken to London, to be touched for the evil by Queen Anne. My mother was at Nicholson's, the famous bookseller, in Little Britain. My mother, then with child, concealed her pregnancy,° that she might not be hindered from the journey. I always retained some memory of this journey, though I was then but thirty months old. I remembered a little dark room behind the kitchen, where the jack-weight fell through a hole in the floor, into which I once slipped my leg. I seem to remember that I played with a string and a bell, which my cousin Isaac Johnson gave me; and that there was a cat with a white collar, and a dog, called Chops, that leaped over a stick: but I know not whether I remember the thing, or the talk of it.

I remember a boy crying at the palace when I went to be touched. Being asked 'on which side of the shop was the counter?' I answered, 'on the left from the entrance,' many years after, and spoke, not by guess, but by memory. We went in the stage-coach, and returned in the wagon,° as my mother said, because my cough was violent. The hope of saving a few shillings was no slight motive; for she, not having been accustomed to money, was afraid of such expenses as now seem very small. She sewed two guineas in her petticoat, lest she should be robbed.

We were troublesome to the passengers; but to suffer such inconveniences in the stage-coach was common in those days to persons in much higher rank. I was sick; one woman fondled me, the other was disgusted. She bought me a small silver cup and spoon, marked SAM. 1. lest if they had been marked S. 1.° which was her name, they should, upon her death, have been taken from me. She bought me a speckled linen frock, which I knew afterwards by the name of my London frock. The cup was one of the last pieces of plate which dear Tetty sold in our distress. I have now the spoon. She bought at the same time two teaspoons, and till my manhood she had no more.

My father considered tea as very expensive,° and discouraged my mother from keeping company with the neighbours, and from paying visits or receiving them. She lived to say, many years after, that, if the time were to pass again, she would not comply with such unsocial injunctions.

I suppose that in this year I was first informed of a future state. I remember, that being in bed with my mother one morning, I was told by her of the two places to which the inhabitants of this world were received after death; one a fine place filled with happiness, called Heaven; the other a *sad* place, called Hell. That this account much affected my imagination, I do not remember. When I was risen, my mother bade me repeat what she had told me to Thomas Jackson. When I told this afterwards to my mother, she seemed to wonder that she should begin such talk so late as that the first time could be remembered.°

This Whitsuntide [1719], I and my brother were sent to pass some time at Birmingham; I believe, a fortnight. Why such boys were sent to trouble other houses, I cannot tell. My mother had some opinion that much improvement was to be had by changing the mode of life. My uncle Harrison was a widower; and his house was kept by Sally Ford, a young woman of such sweetness of temper that I used to say she had no fault. We lived most at uncle Ford's, being much caressed by my aunt, a good-natured, coarse woman, easy of converse, but willing to find something to censure in the absent. My uncle Harrison did not much like us, nor did we like him. He was a very mean and vulgar man, drunk every night, but drunk with little drink, very peevish, very proud, very ostentatious, but, luckily, not rich. At my aunt Ford's I eat so much of a boiled leg of mutton that she used to talk of it. My mother, who had lived in a narrow sphere, and was then affected by little things, told me seriously that it would hardly ever be forgotten. Her mind, I think, was afterwards much enlarged, or greater evils wore out the care of less.

I stayed after the vacation was over some days; and remember, when I wrote home, that I desired the horses to come on Thursday of the first school week; and then, and not till then, they should be welcome to go. I was much pleased with a rattle to my whip, and wrote of it to my mother.

When my father came to fetch us home, he told the ostler that he had twelve miles home, and two boys under his care. This offended me. He had then a watch, which he returned when he was to pay for it.

In making, I think, the first exercise under Holbrook, I perceived the power of continuity of attention, of application not suffered to wander or to pause. I was writing at the kitchen windows, as I thought, alone, and turning my head saw Sally dancing. I went on without notice, and had finished almost without perceiving that any time had elapsed. This close attention I have seldom in my whole life obtained.

———

APRIL 22, 1753. As I purpose to try on Monday to seek a new wife° without any derogation from dear Tetty's memory I purpose at sacrament in the morning to take my leave of Tetty in a solemn commendation of her soul to God.

APRIL 23, EASTER MONDAY. Yesterday as I purposed I went to Bromley where dear Tetty lies buried and received the sacrament, first praying before I went to the altar according to the prayer precomposed for Tetty and a prayer which I made against unchastity, idleness, and neglect of public worship. I made it during sermon which I could not perfectly hear. I repeated mentally the commendation of her with the utmost fervour larme à l'oeil before the reception of each element at the altar. I repeated it again in the pew, in the garden before dinner, in the garden before departure, at home at night. I hope I did not sin. Fluunt lacrymae.° I likewise ardently applied to her the prayer for the Church militant where the dead are mentioned and commended her again to Eternal Mercy, as in coming out I approached her grave. During the whole service I was never once distracted by any thoughts of any other woman or with my design of a new wife which freedom of mind I remembered with gladness in the Garden. God guide me.

APRIL 29, 1753. I know not whether I do not too much indulge the vain longings of affection; but I hope they intenerate° my heart and that when I die like my Tetty this affection will be acknowledged in a happy interview and that in the meantime I am incited by it to piety. I will however not deviate too much from common and received methods of devotion.

JANUARY 23, 1759. The day on which my dear Mother was buried; repeated on my fast with the addition:
Almighty God, merciful Father, in whose hands are life and death, sanctify unto me the sorrow which I now feel. Forgive me whatever I have done unkindly to my Mother, and whatever I have omitted to do kindly. Make me to remember her good precepts, and good example, and to reform my life according to thy holy word, that I may lose no more opportunities of good; I am sorrowful, O Lord, let not my sorrow be without fruit. Let it be followed by holy resolutions and

lasting amendment, that when I shall die like my Mother, I may be received to everlasting life.

I commend, O Lord, so far as it may be lawful, into thy hands the soul of my departed Mother, beseeching thee to grant her whatever is most beneficial to her in her present state.

O Lord grant me thy Holy Spirit, and have mercy upon me for Jesus Christ's sake. Amen.

And, O Lord, grant unto me that am now about to return to the common comforts and business of the world such moderation in all enjoyments, such diligence in honest labour, and such purity of mind, that amidst the changes, miseries, or pleasures of life, I may keep my mind fixed upon thee, and improve every day in grace, till I shall be received into thy kingdom of eternal happiness.

I returned thanks for my Mother's good example, and implored pardon for neglecting it.

I returned thanks for the alleviation of my sorrow.

The dream of my Brother° I shall remember.

JULY 25, 1774.° We saw Hawkeston, the seat of Sir Rowland Hill, and were conducted by Miss Hill over a large tract of rocks and woods, a region abounding with striking scenes and terrific grandeur. We were always on the brink of a precipice, or at the foot of a lofty rock, but the steeps were seldom naked; in many places Oaks of uncommon magnitude shot up from the crannies of stone, and where there were not tall trees, there were underwoods and bushes. Round the rocks is a narrow path, cut upon the stone which is very frequently hewn into steps, but art has proceeded no further than make the succession of wonders safely accessible. The whole circuit is somewhat laborious, it is terminated by a grotto cut in the rock to a great extent with many windings and supported by pillars, not hewn into regularity, but such as imitate the sports of nature, by asperities and protuberances. The place is without any dampness, and would afford a habitation not uncomfortable. There were from space to space seats in the rock. Though it wants water it excels Dovedale, by the extent of its prospects, the awfulness of its shades, the horrors of its precipices, the verdure of its hollows and the loftiness of its rocks. The Ideas which it forces upon the mind are the sublime, the dreadful, and the vast. Above, is inaccessible altitude, below, is horrible profundity. But it excels the Garden of Ilam only in extent. Ilam has grandeur tempered with softness. The walker congratulates his own arrival at the place, and is grieved to think that he must ever leave it. As he looks up to the rocks his thoughts are elevated; as he turns his eyes on the valleys he is composed and soothed. He that mounts the precipices at Hawkeston wonders how he came hither, and doubts how he shall return. His walk is an adventure and his departure an escape. He has not the tranquillity, but the horrors of solitude, a kind of turbulent pleasure between fright and admiration. Ilam is the fit abode of pastoral virtue, and might properly diffuse its shades over nymphs and swains. Hawkeston can have no fitter inhabitants than Giants of mighty bone, and bold emprise, men of lawless courage and heroic violence. Hawkeston should be described by Milton and Ilam by Parnel.

Miss Hill showed the whole succession of wonders with great civility.

The House was magnificent compared with the rank of the owner.

APRIL 13, 1775. MAUNDY THURSDAY. Of the use of time or of my commendation of myself I thought no more, but lost life in restless nights and broken days, till this week awakened my attention.

This year has passed with very little improvement, perhaps with diminution of knowledge. Much time I have not left. Infirmities oppress me. But much remains to be done. I hope to rise at eight or sooner in the morning.

APRIL 14, 1775. GOOD FRIDAY. Boswel° came in, before I was up. We breakfasted. I only drank tea without milk or bread. We went to Church, saw Dr Wetherel in the pew, and by his desire took him home with us. He did not go very soon, and Boswel stayed. I had some scruples but Dilly and Miller called. Boswel and I went to Church, but came very late. We then took tea, by Boswel's desire, and I eat one bun, I think, that I might not seem to fast ostentatiously. Boswel sat with me till night; we had some serious talk. When he went I gave Francis some direction to communicate. Thus has passed hitherto this awful day.

10° 30′ p.m.

When I look back upon resolutions of improvement and amendments, which have year after year been made and broken, either by negligence, forgetfulness, vicious idleness, casual interruption, or morbid infirmity, when I find that so much of my life has stolen unprofitably away, and that I can descry by retrospection scarcely a few single days properly and vigorously employed, why do I yet try to

resolve again? I try because Reformation is necessary and despair is
criminal. I try in humble hope of the help of God.

As my life has from my earliest years been wasted in a morning bed
my purpose is from Easter day to rise early, not later than eight.

11° 15′ p.m. D.j.°

SEPTEMBER 18, 1775.° O God by whom all things were created and are
sustained, who givest and takest away, in whose hands are life and
death, accept my imperfect thanks for the length of days which thou
hast vouchsafed to grant me, impress upon my mind such repentance
of the time misspent in sinfulness and negligence that I may obtain
forgiveness of all my offences, and so calm my mind and strengthen
my resolutions that I may live the remaining part of my life in thy fear,
and with thy favour. Take not thy holy Spirit from me, but let me so
love thy laws, and so obey them, that I may finally be received to
eternal happiness through Jesus Christ, our Lord. Amen.

Composed at Calais in a sleepless night, and used before the morn
at Nôtre Dame. Written at St Omers.

OCTOBER 16, 1775° M. The Palais royal very grand, large and lofty, a
very great collection of pictures. Three of Raphael. Two holy family.
One small piece of M. Angelo. One room of Rubens. I thought the
pictures of Raphael fine.

The Tuilleries—Statues. Venus, Aen. and Anchises in his arms.
Nilus, many more. The walks not open to mean persons. Chairs at
night hired for two sous apiece. Pont tournant.

Austin Nuns. Grate. Mrs Fermor° Abbess. She knew Pope, and
thought him disagreeable. Mrs [Canning] has many books, has seen
life. Their frontlet disagreeable. Their hood. Their life easy. Rise
about five, hour and half in Chapel, dine at ten, another hour and half
at chapel, half an hour about three, and half an hour more at seven.
Four times in Chapel. A large garden. Thirteen pensioners. Teacher
complained.

At the Boulevard saw nothing, yet was glad to be there. Rope
dancing, and farce. Egg dance.

OCTOBER 19, 1775. TH. At court we saw the apartments; the king's
Bedchamber and council chamber extremely splendid. Persons of all
ranks in the outward rooms through which the family passes, servants
and Masters. Brunet with us the second time.

The Introductor came to us—civil to me. Presenting. I had

scruples, not necessary. We went and saw the King and Queen° at Dinner. We saw the other Ladies at Dinner. Madame Elizabeth with the Princess of Guimené. At night we went to a comedy. I neither saw nor heard; drunken women. Mrs Th[rale] preferred one to the other.

OCTOBER 20, 1775. FR. We saw the Queen mount in the forest. Brown habit, rode aside. One Lady rode aside. The Queen's horse light gray—martingale. She galloped. We then went to the apartments, and admired them. Then wandered through the palace. In the passages stalls and shops. Painting in Fresco by a great master worn out. We saw the king's horses and dogs. The Dogs almost all English. Degenerate q.°

The horses not much commended. The Stables cool, the Kennel filthy.

At night the Ladies went to the opera. I refused, but should have been welcome.

The king fed himself with his left hand as we.

MARCH 28, 1777. This day is Good Friday. It is likewise the day on which my poor Tetty was taken from me.

My thoughts were disturbed in bed. I remembered that it was my Wife's dying day, and begged pardon for all our sins, and commended her; but resolved to mix little of my own sorrows or cares with the great solemnity. Having taken only tea without milk, I went to church, had time before service to commend my Wife, and wished to join quietly in the service, but I did not hear well, and my mind grew unsettled and perplexed. Having rested ill in the night, I slumbered at the sermon, which, I think, I could not as I sat, perfectly hear.

I returned home but could not settle my mind. At last I read a Chapter. Then went down about six or seven and eat two cross buns, and drank tea. Fasting for some time has been uneasy and I have taken but little.

At night I had some ease. L.D.° I had prayed for pardon and peace. I slept in the afternoon.

DECEMBER 5, 1784.° Almighty and most merciful Father, I am now, as to human eyes it seems, about to commemorate for the last time, the death of thy son Jesus Christ, our Saviour and Redeemer. Grant, O Lord, that my whole hope and confidence may be in his merits and in thy mercy: forgive and accept my late conversion, enforce and accept my imperfect repentance; make this commemoration of him available to the confirmation of my Faith, the establishment of my hope, and the enlargement of my Charity, and make the Death of thy son Jesus effectual to my redemption. Have mercy upon me and pardon the multitude of my offences. Bless my Friends, have mercy upon all men. Support me by the Grace of thy Holy Spirit in the days of weakness, and at the hour of death, and receive me, at my death, to everlasting happiness, for the Sake of Jesus Christ. Amen.

Letters

To Edward Cave°

Sir

As you appear no less sensible than your readers of the defects of your poetical article, you will not be displeased if, in order to the improvement of it, I communicate to you the sentiments of a person who will undertake on reasonable terms sometimes to fill a column.

His opinion is that the public would not give you a bad reception if beside the current wit of the month, which a critical examination would generally reduce to a narrow compass, you admitted not only poems, inscriptions &c. never printed before, which he will sometimes supply you with; but likewise short literary dissertations in Latin or English, critical remarks on authors ancient or modern, forgotten poems that deserve revival, or loose pieces, like Floyer's, worth preserving. By this method your literary article, for so it might be called, will, he thinks, be better recommended to the public than by low jests, awkward buffoonery, or the dull scurrilities of either party.

If such a correspondence will be agreeable to you, be pleased to inform me in two posts what the conditions are on which you shall expect it. Your late offer gives me no reason to distrust your generosity. If you engage in any literary projects beside this paper, I have other designs to impart if I could be secure from having others reap the advantage of what I should hint.

Your letter, by being directed to S. Smith to be left at the Castle in Birmingham, Warwickshire, will reach

Your humble servant.

To Thomas Warton°

Sir

It is but an ill return for the book with which you were pleased to favour me to have delayed my thanks for it till now. I am too apt to be negligent, but I can never deliberately show any disrespect to a man of your character, and I now pay you a very honest acknowledgement for the advancement of the literature of our native country. You have shown to all who shall hereafter attempt the study of our ancient authors the way to success, by directing them to the perusal of the books which those authors had read. Of this method Hughes° and men much greater than Hughes seem never to have thought. The reason why the authors of the sixteenth century are so little understood is that they are read alone, and no help is borrowed from those who lived with them or before them. Some part of this ignorance I hope to remove by my book° which now draws towards its end, but which I cannot finish to my mind without visiting the libraries of Oxford, which I therefore hope to see in about a fortnight. I know not how long I shall stay or where I shall lodge, but shall be sure to look for you at my arrival, and we shall easily settle the rest.

I am, dear Sir, your most obedient and most humble servant

Sam: Johnson°

July 16, 1754

To the Earl of Chesterfield

February 1755

My Lord

I have been lately informed by the proprietor of *The World* that two papers in which my Dictionary is recommended to the public were written by your Lordship. To be so distinguished is an honour which, being very little accustomed to favours from the great, I know not well how to receive, or in what terms to acknowledge.

When upon some slight encouragement I first visited your Lordship, I was overpowered like the rest of mankind by the enchantment of your address, and could not forbear to wish that I might boast myself *le vainqueur° du vainqueur de la terre*, that I might obtain that regard for which I saw the world contending, but I found my attendance so little encouraged that neither pride nor modesty would suffer me to continue it. When I had once addressed your Lordship in public, I had exhausted all the art of pleasing which a retired and uncourtly scholar can possess. I had done all that I could, and no man is well pleased to have his all neglected, be it ever so little.

Seven years, My Lord, have now passed since I waited in your outward rooms or was repulsed from your door, during which time I have been pushing on my work through difficulties of which it is useless to complain, and have brought it at last to the verge of publication without one act of assistance, one word of encouragement, or one smile of favour. Such treatment I did not expect, for I never had a patron before.

The shepherd in Virgil° grew at last acquainted with Love, and found him a native of the rocks. Is not a patron, My Lord, one who looks with unconcern on a man struggling for life in the water and when he has reached ground encumbers him with help? The notice which you have been pleased to take of my labours, had it been early, had been kind; but it has been delayed till I am indifferent and cannot enjoy it, till I am solitary and cannot impart it, till I am known and do not want it.

I hope it is no very cynical asperity not to confess obligation where no benefit has been received, or to be unwilling that the public should consider me as owing to a patron which Providence has enabled me to do for myself.

Having carried on my work thus far with so little obligation to any favourer of learning, I shall not be disappointed though I should conclude it, if less be possible, with less, for I have been long wakened from that dream of hope in which I once boasted myself with so much exultation, My Lord,

Your Lordship's most humble, most obedient servant,

Sam: Johnson

To Miss Hill Boothby°

Honoured Madam

I beg of you to endeavour to live. I have returned your *Law*,° which however I earnestly entreat you to give me. I am in great trouble; if you can write three words to me, be pleased to do it. I am afraid to say much, and cannot say nothing when my dearest is in danger.

The Allmerciful God have mercy on you.

I am, Madam, your
Sam: Johnson

January 8, 1756

To Samuel Richardson

Sir

I am obliged to entreat your assistance. I am now under arrest for five pounds eighteen shillings. Mr Strahan, from whom I should have received the necessary help in this case, is not at home, and I am afraid of not finding Mr Millar. If you will be so good as to send me this sum, I will very gratefully repay you, and add it to all former obligations.

I am, Sir, your most obedient and most humble servant

Sam: Johnson

Gough Square, March 16 [1756]

To Sarah Johnson

Dear honoured Mother

Neither your condition nor your character make it fit for me to say much. You have been the best mother, and I believe the best woman in the world. I thank you for your indulgence to me, and beg forgiveness of all that I have done ill, and all that I have omitted to do well. God grant you his Holy Spirit, and receive you to everlasting happiness, for Jesus Christ's sake. Amen. Lord Jesus receive your spirit. Amen.

I am, dear, dear mother, your dutiful son,

Sam: Johnson

January 20, 1759

To Lucy Porter [*Johnson's stepdaughter*]

You will conceive my sorrow for the loss of my mother, of the best mother. If she were to live again, surely I should behave better to her. But she is happy, and what is past is nothing to her; and for me, since I cannot repair my faults to her, I hope repentance will efface them. I return you and all those that have been good to her my sincerest thanks, and pray God to repay you all with infinite advantage. Write to me, and comfort me, dear child. I shall be glad likewise, if Kitty° will write to me. I shall send a bill of twenty pounds in a few days, which I thought to have brought to my mother; but God suffered it not. I have not power or composure to say much more. God bless you and bless us all.

I am, dear Miss, your affectionate humble servant

Sam: Johnson

January 23, 1759

To Joseph Baretti (Milan) [*an excerpt*]

My vanity, or my kindness, makes me flatter myself that you would rather hear of me than of those whom I have mentioned; but of myself I have very little which I care to tell. Last winter I went down to my native town,° where I found the streets much narrower and shorter than I thought I had left them, inhabited by a new race of people, to whom I was very little known. My playfellows were grown old, and forced me to suspect that I was no longer young. My only remaining friend has changed his principles, and was become the tool of the predominant faction. My daughter-in-law,° from whom I expected most, and whom I met with sincere benevolence, has lost the beauty and gaiety of youth, without having gained much of the wisdom of age. I wandered about for five days, and took the first convenient opportunity of returning to a place where, if there is not much happiness, there is at least such a diversity of good and evil that slight vexations do not fix upon the heart. . . .

May you, my Baretti, be very happy at Milan, or some other place nearer to, Sir,

Your most affectionate humble servant,
Sam: Johnson

London, July 20, 1762

To George Strahan° [*at Abingdon School*]

Dear George

To give pain ought always to be painful, and I am sorry that I have been the occasion of any uneasiness to you, to whom I hope never to do anything but for your benefit or your pleasure. Your uneasiness was without any reason on your part, as you had written with sufficient frequency to me, and I had only neglected to answer then, because as nothing new had been proposed to your study no new direction or incitement could be offered you. But if it had happened that you had omitted what you did not omit, and that I had for an hour, or a week, or a much longer time thought myself put out of your mind by something to which presence gave that prevalence which presence will sometimes give, even where there is the most prudence and experience, you are not to imagine that my friendship is light enough to be blown away by the first cross blast, or that my regard hangs by so slender a hair as to be broken off by the unfelt weight of a petty offence. I love you, and hope to love you long. You have hitherto done nothing to diminish my good will, and though you had done much more than you have supposed imputed to you, my good will would not have been diminished.

I write thus largely on this suspicion which you have suffered to enter your mind, because in youth we are apt to be too rigorous in our expectations, and to suppose that the duties of life are to be performed with unfailing exactness and regularity, but in our progress through life we are forced to abate much of our demands, and to take friends such as we can find them, not as we would make them.

These concessions every wise man is more ready to make to others as he knows that he shall often want them for himself; and when he remembers how often he fails in the observance or cultivation of his best friends, is willing to suppose that his friends may in their turn neglect him without any intention to offend him.

When therefore it shall happen, as happen it will, that you or I have disappointed the expectation of the other, you are not to suppose that you have lost me or that I intended to lose you; nothing will remain but to repair the fault, and to go on as if it never had been committed.

I am, Sir, your affectionate servant
Sam: Johnson

Thursday, July 14, 1763

To James Boswell

My dear Boswell,

I have omitted a long time to write to you, without knowing very well why. I could now tell why I should not write, for who would write to men who publish the letters° of their friends without their leave? Yet I write to you in spite of my caution, to tell you that I shall be glad to see you, and that I wish you would empty your head of Corsica, which I think has filled it rather too long. But, at all events, I shall be glad, very glad, to see you.

I am, Sir, yours affectionately,
Sam: Johnson

Oxford, March 23, 1768

To Mrs Thrale

Dear Madam

Last Saturday I came to Ashbourn; the dangers or the pleasures of the journey I have at present no disposition to recount. Else might I paint the beauties of my native plain, might I tell of 'the smile of Nature and the charms of art',° else might I relate how I crossed the Staffordshire Canal, one of the great efforts of human labour and human contrivance, which from the bridge on which I viewed it passed away on either side, and loses itself in distant regions, uniting waters that Nature had divided, and dividing lands which Nature had united. I might tell how these reflections fermented in my mind till the chaise stopped at Ashbourne, at Ashbourne in the Peak. Let not the barren name of the Peak terrify you; I have never wanted strawberries and cream.° The great Bull has no disease but age. I hope in time to be like the great Bull; and hope you will be like him too a hundred years hence.

In the mean time, dearest Madam, you have many dangers to pass. I hope the danger of this year is now over, and you are safe in bed with a pretty little stranger in the cradle. I hope you do not think me indifferent about you, and therefore will take care to have me informed.

I am, Madam, your most obedient and most humble servant

Ashbourn, July 3, 1771   Sam: Johnson

To Mrs Thrale [*an excerpt*]

Ostig in Skye. September 30, 1773°

Dearest Madam

I am still confined in Skye. We were unskilful travellers, and imagined that the sea was an open road, which we could pass at pleasure, but we have now learned with some pain that we may still wait for a long time the caprices of the equinoctial winds, and sit reading or writing as I now do, while the tempest is rolling the sea, and roaring in the mountains. I am now no longer pleased with the delay; you hear from me but seldom, and I cannot at all hear from you. It comes into my mind that some evil may happen, or that I might be of use while I am away. But these thoughts are vain. The wind is violent and adverse, and our boat cannot yet come. I must content myself with writing to you, and hoping that you will sometime receive my letter. Now to my narrative.

Sept. 9. Having passed the night as is usual, I rose and found the dining room full of company; we feasted and talked and when the evening came it brought music and dancing. Young Macleod, the great proprietor of Skye, and head of his clan, was very distinguishable; a young man of nineteen, bred a while at St Andrews, and afterwards at Oxford, a pupil of G. Strahan. He is a young man of a mind as much advanced as I have ever known, very elegant of manners and very graceful in his person. He has the full spirit of a feudal chief, and I was very ready to accept his invitation to Dunvegan. All Raarsa's children are beautiful. The ladies, all except the eldest, are in the morning dressed in their hair. The true Highlander never wears more than a riband on her head till she is married.

On the third day Boswel went out with old Malcolm to see a ruined castle, which he found less entire than was promised, but he saw the country. I did not go, for the castle was perhaps ten miles off and there is no riding at Raarsa, the whole island being rock and mountain, from which the cattle often fall and are destroyed. It is very barren, and maintains as near as I could collect about seven hundred inhabitants, perhaps ten to a square mile. In these countries you are not to suppose that you shall find villages, or enclosures. The traveller wanders through a naked desert, gratified sometimes, but rarely, with the sight of cows, and now and then finds a heap of loose stones and turfs in a cavity between rocks, where a being, born with all those powers which education expands, and all those sensations which culture refines, is condemned to shelter itself from the wind and rain. Philosophers there are who try to make themselves believe that this life is happy, but they believe it only while they are saying it, and never yet produced conviction in a single mind; he whom want of words or images sunk into silence still thought, as he thought before, that privation of pleasure can never please, and that content is not to be much envied when it has no other principle than ignorance of good.

This gloomy tranquillity which some may call fortitude, and others wisdom, was I believe for a long time to be very frequently found in these dens of poverty; every man was content to live like his neighbour, and never wandering from home saw no mode of life preferable to his own, except at the house of the Laird or the Laird's near relations, whom he considered as a superior order of beings, to whose luxuries or honours he had no pretensions. But the end of this reverence and submission seems now approaching. The Highlanders have learned that there are countries less bleak and barren than their own, where instead of working for the Laird, every man may till his own ground, and eat all the produce of his own labour. Great numbers have been induced by this discovery to go every year for some time past to America. Macdonald and Macleod of Skye have lost many tenants, and many labourers, but Raarsa has not yet been forsaken by a single inhabitant. . . .

To James Macpherson°

Mr James Macpherson—I received your foolish and impudent note. Whatever insult is offered me I will do my best to repel, and what I cannot do for myself the law will do for me. I will not desist from detecting what I think a cheat from any fear of the menaces of a ruffian.

You want me to retract. What shall I retract? I thought your book an imposture from the beginning, I think it upon yet surer reasons an imposture still. For this opinion I give the public my reasons, which I here dare you to refute.

But however I may despise you, I reverence truth and if you can prove the genuineness of the work I will confess it. Your rage I defy, your abilities since your Homer° are not so formidable, and what I have heard of your morals disposes me to pay regard not to what you shall say, but to what you can prove.

You may print this if you will.

Sam: Johnson

January 20, 1775

To the Revd William Dodd°

Dear Sir

That which is appointed for all men is now coming upon you. Outward circumstances, the eyes and the thoughts of men, are below the notice of an immortal being about to stand the trial for eternity before the Supreme Judge of heaven and earth. Be comforted: your crime, morally or religiously considered, has no very deep dye of turpitude. It corrupted no man's principles; it attacked no man's life. It involved only a temporary and reparable injury. Of this, and of all other sins, you are earnestly to repent; and may God, who knoweth our frailty and desireth not our death, accept your repentance, for the sake of his Son JESUS CHRIST our Lord.

In requital of those well-intended offices which you are pleased so emphatically to acknowledge, let me beg that you make in your devotions one petition for my eternal welfare.

I am, dear Sir, your affectionate servant,

Sam: Johnson

June 26, 1777

To Mrs Thrale°

Madam

If I interpret your letter right, you are ignominiously married; if it is yet undone, let us once talk together. If you have abandoned your children and your religion, God forgive your wickedness; if you have forfeited your fame, and your country, may your folly do no further mischief.

If the last act is yet to do, I, who have loved you, esteemed you, reverenced you, and served you, I who long thought you the first of human kind, entreat that before your fate is irrevocable, I may once more see you. I was, I once was,

Madam, most truly yours.

Sam: Johnson

July 2, 1784

I will come down if you permit it.

From Mrs Thrale

4 July 1784.

Sir—

I have this morning received from you so rough a letter, in reply to one which was both tenderly and respectfully written, that I am forced to desire the conclusion of a correspondence which I can bear to continue no longer. The birth of my second husband is not meaner than that of my first, his sentiments are not meaner, his profession is not meaner—and his superiority in what he professes acknowledged by all mankind. It is want of fortune then that is *ignominious*; the character of the man I have chosen has no other claim to such an epithet. The religion to which he has been always a zealous adherent will I hope teach him to forgive insults he has not deserved—mine will I hope enable me to bear them at once with dignity and patience. To hear that I have forfeited my fame is indeed the greatest insult I ever yet received; my fame is as unsullied as snow, or I should think it unworthy of him who must henceforward protect it.

I write by the coach the more speedily and effectually to prevent your coming hither.

Perhaps by my fame (and I hope it is so) you mean only that celebrity which is a consideration of a much lower kind: I care for that only as it may give pleasure to my husband and his friends.

Farewell, dear Sir, and accept my best wishes: you have always commanded my esteem, and long enjoyed the fruits of a friendship never infringed by one harsh expression on my part, during twenty years of familiar talk; never did I oppose your will, or control your wish: nor can your unmerited severity itself lessen my regard—but till you have changed your opinion of Mr Piozzi—let us converse no more. God bless you!

To Mrs Thrale

Dear Madam

What you have done, however I may lament it, I have no pretence to resent, as it has not been injurious to me. I therefore breathe out one sigh more of tenderness perhaps useless but at least sincere.

I wish that God may grant you every blessing, that you may be happy in this world for its short continuance, and eternally happy in a better state. And whatever I can contribute to your happiness, I am very ready to repay for that kindness which soothed twenty years of a life radically wretched.

Do not think slightly of the advice which I now presume to offer. Prevail upon Mr Piozzi to settle in England. You may live here with more dignity than in Italy, and with more security. Your rank will be higher, and your fortune under your own eyes. I desire not to detail all my reasons; but every argument of prudence and interest is for England, and only some phantoms of imagination seduce you to Italy.

I am afraid, however, that my counsel is vain, yet I have eased my heart by giving it.

When Queen Mary° took the resolution of sheltering herself in England, the Archbishop of St Andrews, attempting to dissuade her, attended on her journey and when they came to the irremeable° stream that separated the two kingdoms, walked by her side into the water, in the middle of which he seized her bridle, and with earnestness proportioned to her danger and his own affection, pressed her to return. The Queen went forward.—If the parallel reaches thus far, may it go no further. The tears stand in my eyes.

I am going into Derbyshire, and hope to be followed by your good wishes, for I am with great affection

Your most humble servant,
Sam: Johnson

London, July 8, 1784

Any letters that come for me hither will be sent me.

NOTES

WORDS found in standard dictionaries, and individuals and historical events listed in the usual works of reference, are not annotated, unless they have some special significance for the interpretation of the text. For the circumstances surrounding the composition of many of the works in the volume, the Introduction should be consulted.

GM = Gentleman's Magazine

POETRY

2 *London.* l. 2. *Thales.* He has been identified with Richard Savage, who did leave London for Cambria (Wales) (see p. 152). The identification has been disputed.

l. 23. *Eliza.* Queen Elizabeth I, whose military successes over the Spanish made her the heroine of the Opposition to Walpole.

l. 30. Walpole's abortive attempt to increase excise taxes, and his alleged failure to protect British merchant ships from depredations by Spanish coast guards, were standard topics of Opposition rhetoric. Masquerade balls were denounced by moralists as encouragements to vice.

3 l. 50. Johnson may be paraphrasing a line by Boileau, in which the blanks are filled by 'George'.

l. 59. Italian *castrati* opera singers were deplored by patriotic Britons. The Stage Licensing Act, 1737, required plays to be approved and licensed by the Lord Chamberlain's office before they could be publicly performed. See p. 71.

l. 72. The *Daily Gazetteer* was the newspaper organ of the Walpole administration.

4 l. 74. H——y's. Probably the Revd John 'Orator' Henley, a public buffoon and a supporter of Walpole.

l. 86. *Villiers.* George Villiers, 2nd Duke of Buckingham, who wasted a fortune and died in squalor.

l. 94. *shore.* Sewer. Johnson transfers Juvenal's imprecations against the baleful influence of Greek immigrants in Rome to the French.

7 l. 213. The country house of some peer or MP who has a government appointment in Westminster.

8 l. 245. The Committee of Ways and Means of the House of Commons proposes measures of taxation. Johnson goes on to satirize George II's frequent visits to his mistress, Amalie von Wallmoden, in Hanover.

l. 252. Special juries, drawn from a panel of wealthier citizens than ordinary juries—and therefore presumably more in favour of preserving the *status quo*—were said to be used by the ministry to obtain convictions of Opposition printers and writers for sedition.

9 *On Colley Cibber*. Walpole's appointment as Poet Laureate of Cibber, who was an execrable poet (though an admirable comedian and memoirist), raised a furore in Opposition circles. Pope made him the hero of *The Dunciad*. *Maro* is Virgil.

10 *Prologue*. When the Theatre Royal, Drury Lane, reopened in 1747 under the new management of David Garrick, he commissioned this prologue for the occasion.

11 l. 36. Farces based on the Faust legend were popular with the uneducated.

l. 46. A noted boxer and rope-dancer of the time.

12 *The Vanity of Human Wishes*. l.2. On a map of the world with Britain in the centre, China, reputedly the home of a high civilization (see p. 41), is in one corner, and Peru, the scene of the massacres and enslavement of the natives by the Spanish under Pizarro, in the diagonally opposite one. The phrase implies a survey of human behaviour from its best to its worst.

l. 15. The feathers on an arrow enable it to maintain its course accurately.

l. 20. This obscure image may be derived from alchemy, in which 'precipitate' was a technical term.

13 l. 49. *Democritus*. Known as 'the laughing philosopher'. The gist of the passage is 'If Democritus could find much to ridicule in the primitive simplicity of ancient Greece, he would find much more in modern Britain'.

14 l. 76. Perhaps an image from fireworks. In the same month as this poem was published, Johnson printed in the *GM* a 'Letter on the Fireworks'—the great fireworks display in Green Park, for which Handel wrote his *Royal Fireworks Music*, to celebrate the Peace of Aix-la-Chapelle, ending the War of the Austrian Succession. Johnson sarcastically likens the war and the peace, pointless as he thinks, to this 'blaze, so transitory and so useless'.

l. 84. *Palladium*. An image of Pallas Athene, which, while it remained in Troy, preserved the city from destruction.

l. 97. *weekly libels*. Political journals. The Septennial Act, 1716, set the maximum duration of a Parliament at seven years. At the end of that period a general election was held, with candidates providing free ale and other treats to prospective supporters.

l. 99. Johnson's account of Wolsey may owe something to Shakespeare's *Henry VIII*.

15 l. 124. A country Justice of the Peace in the Midlands. The Trent is the chief river of Johnson's Staffordshire.

l. 129. *Villiers*. George Villiers, 1st Duke of Buckingham, James I's favourite, assassinated in 1628. Robert *Harley*, 1st Earl of Oxford, leader of a Tory ministry under Queen Anne. After the accession of George I, he was imprisoned in the Tower for two years, and his health suffered. Thomas *Wentworth*, Earl of Strafford, Charles I's minister, attainted by Parliament and executed. Edward *Hyde*, Earl of Clarendon, Charles II's minister, condemned to exile in France. His daughter married the Duke of York, later James II, and became the mother of Queen Mary II and Queen Anne; hence, 'to kings allied'.

l. 139. The Bodleian Library at Oxford will be filled with the books the ambitious scholar will write. *Bacon's mansion*: a structure built over Folly Bridge, Oxford, supposed to have been inhabited by Roger Bacon, the medieval scholar. Legend had it that if a scholar greater than Bacon should pass under it, it would collapse.

16 l. 160. *patron*. Johnson originally wrote 'garret'. After the affair with Chesterfield (p. 782), he changed it to this.

l. 164. *Lydiat*. A distinguished Oxford scholar, who died in poverty.

l. 168. William *Laud*, Charles I's 'High Church' Archbishop of Canterbury, was impeached by the Long Parliament and beheaded in 1645. Although not a great scholar himself, as Chancellor of Oxford University he did much to advance scholarship there. For a different view of him by Johnson, see p. 478.

l. 179. *rapid Greek*. Alexander the Great. On him and the other military 'heroes' mentioned here, see *The Adventurer*, no. 99 (p. 273).

17 l. 192. *Charles XII*. The young King of Sweden, whose early military triumphs ended with a disastrous defeat by Russia in 1709 at the battle of Pultawa or Poltava.

l. 203. *Gothic*. The official name of Sweden is 'the Kingdom of the Swedes, Goths, and Wends'.

l. 214. After his defeat, Charles sought assistance at the court of the Sultan of Turkey. The picture seems to be that of Charles waiting for an audience in an ante-room (as Johnson did in Chesterfield's—see p. 782), while the Sultan's favourites are given priority, and his ministers or attendants deliberate about what is to be done with Charles. The suggestion that 'ladies interpose' refers to a diplomatic intervention by the Russian Empress seems far-fetched—why the plural, 'ladies'?

l. 220. *dubious hand*. Rumour had it that Charles was shot by one of his own officers at the siege of an obscure fortress.

l. 224. Xerxes the Great and the Elector Charles Albert of Bavaria. The latter, when Frederick the Great of Prussia invaded Silesia in the War of the Austrian Succession, joined in in the hope of acquiring other Austrian territory. He was quickly defeated and discredited.

18 l. 232. When Xerxes attempted to cross from Asia to Europe over the

Hellespont, a storm on the ocean destroyed his bridge of boats. In anger, he ordered the sea to be punished by being whipped with chains.

l. 239. The reference seems to be to the naval battle of Salamis. The land battle mentioned earlier ('heap their valleys') must be the later battle of Plataea; it cannot be Thermopylae, where the Persians overcame the small band of Spartans who resisted them.

l. 245. *fair Austria*. Maria Theresa, Queen of Hungary, and heiress to her father Charles VI, Holy Roman Emperor. Frederick of Prussia's invasion of her territories precipitated the War of the Austrian Succession.

l. 249. These irregular troops, from distant parts of the Austrian Empire, were a novelty at the time, and had a reputation for ferocity.

20   l. 313. *Lydia's monarch*. The wealthy Croesus, whose life ended in disaster, despite warnings given him by the Athenian sage Solon.

l. 317. The great Duke of Marlborough, victor of the battle of Blenheim, had a stroke in 1716 and remained incapacitated until his death in 1722. Swift was senile for three years before his death in 1745. There were rumours—which have been discounted—that his servants used to exhibit him to tourists for money.

l. 319. *teeming*. prolific.

l. 321. Anne *Vane*, mistress of Frederick, Prince of Wales, and Catherine *Sedley*, mistress of James II. In fact, neither was particularly beautiful, nor, in the worldly sense, unfortunate.

l. 344. *Suspense*. The regular translation of the Stoic term *epoche*, the refusal to commit oneself to one position or another. The contemptuous dismissal of Stoicism here should be noted. See also pp. 186, 372.

21   *Irene*. The point of this scene is the conversion of Mahomet from his view of women as an inferior species by Irene's intelligence and assertiveness. The Arab chief who kidnaps Pekuah in *Rasselas* seems to have a similarly low view, until Pekuah converts *him* (p. 400). George Sale, the translator of the *Koran*, comments in his 'Preliminary Discourse' (sec. iv) on 'a vulgar imputation on the Mohammedans, who are by several writers reported to hold that women have no souls, or, if they have, that they will perish, like those of brute beasts, and will not be rewarded in the next life', and goes on to controvert it. Sale published this in 1734, possibly after Johnson had drafted the scene (although he owned a copy of Sale's *Koran* at the time of his death). Perhaps Johnson got the idea from the two writers mentioned in his draft of the scene, Humphrey Prideaux (*The True Nature of Imposture in the Life of Mahomet*) and Barthélemy d'Herbelot (*Bibliothèque Orientale*). Irene is pronounced with three syllables—'I-rē-nē'.

24   *A New Prologue . . . Comus*. In 1750 Johnson learned with indignation from his schoolfellow Bishop Thomas Newton's edition of *Paradise Lost* that Milton's granddaughter, Elizabeth Foster, was in want. He publicized the fact, and persuaded Garrick to stage a benefit performance

of *Comus*, which brought her £130. The prologue was advertised as 'by the Author of *Irene*'.

l. 4. The sense seems to be that, whereas Virgil and Horace had to flatter Augustus and Maecenas in their poetry to attract their patronage, Milton's admirers need no such incentive. 'Augustan' is probably also a veiled slur on George Augustus, King George II. There may be some irony in 'patriot' (see p. 580).

25 *Verses for Baretti*. Johnson wrote this comment on extempore poetry (which was itself written extempore) in reply to some verses of his friend Giuseppe Baretti, to whose books on the Italian language he contributed.

Parodies of Modern Ballad Imitations. Wordsworth was unfair to Johnson when, in his *Supplementary Essay*, 1815, he accused him of scorning the old ballads and carrying on a campaign of detraction against them. In fact, Johnson spent two months with Thomas Percy helping to prepare the *Reliques of Ancient English Poetry* for publication (and to find a publisher for it), provided it with a dedication, and gave it considerable publicity in his notes to Shakespeare's plays. But when Percy sought to profit from the publicity by composing a feeble pseudo-ballad of his own, Johnson thought little of it. These quatrains are the result.

l. 1. *Renny*. Frances Reynolds, Sir Joshua's sister, at whose tea-table Johnson composed this extempore.

26 *Impromptu Translation*. The American actress Ilka Chase wittily entitled her memoirs *In Bed We Cry*.

Epitaph on Hogarth. Garrick had written an epitaph on Hogarth which Johnson disliked, and he composed this as an alternative. The text of the first stanza is that which he dictated to Mrs Thrale. There are other versions which seem inferior poetically: 'traced' and 'waved' for 'drew' in the second line assonate somewhat unpleasantly with 'grace'.

ΓΝΩΘΙ ΣΕΑΥΤΟΝ. This (transliterated as GNOTHI SEAUTON), meaning 'know thyself', was the famous exhortation written in the Temple of Apollo at Delphi. The poem, written after the drudgery of the revision of the *Dictionary* in 1773, is a remarkable, indeed rather chilling, piece of introspection and analysis of Johnson's melancholia. The alliterative verse of John Wain's rendering is a satisfying approximation to the roll of the Latin dactylic metre.

30 l. 57. The spaced stops are Wain's. They do not represent an ellipsis; this is the end of the poem.

Skia. Composed while Johnson was in Skye in September 1773.

31 *To Mrs Thrale*. Johnson said of these extempore verses, 'You may see what it is to come for poetry to a dictionary-maker; you may observe that the rhymes run in alphabetical order exactly'. In fact, they do not: note ll. 7 and 9.

32 *Lines in . . . The Rival*. Johnson substituted this couplet for one at the end of an act of a lost play by his friend John Hawkesworth. The thought is central to Johnson's own view of mental health.

On Archaism in Poetry. For Johnson's hostility to artificial language and 'revivals' of outmoded forms in poetry, see his critiques of Collins (p. 761) and Gray (p. 768). The Wartons, Joseph and Thomas, were assiduous practitioners of archaic diction and inverted sentence-order ('uncouth words in disarray'), and so used to be hailed as precursors of Romanticism. Johnson composed the parody of Thomas extempore in Boswell's presence. '"*Gray evening* is common enough," said Johnson; "but *evening gray* he'd think fine."' 'BOSWELL. But why smite his bosom, Sir? JOHNSON. Why, to show he was in earnest (smiling).'

33 *Prologue . . . A Word to the Wise*. This comedy by the minor playwright Hugh Kelly had been hooted down by his enemies when it was first performed in 1770. Johnson's prologue was written for a revival of it, after Kelly's death, as a benefit for his widow and children. Those who accuse Johnson of having no ear should note in particular ll. 9–10.

l. 4. The quotation is from Pope's translation of the *Iliad*, vii. 485, where Agamemnon grants the Trojans' request for a truce to bury their dead.

An Extempore Elegy. Fanny Burney recorded that she, Mrs Thrale, and Johnson jointly produced this mock ballad. As chronology seems to require, the order of the second and third stanzas has been reversed from that given in Joyce Hemlow's *History of Fanny Burney*. Some stanzas between the third and fourth, narrating the lady's progress from the country squire's house to 'the town', seem needed.

34 *To Sir John Lade*. Lade, the posthumous son of Mrs Thrale's brother-in-law, Sir John Lade, Bt., inherited his father's fortune and baronetcy at birth. During his minority he was under the control of guardians; when freed of it, he took Johnson's sardonic advice and became a notorious rake.

35 l. 17. To protect his name, Mrs Thrale, when she first published the poem, substituted 'my lad' for 'Sir John'. The version thus altered is said to have influenced A. E. Housman when writing *A Shropshire Lad*.

On the Death of Dr Robert Levet. Levet, who shared Johnson's house for many years, was an unqualified medical practitioner, who worked among London slum-dwellers who could not afford the services of a qualified doctor. Johnson's better educated and socially higher friends wondered at his friendship with such a 'low' individual. This is his reply. The persistent image of the prisoner in the nine should be noted.

l. 7. *officious*. helpful; 'kind, full of good offices' (Johnson's *Dictionary*).

36 *In Rivum . . . Diffluentem*. Probably written during Johnson's last visit to Lichfield in 1784, shortly before his death.

l. 12. *Nisus*. Nisus and Euryalus, in Virgil's *Aeneid*, were intimate friends. By Nisus, Johnson may mean his old schoolfellow Edmund Hector, with whom, on his last visit to him, he reminisced about their boyhood.

39 *A Latin School Exercise.* Here first printed from the manuscript in the possession of Arthur A. Houghton, Jr. The handwriting is the same as that in two Latin prose exercises in the Bodleian Library (MS Eng. Letters c. 275), one of which is dated by Johnson '1725' (reproduced in facsimile as the frontispiece to vol. i of R. W. Chapman's edition of Johnson's *Letters*, 1952). The present piece is written on a sheet of paper of the same size as the other Bodleian MS, the 'theme' of which (from Macrobius, *Saturnalia*, iii. 17. 10) is underlined with a row of carets in the same way as the theme of this. Hence this is probably another example of Johnson's school work at either Lichfield or Stourbridge. Letters in brackets supply places where the MS is damaged, except at the beginning of the penultimate sentence, where Johnson wrote 'Si', probably in mistake for 'Sic'.

The theme here is from Juvenal, *Satires*, x. 141–2, translated by Dryden (more exactly than Johnson was to do in 'The Vanity of Human Wishes', 183–4) as 'For who would Virtue for herself regard, / Or wed, without the portion of reward?' On the MS some graffitist, outraged at this cynicism, has scribbled 'Quisquis'—'Anyone'—and, in Roman letters, the Greek 'Andres'—'Men'. Johnson, however, in his little essay, takes a different tack, applauding the fact that reward and recognition are incentives to virtue and achievement, and urging those in authority to make use of them. Is the sixteen-year-old schoolboy seriously challenging Juvenal's pessimism, or is he, as clever schoolboys do, merely showing off his intellectual originality to his master? Or is there some hint of the exuberant confidence of literary fame found in his version of Horace made about the same time (p. 1)?

41 *A Voyage to Abyssinia. basilisks.* Lobo does indeed investigate and disprove these travellers' tales.

42 *Geddes.* Michael Geddes, a Scottish Anglican clergyman, defended the authenticity of Abyssinian Christianity and condemned the activities of the Jesuits.

Le Grand. Joachim LeGrand, the French translator of the work and author of the 'Dissertations' in it, was an Oratorian, and not entirely friendly to the Jesuits.

France. Cardinal Fleury, Prime Minister of France during Louis XV's minority, was a supporter of the Jesuits.

Oviedo. André de Oviedo, first leader of the Jesuit mission to Abyssinia.

43 *Ludolfus.* In his *History of Abyssinia*, Hiob Ludolf, a German Lutheran, vigorously combated the Jesuit contention that the Abyssinian church was not really Christian.

Scriptures. See Article VI of the Church of England: 'Holy Scripture containeth all things necessary to salvation'.

44 *The State of Affairs in Lilliput.* From the *GM*, June 1738.

Felix . . . argumentum. 'Happy is the intellect to which so great a subject is presented; happy is the subject to which so great an intellect is brought.' Not traced; perhaps Johnson's own invention.

45 *Blefuscu.* In *Gulliver's Travels*, France, as Lilliput is Great Britain. Mildendo, the capital of Lilliput, is London.

47 *form.* That is, flat.

pontiff. In 1493 Pope Alexander VI issued a famous bull, granting to Spain all newly discovered lands west of a line drawn west of Cape Verde, and to Portugal all those discovered east of it.

human nature. For a memorable denunciation of European activities in the Western Hemisphere, see *The Idler*, No. 81 (p. 296).

Iberia. Spain.

48 *prisons . . . Columbia.* Transportation to the American colonies was a frequent punishment for criminals. But ten thousand is a gross exaggeration.

tortured . . . seamen. In March 1738, Robert Jenkins, master of a British merchant vessel trading (illegally, according to the Spanish) in American waters, exhibited to the House of Commons an ear which he said had been severed from his head by a Spanish *guarda costa*. Britain's formal declaration of 'the War of Jenkins's Ear' took place in October.

49 *Hurgoes.* 'Hurgo'—'a great lord'—is from *Gulliver's Travels*, bk. i, ch. 1.

seven moons. A reference to the Septennial Act; see note to p. 14, l. 97.

392 moons. Lemuel Gulliver arrived in Lilliput on 5 November 1699. With twelve calendar or thirteen lunar months in a year, this would place Gulliver junior's visit in the 1730s.

venality . . . assemblies. Agitation for more frequent general elections was a recurrent cry of oppositions throughout the eighteenth century.

50 *debate . . . Second.* A report immediately follows of a Parliamentary debate, which indeed took place in the fourth session of the eighth Parliament of Great Britain in the eleventh year of the reign of George II. 'Belfaborac' is presumably Westminster.

51 *On Gay's Epitaph.* One of two letters signed 'Pamphilus' ('friend to all') printed in the *GM* in 1738, this one in October, now attributed convincingly to Johnson. 'Sylvanus *Urban*' (Country City): the supposed compiler of the *GM*.

Παντα . . . μηδεν. 'All is laughter, all is dust, all is nothingness.' The second line of this epigram by Glycon in the Greek *Anthology* continues, 'All is spawned by unreason'. The *GM* prints no accents or breathings in the Greek.

52 *Sesostris*. Johnson did forget. Herodotus (ii. 141) assigns the epitaph to a later legendary Egyptian king, Sethos, renowned for his piety.

Dryden. From *Oedipus*, iii. 1, by Dryden and Nathaniel Lee.

53 *knowledge . . . existence*. That is, if, as the epitaph seems to imply, death brings annihilation, the power of knowing will also be destroyed.

54 *The Life of Dr Herman Boerhaave*. The title and the first paragraph here are taken from the first publication of the work in the *GM* from January to April 1739. The body of the text, however, is that of the version in Robert James's *Medicinal Dictionary*, 1742, into which Johnson introduced a number of corrections and stylistic improvements. Johnson took the bulk of his facts from the Latin memorial oration for Boerhaave by his friend and colleague Albert Schultens, but many of the moral generalizations are, as usual, Johnson's. There are a few factual errors in the account, corrected in the standard modern biography by G. A. Lindeboom.

64 *Asiatica*. This prescription, in medical Latin, of a mixture of various vegetable juices is not in the *GM* version, and may have been James's addition.

Lipsius. Johnson probably took the story of Lipsius's deathbed, which is not in Schultens, from the life of Lipsius by his friend Aubert LeMire prefixed to the 1637 edition of Lipsius's works, which Johnson owned. A translation of LeMire's story reads, 'When one of those standing around suggested Stoic *apathia* to him, he answered, "Those things are vain", and pointing his finger at the crucifix near his bed, added, most truly, "That is true patience".'

66 *Aetas . . . unice*. Some of the symptoms in this technical description of Boerhaave's illness—difficulty in breathing, dropsy, insomnia—correspond to some of Johnson's in later life.

69 *Moses*. Deuteronomy 6:5, Leviticus 19:18. Quoted by Jesus in 'the great commandment', Matthew 22:37-40.

70 *infancy*. This is followed by a list of Boerhaave's publications, and, in the *Medicinal Dictionary*, by a further commentary chiefly on Boerhaave's contributions to botany, different in style from the foregoing and more likely to be by James.

71 *A Complete Vindication of the Licensers of the Stage*. Published in May 1739 as a separate pamphlet. Henry Brooke's *Gustavus Vasa*, recounting a patriotic revolt in Sweden against a usurping Danish king and his corrupt Prime Minister (no doubt intended to remind the audience of the Hanoverian George II and Walpole), was refused a licence by the Lord Chamberlain's licensers of plays. Brooke then printed it by subscription, with a preface protesting against his treatment. 'Impartial Hand' is of course heavily ironic: the speaker is a dedicated *apparatchik* of a tyrannical and obscurantist administration.

72 *at court*. Among the administration.

L—— and P——. George Lyttelton, later 1st Lord Lyttelton, and William Pitt the elder, then voluble young members of the 'patriots' of the Opposition. Johnson later changed the high opinion of them expressed here.

special jury. See note to p. 8, l. 252.

riband. Walpole's revival in 1725 of the defunct Order of the Bath (with its red ribbon), in order to provide an inexpensive reward for his supporters, was much satirized.

ancient barons. Such as those who forced King John to grant Magna Carta.

73 *Who . . . age.* This and subsequent quotations of verse are from *Gustavus Vasa.*

75 *Boni . . . auctoritatem.* 'It is the part of a good judge to enlarge his authority.' An old legal maxim, of dubious validity.

great man. A phrase often applied satirically to Walpole.

76 *standing army.* Authority to continue the regular army in existence from year to year was given by Parliament in the passage of an annual Mutiny Act. This enabled the Opposition to declaim against 'standing armies', an old bugbear from the time of Cromwell. See note to p. 103.

gin. Several ineffective and unpopular measures for the control of the sale of cheap gin were passed in the early eighteenth century. See also p. 513.

78 *ambassadors.* 'Old Horace' Walpole, Robert Walpole's brother, ambassador to France and to Holland, was sneered at by the Opposition as uneducated and uncouth.

Anderson. In the play, a supporter of the hero, Gustavus Vasa.

79 *Arvida.* 'Of the royal blood of Sweden, friend and cousin to Gustavus.'

80 *Laureate.* Colley Cibber. See note to p. 9.

81 *Gazetteer.* The *Daily Gazetteer,* Walpole's newspaper. See note to p. 3, l. 72.

great actions of ——. No doubt 'the King'.

82 *But these . . . secrets of state.* Compare this paragraph with the opening of *Observations on the Present State of Affairs,* p. 501.

84 *Annotations to Crousaz.* Published in 1739 (just when is not known). Crousaz's earlier attack on Pope, the *Examen,* was based on a prose translation of the *Essay on Man* by Etienne de Silhouette. In the *Commentaire* he uses Jean-François du Bellay du Resnel's translation into French verse. (There is a suggestion that it was Voltaire who, for his own purposes, encouraged Du Resnel to make it.) Johnson's interlinear retranslation into English of Du Resnel is omitted here. The English version of Crousaz's own remarks is of course by Johnson. This is a selection from the more substantial annotations, most of which are found in the first of the four parts of the *Commentaire* (one devoted to each part

of Pope's *Essay*). No attempt is made here to supply the French accents which Johnson's printer ignored, or to modernize the French.

Roscommon's. In his *Essay on Translated Verse*, 1684.

93 *Geometrician.* Johnson's comment is based on the derivation of the word from *ge*, earth.

94 *love.* See a similar comment on love as the main subject of imaginative literature in the *Preface to Shakespeare*, pp. 421–2.

Du Resnel. The volume also includes a translation by Johnson of Du Resnel's preface to his translation of the *Essay*, which is quoted here.

96 *An Essay on Epitaphs.* From the *GM*, September 1740. In 1756 Johnson also wrote a 'Dissertation on Pope's Epitaphs', which he later appended to his 'Preface' to Pope ('Life of Pope'). Wordsworth has some criticism of Johnson's essays in his own 'Essay on Epitaphs'.

97 *Antipodes.* 'Here lies Pico de Mirandola; the rest of his story is known by the Tagus and the Ganges, even the Antipodes.'

98 *hic quiescit.* 'Here rests Isaac Newton, who searched out the laws of nature.'

Minutius Felix. (Also spelled Minucius.) An early Roman Christian, who wrote his dialogue *Octavius* in defence of Christianity against its pagan enemies. Johnson's quotation is from chapter xxxviii.

99 *immobile saxum.* 'While your golden writings fly far and wide throughout the world, and you live eternally in fame, divine poet, may you lie here in peaceful rest; may grey-haired Faith guard your urn, and the Muses keep watch over it with their eternal torch! May this place be holy, and may no one be so bold as to venture to disturb this venerable bust with sacrilegious hand. Let the ashes of Cowley remain untouched, remain through kindly ages, and keep the tombstone unmoved.'

Angelo. The reference is to Michelangelo's great painting of the Last Judgement in the Sistine Chapel, where Charon and his boat do indeed appear (they also appear in Dante's *Inferno*).

Sannazarius. The tomb of the Renaissance poet Sannazaro in the church of Santa Maria del Parto in Naples was 'defaced' by the addition of the names 'David' and 'Judith' to the pedestals of the flanking statues of Apollo and Minerva.

Passeratius . . . regum vices. The French poet Jean Passerat wrote the following epitaph on his murdered master, Henri III:

'Stay, wayfarer, and mourn the fates of kings. Buried beneath this marble is the heart of a king who gave laws to the French and to the Poles. A murderer hidden beneath a cowl laid him low. Go, wayfarer, and mourn the fates of kings.'

100 *Orate . . . peccatoris.* 'Pray for the soul of X, a most miserable sinner.' The blank is to be filled with the name of the deceased.

per ora virum. 'Let no one honour me with tears, nor have buried me with weeping. Why? I fly alive through the mouths of men.' Ennius was famed as the earliest Roman epic poet.

101 *Greek inscriptions.* Johnson has translated these two epitaphs from the *Anthology* into Latin elegiacs as well as English prose. The Greek in the *GM* has some breathings (which have been regularized here), but no accents.

The poor . . . at rest. Matthew 11: 28, 'Come unto me, all ye that labour and are heavy laden, and I will give you rest'; Job 3: 17, 'There the wicked cease from troubling, and there the weary be at rest.'

103 *Debates in the Senate of Lilliput.* On 13 February 1741 the Whig and 'patriot' opposition to Walpole in Parliament made a concerted effort to get rid of him. Although the *GM* printed the debate in the House of Lords in its July and August numbers of that year, the debate in the Commons was not printed until its February, March, and April numbers in 1743, when Walpole was safely out of office. What is given here is most of the opening attack by Samuel Sandys, a perpetual Opposition gadfly, and the whole of Walpole's masterly final reply. In between, attacks as virulent as that of Sandys had been delivered by Pitt, Lyttelton, and Pulteney. Interestingly, the Tories such as Edward Harley, later 3rd Earl of Oxford, and William Shippen, either supported Walpole or abstained. This debate has not hitherto been printed in a collection of Johnson's works; for some reason, it was omitted from the volumes of his *Debates* published in 1787 and reprinted in 1825.

Sir. All speeches in the House of Commons are addressed to the Speaker.

annual advocates. The passage by Parliament of the annual Mutiny Act, formally authorizing the continuation of a regular army, gave orators like Sandys an opportunity for warning the country against the danger of the administration's using a 'standing army' to overthrow the constitution and establish a dictatorship—as, of course, Oliver Cromwell had done.

112 *sprugs.* pounds. Walpole refers to his house in Chelsea, given by the King.

little ornament. The insignia of the Order of the Garter, generally reserved for royalty and the higher ranks of the peerage, and seldom conferred on a commoner. 'Another place' is parliamentary jargon for the House of Lords.

Clinabs. Commons.

290 to 106. The report is followed without a break by a defence, presumably by Johnson, of the action of the Tories in refusing to support the attack on Walpole.

113 *Memoirs of the Duchess Dowager of Marlborough.* The memoirs of old Sarah Churchill, dowager Duchess of Marlborough (composed with the help of Nathaniel Hooke) were a *succès de scandale* when they were published in 1742, two years before her death at the age of eighty-four (her husband, the great Duke, had died twenty-two years earlier). Their

intimate and usually hostile vignettes of the royal family, when Sarah was the prime favourite of Princess (later Queen) Anne, and the detailed and harrowing account of her great quarrel with her, with its far-reaching political and military consequences, were, as Johnson writes, 'eagerly received', and Cave and Johnson lost no time capitalizing on the publicity: this piece appeared in the March 1742 number of the *GM*, only a month or so after the book appeared. Johnson's high praise (at the end of the eighth paragraph) of the Duchess's racy, informal style, and his conclusion that, although 'Distrust is a necessary qualification of a student in history', yet 'Truth, though not always obvious, is generally discoverable', are notable.

117 *An Account of the Harleian Library*. The origin of this and the two following pieces is described in the Introduction. The 'Account' appeared as 'Proposals' for the sale by subscription of the *Harleian Catalogue*, and as the preface to its first volume.

Thuanian . . . libraries. The seventeenth-century catalogues of the famous collections of the French historian Jacques de Thou, the Dutch scholar Daniel Heinsius (or perhaps his son Nicolaas), and the Roman Cardinal Francesco Barberini.

118 *Fabricius*. Johann Albert Fabricius, German librarian and scholar. Johnson owned his voluminous bibliographies of Greek and Latin literature.

119 *English critic*. Richard Bentley, who had recently died. Johnson, in his 'Preface' to Milton, censures him for supposing a faithless editor who wantonly corrupted the text of *Paradise Lost*. Had Bentley consulted the life of Milton by his nephew Edward Phillips, to which a library catalogue might have directed him, he would have found that the existence of such an editor was impossible.

120 *fugitive piece*. Translations of the French terms *feuille volante* and *pièce fugitive*. It seems likely that Johnson here was responsible for introducing into English the term 'fugitive' for an ephemeral literary production. The earliest citation in the *OED* for this sense is 1766.

121 *I*. That is, Thomas Osborne.

125 *Introduction to the Harleian Miscellany. charter*. Johnson adds a footnote: 'Which begins thus, "Know ye, that We, considering and manifestly perceiving that several seditious editions and heretical books or tracts— against the faith and sound catholic doctrine of holy mother, the Church", &c.'

127 *Photius*. A medieval Patriarch of Constantinople, whose *Bibliotheca* (which Johnson owned) is an immensely valuable collection of extracts from older Greek writers, many of whose writings exist nowhere else.

128 *The Life of Richard Savage*. This abridgement of the *Life of Savage* contains about half the complete text. Short summaries of omitted passages attempt to provide the reader with some continuity.

confession of adultery. In fact, Lady Macclesfield protested her innocence; Johnson took this false account from an anonymous *Life of Savage*, 1727. Scholars are not yet agreed whether Savage's account of his parentage and childhood has any truth in it.

138 *Page*. Sir Francis Page was notorious as a 'hanging judge'. See Pope, *Dunciad*, iv. 30, and the imitation of Horace, *Satires*, II. i. 182.

165 *The Vision of Theodore*. This apologue, with two others, 'The Choice of Hercules' and 'The Table of Cebes', forms the concluding section, 'On Human Life and Manners', of *The Preceptor*, 1748, a large manual of 'self-education' which Johnson may have helped to organize. Mount Tenerife in the Canary Islands, rising directly from the sea, made a strong impression on the earlier European imagination; it was sometimes thought to be the highest mountain in the world.

169 *dictates*. All texts read 'documents', which makes little sense. 'Dictates' is only a guess, but in Johnson's difficult hand, the word could be read as 'documents'. 'Dictates of Education' occurs in the next paragraph.

175 *The Rambler*. The 'titles' of the following essays have been supplied by the editor, as somewhat more succinct descriptions of their subjects than the traditional ones given in Tables of Contents of early collected editions, with which Johnson may have had nothing to do. The epigraphs from classical poets printed at the head of individual essays have been omitted. This was a convention that was beginning to be outmoded in Johnson's time; he supplies them for only a handful of *Idlers*. They would probably add little to the modern reader's appreciation of the essays.

178 [*The New Realistic Novel*] *Roman tyrant*. The motto of Caligula was said to be *oderint dum metuant*. See also the conclusion of *The Rambler*, no. 142, p. 228.

189 [*Stoicism*] *bless the name . . . away*. Job 1: 21.

203 [*Sorrow*] *variety of objects*. Here Johnson quotes from a Latin poem of Grotius, and Francis Lewis's translation: ''Tis long ere time can mitigate your grief / To Wisdom fly, she quickly brings relief.'

207 [*Biography*] *Hale*. Sir Matthew Hale, a much admired seventeenth-century jurist.

209 [*Marriage (3)*] *Misothea*. 'Hater of God, atheist.' Throughout Johnson's moral writings there runs his hatred of Stoic or general pagan fatalism, which negates divine Providence and human free-will.

211 *Hymenaeus*. From 'Hymen', the god of marriage.

215 [*Capital Punishment*] *More*. The view is expressed in several passages in *Utopia*.

[*Literary Imitation*] *elegies and sonnets*. See also the verses 'Whereso'er I turn my view', p. 32, and the criticisms of Gray and Collins, pp. 761, 765.

216 *Mantuan poet*. Virgil.

218 *Spenser*. Among the best known imitations of Spenser during the century are James Thomson's *Castle of Indolence* and William Shenstone's *Schoolmistress*.

play. Shakespeare, *Troilus and Cressida*, II. ii. 106.

226 [*A Rural Tyrant*] *Squire Bluster*. He is supposed to have been based on Sir Wolstan Dixie of Market Bosworth, Leicestershire, 'an abandoned brutal rascal' with whom Johnson spent a few miserable months in 1732.

228 *hated . . . feared*. See note to p. 178.

229 [*Journalists*] See also 'Of the Duty of a Journalist', p. 544.

231 *hackneyed . . . men*. Misquoted from I *Henry IV*, III. ii. 40.

232 [*Parental Tyranny*] *Politicians*. In the eighteenth century the word meant a theorist rather than a practitioner of politics (the latter was usually a 'statesman').

234 *law of social beings*. The 'Golden Rule': 'Therefore all things whatsoever ye would that men should do to you, do ye even so to them: for this is the law and the prophets' (Matthew 7: 12).

235 *officiousness*. See note on 'officious', p. 35, l. 7.

['*Rules*' *of Writing*] With this essay, compare the *Preface to Shakespeare*, especially pp. 423–4.

240 [*A Rooming-House Chronicle*] *cheapened*. bargained for.

243 [*Marriage (4)*] A sequel to *Rambler*, no. 113, p. 207.

245 *concordia discors*. See note to p. 678.

246 [*Congruent Diction*] *Boileau*. *Refléxion* ix.

247 *Macbeth*. The passage (I. v. 48–52) is actually spoken by Lady Macbeth.

248 *dun*. Some of Johnson's 'low' associations still remain with the word. Two of the three definitions in the *Concise Oxford English Dictionary* are '(of) dull greyish-brown colour, as of ass or mouse' and 'Dun horse; dark fishing-fly'. The meaning 'dark, dusky' is classified as '(poet.)'. Johnson's sole definition of 'knife' in his *Dictionary* is 'An instrument edged and pointed, wherewith meat is cut, and animals killed'. The first illustration he gives, no doubt to point up its inappropriateness, is this passage from *Macbeth*.

250 [*A Prostitute's Story (1)*] *wiped them soon*. From the conclusion of Milton's *Paradise Lost*. Adam and Eve have just been expelled from Eden.

252 *Misella*. 'unhappy one' (feminine).

271 [*The Role of the Scholar*] *Pope*. *Dunciad*, iii. 182.

277 ['*Projectors*'] *canal*. Extensive building of canals, as well as the invention of practical steam engines, took place in England in the eighteenth century.

[*A Female Army*] *military operations. The Idler* was published in the years when the Seven Years War was at its height, and sometimes (as in nos. 5, 81, and original no. 22) reflects Johnson's opposition to the war, hostility to military aggression, and general distrust of the military.

279   *Braddock*. Johnson refers to three notorious military fiascos earlier in the war: Braddock's disastrous defeat in the forests of what is now Pennsylvania; the loss of Minorca (with the subsequent court martial and execution of Admiral Byng, an innocent scapegoat), and an abortive amphibious attack on Rochefort on the French coast. His comments on the last two are found in vol. x of the Yale Edition of Johnson's *Works*.

280   [*Political Partisanship*] *Cartesian*. Descartes' teaching that animals are automata which have no feeling is also pilloried in *The Idler*, No. 22 (original numbering) (p. 282).

Berkeley. Berkeley taught no such thing, but Johnson was not the only one to misunderstand him.

281   *Whitehall*. The palace of Whitehall was destroyed, except for the Banqueting Hall, in 1698, by a fire supposedly started by a maid carelessly drying linen before a fireplace.

Tillotson. John Tillotson, Archbishop of Canterbury, was accused (and sometimes still is) of being so great a latitudinarian as not to be a Christian at all. What Johnson thought of the charge is apparent.

broad wheels. In an effort to improve the condition of roads, Parliament placed restrictions on the weight of vehicles and set minimum widths for their wheels (A. S. Turberville, ed., *Johnson's England*, 1933, i. 131).

Sneaker. Contemporary political slang for a turncoat, or someone without political principle. Johnson (probably) reports that the Tories who refused to vote for the motion for Walpole's removal in February 1741 were so called (see note to p. 103).

electoral dominions. Those of Hanover. A standard Opposition charge was that George I and II and their ministers subordinated the interests of Great Britain to those of their native Hanover.

282   *nonjurors*. Clergymen and others who refused to take the required oaths of allegiance to William and Mary after the Revolution of 1688, on the grounds that James II was still the legitimate sovereign. Jack Sneaker suspects them (unjustly, Johnson implies) of being Jacobite plotters.

Jews. Although there was on the whole little anti-semitism in Britain in the eighteenth century, the passage by Parliament in 1753 of an act facilitating the naturalization of Jews aroused a storm of opposition— 'the opponents of the ministry were casting about for a useful cry for the approaching general election' (William Hunt, *Parliamentary History of England*, ix. 428)—and Newcastle was forced to repeal it.

The Idler, No. 22. This powerful Swiftian indictment of human aggression was omitted from the first collected edition of *The Idler*, and the following *Idlers* were renumbered—an unfortunate practice still followed in current editions (in the *Idlers* reprinted below, the revised numbering is given first, and then the original numbering). In the same number of the *Universal Chronicle* in which it appeared, Johnson published an 'Observation'—the fourth and last of those he was permitted to publish there—on the progress of the war, this one denouncing a government-sponsored service of thanksgiving at St Paul's Cathedral for the British victory at Louisbourg, which he maintained was a government-sponsored fraud on the people. 'Surely our understandings are treated with too much contempt,' he wrote there, 'when these fallacies are practised upon us, when we are entertained with such despicable processions, as equivalent to the expense of millions, and the death of thousands.'

284 *appearance of animal life*. A satire of Descartes' theory about the nature of animals. See note to p. 280.

288 [*Debtors' Prisons* (2)] *trained bands*. The militia, in which Johnson is said to have been drawn to serve.

290 [*How to Become a Critic* (1)] *Minim*. From Latin *minimus*, smallest.

292 *Barbarossa*. By John Brown, 1754. *Cleone* by Robert Dodsley, 1758.

293 *echo to the sense*. See Johnson's 'Preface' to Pope, pp. 741–2.

296 *The Idler, No. 81*. This tremendous indictment of the European impact on the Americas was written shortly after the news reached London of James Wolfe's capture of Quebec—and so, ultimately, Canada—from the French on 13 September.

297 *dig metals*. The reference is to Spanish exploitation of the native Indians in the silver mines of Mexico and Peru.

another colour. Negro slaves, such as those brought to work the sugar plantations in the West Indies. 'Jamaica . . . a place of great wealth and dreadful wickedness, a den of tyrants and a dungeon of slaves' (Johnson, 'Introduction to the Political State of Great Britain,' Yale *Works*, x. 137). 'Upon one occasion, when in company with some very grave men at Oxford, his toast was "here's to the next insurrection of the negroes in the West Indies"' (Boswell, *Life*, ed. Hill-Powell, iii. 200). Johnson virtually adopted a young Negro former slave from Jamaica, Frank Barber, tried to give him an education, and made him the residuary legatee of his estate.

such contracts. See p. 501.

written law. The Bible, especially the Gospels.

298 *The Idler, No. 84*. This essay should be read as a sequel to *Ramblers* nos. 4 and 60 (pp. 175, 204).

299 *French prince*. The saying is attributed to a Prince de Condé.

300 [*Limitations of Human Achievement*] *real character*. Bishop John Wilkins's *Essay towards a Real Character and Philosophical Language*, 1668, proposed the invention of a perfectly unambiguous language.

What have ye done? Perhaps an allusion to the General Confession in the Book of Common Prayer: 'We have left undone those things which we ought to have done', derived from Matthew 23: 23 and Luke 11: 42. The use of the archaic 'ye' seems to indicate a biblical source. See also the beginning of the sixth paragraph.

302   *Augustus.* From Suetonius, *Divus Augustus,* 99.

306   ['*This Is the Last*'] *solemn week.* Holy Week, the week before Easter, which in 1760 fell on April 6.

307   *Preface to A Dictionary of the English Language. pioneer.* 'One whose business is to level the road, throw up works, or sink mines, in military operations'—*Dictionary.*

308   *de pluribus una.* 'Why rejoice at having rid yourself of only one out of so many faults?'—Horace, *Epistles,* II. ii. 212.

310   *Hooker. Ecclesiastical Polity,* bk. iv, chap. 14: 'True withal it is, that alteration, though it be from worse to better, hath in it inconveniences, and those weighty.'

     words . . . heaven. Samuel Madden's *Boulter's Monument* (which Johnson revised) has (line 377) 'Words are men's daughters, but God's sons are things'.

311   *Junius and Skinner.* The *Etymologicon Anglicanum* of Francis Junius (du Jon), a seventeenth-century philologian, was published in 1743, Stephen Skinner's *Etymologicon Linguae Anglicanae* in 1671.

312   *votaries . . . muses.* Students, such as Thomas Gray, of Norse and other early Germanic literature.

     alone. Here Johnson inserts a footnote in which he cites several other examples of Junius's 'etymological extravagance'.

316   *fall.* Early editions of the Preface read *full,* to which, as a verb, Johnson accords only one entry in the *Dictionary,* 'To cleanse cloth from its oil or grease.' The verb *fall* has sixty-nine entries (see pp. 331–4).

319   *favourite name.* As well, Johnson sometimes uses quotations from his own works.

     undefiled. 'Dan Chaucer, well of English undefyled'—Spenser, *The Faerie Queene,* IV. ii. 32.

324   *academies.* Johnson's work on the *Dictionary* was inspired by the pioneering Italian dictionary of the Accademia della Crusca, published in 1612, and the great French dictionary of the Académie française, in 1694.

     enchain . . . wind. See note to p. 18, l. 232.

326   *treatise. A Proposal for Correcting, Improving, and Ascertaining the English Tongue,* 1712.

329   *A Dictionary of the English Language.* It is impossible to reproduce photographically a page from the folio editions of the *Dictionary* so as to be legible on a page of the present size. The specimen here is made up from columns of the popular one-volume edition, 'verbatim from the author's last folio edition', published by H. G. Bohn, London, 1828, and

often reprinted, whose reduced print and space make it possible to give the reader a substantial continuous sampling of Johnson's lexicography. Generally, it follows the 1773 folio faithfully, though sometimes, to save space, it abbreviates references to Shakespeare's plays and other sources.

335 *The History of Rasselas. Father of waters*. The Nile, for thousands of years the source of life and fertility in Egypt. It becomes a recurring symbol in the story. When Rasselas and his companions escape from the Happy Valley (ch. xiv), they find themselves overlooking the beginning of the Nile; in their search of 'the choice of life' (chs. xix–xxi) they travel up the Nile as far as the first cataract, then the limit of navigation; their final reflections (ch. xlix) take place when the annual inundation of the Nile, which 'pours down the streams of plenty, and scatters over half the world the harvests of Egypt', confines them to their house. The source of the Blue Nile, which is referred to here, is Lake Tana in northern Ethiopia, and was described by Father Lobo and other early travellers; the source of the White Nile remained a mystery and the subject of much speculation from the time of Herodotus until its discovery in the mid-nineteenth century.

valley . . . Amhara. As Johnson knew from Lobo's *Voyage to Abyssinia* and other travel books, it is historically true that early emperors immured their younger offspring on a mountain in the province of Amhara; Johnson makes it a valley enclosed by mountains. The references by Milton ('where Abassin kings their issue guard, / Mount Amara') and Coleridge ('an Abyssinian maid . . . singing of Mount Abora') are well known.

336 *subterranean passages*. These mysterious secret places with their locked records of human memory have sometimes been interpreted as Johnson's pre-Freudian symbols of the hidden and ominous recesses of the human 'unconscious' that lie beneath the surface of ordinary life. See also the description of Lilinet's cavern in 'The Fountains' (p. 561).

337 *Rasselas*. 'Ras' is a title—'prince' or 'chief'. Johnson seems to have taken the word from the abbreviated form of the name of a nobleman mentioned by Lobo and other historians of Abyssinia, 'Ras Sela Christos'. According to Ludolf (see note to p. 43), the last two words mean 'image of Christ'.

344 *The labour . . . ground*. It is noteworthy that Rasselas has accurately formulated the fundamental problem of aerodynamics that made heavier-than-air flight impracticable until the invention of the internal combustion engine provided a source of adequate power, and that the artist (=artisan) states the principle which made travel in outer space possible in the 1950s. In the last year of his life Johnson displayed much interest in the pioneering balloon flights of the time.

346 *Imlac*. Imlach or Imlah was the father of the prophet Micaiah (1 Kings 22 and 2 Chronicles 18), who declared, 'As the Lord liveth, what the Lord shall speak unto me that will I speak.' The name, or a variant of it, occurs in Lobo and elsewhere as that of an emperor of Ethiopia.

352   *streaks of the tulip.* It needs to be kept in mind (1) that this much-quoted passage emanates from Imlac, not from Johnson (and that Rasselas goes on to express scepticism about Imlac's ideal of the poet); (2) that 'general' here does not mean 'abstract', a word not in Johnson's critical vocabulary, but, as the continuation makes clear ('recall the original to every mind'), 'accessible from the experience of many'. The best known poetic flowers, such as Blake's sick rose and Wordsworth's daffodils, are very general and do not have their streaks numbered.

353   *legislator of mankind.* An interesting anticipation of Shelley's 'poets are the unacknowledged legislators of the world'. Sir Philip Sidney had written to much the same effect in his *Defence of Poetry*.

367   *daughter ... restored.* The story of the man who preaches Stoic detachment and then breaks down when a loved one dies is an old one. It can be found in Fielding's *Joseph Andrews*, 1742, bk. iv, ch. 8, and in Voltaire's *conte*, *Les Deux Consolés*, 1756.

372   *to live according to nature.* One of the oldest and most fundamental doctrines of Stoicism—in Greek, *to homologoumenos tei physei zen*. Diogenes Laertius, *The Lives of the Philosophers*, attributes it to Zeno of Citium, the founder of the school.

      equability of temper. Compare Johnson's rejection of such Stoic imperturbability in 'The Vanity of Human Wishes', ll. 344-9 (p. 20).

376   *In families ... commonly discord.* On this, see *The Rambler*, no. 148 (p. 232).

394   *monastery of St Anthony.* St Anthony of Egypt (3rd century) was the reputed founder of the anchoritic life.

399   *diversions of the women ... childish play.* On the attitude towards women attributed to the Mahometans, see the scene from *Irene* given above (pp. 21-3).

401   *The History of a Man of Learning.* Kathleen M. Grange, 'Dr Samuel Johnson's Account of a Schizophrenic Illness in *Rasselas*', *Medical History*, vi (April 1962) demonstrates the modernity of Johnson's approach to mental illness in the story of the astronomer.

405   *The Dangerous Prevalence of Imagination.* The title of this chapter does not mean that Johnson disapproves of imagination: it is, after all, Rasselas's imagination that leads him, rightly, to escape from the stultification of the Happy Valley. The title refers to the danger when fantasy, as in the astronomer, prevails over contact with reality.

415   *Imlac Discourses on the Nature of the Soul.* On the intellectual background of this chapter, see Robert G. Walker, *Eighteenth-Century Arguments for Immortality and Johnson's Rasselas* (University of Victoria [British Columbia] English Literary Studies, 1977).

418   *sublunary.* In the Ptolemaic system of astronomy, things in the circle of the moon and higher are unchanging; below it—that is, on the earth—things are transitory.

return to Abyssinia. Not, it should be noted, to the Happy Valley, where the one thing guaranteed is unhappiness ('I know not one of all your attendants who does not lament the hour when he entered this retreat' (ch. xii)). They will return to their native country and there presumably embark on their careers in education and government, with the healthy realization that their ideals of perfection can never be fully attained, but continuing to strive towards them. On this, as on other pieces of moral teaching by Johnson, the conclusion of *The Adventurer*, no. 85 (p. 273) is important.

419 *Preface to the Plays of William Shakespeare*. It may be useful to consider the Preface as falling into four sections: (1) (pp. 419–26) Shakespeare's virtues (the longevity of his popularity, the realism of his characterization, a defence of his mingling the *genres* of tragedy and comedy, the naturalness and modernity of his 'familiar dialogue'); (2) (pp. 427–9) Shakespeare's 'faults', which are 'sufficient to obscure and overwhelm any other merit' (like a skilled advocate, Johnson concedes to his opponents whatever may be plausibly conceded, in order to convince the impartial reader of the rightness, on balance, of his thesis of Shakespeare's greatness); (3) (pp. 429–41) a defence of Shakespeare (*a*) specifically, from the charge of not observing the unities of time and place, which Johnson argues are worthless; (*b*) a general defence, based on the differences of culture and taste between Shakespeare's time and the present; the question of Shakespeare's learning; (4) (pp. 441–56) a history of the editing of Shakespeare before Johnson, and a statement of Johnson's own editorial principles. (Some of the views in the Preface Johnson had earlier expressed in his dedication of Charlotte Lennox's *Shakespear Illustrated*, 1753, and his proposals for his own edition, 1756.)

421 *mirror*. A conscious echo of *Hamlet*, III. ii, 'The purpose of playing, whose end, both at the first and now, was and is to hold, as 'twere, the mirror up to nature.' See also *The Rambler*, no. 156, p. 235.

422 *approximates the remote*. Brings the remote near. See *The Rambler*, no. 60, where the same phrase occurs (p. 204) and *The Rambler*, no. 4.

423 *Dennis and Rhymer*. John Dennis's *Essay on the Genius and Writings of Shakespear*, 1712, and Thomas Rymer, *A Short View of Tragedy*, 1692. Voltaire's criticisms of Shakespeare are found in many parts of his works, beginning with his *Lettres Philosophiques*, 1734, based on his experiences in England in the 1720s.

petty minds. Voltaire was understandably annoyed by this gibe, which he quoted ('petits esprits') in a counter-attack on Johnson in his *Dictionnaire Philosophique*.

424 *contrary to the rules of criticism*. The objectors to the mingling of tragedy and comedy included Horace and Sir Philip Sidney.

instruct by pleasing. A notable variation from Horace's *aut prodesse aut delectare* (*Art of Poetry*: 'The aim of the poet is either to be useful or to please').

427 *a disapprobation of the wicked.* If this condemnation implies the breach of 'poetic justice' he deplores in the treatment of Cordelia (p. 465), Johnson fifteen years later performed a spectacular *volte face* in his critique of Addison (p. 671).

429 *quibble.* pun, play on words.

430 *Corneille.* His *Discourse on the Three Unities*, 1660.

433 *Non usque ... a Caesare tolli.* Lucan, *Pharsalia*, iii. 138–40. Roughly, 'Things are not yet so confused that, if the laws were preserved by the voice of Metellus [a minor politician], they would not prefer to be suppressed by Caesar.'

     reverential silence. This extravagant declaration, with its clichés from the classics, is probably ironic: Johnson has certainly shown no disposition to sink down in reverential silence before Voltaire and Corneille.

439 *dewdrops from a lion's mane. Troilus and Cressida*, II. iii. 224.

441 *vale of years. Othello*, III. iii. 169–70.

445 *last editor.* William Warburton, bishop of Gloucester. His edition of Shakespeare was published in 1747.

447 *authors.* Respectively, Thomas Edwards and Benjamin Heath.

448 *small things ... proud.* 2 *Henry VI*, IV. i. 106.

454 *Bishop of Aleria.* Joannes Andreas, a noted classical scholar.

     Illudunt ... incidimus. 'Our conjectures make sport of us, and we are ashamed of them when we later find better manuscripts.'

     Ut olim ... laboratur. 'It used to be the errors, now it is the corrections that cause trouble.'

456 *Dryden.* The passage is from the *Essay of Dramatic Poesy.*

     Quantum ... cupressi. Virgil, *Eclogues*, i. 25: 'as cypresses do among the slow viburnums.'

457 *Specimen of Annotation.* As with the *Dictionary*, it is important to see just what Johnson was doing in his edition of Shakespeare. These facsimile pages are reproduced from the Huntington Library's (formerly the Bridgewater Library's) copy of vol. i of the first edition, 1765. Two of the leaves reproduced were substituted before publication for cancelled ones in which the criticism of Warburton was even harsher.

462 *Concluding Notes.* To the end of each play Johnson appends a general note on the play, sometimes short, sometimes long, recording his own response to it. This is a brief sampling.

467 *Sermon 5.* This is the fifth in the collection of twenty-four *Sermons on Different Subjects Left for Publication by John Taylor, LL.D.*, 1788. Taylor, Johnson's old schoolfellow, was rector of Ashbourne and prebendary of Westminster, as well as holding other well-paid benefices. Except for one whole sermon and part of another, it is generally agreed

that they were written by Johnson. They cannot be dated. This, on the nature and origin of evil, should be read in connection with the review of Soame Jenyns (p. 522). It contains (pp. 472–4) what might be called the only 'Utopia' described by Johnson.

472   *perfect, even as . . . is perfect.* Matthew 5: 48.

476   *The Life of Dr Francis Cheynel.* Published in *The Student, or Oxford and Cambridge Miscellany*, edited by Johnson's friend Christopher Smart, 1751. Johnson has several footnotes referring to Anthony Wood's *Athenae Oxonienses*, his chief source.

      Hammond or Chillingworth. Henry Hammond and William Chillingworth were two of the most eminent Anglican theologians of the seventeenth century. Johnson often quotes Hammond in the *Dictionary*.

      grace. Formal conferring of the degree.

      centum plagas . . . concoquere. 'To endure a hundred blows with Spartan nobility.'

478   *Calamy.* Edmund Calamy, biographer of the dissenting ministers ejected by the Act of Uniformity, 1662.

      greatness. high and powerful position.

479   *brutality.* not 'cruelty' but 'boorishness'.

      Chichester. The text mistakenly reads 'Colchester'.

488   *Review of Warton, An Essay on . . . Pope.* From the *Literary Magazine*, no. i, 15 April–15 May, 1756. Warton, later headmaster of Winchester College, was a friend of Johnson's, and is treated here perhaps more leniently than he might otherwise have been, since it was he who first raised the question, 'Whether Pope was a poet?' (p. 752). It is well to recall that Pope had been dead only twelve years when this was written.

      anecdotes. In the original sense of 'something yet unpublished' (*Dictionary*).

489   *Somerville's.* William Somerville, *The Chase*, 1735.

      effort. The *Literary Magazine* text reads 'effect'. The two words are easily confused in Johnson's hand. Warton has 'effort'.

      Lycidas. It is worth noting that Johnson here calls Warton's description of *Lycidas* as a 'most exquisite piece' 'a just observation' (see p. 699).

490   *Colin's Complaint.* By Nicholas Rowe.

      grossest fault. Johnson's complaint has some justification. In the aria Handel sets the word 'cries' to a long, elaborate roulade. This, however, was a convention in baroque vocal music: the floridity of the setting was supposed to represent 'crying', even though, as Johnson recognized, this was hardly the sense of the word here. It is amusing to find Johnson opposing what might be called a Wagnerian to a Handelian approach to music drama: perhaps he was not so unmusical as is generally thought.

Flatman. Thomas Flatman, 1637–88.

491   *Baillet*. Adrien Baillet, *Des Enfans devenus célèbres par leurs études et par leurs écrits*, 1688.

idea. As generally in Johnson's criticism, a mental picture, a visual image. The word is derived from the Greek verb meaning 'to see', cognate with Latin *video*.

first. The text reads 'past'.

492   *Robert of Gloucester's verse*. The metrical *Chronicle* of the thirteenth-century Robert of Gloucester is written in 'fourteeners'. When the review was first reprinted in 1789, the compositor ludicrously misread 'verse' as 'wife', and subsequent reprints have followed him.

Tassoni . . . Garth. The 'mock-epics' referred to are Alessandro Tassoni's *La Secchia Rapita*, Boileau's *Le Lutrin*, and Samuel Garth's *The Dispensary*. The text mistakenly gives 'Fassoni', followed by most reprints.

493   *inform us*. The second and last volume of Warton's *Essay* was not published until 1782.

495   *Review of Blackwell, Memoirs of . . . Augustus*. From the *Literary Magazine*, no. i, 15 April–15 May, 1756, and no. v, 15 August–15 September, 1756.

496   *vile . . . Sabinum*. Horace (*Odes*, i. 20) humbly invites his wealthy patron Maecenas to visit him and drink some of his poor home-made Sabine wine.

497   *We know not . . . continuation*. The second instalment of the review begins here.

501   *Observations on the Present State of Affairs*. This article, published in the *Literary Magazine*, no. iv, 15 July–15 August, 1756, is a continuation of Johnson's 'Introduction to the Political State of Great Britain', the opening piece in the first number of the magazine. Like it, its aim is to condemn the purposes for which the French and the British have begun their deadly war for empire. On this, see *The Idler*, no. 81 (p. 296).

505   *New Scotland*. Nova Scotia, the British settlement of which took place after the end of the War of the Austrian Succession in 1748.

508   *(To be continued)*. No continuation was published. In the next number of the *Literary Magazine* the political commentary was pro-Pitt and pro-war.

509   *Review of* [*Hanway*], *A Journal . . .* Jonas Hanway was a good-hearted merchant and philanthropist, a benefactor of (among other institutions) the recently established Foundling Hospital for abandoned children. He wrote a silly book, however, and Johnson had fun taking it to pieces. This, the second of three pieces on the subject by Johnson, appeared in the *Literary Magazine*, no. xiii, 15 April–15 May, 1757.

510   *consequences of such a trade*. Some social historians have maintained that

the reduction in the price of tea in the mid-eighteenth century caused it to become the chief drink of the English, displacing gin, and accounting for the notable drop in the death rate in the 1750s.

512   *cicuta.* hemlock.

513   *Paulli.* Simon Paulli, a German/Danish botanist, published *Commentarius de abusi tabaci et herbae theae* [Commentary on the abuse of tobacco and tea] in 1666.

515   *crimes.* This paragraph led to an application by the governors of the Foundling Hospital to the attorney-general for a prosecution of the anonymous writer. The proprietors of the *Literary Magazine* refused to disclose his name, and Johnson replied defiantly the next month (p. 517). See Ruth K. McClure, 'Johnson's Criticism of the Foundling Hospital and Its Consequences,' *Review of English Studies*, NS xxviii (1976), 17–26.

517   *Reply to ... the Gazetteer.* This retort to the threat of prosecution appeared in the *Literary Magazine*, no. xiv, 15 May–15 June, 1757. Hanway had printed a denunciation of Johnson's review in the *Daily Gazetteer*; it does not, however, seem to have survived. Johnson's reply is a masterpiece of sarcasm.

   Le Sage's. The *Literary Magazine* and some early reprints read 'the sage'. This conjectural emendation by an early editor seems plausible. The reference is to a famous incident in the novel where Gil Blas is asked by his employer to criticize a piece of his writing, and, when he tries to do so honestly, receives a torrent of abuse and is discharged.

518   *him who burst the box.* Johnson surely knew that Pandora, who opened the famous box, was female. It would not be hard for a compositor to misread Johnson's 'her' as 'him'.

519   *East India company.* Johnson was later involved in some obscure transaction connected with a Parliamentary investigation of the Company. The reasons for his distrust of it need further research.

522   *Review of [Jenyns], A Free Inquiry ...* From the *Literary Magazine*, nos. xiii–xv, April–July 1757. Soame Jenyns was a wealthy dilettante poet, essayist, and politician. His book was an amateurish attempt to solve the age-old problem of Christians and other monotheists: 'We assume a God who is both omnipotent and benevolent. How then does there come to be evil in the world? If God is powerless to prevent it, then he is not omnipotent; if he can prevent it but will not, it is hard to believe that he is benevolent.' Many of Jenyns's arguments are found in Archbishop William King's *De Origine Mali*, 1702, and Pope's *Essay on Man*. For Johnson's opinion of Pope's *Essay*, see pp. 748–9.

   Manichean system. The belief that the universe is controlled by two equally powerful Gods, one good, one evil, at strife with each other.

523   *effect.* The text reads 'effort'. Only a practised reader of Johnson's hand could distinguish the two words in it.

system of subordination. A. O. Lovejoy, in his classic *The Great Chain of Being*, 1936, traces the concept back to Plato. It postulates that all creation forms a hierarchical continuum, from God (infinity) at the top, descending through the nine grades of angels, to man, and then through animal creation to the lowest forms of life, and finally to non-existence (zero). Johnson disproves this by use of the mathematical concept of infinity. Arabian philosophers such as Avicenna had a similar theory, and the idea of 'plenitude' in Milton's *Paradise Lost* is also relevant.

525 *Cheyne*. George Cheyne (1671–1743), physician and philosopher.

526 *Qui pauca considerat, facile pronunciat*. 'He who considers few things easily gives a decision.' Johnson repeats the phrase in the Chambers/Johnson Vinerian law lectures, part I, lecture 6. The source has not been traced.

527 *species of poverty*. Among the many definitions of 'poor' in his *Dictionary*, Johnson includes 'the *poor* (collectively). Those who are in the lowest rank of the community; those who cannot subsist but by the charity of others; but it is sometimes used with laxity for any not rich'.

poverty and riches. That is, hope inseparably connected with poverty, and fear with riches.

tearing his flesh. This gruesome imagery, *pained, mutilation, pincers*, alludes to a recent event much in the public eye at the time, the dreadful torture and execution (with red-hot pincers tearing his flesh and molten lead poured into the wounds) of Robert-François Damiens for inflicting a superficial wound on Louis XV of France.

528 *dangerous thing*. Pope, *Essay on Criticism*, l. 215.

532 *latter end . . . the beginning*. Shakespeare, *The Tempest*, II. i. 158. Antonio is mocking Gonzalo's utopia.

angels fear to tread. Pope, *Essay on Criticism*, l. 682.

534 *decisions*. The *Literary Magazine* text reads 'derisions'.

omnipotence. See note to p. 542.

535 *Prague*. In the battle of Prague, April 1757, between the Prussian and Austrian armies, more than 20,000 were killed on both sides.

philosopher . . . air pump. 'Philosopher' = 'scientist' (here amateur). Cruel experiments with air pumps and animals were apparently a popular amusement at the time.

539 *artificially*. artistically, ingeniously.

Si sic omnia dixisset! 'Would that he had spoken everything thus!'

540 *wand'ring mazes lost*. Milton, *Paradise Lost*, ii. 561.

542 *Chrysippus's untractableness of matter*. Chrysippus (3rd century BC) was the third leader of the Stoic school of philosophy. The Stoics argued that the God who made the world was unable to overcome the intractable

nature of the matter from which he created it—a 'dogmatical limitation of omnipotence' (p. 534)—and that this accounted for the existence of imperfection and evil in the world. This doctrine, as Johnson suggests, is a form of dualism or Manicheanism and a contradiction of the monotheism of Christianity and other religions. Johnson quotes the phrase 'untractableness of matter' from Jenyns, although Jenyns does not attribute it to Chrysippus. Both Jenyns and Johnson here are drawing on Justus Lipsius's *Physiologia Stoicorum*, 1604.

543 *the hand ... a temple.* Not traced, although the *Literary Magazine* has a footnote, *New Practice of Physick*. A book with the subtitle *New Practice of Physic*, by Thomas Marryat, is said by the *DNB* to have been published in Latin in 1758; its first edition in English, 1764, does not contain Johnson's quotation, and both dates are too late for this 1757 essay. *A New Practice of Piety*—in case the compositor misread Johnson's hand—was published in 1704 (an expansion of Benjamin Bridgwater's *Religio Bibliopolae*, 1691), but the quotation is not found in it.

544 *Of the Duty of a Journalist.* One of several opening manifestoes Johnson was commissioned to write for new periodicals—this for *Payne's Universal Chronicle*, the weekly in which Johnson's *The Idler* and 'Observations' on the Seven Years War were published. See also *The Rambler*, no. 145 (p. 229).

547 *Introduction to Proceedings ... French Prisoners of War.* Johnson was commissioned (through the efforts of Thomas Hollis) to provide this preface to the pamphlet in which a voluntary group of citizens accounted for the money they had collected to provide clothing for the many French prisoners of war interned in England towards the end of the Seven Years War. Published in August 1760.

their works praise them. 'All thy works shall praise thee, O Lord'—Psalm 144: 10.

548 *The rage of war ... horror.* Not to be read as an affirmation by Johnson that there will always be wars: rather that, *while* there are wars, however their effects are mitigated, they will always produce calamity and horror.

do good to them that hate us. Luke 6: 27.

549 *The Bravery of the English Common Soldiers.* First known to have been published in the *British Magazine*, January 1760. The *British Magazine* was edited by Tobias Smollett; conceivably Johnson contributed this piece as a token of gratitude for Smollett's recent help in procuring a discharge from the Royal Navy for Johnson's young black protégé Frank Barber. The 'wonderful year' 1759, as Garrick called it, had seen important British military and naval victories in the Seven Years War.

Cartesians. Johnson (like Swift) frequently pillories Descartes' doctrine that animals are senseless automata, and especially (as in *The Idler*, no. 17) the practice of vivisection that it seems to authorize. See notes to pp. 280, 284.

Russian Empress and Prussian Monarch. The Czarina Elizabeth and Frederick II ('the Great').

550 *freedom of our tenures.* Feudal tenure of land in England was abolished in 1660.

French Count. Comte Turpin de Cressé, *Essai sur l'Art de la Guerre,* 1754.

551 *Review of [Tytler], An Enquiry into . . . Mary, Queen of Scots.* From the *GM,* October 1760. Tytler's book was an important contribution to the controversy over the 'casket letters' that continued for the next century and a half. Modern scholars, such as Mary's most recent biographer, Lady Antonia Fraser, tend to agree with Tytler and Johnson in thinking them spurious. It seems odd to find Hume, supposedly friendly to the Stuarts, on the other side. In a subsequent edition of his *History of England* (vol. v, note N), he denounced Tytler as a 'Scotch Jacobite' who 'must be considered as . . . beyond the reach of argument or reason'.

552 *Goodall.* Walter Goodall's *Examination of the Letters said to be written by Mary, Queen of Scots, to James, Earl of Bothwell,* 1754, was the first work to throw doubt on the authenticity of the letters. They were defended by William Robertson in 'A Critical Dissertation concerning the Murder of King Henry [Darnley] and the Genuineness of the Queen's Letters' appended to his *History of Scotland,* and in Hume's *History of England.*

558 *The Fountains.* From Anna Williams, *Miscellanies in Prose and Verse,* 1766.

Boethius. From his *De Consolatione Philosophiae* ('Of the Consolation of Philosophy'). bk. iii, Metre 12. Translated by Johnson as 'Happy he whose eyes have viewed / The transparent fount of good.'

570 *Robert Chambers's Vinerian Lectures . . .* From British Library King's MS 87, ff. 2–35. Some excerpts have been published in E. L. McAdam, Jr., *Dr Johnson and the English Law,* 1951. This lecture was probably composed and delivered in 1767.

571 *Pompey.* According to Cicero, *Letters to Atticus,* ii. 19. 3, an actor shouted this to Pompey, with great applause from the audience. The context seems to indicate that Johnson read it as 'Through our wretchedness you are great', although a modern translation gives the first phrase as 'To our misfortune'. The whole sentence (or paragraph) in which it is quoted here is one of Johnson's most astonishing examples of baroque prose.

Lucullus . . . Apicius. Wealthy Romans, famous for their extravagant spending. Apicius was especially noted for his gourmet cuisine.

572 *Jura neget sibi nata.* Horace (*Art of Poetry,* l. 122) counsels a dramatist how to represent Achilles: 'He should deny that any laws applied to him.'

573 *mutum et turpe pecus.* 'A dumb, vile herd': Horace, *Satires,* i. iii. 100.

574 *Lex Talionis*. Law of retaliation: 'an eye for an eye, a tooth for a tooth'.

576 *late writer*. Henry Home, Lord Kames, in Tract 1, 'Criminal Law', of his *Historical Laws—Tracts* (Edinburgh, 1758; 2nd edn, London, 1762).

quasi utile. 'Let revenge be as something not pleasant but something useful.'

577 *Grotius*. The references are to Grotius, *Of the Law of War and Peace*, and Samuel von Pufendorf, *Of the Law of Nature and Nations* and *Of the Duty of Men and Citizens*.

580 *The Patriot. Milton*. From the second sonnet 'On the Detraction Which Followed on My Writing Certain Treatises'.

This happy day has now arrived. The general election of 1774, for which Johnson wrote this pamphlet. The previous general election had been in 1768, and under the Septennial Act (see note to p. 14, l. 97) the next need not have been held until 1775.

Court. That is, the current administration.

581 *many made for one*. Pope, *Essay on Man*, iii. 242.

remonstrance. William Beckford, Lord Mayor of London, so 'insulted' George III in 1770.

582 *last peace*. The Peace of Paris, 1763, which ended the Seven Years War. It was concluded by the Prime Minister, the Earl of Bute, whom the opposition slanderously accused of being the lover of young George III's mother, Augusta, Princess of Wales.

Popery ... Quebec. By the Quebec Act, 1774, French civil law was continued in Quebec, and certain privileges of the Roman Catholic clergy were retained. Although it is now generally regarded by historians as a remarkably liberal and tolerant measure for its time, it caused a furore in the Thirteen Colonies, where it was made one of the charges against the British government in the Declaration of Independence.

dragoons ... galleys. The persecution of Protestants in Louis XIV's France after the revocation of the Edict of Nantes in 1685.

toleration. By the Act of Toleration, 1689, Protestant dissenters (but not Roman Catholics) in England were granted the right to worship in their own way. Some of the opponents of the Quebec Act were dissenters.

583 *companions*. 'A man is known by the company he keeps.'

boot. Opposition demonstrations sometimes included the ceremonial burning of a boot (Lord Bute) and a petticoat (the Princess of Wales).

Mile-end ... Lumber-troop. The Assembly Rooms at Mile End, near London, were a favourite meeting place for supporters of Wilkes; the Lumber Troop was one of their clubs.

584 *barren spot*. The Falkland Islands. See Introduction, p. xxiii.

585 *Bostonians*. Earlier in 1774, Parliament had passed an act closing the port of Boston, in retribution for the 'Boston Tea Party'.

586 *resignation of protections.* A statute of 1770 limited the immunity from civil prosecution hitherto enjoyed by members of Parliament.

trial of elections. Grenville's Elections Act, 1770, removed jurisdiction over disputed elections from the partisanship of the whole House of Commons to a small, impartial select committee.

587 *bad eminence.* Milton, *Paradise Lost*, ii. 5–6.

588 *Preface to Maurice, Poems . . . Sophocles.* Published in 1779.

589 *Phœbi reus.* The accused of Phoebus. Johnson's Christian rejection of pagan fatalism results in a notable modification of Aristotle's theory of tragedy.

Franklin. Thomas Francklin's translation of Sophocles appeared in 1759.

591 *Dedication of Burney, An Account . . . in Commemoration of Handel.* The spectacular series of concerts, given in May and June 1784, are said to have been the first 'festival' in honour of a single composer. Burney was anxious to keep Johnson's authorship of the dedication (and the dedication, to Queen Charlotte, of his *History of Music*) a secret, and it was not disclosed until 1934. For another reference to Handel by Johnson, see p. 490. The use of capitals in the original text has been preserved here, as suitable to a ceremonial occasion. George III, like his two predecessors, was a passionate devotee of Handel's music—indeed, a performer of it on the organ at Windsor Castle.

naval investigation. The reference is to George III's patronage of Cook's voyages of exploration in the Pacific.

592 *knowledge.* George III's activities as a patron of art, science, and literature are recounted in John Brooke's biography of him, 1972. In 1768, Johnson, presumably by request, sent a long letter of advice to the King's librarian on developing his great book collection, which on his death passed to the British Museum.

593 *A Journey to the Western Islands of Scotland.* This abridgement contains about one-third of the text of the original. As in the *Life of Savage*, short summaries of omitted sections attempt to preserve the continuity of the narrative.

596 *Beatoun.* David Beaton, Cardinal Archbishop of St Andrews. Johnson omits to mention that his assassination was in revenge for his condemnation for heresy of George Wishart, an early Reformer, who was burnt at the stake.

599 *Davies.* Sir John Davies, *Discovery of the True Causes why Ireland was not Entirely Subdued . . .* , 1612.

604 *unregarded dilapidation.* Johnson originally had a denunciation here of those who were 'longing to melt the lead of an English cathedral'—that of his native Lichfield—and suggested (facetiously, one hopes) that they should be made to swallow it. But he thought better of it, and cancelled the passage.

606 *kail*. cabbage.

Scotorum. An anthology of Latin verse by Scots, edited by Arthur Johnston, 1637. Thomas May wrote a Latin verse continuation of Lucan's *Pharsalia*.

607 *the Peak*. A wild, rocky region in Derbyshire. Ashbourne, the home of Johnson's friend John Taylor, often visited by Johnson, is near by.

609 *Wade*. George Wade, later field marshal, built roads in the Highlands in the 1720s when he commanded the British troops there.

614 *Proctors*. The two officers of Oxford University chiefly responsible for discipline. The River Trent roughly divides England into north and south.

620 *law*. As part of the aftermath of the Jacobite uprising of 1745, a law was passed forbidding the wearing of traditional Highland dress.

Hardwicke. Philip Yorke, 1st Earl of Hardwicke, Lord Chancellor of England, presided at the treason trials of Scottish lords involved in the '45.

622 *Apicius*. See note to p. 571.

empyreumatic. burnt.

626 *proceleusmatic*. giving time. The *keleustes* was the man who called out the time for the rowers of a Greek galley.

627 *Phaeacia*. Where Ulysses was entertained by King Alcinous and his daughter Nausicaa before his return to Ithaca.

628 *degree*. of north latitude.

632 *Crowley*. Sir Ambrose Crowley, an important early manufacturer of iron. He was distantly related to Johnson by marriage.

636 *father of Ossian*. James Macpherson. See p. 789.

637 *Martin*. Martin Martin, *Description of the Western Islands of Scotland*, 1703.

638 *Patagons*. Early explorers reported that Patagonia was populated by men of gigantic size.

640 *Baker*. Henry Baker developed a method of teaching the deaf, but did not publish it.

643 *Addison. Corbet*. A schoolfellow of Johnson's at Lichfield Grammar School.

Chartreux. Better known as the Charterhouse school in London, originally the site of a Carthusian monastery.

644 *execution*. Of a court judgment empowering Steele's possessions to be seized in payment of the debt.

Musae Anglicanae. A collection of Latin verse by various English authors.

Tickell. Thomas Tickell, minor poet, friend, editor, and biographer of Addison; subject of one of Johnson's Prefaces.

645 *Pygmies and Cranes.* Which Johnson translated in English heroic couplets when he was about seventeen.

Montague. Charles Montagu, later 1st Earl of Halifax, a leading Whig politician, and co-author, with Matthew Prior, of *The Country Mouse and the City Mouse,* a burlesque of Dryden's *The Hind and the Panther.*

Somers. Lord Chancellor, another prominent Whig leader. Swift dedicated *A Tale of a Tub* to him.

646 *Smith.* Edmund ('Rag') Smith, minor poet and friend of Addison, another subject of a 'Preface' by Johnson.

647 *Godolphin.* Lord Treasurer; in effect Prime Minister.

simile of the Angel. This celebrated passage in the poem ('The Campaign'), describing Marlborough's direction of the Battle of Blenheim, reads

> So when an angel by divine command
> With rising tempests shakes a guilty land,
> Such as of late o'er pale Britannia passed,
> Calm and serene he drives the furious blast,
> And, pleased th' Almighty's orders to perform,
> Rides in the whirlwind and directs the storm.

Duchess of Marlborough. See p. 113.

649 *Queen.* Anne.

Casa. Giovanni della Casa's *Il Galateo* was published in 1558. Castiglione's *Il Cortegiano* is well known. Both circulated widely in English translation.

650 *Budgell.* Eustace Budgell, Addison's cousin, a miscellaneous writer.

651 *yo para el.* 'Don Quixote was born for me alone, and I for him.'

652 *tax.* The stamp tax, effective from 1 August 1712, was one halfpenny for each copy of the journal.

Hughes. John Hughes, minor poet, subject of still another of Johnson's Prefaces.

653 *Dennis.* John Dennis, the most prominent and controversial literary critic of the time.

Heavily in clouds . . . day. Quoted from *Cato.*

Distrest Mother. By Steele.

dictator. The Duke of Marlborough, who sought the appointment of Commander-in-Chief for life.

Mrs Porter. An actress who played in *Cato.*

654 *Jeffreys.* George Jeffreys, minor writer.

Sewel. George Sewell, physician and miscellaneous writer.

655 *policy.* politics.

Lizards. A fictional family; the writer of the essays is guardian to one of their sons.

657 *dispatch the message.* This pleasant story is denied by modern scholars.

Jacobaei . . . regis. 'A hundred jacobuses [a coin], the entrails of the purse of an exiled king': from *Pro Populo Anglicano Defensio.*

658 *Tonson.* Jacob Tonson, the leading publisher of the time.

659 *nearer way.* That is, by political string-pulling.

Tillotson. See note to p. 281. The prose style of his sermons was much admired.

of use. In compiling his *Dictionary.*

at variance. Homer, *Iliad* (tr. Pope), i. 9–10: 'Declare, O Muse! in what ill-fated hour / Sprung the fierce strife, from what offended pow'r.' A humorous reference to the quarrel between Achilles and Agamemnon which set off the action of the *Iliad.*

660 *seven.* See note on 'weekly libels', p. 14, l. 97.

little Dicky. Macaulay maintained that Addison referred, not to Steele, but to an actor who had this nickname.

Bellum plusquam civile. 'More than a civil war.'

Biographia Britannica. A pioneering dictionary of national biography: 1st edn., 1747–77; 2nd edn., by Andrew Kippis, 1778–93.

661 *extinguished.* The two quotations, or rather paraphrases, are from, respectively, Horace, *Odes,* ii. 1 and Cicero, *De Oratore.*

Warwick. The 8th Earl of Warwick, Addison's stepson, then twenty-two years old.

664 *Brett.* He married Savage's putative mother, Lady Macclesfield, after her divorce (see p. 129)

tie-wig. That is, dressed as a layman. Clergymen wore full-bottomed wigs.

665 *Roman fame.* Pope, *Imitations of Horace,* Epistle ii. 1. 26.

righteousness. Daniel 12: 3.

666 *great writer.* William Warburton, Bishop of Gloucester. 'Great', as usual in Johnson, means not 'excellent' but 'of high station'.

667 *Gazette.* The *London Gazette* is still the official government publication that carries news of appointments, dispatches from theatres of military activity, and the like.

fiction. The use of pagan supernatural 'machinery'—Mars, Jupiter, and the rest.

The well-sung woes . . . feel them most. Pope, *Eloisa to Abelard,* l. 365.

the Angel. See note to p. 647.

668   *Madden*. Samuel Madden, Irish clergyman and writer; supposed to have given Johnson ten guineas to revise his poem *Boulter's Monument*.

669   *late collection*. The anthology for which Johnson wrote these prefaces. Dramatic poetry was generally excluded.

671   *imitation of reality*. An approximation to Aristotle's definition of tragedy in the *Poetics*.

      mirror of life. Johnson's repetition of this phrase, which he uses so strikingly in the Preface to Shakespeare (p. 421), seems to indicate a conscious retraction of what he had written fifteen years earlier on the subject of 'poetic justice' (p. 427).

672   *delight in critical controversy*. Johnson's may have been greater than that of the modern reader, and so only the beginning and end of Dennis's rambunctious, though amusing, strictures are given here.

      Bayes. Dryden, the poet laureate (laurel = bay), as burlesqued in *The Rehearsal*.

674   *taste rather than principles*. Johnson is clearly on the side of 'taste'. Of those who complained that Pope's poetry was 'too uniformly musical', he comments (p. 751), 'I suspect this objection to be the cant of those who judge by principles rather than perception.'

675   *Tom Thumb*. A child's book which Johnson enjoyed. *A Comment on the History of Tom Thumb* burlesques Addison's critique of *Chevy Chase*. It was attributed to one 'William Wagstaffe', clearly a pseudonym (indeed, 'Wagstaffe' was one used by Swift).

      outsteps . . . nature. *Hamlet*, III. ii. 21.

      enthusiastic . . . superstitious. 'Enthusiastic', in its literal meaning of 'claiming to speak by direct inspiration of the Holy Spirit', was often applied pejoratively to Protestant extremists; 'superstitious' was likewise applied to Roman Catholics.

676   *Mille . . . habet*. Tibullus, iv. 2. 14. Translated in the previous sentence.

677   *Cowley. metaphysical*. Johnson seems to mean something like 'practitioners of abstruse philosophy'. Possibly the best single modern equivalent here is 'cerebral', defined in the *Concise Oxford English Dictionary* as 'appealing to the intellect rather than to the emotions'.

      father of criticism. Aristotle, in the *Poetics*. The quotation is not exact.

      so well expressed. Pope, *Essay on Criticism*, l. 298.

678   *discordia concors*. Harmonious disharmony, a phrase used by various Roman critics. For a poetic expression, see 'To Miss ———', p. 10, ll. 25–36. See also the variant, *concordia discors*, p. 245.

      yoked by violence together. It should be noted that this is not an account, as has sometimes been said, of 'conceit' or 'metaphysical conceit', but of 'wit'.

      general. See note on *Rasselas*, ch. x (p. 352).

686 *Dryden's Night*. The passage in *The Indian Emperor*, III. ii, beginning 'All things are hushed as Nature's self lay dead'. Johnson quotes it with similar praise in his *Miscellaneous Observations on Macbeth*, 1745.

689 *Aspice . . . flamma meas*. Jacopo Sannazaro, 'Ad Vesbiam': 'See, Vesbia, by what different torments I am racked! I burn, and, alas, liquid flows from my fire. I am Nile; at the same time I am Etna: restrain my flames, O tears, or, flames, drink up my tears.' It should be noted that Johnson here declares that Cowley and the metaphysical poets were *not* responsible for inventing such 'confusion of images': it was 'full-blown' in classical and in Renaissance Latin poetry.

691 *Musae Anglicanae*. See note to p. 644.

693 *arvis*. *Aeneid*, xii. 896: 'Looking around, he saw a huge stone, a huge old stone, lying by chance on the ground, placed there to mark the boundary of a farm, to settle disputes about fields.'

694 *sentiments*. See note to p. 706.

699 *Milton. fiction*. pagan mythology. See p. 667 and note.

vulgar. common, ordinary, hackneyed. *disgusting*: distasteful, boring. Both words were milder ones than they are now.

Lycidas. For a different verdict by Johnson on *Lycidas*, see p. 489.

703 *vindicate*. Johnson, quoting from memory, gives us Pope's 'vindicate the ways of God to man' (*Essay on Man*, i. 16) instead of Milton's 'justify the ways of God to man' (*Paradise Lost*, i. 26).

705 Θεὸς ἀπὸ μηχανῆς. 'A god from the machine': the practice in some Greek plays in which one of the Olympian gods descends on the stage from above to bring about the denouement.

706 *success and virtue . . . together*. Another rejection, like that in the 'Preface' to Addison (p. 671), of Johnson's earlier stand on 'poetic justice' in his edition of Shakespeare (pp. 427, 465).

sentiments. 'Sentiment. (1) Thought; notion; opinion. (2) The sense considered apart from the language or things; a striking sentence in a composition'—*Dictionary*. 'Sentence. (3) A maxim; an axiom, generally moral'.

707 *sublunary*. See note to p. 418.

loftiness. Johnson here adds a footnote, 'Algarotti terms it *gigantesca sublimità Miltoniana*'.

715 *ingenious critic*. Johnson told a friend that it was William Locke of Norbury Park, Surrey.

718 *Dryden. Rymer*. Thomas Rymer, lawyer, antiquarian, and critic, best known for his severe strictures on Shakespeare's tragedies.

719 *Trapp*. Joseph Trapp, first Professor of Poetry at Oxford. This passage from his lectures (*Praelectiones*), somewhat misquoted by Johnson, was translated (using the correct text) in 1742: 'We know our countryman

Mr Dryden's judgement about a poem of Chaucer's, truly beautiful and worthy of praise; namely, that it was not only equal, but even superior to the *Iliad* and *Æneid*. But we know likewise that his opinion was not always the most accurate, nor formed upon the severest rules of criticism. What was in hand was generally most in esteem; if it was uppermost in his thoughts, it was so in his judgement too.'

Sewel. See note to p. 654.

Quae . . . colosso. Statius, *Silvae*, i. 1: 'What is this doubled mass with a colossus raised upon it?' The reference is to a new equestrian statue of the Emperor Domitian. The 'thundering' sound of the line is intended to be an 'echo to the sense'.

720 *condemned . . . straw*. Committed to an insane asylum, where the bedding was the straw on the floor.

721 *Charles*. The following quotation is from Dryden's *Threnodia Augustalis*, on the death of Charles II.

724 *lateritiam . . . reliquit*. Suetonius, *Life of Augustus*, 29. The translation immediately follows.

725 *Pope*. Included here are the second section (general 'character') and third section (detailed criticism) of the 'Preface'.

726 *ring*. In Juvenal's *Satire* x, Hannibal, after all his military triumphs, is done to death by a poisoned ring. In Johnson's 'imitation', 'The Vanity of Human Wishes', ll. 219–20, the account of Charles XII's obscure death takes the place of this.

727 *unjustifiable impression*. Unauthorized printing.

horresco referens. 'I shudder to tell it'—Virgil, *Aeneid*, ii. 204. Samuel Patrick published revised editions of a Latin and a Greek dictionary.

739 *numeris lege solutis*. 'In lawless metres'—Horace, *Odes*, iv. 2.

Cobb. Samuel Cobb, minor poet and translator.

740 *can show*. See p. 491.

744 *curiosa felicitas*. 'Painstaking felicity'—Petronius, *Satyricon*, 118, discussing Horace.

Essay . . . Pope. Joseph Warton. See p. 488.

747 *Impune . . . Telephus*. 'Unchastised, an enormous *Telephus* would consume a whole day'—Juvenal, *Satires*, i. 4. *Telephus* is a lost tragedy by Euripides.

Priam. Virgil, *Aeneid*, ii. 544–6.

748 *Essay on Man*. See also Johnson's translation of Crousaz (pp. 84–95) and his review of Soame Jenyns (p. 522).

752 *Lo, where Maeotis . . . waste of snows*. Dunciad, iii. 87.

Pope was a poet. See the review of Joseph Warton, p. 488.

755 *Watts. Foster*. James Foster, a celebrated Nonconformist preacher.

756 *Le Clerc.* Jean Le Clerc, French polymath.

760 *Collins. character.* Johnson's 'character' was first printed in *The Poetical Calendar*, 1763.

761 *John Hume.* Now usually spelled 'Home'. Scottish playwright, author of the popular *Douglas*.

765 *Gray. buxom.* '(1) Obedient; obsequious'—*Dictionary*.

 redolent. 'Sweet of scent'—*Dictionary*.

 O Diva . . . Antium. Horace, *Odes*, i. 35.

767 *Incredulus odi.* 'Unable to believe it, I dislike it'—Horace, *Art of Poetry*, l. 188.

768 *suicide.* At the end of the poem, the bard plunges to his death from the cliff.

 Double . . . trouble. Macbeth, IV. i. 10.

771 *Annals.* Johnson seems to have composed these recollections of his youth in the 1760s, perhaps as part of a programme of 'self-psychoanalysis' to mitigate the deep depression he suffered about this time. His insistence on distinguishing between what he personally recollects and what he may have reconstructed from what others have told him should be noted.

 Hector. Father of Edmund Hector, Johnson's schoolfellow and lifelong friend.

 Swinfen. Dr Samuel Swinfen or Swynfen, Johnson's godfather, and father of Elizabeth Desmoulins, who made her home with Johnson for many years.

772 *breach of duty.* Until quite recently, Sunday travel, as a breach of the Fourth Commandment, was frowned on by devout Protestants.

773 *pregnancy.* With Johnson's younger brother, Nathanael.

 wagon. 'Caravans or stage-wagons drawn by four or five horses carried a score or so of passengers, unable to pay for better and faster accommodation': E. L. Beale, 'Travel and Communications', in *Johnson's England*, ed. A. L. Turberville (1933), i. 137. Presumably their passengers would be less likely to complain of the child's coughing than the higher-paying and more closely seated ones of the stage coach.

 S. I. 'I' and 'J' were regarded as the same letter. Words beginning with them are alphabetized together in Johnson's *Dictionary*.

 tea . . . expensive. See the review of Hanway, p. 510.

774 *remembered.* There follows a gap of thirty-eight pages in the manuscript. Most of the continuation is a detailed account of the curriculum of the Lichfield Grammar School.

775 *new wife.* Elizabeth ('Tetty') Johnson died on 17 March (28, New Style) 1752. The most likely candidate for the 'new wife' is Hill Boothby, a pious and learned lady, with whom Johnson exchanged some touching letters before her death in 1756 (see p. 783).

Fluunt lacrymae. 'My tears flow.'

intenerate. Make tender.

776 *my Brother.* Nathanael Johnson died suddenly and mysteriously at the age of twenty-four, just at the time Samuel and David Garrick left for London; suicide has been suspected. His one surviving letter, written not long before his death, complains of his harsh treatment by his brother.

July 25, 1774. From Johnson's journal of his tour to Wales with the Thrales.

777 *Boswel.* Johnson made a point of not doubling final consonants in names (likewise 'Cheynel', p. 476, and 'Levet', p. 35). Boswell, of course, when printing Johnson's letters to him, supplied the extra *l*.

778 *D. j. Deo juvante*—'God helping'.

September 18, 1775. Johnson's sixty-sixth birthday, an anniversary usually marked in his diaries with a self-examination and a prayer for improvement. It will be noted how closely Johnson modelled this and other prayers on the Collects of the *Book of Common Prayer*.

October 16, 1775. This and the two following entries are from Johnson's journal of his tour to France with the Thrales.

Fermor. A niece of Arabella Fermor, the original of Belinda in Pope's *Rape of the Lock*.

779 *King and Queen.* The young Louis XVI and Marie Antoinette. Madame Elizabeth was Louis's sister.

Degenerate q. Mrs Thrale, in her diary of the tour, comments on the unprepossessing appearance of the horses in the royal stables. She and Johnson would have been familiar with the large, powerful drayhorses of the Thrale brewery. The *q* may be the usual abbreviation of '*quaere*' ('query').

L. D. Laus Deo—'God be praised'.

December 5, 1784. Composed for Johnson's last communion; he died on 13 December. The silent editing in the version given in Boswell's *Life*, which omits the petition 'forgive and accept my late conversion', should be noted.

781 *To Edward Cave.* Proprietor of the *Gentleman's Magazine*, which he had founded in 1731. This supremely cheeky (if anonymous) letter from an unknown young man in the provinces understandably brought no answer, but it foreshadows the high standards of journalism Johnson was to maintain when, four years later, he was at last taken on the staff of the *GM*. See also 'Of the Duty of a Journalist', p. 544.

To Thomas Warton. The book for which Johnson thanks him was his *Observations* on Spenser's *Faerie Queene*. He is best known for his pioneering *History of English Poetry*. He was brother to Joseph Warton (see p. 488).

782 *Hughes*. John Hughes, an earlier editor of Spenser. In his Preface to the works of Hughes, Johnson complains of his want of 'an antiquary's knowledge of the obsolete words'.

my book. His *Dictionary of the English Language*, published the next year.

Sam: Johnson. The colon should be noted. It is a sign of abbreviation. Until quite recently given names in signatures were often so abbreviated, as 'Jas:' for 'James' and 'Geo:' for 'George'. Samuel Johnson did not expect to be addressed as 'Sam', and there is no evidence that anyone ever did so after his boyhood.

To the Earl of Chesterfield. le vainqueur. Alaric the Goth, who conquered Rome. This is from the first line of Georges de Scudéry's poem, 'Alaric'.

783 *shepherd in Virgil*. For the passage referred to, from Virgil, *Eclogues*, viii, 43–5, see p. 196. The point is that 'love' such as Chesterfield professed towards Johnson produced misery.

Hill Boothby. See note to p. 775.

Law. Presumably a work by William Law, whose *Serious Call to a Devout and Holy Life*, 1728, Johnson said, 'was the first occasion of my thinking in earnest about religion'.

784 *To Lucy Porter. Kitty*. Catherine Chambers, the devoted servant of Sarah Johnson.

785 *To Joseph Baretti. native town*. Lichfield; Johnson's first visit to it in more than twenty years.

daughter-in-law. Stepdaughter—Lucy Porter, daughter of Tetty and her first husband.

Strahan. Son of Johnson's friend, the printer and MP William Strahan, George was then nineteen. He seems to have quarrelled frequently with his father, as well as taking offence (as this letter indicates) at Johnson. He became a clergyman, administered the last communion to Johnson, and edited his prayers and religious meditations, heavily censoring them.

786 *To Boswell. publish the letters*. As Boswell had done with Johnson's in his *Account of Corsica*.

787 *To Mrs Thrale. charms of art*. From Addison's *Letter from Italy*. Johnson is making fun of the pomposity of travel writers.

strawberries and cream. Johnson and Mrs Thrale had a number of private jokes that they alluded to in their letters, such as her alleged unwillingness to give him enough strawberries, and the pride of the Revd John Taylor, Johnson's host at Ashbourne, in his prize bull.

September 30, 1773. One of a series of long letters to Mrs Thrale during Johnson's Highland tour, constituting virtually a diary of it, on which he drew heavily when writing the *Journey to the Western Islands*. This excerpt has to do with his visit to Raasay (see p. 624).

789 *To Macpherson*. The author of the *Ossian* poems, which Macpherson

maintained were translated from Gaelic originals, but which Johnson and many others believed were 'impostures', composed by Macpherson himself. See pp. 636–8.

Homer. Macpherson's translation of the *Iliad*, 1773, was poorly received.

To Dodd. The Revd William Dodd, a prominent and fashionable clergyman, once a royal chaplain, was convicted of forging the name of his former pupil, the 5th Earl of Chesterfield, to a bond for £4,000, and sentenced to be hanged, as conviction for forgery then entailed. For many weeks Johnson conducted a high-pressured campaign against what seemed to him this barbarous penalty, composing petitions, memorials, and even a sermon in the name of Dodd. Sir Leon Radzinowicz, in his *History of the English Criminal Law*, 1948, devotes a chapter to the incident, and sees Johnson's efforts as the beginning of the movement for the reform of the brutality of eighteenth-century criminal law. In the end, the campaign was unsuccessful, and this letter is Johnson's farewell.

790 *To Mrs Thrale*. She had formally announced her intention to marry Gabriel Piozzi. As an Italian, a Roman Catholic, and a professional musician, he was regarded as an ineligible *parti* for a wealthy brewer's widow, and Mrs Thrale was subjected to a barrage of abuse from all sides. Johnson was old, sick, and lonely, but his outburst can only be excused, if at all, by a more than Platonic feeling towards her. In this memorable exchange, she gives him back as good as she got, or better, and Johnson backs down. Her second marriage did indeed bring her the happiness that her first had not.

792 *Queen Mary*. Mary, Queen of Scots, whose flight to England led in the end to her execution.

irremeable. 'Admitting no return'—*Dictionary*.

FURTHER READING

EDITIONS

The only reliable collected edition of Johnson's works is that which began to be published by the Yale University Press in 1958. So far eleven volumes have appeared: they include Johnson's *Diaries, Prayers, Annals*; *The Rambler, The Adventurer*, and *The Idler*; his *Poems* and *Sermons*; most of his Shakespeare criticism; the *Journey to the Western Islands of Scotland*; and a selection of his political writings. Perhaps thirteen to fifteen volumes are still to come. Important corrections to vol. i were made by J. D. Fleeman, in the *Review of English Studies*, NS xix (May 1968), from new readings of the manuscripts of 'Prayers and Meditations'.

A 'collected edition' in eleven volumes was published in 1787, with four supplementary volumes, 1787–9, and was often reprinted, with some additions and deletions, throughout the nineteenth century (the last such reprinting took place in 1903). These editions are incomplete and textually untrustworthy; the so-called 'best edition', Oxford, 1825, is no better, and sometimes worse, than earlier ones. For most of Johnson's journalistic writings, including the *Debates in the Senate of Lilliput*, the serious student has to go back to their first appearance in the *Gentleman's* and *Literary Magazines* and other eighteenth-century publications—which, thanks to microfilming and facsimile reproduction, are now not difficult of access. Facsimiles of the first and fourth editions of the *Dictionary*, of the edition of Shakespeare, of Johnson's early biographical writings, of his version of Crousaz's *Commentary* on Pope's *Essay on Man*, and of the manuscripts of his 'Prayers and Meditations' are now available.

Other useful editions are those of *The Lives of the Poets* (better, *Prefaces, Biographical and Critical, to the Works of the English Poets*) by G. Birkbeck Hill (Oxford: Clarendon Press, 1905; repr. New York: Octagon Books, 1967); *Rasselas*, by R. W. Chapman (Oxford: Clarendon Press, 1927); Johnson's *Prefaces and Dedications*, by Allen T. Hazen (New Haven: Yale University Press, 1937; repr. Port Washington, NY: Kennikat Press, 1973); *Poems*, by D. Nichol Smith and E. L. McAdam, Jr. (Oxford: Clarendon Press, 1941; 2nd edn., revised by J. D. Fleeman, 1974), and by J. D. Fleeman (Harmondsworth, Middx.: Penguin Books, 1971); the *Life of Savage*, by Clarence Tracy (Oxford: Clarendon Press, 1971).

The standard edition of Johnson's *Letters* (including those of Mrs Thrale to him) is by R. W. Chapman (Oxford: Clarendon Press, 1952). Some corrections to this edition were published by T. M. Knox in *Notes and Queries*, July 1962, and important additions were made by Mary Hyde, 'Not in Chapman', *Johnson, Boswell, and Their Circle*, (ed. Mary Lascelles *et al.* (Oxford: Clarendon Press, 1965) and by Duncan Isles, 'The Lennox Collection', *Harvard Library Bulletin*, 1970–1.

BIBLIOGRAPHY

To ascertain just what was written *by* Johnson is still a difficult task, since much of it was anonymous journalism and contributions to works of others. The standard bibliography, by W. P. Courtney and D. Nichol Smith (Oxford: Clarendon Press, 1915), though still indispensable, has been long outdated. Donald Greene, 'The Development of the Johnson Canon', in *Restoration and Eighteenth-Century English Literature*, ed. Carroll Camden (University of Chicago Press, 1963) provides a list of recent additions, and possible additions, to the canon. J. D. Fleeman, *A Preliminary Handlist of Documents and Manuscripts of Samuel Johnson* (Oxford: Oxford Bibliographical Society, 1967) is an invaluable guide to the manuscript material.

For writings *about* Johnson, James L. Clifford and Donald Greene, *Samuel Johnson: A Survey and Bibliography of Critical Studies* (Minneapolis: University of Minnesota Press, 1970) gives a selective list of about 4,000 titles published between Johnson's lifetime and 1969. For more recent studies, the annual bibliography of eighteenth-century studies formerly published in *Philological Quarterly* and now independently as *The Eighteenth Century: A Current Bibliography* should be consulted.

BIOGRAPHY

The Early Biographies of Samuel Johnson, ed. O M Brack, Jr., and Robert E. Kelley (Iowa City: University of Iowa Press, 1974), reprints fourteen biographical accounts of Johnson that appeared between 1762 and 1786. Mrs Piozzi's *Anecdotes of the Late Samuel Johnson*, 1786, has most recently been edited by Arthur Sherbo (London: Oxford University Press, 1974), and Sir John Hawkins's *Life of Samuel Johnson*, 1787, slightly abridged, by Bertram H. Davis (New York: Macmillan, 1961). The standard edition of James Boswell's *Life of Johnson* (1st edn., 1791) and of his *Journal of a Tour to the Hebrides with Samuel Johnson* (1st edn., 1785) is that edited by G. Birkbeck Hill and revised by L. F. Powell (6 vols., Oxford: Clarendon Press, vols. i–iv, 1934, vols. v–vi (2nd edn.), 1964). Arthur Murphy's *Essay on the Life and Genius of Samuel Johnson* replaced Hawkins's *Life* in the first volume of the collected *Works* of 1792; it is in need of a good modern edition. Reports of detailed research into the first forty years of Johnson's life occupy ten volumes of Aleyn Lyell Reade's *Johnsonian Gleanings* (privately printed, 1909–46; index vol. xi, 1961; the whole reprinted in facsimile, New York: Octagon Books, 1968). Reade's work formed the basis for James L. Clifford's detailed biography of those years, *Young Sam Johnson* (New York: McGraw-Hill, 1955; as *Young Samuel Johnson*, London: Heinemann, 1955). A second volume by Clifford, *Dictionary Johnson* (New York: McGraw-Hill; London: Heinemann, 1979), provides a similarly detailed study of his life between 1749 and 1762. Popular, derivative biographies include those by Joseph Wood Krutch, 1944, John Wain, 1974, and W. J. Bate, 1977. *Johnsoniana*, ed. J. W. Croker, 1836, and *Johnsonian Miscellanies*, ed. G. Birkbeck Hill, 1897, print a large number of contemporary reminiscences of Johnson.

CRITICISM

Donald Greene, *Samuel Johnson* (New York: Twayne Publishers (Twayne's English Authors), 1970; 2nd rev. ed., 1989) attempts a general introduction to Johnson's thought and writings. On special aspects of them, the following are useful:

Paul K. Alkon, *Samuel Johnson and Moral Discipline* (Evanston, Ill., 1967).
Bertrand H. Bronson, *Johnson Agonistes and Other Essays* (Cambridge, 1946; originally published Berkeley, Cal., 1944; repr. Cambridge, 1966, with the addition of his important essay 'The Double Tradition of Dr Johnson').
Joseph Epes Brown, *The Critical Opinions of Samuel Johnson* (Princeton, 1926; repr. New York, 1961). A highly useful finding list for Johnson's critical remarks, although the generalizations in Brown's introduction are not to be trusted.
Chester F. Chapin, *The Religious Thought of Samuel Johnson* (Ann Arbor, Mich., 1968).
J. D. Fleeman, *The Sale Catalogue of Samuel Johnson's Library: A Facsimile Edition* (Victoria, BC, 1975). Reproduces a copy—probably the auctioneer's file copy—that records the purchasers and the prices of the books.
Robert Folkenflik, *Samuel Johnson, Biographer* (Ithaca, NY, 1978).
James Gray, *Johnson's Sermons: A Study* (Oxford, 1972).
Donald Greene, *The Politics of Samuel Johnson* (New Haven, 1960; repr. Port Washington, NY, 1973; 2nd rev. ed., Athens, Georgia, 1989).
Donald Greene, *Samuel Johnson's Library: An Annotated Guide* (Victoria, BC, 1975).
Jean H. Hagstrum, *Samuel Johnson's Literary Criticism* (Minneapolis, 1952; 2nd edn., Chicago, 1967).
Benjamin B. Hoover, *Samuel Johnson's Parliamentary Reporting* (Berkeley, Cal., 1953).
E. L. McAdam, Jr., *Dr Johnson and the English Law* (Syracuse, NY, 1951).
Richard B. Schwartz, *Samuel Johnson and the New Science* (Madison, Wis., 1971).
Richard B. Schwartz, *Samuel Johnson and the Problem of Evil* (Madison, Wis., 1975). Includes a facsimile reprint of the review of Soame Jenyns.
Arthur Sherbo, *Samuel Johnson, Editor of Shakespeare* (Urbana, Ill., 1956).
James H. Sledd and Gwin J. Kolb, *Dr Johnson's Dictionary* (Chicago, 1955).
W. K. Wimsatt, Jr., *Philosophic Words: A Study of Style and Meaning in the 'Rambler' and 'Dictionary' of Samuel Johnson* (New Haven, 1948; repr. Hamden, Conn., 1968).
W. K. Wimsatt, Jr., *The Prose Style of Samuel Johnson* (New Haven, 1941; repr. Hamden, Conn., 1966).

A number of collections of essays by various hands contain important studies of Johnson: *The Age of Johnson*, ed. F. W. Hilles (New Haven, 1949; repr. 1964; a *Festschrift* for Chauncey Brewster Tinker); *New Light on Johnson*, ed. F. W. Hilles (New Haven, 1959); *Johnsonian Studies*, ed. Magdi Wahba (Cairo, 1962); *Johnson, Boswell, and Their Circle*, ed. James L. Clifford, Mary

Lascelles, *et al.* (Oxford, 1965; a *Festschrift* for L. F. Powell); *English Writers of the Eighteenth Century*, ed. John H. Middendorf (New York, 1971; a *Festschrift* for James L. Clifford); *The Unknown Samuel Johnson*, ed. John J. Burke and Donald Kay (Madison, Wis., 1983).

Samuel Johnson: The Critical Heritage, ed. James T. Boulton (London, 1971; New York, 1972), is a useful collection of comment on Johnson in the eighteenth and early nineteenth centuries. Helen Louise McGuffie, *Samuel Johnson in the British Press, 1749–1784* (New York, 1976) lists some 4,000 references to Johnson during the period stated, a large number of them hostile. *Samuel Johnson: A Collection of Critical Essays* (*Twentieth Century Views*), ed. Donald Greene (Englewood Cliffs, NJ, 1965), reprints excerpts from some of the books listed above, as well as other modern essays on Johnson. The quarterly *Johnsonian News Letter*, founded by James L. Clifford in 1941 and now edited at Columbia University by John H. Middendorf, is indispensable for keeping up with scholarly work on Johnson. *The New Rambler* (now annual) of the Johnson Society of London, the annual *Transactions of the Johnson Society* [of Lichfield], and the occasional *Transactions* of the Johnson Society of the North West [of Canada and the United States] often print useful articles on special aspects of Johnson.

INDEXES

POETRY: TITLES AND FIRST LINES

PROSE

INDEX OF RECIPIENTS OF LETTERS

OXFORD

MORE OXFORD PAPERBACKS

This book is just one of nearly 1000 Oxford Paperbacks currently in print. If you would like details of other Oxford Paperbacks, including titles in the World's Classics, Oxford Reference, Oxford Books, OPUS, Past Masters, Oxford Authors, and Oxford Shakespeare series, please write to:

UK and Europe: Oxford Paperbacks Publicity Manager, Arts and Reference Publicity Department, Oxford University Press, Walton Street, Oxford OX2 6DP.

Customers in UK and Europe will find Oxford Paperbacks available in all good bookshops. But in case of difficulty please send orders to the Cash-with-Order Department, Oxford University Press Distribution Services, Saxon Way West, Corby, Northants NN18 9ES. Tel: 01536 741519; Fax: 01536 746337. Please send a cheque for the total cost of the books, plus £1.75 postage and packing for orders under £20; £2.75 for orders over £20. Customers outside the UK should add 10% of the cost of the books for postage and packing.

USA: Oxford Paperbacks Marketing Manager, Oxford University Press, Inc., 200 Madison Avenue, New York, N.Y. 10016.

Canada: Trade Department, Oxford University Press, 70 Wynford Drive, Don Mills, Ontario M3C 1J9.

Australia: Trade Marketing Manager, Oxford University Press, G.P.O. Box 2784Y, Melbourne 3001, Victoria.

South Africa: Oxford University Press, P.O. Box 1141, Cape Town 8000.

THE OXFORD AUTHORS

General Editor: Frank Kermode

THE OXFORD AUTHORS is a series of authoritative editions of major English writers. Aimed at both students and general readers, each volume contains a generous selection of the best writings—poetry, prose, and letters—to give the essence of a writer's work and thinking. All the texts are complemented by essential notes, an introduction, chronology, and suggestions for further reading.

Matthew Arnold
William Blake
Lord Byron
John Clare
Samuel Taylor Coleridge
John Donne
John Dryden
Ralph Waldo Emerson
Thomas Hardy
George Herbert and Henry Vaughan
Gerard Manley Hopkins
Samuel Johnson
Ben Jonson
John Keats
Andrew Marvell
John Milton
Alexander Pope
Sir Philip Sidney
Oscar Wilde
William Wordsworth

THE OXFORD AUTHORS
SAMUEL TAYLOR COLERIDGE
Edited by H. J. Jackson

Samuel Taylor Coleridge, poet, critic, and radical thinker, exerted an enormous influence over contemporaries as different as Wordsworth, Southey, and Lamb. He was also a dedicated reformer, and set out to use his reputation as a public speaker and literary philosopher to change the course of English thought.

This collection represents the best of Coleridge's poetry from every period of his life, particularly his prolific early years, which produced *The Rime of the Ancient Mariner*, *Christabel*, and *Kubla Khan*. The central section of the book is devoted to his most significant critical work, *Biographia Literaria*, and reproduces it in full. It provides a vital background for both the poetry section which precedes it and for the shorter prose works which follow.

THE OXFORD AUTHORS
JOHN DRYDEN
Edited by Keith Walker

Keith Walker's selection from the extensive works of Dryden admirably supports the perception that he was the leading writer of his day. In his brisk, illuminating introduction, Dr Walker draws attention to the links between the cultural and political context in which Dryden was writing and the works he produced.

The major poetry and prose works appear in full, and special emphasis has been placed on Dryden's classical translations, his safest means of expression as a Catholic in the London of William of Orange. His versions of Homer, Horace, and Ovid are reproduced in full. There are also substantial selections from his Virgil, Juvenal, and other classical writers.

THE OXFORD AUTHORS
RALPH WALDO EMERSON
Edited by Richard Poirier

Ralph Waldo Emerson (1803–82) was one of the most influential figures in American life and thought, as well as the most renowned public speaker of his time. Even his detractors recognize the importance of his role in representing both the best and worst of American culture. In his lectures and essays, he cultivated the art of not arriving at intellectual conclusions, encouraging readers (and listeners) to think for themselves.

This volume contains a full selection from the numerous essays and lectures, including 'Nature', 'The American Scholar', 'Self-Reliance', 'The Poet', and his tribute to Thoreau, as well as many less familiar pieces, rarely found in print. In addition, the generous selection of poems and the supporting notes make this the most comprehensive and useful edition of Emerson's work currently available.

THE OXFORD AUTHORS

BEN JONSON

Edited by Ian Donaldson

Ben Jonson's literary reputation with his contemporaries rivalled, and perhaps surpassed, that of Shakespeare. This edition presents the full texts of Jonson's two most popular comedies, *Volpone* and *The Alchemist* and of his commonplace book *Discoveries*, his *Conversations with William Drummond of Hawthornden*, and all his non-dramatic poetry. To this is added a generous selection of songs and poems from the plays and masques, and a number of poems doubtfully attributed to Jonson.

THE OXFORD AUTHORS
JOHN KEATS
Edited by Elizabeth Cook

This volume contains a full selection of Keats's poetry and prose works including *Endymion* in its entirety, the Odes, 'Lamia', and both versions of 'Hyperion'. The poetry is presented in order of composition illustrating the staggering speed with which Keats's work matured. Further valuable insight into his creative process is given by reproducing, in their original form, a number of poems that were not published in his lifetime. A large proportion of the prose section is devoted to Keats's letters, considered among the most remarkable ever written. They provide not only the best biographical detail available, but are also invaluable in shedding light on his poetry.

THE OXFORD AUTHORS

SIR PHILIP SIDNEY

Edited by Katherine Duncan-Jones

Born in 1554, Sir Philip Sidney was hailed as the perfect Renaissance patron, soldier, lover, and courtier, but it was only after his untimely death at the age of thirty-two that his literary achievements were truly recognized.

This collection ranges more widely through Sidney's works than any previous volume and includes substantial parts of both versions of the *Arcadia*, *A Defence of Poesy*, and the whole of the sonnet sequence *Astrophil and Stella*. Supplementary texts, such as his letters and the numerous elegies which appeared after his death, help to illustrate the wide spectrum of his achievements, and the admiration he inspired in his contemporaries.